Law on Civil Appeals

First Edition	2015
Second Edition	**2018**

Law on Civil Appeals

Second Edition

Y.P. Bhagat
Advocate, Supreme Court of India

and

Kumar Keshav
LL.M., Advocate

Universal Law Publishing
an imprint of LexisNexis

LexisNexis

This book is a publication of LexisNexis
(A Division of RELX India Pvt Ltd)
14th floor, Building No 10, Tower-B, DLF Cyber City, Phase-II,
Gurgaon-122002, Haryana, India.
Tel : + 91 124 4774444 Fax: + 91 124 4774100
Website : www.lexisnexis.co.in / E-mail : help.in@lexisnexis.com

---

Y P Bhagat : *Law on Civil Appeals*, Second Edition 2018

ISBN: 978-81-3125-383-0

Printed by: Sanat Printers, 312, Kundli, Haryana-131 028

Printed and bound in India.

PREFACE TO THE SECOND EDITION

The first edition of Law on Civil Appeals exhausted very quickly and people laid persistent demand for updated version with latest developments in the field. All latest important case law have been included in this edition of book with full discussion which could make easy the complex questions of law including the theory of 'substantial question of law'. First edition of this book was published by LexisNexis in the year 2015. Readers strongly demanded some specialized studies on important parts of Civil Law. The legal activists insisted on topic wise presentation and our concern decided to place the subject of civil procedure with more elaborate discussion as topic wise specialized studies has become demand of the day. Easy handling and convenient portability along with exhaustive studies on legal topics is considered an important aspect in this book. We are sure that this book may be much beneficial for the legal activists including the judges and the lawyers.

Y P Bhagat

PREFACE TO THE FIRST EDITION

After success of other publications, the readers strongly demanded for specialized studies on the laws relating to appellate jurisdiction. Although some other books were also ready for publication, but because of persistent demand, particularly from the lawyers and for other reasons and convenience our publishers, who are concern of repute also preferred to publish this book now and that is how it came to you.

Although the subject has already been covered by the earlier comments on CPC, presented by me and published by Universal Law Publishing, yet there were some constraints in going in further details on the subject. Easy handling and convenient portability of the books is an important thing which has to be kept in mind while preparing a book and at the same-time, exhaustive studies on legal topics is also an important aspect of the legal profession. Hence, subject-wise specialized book has become demand of the day.

In course of completing other books, I felt that hardly any author has considered the desirability of presenting such book with concentrated discussion. I have tried my best to meet the demand of the legal activists, and it is for you the readers to judge how far it could serve you.

July 2015 **Y P BHAGAT**

INTRODUCTION

As we know, the law of civil procedure is a vital bridge connecting two disparate wards. The substantive law that defines the rights and liabilities of Judiciary, on the one hand and the day-to-day of judicial officers and law officials who administer the law, on the other that is the rules of procedures.

Having long experience as a legal practitioner and as a judicial officer, I feel that the part of CPC covering the laws and rules of procedures regarding civil appeals has been the most vexing subject for all and have very often drawn attention of the law courts. Hence, concentration on the subject was required like anything.

For long, I had the vision of such a book which could explain the complex questions in simple way. I am confident that the present book entitled "Law on Civil Appeals" may significantly serve the purpose. Every page of this book is crammed full of useful laws and tips which may benefit not only the lawyers but the judges as well. The first and most important benefit of this work is its capacity to promote consistency and predictability in judicial decision-making. These attributes are the very hallmarks of the rule of law and they are no less important in the realm of procedural law than in the realm of substantive law. Judges should aim to apply principles of civil procedures with reasonable consistency and the task is made much easier if legal practitioners have a fuller understanding of the background of each rule and its application. I feel that this book has the merit of being specifically tailored to the unique features of the law and courts. It places this book in a class of its own. It is rare enough to find a legal publication like the present one having potentiality to focus on laws.

I have already presented other books on civil laws. Those books have covered much comments on the law relating to civil appellate jurisdiction. Yet certain aspects could not be touched. While making comments on CPC I had to go provision-wise, but some thing yet was to be studied to have a complete grip over the subject. Moreover, persistent demands were coming from different corners for specialized book on the subject.

Section 109 and Order XLV deal with provisions for appeal before the Supreme Court. But that is not all about a civil appeal before the apex Court. Therefore, in this book I have placed the comparative studies of these provisions of CPC and the provisions of articles 133 and 136 of the Constitution of India as also the Supreme Court Rules. I Have tried to make it clear in this book why people prefer to go under article 136, though there are specific provisions for such appeals under article 133 of Constitution besides the various provisions of CPC. I am sure that this is the exclusive book in the market which places comparative studies of various provisions relating to civil appeals. Besides the provisions contained in the Code of Civil Procedure and the Constitution. I have also referred to the provisions of the Supreme Court Rules regarding civil appeal before it.

This book has two purposes, *first,* to serve as a text of law and *second,* to provide a reference manual and it is certainly a significant achievement by me for the fuller advantages to all the legal activists, the credit going to the legal luminaries all around and near me who always played role of guides and inspirators. The judicial activists of outstanding and established repute are of the view that providing such books is in itself a great service to all.

Unlike others, this book places details of the provisions as it existed earlier and have explained how the provisions for the same subject as it stood in the Code of Civil Procedure differed from that existed in the Constitution of India. I have also discussed how by necessary amendments the different provisions were kept at par with each other.

Many legal luminaries including senior lawyers of higher Judiciary have opined that this is the solitary book in the market which may be a good friend and guide for the legal activists. Taking into view the facts stated above, I am sure that this book may successfully serve our purposes.

CONTENTS

PART I

SUBSTANTIVE PROVISIONS OF CIVIL APPEALS

PART II

RULES OF PROCEDURE

ORDER XLI

TABLE OF CASES

A

B

C

D

E

H

I

J

L

M

N

O

P

R

S

T

U

V

W

Y

Z

PART I

SUBSTANTIVE PROVISIONS OF CIVIL APPEALS

CHAPTER I

APPEALS FROM ORIGINAL DECREE

CIVIL APPEALS

***96. Appeal from original decree.*—(1) Save where otherwise expressly provided in the body of this Code or by any other law for the time being in force, an appeal shall lie from every decree passed by any Court exercising original jurisdiction to the Court authorized to hear appeals from the decisions of such Court.**

(2) An appeal may lie from an original decree passed *ex parte.*

(3) No appeal shall lie from a decree passed by the Court with the consent of parties.

(4) No appeal shall lie, except on a question of law, from a decree in any suit of the nature cognizable by Courts of Small Cause, when the amount or value of the subject-matter of the original suit does not exceed ten thousand rupees.

SYNOPSIS

Comments

1. Scope and Application

The provisions contained under section 96 should be examined along with the provisions of Order XLI. The word 'appeal' has not been defined in the Code. We have to take the ordinary meaning of the term. The matter was examined by a Full Bench of the High Court of Rajasthan which held that any application by a party to an Appellate Court, asking it to set aside or reverse a decision of a subordinate court, is an appeal within the ordinary acceptation of the term; *Namamal* v. *Radhey Shyam,* AIR 1970 Raj 26 (FB).

It was examined by the Supreme Court also in the case of *Shanker Ramchandra.* The Supreme Court held that it is a proceeding for review to be carried out by a higher authority of a decision given by a lower one; *Shanker Ramchandra Abhyankar* v. *Krishnaji Dattatraya Bapat,* AIR 1970 SC 1: (1970) 1 SCR 322: 72 Bom LR 179; *see* also *Dayawati* v. *Inderjit,* AIR 1966 SC 1423: 1966 (2) SCJ 784: (1966) 3 SCR 275.

A party does not have inherent right to appeal. Hence, he may not assert any such right, unless specifically provided. Section 96 lays down provision for a first appeal against the original decree and hence, by virtue of the provisions of this section, the party gets a valuable right to present a first appeal and to be heard, both on questions of law and fact and decided by giving reasons of its findings; *Madhukar* v. *Sangram,* AIR 2001 SC 2171: (2001) 4 SCC 756: JT 2001 (5) SC 72: 2001 AIR SCW 1804: (2001) 2 LRI 1126.

Any change in the law during the pendency of an appeal has to be taken into account and will govern the rights of the parties; *Lakshmi Narayan Guin* v. *Niranjan Modak,* AIR 1985 SC 111: (1985) 1 SCC 270: (1985) 2 SCR 202.

The provisions of section 96 were amended by the Amendment Act of 1976 when sub-section 4 was inserted. By the Amendment Act, 1999 the words 'three thousand rupees' were replaced by the words 'ten thousand rupees' which took effect from 1-7-2002. The provisions of amended section 96 shall not apply or affect any appeal from an original decree admitted before the commencement of the amended section 96 and every such admitted appeal shall be dealt with as if the amended section has not come into force.

2. Bar to Decree-Principle of Merger

Once a decree is appealed against, the theory of merger comes into operation and all the principles applicable to pendency of the suit will apply. It was examined in the case of *Sadhu Singh*. A decree was appealed against which was passed before coming into force of the provisions of Punjab Pre-emption (Repeal Act 1973) which came into force during pendency of the appeal. The said Act provided that 'no court shall pass a decree in any suit for pre-emption'. It was held that the trial courts decree merged in appeal and the statutory prohibition would apply; *Sadhu Singh* v. *Dharam Dev,* (1981) 1 SCC 510: AIR 1980 SC 1654.

3. Whether Consent Decree can be Set Aside in Appeal

A consent decree cannot be set aside in appeal, or review, or rule obtained by motion; *Hudder Field Banking Company* v. *Lister,* (1895) Ch 273; *J.C. Galstaun* v. *Pramatha Nath Roy,* AIR 1929 Cal 470: 33 Cal WN 883: ILR 57 Cal 154; *Yusuf Ismail Bhai* v. *Abdullabhai Lalji,* AIR 1932 Bom 615: 34 Bom LR 880: ILR 56 Bom 231. It is clear that section 96 deals with appeal against an original decree. It may be noted that an order under section 47 is a deemed decree, but it is not appealable as such and section 96 is not, therefore, attracted; *B. Nookaraju* v. *M.S.N. Charities,* AIR 1994 AP 334: 1994 (3) Civ LJ 382: 1994 (2) Cur CC 414.

4. *"Ex parte"* Decree

A defendant against whom a decree has been passed *ex parte,* and who has not adopted the procedure provided by Order IX, can appeal: 9 M. 445. Appealability of Order under Order XVII, rule 97 (1937) N. 519.

5. Adverse Finding

The High Court of Madras considered whether an adverse finding on a single issue can be appealed against. The Court said that an adverse finding on any single issue or issues is not appealable unless such finding is incorporated in the decree: 6 MLJ 86; 44 IC 723. According to the High Courts of Assam and Punjab a party in whose favour a decree has been passed may appeal against a finding adverse to him – the test to be applied being whether the finding is one to which the rule of *res judicata* may be held to be applicable so as to disentitle the aggrieved party to agitate the question covered by the finding in any other proceeding: 42 CWN 492; *Bhubindra Narayan Bhattacharjya* v. *Tarupriya Debya,* AIR 1950 Assam 119: ILR (1950) 2 Assam 225; *Ali Ahmad* v. *Amarnath* AIR 1951 Punj 444: 53 PLR 96.

6. Section 96(3): Consent Decree

The High Court of Patna examined the procedures contained in section 96(3) and held that section 96(3) applies only to suits and not to proceedings in execution. Consent decrees are not appealable: 43 C. 85. So too a decree on compromise: 12 Pat. 359: 1993 P. 306, even in a suit under section 92, C.P. Code: 26 Pat. 83: 1948 Pat 97. But they can be set aside for proper grounds by a separate suit: 15 B. 594. For a consent decree to come within the prohibition of section 96(3), it is not necessary that the consent should continue till the passing of the decree: 12 P. 359: 1933 Pat 306. About a decree passed against a minor, the High Court of Allahabad held that in as much as a decree passed upon a compromise against a minor, for which leave of the court was not obtained under the provision of Order XXXII 32, rule 7, cannot be said to be a valid consent decree. The minor can appeal against the decree and section 96 cannot be pleaded as bar of the appeal; [*Chhabbalal* v. *Kallu Lal*, AIR 1946 PC 72: 1946 ALJ 254 (PC), appl.]; *Sagwa* v. *Dalwa*, (1951) 2 All LJ 633: 1951 All WR 673: AIR 1952 All 97; *A.K. singh* v. *Durjansingh*, (1952) 3 Raj LW 396: AIR 1953 Raj 153: ILR (1952) 2 Raj 470.

Where a compromise has been recorded and it has not been challenged in any way in lower court, the recording of the compromise must be held to have been done by consent and no appeal lies from the Order: 57 B 206: 35 Bom LR 127: 1933 B 203; but person denying the compromise can appeal: 114 LC 101: 1929 Sind 32; 156 LC 1035. There is a distinction between a decree passed by consent of parties to which section 96 applies and a compromise of suit under Order XXIII, rule 3. Section 96 does not in all cases bar an appeal which involves a consent decree. Where an order recording a compromise is passed under Order XXIII, rule 3, an appeal lies from it under Order XLIII, rule 1, clause (m) and section 96(3) is not a bar to such a appeal. (1993 B. 205, not foll.): 29 SLR 437: 1936 Sind 59. Since a consent decree merely embodies the forms of the contract between the parties and is a mere capture of argument on which it is founded, a right of appeal from this decree is not given. Where, however, the terms of the decree not agreed to by the parties are imposed upon them by court, the court does not and could not have acted under Order XXIII, rule 3, C.P. Code when passing the decree.

The High Court of Ajmer had said that an agreement to accept the decision of a court as that of an arbitrator will bar an appeal: 15 L 726: 1934 L 176(2); AIR 1953 Ajmer 31 (36). Where parties to a suit come to an agreement that the ultimate decision of the court will be final and it would not be open to appeal, the decree passed in such circumstances would in essence, amount to a consent decree based on agreement arrived at between the parties and would not be appealable. But where the agreement provided, that 'the parties empower the court to grant permission to the Commissioner to take additional evidence if the latter thinks it necessary, the High Court of Allahabad said that the court may after hearing the parties pass order which it may deem suitable and the order will not be appealable or subject to revision. These words related only to the grant of permission to Commissioner to take additional evidence, if necessary. It was not in respect of the ultimate decision of the suit and the agreement did not preclude the parties from preferring an appeal from the ultimate decision of the case: AIR 1934 All 789. In a suit filed in normal course in a court having jurisdiction, a Commissioner was appointed who, after inspecting the locality submitted his plans and reports. The parties dispensed with oral evidence and invited the judge to make a local inspection and he accordingly inspected the locality. Both the parties agreed to abide by the decision of the court after his personal inspection. The judge gave his decision of the court after his personal inspection. The judge gave his decision on the basis of Commissioner's plans and reports and the notes of his personal inspection. A full and complete Judgment recording his findings on the issue with reasons, therefore, was given and was followed by a decree. It was held that the proceedings were not in any sense *extra cur sum curiae*. The suit was one triable by the court in the normal course. The only deviation from the normal procedure was that the observations of the judge in the course of his local inspection were substituted for the local evidence of witness, with the consent of the parties. It was not, therefore, (1) a consent decree and section 96(3) did not bar an appeal from it. The decision was not also in the nature of an award; (2) that if, on the basis of the notes of local inspection and the commissioner's plans and reports alone, without more, the decision of the court could be shown to be erroneous in fact or in law, the appellant was entitled to do so, unless he had agreed expressly or by necessary implication to give up the right of appeal; (3) that the words "abide by the decision", without more, did not imply an abandonment or giving up of the right of appeal: 1956 AWR 517. According to the High Court of Patna, an agreement between the parties that they would not adduce any oral evidence and the court would write out a judgment and the party who had the *onus* to prove the case would lose, does not amount to an agreement that even when the decision was wrong in law as to the question of *onus* of proof they will not appeal against the decision. In all such cases, the question is whether the parties had agreed to abide by the decision. If not, their right to appeal from decision of the court is not taken away; *Dulhin Mahabati Kuer* v. *Raghunandan Prasad Singh*, 1957 BLJR 658: AIR 1958 Pat 249.

7. A Suit where Several Issues were Framed

Where in a suit several issues were framed on the pleadings, but there had been a statement by counsel for the parties to the effect that only decision on issue No. 1 might be arrived at and if the decision was in favour of the plaintiff then the suit should be decreed irrespective of the other defences and if the decision on that issue was against the plaintiff then the plaintiff's suit should be dismissed, and the trial court, deciding the issue in the favor of plaintiff, decreed the suit, the High Court of Allahabad examined the nature of a consent decree and held, that the decree was not a consent decree, but was one passed on merits after certain pleas had been given up, and, therefore, the appeal from the decree to the lower appellate court was a proper appeal: *Sat Narain Pandey* v. *Dhurva Narain*, 1958 All LJ 526: AIR 1959 All 22: 1958 All WR (HC) 631, where the parties to a suit agree and say that the determination of their disputes by a third person is to be final between them, it is to be regarded as an undertaking not to appeal: 69 OLJ 173: 62 O. 229: 1935 C 239. When a party offers to be bound by a statement it becomes conclusive under the Indian Oaths Act and it is on that the court decides. The decree in such a case is not a consent decree: 15 L 305: 1934 L 67 (1). The case in which an appeal is barred under section 96(3). C.P. Code, are those in which the decree is passed on consent of parties. It is not necessary for the application of section 96(3) that there should have been a compromise duly recorded under Order XXIII, C.P. Code. But there must be consent of the parties to the particular decree. The fact that the parties make certain admissions of fact and even express their view of the law, would not make the decree a consent decree, when they leave the decision to court and do not intimate either expressly or impliedly that they would accept that decision. Hence, an appeal is not barred in such a case under section 96(3): ILR (1949) A. 604. Where the plaintiff accepted the statement of the defendant admitting almost the whole claim of the plaintiff and the court instead of passing a decree in terms of the statement of the parties which it recorded, proceeded to deliver judgment and purported to pass a decree on the merits of the case, although in view of these statements it cut short the discussion regarding evidence: the High Court at Bilaspur held, (i) that an appeal to the District Judge was not barred under section 96(3) as no consent decree had been passed; (ii) Held further, that if a consent decree had been passed an appeal would not have been competent under Order XLIII, rule 1(m) because after parties statements were recorded there was no contest before the court: AIR 1954 Bilaspur 4. A person not party to the suit can appeal against the compromise decree: 22 CLJ 333: 20 CWN 178. A consent decree in a partition suit as between some of the parties is not binding on any of the parties: 27 J.C. 242. An appeal lies against a decree passed on a compromise entered into by a Vakil without reference to his client. 41 M. 233 (23 MLJ 381, Distt.; 21 M. 274, foll.) About appointment of a Commissioner with consent, it was held that an order directing the appointment of a Commissioner with the consent of parties does not come under clause (3) of the section: 29 MLJ 219; also *see* 27 MLJ 173. The fact that defendant does not raise any objection to a particular relief is eventually decreed; 49 LC 840: 15 NLR 39.

8. Consent Decree Passed in Appeal – Not Appealable

In order that an appeal may be barred under section 96(3) against a consent decree, the consent decree must be a valid one. High Court of Allahabad held that the contention that even if a consent decree passed by appellate court was a valid decree, a valid appeal would lie against it because section 96(3) would apply to appeals from consent decree passed in appeal by virtue of section 108, and furthermore, the principle of *estopple* upon which section 96(3) is based applies equally to appellate decrees which have been passed on consent of the parties; *Audh Behari Lal* v. *Faqir Rai,* AIR 1951 All 236: 1951 AWR (HC) 488. (Overruled): *Baqridan* v. *Bashir Ahmad Khan,* 1955 All LJ 850: AIR 1956 All 94: ILR (1956) 1 All 586.

9. Question of Limitation not Decided by the Trial Court

The High Court of Gujarat said that where a question of limitation is not decided by the trial court the appellate court cannot decide the issue and decide against the plaintiff without giving him an opportunity to produce evidence; *Abdul Matin* v. *Abdul Aziz,* AIR 1990 Gau 70: (1990) 1 Cur CC 438.

10. Determination of Maintainability of Appeal

In the case of Raja Kulkarni, the Supreme Court laid down the principles for deciding the question of maintainability of an appeal. The Court held that it is for appellate court to determine the competence of appeal. A party cannot be prevented from filing an appeal. Ordinary consequences of filing of appeal follow even if the appeal is not valid or competent. Whether the appeal is valid or competent is a question entirely for the appellate court before whom the appeal is filed to determine, and this determination is possible only after the appeal is heard, but there is nothing to prevent a party from filing an appeal which may ultimately be found to be incompetent, *e.g.*, when it is held to be barred by limitation or that it does not lie before that court or is concluded by a finding of fact under section 100 of the Civil Procedure Code. From the mere fact that such an appeal is held to be not maintainable for any ground whatsoever, it does not follow that there was no appeal pending before the Court; *Raja Kulkarni* v. *State of Bombay*, AIR 1954 SC 73: 1954 SCJ 50: 1954 SCR 384: 1954 (1) Mad LJ.

11. Negligence by Counsel

In the case of Bihar Electricity Board the Supreme Court examined the consequence of negligence by the counsel and said that failure to file Vakalatnama in spite of directions by court, dismissal of appeal due to negligence of Counsel is not proper; *Bihar State Electricity Board* v. *Bhowra Kankanee Collieries Ltd.*, AIR 1982 SC 60: 1984 (Sup) SCC 597: 1982 Pat LJR 22 (SC): 1982 Guj LH 168.

12. Appeal—Condonation of Delay

In the case of R.K. Ramachandran appeal was filed after delay of 565 days ignoring opinion of District Government Pleader. No reasonable or satisfactory explanation for inordinate delay in filing appeal was offered. Discretion exercised by High Court in condoning delay was held to be neither proper nor judicious. Order condoning delay was unsustainable and was set aside. The Supreme Court held that the High Court does not appear to have examined the reply filed by the appellant as reference to the same is conspicuous by its absence from the order. The Court said that we are not satisfied that in the facts and circumstances of this case, any explanation, much less a reasonable or satisfactory one had been offered by the respondent-State for condonation of the inordinate delay of 565 days. The discretion exercised by the High Court was thus neither proper nor judicious. The order condoning the delay cannot be sustained. This appeal, therefore, succeeds and the impugned order was set aside; *P.K. Ramachandran* v. *State of Kerala*, AIR 1998 SC 2276: 1997 (3) Mad LW 428: (1997) 7 SCC 556: 1997 (2) Ker LT 647: (1997) 6 SCALE 209.

13. Appeal—Suit for Declaration of Title

The Supreme Court in *Monoji Rao* v. *T. Krishna*, examined the case where claim made on the basis of allotment letter and possession certificate issued by Development Authority. Defendant a trespasser in suit premises admitted title of plaintiff. It was held that order of first appellate court holding that documents clearly establish claim made by plaintiff and declaration had to be given in favour of plaintiff fell within region of appreciation of material on record. Therefore, no interference was called for with finding of High Court that trial court ought to have decreed the suit; *Manoji Rao* v. *T. Krishna*, AIR 2001 SC 623: (2001) 2 SCC 384: JT 2001 (1) SC 621.

In *Santosh Hajari* v. *Purushottam Tiwari*, the trial court found that ownership of suit property vested in plaintiff and negatived plea of adverse possession holding that he forcibly occupied disputed area, reversed by first appellate court The High Court dismissed second appeal *in limine* holding that no substantial question of law arose for determination.—Defendant's plea of adverse possession raised substantial question of law as plaintiff's suit was barred by limitation under article 65 of Limitation Act.—High Court order suffered from legal infirmity.—Case was remanded back for fresh decision uninfluenced by observations made; *Santosh Hazari* v. *Purushottam Tiwari (dead) by LRs.*, AIR 2001 SC 965: (2001) 2 SCC 179: JT 2001 (2) SC 407.

14. Sections 96 and 47—Maintainability of Appeal from Execution

Mortgage decree passed.—Failure by mortgagor to carry out the terms of decree.—Mortgagee applying for execution of decree.—Application for execution not properly couched and moved as application in the suit.— The Supreme Court held that applications in substance were seeking execution.—Appeal against the order passed on application was held maintainable; *Smt. Ashalata Debi* v. *Sri Jadu Nath Roy*, AIR 1954 SC 409: 1954 SCA 635: 1954 SCJ 690: (1955) 1 SCR 150.

Appeal against an order passed under Order XXI, rule 58 – Whether a regular appeal or a miscellaneous appeal—

Andhra Pradesh High Court examined whether a miscellanous appeal lies against an order passed under Order XXI, rule 58. This Miscellaneous Appeal was filed 'against an order passed in an Execution Application filed under Order XXI, rule 58(1) of the Civil Procedure Code by the appellant herein holding that he has not established his claim over the petition schedule property.

At the inception stage, the simple question that arose for consideration in this matter was whether it is a 'regular Appeal' or a 'Miscellaneous Appeal' that lies against an order passed after adjudication in a claim petition filed under Order XXI, rule 58 of the Civil Procedure Code as amended in 1976. In the court below the claim petition was rejected on merits holding that the appellant did not establish his claim over the property in question.

It was held that against an order made under rule 58(3) Order XXI only a Miscellaneous Appeal lies and not a Regular Appeal, since the application made under Order XXI, rule 58(1) can in no way be treated as a regular suit. In the light of these two decisions and the different provisions of the Code referred to hereinbefore, the court observed we are of the firm opinion that the order made under rule 58(3) of Order XXI of the amended Code has only the status of 'deemed decree' and not a 'decree' by itself and that such orders are not covered by the definition under section 2(2) namely of 'decree' so as to attract the provisions of section 96 of the Civil Procedure Code and therefore, only a 'Miscellaneous appeal' lies against such 'order' and not a 'Regular appeal'. *B. Nookaraju* v. *M.S.N. Charities*, AIR 1994 AP 334: 1994 (2) ALT 125: 1994 (3) Civ LJ 382.

15. Section 96 and Section 115

A Full Bench of the Madhya Pradesh High Court considered whether simply a revision or an appeal is maintainable against an order passed under rule 58 of Order XXI. The material facts giving rise to this reference, briefly, are as follows: In a suit instituted by the applicants against the opponents in the Court of the Civil Judge, II Class, Neemuch, an application for the grant of temporary injunction, submitted by the applicants was rejected. Aggrieved by that order, the applicants preferred an appeal in the Court of Addl. Judge, Neemuch to the Court of District Judge, Mandsaur, but that appeal was also dismissed. Hence, the applicants preferred a revision petition under section 115, C.P.C. before this court on 5-11-1984. Prior to that date section 115, C.P.C. was amended by the Code of Civil Procedure (Madhya Pradesh Amendment) Act 29 of 1984 (hereinafter referred to as 'the Amending Act'), which came into force on 14-8-1984. The effect of the amendment made in section 115. C.P.C. was considered by a Division Bench of this Court in *Pirbux's* case and it was held that as a result of the amendment, the jurisdiction of the High Court under section 115, C.P.C. to revise an order passed in appeal by a District Court was taken away irrespective of the fact that the suit which gave rise to the appeal before the District Court was pending when the Amending Act 29 of 1984 came into force. The Division Bench held that its view was supported by the decision of the Division Bench at Gwalior in C.R. No. 942 of 1984 (*Gayaprasad* v. *Deepchand*) (reported in 1985 Cur Civ LJ 91) when these decisions were brought to the notice of the learned Single Judge, who heard this revision petition, the learned Judge doubted the correctness of those decisions. Hence, he referred the matter to the Chief Justice. That is how this Full Bench had been constituted to decide the question of the maintainability of this revision petition.

It was held that in the absence of any express provision to the contrary, in the Amending Act supervisory or revisional power under section 115, CPC has to be exercised in accordance with the provisions of law in force at the time when the power is sought to be exercised. It, therefore, follows that after 14-8-1984 when the Amending Act 29 of 1984 came into force, the High Court is empowered to exercise only such powers as are conferred on the High Court by the provisions of section 115, CPC as amended. In this view of the matter the Court did not see any cogent reason to differ from the view taken in the Division Bench decisions of this Court in Civil Revn. No. 6 of 1985 (reported in (1986 Cur Civ LJ 36) *Pirbux* v. *Babulal* and in Civil Revn. No. 942 of 1984 (*Gayaprasad* v. *Deepchand* (reported in 1985 Cur Civ LJ 91). The Court further said that as the revision, petition in the instant case was directed against an order passed by a district court in appeal, arising out of a suit of the value of less than twenty thousand rupees, it is not maintainable under section 115, CPC. The revision petition, therefore, failed and was accordingly dismissed; *Ramchandra* v. *Dattatraya,* 1986 Jab LJ 344: 1986 MPLJ 406: AIR 1986 MP 191 (FB).

The High Court of Madhya Pradesh in the case of *Sawal Singh* examined whether a revision lies under section 115 against a decree passed in original jurisdiction.

As held by the Supreme Court in *Smt. Ganga Bai* v. *Vijay Kumar,* AIR 1974 SC 1126: 1974 Mah LJ 602: 1974 MPLJ 629: (1974) 2 SCC 393: (1974) 3 SCR 882, it is well-settled that though there is an inherent right in every person to bring a suit of a civil nature, a right of appeal inheres in no one and an appeal for its maintainability must have the clear authority of law. The right of appeal is thus a creature of statute. Similarly, if a right of revision is claimed, it should be conferred by a provision of law. In this connection difference in the language used in section 96, CPC and section 115, CPC is noteworthy. Section 96, CPC provides that an appeal shall lie from every decree passed by any Court exercising original jurisdiction, to the Court authorised to hear appeals from the decrees of such Court. Section 96, CPC thus confers a right of appeal. On the other hand, section 115, CPC which deals with revisions provides that the High Court may call for the record of any case and if certain conditions are fulfilled, may make such order as it thinks fit. It is true, as urged on behalf of the petitioner, that the use of the word "may" in section 115, CPC does not mean that the High Court has an unfettered discretion in dealing with a case under section 115, CPC. But the fact that the discretion of High Court under section 115, CPC is controlled by that provision does not lead to the conclusion that a substantive right is conferred on a litigant by section 115, CPC; *Sawal Singh* v. *Ramsakhi,* 2002 (4) MPHT 200: 2003 AIHC 1737: (2002) 2 MPJR 169.

16. Nature of Appeal and Revision – Sections 96 and 115

The Supreme Court examined the difference between an appeal under section 96 and a revision petition under section 115 and said that appeal and revision petition are separate proceedings. A revision petition was filed during pendency of first appeal and was dismissed. Appeal was filed before Supreme Court against orders passed by the High Court in revision. It was held that the appellate court is not to be influenced by the observations recorded in revision during pendency of appeal; *Shrinarayan Singh* v. *Surajnarayan Gupta,* (2005) 12 SCC 417.

17. Nature of First Appeal – It is a Continuation of Suit

The Supreme Court in the case of *Bhogmal* held that appeal is a continuation of suit. *Purshotam Reddy* v. *K. Satish,* (2008) 8 SCC 505. It has been held by the apex Court that an appeal is a continuation of the suit; *Bhagmal* v. *Munsi,* (2007) 1 SCR 1114.

18. Section 104 and Order XLIII(1)

Andhra High Court in the case of Elisha examined the relative provisions under section 96 and Order 43(1), in the case of *Elisha*. The note of the Registry stated that the L.P.As. of the present nature were barred under the provisions of section 104(2) of the Civil Procedure Code. Mr. S.A. Chari, learned counsel for the appellants raised the question that the appeals were never preferred under Order XLIII, rule 1, C.P.C., but were filed under section 96 of C.P.C. read with section 11 of the Andhra Pradesh (Telangana Area) Societies Registration Act, 1850 Fasli (hereinafter shortly referred to as "the Act'). In as much as the decision of the learned Principal District Judge was a decree as defined under section 2(2) of the C.P.C., it is appealable as provided under section 96 of C.P.C.

The Court said that there was no dispute about the fact that the first respondent was a Society registered under the Act. The second respondent was its Chairman and official representative. The dispute between the parties related to its management for redressal of which the application was filed by the appellants before the Principal District Judge, Rangareddy District, which is the designated Court for the purpose. The application was dismissed on merits. As the application had been filed under section 11 of the Act, it is submission of Mr. Chari that the decision of the District Judge finally adjudicated the rights of the parties as were claimed in the application and hence the decision is in the nature of a decree from which the appeal shall lie to this Court as any other appeal from the decrees passed by the District Judge.

It may be noted that Order XLIII, rule 1 of C.P.C. itself specifies the nature of the orders which are appealable. An appeal to be maintainable under Order XLIII, rule 1 of C.P.C. must be from the orders which are contemplated under that provision, as has been considered in *Varalakshmi* v. *Veerareddi,* cited at (supra). All orders passed by the Court are not *ipso facto* appealable, under the provisions of Order XLIII, rule 1 of C.P.C., but may be under the provisions of a special statute itself.

In the result, the Court held that the learned Single Judge had rightly held that the appeals were not maintainable. Consequently, the present appeals were dismissed with costs; *S. Elisha* v. *World Missionary Evangelism,* 1997 (3) ALT 155.

19. Sections 96, 100, 104, 105—Appeal—Permissibility

No appeal lies on a mere finding of the court unless provided under the provisions of the Code; see *Ganga Bai* v. *Vijay Kumar,* AIR 1974 SC 1126: 1974 Mah LJ 602: 1974 MPLJ 629: (1974) 2 SCC 393: 1974 (3) SCR 882.

20. Challenge to Preliminary Decree along with the Final Decree is not Permissible

Section 97 provides that the correctness of the preliminary decree cannot be challenged if no appeal is preferred against it. It clearly provides that if it is not challenged in appeal, it would be treated as correct and binding on the parties. In such a case an appeal against the final decree would inevitably be limited to the points arising from proceedings taken subsequent to the preliminary decree and the same would be dealt with on the basis that the preliminary decree was correct and is beyond challenge; *Kaushalya Devi* v. *Baijnath Sayal,* AIR 1961 SC 790: 1962 (1) SCJ 684: 1961 (3) SCR 769.

21. First Appeal is a Matter of Valuable Right

The Supreme Court has made it clear in the case of Madhukar that duty of High Court is to deal with all issues and evidence led by parties before recording its findings.—Parties have a right to be heard both on questions of law and fact. High Court order being cryptic ignoring relevant aspects was set aside. Case was remanded back for fresh disposal according to law. In the case of Madhukar the Supreme Court held that sitting as a Court of first appeal, it was the duty of the High Court to deal with all the issues and the evidence led by the parties before recording its findings. It has failed to discharge the obligations placed on a first appellate court. The Court said that judgment under appeal is so cryptic that none of the relevant aspects have been noticed. The appeal has been decided in a very unsatisfactory manner. First appeal is a valuable right and the parties have a right to be heard both on questions of law and facts and the judgment in the first appeal must address itself to all the issues of law and fact and decide it by giving reasons in support of the findings; *Madhukar* v. *Sangram,* AIR 2001 SC 2171: (2001) 4 SCC 756: JT 2001 (5) SC 72.

22. *Locus Standi* of Appeal from Original Decree

The Supreme Court held in *Baldev Singh* v. *Surinder Mohan Sharma,* AIR 2003 SC 225 that only the appeal of a person aggrieved by and dissatisfied with the judgment and decree is maintainable. (2003) 1 SCC 34: AIR 2003 SC 225: 2002 AIR SCW 4674. The Supreme Court again examined the question of right to appeal; *see* 2004 SCC (Cri) 1681; *Transmission Corporation of Andhra Pradesh* v. *Ch. Prabhakar,* (2004) 5 SCC 551: 2004 AIR SCW 3223: AIR 2004 SC 3368; *See* also *Tirupati Balaji Developers Pvt. Ltd.* v. *State of Bihar,* AIR 2004 SC 2351: 2004 AIR SCW 2522: (2004) 5 SCC 1.

The High Court of Rajasthan discussed the availability of the right to appeal and said that as a rule it is only a party to the proceeding in the primary court or tribunal who has the right to prefer an appeal against the order of that Tribunal provided of course he is aggrieved by it, and if any other person happens to be aggrieved by that order, and his interests are affected thereby, he can file an appeal against it only by leave of the court of appeal but not otherwise. The grant of leave to file an appeal to voters who had not made an election petition themselves and who were, therefore, not a party before the tribunal may well be fraught with the gravest danger, and lead to untold harassment of successful candidate or candidates, and occasion endless prolongation of enquiries into matters related to their election. The High Court would, therefore, be extremely loath to allow such persons to file an appeal, against the order of the election Tribunal except perhaps under rare and most exceptional circumstances: *Heersingh* v. *Veerka,* 1958 Raj LW 251: AIR 1958 Raj 181: ILR (1958) 8 Raj 380. A party cannot appeal against a decision in his favour on the ground that one of the findings is against him: 24 LC 36: 51 IC 622; *See* also 2 LW 101: 27 IC 861: 3 Al 52 (FB). When a suit is dismissed for want of cause of action, there cannot be an appeal by the defendant on a finding: 20 CWN 1354. The High Court of Madras said that though a suit is dismissed, a defendant has a right of appeal and for that purpose it is open to the parties to go behind the decree and see really what the adjudication is: 25 MLJ 379: 36 MLJ 641: 30 Mad 447; 9 CWN 584. If a person who ought not to have been made a defendant as such, he cannot appeal. An order directing the removal of a party's name from array of parties is in substance though not in form, a decree and an appeal lies therefrom: *Shair Ali* v. *Jagmohan Ram,* AIR (18) 1931 All 333 (2): 53 All 466. The said Court further said that any plaintiff or a defendant has a right to appeal without the recurrence of the other parties to the suit: 22 B. 718. The representative of a deceased person can appeal from the decree, although he may not have been brought on the record: 12 MLJ 435.

The right of appeal can be exercised only by those in whom the power is vested expressly or impliedly by the statue. In a suit under Order XXI, rule 103, against the official receiver, a decree was passed in favor of the plaintiff. The official receiver did not prefer an appeal. The appellant, who was one of the creditors, appealed against the decree insofar as it related to the official receiver. The said Court held that the appellant not having been party to the suit, was incompetent to prefer the appeal: 57 M. 360: 66 MLJ 532. Agent authorized to defend suit was authority to file appeal – Not necessary: PLR 470: ILR 1957 Punj 1443.

23. Powers of First Appellate Court

The Supreme Court has made it clear that first appellate court is within its powers in interfering with findings of fact reached by trial court, but only after considering the matter both on facts and on law. *Tarak Nath Shah* v. *Bhutoria Bros. Pvt. Ltd.*, AIR 2002 SC 2063: 2002 AIR SCW 2120: (2002) 5 SCC 15; *See* also *Banarsi* v. *Ram Phal*, AIR 2003 SC 1989: 2003 AIR SCW 1494: (2003) 9 SCC 606 and *Shiv Shakti Co-op. Housing Society, Nagpur* v. *Swaraj Developers*, AIR 2003 SC 2434: 2003 AIR SCW 2445: (2003) 6 SCC 659. The Supreme Court has held in the case of Meenakshi also that a court of appeal should not ordinarily interfere with the discretion used by the trial court. *M. Meenakshi* v. *Metadin Agrawal*, AIR 2007 SC (Supp) 1848: 2006 AIR SCW 4323; *See* also *Chintamani Ammal* v. *Nand Gopal Gounder*, (2007) 4 SCC 163: AIR 2007 SC (Supp) 593: 2007 AIR SCW 1629, in which the apex Court stressed that the appellate court while doing so must assign reasons.

In the case of *Arundhati* the Supreme Court mandated how a first appeal should be disposed off. The Court held that a first appeal can not be dismissed at the admission stage. The Supreme Court held that the High Court erred in dismissing the first appeal at the admission stage itself without issuing notice to the respondent and without looking into the evidence. *Arundhati* v. *Irnna*, (2008) 3 SCC 181: AIR 2008 SC (Supp) 1570; *See* also *Thota Laxmi Vankat Bala* v. *Muttam Setti Seethamma*, (2008) 11 SCC 218; *B.K. Shri Harsha* v. *Bharat Heavy Electricals*, AIR 2008 SC 1267: 2008 AIR SCW 1301: (2008) 4 SCC 48; *Brihanmumbai Mahanagar Palika* v. *Akruti Nirman Pvt. Ltd.*, AIR 2008 SC (Supp) 1415: (2008) 3 SCC 78; *Ramniwas Gupta* v. *Mumtaj Hasan*, (2008) 17 SCC 362; *Payappar Sree Dharmasastha Temple A. Com.* v. *A.K. Joseph*, (2009) 14 SCC 628: 2010 AIR SCW 3187 and *Indian Oil Corpn. Ltd.* v. *Raja Transport Pvt. Ltd.*, (2009) 8 SCC 520: 2009 AIR SCW 7354: 2010 (1) ALJ 751. The Supreme Court has directed that where there are triable issues, the first appeal should not be disposed off summarily *B.K. Sriharsa* v. *Bharat Heavy Electrical Ltd.*, AIR 2008 SC 1267: 2008 AIR SCW 1301: (2008) 4 SCC 48; *Naga Shelly* v. *Vijay Kumar*, (2009) 10 SCALE 124.

24. Forum

In a case *A* sued *B* for redemption of a house on payment of Rs. 1000. *B* pleaded that *A* had admitted *B* as owner and that he had rebuilt the house, incurring a cost of Rs. 10,000, which *A* must pay in addition to the mortgage money. The subordinate judge passed a preliminary decree for redemption of mortgage on payment of Rs. 9050. *B* filed an appeal to the High Court and not to the District Judge as the value of the subject-matter in a redemption suit was the amount adjudicated by the trial court, Rs. 9050, and not the valuation given by the plaintiff, Rs. 1000. [1926 L 370 (FB), foll. 106 PR 1895 (FB), held overruled.]: 148 IC 324: 1933 L 155. Where a suit for declaration valued at

Rs. 6000, the court has to find whether there was a valid subsisting mortgage debt of Rs. 21,000 in favor of plaintiff and the suit is tried by a senior subordinate judge, the suit being a declaratory suit will not be governed by S. S, Suits Validation Act and the proper valuation for purposes of jurisdiction being Rs. 21,000 the appeal in the suit will lie to the High Court and not to the district court: AIR 1955 HP 50. In a case the suit was valued at Rs. 150. Trial court decided that suit was undervalued – No definite decision was given as to what should be correct value. Appeal lay to District Judge: AIR 1953 Sau 65. According to the High Court of Patna an appeal from a decree of a subordinate judge will not lie straight to the High Court where the value of the original suit in which the decree was made did not exceed Rs. 5000 on the allegation made by the appellant that the original suit should have been valued at more than Rs. 5000, and in such a case the High Court cannot direct an independent enquiry to verify that allegation and thereafter to admit the appeal on the verification of the same; (*Amir Nawab* v. *Wajeda Begum,* ILR 6 Pat 420: AIR 1927 Pat 289, Overruled.): ILR 1958 BLJR 246.

25. Section 96 and 100, Order I, Rule 1

Relief to party not having preferred appeal-Against the judgment – The Supreme Court held that relief to the party which did not prefer appeal is not permissible; *Chokalingaswami Idol* v. *Gnanapragasam,* AIR 2008 SC 2025: 2008 AIR SCW 2676: (2008) 4 SCC 219.

Sections 96 and 92(1)(f) – *Locus Standi* of Appeal by third party against decree allowing sale of trust property by District Court – Third Party, if "aggrieved" – If a third party established that he is interested in the welfare of the Trust, held he would be an "aggrieved party" having *locus standi* to prefer an appeal; *Swami Shankaranand* v. *Mahant Sh. Sadguru Sarnanand,* AIR 2008 SC 2763: 2008 AIR SCW 4595: (2008) 8 SCALE 698.

26. Sections 96 and 105

Memorandum of appeal – It has been held in the case of *Wada Arun Asbestos* that any error, defect and irregularity in any order affecting the decision may be set-forth in the memorandum; *Wada Arun Asbestos P. Ltd.* v. *Gujarat Water Supply and Sewerage Board,* AIR 2009 SC 1027: 2009 AIR SCW 156: (2009) 2 SCC 432.

27. Section 96 Order XLI, Rule 31

The Supreme Court has laid down that the appellate court should state the points for determination, decision thereon, reasons for the decision and the relief granted; *B.V. Nagesh* v. *H.V. Srinivasa Murti,* 2010 (7) Supreme 438: JT 2010 (10) SC 551: 2010 AIR SCW 6184: (2009) 2 SCC 432: (2010) 10 SCALE 222.

28. Section 54 of LA Act and Section 96 of CPC

Allahabad High Court considered the maintainability of a subsequent writ petition while an appeal under section 96, CPC was already dismissed as withdrawn in the case of *Major Jasbinder Singh Bala* v. *IInd Additional District Judge.* In the said case simultaneously the present writ petition being Writ Petition No. 38064 of 2002 reported on 5.9.2002 was filed on 5.9.2002 itself. Thus two options were exercised by the petitioner on the same date. It is really speaking, a case of forum hunting. The petitioner had already availed the statutory remedy of filing a First Appeal under section 96 of the Code of Civil Procedure (hereinafter referred to as the C.P.C.) read with section 54 of the Act against the judgment and order dated 29.4.2002 as the order passed under section 30 of the Act amounted to a decree within the meaning of section 2(2) C.P.C. and had attained finality and would remain alive unless set aside by the superior Court. The petitioner being conscious of this, had availed of his statutory remedy under section 96, C.P.C.

It is also abundantly clear that the petitioner was having full knowledge of the fact that he had availed of the statutory remedy by way of availing first appeal against the judgment and order dated 29.4.2002 passed under section 30 of the Act. The plea taken by the petitioner in para 42 of the writ petition is that it was not possible for him to file first appeal on account of the fact that it would incur heavy Court fees. From a plain reading of para 42 of the writ petition, it is clear that the facts as stated do not disclose that in fact the petitioner had already availed of the statutory remedy under section 96, C.P.C. The petitioner had given the reference of the judgment of this Court in *Shyamlata Jauhari* (supra) wherein it has been held that the award given by the learned Land Acquisition Collector is not a decree under section 2(2) of the C.P.C. and therefore not appealable.

In the instant case, the judgment and order under challenge was by the Court deciding a reference under Section 30 of the Act. Therefore reference to the said judgment of this Court was totally misplaced and the ratio of the said judgment had no bearing in that case. It was contended that when the first appeal was dismissed as withdrawn on 17-12-2003 a simple order of dismissal for withdrawal was passed. The appellant in that appeal did not get the appeal dismissed as withdrawn with liberty to file a fresh matter and, therefore, the petitioner had acquiesced and the decree against which the first appeal was filed also had become final and had attained finality. Thus, the writ petition is not maintainable.

The contents reveal that the petitioner had full knowledge of what he was doing. Petitioner has clearly indulged in an activity, which is nothing but an abuse of the process of the Court and, therefore, he is not entitled to any equitable relief in extraordinary discretionary jurisdiction of the Court. He has not come with clean hands. He has in fact suppressed the material facts about filing of the appeal simultaneously.

In view of the above, the Court expressed the considered opinion that the petitioner had not approached this Court with clean hands and he was guilty of suppressing material information. He had filed an appeal against the impugned decision and had voluntarily withdrawn the same without seeking any liberty to approach any other forum or file the present writ petition. The conduct of the petitioner in proceeding in such a manner amounted to abuse of process of the Court and was thus, held to be reprehensible. It further justified no interference at his behest under this Writ Petition; 2006 (2) AWC 1545.

29. Section 96, CPC and Section 49(1) of LA Act

The Supreme Court of India, in the case of *Deepchand* examined whether an adjudication by the civil court in a reference under section 49(1) of the LA Act amounts to a decree and consequently an appeal under section 96 lies.

The facts lie in a short compass. Notification under section 4(1) and declaration under section 6, of the Act were published in the State Gazette acquiring land measuring 2 acres 46 cents (approximately) on Biaora village in Rajgarh District. The appellant had objected under section 49(1) of the Act to the acquisition, contending that the entire land including his factory and office building should be acquired, without which the Act should not be put in operation. Thereon, reference under section 49(1) was made to the Civil Court which by order dated April 29, 1969 held that the land proposed to be acquired did not form an integral part of appellants' factory and office buildings and answered the reference accordingly. The appellants carried the matter in appeal to the High Court. In the High Court, when an objection was raised on behalf of the State that the order of the Civil Court is not a decree and as such it is not appealable obviously under section 96 of CPC, it upheld the objection and dismissed the appeal as not maintainable. Therefore, the Court held that the determination under section 49(1) of the Act is not a decree within the meaning of section 2(2), CPC and that an appeal under section 96, CPC does not lie. The appeal is accordingly dismissed, but in the circumstances, without costs; *Deep Chand* v. *Land Acquisition Officer*, AIR 1994 SC 1901: JT 1994 (3) SC 319: (1994) 108 PLR 197.

Section 96 – Appeal filed by the LRs. who were not impleaded as party to the suit—

Supreme Court of India decided the question of appeal filed by the LRs. in the case of *Krishna Murti*. This civil appeal arises out of judgment and decree rendered by Karnataka High Court on 22-3-1999 filed under section 96, CPC against judgment and decree dated 11-10-1996 passed in O.S. No. 3656/81 on the file of City Civil Judge, Bangalore, decreeing the suit for declaration. By the impugned judgment, the High Court was set aside the judgment and decree dated 11-10-1996. Hence, the civil appeal was filed by the LRs. of deceased Krishnamurthy S. Setlur (original plaintiff).

According to the trial court, therefore, between 1946 and 1962-63, K.S. Setlur was in possession. He had possessory title. He was in possession till 1970 when he was unlawfully dispossessed and in view of the judgment of the High Court dated 14-8-1981 possessory title in the suit lands had vested in K.S. Setlur (plaintiff). In the circumstances, the trial court decreed the suit in favour of the plaintiff. The trial court declared that Narsimha Setty did not derive title from the LRs. of Iyengar under the above two sale deeds dated 21-5-1970 and 7-9-1970. Aggrieved by the said decision of the trial court dated 11-10-1996, the matter was carried in appeal by the LRs. of Iyengar and their alienees to the High Court under section 96, CPC *vide* RFA No. 672/96. By the impugned judgment dated 22-3-1999, the appeal filed by the defendants stood allowed and the impugned judgment of the trial court was set aside. Hence, this civil appeal. As stated at the outset, the present civil appeal was filed by the LRs.

of the deceased K.S. Setlur, the original plaintiff. This civil appeal arose out of the judgment of the High Court dated 22-3-1999 in RFA No. 672/96 filed under section 96, CPC.

It was urged on behalf of the appellants-plaintiff that the suit was based on adverse possession. According to the appellants, Shyamala Raju was the tenant of K.S. Setlur since deceased. According to the appellants, Shyamala Raju had attorned the tenancy in 1946 in favour of K.S. Setlur. According to the appellants, Shyamala Raju had surrendered possession to K.S. Setlur on 23-4-1962. According to the appellant, the High Court had categorically declared *vide* judgment dated 14-8-1981 in RSA No. 545/73 that the possessory title stood vested in K.S. Setlur. It is urged on behalf of the appellants that Iyengar had also instituted a suit for permanent injunction being Suit No. 79/49 in which it has been held that Iyengar was not in possession of the suit lands but he was certainly entitled to file a separate suit for declaration of his title. It was urged on behalf of the appellants that despite liberty being given to Iyengar to institute a separate suit for declaration of title, neither Iyengar nor his LRs. ever instituted a suit for title and, therefore, the possessory title found by the High Court *vide* judgment dated 14-8-1981 in favour of K.S. Setlur cannot be allowed to be reopened in the present proceedings. It was urged on behalf of the appellants that the trial court was right in coming to the conclusion that the possessory title stood vested in K.S. Setlur. In this connection, reliance was placed on judgment dated 14-8-1981 in RSA No. 545/73. According to the appellants, the LRs. of Iyengar, in the above circumstances, had lost their right to recover possession. In this connection, the appellants placed reliance on section 27 of the Limitation Act, 1963. It was urged on behalf of the appellants that the impugned judgment is full of contradictions and inconsistent findings. It was urged on behalf of the appellants that the matter needs to be remitted back since there are fundamental errors in the impugned judgment.

On the other hand, it was urged on behalf of the respondents-defendants that the trial court had failed to appreciate that the judgment of the High Court dated 14-8-1981 in RSA No. 545/73 arose from proceedings/Suit No. 89/63 filed by K.S. Setlur against his alleged tenant, Shyamala Raju. In that suit, the LRs. of K.S. Setlur were not made party defendants. According to the respondents, the present Suit No. 3656/81 filed by K.S. Setlur was a title suit for a declaration that the LRs. of Iyengar had no right, title or interest in the suit lands and that they had no right to transfer/alienate the suit lands in favour of Narsimha Setty and others. According to the respondents, the trial court has erred in treating the present suit as a suit based on adverse possession. According to the respondents, the suit was based on title, it was subsequently amended falsely alleging that the plaintiffs were forcibly dispossessed. According to the respondents, K.S. Setlur was in fact dispossessed in 1953. According to the respondents, the trial court had erred in holding that K.S. Setlur was dispossessed in 1969-70. According to the respondents, the trial court had erred in holding that the tenant's possession during 1946-1963 was the plaintiff's possession, which, according to the respondents, was a fundamental error in the judgment of the trial court. According to the respondents, the judgment of the High Court dated 14-8-1981 was between K.S. Setlur and Shyamala Raju. In that proceedings, LRs. of Iyengar were not party defendants and, therefore, the judgment of the High Court dated 14.8.1981 was not binding on them.

It is true that the litigation was pending for the last several years, however, the Court agreed with the contention advanced on behalf of the appellants that there were serious errors in the impugned judgment which warrants interference under article 136 of the Constitution of India. For the reasons indicated above, without expressing any opinion on the merits of the case, the Court allowed this civil appeal, set aside the impugned judgment of the High Court dated 22-3-1999 in RFA No. 672/96 and remitted the case back to the High Court to decide the said RFA No. 672/96 *de novo* in accordance with law; *Krishnamurthy S. Setlur* v. *O.V. Narasimha Setty,* AIR 2007 SC 1788 on 23 February, 2007.

30. Waiver

Where the plea of limitation is waived, though the suit is time-barred, the decree following is a consent decree and thus not appealable: 39 MLJ 68: 24 CWN 1055 (PC). Agreement to abide by decision of court – Appeal, if lies: 1926 A. 90: 89 IC 586.

31. Decree on Appeal

The High Court of Madras held that an appeal being a continuation of original proceeding, the appellate court's decree is the decree in the suit: 30 M.L.J. 379.

32. Section 96 – Whether the Business was a Joint Venture is not a Question of Fact

In *Gannamani Anasuya* v. *Mrs. Parvathi Amarendra Chowdary,* 2000 1 ALD 533: 2010 6 ALT 518: 2011 2 Civ CC 130 (AP), One of the questions for examination was whether the business was a joint venture is a question of facts.

In the case under reference parties on both the sides were closely interrelated. For convenience sake, they are referred to as arrayed in the Court below. The respondents 1 and 2/the plaintiffs filed the suit inter alia seeking for partition of the plaint 'A' schedule property into 3 equal shares by metes and bounds and to allot two such shares to them and for partition of plaint 'B' schedule properties into 9 equal shares by metes and bounds and to allot 4 such shares to them through the process of Court and directing the defendants 1 to 3 to render accounts in respect of poultry business, which was allegedly run in the plaint 'B' Schedule property from the year 1968 till the date of filing of the suit and for awarding future profits and costs.

Aggrieved by the said Judgment and decree, which was dated 23-4-1993 earlier this very appeal was filed in A.S. No. 1930 of 1993 in this Court. However, this Court did not find in favour with any of the contentions urged on behalf of the appellants, and the same was dismissed as per the judgment and decree dated 29-10-1999, confirming the decree of the Court below.

Thereafter, the appellants filed further appeal to the Supreme Court in Civil Appeal No. 7318 of 2000, which was allowed as per the orders dated 17-5-2007 remanding the appeal to this Court for fresh disposal on the directions as pointed out therein. It is needless to mention that in regard to the issue No.1 the Hon'ble Supreme court held as under:

The Hon'ble Supreme Court held that the question as to whether the business was a joint venture is not being a question of fact, the court should not exercise discretionary jurisdiction under Article 136. Insofar as the immovable property was concerned, having regard to the provisions contained in Section 45 of the Transfer of Property act, it was conceded that Narasimha Murthy had half share. At paragraph 21, the Hon'ble Supreme Court observed that the reasoning of the High Court in regard to Ex.B.8 was not acceptable, dealing of affairs by Defendant No.1 will have a direct bearing on issues. An Admission by Karta H.U.F. would be relevant. There was an admission by Narasimha Murthy of the Hindu undivided family, who was managing the family property, that in terms of Section 58 of the Indian Evidence Act, admitted need not be proved, the document is admitted (Ex.B8) and having regard to the provisions of section 145 of the Indian Evidence Act, the Hon'ble Supreme Court held that the relevant factors have not been considered. That no signatures as such is required on Ex.B.8 in view of the admission made by defendant No.1, and such admission should have been taken into consideration. In paragraph 25 of the said judgment, there is a discussion about the partnership and .... Joint ventures and that the conduct of the parties and how they dealt with the business of the partnership is relevant. ...in view Section 3 of the Limitation Act was relevant and D1 had to explain Ex.B.8 figures and that it was not for appellants... that it is for this Hon'ble Court to frame the points for determination in the light of the submissions made on behalf of the appellants and apart from this, issue Nos.1 and 4 should be decided afresh.

On remand the Court settled fresh issues. The Court found, the main contention on behalf of the appellant apparently runs on the same lines as set forth on a broader perspective denying about the existence of any joint-ness either by investment or by participation about the aforesaid businesses. Having regard to the findings of facts, which remained un-assailed in respect of schedule 'A' property, it is not necessary to delve into the said aspect. Therefore, both the counsel did not make any effort to canvass on the said aspect, hence, as restricted by themselves the question now, which boils down is only to the schedule 'B' the business and Ex.B8.

33. An Admission can be Used against the Maker

The Hon'ble Supreme Court However, observing on Ex.B.8, it was proceeded to the following effect:

> "However, it is difficult for us to accept the reasoning of the High Court in regard to Ex.B.8. Plaintiffs (Respondent Nos.1 and 2) were claiming the property as members of the Hindu undivided family. Admittedly, the interest of the Hindu undivided family was being looked after by Narasimha Murthy and after his death by Defendant No.1 (Respondent No.3). Correspondences were exchanged by and between Appellant Nos.1 and 2 only with Narasimha Murthy and Defendant No.1 (Respondent No.3). Yet again admittedly, Defendant No.1 (Respondent No.3) was the

manager of the Hindu undivided family. His dealing with the appellant in regard to the affairs of the business will have a direct bearing in the matter of determination of the issues raised before us.

An admission made by a party can be used against him. When such admission is made by a Karta of the Hindu undivided family, who is managing the family property as well as family business affairs, the same would be a relevant fact. When a claim was made by the plaintiffs for rendition of accounts in the lis, issuance of a document purported to have been authored by one of the parties, in our opinion, was required to be taken into consideration.

In terms of Section 58 of the Indian Evidence Act, 1872, a thing admitted need not be proved. (See *Shreedhar Govind Kamerkar* v. *Yeshwant Govind Kamerkar*, 2006 (14) SCALE 174: (2006) 13 SCC 481.

It is also a trite law that when in cross-examination a witness accepts the correctness of a document, the same would be relevant. A pleading in regard to existence of a document may be necessary for advancing the case of a party, but when a witness admits a document to be in his own handwriting without anything more, the effect thereof may have to be considered having regard to the provisions contained in Section 145 of the Indian Evidence Act in terms whereof the only requirement would be that his attention is drawn before a writing can be proved. These relevant facts have not been considered by the High Court. The High Court merely proceeded on the basis that Ex.B.8 did not contain any anybody's signature. If the Defendant No.1 accepted the contents of the said document, which, according to him, were noted by him from the books of accounts, authenticity thereof is not in question, and, thus, even in absence of books of accounts, relevant pages whereof were found to have been torn. The High Court ought to have taken the same into consideration as well as the admission on the part of the Defendant No.1 and the effect thereof. Such an admission could be taken into consideration both for the purpose of arriving at a finding in regard to the fact as to whether a full and final settlement of accounts had been arrived at, which was a relevant fact as also for determining the question of limitation.

34. Section 96 – Ist Respondent could not Convey a Better Title to his Wife

In *Sai Kommoju Durga Prasada Rao* v. *Patnala Babu Rao*, 2011 6 ALD 26: 2011 6 ALT 756 (AP), the High Court of Andhra Pradesh held, though the 1st appellant is said to have executed a gift deed, being Ex.B.6, on 10.04.2003, in favour of his wife, the 2nd appellant, in respect of the property. It is already held that the 1st respondent did not derive any title to the property and he cannot convey a better title to his wife, the 2nd appellant. In addition to that, it was elicited from the 1st appellant as DW.1 that there are no documents to show that Ratnayamma purchased the plaint schedule property from the father of the 1st respondent, and that the Will marked as Ex.B.10 is in respect of a different item of property. He admitted that the property mentioned therein i.e. House bearing No. 46-15-11 has fallen to the share of Ratnayamma. He was not entitled to lay any claim to the suit schedule property, on the basis of the said document.

35. An Agent cannot Plead a Case of Adverse Possession

The High Court further held, The appellants could have taken the plea of adverse possession, but for the fact that they have specifically pleaded that Ratnayamma purchased the property. Added to that, Ratnayamma was appointed as power of attorney under Ex.B.1 by the 1st respondent. An agent much less his/her legal representative can never be permitted to plead any rights adverse to the interests of the principal. As a matter of fact, there is nothing on record to disclose that Ratynayamma had ever asserted any rights over the property, in herself. It is only the 1st appellant that made an attempt in this regard. When the possession of the property by Ratnayamma cannot be treated to be adverse, to the interest, of the 1st respondent, the question of the 1st appellant claiming through Ratnayamma, that too, under a Will, taking the plea of adverse possession, does not arise. Therefore, the inescapable conclusion is that the 1st respondent was entitled to recover the possession of the property.

36. Section 96 – A Contract is Completed when an Offer Made is Accepted

In *Malaprabha Co-Operative, Rep by its Incharge Managing Director* v. *Buildmet Pvt. Ltd., Rep by its Director H.N. Varadarajan*, 2012 5 Kar LJ 445: 2012 3 KCCR 2304 (Kar), the High Court of Andhra Pradesh said, On re-appreciation of pleadings, oral and documentary evidence available on record, it is seen that the tender for construction of building was called for by the defendant – Society from its office situated at Saundatti in Belgaum District. It is also seen that the tender for accepting the contract was submitted within the territorial jurisdiction of the said Court. The contract was also entered between the parties and the same was executed within the jurisdiction of Saundatti vide Ex.P-2 and the terms and conditions which was agreed between the parties which was made as part of the agreement Ex.P-4 is the only document, which is written by plaintiff from its office and addressed to defendant. Except this document, all other documents are executed by the parties within the territorial jurisdictional Court at Saundatti. In that view of the matter, the finding of Trial Court on Issue No.4 to the effect that there are several correspondence taken place between plaintiff and defendant, some of them originating from the branch office of plaintiff, which is situated at Bangalore and therefore the plaintiff has cause of action to initiate the suit within the territorial jurisdiction at Bangalore, cannot be sustained. The finding of the Trial Court to that effect is contrary to Section 20 of CPC and also Section 4(2) and 4(3) of the Contract Act, 1872 as held by this Court in the matter of *Republic Medico Surgical Company, Bangalore* v. *Union of India* reported in AIR 1980 Karn 168: 1979 (2) Kar LJ 410, which reads as under:

> "The contract is completed when an offer made is accepted. It is the acceptance that gives rise to the cause of action and not merely an offer. Hence, even though an offer is made from Bangalore, it cannot be said that a part of the cause of action arises in Bangalore. In a suit the cause of action will consist of making of the contract and its breach at the place where it is to be performed. Therefore, a suit for breach of contract can, at the option of the plaintiff be brought either at the place where the contract was made or at the place where the breach was committed. It can also be said that the place where money is to be paid or goods are

to be supplied are also the places where parts of the cause of action arise, but certainly not the place where offer is made."

Which position is accepted by the decision of the Apex Court in the matter of *C.V. Subba Rao* v. *B. Ramachandra Rao,* reported in AIR 1966 SC 543. It is seen that mere making of an offer does not form part of the cause of action for suit for damage for breach of contract which has resulted from acceptance of the offer in terms of the ratio laid down by the Apex Court.

In that view of the matter, this Court found that the finding of the Trial Court on issue No.4was not sustainable and the same was required to be set aside. Consequently the Judgment and Decree dated 18.08.2003 passed in O.S. No. 6949/1991 on the file of Additional City Civil Judge, Bangalore (CCH-14),was required to be set aside.

37. Section 96 – Whether the Defendants were Required to Pay the Balance Sale Consideration of Rs. 15,50,000 a day Prior to Completion of 90 day

In *T.N. Arun Kumar* v. *Shivanna,* 2012 3 AIR (Kar) (R) 512: 2012 6 Kar LJ 149: 2012 3 KCCR 1757 (Kar), the following pointswere not in dispute in this appeal that the parties were not disputing the execution of agreement of sale dated 16.06.2006. The defendants are also not disputing the receipt of Rs. 10,00,000/- by them as advance sale consideration from the plaintiffs. They were also not disputing the time stipulated for completion of the agreement as 90 days from the date of agreement. But their main contention before the Court below was that the defendants were required to pay the balance sale consideration of Rs. 15,50,000/-a day prior to completion of 90 days and that the plaintiffs did not pay the amount. Now we have to examine whether the plaintiffs were ready to pay the balance sale consideration within the time stipulated.

The High Court held, in the overall circumstances, this Court is of the opinion that even if the plaintiffs have obtained a decree for specific performance they are unable to pay the amount or deposit the balance sale consideration for two years. Considering the conduct of the plaintiffs we have to hold that the plaintiffs were never ready and willing to perform their part of the contract and the decree passed by the Court below has not been utilized by the plaintiffs – respondents and they cannot be permitted to contend that when once the decree is passed they are entitled to deposit money at their whims and fancies. In view of the conduct of the plaintiffs – respondents the Judgment passed by the Court below has to be set-aside by us. Accordingly we answer point No.(i).

When we hold that the respondents-plaintiffs are not entitled for decree for specific performance it is the duty of the Court to mould the relief and the advance sale consideration paid by the plaintiffs has to be refunded because there is no dispute in regards to the payment of Rs.10,00,000/-as advance sale consideration and now the value of the land in and around Devenahalli has been escalated by many folds. On account of this the appellants have been benefited. In the circumstances, we are of the view that Rs.10,00,000/-received as advance sale consideration shall carry interest at 24% per annum from the date of agreement till the date of payment.

In the result the appeal is allowed. The judgment and decree passed by the Civil Judge (Sr.Dn.). Devenahalli in OS No. 314/2007 dated 23rd March 2010 is hereby set-aside and in modification of the decree the suit of the plaintiffs has been decreed directing the defendants to refund Rs. 10,00,000/-which was received as advance sale consideration with interest at 24% per annum from 16.06.2006 till the date of payment. Parties to bear their costs.

38. Section 96 – Money Suit Filed within Six Months of Accrual of Cause of Action – Whether Barred by Limitation

In *P. Vishwanath Shetty* v. *K. Balachandra Shetty,* 2009 6 AIR (Kar) (R) 108: 2010 1 KCCR 676 (Kar), the plaint initially was not signed by pltfs. No. 2 to 18, The averment in the plaint did not suggest that the pltfs. No. 1 was authorised to prosecute the suit on behalf of pltfs. No. 2 to 18. On the other hand, the plaint suggested that, it was a case of joinder of plaintiffs and joinder of causes of action. Each one of the plaintiffs asserted that the suit was instituted in their individual capacity jointly with other plaintiffs. (b) The amendment to the cause title is effected describing first plaintiff as the power of attorney to the pltfs. No. 2 to 18 after three years of the institution of the suit. The amendment effected was after the expiry of the limitation. Hence, there was no valid institution of the suit by pltfs. No. 2 to 18. (c) The agreement at Ex. P. 2 disclosed that the amount was to be payable on or before 31-3-89 the suit was filed on 4-7-92 which is beyond the period of limitation. The first plaintiff suppressed the material facts regarding the financial status of the company. The company at the time of Ex. P. 1 was a sick industry. The BIFR proceedings were instituted for rehabilitation. The appellant because of misrepresentation and fraud purchased the shares. In that view the contract under Ex. P. 1 is void.

39. Absence of Signatures of Some of the Plaintiffs in the Plaint would not Invalidate the Plaint

SRI K. Ramakrishna Bhat, counsel for respts. No. 1 to 18 per contra, relied on the ruling of Privy Council *Mohini Mohun Das* v. *Bungsi Buddan Saha Das,* ILR 17 Cal 580 (PC), ruling of the bombay High Court in *AIR* v. *Ramachandra dhondo Datar,* AIR 1961 Bom LR 292: ILR (1961) Bom 257, and the decision of the Patna High Court in *Bibi Asghari* v. *Muhammad Kasim,* AIR 1951 Pat 323: ILR 54 All 57, to bring home the point that the absence of signatures of some of the plaintiffs in the plaint would not invalidate the plaint and does not render suit bad in law. Further it is held that the making signatures belatedly in the plaint would not make the suit barred by limitation. ON the facts it is submitted that, the first plaintiff had filed the photocopy of the power of attorney of pltfs. No. 2 to 18 dt. 26-3-1982 along with the plaint. Upon the technical objection by the defendants an application was filed for amendment of the cause title. The court after hearing both the parties allowed the application. Accordingly the amendment is effected describing the plaintiff as power of attorney of pltfs. No. 2 to 18 and original power of attorney is also produced. Hence, it is argued that the technical defects on the plaint are properly cured by the necessary amendment. Therefore, it cannot be argued that the suit is validly instituted and barred by time.

In the decision of the Privy Council the facts disclose that, the suit is when instituted by three plaintiffs jointly for recovery of money. One Mohini Mohun

Das was the Manager for three brothers who had lent loan to the defendant. The suit was instituted on behalf of three brothers (Creditors) the plaint was verified and signed by Mohini Mohun Das the petition was filed by Mohini Mohun Das to amend the cause title to implead him as co plaintiff. The trial Court dismissed the suit on the ground that Mohini Mohun Das who signed and verified the pleadings had no authority and the application to come on record is filed after the expiry of the period of limitation. In the context of the said facts The privy Council while allowing the appeal, has made the following observations:

> "on the face of the plaints the three joint creditors are named as co-plaintiffs. The names of Gobind Rani and Khetter Mohun have not been struck out, nor did they, or either of them, attempt to repudiate the suits. But still it was contended that Mohini Mohun was the sole plaintiff, or, at any rate, that khetter Mohun ought not to be treated as a co-plaintiff from the commencement of the litigation. "

The Bombay High Court in *AIR* v. *Ramchandra Dhondo Dattar*, AIR 1961 Bom 292: ILR (1961) Bom 257, has made the following observations: (18) Their Lordships of the Privy Council observed in ILR 17 Cal 580 (PC) that there was ho rule that a person named as co-plaintiff in the plaint was not to be treated as a plaintiff unless he signed and verified the plaint. Order VI, Rule 14, which requires that every plaint should be signed by the plaintiff and his pleader, if any, has, in view of the Privy council decision to be interpreted so as to mean that a plaint should be signed by at least one plaintiff. See also *Bibi Ashari* v. *Muhammad Kasim*, AIR 1951 Pat 323 and ILR 54 All 57: AIR 1931 All 507 (SB) 25 As regards the verification of the plaint in the instant case it was verified by Chushey as agent of the ARI Limited (plaintiff No. 1). It was not verified by plaintiff No. 2. Order VI, rule 15 of the Civil Procedure Code requires that the plaint should be verified by the plaintiff or one of the plaintiffs or by some other person proved to the satisfaction of the Court to be acquainted with the facts of the case. Order VI, Rule 15, does not refer to persons authorized by the plaintiff or any of the plaintiffs. If the plaint is not verified by a plaintiff or by any one of the plaintiffs, it can be verified only by a person proved to the satisfaction of the Court to be acquainted with the facts of the case. It is true that there are several authorities in favour of the view that omission to verify a pleading is a mere irregularity and that a pleading which is not verified as required by Order VI, Rule 15, may be verified at any later stage of the suit, even after the expiry of the period of limitation.

Examining the cases referred to the Court held, the ratio laid down in the above decision squarely applies to the facts on hand. In the instant case, pltfs. No. 1 to 18 had filed the suit, the plaint was signed and verified by pltf. No. 1. At the time of filing of the suit the photo copies of the powers of attorney of pltfs. No. 2 to 18 were filed. Upon the objection by the other side, formal defect was noticed, an application was filed to amend the cause title to describe the 1st plaintiff as power of attorney of pltfs. No. 2 to 18. The amendment is allowed. The request for amendment is granted, accordingly the cause title is amended. The contents of Ex. P. 1 and Ex. P. 2 disclose that the pltf. No. 1 is entered into transaction with the appellant on behalf of pltfs. No. 2 to 18 whose shares were being sold. In Ex P. 2 it is also specifically stated that, the appellant should not question the authority of first plaintiff to effect the transfer of shares of pltfs. No. 2 to 18 in the future course of time. The fact that the first plaintiff acted as agent of pltfs. No. 2 to 18 is borne on record in Ex. P. 1 and P. 2, the photo copies of the powers of attorney filed along with the plaint and the original powers of attorney. The appellant had acknowledged the fact that the pltf. No. 1 is acting as agent of pltfs. No. 2 to 18 when he was entering into a contract for purchase of shares of pltfs. No. 2 to 18. In that view, it becomes explicit that plaintiff No. 1 had a valid authority to represent pltfs. No. 2 to 18. The amendment effected to cause title although belated fully cures the technical defects if any. In view of the ratio laid down by privy Council and the Bombay High Court, it cannot be said that the suit is invalid and barred by time.

40. Section 96 – First Appeal – Suit for Declaration that the Asthal and the Temple with Properties are Public Trust Properties

In *The Bihar State Board of Religious Trust* v. *Mahanth Shyam Sunder Das,* 2012 3 BBCJ 9 Patna High Court held, performance of pooja on special occasion will not mean that the Asthal is a public trust.

In the said case the defendant filed contesting written statement. According to the defendant's case in short is that Galama Asthal was founded by Mahanth Gopal Das, brother of great grandfather of this defendant. He was a Grihasth who had inherited ancestral lands. Subsequently, Gopal Das who was a Sadhu of great fame got presents from his followers and he purchased other lands. His Chela Gangaram Das also acquired some lands out of usufruct of the land left by Gopal Das. The lands about 40 - 42 Bigha were recorded in the name of Gangaram Das during last cadastral survey. He also sold 2 or 3 Bigha lands. He nominated Sukhram Das as his Chela. He also acquired some lands and sold some lands. The properties belonging to the Asthal have all along been the personal properties of Mahanth and was being utilized as such. Gopal Das became Birakt Vaisnab and he came out of his ancestral house. He installed idols of Sri Ram Janki and Laxmanji for his personal worship. He also installed idol of Saligram for his personal worship. There was neither temple nor any place for general public. Gopal Das and his followers were worshiping the deities personally. The general public had no access or have Darshan to deities. When mud wall house fell down a brick wall house with tiles over it was constructed and the deities have been kept in a room of the house.

The Court further said, according to the pleadings of the plaintiff itself the property is not dedicated to the deities. The properties devolved from one Mahanth to his Chela who is nominated by Guru i.e. devolution is from Guru to Chela and the Asthal is of Vaisnab Sampradaya. The succession of Mahanthship is from Guru to Chela. The plaintiff also admitted that the properties were given to the founder and also to the subsequent Mahanths and subsequently Mahanths have been acquiring the properties out of the income from the original grant.

It is admitted fact that there is no document of dedication or Samarpannama in favour of the deities and likewise there is no document to prove that the properties were ever dedicated. Therefore, the fact becomes admitted that the deities are not the owner of the properties. Therefore, the burden is on the part of plaintiff to prove that the properties appertaining to the Galma Asthal is public trust properties. In support of their cases the plaintiff has only filed one document i.e. Ext.-1 which is certified copy of the sale deed executed by Mahanth Sukhram Das in favour of Nand Lal Missir in the year 1913 wherein Mahanth Sukhram Das has described himself as Vairagi and profession as Fakiri. The learned counsel Mr. Trivedi on the basis of this description submitted that a Vairagi cannot be said to have got any attachment of the property and, therefore, he was holding the property on behalf of the public in general. In other words, according to the learned counsel the properties were held by the Mahanth for charitable purposes and for religious purposes.

The plaintiff appellant's case is that the public used to perform Pooja in the temple of Asthal and there was no restriction for performance of Pooja by general public and examined witnesses. PW 1 to 8 and 10 to 20 have stated that general public used to perform Pooja without there being any restriction. PW 5, 6, 8, 12, 15, 16, 18 and 20 have again stated that Sadhus and Abhyagat used to come to Asthal who have been entertained by Mahanth. This fact is admitted by DW 6 and DW 11 and DW 12 also. The other witnesses of the defendants i.e. DW 1, 2, 3, 6, 9, 11 and 12 have stated that general public have no liberty to perform Pooja in Asthal. DW 1, 10 to 12 have stated that the temple of the Asathal is inside the Angan and, therefore, Darshan by every person is not possible. Some documentary evidences have also been produced by the defendants. The sale deeds have been marked as Ext.-C series and rent receipt Ext. A series whereas Khatiyan as Ext. B series. These documents have been filed by the defendants to prove that the properties have been recorded in the name of Mahanth and the Mahanths were dealing the properties exclusively. These are the evidences adduced on behalf of the parties.

In view of the above clear position the onus to prove that the respondent Mahanth held the properties of trust for charitable character was clearly on the appellant Board who alleged that it was public trust. Here admittedly there is no document showing Samarpannama or dedication. The Board has tried to establish the nature of the trust as public trust on the basis of oral evidences. We have seen above that some of the witnesses have stated that the public used to worship without there being any hindrances. However, it appears that none of the witnesses have stated that the original founder Mahanth Gopal Das Ji or any of the succeeding Mahanth at any time dedicated the properties to the deities.

41. Section 96 – First Appeal – Dismissal without Discussing or Appreciating the Evidence – Illegal

In *Leela Krishnarao Pansare* v. *Babasaheb Bhanudas Ithape,* 2014 (4) JT 606: 2014 3 RCR (Civ) 602: 2014 4 SCALE 665: 2014 15 SCC 821; the Apex Court held, dismissal order passed by the High Court without discussing or appreciating the evidence is illegal.

In short, the facts of the case were that the appellants had filed a suit against the respondents for a declaration to the affect that the agreement to sell entered into between the appellants and the respondents should be cancelled and the appellants should be put in possession of the land in question.

The aforesaid agreement to sell had been entered into and in pursuance of the said agreement, possession of the land in question had been handed over to the respondents upon a payment of Rs. 1 lac, which was part of the consideration. The consideration for sale was Rs.10 lacs. The remaining amount of Rs.9 lacs was to be paid in two installments of Rs. 4 lacs and Rs. 5 lacs each. Rupees 4 lacs were to be paid by the respondents by the end of 30.01.1996 and the remaining Rs.5 lacs were to be paid at the time of execution of the sale deed.

It was also agreed that before execution of the sale deed the appellants had to get an entry "Deosthan Inam" removed from the revenue record. The land in question was shown as "Deosthan Inam" and the said entry was to be deleted as it was said on behalf of the appellants that the land in question was not "Deosthan Inam" land and needful was to be done by the appellants for removal of the said entry.

The suit filed by the appellants had been dismissed and First Appeal filed in the High Court by the present appellants has been dismissed.

The Supreme Court held, upon perusal of the impugned judgment delivered by the High Court, it is clear that the entire sale consideration had not been paid but at the same time it is also an admitted fact that the appellants did not get the entry with regard to the "Deosthan Inam" deleted. There is no discussion about the efforts made by the appellants for getting the said entry deleted. The High Court has also not discussed the consequences of non-deletion of the said entry and the efforts made by the appellants for not getting it deleted. Similarly, there is no definite finding as to how much consideration was paid and at what time or stage.

Even the amount payable by the respondent towards purchase price had not been paid in full to the appellants and the said thing has not been properly discussed.

We find that the relevant evidence has neither been discussed nor been properly appreciated by the High Court. It was very much necessary for the High Court to decide whether the appellants and the respondents had performed their respective duties, which they had to perform in pursuance of the agreement with regard to sale of the land in question.

In our opinion, without appropriate appreciation of the evidence, the High Court should not have dismissed the appeal and therefore, we allow the present appeal and remand the matter to the High Court so that after hearing the concerned parties, the High Court would take a fresh decision. As the agreement with regard to sale of the land had been executed before several years, we hope that the High Court would hear and decide the appeal as expeditiously as possible.

42. Section 96 – Appreciation of Evidence – Jurisdiction of the Appellate Court

In *Sh. Prem Sagar* v. *Sh. Qamaruddin*, 2011 176 DLT 52 (Del) the High Court said, sitting as an Appellant Court, I can interfere with the findings of the trial court only if the same are perverse or illegal. Merely because two views are possible on the basis of the facts which have come on record and the evidence which has been led would not entitle to this Court to interfere with the findings and conclusions of the trial court. In view of the detailed discussions in paras 11 to 38 of the judgment, and some of the paragraphs which I have reproduced above, it cannot be said that the findings and the conclusions are in any manner illegal or perverse. In fact, in my opinion, grave prejudice and harm will be caused to the defendant/respondent who not only purchased the property and paid the price, but who thereafter was forced to file a suit for specific performance which was subsequently decreed. No doubt, the plaintiff was not a party to the said suit, however, it otherwise has been proved before the trial court that the father of the plaintiff was the actual owner of the property and also that the father of the plaintiff/appellant acted with the active consent of the plaintiff/appellant/son to enter into an agreement to sell.

In the case on hand the learned counsel for the appellant very strenuously argued that the tests laid down for proving that the son was only a benami owner and the father was the real owner, have not been proved and which tests are those as laid down by the Supreme Court in the judgment of *Jaydayal Poddar (Deceased) through LRs.* v. *Mst. Hazara*, AIR 1974 SC 171: 1974 (1) SCR 70. Great stress was laid on the fact that no intention has been proved for the benami transaction and nor has it been proved that the consideration flowed from the father to the original seller of the property. It has also been argued that since the agreement to sell states that possession will be delivered at the time of the execution of the sale deed, this was indicative of lack genuineness of agreement because the respondent/defendant was already in possession claiming to be a tenant of the property. It is also argued that there is no presumption that when a property is purchased in the name of minor the same should automatically be taken as a benami property.

The High Court held, I am afraid that I am unable to agree with any of the contentions as raised by the counsel for the appellant. A decision in a civil case is based on balance of probabilities. There are always pros and cons in every case, meaning thereby, there is always something for and against each of the parties as per the evidence which comes on record. Further, the court ultimately puts the same in a melting pot and thereafter arrives at a decision on the balance of probabilities. The balance of probabilities clearly show that the claim of respondent/defendant in this case, who has paid the price of the plot, should not be defeated by the act of the plaintiff in claiming possession of the property which was sold by the father of the plaintiff/appellant when admittedly there are no bad or strained relations between the plaintiff/appellant son and his father Sh. Sarda Ram. Also the agreement to sell nowhere states that the monies paid for the property purchased in the name of the plaintiff/appellant were not paid by the father, and in fact, the agreement to sell uses the expression "through father" and which, in my opinion, is an indication of the father having paid the price for the property. Also, the trial court has not acted illegally or perversely in finding nothing on record that it was not from the funds of the grand-mother of the plaintiff that the price for the subject property was paid and thus the property was accordingly purchased in the name of the plaintiff/appellant.

In *AMCO Vinyl Ltd.* v. *Classic Industries,* 2012 190 DLT 35, Delhi High Court held, in my opinion, the trial Court has fallen into an error in holding that the suit has not been properly filed allegedly because the resolution Ex.PW1/2 & Ex.PW1/3 (being the extract and complete resolution respectively) does not mention with regard to signing and verification of the plaint. When we look at the resolution dated 29.1.2001 (wrongly mentioned dated 29.1.2002), it is seen that Mr. Anchal Bhargava has been authorized to appoint a lawyer and sign all the documents on behalf of the company including making any statement in the Court. In my opinion, this is sufficient authorization and it cannot be said that the suit has not been validly instituted and filed because signing of documents will include signing of pleadings and thus filing of the suit. In fact, the Supreme Court has in the judgment reported as *United Bank of India* v. *Naresh Kumar,* 1996 (6) SCC 660: AIR 1997 SC 3 held that the suits filed by companies should not be dismissed on technical grounds once they are pursued to the hilt. I therefore set aside the findings of the trial Court with respect to issue No.1 and hold that the suit has been validly instituted and filed.

43. Section 96 – Filing Ist Appeal is to the Impugned Judgment of the Trial Court

In *United Bank of India* v. *Smt. Shakuntala Yadav,* 2012 187 DLT 64 (Del) The Trial Court noted that rents had fallen during the relevant period, and therefore, instead of granting Rs. 43/- per square feet, mesne profits have been granted at Rs. 25/- per square feet. In every case of determination of mesne profits, some amount of honest guess work is always involved. Obviously, there cannot be complete exactness of evidence led with respect to rate of rents/mesne profits, and the Courts have to make a best judgment assessment on the basis of the evidence which is led before it. I have already stated above that the suit premises are situated on the main road, and surely, premises on the main road have far higher rents than premises located in the interiors.

The High Court said, I therefore do not feel that the Trial Court has committed any illegality or perversity in granting mense profits at Rs.25/- per square feet and therefore there is no ground for interference in this appeal so far as the awarding of the rate of mesne profits are concerned. In fact I find that the Trial Court has been more than liberal to the appellant/bank inasmuch as the rate of mesne profits should ordinarily undergo an increase each year, however, the rate of mesne profits which has been granted continues to be for a fixed amount for the entire period from 1.10.1997 to 31.12.2003, i.e. a period of about 6 years.

At this stage, it is however necessary to point out a seeming illegality in the impugned judgment which allows interest at 9% per annum pendent lite and future till realization. I may note that the suit has been filed on 20th October, 1997 and therefore there would hardly be any mense profits which would be payable with respect to the pre suit period. The mesne profits have only accumulated pendent lite and till 31.12.2003 when the premises were vacated.

Therefore it cannot be said that interest at 9% per annum can be granted on the total amount of the money decree on mesne profits from the date of filing of the suit. Obviously, interest has to be calculated only from the end of the month for which the mesne profits became payable. Learned counsel for the respondent could not very seriously dispute this illegal position. I therefore clarify the impugned judgment by observing that when the Trial Court has granted interest at 9% per annum pendent lite and future, interest will only be calculated from the end of the month from which the mesne profits would be payable, and it will not be that interest will be paid from the date of filing of the suit on the total amount of mesne profits decreed.

44. Section 96 – Impugning the Judgment of the Trial Court

In *Hindustan Roller Supply Co.* v. *State Of Uttar Pradesh*, III (2006) BC 290: 119 (2005) DLT 602 learned counsel for the appellant/plaintiff firstly argued before this Court that once there is a subsequent judgment of the trial Court dated 18.5.2010 holding the suit to be within limitation, the appeal must automatically succeed. It was secondly argued that in any case the appeal is liable to succeed because the appellant in fact had given the bills stated in Annexure-A to the plaint to the respondents/defendants and which is proved from the letter dated 28.10.1997, Ex.PW1/12 sent by the appellant/plaintiff to the respondents/ defendants.

The High Court said, in my opinion, the original judgment dated 13.1.2003 is correct and the suit was rightly dismissed by the trial Court.

The next issue thereafter to be looked into as to whether the bills which are the subject matter of Annexure-A; including two bills Nos.2908 and 2909; were ever raised upon/delivered to the respondents. The trial Court, in this regard, has held as under:

> "14. In order to prove the claim for these two bills the plaintiff has to serve the bills upon the defendants for the payment, and in his examination-in-chief though he has deposed in his affidavit filed in lieu of examination-in-chief that he has submitted the bills; but on cross-examination he had specifically stated that he had not taken the receipt of the bills which he had submitted in the department and that he had sent the bills Ex.PW1/5 to Ex.PW1/11 to the department through post and he has further deposed that he has not filed the postal receipts of the same in the Court file. Therefore, in view of this statement made by the PW-1 on cross-examination, it appears that the bills have been sent to the defendant by post but no document has been placed on record to prove the service of such bill upon the defendant. The document Ex.PW-1/12 has been relied by the plaintiff to prove that the bills has been submitted to the defendant no.2, and on argument it is submitted that the said document Ex.PW1/12 was bearing the receipt of the said bill. Once the witness has specifically admitted that he had taken no receipt regarding the submission of the bills form the department and that he has sent these bills by post but no postal receipt in that regard has been proved for sending the said bills to the defendant and receipt thereof through the

postal authorities, I find that the said document Ex.PW-1/12 relied by the plaintiff cannot be relied as a conclusive proof to submit the bills with the defendant. Therefore, I find that in absence of receipt of the said letter duly executed by a competent person on behalf of the defendant No.1 or 2 either on the said letter and in the absence of any postal receipt produced and proved on record to prove the transmission of that letter and receipt thereto by the defendant, I find that the plaintiff bitterly failed to prove the service of these bills upon the defendant. Therefore, I find that the plaintiff cannot be held entitled to recover the amount of Ex.PW1/9 and Ex.PW-1/11 unless he proves by reliable evidence the service of these bills upon the defendants which he bitterly failed, as found above, and, therefore, I find that the plaintiff cannot be held entitled to claim that amount from the defendant unless the bill has been duly served upon the defendant with the log book of the driver concerned. So the claim of the plaintiff for that amount remains pre-mature, and, therefore he cannot be held entitled to recover ` 1,55,700. So this issue stands decided in favour of the defendants and against the plaintiff."

The High Court said, I agree with the aforesaid findings and conclusions of the trial Court inasmuch as once the appellant/plaintiff takes up a case that bills were sent by post and he fails to file and prove any postal receipts for service of these bills, it is rightly held that these bills were never submitted to the respondent No.1/State of U.P. In the examination in chief, it was submitted on behalf of the appellant/plaintiff that no receipts were taken with respect to the bills submitted inasmuch as the bills were sent by post. Once the appellant/plaintiff therefore failed to prove that the bills, Ex.PW1/5 to Ex.PW1/11, the subject matter of Annexure-A to the plaint were ever served on the respondents, obviously it must be held that they would not be genuine bills for which payment had to be made by the respondent No. 1/State of U.P. This aspect of the bills not having been supplied is strengthened by the fact that if really work under these bills was done, then, surely the appellant/plaintiff would have filed and proved on record the log books containing the signatures of the driver and possibly the counter-signatures on behalf of the respondents/defendants showing that road rollers in fact were supplied for the period which are the subject matter of the bills stated in Annexure-A to the plaint. After all, a substantial monetary liability of Rs. 3,20,600/- as the principal amount alongwith interest thereon @ 18% per annum as claimed by the appellant/plaintiff cannot be fastened on the respondents/defendants unless it is proved quite clearly that road rollers were in fact supplied for the periods which.

45. Section 96 – Dispute Over Plot of Land between Union of India (Railways) and Defendant

Union of India v. *K.V. Lakshman*, 2016 (3) RCR (Civil) 1019: 2016 AIR (SCW) 3139: 2016 (5) MLJ 504 (SC) the Supreme Court held, It is a settled principle of law that a right to file first appeal against the decree under Section 96 of the Code is a valuable legal right of the litigant. The jurisdiction of the first appellate Court while hearing the first appeal is very wide like that of the Trial Court and it is open to the appellant to attack all findings of fact or/and of law in first appeal.

It is the duty of the first appellate Court to appreciate the entire evidence and may come to a conclusion different from that of the Trial Court.

Similarly, the powers of the first appellate Court while deciding the first appeal are indeed well defined by various judicial pronouncements of this Court and are, therefore, no more res integra. It is apposite to take note of the law on this issue.

As far back in 1969, the learned Judge - V.R. Krishna Iyer, J (as His Lordship then was the judge of Kerala High Court) while deciding the first appeal under Section 96 of the CPC in *Kurian Chacko* v. *Varkey Ouseph,* AIR 1969 Ker 316, reminded the first appellate Court of its duty to decide the first appeal. In his distinctive style of writing with subtle power of expression, the learned judge held as under:

> "1. The plaintiff, unsuccessful in two Courts, has come up here aggrieved by the dismissal of his suit which was one for declaration of title and recovery of possession. The defendant disputed the plaintiff's title to the property as also his possession and claimed both in himself. The learned Munsif, who tried the suit, recorded findings against the plaintiff both on title and possession. But, in appeal, the learned Subordinate Judge disposed of the whole matter glibly and briefly, in a few sentences.
>
> 2. An appellate court is the final Court of fact ordinarily and therefore a litigant is entitled to a full and fair and independent consideration of the evidence at the appellate stage. Anything less than this is unjust to him and I have no doubt that in the present case the learned Subordinate Judge has fallen far short of what is expected of him as an appellate Court. Although there is furious contest between the counsel for the appellant and for the respondent, they appear to agree with me in this observation....."

In this case the dispute in this case related to a plot of land situated near Krishnarajapuram Railway Station, which is around 14 KMs away from Bangalore city- details of which are mentioned in the plaint (herein after referred to as "the suit land").

The appellant filed the suit bearing Civil Suit No. 5588/1976 against the respondents in the Court of Ist Additional City Civil and Session Judge, Bangalore for a declaration that they (appellant) are the owners of the suit land and that the respondents whose ancestral claims to have interest in the suit land have no right, title and interest in the suit land. The appellant in order to prove their title over the suit land filed certain documents.

The respondents filed their written statements and while denying the appellant's title asserted their own title over the suit land through their predecessors. According to them, their predecessors acquired occupancy rights under the State Tenancy Laws over the suit land in revenue proceedings. It was contended that by virtue of these proceedings, their ancestral acquired superior title over the suit land to the exclusion of every one including the appellant and the same devolved on them after the death of their predecessor in title. The respondents also raised a plea that the suit is barred by limitation. The

Trial Court on the basis of the pleading framed issues arising in the civil suit. Parties adduced evidence.

Therefore, the dispute that essentially arose between the parties was who is the owner of the suit land-the appellant (Union of India-Railways) or the respondents' predecessor in title?

46. Section 96 and Question of Title and the Question of Limitation

In *Chandraprabha Devi* v. *Ram Chandra Prasad Singh*, 2016 (2) BL JUD 279 (Patna) the High Court of Patna examined in a first appeal question of title and limitation. Admittedly, in this case, the plaintiffs never paid the entire consideration amount of Rs.1,43,998/-. I have found that only Rs.41,400/- was paid. It is also admitted that delivery of possession of the mortgage property more than hundred acres of land was not given to the plaintiffs. The registration receipt were not given to the plaintiffs rather it was kept by the defendants themselves and the original registered mortgage deeds, ext.'H' series, have been produced by the appellants. Now, let us examine the case as to whether the mortgagee, i.e., the plaintiffs have got right to file mortgage suit and pray for sale of the mortgage property.

27. From bare perusal of the ext. 'H' series, it becomes clear that the mortgage is an usufructuary mortgage. Neither the appellant nor the respondent disputed this position. The usufructuary mortgage is defined as follows:—

> "Where the mortgagor delivers possession or expressly or by implication binds himself to deliver possession of the mortgaged property to the mortgagee, and authorizes him to retain such possession until payment of the mortgage money, and to receive the rents and profits and to appropriate the same in lieu of interest, or in payment of the mortgage money, or partly in lieu of interest or partly in payment of the mortgage money, the transaction is called a usefructuary mortgage and the mortgagee a usefructuary mortgagee."

28. In view of the above definition, the ingredients of usufructuary mortgage are (i) There is delivery of possession to the mortgagee. (ii) the mortgagee is to retain possession until the money is repaid and is entitled to appropriate income thereof. (iii) if the loan is repaid or discharged then the property is redeemed and (iv) in this usefructuary mortgage, there is no personal liability and there is no remedy available either by sell or for closure. No doubt, in the present case, there is undertaking to delivery of possession but the plaintiff themselves did not pay the entire consideration amount of Rs.1,43,998/-. Therefore, the plaintiffs are at fault.

29. In the Transfer of Property Act, the mortgagees have two rights. One against the person of the mortgagor and the other against the mortgaged property. So far the rights against the persons of the mortgageor is concerned, it is dealt with in Section 68 of the Transfer of Property Act whereas the right against mortgaged property is concerned, it is dealt with in Section 67, 69 and 69A. The Court below in the present case has held that the suit is maintainable under Section 68 of the Transfer of Property Act. The plaintiffs also filed the suit for availing the rights against the person of the mortgagor.

Section 68 of the Transfer of Property Act reads as follows:—

> ***68. Right to sue for mortgage-money***—(1) The mortgagee has a right to sue for the mortgage-money in the following cases and no others, namely,
>
> (a) where the mortgagor binds himself to repay the same;
>
> (b) where, by any cause other than the wrongful act or default of the mortgagor or mortgagee, the mortgaged property is wholly or partially destroyed or the security is rendered insufficient within the meaning of section 66, and the mortgagee has given the mortgagor a reasonable opportunity of providing further security enough to render the whole security sufficient and the mortgagor has failed to do so;
>
> (c) where the mortgagee is deprived of the whole or part of his security by or in consequence of the wrongful act or default of the mortgagor;
>
> (d) where, the mortgagee being entitled to possession of the mortgaged property, the mortgagor fails to deliver the same to him, or to secure the possession thereof to him without disturbance by the mortgagor or any person claiming under a title superior to that of the mortgagor
>
> (2) Where a suit is brought under clause (a) or clause (b) of sub-section (1), the Court may, at its discretion, stay the suit and all proceedings therein, notwithstanding any contract to the contrary, until the mortgagee has exhausted all his available remedies against the mortgaged property or what remains of it, unless the mortgagee abandons his security and, if necessary, re-transfers the mortgaged property.

47. Section 96, Order XXIII, Rule 3A read with Section 151, Order XLIII, Rule 1 and Order XLVII

In *Harbhajan Kaur* v. *Veer Kaur*, 2016 (4) PLR 15 (P&H): 2016 (167) AIC 777, the sole question that called for determination was whether the order dated 23.07.2014 passed by the Civil Judge (Senior Division) Kurukshetra, allowing the application filed by the petitioners under Order XXIII, Rule 3A read with Section 151 CPC and setting-aside the award dated 07.03.2009 passed by the Lok Adalat is amenable to challenge in regular civil appeal filed before the First Appellate Court at Kurukshetra.

Counsel for the petitioners would contend that as the trial Court has not passed any judgment much less a decree while disposing of application filed by the petitioners under Order XXIII, Rule 3A read with Section 151 CPC, the order passed by the trial Court cannot be challenged in appeal by invoking Section 96 CPC. It is further submitted that even if the respondent has any grievance to express against the said order, she may be entitle to file a revision petition before this Court. It is further argued that the First Appellate Court committed a serious error rather illegality by holding that the application filed by the petitioner for setting-aside the award of Lok Adalat dated 07.03.2009 is to be considered as an application for review and, therefore, the appeal is maintainable under Order XLVII, Rule 7 (1) CPC.

Counsel for the petitioners would contend that as the trial Court has not passed any judgment much less a decree while disposing of application filed by the petitioners under Order XXIII, Rule 3A read with Section 151 CPC, the order passed by the trial Court cannot be challenged in appeal by invoking Section 96 CPC. It is further submitted that even if the respondent has any grievance to express against the said order, she may be entitle to file a revision petition before this Court. It is further argued that the First Appellate Court committed a serious error rather illegality by holding that the application filed by the petitioner for setting-aside the award of Lok Adalat dated 07.03.2009 is to be considered as an application for review and, therefore, the appeal is maintainable under Order XLVII, Rule 7 (1) CPC.

7. Counsel for the respondent, on the other hand, has supported the impugned order with the submissions that as an independent suit to challenge the award passed on the basis of compromise is barred by the provisions of Order XXIII, Rule 3 CPC, the application filed by the petitioners to assail the said award of the Lok Adalat on any score whatever including that of fraud would amount to review of the earlier judgment and decree dated 07.03.2009, therefore, the appeal is maintainable before the Court of Additional District Judge by invoking the provisions of Order XLVII, Rule 7 CPC, as has been held by the First Appellate Court. In support of his contention, he has referred to judgment of the Kerala High Court *Anandan* v. *Nanu,* 2007 (5) RCR (Civil): AIR 2007 Ker 146, judgment of this Court *Balwinder Singh* v. *Karnail Singh,* 2000 (3) RCR (Civil) 229: AIR 2005 P&H 183, *Wassan Singh* v. *Lakha Singh,* 2005 (2) RCR (Civil) 791: (2005) 141 PLR 63, judgment of Allahabad High Court *Harendra Prasad* v. *Smt. Parshottama,* AIR 1995 All 30, judgment of Bombay High Court *Waman Ramchandra Bhayde* v. *Kanta Narayan Patel,* 2013 (1) ALL MR 62: 2013 (1) Bom CR 200, judgment of Madhya Pradesh High Court *Thakur Prasad* v. *Bhagwandas,* 1985 MPLJ 149: AIR 1985 MP 171. Further reliance has been placed upon judgment of Hon'ble the Supreme Court of India *Sushil Kumar Sen* v. *State of Bihar,* 1975 (1) SCC 774: AIR 1975 SC 1185.

The Court said, I have heard counsel for the parties, perused the paper book and the judgments cited at bar with the able assistance of counsel for the parties.

9. Before dealing with rival submissions made by counsel for the parties, a brief reference to the operative part of the order passed by the trial Court while disposing of the application filed by the petitioners under Order XXIII, Rule 3A read with Section 151 CPC for setting-aside the award dated 07.03.2009 is pertinent. The trial Court in Para 13 of the order dated 23.07.2014 has held, reads thus:—

> "As a sequel to my aforesaid findings especially rendered on Issue No.1, the application filed by the applicants/defendants stands allowed and the award dated 07.03.2009 passed by the predecessor of this Court is hereby set-aside. However, there is no order as to costs. Paper be tagged with main case file and after due compliance same be sent back to the Record Room."

10. Subsequent to the passing of this order, it appears that the respondent/ plaintiff did not file an application before the trial Court for revival of the suit titled *Smt. Veer Kaur* v. *Harbhajan Kaur*, (2016) 184 PLR 15 or its decision on merits. However, she preferred an appeal before the District Judge, Kurukshetra by invoking the provisions of Section 96 CPC. Section 96 CPC provides for appeal from original decree and a relevant extract therefrom, germane to the controversy, is extracted herein below for ready reference:

> The Court further referred to the provisions of section 96 and said, A conjoint reading of the aforesaid extracts i.e. operative part of the order passed by the trial Court for setting-aside the award dated 07.03.2009 and Section 96 CPC, it becomes crystal clear that the respondent cannot maintain a regular appeal by invoking the provisions of Section 96 CPC to assail the order dated 23.07.2014 passed by the trial Court. By way of order dated 23.07.2014, the trial Court only set-aside the award dated 07.03.2009 passed by the Lok Adalat but never decided the suit on merits, therefore, the order passed by the trial Court neither amounts to a judgment much less a decree amenable to challenge by invoking Section 96 CPC. In this view of the matter, I have no hesitation to hold that the First Appellate Court committed a gross error rather illegality by holding that the appeal filed under Section 96 CPC is maintainable.

***97. Appeal from final decree where no appeal from preliminary decree.*—Where any party aggrieved by a preliminary decree passed after the commencement of this Code does not appeal from such decree, he shall be precluded from disputing its correctness in any appeal which may be preferred from the final decree.**

SYNOPSIS

Comments

1. Preliminary Decree

The High Court of Allahabad discussed the nature of a preliminary decree. The Court said that where in a suit for contribution, the lower court decided the defendant's liability to contribute and also the extent and it only remained to work out the amount of the decree: held, that the findings amounted to a preliminary decree from which an appeal was competent: 9 Luck. No appeal lies from an order passed in a partition suit after the preliminary decree and before the passing of the final decree: 1937 ALJ 809: 1937 All 694. The question whether adjudication is a decree or an order, is one of substance: 42 C. 914 (PC); 9 Luck 701: 1934 Order 307. The right to appeal lies only from a preliminary decree and not from a preliminary finding in a suit directing accounts to be taken: 38 B.331; 39 B. 339 (FB). Where there is only a preliminary finding and no decree is drawn up, there is no preliminary decree and no appeal under section 97.

2. Interim Final Decree

Interim final decree is neither a final decree, nor a preliminary decree. According to the High Courts of Allahabad and Madras, between the preliminary decree and the final decree, the lower court can pass many interim final decrees. In such a case it is open to the plaintiff to file an appeal against the interim final decree if so advised, or it is open to the trial court to take this up as a part of the final decree itself in case there is no urgency and in that case an appeal can be filed against the final decree itself; 35 All 159; *Babburu Basavayya* v. *Babburu Guravayya*, ILR 1952 Mad 173: (1951) 2 Mad LJ 176: AIR 1951 Mad 938 rel. on); *Nallasivam Chettiar* v. *Avudayammal*, (1958) 1 Mad LJ 181: ILR (1958) Mad 417: AIR 1958 Mad 462.

It is the duty of a party aggrieved by a direction in a preliminary decree for accounts passed by the courts to appeal against it; if he does not do so, he cannot be permitted afterwards to go behind the direction in question at the time of taking accounts. Section 97, C.P.C., is a bar to such a course: ILR 1945 Kar 368: 1946 Sind 28. Where the preliminary decree provides that if the net proceeds of the sales are insufficient the plaintiff shall be at liberty to apply for a personal decree, such a provision is an award of a personal decree; and if the defendant does not appeal from it, he is precluded under section 97, C.P.C., from afterwards disputing its correctness.

The High Court of Madras examined the consequence of an appeal against a preliminary decree and held that if an appeal from a preliminary decree succeeds, the final decree passed later on falls to the ground: 34-A. 493; 36-A. 532; 35 MLJ 361. The legislature in enacting section 97 intended to prevent preliminary questions being raised in the form of an appeal after a case has been decided upon merits: 36B. 536; 1937 R 494. Where a final decree is passed, no appeal will lie against a preliminary decree; 48 C 1036: 1921 C 109; 1928 L. 73; 107 IC 610.

3. Final Decree Passed During Appeal Against Preliminary Decree

An appeal was preferred against a preliminary decree in a suit for partition. During pendency of the said appeal, a final decree was passed. It was held that the final decree is dependent on the preliminary decree and must fail if the preliminary decree is reversed in appeal. *Baswant* v. *Kallappa*, AIR 1938 Bom 222: 175 IC 43; *See* also *Kankayya* v. *Lakshmayya*, AIR 1950 Mad 218 and *Uppala Subbiah* v. *Chitrala Narasimhuloo*, AIR 1956 Hyd 161: ILR (1956) Hyd 45.

A preliminary decree in a partition suit was passed by consent without complying with the provisions of Order XXXII, rule 7(1), but no appeal was preferred against it. It was held by the Supreme Court that its validity could not be questioned in an appeal against the final decree; *Kaushalaya Devi* v. *Baijnath Sayal*, AIR 1961 SC 790: 1962 (1) SCJ 684: (1961) 3 SCR 769.

4. Practice and Procedure

It is a salutary rule that where the issue is simple and straightforward and the only question is which set of witnesses is to be believed, the findings of fact of the trial judge should not be lightly disregarded: 49-C. 132: 1922 C. 260. Small cause suit tried on the original side – appeal from decree: 51 IC 967. An appeal lies from a decree in a suit transferred from the small cause court to the original side under section 23 of the provisions of Small Cause Courts Act and the appellate court can remand the suit 45 IC 645.

5. Section 97 – Appeal against Final Decree – No Appeal Filed against Preliminary Decree

In *Ishaque Mohd.* v. *(Smt.) Saini Begam*, 2010 3 MPHT 370: 2010 3 MPJR 93: 2010 3 MPWN 63: 2010 0 Supreme (MP) 290. To appreciate the contention of the parties, firstly, legal position in respect of objections of the respondent may be looked into. Section 97 of the Civil Procedure Code, 1908 reads as under:

> *97. Appeal from final decree where no appeal from preliminary decree*— Where any part aggrieved by a preliminary decree passed after the commencement of this Code does not appeal from such decree, he shall be precluded from disputing its correctness in any appeal which may be preferred from the final decree.

The aforesaid provision specifically provides that where any party has not filed any appeal against the preliminary decree, he shall be precluded from disputing its correctness in any appeal which may be preferred from the final decree.

The apex Court considered the scope of section 97 -in *Venkatrao Anantdeo Joshi* v. *Sau. Malatibai*, AIR 2003 SC 267: 2003 (3) AWC 2196 (SC), wherein the apex Court held that in a suit for partition where preliminary decree is passed, at the time of passing of final decree it is not open to the respondents to raise objection that he was a tenant of the suit premises. Section 97 of CPC specifically provides that where any party aggrieved by the preliminary decree does not appeal from the said decree, he is precluded from disputing its correctness in any appeal which may be preferred from the final decree. The apex Court referred an earlier judgment in *Moolchand* v. *Dy. Director, Consolidation*, AIR 1995 SC 2493: 1995 (2) UJ 799, in this regard. The Division Bench of this Court in *Devi sahai* v. *Sardar Govindaro Mahadiak*, AIR 1992 MP 13, held that a preliminary decree passed in partition suit is not a tentative decree but should be regarded as conclusive in respect of the matters dealt with in the preliminary decree. Although when the Legislature provided for a preliminary decree, a final decree is to be passed and the final decree has been made executable but that would not mean that a preliminary decree is a tentative decree on an interlocutory order. The provisions of section 97, CPC, attained finality to a preliminary decree in respect of the matters decided by it. A party aggrieved by a preliminary decree does not appeal from it then he is precluded from disputing its correctness in an appeal from the final decree.

The High Court held, in view of the specific provisions as contained in section 97 of the Code and the law laid down by the apex Court and this Court, there is no iota of doubt that the appellant is precluded from raising correctness of the preliminary decree in this appeal. Though appellants in this appeal has also challenged the preliminary decree but has not filed any application seeking condo-nation of delay in filing appeal. Apart from this, along with the memo of appeal, a certified copy of the preliminary decree is also not filed. Agai11st the preliminary decree dated 24.2.2004, this appeal was barred by limitation on 19.1.2006 when this F.A. No. 112/06 was filed. In absence of application or certified copy of the decree this appeal cannot be found as an appeal against preliminary decree, so no interference can be made in the preliminary decree.

6. Section 97 – Partition – Preliminary Decree – Second Appeal – Preliminary Decree Attained Finality

In *Yad Ram* v. *Rattan Singh,* 2010 4 Law Herald 2927 (P&H) the plaintiff-respondent was also held entitled to separate possession by partition of the suit land to the extent of 3/16th share vide judgment and decree dated 13.03.2002. Thereafter, plaintiff-respondent filed an application for preparation of final decree. The trial Court appointed the Local Commissioner to suggest mode of partition. However, the aforesaid decree was challenged by the appellants by filing Civil Appeal No. 25 of 09.04.2004\07.06.2004. The aforesaid appeal was accepted and the judgment and decree dated 03.04.2004 was set aside vide judgment and decree dated 27.01.2005 passed by Additional District Judge, Gurgaon and the matter was remanded back to pass appropriate judgment and decree after giving due opportunity of being heard to the parties.

After the remand, parties were granted opportunities to lead their evidence. However, appellant, except examining himself adduced no further evidence. While passing the final decree, vide judgment dated 19.02.2010, the trial Court observed as under:

> "Admittedly, as per judgment passed in the suit the plaintiff-decree holders are owners to the extent of 3/16th share in the suit land which is shown in a site plan attached with the main suit. Now, on the basis of evidence on file there is nothing that would not call for the appointment of local commission to partition the suit land as per the share of the parties and hence, finding merit in the application filed, the same is allowed and the plaintiff-decree holders are entitled for the final decree for partition of the suit land as per subsequent report of the local commission. The report thus submitted by the local commission be made a part of the

final decree sheet. The present application for preparation of final decree is accordingly allowed."

Aggrieved from the aforesaid judgment and decree dated 19.02.2010, the appellant preferred an appeal before the Lower Appellate Court which was also dismissed vide impugned judgment and decree dated 19.02.2010.

While dismissing the appeal, the Lower Appellate Court observed as under:

> "It is for the appellants to prove that decree for partition and report of local commissioner is against record and without evidence. Learned counsel for the appellant has failed to show how the final judgment and decree is against record and without evidence whereas from the statement of Rattan Singh PW1, order and decree dated 03.04.2004 passed by Sh. Gopal Krishan, the then Addl. Civil Judge (Sr. Divn.), Nuh, it is proved that the learned lower Court appointed Sh. S.C. Gupta, Advocate, as Local Commissioner. He submitted his report dated 09.10.2003. On the local commissioner report, objections were invited and on hearing the final judgment and decree is passed. The final judgment and decree is in accordance with law and as per local commissioner report. Learned counsel for the appellant has failed to point out any illegality in the judgment and decree under challenge. The judgment under challenge is reasoned, speaking, as per pleadings and evidence on record."

The Court held, There is no dispute that the preliminary decree dated 13.03.2002 passed in Civil Suit No. 82 of 09.06.2000 between the parties wherein the plaintiff-respondents were held entitled to 3/16th share by way of partition has become final. Before the trial Court, which prepared the final decree of partition, it was for the appellant to prove that decree for partition determining the share of defendant-respondent and report of the Local Commissioner suggesting the mode of partition was against law. The courts below have recorded a finding of fact that appellant has failed to place on record any evidence on the basis of which, it can be pointed out that the preliminary judgment and decree dated 13.03.2002 suffers from any infirmity. Even before this Court, learned counsel appearing on behalf of the appellant was unable to show any such illegality in the aforesaid judgment and decrees dated 13.03.2002.

7. Partition Suit – Preliminary Decree – The Suit for Partition is not Disposed Off by Passing of the Preliminary Decree

In *Ganduri Koteshwaramma* v. *Chakiri Yanadi,* 2012 1 All MR (SC) 443: 2011 Supp 2 ANJ (SC) 121: 2012 1 BBCJ (SC) 338: 2012 4 Bom CR (SC) 821 the Supreme Court held, a preliminary decree determines the rights and interests of the parties. The suit for partition is not disposed of by passing of the preliminary decree. It is by a final decree that the immovable property of joint Hindu family is partitioned by metes and bounds. After the passing of the preliminary decree, the suit continues until the final decree is passed. If in the interregnum i.e. after passing of the preliminary decree and before the final decree is passed, the events and supervening circumstances occur necessitating change in shares, there is no impediment for the court to amend the preliminary decree or pass another preliminary decree redetermining the rights and interests of the parties having regard to the changed situation. We are fortified in our view by a 3-Judge Bench decision of this Court in the case of *Phoolchand* v. *Gopal Lal,* AIR 1967 SC 1470: [1967] 3 SCR 153, wherein this Court stated as follows:

> "We are of opinion that there is nothing in the Code of Civil Procedure which prohibits the passing of more than one preliminary decree if circumstances justify the same and that it may be necessary to do so particularly in partition suits when after the preliminary decree some parties die and shares of other parties are thereby augmented. . . . .. So far therefore as partition suits are concerned we have no doubt that if an event transpires after the preliminary decree which necessitates a change in shares, the court can and should do so; .... there is no prohibition in the Code of Civil Procedure against passing a second preliminary decree in such circumstances and we do not see why we should rule out a second preliminary decree in such circumstances only on the ground that the Code of Civil Procedure does not contemplate such a possibility. . . for it must not be forgotten that the suit is not over till the final decree is passed and the court has jurisdiction to decide all disputes that may arise after the preliminary decree, particularly in a partition suit due to deaths of some of the parties. . . . .a second preliminary decree can be passed in partition suits by which the shares allotted in the preliminary decree already passed can be amended and if there is dispute between surviving parties in that behalf and that dispute is decided the decision amounts to a decree..... ...."

This Court in the case of *S. Sai Reddy* v. *S. Narayana Reddy,* (1991) 3 SCC 647 had an occasion to consider the question identical to the question with which we are faced in the present appeal. That was a case where during the pendency of the proceedings in the suit for partition before the trial court and prior to the passing of final decree, the 1956 Act was amended by the State Legislature of Andhra Pradesh as a result of which unmarried daughters became entitled to a share in the joint family property. The unmarried daughters respondents 2 to 5 therein made application before the trial court claiming their share in the property after the State amendment in the 1956 Act. The trial court by its judgment and order dated August 24, 1989 rejected their application on the ground that the preliminary decree had already been passed and specific shares of the parties had been declared and, thus, it was not open to the unmarried daughters to claim share in the property by virtue of the State amendment in the 1956 Act. The unmarried daughters preferred revision against the order of the trial court before the High Court. The High Court set aside the order of the trial court and declared that in view of the newly added Section 29-A, the unmarried daughters were entitled to share in the joint family property. The High Court further directed the trial court to determine the shares of the unmarried daughters accordingly. The appellant therein challenged the order of the High Court before this Court. This Court considered the matter thus;

> ".........A partition of the joint Hindu family can be effected by various modes, viz., by a family settlement, by a registered instrument of partition,

by oral arrangement by the parties, or by a decree of the court. When a suit for partition is filed in a court, a preliminary decree is passed determining shares of the members of the family. The final decree follows, thereafter, allotting specific properties and directing the partition of the immovable properties by metes and bounds. Unless and until the final decree is passed and the allottees of the shares are put in possession of the respective property, the partition is not complete. The preliminary decree which determines shares does not bring about the final partition. For, pending the final decree the shares themselves are liable to be varied on account of the intervening events. In the instant case, there is no dispute that only a preliminary decree had been passed and before the final decree could be passed the amending Act came into force as a result of which clause (ii) of Section 29-A of the Act became applicable. This intervening event which gave shares to respondents 2 to 5 had the effect of varying shares of the parties like any supervening development. Since the legislation is beneficial and placed on the statute book with the avowed object of benefitting women which is a vulnerable section of the society in all its stratas, it is necessary to give a liberal effect to it. For this reason also, we cannot equate the concept of partition that the legislature has in mind in the present case with a mere severance of the status of the joint family which can be effected by an expression of a mere desire by a family member to do so. The partition that the legislature has in mind in the present case is undoubtedly a partition completed in all respects and which has brought about an irreversible situation. A preliminary decree which merely declares shares which are themselves liable to change does not bring about any irreversible situation. Hence, we are of the view that unless a partition of the property is effected by metes and bounds, the daughters cannot be deprived of the benefits conferred by the Act. Any other view is likely to deprive a vast section of the fair sex of the benefits conferred by the amendment. Spurious family settlements, instruments of partitions not to speak of oral partitions will spring up and nullify the beneficial effect of the legislation depriving a vast section of women of its benefits".

8. Section 97 – Preliminary Decree – Would not Convert Automatically into a Final Decree after Expiration of the Period of Limitation of Preferring an Appeal

In *Kasturi Devi Jain* v. *Union Bank of India,* 2011 (1) JLJ 95 (MP), the High Court said, the scope of preferring an appeal against the preliminary decree is envisaged in section 97 of CPC, which provide that when no appeal is preferred against the preliminary decree, the party is precluded from disputing the correctness of the preliminary decree, but this fetter could not be pressed into service to demonstrate that after expiration of the period of limitation of preferring an appeal, the plaintiff would not be required to obtain a final decree. This controversy has been analyzed by the Supreme Court in its judgment reported as, *Mool Chand* v. *Deputy Director,* (1995) 5 SCC 631: AIR 1995 SC 2493, where paragraphs No. 25 to 29 of this judgment throw adequate light on the controversy in the following manner:

25. Preliminary decree is an appealable decree. Section 97 of the Code of Civil Procedure provides as under:

> "97. *Appeal from final decree where no appeal from preliminary decree.*— Where any party aggrieved by a preliminary decree passed after the commencement of this Code does not appeal from such decree, he shall be precluded from disputing its correctness in any appeal which may be preferred from the final decree."

Thus, if an appeal is not filed against the preliminary decree and its correctness is not challenged, it becomes final and the party aggrieved thereby will not be permitted to challenge its correctness in an appeal against final decree.

The Privy Council in *Ahmed Musaji Saleji* v. *Hashim Ebrahim Saleji,* (1916) ILR 42 Cal 914 (924): 17 Bom LR 432, held that failure to appeal against a preliminary decree would operate as a bar to raising any objection to it in an appeal filed against final decree. This Court in *Venkata Reddi* v. *Pothi Reddi,* AIR 1963 SC 992: 1963 (2) An WR 126, has held that the impact of section 97 is that the preliminary decree, so far as the matters covered by it are concerned, is regarded as embodying the final decision of the Court passing that decree. It observed as under:

> "A preliminary decree passed, whether it is in a mortgage suit or a partition suit, is not a tentative decree but must, insofar as the matters dealt with by it are concerned, be regarded as embodying, the final decision of the Court passing that decree."

This decision was relied upon in *Gyarsi Bai* v. *Dhansukh Lal,* AIR 1965 SC 1055: [1965] 2 SCR 154 in which it was observed as under:

> "It is true that a preliminary decree is final in respect of the matters to be decided before it is made .... it is indisputable that in a mortgage suit there will be two decrees, namely, preliminary decree and final decree, and that ordinarily the preliminary decree settles the rights of the parties and the final decree works out those rights."

9. Order 22, Rule 4, Order 22, Rule 9, Section 97 – Appellant not Party to the Suit

In *Md. Asgar Hussain, Md. Nepali, Bibi Sabra and Bibi Guljaha* v. *Md. Safique Alam,* 2011 (2) JCR 204 (Jhk): AIR 2011 Jhar 63, the Appellants were not the parties to the suit. Their case was that a partition suit was instituted by one Mossomat Jumni, Mostt Bratan and Rafique Alam claiming partition of the suit property. The mother of the Appellants namely Bibi Zubeda and Abul Hussain, elder brother of the Appellants, were Defendants – second party. They had also claimed their share. The parties had adduced their evidences and on appraisal of the evidences of the parties, partition suit was decreed in favour of the Plaintiffs holding that the Appellants' mother Bibi Zubeda and the Appellants' brother Abul Hussain have absolute no right, title and interest in the suit property and they were rank outsiders.

The Plaintiffs' mother had preferred appeal against the said judgment and decree of the trial court, which was dismissed. The second appeal filed against the said judgment being S.A. No. 420/1998 was also dismissed. Thereafter Special Leave to Appeal was filed before the Supreme Court being S.L.P. (Civil) No. 17036/2000. The same was also dismissed by Hon'ble Supreme Court. Final decree, thereafter, was prepared on the basis of the preliminary decree.

The High Court said, It is an admitted fact that the mother of the Appellants-Bibi Zubeda was a party to the Partition Suit. She had contested that suit but her claim was rejected on the ground that she is not a co-share'. She filed appeal against the said decree. The appeal was dismissed. She preferred second appeal which was also dismissed She had, therefore, filed Special Leave Petition before the Supreme court, that too was dismissed. Once the claim of share of Bibi Zubeda was adjudicated upon and dismissed by a decree of competent civil court, confirmed up to the Hon'ble Supreme Court, heirs and successors in interest are bound by the same. Learned lower appellate court has considered the said legal position and has rightly held that the claim of Appellants are barred by res-judicata. Since in the said preliminary decree, it was held that the Plaintiffs' mother and brother had no right, title and interest in the suit property, non-substitution of the Appellants after death of their mother in the final decree proceeding does not at all affect the decree.

The final decree proceeding is based on the right declared in the preliminary decree. When the right claimed by Appellant's mother was negated in preliminary decree, non-substitution of the Appellants as her legal heirs in the final decree proceeding does not in any way affect the final decree and the Appellants are not entitled to the reliefs prayed for, as rightly held by learned lower appellate court.

I, therefore, find no error or any ground, much less any substantial question of law in this second appeal.

10. Section 97 and 96 – Preliminary Decree and Final Decree

In *Prabhakar Panigrahy* v. *Subash Chandra,* 2016 Supp 1 OLR 236 (Ori) the High Court said, the decree is defined in Section 2 (2) of the Code of Civil Procedure Under the explanation, it is explained that a decree is preliminary decree when further proceeding is taken before the suit can be completely disposed of and it is final when such adjudication completely disposes of the suit. The settled position thus is that a preliminary decree is one which declares the rights and liabilities of the parties leaving the actual result to be worked out in further proceedings when as a result of further inquiries conducted pursuant to the preliminary decree, the rights of the parties are fully determined and a decree is passed in accordance with such determination which is final. Both the decrees are in the same suit. Final decree may be said to have attained its finality in two ways: (i) when the time for appeal has expired without any appeal being filed against the preliminary decree or the matter has been decided by the highest Court, (ii) When, as regards the Court passing the decree, the same stands completely disposed of.

Section 96 of the Code provides that save as otherwise expressly provided in the body of the Code or by any other law for the time being in force, an appeal shall lie from every decree passed by any Court exercising original jurisdiction to the Court authorized to hear appeals from the decision of such Court. So, an appeal certainly lies against the final decree subject to the restriction contained in Section 97 of the Code that where any party aggrieved by a preliminary decree does not appeal from such decree, he shall be precluded from disputing its correctness in any appeal which may be preferred from the final decree.

11. Appeal without Copy of Decree

The High Court said,

> "6A: Last paragraph of judgment to indicate in precise terms and reliefs granted:—(1) The last paragraph of the judgment shall state in precise terms the relief which has been granted by such judgment.
>
> (2) Every endeavour shall be made to ensure that the decree is drawn up as expeditiously as possible, and, in any case, within fifteen days from the date on which the judgment is pronounced; but where the decree is not drawn up within the time aforesaid, the Court shall, if requested so to do by a party desirous of appealing against the decree, certify that the decree has not been drawn up and indicate in the certificate the reasons for the delay, and thereupon—
>
> (a) an appeal may be preferred against the decree without filing a copy of the decree and in such a case the last paragraph of the judgment shall, for the purpose of Rule 1 of Order XLI, be treated as the decree, and
>
> (b) so long as the decree is not drawn up, the last paragraph of the judgment shall be deemed to be the decree for the purpose of execution and the party interested shall be entitled to apply for a copy of that paragraph only without being required to apply for a copy of the whole of the judgment; but as soon as a decree is drawn up, the last paragraph of the judgment shall ceased to have the effect of a decree for the purpose of execution or for any other purpose;
>
> Provided that, where an application is made for obtaining a copy of only the last paragraph of the judgment, such copy shall indicate the name and address of all the parties to the suit."

Thus, Rule 6-A enjoins as it was then:—

> "that the last paragraph of the judgment shall state in precise terms the relief which has been granted by such judgment. It has fixed the outer time limit of 15 days from the date of the pronouncement of the judgment within which the decree must be drawn up. In the event of the decree not so drawn up, clause (a) of sub-rule (2) of Rule 6A enables a party to make an appeal under Rule 1 of Order XLI C.P.C. without filing a copy of the decree appealed against and for that purpose the last paragraph of the judgment shall be treated as a decree."

However, the same has been substituted by Amendment Act No.46 of 1999 in Section 28 which has come into force w.e.f. 1.7.2002 which reads as follows:—

(2) An appeal may be preferred against the decree without filing a copy of the decree and in such a case the copy made available to the party by the Court shall for the purposes of Rule 1 of Order XLI be treated as the decree. But as soon as the decree is drawn, the judgment shall cease to have the effect of a decree for the purpose of execution or for any other purpose."

Decree becomes enforceable the moment the judgment is delivered—

It therefore follows that the decree becomes enforceable the moment the judgment is delivered and merely because there will be delay in drawn up of the decree, it cannot be said that the decree is not enforceable till it is prepared. Similarly, an appeal may be preferred against the decree without it being formally drawn up and without filing a copy of decree.

So here the question arises as to which order is the order of passing of the final decree so that said date will be taken to be the date of passing of final decree; whether the date on which the report of the Civil Court Commissioner was accepted or the date thereafter that again formally in order of final decree is passed when as already stated that the first order was not a conditional one as regards acceptance of the Civil Court Commissioner report nor dependent upon any further inquiry whatsoever on any subject relating to the suit either directly or indirectly or even as ancillary or incidental thereto. At the cost of reputation, it may be stated that the order stating about the payment of money to be made by the parties inter se is just as was indicated in the report of the Civil Court Commissioner which had already been accepted in its entirety for all purposes .The report of the Civil Court Commissioner had been accepted in toto by order dated 5.12.2013 and that has been subsequently restated in the order dated 23.6.2014.So after order dtd. 05.12.2013, the parties were left with no option of questioning the legality or propriety of the report of the Commissioner on any of the aspects as indicated there and the only option was to question it by carrying it before the superior Court in a legally constituted proceeding as permissible in law within the prescribed period of limitation.

12. Question of Limitation in Filing Appeal

Now, Article 116 of the Limitation Act is required to be gone through and that says that the time for filing appeal under the Code of Civil Procedure to any Court other than High Court from a decree or order is thirty days and the time begins to run from the date of decree. It is the settled position of law that the date of decree is the date of judgment, though in fact decree may have been signed on a different date. The date of decree is the date on which the judgment is pronounced and not the date when the decree is signed.

The position of law has by now been well settled in case of *Dr. Charanji Lal (D) by L.Rs.* v. *Hari Das (D) by L.Rs.*, AIR 2005 SC 2564: (2005) 10 SCC 746, referring to the earlier decisions in case of *West Bengal Essential Commodities Supply Corporation* v. *Swedesh Agro Farming and Storage Pvt. Ltd.*, AIR 1999 SC 3421: 1999 (37) ALR 340; *Shankar Balwant Lokhane (dead) by LRs.* v. *Chandrakant Shankar Lokhande,* AIR 1995 SC 1211 and *Hameed Joharan* v. *Abdul Salam,* AIR

2001 SC 3404 that engrossment of the final decree on stamp paper in a suit for partition would relate back to the date of the decree. The enforceability of the decree does never get suspended for such non-engrossment of the final decree on the stamp paper and the time period for filing the appeal would run from the date when the final decree is passed and not from the date when it is engrossed on the stamp paper being supplied by any of the parties. In view of that the party not filing the appeal against the order of passing of final decree within the period prescribed in Article 116 of the Limitation Act cannot do so afterwards after expiry of period of limitation by computing the time period from the date of engrossment of the final decree on the stamp paper and get the benefit of exclusion of said time till engrossment of final decree on stamp paper for the purpose of filing the appeal against the final decree on the ground that since it was no so engrossed, he could not file the appeal. Even to execute the said final decree, the period of 12 years has to be computed from the date of order by which final decree is passed and not from the date of engrossment of the same on stamp paper since as provided in Article 136 of the Limitation Act, the decree becomes enforceable on the day it is passed i.e. the date of order and not on the day it is drawn and engrossed on stamp paper. The drawl and engrossment of the same on stamp paper is to make the decree executable and for fiscal purpose. The executability and enforceability altogether have different connotations. So for filing the execution of the final decree, the requirement is to file the final decree engrossed on stamp paper but to file appeal that is not the requirement and the certified copy of the order passing the final decree will suffice the purpose and if no appeal is filed within the time period from that order, the same would be final. The running of time period for appeal will not remain under suspension till its engrossment on stamp paper.

13. Section 97 and Partition Act: Section 2 and 3 – The Division of Property by Metes and Bounds is the Rule and Grant of Money Value is only an Exception

In *K. Vijayalakshmi* v. *K. Sashikanth,* 2015 1 CTC 73: 2014 8 MLJ 272 (Mad), the High Court held, in a suit Partition is a comprehensive legal process in and by which joint ownership and common possession of property is converted into individual property of the respective sharers. Each sharer is allotted a specific item of property of the joint family, after such division by metes and bounds. It is an elementary principle of law that in case there are several co-owners, partition should be effected among them by giving to each sharer his/her share IN SPECIE to the extent possible. In short, if the property is capable of division by metes and bounds, each co-owner should be given a share instead of money value.

In a suit for partition, the Court at the first instance, declares the right of parties and the property available for partition. The decree passed in the suit, which is in the nature of a preliminary decree directs partition of joint property in definite shares.

Section 97 of the Code of Civil Procedure provides that in case a party to the partition suit fails to challenge the preliminary decree, he would be precluded from disputing its correctness in appeal, which may be preferred from the final decree. Therefore it is clear that the rights of the parties are crystalised and conclusively determined by the preliminary decree.

After passing the final decree, it is open to any one of the parties to initiate proceedings for passing a final decree. The Court after taking cognizance of the final decree application is obliged to proceed in accordance with Order XXVI Rule 13 of the Code of Civil Procedure. The Court would appoint an Advocate Commissioner to partition the property by metes and bounds. The Commissioner appointed for such purpose acts as the authorised officer of the Court and as such he is duty bound to distribute the property among the parties taking into account their respective shares and in the light of the direction given by the Court in the warrant of appointment on the basis of the preliminary decree. Rule 14 of Order XXVI contained a legislative mandate that the Commissioner would allot such share to the parties, meaning thereby joint property should be divided in specie and each one of the sharers should be given a specific item. Sub Rule (2) of Rule 14 of Order XXVI mandates that the Commissioner shall prepare and sign the report apportioning the share of each parties by metes and bounds. This makes the position very clear that the Commissioner is obliged to effect physical division of property into two or more shares. Since a co-owner is entitled, as a matter of right, to partition the co-ownership property, he is also entitled to claim allotment of a specified extent of property to him.

The possible difficulty to the other sharers in case the property is divided into two or more shares, cannot be a ground to deny physical division of property and separate allotment to the co-owners in accordance with the share position.

Equitable Partition: The Court while considering the proceedings for passing a final decree would be confronted with a difficult situation in case a request for reservation of residential house or any other kind of superstructure on equitable ground is made by one of the parties to the final decree. The Court in such a case is expected to consider variety of factors. There would not be much difficulty for such equitable allotment of residential house or other superstructure subject to payment of just compensation or owelty to other sharers in case the property is situated in a backward or rural area, where the land value is comparatively less and there is no scope for any kind of fluctuation. That is not the case of property abutting main roads or having commercial value. In case the property is situated in an urban area or within the jurisdiction of Municipality, Municipal Corporation or Metropolitan City, the Court cannot shut its eyes to the ground reality. The land value is increasing considerably in these areas on account of limited supply and more demand. The sharer, who wanted preferential allotment on equity must be directed to pay market value in such cases. The plea of reservation on equitable ground must be a bona fide one. There are cases in which the occupant of the house would be employees of Banks, Corporates or Government employees eligible for house building allowance for the purpose of construction of residential house. However, they would not undertake such a course with a view to claim equitable allotment of co-ownership property with superstructure. The Court in such cases must make a genuine exercise to see as to whether the request for allotment on equitable ground is a ruse for getting preferential allotment and thereafter to sell it to strangers for a fabulous sum. While doing equity to a party, the Court should not do injustice to the opponent. Reservation on equitable ground is therefore not a right. It is a way of equitable partition of property.

There are two stages in the matter of allotment of the entire property or superstructure to one sharer or group of sharers on the ground of equity. The Court at the first stage is expected to take a decision as to whether the party is really entitled for reservation on the ground of equity. The fact that a particular sharer is residing in the house property alone cannot be a ground for preferential allotment of valuable property to him on equitable grounds. The Court must examine the case by taking an overall view of the matter. The financial position of the party claiming preferential right to retain the property on the ground of his occupation of the house property is also a relevant factor. In case any of the other sharers are also not having residential houses of their own and the property is divisible, the same is also a vital factor to deny the claim of one of the sharer to give preferential right to retain the entire suit property or house on the ground that he has been using it for residential purpose. The Court therefore in such cases is bound to exercise its judicial discretion objectively. The entire background facts should be taken note of while deciding the application for allotment of property in its entirety or reservation of house property by directing the other sharers to accept the money value.

14. Section 97A – Preliminary Decree is not a Tentative Decree

In *Ravinder Kaur* v. *Gagandeep Singh,* 2016 156 DRJ 620 (Del): 2016 (156) DRJ 620, the plaintiff and defendant entered into a partnership agreement for carrying out business under the style of "Nu-Nischal's Klick Selection" from property No. 15A/26, (basement), WEA, Karol Bagh, New Delhi (hereafter "suit property"). The suit property is owned and possessed jointly by the plaintiff and the defendant. In the partnership, however, the plaintiff has 50% share while defendant has 25% share.

On 24.04.2008 this Court made an ad-interim order, which was to bind the parties (in OMP 192/2008 and OMP 193/2008). The said order is extracted below:

> "Vide order dated 9.04.2008, an Arbitrator was appointed with the consent of the parties to adjudicate the disputes inter se the parties. The parties were directed to appear before the learned Arbitrator on 28.04.2008. Counsels for the parties state that in the interregnum, during the period when the Local Commissioners were directed to complete the proceedings of commissions in terms of the orders dated 9.04.2008 and 11.04.2008, further disputes have arisen between the parties and that each of them feels threatened by the other, thus hindering the smooth transaction of business at the two shops, subject matter of the present OMPs. Both the parties express an apprehension that the other party may obstruct their ingress and egress into the said shops and create hindrances in the peaceful running of the business from the premises, during the

pendency of the arbitration proceedings. However, neither of the parties disputes the fact that the partnership deed executed between the parties could be dissolved in accordance with the terms and conditions contained therein. While counsel for the petitioner submits that the partnership stands dissolved in view of his notice dated 31.3.2008, counsel for the respondent objects to the modality of the termination. Needless to state that the said issues may be raised before the learned Arbitrator appointed in the case, who shall decide the same."

On 26.02.2014, in the light of submissions and statement on behalf of the parties, the learned Single Judge made the following order, in the suit:

> "1. The learned counsel for the defendant has stated that so far as the plaintiff is concerned, he has 50 per cent interest in the shop in question and accordingly, there is no dispute regarding the shares of both the plaintiff and the defendant. However, it is submitted by him that as the defendant has been appointed as a receiver of the shop in question and the matter is pending before the learned arbitrator, the final decree to that effect may not be passed.
>
> I have considered the submission made by the learned counsel for the defendant as well as the learned counsel for the plaintiff. The case which has been set up by the plaintiff in the plaint is that on 12.10.1998 he had purchased 50 per cent share in the basement of property No. 15A/26 WEA. Ajmal Khan Road. Karol Bagh, New Delhi which is situated on a plot of land measuring 267 square yards. The defendant in his written statement has not denied this averment made by the plaintiff ."

After preparation of final decree controversies arose between the prties. The High Courtsaid, Section 97 of the CPC, which, the plaintiff insists, constitutes a bar to the maintainability of the present appeal, reads as follows:

> "97. Appeal from final decree where no appeal from preliminary decree - Where any party aggrieved by a preliminary decree passed after the commencement of this Code does not appeal from such decree, he shall be precluded from disputing its correctness in any appeal which may be preferred from the final decree."

The Supreme Court had occasion to deal with the finality statutorily imputed by reason of Section 97 in a number of judgments. In *Mool Chand* v *Dy. Director Consolidation* 1995 (5) SCC 631, it held as follows:

> "Thus, if an appeal is not filed against the preliminary decree and its correctness is not challenged, it becomes final and the party aggrieved thereby will not be permitted to challenge its correctness in an appeal against final decree."

The Privy Council in *Ahmed Musaji Saleji* v. *Hashim Ebrahim Saleji*, AIR 1915 PC 116, held that failure to appeal against a preliminary decree would operate as a bar to raising any objection to it in an appeal filed against final decree. Thus Court in *Venkata Reddy* v. *Pothi Reddy*, (1963) Supp 2 SCR 616: AIR 1963 SC 992, 993 has held that the impact of Section 97 is that the preliminary decree, so far as the matters covered by it are concerned, is regarded as embodying the final decision of the Court passing that decree. It observed as under:

> "A preliminary decree passed, whether it is in a mortgage suit or a partition suit, is not a tentative decree but must, in so far as the matters dealt with by it are concerned, be regarded as embodying the final decision of the Court passing that decree,.......................".

This decision was relied upon in *Gyarsi Bai* v *Dhansukh Lal,* AIR 1965 SC 1055 in which it was observed as under:

> "It is true that a preliminary decree is final in respect of the matters to be decided before it is made. It is indisputable that in a mortgage suit there will be two decrees, namely preliminary decree and final decree, and that ordinarily the preliminary decree settles the rights of the parties and the final decree works out those rights."

The only argument, which the appellant/defendant urged in reply to the plaintiff's reliance on Section 97, was that the provision does not preclude a challenge to a preliminary decree after a final decree is made, if the former is a nullity. Now, that, in the Court's opinion is begging consideration. Besides urging Section 5 of the Arbitration Act, the defendant has nothing to show how the suit properly lay, because there is no dispute that the parties own equal share in the suit property. It has not been pleaded or proved that there exists an arbitration agreement, which precludes the disputes that were urged in the partition suit, from the jurisdiction of the civil court; nor was there any document to show that the Court's jurisdiction in the given facts of the case, was ousted. Besides a bland assertion of nullity, there is no explanation why the preliminary decree was never challenged before the final decree. The mere reliance on the interim orders, which in essence worked out the equities of the parties, to arrive at a working solution *pendente lite,* as it were, did not displace the undoubted jurisdiction of civil courts over partition claims. Therefore, the explanation of the appellant is without merit. The appeal is consequently not maintainable.

15. Sections 67 read with Sections 94, 95 and 97 – Suit for Recovery

In *Jai Prakash Hydro Power Ltd.* v. *Misoo Ram (deceased) through LR, (Himachal Pradesh),* 2016 (Latest HLJ) HP 185: 2006 (3) Shim LC 31 the High Court held, Mr. Bhupender Gupta, learned Senior Advocate has drawn the attention of the Court to Ext. DX. Plaintiff while appearing as PW-1 has admitted receipt Ext. DX. It has come in the evidence as discussed herein that the plaintiff was paid final compensation and he has received the same in the presence of DW-2 KBR Dubey and DW-3 S.K. Mitra. It is also duly established from Ext. DW-2/A to Ext. DW-2/G that the plaintiff has received the amount of compensation towards damages of crop on 28.2.2001, 18.2.2001, 25.2.2001, 2.3.2001,18.2.2001, 26.2.2001 and again on 26.2.2001. Once plaintiff has received full and final settlement of compensation for damages, present suit filed by the plaintiff was not at all maintainable. This material aspect has been overlooked by the learned District Judge while decreeing the suit of the plaintiff. Plaintiff was estopped from filing suit after receiving full and final payment.

Plaintiff has been paid due and admissible compensation for the damage caused to his apple trees while erecting HT transmission lines from Karchham to Jhakri. Plaintiff ought to have disclosed that he has received full and final compensation, in the plaint. He has suppressed material facts. Plaintiff has received compensation without any reservation or any protest. He was estopped from instituting suit for recovery of damages. Plaintiff in his replication has also not denied the fact that he has received a sum of Rs. 33,800/-. Photocopies of the document were marked and exhibited in evidence. No objection was raised at the time of marking and exhibiting the documents. In all the receipts as discussed herein above, it has been proved that amount has been paid as compensation as final settlement towards damage to the apple trees while laying transmission lines. Plaintiff has received Rs. 6,905/- from the defendant and Rs. 33,800/- from the Larson & Toubro Ltd. Construction Group.

15. Trial court has gravely erred in discarding testimonies of defendants' witnesses.

16. In view of the discussion and analysis as made herein above, the judgment and decree dated 17.9.2005 rendered by learned District Judge, Kinnaur Civil Division at Rampur Bushahr, Himachal Pradesh in Civil Suit No. 17/2003, is set aside. Suit of the plaintiff is dismissed.

16. Electricity Act, 2003 Sections 67 read with Sections 94, 95 and 97 Suit for Recovery

In *Jai Prakash Hydro Power Ltd.* v. *Misoo Ram (deceased) through LR*, 2006 (3) Shim LC 31 (HP).

17. Sections 97(1) and 100 Second Appeal – Framing of Issues

In *Tulli Ram* v. *Fateh Singh @ Fatehbir*, 2017 (1) PLR 688 (P&H) the High Court said, I have heard the learned counsel for the parties and appraised the paper book and of the view that there is a force and merit in the submissions of Mr. Amit Jain, for, the fact noticed above itself reveals, that there was an apparent collusion as Gulab Singh had caused a breach of trust reposed in him by the principal/appellant(s). His attorney had already been cancelled and earlier sale deed executed on that basis had as per the judgment and decree dated 29.04.2005 been set aside. Nothing prevented Gulab Singh-attorney-holder, who was the defendant in the earlier round of litigation, to disclose the factum of the agreement to sell in hand. If at all, the agreement to sell was entered on 18.09.2000, nothing prevented the respondent(s)-plaintiff(s) to examine the stamp vendor or his register. Even the scribe produced did not bring, on record, the register. All these factors are key for declining the discretionary relief, yet the Courts below did not appreciate the aforementioned facts. The judgment and decree dated 29.04.2005 (Ex.D-4) is part and parcel of the record of the Courts below. The Court ought to have examined the contents thereof by noticing the conduct of the agent. It has also not been proved whether the consideration had allegedly been received by the attorney and passed on to the appellant(s)-defendant(s) or not. In my view, it is a fit case where the Courts below should not have exercised the discretion under Section 20 of the 1963 Act and at the best, once, the respondent(s)-plaintiff(s) have proved the amount of sale consideration of Rs. 2,00,000, they should have been held entitled to recover the amount from Gulab Singh-defendant No. 3.

6. No doubt, this Court on earlier occasions had been framing substantial questions of law while deciding the appeal, but in view of the *ratio decidendi* culled out by five learned Judges of the Hon'ble Supreme Court in *Pankajakshi (dead) through LRs* v. *Chandrika*, AIR 2016 SC 1213: 2016 (1) KLT 851, wherein the proposition arose as to whether in view of the provisions of Section 97 (1) CPC, whether the provisions of Section 41 of the Punjab Courts Act, 1918 would apply or the appeal i.e. RSA would be filed under Section 100 of Code of Civil Procedure. The Constitutional Bench of Hon'ble Supreme Court held that the decision in *Kulwant Kaur* v. *Gurdial Singh Mann (dead) by LRs*, 2001 (4) SCC 262: [2001] 2 SCR 525 applicability of Section 97(1) of CPC was not correct law, in essence, the provisions of Section 41 of the Punjab Courts Act, 1918 had been restored back and therefore, I do not intend to frame the substantial questions of law while deciding the appeal aforementioned.

7. For the foregoing reasons, the judgment and decree of both the Courts below viz-a-viz the grant of discretionary relief i.e. the specific performance of agreement to sell dated 18.09.2000, are hereby set aside and are modified that the respondent(s)-plaintiff(s) are entitled to recover the amount of Rs. 2,00,000/- along with interest @ 6% from Gulab Singh. The suit of the respondent(s)-plaintiff(s) is partly decreed. The decree sheet is ordered to be drawn.

With the aforesaid observations, the appeal stands disposed of.

18. Section 97 and 54 – Decree for Partition – Appeal

In *Manoj Lala* v. *Motilal Lala*, AIR 2017 Gau 62, Mr. Das, learned senior counsel appearing for the appellants submits that his clients are not aggrieved by the preliminary decree dated 24/12/2001 passed by the learned Civil Judge No. 1, Cachar, Silchar but are challenging the final decree dated 19/11/2009, inter-alia, on the ground that the final decree is not in conformity with the preliminary decree dated 24/12/2001. Mr. Das further submits that the "Saham" prepared under the directions of the learned Civil Judge No.1, Cachar, during the pendency of the MC No. 1/2004 preferred by the respondent no. 3 is wholly illegal and has rendered the entire process as null and void. He submits that the Court below ought to have permitted the Collector to take note of the grievances of all the parties before affecting the partition of the immovable properties.

By referring to a decision of the Hon'ble Supreme Court rendered in the case of *Bikoba Deora Gaikwad* v. *Hirabai Marutirao Ghorgare* reported in (2008) 8 SCC 198: 2008 (72) ALR 191 as well as *Muthangi Ayyanna* v. *Muthangi Jaggarao* reported in (1977) 1 SCC 241, Mr. Das submits that the process initiated under Section 54 of the CPC is ministerial function of the Court and if there is any discrepancy between the preliminary decree and the final decree prepared in terms thereof, than in that event, the appeal against the final decree shall be maintainable in the eye of law.

By relying on another the decision of the Supreme Court in the case of *Shankar Balwant Lokhande (Dead) by LRs* v. *Chandrakant Shankar Lokhande*, AIR 1995 SC 1211, Mr. Das submits that till such time the final decree determining the rights of the parties by metes and bounds is drawn up and is engrossed on stamped papers, no executable decree can be said to have been prepared.

It is also the specific case of the appellants that ever since Amaresh Singh has purchased the share of the plaintiff no. 2 in the ancestral property of the appellants, all the legal proceedings have been conducted by him in the name of the plaintiffs and but for the induction of an outsider in the form of Amaresh Singh, the contentious issues arising by and between the parties would have been amicably resolved long back.

He ourt held, From a plain reading of the order dated 30/07/2012 passed by the Apex Court, it is apparent that the appellants have been granted leave to prefer an appeal against the final decree prepared in connection preliminary decree dated 24.12.2001 passed in Title Suit No 23/1987. Therefore, a clear understanding as regard the true identity of "final decree" against which the leave to appeal has been granted will be necessary. Since the present appeal has been preferred against the final decree dated 19/11/2009 whereas only the certified copy of the final decree dated 28/10/2009 is available on record, hence, a query was made by this court seeking clarification in the matter. However, the learned counsel for both the parties could not indicate with any degree of clarity and precision as to which final decree has been permitted to be appealed against by the order dated 30/07/2012.

The aforesaid aspect of the matter assumes great significance for the following reasons. If the decree dated 28/10/2009 is treated as the final decree, then the present appeal would not be maintainable since the final decree dated 28/10/2009 is not under challenge in this proceeding. Moreover, the appellants having unsuccessfully challenged in RFA No 4 / 2010, the judgement and order dated 28/10/2009 directing preparation of final decree, a further challenge to the order dated 28/10/2009 in the present appeal would also not be permissible in the eye of law. In the absence of any challenge to the order dated 28/10/2009, assailment of the final decree prepared thereunder may also not be sustainable. Since, there is no final decree dated 19/11/2009 available on record, the question of impugnment of the same in the present appeal also cannot not arise.

Form an analysis of the submissions made on behalf of the appellants, it appears to this court that in the garb of the present appeal, the appellants are making a veiled attempt to re-agitate the same issues raised in RFA No. 4/2010 which were conclusively decided by the order dated 22/03/2012 passed by the Division Bench. The entire thrust of arguments advances by the appellants' counsel appears to be directed against the involvement of an outsider, viz. Amaresh Singh, who is stated to have purchased the share of plaintiff No.2. It appears that the basic objection of the appellants is not so much as regards either the preliminary decree or the final decree but pertaining to the purchase of the share of the plaintiff no.2 by Amaresh Singh. Even if that be the case, the appellants cannot be permitted to agitate such an issue in the instant appeal preferred in terms of the leave granted by the Hon'ble Apex Court.

For the reasons stated here-in-above, I am of the considered opinion that there is no merit in this appeal and the same is accordingly dismissed.

There would be no order as to costs.

19. Order XX, Rule 18 and Section 97 – Partition Suit – Preliminary Decree – Survey Commissioner Appointed

In *Sri Pranballab Debnath* v. *Minati Debnath, (Tripura)* AIR 2017 Tripura 22 the petitioner filed a written objection against the application of the respondent No. 2 for passing a final decree and at the same time filed an application stating that his mother and sister had gifted their respective shares in the suit land in his favour by the Gift Deed bearing No. 1-2665 dated 16-5-1996. The trial court then directed the petitioner to produce the said Gift Deed, but he could not do so despite exercise of due diligence by him whereupon the trial court drew adverse inference against him and rejected the application so filed by him. The petitioner also filed an application under Order XVIII, Rules 17 and 18 CPC for examining him to prove the said Gift Deed. In the meantime, the respondent No. 2 filed his written objection against the said application on the ground that the applications were after-thought and a device to stall the proceeding and prayed for the rejection thereof. The trial court after hearing the parties passed the impugned order rejecting the said applications. Aggrieved by this, this revision is preferred by the petitioner. It is the contention of Mr. P. Chakraborty, the learned counsel for the petitioner that the petitioner has now become entitled to 3/7th share of the suit land by virtue of the said Gift Deed and the trial court misdirected itself by fixing a date for hearing on the report of the Survey Commissioner without considering his new case vis-a-vis the said Gift Deed; this resulted in irreparable loss to him. He, therefore, submits that there is improper exercise of jurisdiction by the trial court in throwing out his case without hearing him on merit.

The High Court said, I have given my anxious consideration to the contentions advanced by the learned counsel for the petitioner, but do not find any merit thereon. Preliminary decree is undoubtedly an appealable decree. Section 97 of CPC is in the following terms:

> "97. *Appeal from final decree where no appeal from preliminary decree.*— Where any party aggrieved by a preliminary decree passed after the commencement of this Code does not appeal from such decree, he shall be precluded from disputing its correctness in any appeal which may be preferred from the final decree."

The Apex Court had an occasion to consider the provision of Section 97, CPC in *Mool Chand* v. *Dy. Director, Consolidation,* (1995) 5 SCC 631: AIR 1995 SC 2493, and explained the legal position in the following manner:

> "26. Thus, if an appeal is not filed against the preliminary decree and its correctness is not challenged, it becomes final and the party aggrieved thereby will not be permitted to challenge its correctness in an appeal against final decree."
>
> 27. The Privy Council in *Ahmed Musaji Saleji* v. *Hashim Ebrahim Saleji,* AIR 1915 PC 116: 17 Bom LR 432 (SC), held that failure to appeal against a preliminary decree would operate as a bar to raising any objection to it in an appeal filed against final decree. This Court in *Venkata Reddi* v. *Pothi Reddi,* 1963 Supp (2) SCR 616: AIR 1963 SC 992 has held that the impact of Section 97 is that the preliminary decree, so far as the matters

covered by it are concerned, is regarded as embodying the final decision of the court passing that decree. It observed as under:

> "A preliminary decree passed, whether it is in a mortgage suit or a partition suit, is not a tentative decree but must, insofar as the matters dealt with by it are concerned, be regarded as embodying the final decision of the court passing that decree."

This decision was relied upon in *Gyarsi Bai* v. *Dhansukh Lal,* AIR 1965 SC 1055: (1965) 2 SCR 154 in which it was observed as under:

> "It is true that a preliminary decree is final in respect of the matters to be decided before it is made.. It is indisputable that in a mortgage suit there will be two decrees, namely, preliminary decree and final decree, and that ordinarily the preliminary decree settles the rights of the parties and the final decree works out those rights."

In the instant case, the petitioner, admittedly, did not challenge the preliminary decree passed by the trial court. Even when the trial court asked him to produce the Gift Deed in question also, he failed to do so. The effect of Section 97 is that the preliminary decree so passed by the trial court, in so far as the matters covered by it is concerned, is regarded as embodying the final decision of the court passing the decree. There is, therefore, no improper exercise of jurisdiction by the learned Civil Judge in rejecting the series of application filed by the petitioner. Apparently, the petitioner is making a last ditch effort to stall the proceedings lawfully conducted by the trial court so that the respondent is deprived of the fruit of his litigation.

***98. Decision where appeal heard by two or more Judges.*—(1) Where an appeal is heard by a Bench of two or more Judges, the appeal shall be decided in accordance with the opinion of such Judges or of the majority (if any) of such Judges.**

(2) Where there is no such majority which concurs in a judgment varying or reversing the decree appealed from, such decree shall be confirmed:

Provided that where the Bench hearing the appeal is composed of two or other even number of Judges belonging to a Court consisting of more Judges than those constituting the Bench and the Judges composing the Bench differ in opinion on a point of law, they may state the point of law upon which they differ and the appeal shall then be heard upon that point only by one or more of the other Judges, and such point shall be decided according to the opinion of the majority (if any) of the Judges who have heard the appeal including those who first heard it.

Nothing in this section shall be deemed to alter or otherwise affect any provision of the letters patent of any High Court.

SYNOPSIS

Comments

1. Section 98: Scope and Application

With the addition of sub-section (3), section 98, by the repealing and Amending Act of 1928, that section has no application to cases heard by Division Bench of a Chartered High Court, whether on appeals from decrees of subordinate courts or from decrees passed by a judge of High Court on the original side. All cases of difference of opinion among the judges composing the Division Bench are governed by clause 36, Letters Patent, and the Division Bench should state expressly the points of difference: 15 L 425: 1934 L. 371(FB); 34 PLR 584: 1993 L 648 (1); ILR 1938 A. 972. Letters Patent, clause 36 and not section 98, governs the procedure in cases of difference of opinion in revision cases: 32 IC 330: 17 Cr LJ 42. Section 98 applies even to Chartered High Courts subject of letters patent clause 36. The Madras High Court said that the result is that clause 36 applies to chartered High Court and section 98 to courts other than chartered High Courts: *Dhunu Raju* v. *Bulkishen Das Moti Lal Dugu*, ILR 52 Mad 563: AIR 1929 Mad 641: 57 MLJ 264 (FB). If the appellate court Judges agree that a part of the lower court judgment is erroneous, that part must be reversed, and if as to rest, the Judges are equally divided, it is deemed as confirmed: 31 IC 965; 22 CLJ 525; 1928 M. judges differing on a question of law decision to be arrived at with reservation of point of law: 22 IC 383: 18 CWN 33. Where, in an appeal under the Land Acquisition Act, the judges composing Division Bench differ as to the amount of additional compensation, the award of the lower court should be confirmed under section 98: 41 M. 943: 35 MLJ 110.

2. Decree Regarding Several Items

Where the 'decree' contains adjudications regarding several items each adjudication is a decree as defined in section 2(2) and the provisions of section 98 should be applied with reference to the adjudication of each item. Where the judges composing a Bench do not agree in confirming the adjudication made by the lower court in respect of one item, but they agree in reversing the decree of the lower court as regards another item, the decree appealed from should be varied so far as the Bench agree that it should be varied and confirmed (31 IC 965, rel. on); *Harak Narain* v. *Babban*, 55 All 672: 1933 ALJ 1425: AIR (20) 1933 All 473. Where two judges of a Division Bench differ on a point of law and refer the matter to a third judge, the latter must confine his opinion to the specific point and not dispose of the case *de novo* on the merits: *Portab Singh* v. *Bhabuti Singh*, ILR 35 All 487: 40 IA 182: 25 MLJ 492 (PC).

It may be noted here that the new Code has brought considerable changes in the provisions. Under the old Code, when the two judges differed, the whole appeal was referred to a third judge, but under the new code, it is only the point of the law that has to be referred: 39 C. 353: 16 CWN 817. Under the proviso to the section, reference can be made only when there is a difference on a question of law and not on fact: *Gossami Sri Gridhariji* v. *Romanlalji Gossami*, (1889) 16 Ind App 137: ILR 17 Cal 3 (PC). The word 'may' used in the proviso cannot be read as equivalent to the word 'shall'. Under the proviso it is discretionary for the members of the Bench hearing appeal to state the point of law on which they differ. If they do not choose to state the point of law but proceed to give their judgments differing from each other, the decree of the lower court from which the appeal has been filed is to be confirmed. When a Bench differ in opinion on certain points of law, under section 98, they may state those points and the hearing by the other judges is confined to the specific points stated, and cannot cover the whole case again. Section 98 is confined to points of law only but the newly added sub-section (3) makes it subject to the provisions of the letters patent, under clause 27 of which the points of difference may be points of fact as well as points of law. But in both cases only the points of difference should be stated and not the whole case. *Akbari Begam* v. *Rahmat Husain*, 56 All 39: 1993 ALJ 1127: AIR 1933 All 861 (SB); *Kameshwar Singh* v. *Rajbansi Singh*, AIR 1943 Pat 433: 217 Ind Cas 49 (Practice of Patna High Court is to note the point of law on which judges differ in the order sheet). Where in an appeal the case is referred to a third judge on difference between two judges who heard the appeal it is not open to the third judge to adjudicate upon the point on which there is no difference of opinion between two judges. *Zainuddin Hussain Mirza* v. *Sohan Lal Pachisia*, 1958 BLJR 84: 1957 Pat LR 481: AIR 1958 Pat 290. Reference to a third judge – Third judge deciding case on another point – procedure; 26 CWN 985: 1922 C 544.

Section 98(2).—Dissenting views of judges.—Words "consisting of" used in Section 98(2).—Mean and has relevance only to sanctioned strength of judges.—Two judges constituting Division Bench expressed different views and thought it fit to refer matter to third judge.—Matter should await till arrival of third judge.

The words "consisting of" shall mean and also be considered to have relevance only to the sanctioned strength. Therefore, taking to account the fact that for the time being, there were only two judges in position and that the learned Judges who constituted the Division Bench, expressed different views and at the same time thought fit to refer the matter to the opinion of a third judge, the matter should await till the arrival of a third judge. *Sikkim Subba Associates* v. *State of Sikkim*, AIR 2001 SC 2062: (2001) 5 SCC 629: JT 2001 (5) SC 186. The Supreme Court said in the case of *Tej Kaur* that if there is no majority opinion approving or reversing the decree under appeal, it should be confirmed. *Tej Kaur* v. *Kirpal Singh*, AIR 1995 SC 1681: (1995) 5 SCC 119: 1995 (3) SCALE 596: JT 1995 (5) SC 201.

3. Section 98(2) – A general Law – Whether can be Superseded by a Subsequent Act

In *Pankajakshi (dead) through LRs.* v. *Chandrika,* 2011 (1) CHN (SC) 227: 2010 12 JT 151: 2010 4 KLT (SC) 608: 2011 (1) RCR (Civ) 146, learned counsel for the appellant submitted that since there was a difference of opinion between the two Hon'ble Judges of the High Court, the appeal should have been referred to the Hon'ble the Chief Justice for placing it before one or more other Judges. However, learned counsel for the respondent submitted that in view of the proviso to Section98 (2) the reference to one or more other Judges can only be made when there is difference of opinion between the two Judges on a point of law. He submitted that since the difference of opinion was on a question of fact no reference could have been made to one or more other Judges, and the appeal should have been dismissed in view of the main part of Section 98 (2) CPC.

Section 9 of the Kerala High Court Act by which the Travancore-Cochin High Court Act was repealed to the extent of its repugnance may also be extracted. It reads:

> "9. *Repeal.*—The provisions of the Travancore-Cochin High Court Act, 1125 (5 of 1125), insofar as they relate to matters provided in this Act, shall stand repealed."

In our opinion Section 23 of the Travancore-Cochin Act is in the nature of a special provision while Section 98(2) is in the nature of general law. As between the two, the former would apply in preference to the latter. The decision of this *Courtin P.V. Hemlatha* v. *Kattamkandi Puthiya Maliackal Saheeda,* AIR 2002 SC 2445: 2002 (5) ALT 19 (SC) to the extent it takes a contrary view, in our opinion, requires to bere considered. That apart, the question whether in an appeal arising out of an order passed by the High Court to which Section 98(2) of the CPC applies, this Court can in exercise of its power under Article 136 of the Constitution direct the matter to be placed before a third Judge to resolve the conflict arising from two differing judgments, has not been examined either in P.V. Hemlatha's or Tej Kaur's case. We, therefore, consider it appropriate to refer to a larger Bench for consideration and an authoritative pronouncement the following two questions: (1) Whether Section 23 of the Travancore-Cochin Act remains unaffected by the repealing provisions of Section 9 of the Kerala High Court Act. If so, whether Section 23 is in the nature of a special provision vis-a-vis Section 98(2) of CPC.

(2) Whether this Court can under Articles 136 and 142 of the Constitution direct in any appropriate case of reference to a third judge to resolve the conflict arising between two judges of the High Court hearing an appeal, on a question of fact. Let the papers of this case be placed before Hon'ble the Chief Justice for constituting a larger Bench.

4. Order XXII Rule IV(4), Section 98 – No Substitution Made for 18 Years

In *Nazim Khan* v. *Bibi Tohidan,* 2014 (2) PLJR 595 from the facts stated above, it is apparent that though more than 18 years have already elapsed, when by office note dated 11.09.1995 it was pointed out that the respondent No. 13 and 27 are dead, yet no petition has been filed till date seeking substitution of deceased respondent no. 13 and 27.

When this matter has been placed for consideration by office note dated 03.04.2014 on the competency matter, learned counsel appearing on behalf of the appellants submits that the respondent no. 13 and 27 were not the contesting defendants in the court below, therefore, the appellants are not required to take any steps for substitution of their heirs and legal representatives. According to him, the appellants are exempted from filing substitution petition in terms of Order XXII Rule 4(4) C.P.C. In support of the above contention he has placed reliance on a Division Bench judgment of this Court in the case of *Md. S. Imam* v. *Rai Bharat Kumar,* AIR 2000 Pat 321, para-20: AIR 2000 Pat 321. I am afraid, the submissions made on behalf of the appellants cannot be accepted and has to be rejected in view of the latest judicial pronouncements made by the Hon'ble Apex Court in the case of *Budh Ram* v. *Bansi,* (2010) 11 SCC 476.

It is true that Order XXII Rule 4(4) provides that in appropriate cases the Court may exempt the plaintiff from the necessity of substituting the legal representatives of any such defendant, who has failed to file a written statement or who, having filed it, has failed to appear and contest the suit at the hearing. For better appreciation Order XXII Rule 4 (4) C.P.C. is reproduced herein below:

> "The Court whenever it thinks fit, may exempt the plaintiff from the necessity of substituting the legal representatives of any such defendant who has failed to file a written statement or who, having filed it, has failed to appear and contest the suit at the hearing; and judgment may, in such case, be pronounced against the said defendant notwithstanding the death of such defendant and shall have the same force and effect as if it has been pronounced before death took place."

In the present case, admittedly, the respondent no. 13 and 27 are dead. Apparently, in the present first appeal, time was granted to the appellants by order dated 19.10.1995, again by order dated 16.11.1995 and finally by order dated 23.10.1997 for filing substitution petition vice deceased respondent no. 13 and 27. Despite passage of more than 18 years since the first order was passed on 19.10.1995, substitution petition has not been filed on behalf of the appellants. In fact, no petition, at all, has been filed on behalf of the appellants, even for seeking exemption from the necessity of substituting the heirs of the deceased respondent no. 13 and 27.

In view of the fact that the appeal has abated as against the heirs and legal representatives of the deceased respondent no. 13 and 27 and in view of the fact that the present first appeal arises out of the judgment and decree passed in a partition suit, this appeal has become incompetent and it cannot proceed further in view of the law laid down by the Hon'ble Apex Court in the cases of *State of Punjab* v. *Nathu Ram,* AIR 1962 SC 89; *Ram Sarup* v. *Munshi,* AIR 1963 SC 553; *Rameshwar Prasad* v. *Shambehari Lal,* AIR 1963 SC 1901, as also *Budh Ram* v. *Bansi,* 2010 AIR (SCW) 5071.

5. Section 98 – Order XXII, Rule 4 – Abatement Partial if Some of the Persons Representing the Estate on Record

In *Andhra Pradesh Industrial Infrastructure Corporation Limited* v. *Pratap Karan,* 2015 7 JT 595: 2015 10 SCALE 584: 2016 2 SCC 82: 2015 8 SLT 50, the Supreme

Court said, Letters Patent, wherever applicable, shall prevail over section 98, CPC. When the name of the original owner was recorded as owner of the suit property even in Record of right duly prepared in the year 1954-55 as evident from khasra-pahani, sudden removal of his name and substitution with name of State all of a sudden without any proceeding for Survey Settlement proceeding or preparation of record of right is illegal.

Plaintiffs had equal shares in the suit property left by their predecessors joining in the suit. Hence, even after death of any of the plaintiffs, the estate will be fully and substantially represented by the other sharers as owners of the suit property. Therefore, the entire suit will not abate because of non-substitution of the legal representative(s) of plaintiffs dying during pendency of appeal in High Court.

6. Section 98(2) – Read with Clause 36, Letters Patent

Where the two learned Judges of the Division Bench passed separate judgments. One of the learned Judges allowed the appeal and set aside the trial court judgment, whereas another learned Judge affirmed the trial court finding and dismissed the appeal. Both the learned Judges differed not only on the point of facts but also on the point of law. The learned Chief Justice, therefore, referred the matter to the third Judge for deciding the appeal. The learned third Judge, after going through the judgments of the learned differing Judges, formulated various issues and recorded its finding on all the points. The learned third Judge finally upheld the finding recorded by one of the learned differing Judges and allowed the appeal. In our considered opinion, therefore, there has been complete compliance of Clause 36 of the Letters Patent of the Andhra Pradesh High Court and the impugned judgment cannot be vitiated on that account.

7. Sections 98, 114 – Review – Jurisdiction of High Court

In *U.P. State Road Transport Corp.* v. *Indra Raj Verma,* 2017 4 ADJ 752: III (2017) ACC 292 (All), the High Court examined the jurisdiction of the High Court to review.

The Court held, in my humble view, the jurisdiction of review of its own judgements by virtue of Section 114 CPC is inherent in a Court and there is no doubt that the High Court being a Court of record for this purpose would not be a Court. The Tribunals unless such a jurisdiction is conferred cannot exercise the jurisdiction of review. The view taken by this Court finds support from a recent judgment rendered by the Apex Court in *Commissioner of Income Tax, Guwahati-I* v. *Meghalaya Steels Ltd.,* (2015) 279 CTR (Gau) 193: 2013 (4) GLT 254

In view of what has been recorded above, the submission put forth by Sri Shikhar Anand, learned counsel for the other side that such a jurisdiction in absence of an enabling provision being made in the Motor Vehicles Act, 1988 cannot be exercised by the High Court, in my considered opinion, deserves to be rejected. The position does not alter even if the jurisdiction of Civil Court by virtue of Section 175 of the Motor Vehicles Act is excluded for the reason that the High Court nevertheless is empowered to exercise civil appellate jurisdiction.

8. Section 98(3) – Repeal of Act by Subsequent Act

In *Pankajakshi (Dead) Through L.Rs.* v. *Chandrika,* 2016 1 BBCJ (SC) 516: (2016) 6 SCC 157: the Supreme Court said, applying the test laid down by the aforesaid decisions of this Court, namely, that the subject matter of the two statutes must essentially be the same and/or that the main object and purpose of the statutes should be substantially similar, we find that the Travancore-Cochin High Court Act formed the Charter for jurisdiction to be exercised by the said High Court. This jurisdiction is exercised not only in civil matters but criminal and other matters as well. The main object and purpose of the Travancore-Cochin Act is to lay down the jurisdiction and powers of the High Court that was established in the said State. On the other hand, the subject matter of the Code of Civil Procedure is to lay down procedure in all civil matters, and no others. Also, the said Code would apply to all courts which deal with civil matters, subject to the exceptions contained therein, and not only the High Court. For this reason, it is difficult to say that the Code of Civil Procedure corresponds to the Travancore-Cochin High Court Act. Shri Viswanathan's first contention must therefore fail.

9. Section 98(3) – Scope and Object – Section 98(2) of the Code of Civil Procedure to all Courts and in Civil Proceedings Only

In *Pankajakshi (Dead)* v. *Chandrika,* 2016 (161) AIC 157: 2016 (2) MLJ 448: 2016 AIR (SCW) 1213 (SC) (Constitution Bench), the Apex Court held, We now turn to the arguments based on Section 98(3) of the Code of Civil Procedure.

As has been stated herein above, Section 98(3) was introduced in the year 1928 when all the High Courts in British India were governed only by the Letters Patent establishing them. The reason for the introduction of the said Section goes back to the landmark judgment of the Privy Council in Bhaidas' case and various other judgments following the said landmark judgment.

In Bhaidas' case (supra), the Privy Council had to decide whether clause 36 of the Letters Patent would prevail over Section 98 of the Code of Civil Procedure. Clause 36 of the Letters Patent was similar to Section 23 of the Travancore-Cochin High Court Act. The Privy Council, after setting out Section 4 of the Code of Civil Procedure, held:

> "*There is no specific provision in section 98, and there is a special form of procedure which was already prescribed.* That form of procedure section 98 does not, in their Lordships' opinion, affect. The consequence is that the appellant is right in saying that in this instance a wrong course was taken when this case was referred to other Judges for decision, and he is technically entitled to a decree in accordance with the judgment of the Chief Justice. This view of the section is not novel, for it has been supported by judgments in Madras, in Allahabad and in Calcutta."

The controversy which reared its head after the aforesaid judgment was as to whether appeals under the Code of Civil Procedure, being referred to in clause 16 of the Letters Patent, would also be covered by clause 36. In order to appreciate the aforesaid controversy, it is necessary to set out clauses 15, 16 and 36 of the Letters Patent as follows:—

"*Clause 15. Appeal from the courts of original jurisdiction to the High Court in its appellate jurisdiction*:—And we do further ordain that an appeal shall lie to the said High Court of Judicature at Madras, Bombay, Fort William in Bengal from the judgment (not being a judgment passed in the exercise of appellate jurisdiction in respect of a decree or order made in the exercise of appellate jurisdiction by a Court subject to the superintendence of the said High Court and not being an order made in the exercise of revisional jurisdiction, and not being a sentence or order passed or made in exercise of the power of superintendence under the provisions of Section 107 of the Government of India Act, or in the exercise of criminal jurisdiction) of one Judge of the said High Court or one Judge of any Division Court, pursuant to Section 108 of the Government of India Act, and that notwithstanding anything hereinbefore provided, an appeal shall lie to the said High Court or one Judge of any Division Court, pursuant to Section 108 of the Government of India Act, on or after the first day of February, 1929 in the exercise of appellate jurisdiction in respect of a decree or order made in the exercise of appellate jurisdiction by a Court subject to the superintendence of the said High Court where the Judge who passed the judgment declares that the case is a fit one for appeal; but that the right to appeal from other judgments of Judges of the said High Court or of such Division Court shall be to Us, Our heirs or successors in Our or Their Privy Council, as hereinafter provided.

Clause 16. Appeal from Courts in the Provinces:—And we do further ordain that the said High Court of Judicature at Fort William in Bengal shall be a court of Appeal from the Civil Courts of the Bengal Division of the Presidency of Fort William, and from all other Courts subject to its superintendence, and shall exercise appellate jurisdiction in such cases as are subject to appeal to the said High Court by virtue of any laws or regulation now in force.

Clause 36. Single Judges and Division Courts:—And we do hereby declare that any function which is hereby directed to be performed by the said High Court of Judicature at (Madras), (Bombay), Fort William in Bengal in the exercise of its original or appellate jurisdiction, may be performed by any Judge, or by any Division Court thereof, appointed or constituted for such purpose, in pursuance of section 108 of the Government of India Act, 1915; and if such Division Court is composed of two or more Judges and the Judges are divided in opinion as to the decision to be given on any point, such point shall be decided according to the opinion of the majority of the Judges if there shall be a majority, but if the Judges should be equally divided, they shall state the point upon which they differ and the case shall then be heard upon that point by one or more of the other Judges and the point shall be decided according to the opinion of the majority of the Judges who have heard the case including those who first heard it."

It will be seen that clause 36 refers to the "appellate jurisdiction" of the High Court, which jurisdiction would contain appeals both under clause 15 of the Letters Patent and under Section 96 of the Code of Civil Procedure. Despite this, some High Courts took the view that appeals under Section 96 of the Code of Civil Procedure would not be covered by clause 36 of the Letters Patent, and that therefore Section 98(2) and not Clause 36 would be applied in such appeals before the High Courts.

In an instructive Full Bench judgment in *Immidisetti Dhanaraju* v. *Motilal Daga*, AIR 1929 MAD 641: 1929 (29) LW 823, owing to the difference of opinion between two learned Judges of the High Court, the question that had to be decided was whether clause 36 of the Letters Patent would apply or Section 98 of the Code of Civil Procedure. Phillips, J. after referring to the Privy Council judgment in Bhaidas' case, stated:—

> "There is no specific provision in Section 98, and there is a special form of procedure which was already prescribed. That form of procedure Section 98 does not, in their Lordships' opinion, affect."

10. PR Act, 1951, Sections 98(b), 100(1)(b) and 123(1) – Civil Procedure Code, 1908, Order VII, Rule 11(a) – Election Petition – Dismissal of Election Petition on Ground of Want of Cause of Action – Order VII, Rule 11(a)

In *Sri. Neiphrezo Keditsu* v. *Smt. Zeneisiile Ate Loucii*, AIR 2016 Gau 155 (Gau), High Court of Gauhati said, From the aforesaid averments made in paragraph 7, it would appear that payment was made to five named persons not only for securing votes of their clan members but also for casting their own votes and so the five named persons are also recipients of alleged bribe. It has been alleged that such distribution has been made by Peter Kuotsu with the knowledge, consent and connivance of the respondent. It is also mentioned in the same paragraph that one of these five persons informed about the whole episode to the election petitioner and pursuant thereto her proposed share of Rs. 3,000/- was also forwarded to her through one Diezelie Loucii. Payment made to these five persons by Peter Kuotsu on 09.10.2014 at about 7-8 P.M. in Zhadima village, therefore, is a complete incident forming material fact. Whether or not, such facts can be established by adducing evidence by the election petitioner is altogether a different question. Fact remains that specific date, time and place of distribution of money by a particular person to specified persons have been made. The source of information has also been disclosed. The returned candidate in his application for rejection of election petition might have denied the correctness of the statements but his denial cannot be taken into consideration while deciding applicability of the provision of Order VII, Rule 11 of the Code of Civil Procedure. The allegations levelled in paragraph 7 of the election petition if taken at face value whether a triable case has been made out, is to be considered at this stage. Explanation given by the returned candidate is not relevant at this stage. Judged from such angle it cannot be said, in my considered opinion, that a triable case has not been made out by the averments made in the election petition.

Similarly, in paragraph 11 of the election petition the allegation is made that one Vibeilietuo Kets distributed money to voters/electors of Gariphema village in the residence of Kezha Loha at 5 P.M. on 09.10.2014. This was witnessed by Pastor Riiduozhii Yashii and his wife. These two persons informed the election petition that such distribution of money was held at the place and time aforementioned and it was to the knowledge, consent and connivance of the returned candidate. To buttress the allegation of consent, Pastor Riiduozhii Yashii further informed the petitioner that few days prior to the aforesaid distribution of money, the returned candidate had attended a feast in the residence of Kezha Loha where he met the people of Gariphema village. The distribution of money was made thereafter on 09.10.2014 asking for votes in favour of the returned candidate. Prima facie, date, time and place of alleged distribution of money and allegation of consent of the returned candidate has been made in paragraph 11 of the election petition. It is true that the names of voters who were present there have not been disclosed but at the same time it has been stated that 72 voters were present at the aforesaid date and time in the house of Kezha Lohe to receive money at the rate of Rs. 50,000/- per head for casting vote in favour of the returned candidate. When an assembly of 72 persons was allegedly witnessed by Pastor Riiduozhii Yashii and his wife and he disclosed this information to the election petitioner, and it has also been specifically stated that aforesaid Kezha Lohe is originally a resident of Gariphema village, the allegation does not appear to be that bald, vague or unnecessary warranting an inference that they do not give rise to material facts. The number of villagers of a particular village has been mentioned. The place where they had assembled on which date and time have been mentioned and the amount of money received by each of them is also specified and all these things have been allegedly informed to the election petition by an eye witness. If in course of trial of the election petition, the petitioner examines Pastor Riiduozhii Yashii, he being the person who had witnessed the alleged fact shall definitely be a competent witness to prove such fact and so it is possible on the basis of the averments made in paragraph 11 of the election petition to make out a prima facie case of bribery within the meaning of section 123(1)(A)(b) of the Act. The question as to how the knowledge and consent of the returned candidate could be inferred by Pastor Riiduozhii Yashii may, at best, be a subject of cross examination provided he steps inside the witness box. Situated thus, I am not inclined to hold that allegation levelled in paragraph 11 of the election petition do not make out a cause of action for going into trial.

Once it is held that allegations made in paragraph 7 and 11 of the election petition have given rise to cause of action for trial of an election petition on corrupt practise, it would be improper to throw away the election petition at this stage merely for improper verification in the concerned affidavits. The affidavits are apparently in terms of the prescribed form under the Act. Being aware as to the observations made by the Hon'ble Supreme Court in the case of K.K. Ramachandran Master (supra), this court cannot scuttle the election petition at the preliminary stage when allegations of corrupt practise have been levelled. The Hon'ble Supreme Court held that defective verification of affidavit is curable. Such view was expressed by the Hon'ble Supreme Court in the case of *F.A. Sapa* v. *Singora* reported in (1991) 3 SCC 375: AIR 1991 SC 1557 and in *Sardar Harcharan Singh Brar* v. *Sukh Darshan Singh* reported in (2004) 11 SCC 196: AIR 2005 SC 22. A charge of corrupt practise is really a serious one. It cuts at the very root of sanctity of an election. It vitiates the election process not only for the concerned election but also disentitles an offender to be candidate for a further period. This is why even after expiry of the term of election, an election petition involving corrupt practise does not become infructuous. Considering the serious nature of the charge of corrupt practise, the Hon'ble Supreme Court held in paragraph 10 of the case of K.K. Ramachandran Master (supra) that petitioner should not be refused an opportunity to prove the allegations made by him although petition might be clumsily drafted and improperly verified. This court cannot lose sight of the observation made by the Hon'ble Supreme Court in the case of K.K. Ramachandran Master (supra) and so the objection raised in regard to verification of the election petition cannot be based so as to reject the election petition at the threshold without giving a scope to the election petitioner to make amend for the curable defect. Thus, all the points raised by the learned counsel on behalf of the returned candidate in support of his prayer for rejection of election petition under Order VII, Rule 11 of the Code of Civil Procedure are found to be not acceptable and accordingly, this application is devoid of any merit. The application stands dismissed.

11. Sections 98 and 114 – Order XLVII – Review

In *U.P. State Road Transport Corp. Thru. Its M/D* v. *Indra Raj Verma*, 2017 (4) ADJ 752: 2017 (2) TAC 350: 2017 (3) ACC 292 (All) (Lucknow Bench) the High examined the scope of section 98 of the code and said, a conjoint reading of Chapter V Rule 2 (c) and Rule 8 of the High Court Rules read with Section 98 CPC would lead to a corollary that a matter cognisable by learned Single Judge may be decided as per the rules of procedure or other law or special order of the Chief Justice. Rules of procedure made by the High Court import the procedure what it is provided under Section 98 CPC.

Addressing on the question of maintainability of review petitions, learned counsel for the petitioner has argued that the statutory rules framed in exercise of power under Article 225 of the Constitution of India provide two special remedies; (i) the remedy of special appeal under Chapter VIII Rule 5; and (b) review under Chapter V Rule-12. The distinction in the two remedies, as pointed out by learned counsel for the review petitioner is that no special appeal lies, if a person is aggrieved against the judgement of Single Judge of the High Court which arises out of judicial/*quasi* judicial proceedings decided by a court/authority; but, there is no such restriction placed upon the jurisdiction of this Court insofar as the review of its own judgement passed by the High Court is concerned.

Whatever the distinction may be, it is well settled that the remedy of appeal, revision or review unless provided for under law cannot be exercised. In the present case, the question is whether review of its own judgement passed by the High Court in exercise of civil appellate jurisdiction provided under Section 173 of the Motor Vehicles Act is permissible or not. The procedure provided under Chapter V Rule 12 of the High Court Rules is reproduced below:

> "12. *Application for review*:—An application for the review of a Judgement shall be presented to the Registrar General, who shall endorse

thereon the date when it is presented and lay the same as early as possible before the Judge or Judges by whom such judgment was delivered along with an office report as to limitation and sufficiency of court fees. If such Judge or Judges or any one or more of such Judges be no longer attached to the court, the application shall be laid before the Chief Justice who shall having regard to the provisions of Rule 5 Order XLVII of the Code, nominate a Bench for the hearing of such applications:

Provided that an application for the review of a judgment of one Judge who is precluded by absence or other cause for a period of six months next after the presentation of the application from considering the decree or order to which the application refers, shall be heard or disposed of by a single Judge, and that an application for the review of a judgment of two or more Judges, any one or more of whom is or are precluded by absence or other cause for a period of six months next after the presentation of the application from considering the decree or order to which the application refers, shall be heard or disposed of by a Bench consisting of the same or a greater number of Judges."

The above Rule merely regulates the procedure as to how an application for review is to be dealt with.

It may be gainful to note that the provisions of Section 114 CPC are available to a court irrespective of the nature of civil jurisdiction it exercises; the conditions, however, subject to which the review jurisdiction can be exercised are that the decree or order must not be appealed against or there is absence of any such remedy under law. In the present case, the certificate under Article 134-A of the Constitution of India does not seem to have been prayed for nor the High Court of its own motion has granted any. The bar of Article 133 (3) also applies. Appeal under Article 136 of the Constitution of India has also not been filed. Thus, there is no impediment coming in the way of filing review petitions.

In my humble view, the jurisdiction of review of its own judgements by virtue of Section 114 CPC is inherent in a court and there is no doubt that the High Court being a court of record for this purpose would not be a court. The Tribunals unless such a jurisdiction is conferred cannot exercise the jurisdiction of review. The view taken by this Court finds support from a recent judgment rendered by the apex court reported in *Commissioner of Income Tax, Guwahati-I* v. *Meghalaya Steels Ltd.*, (2011) 241 CTR (Gau) 384: 2014 (2) GLT 33

16. In view of what has been recorded above, the submission put forth by Sri Shikhar Anand, learned counsel for the other side that such a jurisdiction in absence of an enabling provision being made in the Motor Vehicles Act, 1988 cannot be exercised by the High Court, in my considered opinion, deserves to be rejected. The position does not alter even if the jurisdiction of civil court by virtue of Section 175 of the Motor Vehicles Act is excluded for the reason that the High Court nevertheless is empowered to exercise civil appellate jurisdiction.

From a plain reading of Chapter V Rule 12 of the High Court Rules, it is gathered that the Rules merely regulate the procedure so as to carry out the object of Section 114, CPC. In other words, the power of review being inherent in a Court necessitates laying down the procedure to deal with review applications and it is i this context that Chapter-V Rule 12 has come to be framed under Article 225 of the Constitution of India. The High Court being a court of record hence the power of review of its judgements is inherent by virtue of Section 114 CPC.

12. Valuation of Appeals for Determination of Pecuniary Jurisdiction

The High Court also considered the question of valuation of appeal for deciding jurisdiction and said, The next vital question is as regards the valuation of appeals for determination of pecuniary jurisdiction of learned Single Judge exercising appellate powers under Section 173 of Motor Vehicles Act. Reference may be made to Chapter VIII Rule 40 of the High Court Rules which for ready reference is extracted below:

> "40. Court fee to be paid in cases coming up before the Court:- Court fees shall be payable in cases coming before the Court in the exercise of its ordinary original civil jurisdiction or in the exercise of its jurisdiction as regards appeals from judgment passed by it in the exercise of its ordinary civil jurisdiction to the extent to, and the manner in which they are payable in similar classes of cases coming before it, under the provisions of Section 4 of the Court Fees Act, 1870."

The aforesaid rule by reference makes Section 4 of the Court Fees Act, 1870 applicable insofar as the money claims are concerned. Right to claim compensation is essentially a money claim, therefore, the Court would hasten to refer to the Court Fees Act, 1870. The relevant part of Section 7 of the Court Fees Act which relates to money claims, is reproduced as under:

> "7. *Computation of fees payable in certain suits.*—The amount of fee payable under this Act in the suits next hereinafter mentioned shall be computed as follows:—
>
> *For money.*—(i) In suits for money (including suits for damages or compensation, or arrears of maintenance, of annuities, or of other sums payable periodically)-according to the amount claimed."

The aforesaid provision clearly demonstrates that a money claim read in the Statutes for damages or compensation etc. is to be valued according to the main claim. Insofar as the valuation of appeals is concerned, reference may also be made to Section 8 of the Court Fees Act, 1870, which is reproduced hereunder:

> "8. *Fee on memorandum of appeal against order relating to compensation.*— The amount of fee payable under this Act on a memorandum of appeal against an order relating to compensation under any Act for the time being in force for the acquisition of land for public purposes, shall be computed according to the difference between the amount awarded and the amount claimed by the appellant."

A plain reading of Section 8 of Court Fees Act, 1870 demonstrates that the same would apply only in relation to the matters of claim of compensation under Land Acquisition Act but guidance insofar as the valuation of appeals filed before this Court is concerned, can be derived from the above provision so far as money claims whether in a suit or appeal before this Court is concerned.

This Court in view of the provisions quoted above, is of the considered opinion that the valuation of appeals filed before this Court would be determinable on the amount as it is set out in the claim filed before the Tribunal. The court fee under the Motor Vehicles Rules, 1998 is fixed, therefore, nothing turns on the question of payment of court fee but pecuniary jurisdiction of this court has to be viewed in the light of valuation of appeal mentioned therein. The appeal for enhancement of compensation clearly mentions the valuation of appeal at Rs. 45,09,950/- after deduction of the amount allowed by the Tribunal. Thus, even if the appeal subsequently filed by UPSRTC was valued at Rs. 4,90,050/-, the same ought to have been heard along with the appeal for enhancement and the two appeals were thus cognisable by a Division Bench. The position in money claims would be different, if the appeal was filed by UPSRTC alone. A respondent against whom a money claim is allowed, would maintain an appeal on the quantum of amount allowed, being it cause arising against the judgment

***99. No decree to be reversed or modified for error or irregularity not affecting merits or jurisdiction.*—No decree shall be reversed or substantially varied, nor shall any case be remanded in appeal on account of any misjoinder or non-joinder of parties or causes of action or any error, defect or irregularity in any proceedings in the suit, not affecting the merits of the case or the jurisdiction of the Court.**

Provided that nothing in this section shall apply to non joinder of a necessary party.

SYNOPSIS

Comments

1. Section 99: Scope and Application

Justice Beg discussed the relative scope of sections 99 and 105 of the Code of Civil Procedure and said that both are not in conflict with each other. According to him, section 105 does not affect merit of the case.

2. Per Beg, J.

Section 99 is not in conflict with section 105 as the latter relates to matters not affecting the merits of the case and the former relates to matters affecting the merits of the case or jurisdiction of the court: *District Board, Muzaffarnagar* v. *Upper India Sugar Mills Ltd.*, AIR 1957 All 527. The section applies only to errors or defects or irregularities in the suit or proceedings out of which the appeal then being heard arises; and not to provisions of suits or proceedings which have come to an end: 23 A. 499 (500); 1938 NLJ 392 1938.

A trial court cannot assume the role of an appellate court and condone material faults in its own procedure with help of section 99, C.P.C.; *A.S. Metal Mart* v. *First National Bank, Ambala*, ILR 1953 Patiala 615: AIR 1954 Pepsu 115. Section 99 undoubtedly relates to the powers of an appellate court but it shows that distinction between lack of jurisdiction and wrong exercise of it has been recognized by the Code: *Inder Pal Singh* v. *Babu Singh*, 1956 All LJ 228: 1955 All WR (HC) 637: AIR 1956 All 218. Section 99 refers only to decrees that is, decrees of civil courts. It does not refer to any award and the procedure followed by the arbitrators in giving the award: *Firm Jaidev Madanlal Sarrafs* v. *Kanhaiyalal Heda*, 1953 AIMJ 94: AIR 1953 Ajmer 49. Where it turns out that a *vakalatnama* on behalf of a party to an appeal under a disability (insanity) bore the thumb mark not of the lunatic but of another person, it cannot be said that the whole proceedings are invalid and that the decree passed in the appeal, is void and of no effect when there was a next friend on behalf of the insane person who also signed the vakalatnama and represented the insane person in appeal. At the most it is only an irregularity not affecting the merits: 53 Mys HCR 111. The best test to ascertain whether an erroneous interlocutory order has affected the ultimate decision on the merit is to see whether the court would have come to the same decision had the erroneous order not been passed: 2 CIR 257. Where the appellate court did not apply its mind to the case fully and proceeded on an entire misapprehension of the trial court's decision, a remand for a fresh disposal of appeal would be justified: 1931 C. 164: 52 CLJ 566. A decree can be varied on appeal on grounds which have come into existence since it was passed: 1931 B. 280: 33 Bom LR 266. The successor of a deceased or resigned *mutawalli* has no *locus standi* on a litigation pending until his name is actually brought on the record in place of former *mutawalli*. No order or decree in his favor could be passed till then. But if a decree were to be passed prior to such bringing on record, the irregularity affects the merits of the case fundamentally and is not covered by section 99: 1940 RD 402: 1940 AWR (BR) 214.

3. Extent of Prejudice where the Copies of Statements were not Furnished

Supreme Court of India in the case of *State Bank of Patiala*, examined the extent of prejudice. In the said case copies of statements of witnesses were not furnished and the plaintiff's case was decreed mainly on the ground of the non-furnishing of the copies of the statements of witnesses and documents, the factual position as found by the appellate court is to the following effect: though a list of documents/witnesses was furnished to the respondent before the commencement of the enquiry, the copies of the documents and statements recorded during the preliminary enquiry were not supplied to the respondent. Half an hour before the commencement of the enquiry proceedings, the respondent was advised to peruse the said documents and the statements of witnesses which he did. Balwant Singh was not examined at the regular enquiry.

The other witness who was examined during the preliminary enquiry, Kaur Singh, Patwari, was examined at the regular enquiry. The question is whether on the above facts, it can be held that there is a violation of Regulation 68 and whether the violation, if any, vitiates the enquiry. Regulation 68 insofar as is relevant, reads thus:

"(a) The inquiring authority shall where the officer does not admit all or any of the articles of charge furnisd to such officer a list of documents by which and a list of witnesses by whom, the articles (b) the inquiring authority shall also record an order that the officer may for the purpose of preparing his defence:

(i) Inspect and take notes of the document listed within five days of the order or within such further time not exceeding five days as the inquiring authority may allow:

(ii) submit a list of documents and witnesses that he wants for enquiry.

(iii) be supplied with copies of statements of witnesses, if any, recorded earlier and the Inquiring Authority shall furnish such copies not later than three days before the commencement of the examination of the witnesses by the Inquiring Authority.

The Court observed that where the enquiry is not governed by any rules/regulations/statutory provisions and the only obligation is to observe the principles of natural justice or, for that matter, wherever such principles are held to be implied by the very nature and impact of the order/action the Court or the Tribunal should make a distinction between a total violation of natural justice [rule of *audi alteram partem*] and violation of a facet of the said rule, as explained in the body of the judgment. In other words, a distinction must be made between "no opportunity" and no adequate opportunity, *i.e.*, between "no notice"/"no hearing" "no fair hearing". (a) In the case of former, the order passed would undoubtedly be invalid, one may call it "void" or a nullity if one chooses to. In such cases, normally, liberty will be reserved for the Authority to take proceedings afresh according to law, *i.e.*, in accordance with the said rule [*audi alteram partem*. But in the latter case, the effect of violation [of a facet of the rule of *audi alteram partem*] has to be examined from the standpoint of prejudice; in other words, what the Court or Tribunal has to see is whether in the totality of the circumstances, the delinquent officer/employee did or did not have a fair hearing and the orders to be made shall depend upon the answer to the said query. It is made clear that this principle does not apply in the case of rule against bias, the test in which behalf are laid down elsewhere. While applying the rule of *audi alteram partem* the primary principle of natural justice, the Court/Tribunal/Authority must always bear in mind the ultimate and over-riding objective underlying the said rule, *viz.*, to ensure a fair hearing and to ensure that there is no failure of justice. It is this objective which should guide them in applying the rule to varying situations that arise before them.

There may be situations where the interests of state or public interest may call for a curtailing of the rule of *audi alteram partem*. In such situations, the Court may have to balance public/State interest with the requirement of natural justice and arrive at an appropriate decision. Now, in which of the above principles does the violation of sub-clause (iii) concerned herein fall? In our opinion, it falls under Principles No. 3 and 4(a) mentioned above. Though the copies of the statements of two witnesses [Kaur Singh, Patwari and Balwant Singh] were not furnished, the respondent was permitted to peruse them and take notes therefrom more than three days prior to their examination. Of the two witnesses, Balwant Singh was not examined and only Kaur Singh was examined. The respondent did not raise any objection during the enquiry that the non-furnishing of the copies of the statements is disabling him or has disabled him, as the case may be, from effectively cross-examining the witnesses or to defend himself. The trial court has not found that any prejudice has resulted from the said violation. The appellate court has no doubt said that it has prejudiced the respondent's case but except merely mentioning the same, it has not specified in what manner and in what sense was the respondent prejudiced in his defence. The High Court, of course, has not refereed to aspect of prejudice at all.

For the above reasons, the Court held that no prejudice had resulted to the respondent on account of not furnishing him the copies of the statements of witnesses. The Judges felt satisfied that on account of the said violations it cannot be said that the respondent did not have a fair hearing or that the disciplinary enquiry against him was not a fair enquiry. Accordingly, we allow the appeal and set aside the judgment of the High Court affirming the judgments of the trial court and appellate court the suit, filed by the respondent shall stand dismissed; *State Bank of Patiala* v. *S.K. Sharma,* AIR 1996 SC 1669: (1996) 3 SCR 972: (1996) 3 SCC 364.

4. Effect of Error Committed by the Trial Court on the Second Appeal

Bombay High Court in the case of *Subhash Vithalrao Gatlewar* examined the error committed by the district Judge in making available to the plaintiff a decree for possession.

This second appeal was filed by unsuccessful defendants No. 3 to 8 who had succeeded in the trial court, however, failed in the first appellate court. The question was do defendants 3 to 8 prove that they acquired the ownership of the suit site by way of adverse possession for more than 12 years?

Learned trial court held the Issue No. 3 in favour of the defendants No. 3 to 8. While holding so, learned trial judge disbelieved the plaintiffs evidence of the defendant being the lessee and their having paid the rent which were Exh. 65 and 68. The suit No. 52 of 1981 was dismissed by the Judgment and decree dated 12-11-1982.

The aggrieved plaintiff filed appeal before the District Court which was registered as Regular Civil Appeal No. 38/1983. The said appeal was heard and decided by District Judge, Yavatmal who allowed the appeal, reversed the decree of the trial court and decreed the suit.

Present second appeal was admitted on ground No. 1 of memo of appeal namely:—

> "1. That the learned District Judge was in error in seeking to make available to the plaintiff a decree for possession particularly when it was

evident that he had failed to establish his possession within 12 years from the date on which the suit came to be filed."

The Court said that judgments are relied upon to bring home the point as to what are the ingredients which the appellant does not dispute the proposition that the appellants had to establish and prove occupation hostile to the owners right and urged and repeated that whatever was the evidence brought by the appellants to prove their animous and possession being hostile was sufficient. It is, therefore, not necessary to deal with all the citations in details. In view of the discussion hereinbefore, being unpursuaded by the submission of the appellants that the substantial question of law framed by this Court at the time of admission and at the time of hearing is liable to be answered in the negative holding that the appellants having failed to prove their possession being adverse and that the District Judge was not in error in allowing the appeal. The appeal before the High Court, therefore, was dismissed with costs; *Subhash Vithalrao Gatlewar* v. *Dattatraya Keshavrao Shinde*, 2005 (1) Mh LJ 43.

5. Additional Plaintiff Added after Remand of the Case

Additional plaintiffs impleaded after the case was remitted back – After remand, an application was moved by the power-holder, Veeraraghava Iyer, to implead the wife and daughters of Krishna Iyer as suppl. plaintiffs. That application, I.A. 2948 of 1990, was allowed and the wife and children were brought on record as suppl. plaintiffs 2 to 4.—The High Court of Kerala examined a case where the additional plaintiffs were impleaded after the case was remanded back.

The appeal was directed impugning the judgment and decree passed by the learned Additional Sub-Judge, Palakkad in O.S. No. 238 of 1979. One Chami Narayanan-defendant is the appellant. One Krishna Iyer represented by his Power of Attorney-holder Veeraraghava Iyer is the first plaintiff and supplemental plaintiffs 2 to 4 are the wife and daughters of Krishna Iyer, who are Respondents 2 to 4 in this appeal.

The common grounds of both the appellant and the respondents were as follows: Suit was originally filed by Veeraraghava Iyer representing as Attorney of Krishna Iyer for recovery of a sum of Rs. 8,004 borrowed by the appellant by executing Ext. A-1 promissory note dated 26-7-1976. Apart from the above common grounds of both the sides, it is the further contention of the respondents that prior to the execution of Ext. A-1 pronote, Krishna Iyer executed Ext. A-2 general power deed dated 5-5-1975. Krishna Iyer left his family in the year 1977 and his whereabouts were not known for more than 7 years. However, once he was seen by Veeraraghava Iyer, the Attorney, when the period of limitation for claiming the amount under the pronote was nearing. Veeraraghava Iyer in his capacity as donee of the power conferred on him under Ext. A-2 filed the suit before the expiry of the period of limitation. It is also the admitted ground as culled out from the records that the suit was originally dismissed by the Court below holding that the donee of the power, Veeraraghava Iyer, is not clothed with the right of laying a claim under the pronote. Aggrieved by the judgment of dismissal of the suit, an appeal was preferred before this Court as A.S.

No. 422 of 1982. This Court remanded the matter to the Court below for fresh trial with a direction to render a finding on the validity of the power deed, Ext. A-2, after framing an issue in that regard. After remand, an application was moved by the power-holder, Veeraraghava Iyer, to implead the wife and daughters of Krishna Iyer as suppl. plaintiffs. That application, I.A. 2948 of 1990, was allowed and the wife and children were brought on record as suppl. plaintiffs 2 to 4.

To uphold or uproot the judgment of the trial court the following points were raised: (1) Whether Ext. A-2 is a general power deed or it is a specific power deed conferring authority on Veeraraghava Iyer; (2) Barring whether Ext. A-2 is a general or a specific power deed, could Veeraraghava Iyer lay the claim under the pronote under the doctrine of 'agency by necessity'? (3) Whether the impleadment of suppl. plaintiffs 2 to 4 is legally correct and proper? (4) Apart from the decision whether the impleadment is correct or not, if the suit is barred by limitation? and (5) The order passed by the Court below in the application. I.A. 2948 of 1990, impleading suppl. plaintiffs 2 to 4 can be challenged in this appeal as per the statutory provisions enjoined in section 105, CPC?

The Court observed that when appointing a Second Commissioner and accepting his proceeding, the Court must have taken a clear view as to why the first Commissioner's report and proceeding were not accepted and set aside. But the above principle will not render any assistance to the case of the appellant before me. For, in the instant case before me I have found above that the order of impleadment is not illegal and the Court does not lack jurisdiction while passing the said order and the application, in fact, has been filed by the legal representatives within the right time and in accordance with the statutory provisions of law.

Finally, it was held that the impleadment of suppl. plaintiffs 2 to 4 is legal, correct and proper that the suit is not barred by limitation and that the impleadment of suppl. plaintiffs 2 to 4 cannot be challenged in this appeal under the provisions of section 105, CPC. In the result, the appeal was dismissed. However, the parties were directed to suffer their respective costs. Order on C.M.P. No. 3937 of 1991 in A.S. No. 377 of 1991 stood dismissed; *Chami Narayanan* v. *V.R. Krishna Iyer*, AIR 1998 Ker 365: 1998 (2) Ker LT 420: 1999 (2) Land LR 350.

6. Dispute where the Tenant Defendant Claimed Ownership-Statutory Objection against Claim of Possession was Raised

The Bombay High Court in the case of *Vatsalabai Wd/O Vishwanath* v. *Madhaorao Laxmanrao Thakare*, (2005) 1 Mah LJ 980 examined the status of the defendant claiming to have acquired status of owner. The second appeal was filed by legal heirs of original defendant No. 1. The suit was decreed and the decree has been confirmed by the first appellate court.

According to the plaint, the suit lands were let out to the defendant No. 1 for the period upto 1-3-1957 and it is alleged that the defendant No. 1 sub-let Survey No. 105/2 to the defendant No. 2 soon and after the lease period was over, the defendants re-delivered the suit lands in possession of the owner

Ahilyabai who thereafter cultivated the land personally. Thereafter Ahilyabai was dispossessed sometime at the end of April, 1957.

Consequent upon the death of the original owner Ahilyabai, the plaintiff Madhaorao Thakare became the owner and, therefore, filed suit for possession of the suit land and also claimed *mesne* profit. The defendant No. 1 contested the suit by filing the written statement and specifically admitted the lease of one year and further pleaded that he, however, continued to cultivate as tenant. As he claimed the tenancy, prayed for referring the dispute as to his status as tenant, to the Tenancy Court for adjudication. He also pleaded that he had become the owner of the suit land on tiller's day.

The crucial question which was posed as main hindrance and the statutory objection to the claim for possession related to the issue of tenancy. The learned trial court observed as regards tenancy at page 18 of print as follows:

> "So far as the question of tenancy is concerned this right is negatived to the Defendant upto the highest Tribunal of our nation. The copy of order of M.R.T. is at Exh. 74. I have no jurisdiction to entertain this plea and therefore, in view of finding of competent Court, this issue is answered in negative.
>
> It is, thus, obvious that a judgment of 1st appellate court as well is not liable to be set aside on account of any error or defect or irregularity in any suit or appellate proceedings or judgment "not affecting the merits of the case or the jurisdiction of the Court." Section 99, Civil Procedure Code has been interpreted by various High Courts from Privy Council and the Hon'ble Supreme Court, as well. The construction thereof is impelled for avoiding unnecessary cost and inconvenience to the litigant as well as avoiding the situation of setting aside the judgment on account of technicality when the judgment and decree otherwise does not affect the merits of the case, It shall be useful to simply refer to the judgment on this point and shall not be necessary to discuss each one in detail.
>
> According to the Court, it is, therefore, liable to be held that in the present case, the appellate Court's judgment is not liable to be regarded as illegal or otherwise contrary to the principles of justice and suffering from non-application of mind on account of its failure to comply with Order XLI, rule 31 of Civil Procedure Code. It is also considered necessary to record that in view of section 99 of Civil Procedure Code, the judgment impugned is not liable to be reversed on account of the said failure as the appellant has failed to demonstrate that the judgment and decree under appeal are wrong on merits and resulting in injustice. No substantial question of law is involved in this case on which the impugned judgment can be reversed. In the result, the appeal fails. Same is dismissed with costs throughout"; 2005 (1) Mh LJ 980.

7. Meaning and Scope of the Term 'Jurisdiction'

The term 'jurisdiction' is used in the sense of pecuniary or local jurisdiction or jurisdiction relating to the subject-matter of the suit: 28 C 324: 5 CLJ 71: 5 CLJ 329. A Full Bench of the High Court of Patna examined the jurisdiction of the appellate court and said that the word 'jurisdiction' in section 99 judged from the point of view of locality pecuniary value or the subject-matter of a suit, means competency to try. When there is a want of jurisdiction an appellate court will interfere even if there is no miscarriage of justice: 95 IC 406: 1926 A. 650; 1937 P. 147. District Judge entertaining incompetent appeal – second appeal lies; *Arjun Rautura* v. *Krishna Chandra Gajpati Narayan Deo,* AIR 1942 Pat 1: ILR 21 Pat 1 (FB).

8. Trial Court Discarding Report of the First Commissioner—Its Legality

The trial court discarded the report of the first Commissioner. The High Court of Kerala examined the legality of the findings.

The main point involved in these appeals was relating to the accounts and the liability of the first defendant. The Supreme Court directed the appointment of a Commissioner and had given specific directions relating to that matter. Counsel for the first defendant, Mr. C.K. Sivasankara Panicker, very vehemently attacked the approach and the basis of the decision of the lower court. The court below discarded Ext. C5 report (1st Commissioner's report) altogether and placed reliance on the second Commissioner's reports (Exts. C6 and C10). Counsel attacked the approach made in this regard as unjustified and unsustainable. Counsel for the first plaintiff, Mr. P. Sukumaran Nair, was not able to successfully substantiate the approach and basis adopted by the lower court in eschewing Ext C5 totally, and also in setting aside Ext. C5 (first Commissioner's report), after obtaining the second report (Exts. C6 and C10). However, counsel submitted in the alternative, that in view of prior proceedings, the court below could place reliance on Exts. C6 and C10 (second Commissioner's reports) to the extent they do not militate against the findings contained or dealt with in Ext. C5. On this aspect, counsel stressed the terms of the order of the trial court dated 21-12-1974 as affirmed in C.R.P. No. 41 of 1975.

The Court held that on the facts of this case, the Court below acted illegally and totally in excess of or without jurisdiction in appointing a second commissioner and in placing reliance on Exts. C6 and C10 reports. The judgment of the trial court shows that the entire reasoning and conclusion is based on Exts. C6 and C10. The judgment of the trial court cannot stand. In view of our conclusion Ext. C5 will hold good, till it is set aside, for reasons stated, Exts. C6 and C10 should be eschewed from consideration. The trial court will consider Ext. C5 report and the evidence of the Commissioner recorded on 15-1-1972. If the court finds for valid and sufficient grounds, that Ext. C5 report is not acceptable or otherwise infirm, then and then alone, it will appoint another Commissioner and proceed further in accordance with law. In case the court finds that Ext. C5 report is proper and acceptable, it will proceed to decide the suit in the light of that report and evidence recorded in the case.

For the reasons stated above, the judgment and decree of the court below were set aside. The appeals were allowed. The matter was remitted back to the court below for fresh consideration in accordance with law and in the light of the observations contained herein. The matter was directed to be posted in the court below for appearance of parties on 7-1-1985; *Swami Premananda Bharathi* v. *Swami Yogendra Bharathi,* AIR 1985 Ker 83: 1985 Ker LT 144: 1985 Ker LJ 225.

Whether the judgment and decree of the Court below are vitiated for non-compliance with the provisions contained in Order I, rule 3B and Order VI, rule 4A, Civil Procedure Code, the Madhya Pradesh High Court referred to the views of Fransis Bacon in the case of *Brijrajsingh* that Judges must be beware of hard constructions and strained inferences; for there is no worse torture than torture of laws – said Francis Bacon. Should the law be so interpreted and implemented as to let the litigation go into a circuitous and torturous path of journey or should it be so interpreted as to cut-short litigation keeping in view the purpose and object behind its enactment, is the question staring at the Court hearing this reference.

The Code of Civil Procedure (M.P. Amendment) Act, 1984 (Act No. 29 of 1984) introduced rule 3B, in Order I, and rule 4A, in Order VI, in the body of the Code of Civil Procedure, 1908, as applied to the State of Madhya Pradesh. Of late, it has come to the notice of this Court that the provision is being utilised by the appellate courts as a tool for earning easy disposal of appeals by making orders of remand unmindful of the fact that a convenient resort to that provision has the result of setting at naught the concluded decrees of competent courts, well merited otherwise, and thereby throwing down the litigants to retread the arduous path of tiresome litigation.

The facts in brief were that the plaintiff/respondent No. 1 instituted a suit for declaration of title and partition relating to an agricultural holding. The suit was instituted on 20-10-1976 and came to be decided on 28-8-1980. The suit was decreed on 2-9-1980. The defendants preferred an appeal before the lower appellate court which was heard on merits and dismissed by the lower appellate court *vide* its judgment and decree dated 17-4-1990. In between, on 14-8-1984, had come into force the Amending Act of 1984. The provisions of Order I, rule 3B, and Order VI, rule 4A, Civil Procedure Code were not complied with by the defendant as appellant before the lower appellate Court nor did that Court advert its attention at securing compliance therewith. The losers in litigation, *i.e.*, the defendants, have come up to this court now seriously complaining of jurisdictional incompetence in the lower appellate court for failure of compliance thereat with the provisions contained in Order I, rule 3B, and Order VI, rule 4A, suggesting that the decree passed in appeal was vitiated and forcefully pressing for a remand so as to secure a rehearing of the appeal at the hands of the lower appellate Court after compliance with the said provisions of law. This Court admitted the appeal for hearing parties on the following question:

> "Whether the judgment and decree of the Court below are vitiated for non-compliance with the provisions contained in Order I, rule 3B and Order VI, rule 4A, Civil Procedure Code."

For the foregoing reasons the Court answered the questions referred as under:—

(1) the non-compliance with the provisions contained in Order I, rule 3B, Civil Procedure Code does not create jurisdictional incompetence in the Court hearing the suit or appeal solely on account of non-compliance therewith;

(2) the defect as to non-compliance with the provisions contained in Order I, rule 3B, Civil Procedure Code can be rectified by joining the State as party to the proceedings and noticing it at that very stage at which the defect is detected or pointed out to the Court;

(3) the party on whom lay the primary duty of impleading the State as party to the case having defaulted in doing so, cannot plead the defect at subsequent stage of the proceedings to its own advantage so as to get rid of a decree against it, otherwise well merited. No such decree shall be set aside unless the State be in a position to point out that merits of the case or jurisdiction of the Court have been affected on account of non-compliance with the provisions contained in Order I, rule 3B, and Order VI, rule 4A, Civil Procedure Code.

Accordingly, the Court directed the matter to be placed before the Single Judge as per Roster for disposal of Second Appeal in accordance with law. *Brijrajsingh* v. *Bitto Devi,* 1994 (0) MPLJ 192.

9. Misjoinder of Parties and Causes of Action

The words 'any misjoinder of parties or 'cause of action' have been inserted to supersede the ruling. An objection as to misjoinder cannot be taken for the first time on appeal, especially when the suit is decided on the merits in the first court: (17 IC 97) when the alleged misjoinder has affected neither the merits of the case nor the jurisdiction of Court. The Privy Council did not interfere, though the High Court may have acted erroneously in not giving effect to a plea of misjoinder: *Mahomed Hussain Khan* v. *Kishva Nandan,* ILR 1937 All 655: AIR 1937 PC 233. *See* also N. 418: 1937 PC 42. In a case to set aside father's alienations on grounds of immorality, several alienees parties pleaded misjoinder but did not press. The Privy Council examined the case where in spite of the misjoinder of the plaintiff as also the causes of action, the trial court has proceeded to take evidence on all the issues settled in the suit and the defendants have, apart from pointing out that they have been inconvenienced and harassed in leading evidence, not been able to show how they have been prejudiced by the mode of the trial and further in spite of the questions having been raised in the written statement and having been put in issue, it was not pressed for decision at early stage before the trial court of the case, it is not a fit case for the High Court to exercise its discretion against the plaintiffs and force them to start all over again with the suits: (1937 PC 42, foll.) *Madan Lal L. Raja Ram* v. *Munshi Datu,* AIR 1956 Pepsu 80. It was further held that where parties do not appear to have been prejudiced in any manner by an alleged misjoinder of defendants or causes of action, the defect if any is completely cured by section 99 CPC: 1949 RD 91.

10. Procedural Error – Omission to Bring Legal Representative on Record – Correction of Error – Payment of Costs

Where the procedural error has been brought to the notice of the trial court the error and mistake should be rectified and the rectification should be made even if no actual prejudice has been caused. Held, that in the circumstances of case, the omission to bring the legal representatives of the deceased defendant on record was a procedural mistake which had to be rectified but as there was great delay in bringing the error to the notice of the court the rectification should be made on payment of substantial costs; *Bengalilal Kanhiyalal Agarwal* v. *Gokal Chand Narain Das*, AIR 1954 Ajmer 80.

11. Illustrative Cases

Decree passed cannot be reversed simply because it was passed without hearing arguments. Where a person who is necessary party is not impleaded as defendant in spite of such objection being taken at the very start, the suit should be dismissed: *Subbaraya Sastri* v. *Seetha Ramaswami*, AIR 1933 Mad 664: 65 MLJ 290. Striking out names from the plaint and amending issues are not errors affecting the merits of the case. Where an irregularity in the matters of a transfer is owing to an administrative order, the irregularity is curable under section 99 CPC.; 1950 Ajmer 33. If a decree-holder instead of moving court which passed the decree moves the transferee court to proceed under section 50 against the legal representatives of the judgment-debator who dies pending execution, the defect in the procedure, is an irregularity and if it is not shown that this irregularity has affected the merits of case and the appellate court is prohibited from interfering with the order of transferring court impleading the legal representatives in view of section 99 read with section 141, when the objection was not raised at the appropriate stage: [*Debendra Nath* v. *G.A. Aratoon*, ILR 19 Pat 838: AIR 1941 Pat 139 and *Sham Lal Pal* v. *Modhu Sudan Sircar*, ILR 22 Cal 558, rel. on]; *Nilawwa Komm Malashiddappa* v. *Virupaxappa Mahantappa*, AIR 1959 Mys 99. The question of plaintiff's good faith is one of the facts and where it is material for his case it is necessary for him to raise that question in his pleadings and at any rate by asking the court to frame an issue on the point. According to the High Court of Bombay if he fails to do so, he cannot in appeal be allowed to say that there should have been an issue upon the point and as that question was not decided the dismissal of his suit cannot be upheld: 56 Bom LR 394: ILR (1954) Bom 463. The High Court of Rajasthan said that if the parties have not been prejudiced by the omission to frame issues and substantial justice has been done in case, notwithstanding the omission to frame issues, the decision will not be set aside, and the case will not be remanded for a new trial: 1951 Raj 56. An objection that there cannot be a decision in a partition suit of rights subordinate to that of the co-sharers, cannot be gone into for the first time in appeal; *Midnapore Zemindary Co. Ltd.* v. *Kumar Nares Narain Roy*, AIR 1921 Cal 368: 33 Cal LJ 317. An error in the valuation of the claim is not one which affects the merits of case: 1 BHCR 163.

12. Set-off – Court Fee not Paid

The High Court of Patna decided the effect of decision on point without raising issue 198 IC 390: 1942 Pat 366. Form of an issue, throwing *onus* on the wrong party, is not a ground in appeal for setting aside the decree provided the parties were not misled and the evidence fully gone into: 17 CLJ 38: 17 CWN 280. Where the plaintiff, in disregard of the provisions of Code, has united in the same suit, several suits against separate defendants, with the result that the litigation is conducted as though the defendants were a community with common interest, the procedure, though highly irregular, prevents the plaintiff from objecting to the use of evidence given in the case of some defendants as evidence in favor of all the parties. The deposition of a handwriting expert, signed by him and admitted in evidence does not vitiate the trial though it is not signed by the judge: 68 IC 664: 1923 N 7 (1). The exclusion of evidence in the lower court is not a sufficient ground for reversing that court's decision, unless the appellate court comes to the conclusion that the evidence referred, if it had been received ought to have varied the decision: 8 B. 408. Remand order consequent on error in rejecting documents already admitted by the predecessor judge is not one affecting the merits: 13 B. 499. The High Court of Madras following 36 M. 477, held that the second appellate court cannot set aside the decree of the first appellate court on the ground of improper admission of additional evidence unless it is satisfied that the decision on the merits is wrong, and that the additional evidence might have resulted in the wrong decision: 26 IC 50: 1914 MWN 864.

***99A. No order under section 47 to be refused or modified unless decision of the case is prejudicially affected.*—Without prejudice to the generality of the provisions of section 99, no order under section 47 shall be reversed or substantially varied, on account of any error, defect or irregularity in any proceeding relating to such order, unless such error, defect or irregularity has prejudicially affected the decision of the case.**

SYNOPSIS

Comments

1. Section 99 – Petition for Substitution Filed After Period of Limitation

In *Shrimati Panna Bala Manna* v. *Basudeb Manna,* 2011 (2) CHN 395: 2011 (2) CLJ 471 (Cal) the high Court examined the effect of limitation on an application for substitution. THE plaintiff initially instituted the suit against one Binoy Krishna Manna. Binoy Krishna Manna died during the pendency of the suit. Consequently, his heirs and legal representatives were substituted.

One of his heirs, namely, Kashi Nath Manna, who was substituted as defendant no. 1 (c), died intestate on June 6, 2006.

Admittedly, neither any application for substitution was filed nor any order was obtained by the plaintiff for exemption from substituting the heirs and legal representatives of said Kashi Nath Manna.

Mr. Sourav Sen, learned Advocate appearing for the sole respondent, strenuously argues that as the defendant concerned did not file his written statement, the decree passed against him is not a nullity in view of the provisions of Section 99 of the Code of Civil Procedure.

The High Court said, we are unable to accept the submission advanced by Mr. Sen. Abatement is automatic. The defendant No. 1 (c) died on June 6, 2006. After the expiry of the period of limitation for substituting the heirs and legal representatives of the said deceased defendant No. 1 (c), the suit stood abated as against him. However, leave could have been obtained by the plaintiff from exempting the plaintiff from substituting the heirs and legal representatives of the said defendant no. 1 (c) as the said defendant no. 1 (c) did not file his written statement in the suit. Admittedly, no such prayer was made.

Section 99 of the Code of Civil Procedure saves irregularities in respect of non-joinder of parties except where the non-joinder is of necessary party as non-joinder of necessary party is fatal to the suit. The provision is mandatory and, therefore, the Court has no discretion.

In this case the question of non-joinder of party is not involved. Here, on the death of a necessary party the suit stood abated due to the failure of the plaintiff to take steps for substitution.

Therefore, the decree passed against a deceased defendant is a nullity and has to be set aside.

2. Section 99 – In Second Appeal Judgment of ist Appellate Court is Unsustainable – Other Issues Need not be Examined

In *Ratan Lal Saha* v. *Gossaigaon Town Committee,* 2014 5 Gau LT 715 (Gau) the High Court of Gauhati said, having held that the appeal itself is incompetent and as such the appellate judgment is not sustainable in law, there is no necessity of deciding the second substantial question of law, which only relates to validity of the appellate decree for non consideration of certain exhibits. If the appeal itself is incompetent, by questioning, whether the appellate Court did or did not consider those exhibits, is irrelevant? Therefore, the second substantial question of law is abandoned being not relevant. In the result the second appeal is allowed. The impugned appellate judgment passed by the learned Civil Judge Senior Division, Kokrajhar, is set aside and the learned trial court decree passed by the learned Civil Judge Junior Division No. 2, Kokrajhar, in title suit No. 7 of 1994 is restored.

3. Section 99 read with Section 141 – Section 99 Prohibits Reversal or Making Substantial Variations in a Decree in Appeal for Misjoinder or Non-Joinder of Parties

In *Manti Devi* v. *Kishun Sah @ Kishun Deo Sao,* 2017 0 Supreme (SC) 342.

Kurian Joseph, R. Banumathi, JJ. in Civil Appeal Nos. 2014 of 2009 Decided on 23-03-2017 said, no suit can be dismissed in appeal or revision for misjoinder or nonjoinder of parties.

The High Court said, respondents/tenants pursued the matter in revision before the High Court. The High Court took the view that the suit was liable to be dismissed for misjoinder of parties. The relevant consideration reads as follows:—

> "In my view, the present case is not saved for the simple reason that where the plaintiffs had jointly petitioned to be the landlord and it is found that they are not "landlord" for the purposes of the suit in question, then jointly they has no causes of action. Further individually they had distinct causes of action as against distinct properties. The evidence does not distinguish the properties. It deals with the property as co owner which is incorrect. Their suit was instituted on a wrong and misconceived premise of joint/co ownership of premises. They had no joint personal necessity. In my view, it materially affects the merit of the case and is accordingly not saved by Section 99 of the Code of Civil Procedure. The decree of eviction is thus liable to be reversed and is accordingly set aside and the suit is dismissed."

Learned senior counsel, inviting our attention to Section 99 of the Code of Civil Procedure, contends that no decree shall be reversed or varied substantially on account of non-joinder or misjoinder of parties. Section 99 of the Code of Civil Procedure reads as follows:—

> "99. No decree to be reversed or modified for error or irregularity not affecting merits or jurisdiction.—No decree shall be reversed or substantially varied, nor shall any case be remanded, in appeal on account of any misjoinder or non-joinder of parties or causes of action or any error, defect or irregularity in any proceedings in the suit, not affecting the merits of the case or the jurisdiction of the court:
>
> Provided that nothing in this section shall apply to non-joinder of a necessary party."

The provision, in our view, is crystal clear. No decree can be reversed or substantially varied in appeal on account of misjoinder or non-joinder of parties. Under Section 141 of the Code of Civil Procedure, procedure under the Code in regard to suit shall be followed as far as it can be made applicable to proceedings in any Court of Civil jurisdiction. Therefore, what is provided under Section 99 of the Code of Civil Procedure in respect of appeal would apply to revision as well.

4. Order I, Rule 10 read with Section 99 – Plaintiffs Duly Substituted before Trial Court Itself

In *Kuldeep Kumar Dubey* v. *Ramesh Chandra Goyal (D) th LRs.*, 2015 1 ADJ (SC) 785: 2015 1 BBCJ (SC) 551: 2015 4 CivCC 333: 2015 2 JCR (SC) 174 the Su6preme Court said, defect/irregularity which does not affect merits of the case or jurisdiction of the court can be corrected under Order I rule 10 CPC and no suit should be reversed on such ground.

Learned counsel for the appellants submitted that it is undisputed that appellants Nos.1 and 2 are the sole owners of the property in question. It is not disputed that they were substituted as plaintiffs on the death of Shiv Kumar before the trial Court itself. It is also not disputed that they could maintain the suit for eviction. Thus on admitted facts, only defect pointed out is of formal nature in description without, in any manner, affecting the merits or the jurisdiction of the Court. Such irregularity could have been corrected by the Court under Order I Rule 10 and can be corrected even at this stage unless the defendant is in any manner prejudiced. No principle or authority has been brought to our notice which could affect the maintainability of the suit merely on account of wrong description which did not in any manner cause prejudice to the defendant, particularly when no such objection is shown to have been raised before the trial Court.

In our view, the District Judge is, thus, not justified in reversing the decree of the trial Court on such a technicality which did not in any manner affect the merits of the case. Section 99 of the Code of Civil Procedure.

5. Order VI Rule 17, Section 99 – Nature of Amendment is Relevant

In *Bhagwatiprasad* v. *Virendra Bhagwatiprasad Agrawal*, 2014 6 All MR 674: 2014 3 BomCR 736: 2015 2 CivCC 548: 2015 1 MhLJ 403, on behalf of the defendant/ appellant, it is submitted with reference to the ruling in *Abeda Iqbal Patel* v. *Cormorant Investment Pvt. Ltd.* reported in 2009 (3) Bom CR 338 (Para 7): 2009 (2) MhLJ 446, that the amendment proposed in the Written Statement ought to have been allowed by condoning delay to amend the Written Statement. Delay to amend the Written Statement could have been condoned. According to the learned Counsel for the appellant, a new plea can be allowed at the appellate stage. He made reference to the rulings in *Pandit Ishwardas* v. *State of Madhya Pradesh* reported in (1979) 4 SCC 163: AIR 1979 SC 551, and *Estralla Rubber* v. *Dass Estate (P) Ltd.*, (2001) 8 SCC 97 (Paras 5 and 7). The learned Counsel contended that the jurisdiction to decide the application for amendment of the Written Statement was wrongly exercised by the first Appellate Court.

The Court said, in view of Order VI, Rule 17 of the Code of Civil Procedure, on behalf of the respondents (original plaintiffs), it is urged that nature of amendment sought to be introduced is relevant. Learned Counsel for the respondent submitted that, in the Written Statement, there was no dispute about the description or identity of the suit property. Hence, amendment was held unnecessary and mala fide to delay the fruits of proceedings in the suit instituted in the year 1994. The appellant had filed Writ Petition No. 1709 of 2004 in this Court, which was not pressed and withdrawn by the Appellant with liberty to raise contention in the First Appeal. Thus, according to the learned Counsel for the respondent, the much belated attempt at the stage of Second Appeal by the appellant to amend the Written Statement is afterthought & mala fide only with a view to delay the inevitable fruits of the decree in the facts & circumstances of this case.

Section 99 of the Civil Procedure Code contemplates that no decree can be reversed or varied nor the appeal can be remanded for non-joinder of the party or causes of action. There was no any cross-examination of the plaintiffs in respect of the suit filed by Radheshyam pending as First Appeal. There was no any application in the trial Court at or before the date of hearing of the suit to implead Radheshyam. The first Appellate Court had clarified that Radheshyam was not a necessary party to the suit. The suits relating to the agreement to sell the suit property to Radheshyam instituted by or on behalf of Radheshyam and the suit simplicitor filed by the plaintiffs to recover possession from the defendant – appellant are different suits altogether with different causes of action awaiting their results separately. Learned Advocate for the respondent, therefore, supporting the impugned Judgment and Order, has prayed for dismissal of the appeal.

Legal position in this regard must be discussed. The Hon'ble Supreme Court of India in the case of *Salem Advocate Bar Assn.* v. *Union of India*, (2005) 6 SCC 344: AIR 2003 SC 189, has held thus:

> "It is to be noted that the provisions of Order VI Rule 17 CPC have been substantially amended by the CPC (Amendment) Act, 2002. Under the proviso no application for amendment shall be allowed after the trial has commenced, unless in spite of due diligence, the matter could not be raised before the commencement of trial."

The Hon'ble Supreme Court of India in the case of *Rajkumar Gurawara (Dead) Through. L.Rs.* v. *S.K. Sarwagi and Co. Pvt. Ltd.*, (2008) 14 SCC 364, decided on 14.5.2008 has observed thus:

> "It is settled law that the grant of application for amendment be subject to certain conditions, namely, (i) when the nature of it is changed by permitting amendment; (ii) when the amendment would result in introducing new cause of action and intends to prejudice the other party; & (iii) when allowing amendment application defeats the law of limitation. The plaintiff not only failed to satisfy the conditions prescribed in proviso to Order VI Rule 17 but even on merits his claim is liable to be rejected."

The Hon'ble Supreme Court of India in the case of *Chander Kanta Bansal* v. *Rajinder Singh Anand*, (2008) 5 SCC 117: AIR 2008 SC 2234 has observed as follows:—

> "It makes it clear that after the commencement of trial, no application for amendment shall be allowed. However, if it is established that in spite of "due diligence" the party could not have raised the matter before the commencement of trial depending on the circumstances, the court is free to order such application. The words "due diligence" has not been defined in the Code. According to Oxford Dictionary (Edition 2006), the word "diligence" means careful and persistent application or effort. "Diligent" means careful and steady in application to one's work and duties, showing care and effort. As per Black's Law Dictionary (18th Edition), "diligence" means a continual effort to accomplish something, care; caution; the attention and care required from a person in a given situation. "Due diligence" means the diligence reasonably expected from, and ordinarily exercised by a person who seeks to satisfy a legal requirement or to discharge an obligation. According to Words and Phrases by Drain-Dyspnea (Permanent Edition 13-A) "due diligence", in law, means doing everything reasonable, not everything possible. "Due diligence" means reasonable diligence; it means such diligence as a prudent man would exercise in the conduct of his own affairs. It is clear that unless the party takes prompt steps, mere action cannot be accepted and file a petition after the commencement of trial."

The Hon'ble Supreme Court of India in the case of *Ajendraprasad Ji N. Pandey* v. *Swami Keshavprakeshdasji N.*, 2006 (12) SCC 1: AIR 2007 SC 806, in paragraph 57 of the decision, has observed as follows:

> "It is submitted that the date of settlement of issues is the date of commencement of trial."

The Hon'ble Supreme Court of India in the case of *Baldev Singh* v. *Manohar Singh*, 2006 (6) SCC 498: 2006 (5) Supreme 943 in paragraph 17 of the decision, has held and observed as follows:

> "Before we part with this order, we may also notice that proviso to Order VI Rule 17 CPC provides that amendment of pleadings shall not be allowed when the trial of the suit has already commenced."

Order I, Rule 10, Order XXIII, Rule 1, Order XLI, Rule 23, Section 99 – Effect of Law of Benami Property (Transaction) Prohibition Act

In *Yerrapapareddy Polaiah* v. *Yerrapapareddy Ramaniah*, 2016 3 ALT 495 (AP): 2017 (1) ALD 730, initially, after examining P.Ws.1 and 2 on behalf of the plaintiff and marking Exs.A1 to A4 and after examining D.Ws.1 to 4 and marking Exs.B1 on behalf of defendants 1 to 5, after trial, the suit was dismissed on 11.04.2005. Against the said judgment and decree, the plaintiff preferred appeal in AS No. 59 of 2005 before the District court, Nellore, which was allowed on 20.09.2007 by setting aside the judgment and decree of the trial Court and the matter was remanded to the trial Court by the 1st appellant Court by observing as follows:

> "..... the matter is remanded to the lower court for determination of the question as to whether the plea of the defendants is not permissible in view of the Benami Transactions (Prohibition) Act and to determine as to whether the defendants have discharged the burden of proof that the document is sham or nominal, and to further determine in case the mother of the plaintiff is having right in the property, whether the will affects her right or not; the plaintiff also, if interested for a just adjudication of the rights in items No. 1 to 3, should take steps for adding Ramanaiah in whose favour the property under Items No. 1 to 3 is said to have been sold by the 1st defendant and Subbamma and, if no steps are taken, the determination of the suit shall be confined only to Item No. 4 of the property. Both the parties shall be given opportunity to adduce further evidence. Both parties to appear before the lower court on 01.10.2007."

Subsequently, the matter was taken up by the trial Court. The plaintiff impleaded the 6th defendant vide orders dated 28.02.2008 in I.A.No.1335 of 2007. The 6th defendant also filed written statement and additional written statement. After filing of the rejoinder by the plaintiff, the trial Court also framed additional issue on 18.02.2009. In addition to the evidence already on record, P.W.3 was examined and marked Exs. A5 to A7 on behalf of the plaintiff and on behalf of the defendants, in addition to the evidence of D.Ws.1 to 4, they examined D.Ws. 5 and 6 and got marked Exs.B2 to B4. Basing on the pleadings of both parties, after considering the both oral and documentary adduced on either side, the trial Court decreed the suit as follows:

"23. In view of the finding given on issues No. 1 to 4 and the additional issue dated 18.02.2009, the plaintiff, his sister Kuppa Ramanamma and the legal heirs of his other sister Athipati Krishnamma, are each entitled for ?rd share in ½ share of the plaint schedule property. In view of the circumstances prevailing in this case, each party do bear their own costs and a preliminary decree can be passed accordingly. This issue is answered accordingly.

In the result, the suit was decreed, but without costs, directing division of plaint schedule property into 2 (two) equal shares, and out of 1 (one) such share, to allot ?rd share each to the plaintiff, to his elder sister Kuppa Ramanamma and to the legal heirs of his another sister Athipati Krishnamma. Preliminary decree is accordingly passed."

Against the said judgment and decree, the 6th defendant filed A.S. No. 55 of 2010 and the defendants 2 to 5 filed A.S.No.62 of 2010. The 1st Additional District Judge, Nellore, by Common Judgment dated 31.07.2014 allowed both the appeals by setting aside the judgment and decree in O.S. No. 31 of 1998 on the file of the Principal Senior Civil Judge, Nellore dated 11.02.2010 and suit was remanded to trial Court, which shall given an opportunity to the plaintiff to implead all the necessary parties forthwith and adduce further evidence if any in this regard. The trial Court was also directed to dispose of the suit as expeditiously as possible. Against the said common judgment, the present appeals are filed by the plaintiff.

Learned counsel for the appellant submits that the trial Court rightly decreed the suit of the appellant holding that the appellant is entitled to allotment of 50% of the suit schedule property after dividing the suit schedule property into two equal shares and out of one such share, the appellant, his elder sister Kuppa Ramanamma and to the legal heirs of his another sister Athipati Krishnamma were entitled to ?rd share each out of that 50% of the suit schedule property. He would further contend that the trial Court consciously held that the two sisters of the appellant can apply for division of their respective shares at least at the time of passing of final decree safeguarding the interest of other co-parceners, as such, there is no need for remanding the matter back to the trial Court. He also contended that the appeals before the lower appellate Court have been filed against the judgment of the trial Court only on the ground that sisters of the appellant have not been impleaded. He further contended that the trial Court consciously taken care regarding the shares of the sisters of the appellant and there was no need for remanding the matter back to the trial Court. He further contended that even as per Section 99 of CPC, the judgment and decree need not be set aside for misjoinder of parties or of causes of action. Even the merit of the case is not going to be affected. He further submits that the sisters of the appellant can be impleaded at the time of passing of final decree proceedings. He further submits that under Order I Rule 10 CPC, the Court may at any stage of the proceedings, on its own or on application made by a party, direct a third party to be impleaded in the suit or proceeding for complete and effective adjudication of the issue involved in the suit and that there is no impediment for impleading the parties in the final decree proceedings and that there is no valid reason for remanding the matter to the trial Court. In support of his contention, he relied on the judgments reported in *Bayyarapu Narayana Raidu* v. *Pagadala Varalaxmi*, 2014 (4) ALT 808: 2014 (2) ALD 176; *Sannapu Reddy Venkata Reddy* v. *Jillela Bhupal Reddy*, 2014 (4) ALT 339: 2014 (2) ALD 739; *Seth Anand Kumar* v. *Abnash Kaur*, 1969 (2) UJ 115 SC; *T. Chandrasekhar* v. *Sunchu Rajamallu*, 2015 (1) ALT 454: 2014 (6) ALD 58; *Nima Kaur* v. *Surjith Singh*, 1997 (5) ALT 183: 1997 (5) ALD 185 and *Madadi Narasimha Reddy* v. *Madadi Ramachandra Reddy and two Others*, 1975 An WR 227.

On the other hand, learned counsel for the respondents submits that no final decree be passed unless all the co-parceners are added. He further submits that admittedly, the appellant has not made her two sisters as parties in the suit, who are necessary parties and that in a suit for partition, all the co-parceners and legal heirs of the deceased have to be made parties, failing which, the suit is liable to be dismissed. He submits that the lower appellate Court instead of dismissing the suit, remanded back the matter to the trial Court giving an opportunity to the appellant to implead his sisters as parties to the suit. As such, the judgment and decree of the trial court cannot be validated. He further submits that the trial Court allotted the shares to the sisters of the appellant, though they are not parties to the suit, which is erroneous, as such, the lower appellate Court rightly set aside the judgment and decree of the trial Court and remanded the matter back to the trial Court. In support of his contention, he relied on the judgments reported in *Kanakarathanammal* v. *V.S. Loganatha Mudaliar*, AIR 1965 SC 271: [1964] 6 SCR 1; *Ali Amad (deceased represented by L.Rs)* v. *Sindhi Ebrahim Kasam*, AIR 1983 Gujarat 156: 1983 GLH 117; *Kusampudi Subba Raju* v. *Panumatsa Sayi Raju*, 2005 (5) ALT 192: 2005 (1) An WR 604 (AP): 2005 (6) ALD 88 and *K. Bhaskar Rao* v. *K.A. Rama Rao*, 2010 (6) ALT 109: 2010 (5) ALD 339.

The Hon'ble Supreme Court in *Kanakarathanammal* v. *V.S. Loganatha Mudaliar* (supra) observed as follows:

> "15....... .... Once it is held that the appellant's two brothers are co-heirs with her in respect of the properties left intestate by their mother, the present suit filed by the appellant partakes of the character of a suit for partition and in such a suit clearly the appellant alone would not be entitled to claim any relief against the respondents. The estate can be represented only when all the three heirs are before the Court. ...."

(b) In *Ali Amad (deceased represented by L.Rs)* v. *Sindhi Ebrahim Kasam* (supra), the Hon'ble Gujarat High Court held as follows:

> "5.... .... This is the clear exposition of law and even on the first principles also, it is necessary that all persons who are entitled to a share in the property by inheritance must be made parties to the suit for partition.

(c) In *Kusampudi Subba Raju* v. *Panumatsa Sayi Raju* (supra), this Court held as follows:

> "19. It is true that there is some negligence on the part of the plaintiff in not impleading the necessary parties and on that ground the plaintiff is liable to be non-suited and accordingly the suit was dismissed. But,

however, in the light of the peculiar facts and circumstances and especially in the light of the view expressed by this Court in relation to the bar under Order XXIII, Rule 1 of the Code and the applicability thereof to a different cause of action and the subsequent events, this Court is of the considered opinion that it would be just and proper to remand the matter and give an opportunity to the plaintiff to implead all the necessary parties forthwith and also adduce further evidence if any in this regard. It is needless to say that the necessary parties so impleaded also would be given an opportunity and the other parties who are already on record also to be given opportunity to adduce further evidence if any in this regard in view of the order of remand being made by this Court."

(d) In *K. Bhaskar Rao* v. *K.A. Rama Rao*, 2010 (6) ALT 109: 2010 (5) ALD 339 a learned Single Judge of this Court observed as follows:

"22. While the stand of the plaintiff before the trial Court was that it was not necessary, as the sisters were already married and given sufficient share at the time of marriage, in this appeal the appellant has filed an application CMP No. 2141 of 2005 to implead the sisters as parties. In view of the stand of the plaintiff that no share need to go to them and in spite of pointing out that their presence is necessary in the suit, the plaintiff has chosen not to implead them. The defect of non-joinder of necessary parties being fatal, the same cannot be cured by impleading them in appeal. The trial Court, therefore, rightly held that the suit is liable to be dismissed on the ground of non-joinder of necessary parties. I see no reason to take a different view."

In view of above citations relied on by the learned counsel for the respondents, it is well settled law that in a suit for partition, all the heirs are entitled for share in the property including daughters, irrespective of their marital status and any suit without impleading all the legal heirs, is liable to be dismissed. Admittedly, the appellant has two sisters and one of them died. The trial Court had already allotted shares to his two sisters, who are not at all parties to the suit. It is the case of the appellant that his sisters can be added as necessary parties even in final decree proceedings. In view of above legal position, I am of the opinion that the sisters of the appellant, being legal heirs along with appellant, are proper and necessary parties for adjudication of the suit before the trial Court.

The application filed under Order I Rule 10 CPC need not depend upon the existence of absolute rights. It would be sufficient, if the parties have some interest in the property, which is the subject matter of the suit.

Under Order I Rule 10 CPC the Court may at any stage of the proceedings, on its own or on application made by a party, direct a third party to be impleaded in the suit or proceeding for complete and effective adjudication of the issue involved in the suit. Thus, there is no impediment for impleading the parties in the final decree proceedings. The Court has wide discretion in the matter of adding the parties to the proceedings under Order I Rule 10 CPC, if the Court is of the opinion that the proposed party has a right in the subject matter and there is a possibility of his right being affected if he is not added as a party."

(b) In *Nima Kaur* v. *Surjith Singh* (supra), a learned Single Judge of this Court held as follows:

> "7. In *Phoolchand* v. *Gopal Lal*, AIR 1967 SC 1470: [1967] 3 SCR 153, it was held that any partition suit by which the shares allotted in the preliminary decree already passed can be amended and if there is dispute between surviving parties in that behalf and that dispute is decided, the decision amounts to a decree and that there is no prohibition in the Code of Civil Procedure against passing a second preliminary decree in such circumstances. It was also clarified in the said judgment that this can be done so long as the final decree has not been passed and also that such course of action is permissible only in partition suits. It would be appropriate to extract a relevant portion of the said judgment, which is as under:
>
> "(7) We are of opinion that there is nothing in the Code of Civil Procedure which prohibits the passing of more than one preliminary decree if circumstances justify the same and that it may be necessary to do so particularly in partition suits when after the preliminary decree some parties die and shares of other parties are thereby augmented. We have already said that it is not disputed that in partition suits the Court can do so even after the preliminary decree is passed. It would in our opinion be convenient to the Court and advantageous to the parties, specially in partition suits, to have disputed rights finally settled and specification of shares in the preliminary decree varied before a final decree is prepared. If this is done, there is a clear determination of the rights of parties to the suit on the question in dispute and we see no difficulty in holding that in such cases there is decree deciding these disputed rights; if so, there is no reason why a second preliminary decree correcting the shares in a partition suit cannot be passed by the Court. So far therefore as partition suits are concerned we have no doubt that if an event transpires after the preliminary decree which necessitates a change in shares, the Court can and should do so; and if there is a dispute in that behalf, the order of the Court deciding that dispute and making variation in shares specified in the preliminary decree already passed is a decree in itself which would be liable to appeal. We should however like to point out that we are saying must be confined to partition suits".

6. Section 99 – Necessary Party – Meaning of – Effect of Non-joinder of Necessary Party

In *Sri Amal Ghatak* v. *Sri Subrata Dutta*, 2016 (5) Gau LR 212 (Gau) the High Court said, I have gone through the pleadings of the parties, the evidence adduced by them both oral and documentary and the impugned first appellate judgment passed by the learned First Appellate Court as well as the original judgment and decree passed by the learned trial Court.

It is the case of the plaintiffs that the land originally belonged to Haleswar Debalaya and one Abdul Hakim came into possession of the suit land under the Debalaya way back in the year 1937. He thereafter by executing a registered sale deed on 23.01.1947 (Ext-7) sold his possessory right in favour of one Jagadish Chandra Dutta. Till then the Assam State Acquisition of Lands belonging to Religious or Charitable Institution of Public Nature Act, 1959 (Assam Act IX of 1961)(hereinafter referred to as 'the Act IX of 1961') had not been in existence. The Act received the assent of the President on 02.04.1961 being a matter under the Concurrent List under the Seventh Schedule to the Constitution of India and only thereupon it came into force upon publication of notification in the official Gazette. The Act came into effect with effect from 01.01.1963. However, after the Act had come into existence on 01.01.1963 Jagadish Chandra Dutta executed Ext-1 sale deed on 27.12.1963 in favour of the predecessor of the plaintiffs by executing a registered sale deed. As on that date when the Act IX of 1961 came into force Jagadish Chandra Dutta had already acquired possessory right of the suit land by way of purchase from Abdul Hakim vide Ext-7 on the one hand and by deed dated 05.03.1953 (Ext-9) on the other hand from Jagyeswar Sarma of Haleswar Dbalaya. Jagadish Dutta, therefore, was a raiyot of the Debalaya as on 01.01.1961 and so he acquired the status of a tenant under Section 15 of the Act IX of 1961. It is also to be mentioned here that prior to the same by way of operation of Act of 1955, which had come into force on 01.08.1955, Jagadish Chandra Dutta became a 'tenant' within the meaning of Section 3(g) of the Act of 1955 and he having made construction thereof, as has been revealed from the findings of the learned trial Court in respect of Issue Nos.5 and 6, he became entitled to protection from eviction under Section 15 of the Act of 1955. It is, therefore, wrong to hold that Jagadish Chandra Dutta did not acquire any semblance of right, title or interest with respect to the suit land by his purchase on 23.01.1947 or when he sold the same to the predecessor of the plaintiffs on 27.12.1963. Whether he is evictable or not would be a dispute at the instance of Haleswar Debalaya and definitely a third party cannot question the status of the plaintiffs by referring to the provisions of Act IX of 1961. The learned First Appellate Court only considered that by enactment and promulgation of Act IX of 1961 State of Assam became the owner and so Debalaya is a necessary party.

In the case of *Vidur Impex and Traders Private Limited (supra)*, relied on by Ms. B. Choudhury, learned counsel for the appellants, Hon'ble Supreme Court has held in paragraph 41.2 that a necessary party is the person who ought to be joined as a party to the suit and in whose absence an effective decree cannot be passed by the Court. A proper party, on the other hand, is a person whose presence would enable the Court to completely, effectively and properly adjudicate upon all matters and issues though he may not be a person in favour of or against whom a decree is to be made. In Section 99 of the Code of Civil Procedure it has been provided that no decree shall be reversed or substantially varied, nor shall any case be remanded, in appeal on account of any mis-joinder or non-joinder of parties or causes of action or any error, defect or irregularity in any proceedings in the suit, not affecting the merits of the case or the jurisdiction of the Court. In the proviso, however, it has been laid down that nothing in this section shall apply to non-joinder of a necessary party. Addition of proviso to Section 99 goes to show that in case a necessary party is not impleaded in a proceeding bar under Section 99 of the CPC shall not apply. The proviso does not include proper party but it includes only necessary party. This is why before seeking either to allow an appeal or to modify a decree or to remand the case, it is necessary to ascertain as to whether a party is a necessary party or not. This can be examined only by going through the averments made in the plaint and the prayers made therein. A person against whom some relief is claimed can only be a necessary party. This is because unless such party is impleaded and given an opportunity of placing his case no decision can be arrived at contrary to his interest. If any order is passed or action is taken against someone resulting in civil consequence on them and that too by not giving him an opportunity of hearing, in that event, such order passed or action taken become non-est in law by virtue of violation of the principles of natural justice. This is why to ascertain a person or an authority is a necessary party or not it has to be seen whether he has any reply to give against the recital made in the plaint or not. If no reply or view of such person is required for adjudication of the matter raised, in that event, he may not be a necessary party and his presence may not be indispensable although he may be a proper party as his presence may be necessary to ascertain the correctness or otherwise of the respective cases of the two sides in litigation. Having noticed the meaning of the words 'necessary party' within the meaning of proviso to Section 99 of the CPC it has to be seen as to whether in the present case Haleswar Debalaya can be said to be a necessary party and thereupon to decide as to whether the impugned first appellate judgment and decree is violative of Section 99 of the CPC or not.

7. Section 99 – Civil Procedure Code, 1908, Order VII, Rule 14 (3) – Evidence Act, 1872 Sections 63, 65, 76 and 35

In *Antar Singh Darbar* v. *Shri Kailash Vijayvargiya*, 2016 (3) MPLJ 170: 2016 (2) Jab LJ 154 (MP) (Indore Bench) the High Court referred to the provisions of R T I and said, taking these provisions of Indian Evidence Act into consideration, it is apparent that certified copies whether given under section 76 of Indian Evidence Act or under the provisions of Right to Information Act can only be admitted in evidence without examining the author of the documents and without comparing them with the original. For rest of the documents which are not public document, the original should be called before the court and the persons in whose possession such documents are kept, should be called for evidence. So far as the principles laid down in case of *Narayan Singh* (supra), the question before the Co-ordinate Bench of this court was whether a copy obtained under Right to Information Act should be admitted for evidence. In that case, document was a public document. It was a map of the house and building construction permission from the Nagar Nigam. This document falls under the category of the public document, and therefore, the principles laid down in case of *Narayan Singh (supra)* cannot be applied on all the documents in derogation of provisions of Indian Evidence Act.

Accordingly, this application is disposed of with the observation that all the documents which are taken on record by the earlier order of this court referred to above shall be admitted and proved in evidence depending upon their nature whether they are public documents or private documents under the relevant provisions of Evidence Act.

This brought us to the objections raised by the counsel for the respondent against issuance of notice to Shri Shivraj Singh Chouhan the then Chief Minister and leader of Bhartiya Janta Party in the year 2013 when the Vidhan Sabha election took place. The main objection appears to be that the examination of petitioner's witness is still in progress and there is nothing in evidence so far recorded which would justify the naming of any person under Section 99 of R.P. Act, 1951.

This apart, witnesses of respondent are yet to be examined. Thus, at this stage, issuance of notice under Section 99 of R.P. Act is not called for, and therefore, it is prayed that the issuance of notice may be postponed till recording of evidence.

Counsel for the petitioner, however, submits that there are specific allegations against Shri Shivraj Singh Chouhan who gave a speech in a public meeting in which the respondent-Kailash Vijaywargiya was also present on the stage along with Shri Shivraj Singh Chouhan, and therefore, he has likely to be named under section 99 of the Act, and therefore, notice should be given at this stage so that he may have an opportunity to cross-examine the witnesses produced by the petitioner.

The question whether the notice is to be issued under section 99 of R.P. Act after conclusion of trial or during the trial was decided by this court in E.P. No. 23/2014 vide order dated 20.10.2015. In this order after referring to various judgments of Hon'ble Apex Court, it was held that notices are to be issued during the trial and not at the conclusion of the trial, and therefore, if at all, the notice is to be issued to Shri Shivraj Singh Chouhan, it has to be issued at this stage so that the proceedings are concluded simultaneously.

Whether the act alleged in the petition falls within the purview of above provisions of Act needs not be decided and it may be decided at the end of the trial. If at this stage, any inference is given, this may affect decision of this court on merit, and therefore, presently, there appears to be no harm in issuing the notice to Shri Shivraj Singh Chouhan, who may cross-examine the witnesses produced by the petitioner who spoke against him in this petition. In this view of the matter, the objections raised by the counsel for the respondent are rejected. It is directed that the notice under section 99 of R.P. Act be issued on payment of necessary process fee as per law and supply copy of relevant portion of the petition by the petitioner to Shri Shivraj Singh Chouhan by Hamdast as well as by regular mode.

8. Sections 99 and 141 – Misjoinder of Parties

In *Manti Devi* v. *Kishun Sah @ Kishun Deo Sao*, AIR 2017 SC 002: 2017 (4) SCALE 290: 2017 (2) PLJR 314 (SC) the Apex Court examined the effect of misjoinder of parties and held, Section 99 specifically provides that " no decree shall be reversed or varied substantially on account of non-joinder or mis-joinder of parties in appeal.

In the said case learned senior counsel, inviting our attention to Section 99 of the Code of Civil Procedure, contends that no decree shall be reversed or varied substantially on account of non-joinder or misjoinder of parties. Section 99 of the Code of Civil Procedure reads as follows:-

> "99. No decree to be reversed or modified for error or irregularity not affecting merits or jurisdiction.- No decree shall be reversed or substantially varied, nor shall any case be remanded, in appeal on account of any misjoinder or non-joinder of parties or causes of action or any error, defect or irregularity in any proceedings in the suit, not affecting the merits of the case or the jurisdiction of the court:

Provided that nothing in this section shall apply to non-joinder of a necessary party."

The provision, in our view, is crystal clear. No decree can be reversed or substantially varied in appeal on account of misjoinder or non-joinder of parties. Under Section 141 of the Code of Civil Procedure, procedure under the Code in regard to suit shall be followed as far as it can be made applicable to proceedings in any Court of Civil jurisdiction. Therefore, what is provided under Section 99 of the Code of Civil Procedure in respect of appeal would apply to revision as well.

The judgment of the High Court is set aside and the judgment and decree of the Trial Court is restored. The appeal is allowed.

However, the respondents/tenants are granted time till 30.09.2017 to surrender vacant and peaceful possession, subject to their filing usual undertaking within six weeks. If the undertaking, as above, is not filed the respondents shall not be entitled for this extension of time for surrendering vacant possession.

APPEAL FROM APPELLATE DECREES

***100. Second appeal.*—(1) Save as otherwise expressly provided in the body of this Code or by any other law for the time being in force, an appeal shall lie to the High Court from every decree passed in appeal by any Court subordinate to the High Court, if the High Court is satisfied that the case involves a substantial question of law.**

(2) An appeal may lie under this section from an appellate decree passed *ex parte*.

(3) In an appeal under this section, the memorandum of appeal shall precisely state the substantial question of law involved in the appeal.

(4) Where the High Court is satisfied that a substantial question of law is involved in any case, it shall formulate that question.

(5) The appeal shall be heard on the question so formulated and the respondent shall, at the hearing of the appeal, be allowed to argue that the case does not involve such question:

Provided that nothing in this sub-section shall be deemed to take away or abridge the power of the Court to hear, for reasons to be recorded, the appeal on any other substantial question of law, not formulated by it, if it is satisfied that the case involves such question.

SYNOPSIS

Comments

1. General

An execution of decree in part or in full, whether through the court or otherwise does not affect the right of appeal nor the fact that only a separable portion of the decree was appealed against in the lower appellate court can be a bar to an appeal to the court. In as much as this is an appeal against the decree passed by the lower appellate court, the appeal is complete under section 100, CPC (1959) 1 Andh WR 148. Appeal under section 142, Calcutta Municipal Act is in the nature of first appeal, not second appeal: *Corporation of Calcutta* v. *Jalajbasini*, AIR 1928 Cal 450: 32 CWN 378. Section 100 must be read with Order XLI, rule 33. The High Court of Patna held that where a subordinate court wrongly entertains an appeal when it has jurisdiction to do so, a second appeal lies against that order: 1950 Pat 90. The Madras Court said that where the court entertains an appeal which does not lie and decides it on the merits its order may be challenged by a second appeal to the High Court: *Kallalagar Devasthanam Madura* v. *Baskaram Pillai*, AIR 1942 Mad 741: (1942) 2 MLJ 450. Where in a suit by a mortgagee for declaration of amount due under the mortgage and sale of the hypothec on the ground that the claim was barred by limitation and the plaintiff did not appeal against the decree but was content with the declaration of the amount due under the mortgage granted by the trial court, but on appeal by the puisne mortgagee the appellate court declined to grant any declaratory relief to the plaintiff and dismissed the suit. The Privy Council held that in the circumstances the plaintiff could not agitate the question of limitation on second appeal without appealing against the decree of trial court dismissing suit for sale of hypothec. The plaintiff had in effect directly appealed to High Court which course is not permissible. (*Mohammed Khaleef* v. *Les Tanneries*, 53 Ind App 84: AIR 1926 PC 34 (PC): 51 MLJ 570, relied on): *Dhonavakonda Gopalarao* v. *Thatha Venkatadri*, AIR 1957 AP 19: 1956 Andh WR 111: 69 Mad LW (Andh) 27. A second appeal is competent from an order remanding a case for rehearing: 52 CWN 671. A second appeal does not lie in execution proceedings if no second appeal would lie in the suit itself: 43 A. 403, foll.: 52 PLR 13. Decision of Collector under section 20A, Madras Estates Land Act if a decree: ILR (1942) M. 959: 1942 M 599: (1942) 2 MLJ 162. The High Court of Punjab following the Supreme Court held that where the decree was passed after the remand order and during the pendency of the second appeal from that order, it must be taken to subject to the result of the second appeal. If the second appeal fails, then the decree is not affected by the appeal. On the other hand, if the second appeal succeeds then the subsequent proceedings would fall with the remand order and would be of no effect. (*Shiromani Gurdwara Parbandhak Committee, Amritsar* v. *Raja Shiv Rattan Dev Singh*, ILR 1955 Punj 1108: AIR 1955 SC 576 foll.): *Chanan Ram* v. *Kahan Singh*, 59 Punj LR 267: AIR 1958 Punj 81. The Supreme Court said that in a second appeal the memorandum must contain the substantial question of law. The respondent, therefore, has a right to argue that there is no substantial question of law involved in the appeal. Therefore, the existence of a substantial question of law is the *sin quo non* for the exercise of the jurisdiction under section 100; *Panchugopal Barua* v. *Umesh Chandra Goswami*, AIR 1997 SC 1041: 1997 AIR SCW 1035: (1997) 4 SCC 713.

It is the 'substantial question of law' not a mere question of law, which is essential condition for maintaining a second appeal. The phrase 'substantial question of law' has not been defined in the Code. The proper test for determining whether a question of law raised in the second appeal is substantial or not would be whether it directly and substantially affects the rights of the parties and whether it is an open question in the sense that it is not finally settled by the superior courts. If the question has been settled by the highest court, the general principles to be applied in determining the question are well-settled and the question is merely of the application of those principles, the question will not be a substantial question of law; *Damjibhai Bijibhai Basava* v. *Ranchodbhai Zinabhai*, AIR 2000 SC 1000: 2000 AIR SCW 663: (2000) 3 SCC 22.

The Supreme Court of India in *Gurdev Kaur* v. *Kaki*, (2007) 1 SCC 546: AIR 2006 SC 1975: 2006 AIR SCW 2404 (Appeal (Civil) 2083 of 2006) explained the ambit and scope of section 100 and said that the ambit of section 100, C.P.C. has not been properly appreciated and applied in a large number of cases. We are, once again making a serious endeavour to discern legislative intention, ambit and scope of interference under section 100, C.P.C. We plan to carry out this exercise by critically examining important judgments decided before and after 1976 amendment in section 100, C.P.C. This effort is made with the hope that in future the High Courts would decide according to the scope of section 100, C.P.C. and this Court may not be compelled to interfere with the judgments delivered under section 100, C.P.C.

In *Koppisetty Venkat Ratnam (D)* v. *Pamarti Venkayamma*, 2009 AIR SCW 2332 (on 23 February, 2009) reiterated that under section 100, C.P.C. jurisdiction of the High Court to entertain a second appeal is confined only to such appeals which involve a substantial question of law and it does not confer any jurisdiction on the High Court to interfere with pure questions of fact while exercising its jurisdiction under section 100, C.P.C. That apart, at the time of disposing of the matter the High Court did not even notice the question of law formulated by it at the time of admission of the second appeal as there is no reference of it in the impugned judgment. The Court further said that judgments of the courts below are confined to hearing of substantial questions of law. Interference with the finding of fact by the High Court is not warranted if it invokes reappreciation of evidence. This court found that the impugned judgment of the High Court was vulnerable and needed to be set aside. In *Chandrika Singh*

(Dead) by LRs. v. *Sarjug Singh,* (2006) 12 SCC 49, this Court again reiterated the legal position that the High Court under section 100, C.P.C. has limited jurisdiction. To deal with cases having a substantial question of law, this Court observed as under:

> While exercising its jurisdiction under section 100 of the Code of Civil Procedure, the High Court is required to formulate a substantial question.

It may be mentioned that in a first appeal filed under section 96, C.P.C., the appellate court can go into questions of fact, whereas in a second appeal filed under section 100, C.P.C. the High Court cannot interfere with the findings of fact of the first appellate court, and it is confined only to questions of law.

2. Second Appeal – Nature and Scope

The Bombay High Court in *Shivprasad Shankarlal Pardeshi* v. *Leelabai Badrinarayan Kalwar,* AIR 1998 Bom 131: 1998 (2) Bom CR 744: (1998) 1 Bom LR 822 examined the nature and scope of second appeal with reference to an appeal under section 72(4) of the Bombay Public Trust Act, 1950. This appeal of 1979 was placed before the Court pursuant to the order passed by the learned Chief Justice on a reference made by a learned Single Judge on 17th August, 1994 for deciding the following three questions:

(1) Whether an appeal filed under section 72(4) of Bombay Public Trusts Act, 1950 is subject to restrictions and limitations imposed on a "Second Appeal" as prescribed under section 100 of the Code of Civil Procedure? Whether an appeal under section 72(4) of the Act is maintainable even on questions of fact, mixed questions of fact and law or mere question of law?

(2) Whether the trust known as Gangubai's Shri Datta Trust, situate at Solapur created under the Deed of Trust dated 13th November, 1941 is a public trust or a private trust and whether the properties of the said trust including the income thereof are liable to be considered as income of public religious or charitable trust or as private income?

(3) Whether in any event the said trust is a public charitable trust insofar as it provides for utilization of 20% of its income for education of poor students, maintenance of poor widows and for assistance to the poor in connection with marriage or death, If so, whether the said trust is in any event liable to be registered under the Bombay Public Trusts Act, 1950?

The Court observed: "Having regard to the conflicting views expressed by the Single Judges of this Court, it is necessary for us to first address ourselves to the first question as to whether an appeal filed under section 72(4) of Bombay Public Trusts Act, 1950, like the present one, is subject to the restrictions and limitations imposed on a "Second Appeal" as prescribed under section 100 of the Code of Civil Procedure? In other words whether such an appeal, though registered in this Court as a "First Appeal" is maintainable even on questions of fact or whether it can be entertained only if the High Court is satisfied that the case involves a substantial question of law, within the meaning of sub-section

(1) of section 100 of the Civil Procedure Code. We propose to deal with this question before dealing with the merits of this appeal".

Section 2(13) of the Bombay Public Trusts Act, defines a 'public trust' to mean an express or constructive trust for either a public religious or charitable purpose or both and includes a temple, a math, a wakf, church, synagogue, agiary or other place of public religious worship, a dharmada or any other religious or charitable endowment and a society formed either for a religious or charitable purpose or for both and registered under the Societies Registration Act, 1860. Section 18 of the said Act deals with registration of public trusts and sub-section (1) stipulates that it shall be the duty of trustee of a public trust to make an application for the registration of the Pubic Trust. Section 19 deals with the inquiry for registration which is to be made by the Deputy or Assistant Charity Commissioner in the manner prescribed for ascertaining the relevant factors for determining whether a trust exists and whether such trust is a public trust. On completion of the enquiry, the Deputy or Assistant Charity Commissioner has to record his findings, with reasons, as provided in section 20 and section 21 deals with the entries to be made in the register.

The Court observed: In our view, no case has been made out for disturbing the concurrent findings of fact recorded by the Deputy Charity Commissioner and confirmed by the learned Assistant Judge. In this view of the matter our answers to the questions referred to us are as under:—

(1) An appeal filed under section 72(4) of Bombay Public Trusts Act, 1950 is a 'Second Appeal' to this Court and is subject to the restrictions and limitations imposed on a "Second Appeal" as prescribed under section 100 of the Code of Civil Procedure. There is nothing in the scheme of section 72 of the Bombay Public Trust Act or for that matter any other provisions of the said Act which widens the scope of the appeal beyond the limits prescribed by section 100, C.P.C. The Court observed our view therefore, such an appeal is maintainable only if the High Court is satisfied that the case involves a substantial question of law within the meaning of section 100, C.P.C.

(2) The trust known as Gangubai's Shri Datta Trust, situate at Solapur created under the Deed of Trust dated 13th November, 1941 at Exhibit 66, is a private trust and not a public trust. The properties of the said trust including the income thereof were, at all times, the private properties of Gangubai and, on the evidence that has come before us, they clearly appear to have been treated as private properties of Leelabai.

(3) Since the dominant purpose of the trust was of a private nature and since only 20% of its income was being utilised for the education of poor students, maintenance of poor widows and for assistance to the poor in connection with marriage or death, no case has been made out for registration of the said trust in accordance with the provisions of the Bombay Public Trusts Act, 1950. The Court said that in this view of the matter, there is no substance in this appeal which is accordingly dismissed. In the circumstances however, there will be no order as to costs.

3. Right and Nature of Second Appeal

The Supreme Court examined the nature of second appeal also in *Hero Vinoth* v. *Shesamal,* AIR 2006 SC 2234: 2006 AIR SCW 2833: (2006) 5 SCC 545 and *James Joseph* v. *State of Kerala,* (2010) 9 SCC 642: 2010 AIR SCW 5825 and held that it is a substantive statutory right, and neither a natural right nor an inherent right. Hence, it has to be regulated by statutory provisions of law

4. Nature of Second Appeal Against the Order Passed by the Charity Commissioner under the Bombay Public Trust Act

The Bombay High Court in *Sadanand Shantwan Salvi* v. *The Nasik Diocesan Council Reg.,* 1997 (4) Bom CR 39 also examined nature of the appeal. In the said case Mr. P.N. Joshi, the learned counsel for the Bishop contended that the Assistant Charity Commissioner passed the original order as a trial court. Then the parties filed application before the learned District Judge under section 72(1) of the Act. Though it is styled as an application, it virtually is an appeal to the District Judge. Therefore, it was argued that what the District Judge has decided under section 72(1) of the Act is a First Appeal. Even the learned counsel for the appellants have no quarrel with the proposition and in fact there cannot be any dispute on this point. That though the words used are "an application" in section 72(1) of the Act, it is nothing but appeal against the original order of the Charity Commissioner. Mr. P.N. Joshi, the learned counsel for the Bishop contended that the Assistant Charity Commissioner passed the original order as a trial court. Then the parties filed application before the learned District Judge under section 72(1) of the Act. Though it is styled as an application, it virtually is an appeal to the District Judge. Therefore it was argued that what the District Judge has decided under section 72(1) of the Act is a First Appeal. Even the learned counsel for the appellants have no quarrel with the proposition and in fact there cannot be any dispute on this point. That though the words used are "an application" in section 72(1) of the Act, it is nothing but appeal against the original order of the Charity Commissioner.

The apex Court has clearly pointed out that the appeal provision in section 104 of the said Himachal Pradesh Act is wider than section 100, C.P.C. Similarly, we find here, section 72(4) of the Act which provides for an appeal to the High Court is wide and general without any limitation unlike section 100, C.P.C.

5. Nature of Appeal under Section 5(ii) of the Kerala High Court Act

Kerala High Court also examined the nature of an appeal. In *Shankari Amma* v. *State of Kerala,* (1991 (2) KLT 184) a Division Bench of this Court held that in appeal filed under section 5(ii) of the Kerala High Court Act (hereinafter referred to as the Act) it is incumbent upon the appellant to formulate substantial question of law. In the said decision it was held that the principles embodied in section 100, C.P.C. proclaims the policy of the Legislature in the matter of entertaining second appeals and as the said provision is based on public policy they are in substance applicable to section 5(ii) of the Act which is a kindred provision. Another Division Bench took a different view and referred the matter to a Full Bench for decision:

"In our view, the principles embodied in section 100, C.P.C. proclaims the policy of the Legislature in the matter of entertaining second appeals. The said provision is based on public policy. We have held that the provisions of section 100, C.P.C. are in substance applicable to section 5(ii) of the Kerala High Court Act, which is a kindred provision."

"The power of a Division Bench hearing a Letters Patent Appeal under Clause 10 from the judgment of a Single Judge in first appeal is not limited only to a question of law under section 100, C.P.C. but it has the same power which the Single Judge has as a first Appellate Court in respect of both question of fact and of law. The limitations on the power of the Court imposed by sections 100 and 101, C.P.C. cannot be made applicable to an appellate court hearing a Letters Patent Appeal for the simple reason that Single Judge of the High Court is not a Court subordinate to the High Court."

In the above decision an earlier judgment of five Judges Bench of the Supreme Court in *Alapati Kasi Viswanthan* v. *A. Sivarama Krishnayya*, (CA No. 232 of 1961) was referred to, Wanchoo, J. speaking for the Court observed:

"The first contention urged before us on behalf of the appellant is that the Letters Patent Bench was not authorised in law to reverse the concurrent findings of fact of the Subordinate Judge and the learned Single Judge of the High Court. It is submitted that a Letters Patent Appeal stands on the same footing as a second appeal and it was therefore not open to the Letters Patent Bench to reverse the concurrent findings of fact of the two Courts below. We are of opinion that this contention is not correct. A Letters Patent Appeal from the judgment of a learned Single Judge in a first appeal to the High Court is not exactly equivalent to a second appeal under section 100 of the Code of Civil Procedure, and, therefore, it cannot be held that a Letters Patent Appeal of this kind can only lie on a question of law and not otherwise. The matter would have been different if the Letters Patent Appeal was from a decision of a learned single Judge in a second appeal to the High Court. In these circumstances it will be open to the High Court to review even findings of fact in a Letters Patent Appeal from a first appeal heard by a learned Single Judge, though generally speaking the Letters Patent Bench would be slow to disturb concurrent findings of fact of the two Courts below. But there is no doubt that in an appropriate case a Letters Patent Bench hearing an appeal from a learned Single Judge of the High Court in a first appeal heard by him is entitled to review even findings of fact. The contention of the appellant therefore that the letters Patent Bench was not in law entitled in reverse the concurrent findings of fact must be negatived." The Court held, "conclusion which we have arrived at here shall not be interpreted to mean that admission of the appeal under section 5(ii) is automatic and unfettered and that the Court lacks power to consider the admissibility of appeal under other provisions of C.P.C." *Kannachett Venugopalan* v. *Malappuram District Co-operative Milk Supply Union Ltd.*, AIR 1995 Ker 369: 1995 (2) Ker LJ 170: 1995 (2) Ker LT 200.

6. Nature of Appeal where Appellate Decree is without Jurisdiction

Where a decree has been made by the appellate court without jurisdiction, an appeal lies against it precisely in the same manner as if it had been made with jurisdiction: 45C, 926; 1925 C 1932. A question of jurisdiction is one of pure law which though not raised in the lower court, can be entertained and adjudicated upon in second appeal: 57 IC 206: 18 ALJ 923; 9 Luck 365. Where an objection as to jurisdiction is not taken in the lower appellate court, the plea must be deemed to have been waived and cannot be raised in second appeal: Where an amendment was allowed after the expiration of the limitation period, the High Court can take notice of it in second appeal, though the point was not pressed in the lower appellate court: 36 A 370. A second appeal is not maintainable against an order rejecting cross objections; but the court might interfere in revision: 44 IC 812. In a suit of a small cause nature, an order in execution proceedings is not appealable; *Vemuri Pitchayya* v. *Raja Yarlagadda Ankineedu*, AIR 1924 Mad 367: 45 Mad LJ 651.

7. Error in Procedure

The High Court of Allahabad stressed that error of procedure must be an error affecting the merits of the case and the High Court can interfere on the ground of any substantial error or defeat in the procedure which may possibly have produced an error or defeat in the decision of the case upon the merits: 1940 P. 33: 1942 ALJ 671: 1943 All 82. (Finding arrived at in disregard of provisions of law). 1937 ALJ 46: 1937 All 105. The question whether a document, such as a promissory note, is genuine or not is purely a question of fact, and a finding of fact thereon cannot be interfered with in second appeal. But if the lower appellate court requires too high a standard of proof for the establishment of any particular fact, and differs from the trial court's appreciation of evidence, that is an error of law or procedure justifying interference under section 100(i)(c), on a mistaken view as to the standard of proof, the High Court will interfere in second appeal: 1937 MWN 188; *Venkata Rao* v. *Venkayya*, (1942) 2 MLJ 427: AIR 1943 Mad 38(2). Where an obvious point of law arises, the practice of some lower courts, of attempting to shut out a second appeal by the use of the language designed to clothe a decision on a point of law with the appearance of a finding of fact, ought to be deprecated: 18 P. 204: 1939 PWN 37: 1939 P 402. Where proper issues have not been framed and the lower court has not discussed the real question in controversy, the High Court may remand the case for proper disposal: 152 IC 220: 35 PLR 156. Refusal by the appellate court, in the exercise of its discretion, to admit additional evidence given under Order XLI, rule 27, is not a substantial defeat or error in procedure: 33 A. 379. Even if the judgment of the appellate court is meager and not in conformity with the rule, unless a substantial error affecting the merits of the case is shown, the High Court will not interfere: 31 MLJ 870. The refusal of the lower appellate court to act under Order XLI, rule 33, C.P. Code, is not an error of law with which the second appellate court is bound to interfere: *Narasimham* v. *Narasinga Rao*, 123 IC 39: AIR (17) 1930 Mad 707. The High Court will reverse a finding in second appeal if there was substantial error in procedure resulting in a finding not secundum allegata et probate and not sustainable in law: 39 B. 149; 10 Pat IT 589; 1929 P

609; 22 LW 352; 1925 M 973. A decision based on the finding of fact contrary to the case set-up can be questioned in second appeal: 1926 L. 535. Where the appellate court made out a new case not raised by the parties and not warranted by the pleadings or evidence, the High Court will interfere: 104 IC 781; 1927 M 1167; 132 JC 426; 1931 A. 219; 1938 Sind 198. Where the appellate court decides a question of fact, not upon the evidence, but holding that a superior court decided a similar case between different parties in a particular way, it is a defect in procedure: *Balunki Rout* v. *Kunja Behari Deb*, AIR 1927 Pat 209: ILR 6 Pat 698 (FB). Second appeal lies in a case where a preliminary decree for accounts is passed and that decree is set aside by the lower appellate court, though the appellate court did not pass a decree in pursuance of its judgment: 31 PLR 386: 1930 L. 125. A Full Bench of the High Court of Assam held that it is clearly an error of law if the first appellate court reverses the judgment of the trial court without disbelieving the evidence on which the finding of the trail court is based; *Biswanath Rajanikanta Roy Choudhury* v. *Chunilal Kanailal Firm*, ILR (1952) 4 Assam 89: AIR 1952 Assam 69 (FB).

8. Error in *Ex Parte* Hearing of Appeal – Interference

The failure to determine the crucial question between the parties to a suit and to consider the oral evidence adduced on behalf of the defendant is a substantial error of procedure: 56 IC 40. So also, if the lower appellate court gives a decree not based on evidence: 26 IC 240. Where both parties agree to proceed not only on the evidence taken before Munsif, but also on evidence recorded by the Commissioner and the lower appellate court discarded the evidence recorded before the Commissioner, there is a defeat of procedure: 46 CLJ 558: 1928 C 136. The appellate court has no power to go behind a finding of the trial court, when the appellant has accepted it in his ground of appeal. The carelessness of the appellant's counsel in drafting the grounds makes no difference; 59 IC 689: 1921 L 182.

9. Whether a Finding of Fact can be Challenged in a Second Appeal

The High Court of Rajasthan examined the issue in *Chatar Lal* v. *Ramdas*, AIR 1979 Raj 87: (1979) Rent LR 821: (1979) 1 Ren CR 754. The following question of law was referred by one of us (M.C. Jain, J.) to be answered by the Full Bench *vide* order of reference dated 2-9-1978:—

> "Whether the finding recorded by the first appellate court on the issue relating to comparative hardship remitted by this Court, being a finding of fact, is not open to challenge in the second appeal?"

The material facts leading to the present reference may be briefly stated as follows:—

> Mahant Ramdas, plaintiff-respondent, instituted a suit for arrears of rent and ejectment from the disputed premises on the ground of personal necessity and default in the Court of Munsif, Udaipur, who by his judgment dated 30-11-1966 decreed the suit for eviction having found Issue No. 2 regarding personal necessity in favour of the plaintiff. The defendant went in appeal, but his appeal was dismissed by the learned Additional District Judge, *vide* his judgment dated 10th of July, 1968.

The defendant then preferred the second appeal. During the pendency of the second appeal the Rajasthan Premises (Control of Rent and Eviction) (Amendment) Act, 1976, came into force and in view of the amended section 14(2) the following issue of comparative hardship was remitted for trial by this Court to the first appellate court *vide* order dated 31-3-1976:—

"Whether having regard to all the circumstances of the case including the question whether any other reasonable accommodation is available to the landlord or the tenant, greater hardship would be caused by passing a decree than by refusing to pass it?"

The Court observed, "having considered the case-law which was brought to our notice we find ourselves in respectful agreement with the view that when an issue is remitted under Order XLI, rule 25, C.P.C., in second appeal to the first appellate court, the finding of fact sent back by the first appellate court is not open to attack, except on the grounds stated in section 100, C.P.C".

This view appears to be in consonance and harmony with the provisions contained in Order XLII, rule 1 and sections 100, 101 and 103, C.P.C. Even in the amended section 103, C.P.C., we find as to when the High Court can determine the issue of facts. The High Court is empowered to determine any issue necessary for the disposal of the appeal, if the evidence on the record is sufficient, when the same has not been determined by the lower appellate court or by the court of first instance and the lower appellate court, or which have been wrongly determined by such court or courts by reason of a decision on such question of law, as is referred to in section 100. The power to determine the issues on facts, is limited to the situations mentioned in section 103. In case the issue of fact has been determined by the lower appellate court, whether on being remitted in second appeal or otherwise, such a finding of fact given by the lower appellate court cannot be determined by the High Court and the reason appears to be that as a senior and experienced Judge presides over the first appellate court, it will be taken that the findings of facts arrived at by him, are correct. If this would not have been the intention, an exception would have been provided that even in second appeal when issue of fact is remitted to the first appellate court, the findings on that issue can be assailed in second appeal. Rather we find a contrary intention expressed in the language of Order XLII, rule 1, C.P.C, coupled with the legal bar provided in sections 100 and 101, C.P.C, and if these provisions are further read with the provisions of section, 103, the intention in our opinion becomes abundantly clear. The only way out appears to be that in order to obviate such an eventuality or result, the issues of fact should be remitted to the first court in second appeal. In view of what we have discussed above, our answer to the question referred to us, is in the affirmative. The Court ordered to return the answer to the Bench concerned.

The High Court of Calcutta examined the provisions of section 100 and held that where findings are remitted to the High Court by the first appellate court under Order XLI, rule 25 of the Code the appeal in the High Court continues to be a second appeal and in the absence of special provisions in law, the findings of facts, when they are before the High Court, are immune from attack except on the ground of error of law or procedure within the meaning of section 100 of the Code: 91 CLJ 327: AIR 1954 Cal 90. Where there is no error or defect in the procedure, nor any error of law, within the meaning of section 100, the finding of the first appellate court upon the question of fact is final, if that court had before it evidence proper for consideration in support of the finding. A finding of fact, however erroneous, cannot be challenged in a second appeal and, it must stand final, as a second appeal can be entertained only on the specific grounds mentioned in section 100. The Privy Council and subsequently, the Supreme Court as also the High Court of Madras were of the view that the only question, therefore, which the High Court on second appeal may consider in such a case is whether the lower appellate court had before it any evidence proper for its consideration in support of its finding. (AIR 1929 PC 286: 57 Mad LJ 849 and *Arjan Singh* v. *Kartar Singh*, AIR 1951 SC 193: 1951 ALJ SC 78: 1951 (1) MLJ 556: 1951 SCJ 274: 1951 SCR 258: 1951 SCJ 247. The High Court in second appeal is bound by the finding of the trial court but by that of the lower appellate court on a question of fact when there is nothing to show that the finding is vitiated in any way: *Administrator, Corporation City of Lahore* v. *Sampuran Singh*, 226 IC 425: AIR 1947 Lah 172. The High Court of Allahabad said that the High Court in second appeal is entitled to come to a finding of fact where the lower appellate court has omitted to arrive at such finding: 1940 ALJ 366: 1940 All 349. The High Court of Patna said that conclusions of fact by the lower appellate court, however erroneous or unsatisfactory are conclusive in second appeal and cannot be challenged: 22 Pat LT 196; 1937 Sind 263; Similar view was held by a Full Bench of the High Court of Assam *Sehopanit Shah* v. *Chabilal Tewari*, AIR 1952 Assam 52 (FB): 1954 Pat 455; *Fatah Gugan* v. *Sardara*, 59 PLR 501: ILR 1957 Punj 1997: AIR 1958 Punj 333 (Even if the High Court would have decided otherwise). The Courts are consistent of the view that there is no jurisdiction to entertain a second appeal on the ground of erroneous finding of fact, however gross the error may seem to be, nor does the fact that the finding of the first appellate court is based on some documentary evidence make it any less a finding of fact. A Judge of High Court has, therefore, no jurisdiction to interfere in second appeal with findings of fact given by the first appellate court based upon an appreciation of the relevant evidence. Extremely strong grounds are necessary for interfering with the finding of the trial judge, who heard the witnesses, that they were unworthy of belief: 116 IC 432: 1929 N 117. The Courts have stressed the Legislature, rightly or wrongly, decided that the first appellate court is to be trusted and it behooves first appellate judge to bear in mind the fact that their findings of fact are conclusive and they, therefore, have a great responsibility. If they are not careful it may be a matter for administrative discipline, but a second appellate court cannot put the matter right in second appeal: ILR (1939) N 510: 1939 N 221. The High Court should be reluctant in upsetting the finding of fact recorded by the first appellate court on the ground merely that it is against the weight of evidence or on the fact that the judge has not in his judgment referred to all the evidence on the record. The High Court of Ajmer had said that it is only when there is no evidence at all for the fact to be proved or where the evidence is disbelieved for no reason at all that the court will interfere in second appeal: *Bala Sundri* v. *Radha Kishan*, AIR 1955 Ajmer 14. Findings of fact recorded by first appellate court, however, erroneous they may be, cannot be reopened unless it is held that the findings are vitiated. When the appellate court fails to take into consideration evidence on record or misreads some important evidence or omits to pay sufficient attention to some evidence which shifts the burden of proof, commits some mistake in law or omits to consider the evidence of a material witness, the findings of fact may be vitiated and not binding on the second appellate court. The question whether the findings of fact recorded by the first appellate court in any particular case are binding or have been vitiated by some error is a question of fact to be decided on the facts of each particular case: *Lal Singh* v. *Tejmal*, AIR 1954 Ajmer 75. A finding of fact is binding on a second appellate court. 1935 P 42; ILR (1943) I MLJ 14; where there is no error or defect in the procedure, the finding of the first appellate court upon a question of fact is final, if that court had before it evidence proper for its consideration in support of the finding: *Manturabai* v. *Ithal Chiman*, ILR 1954 Nag 96: AIR 1954 Nag 103; *Abdul Shakur* v. *Kotwaleshwar Prasad*, AIR 1958 All 54, relying on 18 C 23 (PC), if there was any failure of the court below to appreciate the real issues involved, the finding of fact is not conclusive in second appeal. (70 IA 225, rel. on): 1949 Oudh 87. The High Court of Karnataka, however, said that where the lower appellate court fails to consider in a proper judicial manner a material piece of evidence, and applies to the case a standard of proof different from, and higher than, that applicable under the Evidence Act, the High Court in second appeal will not accept its findings of fact as final and will interfere: ILR (1946) Kar 246: 1947 Sind 102. The High Court of Calcutta also said that where it appears that all the evidence available is not considered the High Court will and should interfere in second appeal: 51 PLR 70: 1949 EP 342; *Subodh Gopal Bose* v. *Brojendra Kishore Roy*, 91 CLJ 327: AIR 1954 Cal 90. A finding arrived at without considering material evidence which was on record cannot be accepted as a valid finding and the question whether there has been omission to consider material evidence is not a question of fact but question of law: 1958 Ker LJ 396. Where it had been decided by the lower court that a certain wall and a door did not encroach on the plot in suit: held that it was not open in a second appeal to direct the lower court to hold an enquiry, as to the same matter; 40 CWN 449: 1946 PC 83: 70 MLJ 455 (PC).

The High Court of Allahabad relying on the views of the Privy Council, (35 Cal 1039 (PC), held that a finding based on mere conjectures or surmises would be tantamount to a finding on no evidence since conjecture cannot be accepted as a substitute for proof: *Abdul Shakur* v. *Kotwaleshwar Prasad*, AIR 1958 All 54. The High Court of Patna said that a finding of fact which is arrived on certain observations in an order which are not evidence is a finding not based on evidence, and is not conclusive: 1950 Pat 302. According to the High Court of Bombay where the funding arrived at on an important point by the courts below is grossly incompatible with evidence, and then even if the finding is on a question of fact the High Court will be justified in interfering in second appeal: AIR 1956 Bom 155. Interferences of fact which are not unreasonable and are justified by evidence cannot be interfered with in the second appeal: 1931 Sind 20; IC 523; RLR 314 (Rev); 1926 O 522; 95 IC 463 (1): 13 OLJ 146; 39 CWN 303. Where more than one inference is legally open from the evidence, the High Court cannot in second appeal refuse to be bound by that inference drawn in court below: 1923 L. 239 (I); 73 IC 232: 1923 L. 236 (1); 1939 Pat 218; (1954) 1 MLJ 548. Where the lower appellate court based its findings on a sweeping statement that water discharged from latrines in Indian homes should as rule be treated as nuisance held, that the finding was given without reference to the evidence bearing on the point: 1936 OWN 310: 1936 O 211. A finding of fact by the lower appellate court which is contrary to pleading and evidence is not binding in second appeal: *Shaikh Mohammad* v. *Governor-General in Council, Indian Union, Delhi*, ILR (1955) Nag 45: 1955 NLJ 172: AIR 1954 Nag 337. If in arriving at the finding of facts the courts below have committed errors of law and substantial errors of procedure, second appeal would certainly be maintainable: *Basanti* v. *Pohlu*, AIR 1952 Bilaspur 13. Earlier, the High Court of Patna had said that a finding of fact is not binding in second appeal if it is marked by errors of law as that of ignoring to the record of rights; *Bhup Narayan Singh* v. *Hira Lal*, 17 Pat LT 405: AIR 1936 Pat 185; 37 PL.

The Privy Council had stressed that the High Court is not entitled to go behind the findings of fact of District Judge which did not result from misconstruction of a document or the misapplication of law or procedure, but upon the oral evidence in the case: 1919 PC 39: 37 MLJ 199 PC; *Sakaldip Singh* v. *Imrit Barhi*, 10 Pat LT 630: AIR 1930 Pat 71: 120 Ind Cas 292. It was also said that the finding of fact of lower appellate court which proceeds on an erroneous view of the law and which is inconsistent with the facts recited can be interfered with by the High Court: *Murarilal* v. *Balkishan*, 95 IC 636: AIR 1926 Nag 416; *Harihar Prasad* v. *Janak Dulari*, 21 Pat LT 873: 191 IC 275: AIR 1941 Pat 118. Later, the High Court of Patna said that where the court of appeal in reversing the conclusion arrived at by the trial court erred in many respects and the finding given by the court of appeal was partly based on conjecture and on a wrong application of law, is as such perverse and not of a character which can be said to be binding on the High Court in second appeal: *Ram Narain Prasad Singh* v. *Manki Singh*, 1954 BLJR 486: AIR 1954 Pat 562: 33 Pat 638; *See* also *Budhi Jena* v. *Dhobai Naik*, 24 Cut LT 100: AIR 1958 Ori 7: ILR 1957 Cut 574 (Reversing finding of lower appellate court cryptic and without discussion). The High Court of Allahabad, however, said that a finding of fact which has been arrived in complete disregard of legal propositions involved in the consideration of the question in issue cannot be regarded as conclusive: 1935 ALJ 828: AIR 1935 All 774, or in disregard of the presumption provided by any Statute, as was held by the High Court of Patna: *Mehar Din* v. *Hakim Ali*, 157 IC 561: AIR 1935 Lah 912; *Bhup Narayan Singh* v. *Hira Lal*, AIR 1936 Pat 185: 161 IC 709. Relying on the views of the Supreme Court [*Dhirajlal Girdharilal* v. *Commr. of Income-tax, Bombay*, AIR 1955 SC 271: (1954) 26 ITR 736]: the High Court of Punjab said that where in arriving at a finding of fact on the question whether the defendant was the *chela* of last mahant the lower appellate court drew an adverse presumption against the plaintiff under section 114 of the Indian Evidence Act, which it was not entitled to do and used certain documents as substantive pieces of evidence, which also could not be done, and failed to apply its mind to the rule with regard to the admissibility and use of the findings given in the previous judgments *inter partes*, the finding is vitiated by an error of law and is liable to set aside in second appeal. ILR (1958) Punj 1866. As per the High Court of Allahabad finding of fact may be vitiated by error of law, for example, failure to consider important evidence or on misreading or misinterpretation of evidence; *Buddha* v. *Balwanta*, AIR 1958 All 699.

The Supreme Court also stressed that where the lower courts had misunderstood the real point for determination in arriving at a finding of fact that the institution of suit was not for the benefit of the junior, held, that the second appeal had rightly held that the suit was instituted for the benefit of the minor plaintiff: AIR 1958 SC 1042. Where finding of facts is based on additional evidence which ought not to have been admitted and evidence admitted also is inherently defective and it did not prove what party had to prove, the High Court at Bilaspur relying on the view of Supreme Court held that the finding is not binding in second appeal. [*Arjan Singh* v. *Kartar Singh*, AIR 1951 SC 193: 1951 ALJ SC 78: 1951 (1) MLJ 556: 1951 SCJ 274: 1951 SCR 258, rel. on]: AIR 1953 Bilaspur 17. Where the trial court has failed to consider relevant and material evidence on the record in arriving at a conclusion, and the first appellate court which is the final Court of fact has not recorded finding, cannot be final in second appeal: *Bansi Sah* v. *Krishna Chandra*, 30 PIT 231: AIR 1951 Pat 508. Where a decision is based on surmises, when there is evidence on the record which should have been considered, it e-mails a question of law: 1939 AMLJ 116. Inferences not warranted by the evidence and based on surmises cannot be conclusive in second appeal: AIR 1948 Pat 247; *Garibu* v. *Bhagat Lakshami Narain*, AIR 1952 J&K 24: (1952) 10 J&K LR 186. A respondent in second appeal is not debarred from challenging the correctness of the finding of fact of the first dismissed appeal: 179 IC 916: 1936 R 59. The High Court of Lahore had said that where the judgment of the lower court dealing with point of fact is confused and contains mistakes of fact, and material evidence bearing on the disputed matters has not been considered, the findings of fact have not been considered, the finding of fact are not conclusive and binding on the second appeal, and the second appellate court is justified in re-opening those matters and examining the evidence itself: ILR (1941). A 568: 1941 Lah. 10; 1926 O, 353 (Finding on mistaken view of pleadings). Perverse findings, though of fact are good grounds for remand in second appeal: 1931 MWN 102.

The High Court of Patna explained the position where more than one view were possible and said that where the lower courts have taken a view which was open to them as Courts of fact, the High Court cannot be asked to interfere in second appeal, on the ground that another view was possible; *Julum Rai* v. *Jainarain Rai*, 28 Pat 441: AIR 1951 Pat 370. To justify interference with a finding of fact, it must be shown that the finding of the lower appellate court are such that hey have no basis whatsoever on the evidence on record: 1941 AWR (Rev) 356: 1941 OA (Supp) 270; ILR (1945) N 444: 1945 NLJ 172: 1946 N 138. It is neither necessary nor proper for the High Court in second appeal to consider whether the reasoning for a finding of fact is acceptable 1949 Cal 204. Where a lower appellate court, without giving cogent reasons, differs from the finding of the trial court which had the best means of judging the weight to be attached to the evidence tendered before it, can be set aside in second appeal by the Board; 1939 AWR (BR) 277.

Where on a question of fact the findings of the two Courts below are concurrent, the High Court will ordinarily go into the evidence, very minutely. But where the lower appellate court has not taken the trouble of discussing the evidence and has adopted the reasons given by the trial court in support of its finding with slight modifications here and there, the High Court will go into the evidence: ILR (1952) Patiala 151: AIR 1954 Pepsu. The High Court of Kerala said that if an appellate Judge does not apply his mind to the facts of the case before him, but merely records a finding confirming the conclusion reached by the Munsif without himself bestowing any consideration thereon, it can surely be said that his is not a judgment and that notwithstanding the apparent concurrent findings which will ordinarily conclude the High Court to consider the question afresh and dispose of the case as though there had been no judgment in appeals; *Ouseph Ouseph* v. *Mathen Mariyamma*, 1954 Ker LT 78: AIR 1954 Trav Co 297.

10. Illustrations of Question of Fact

Where a custom is alleged to exist the existence or non-existence of such a custom is a question of fact; but it is a question of law whether there is proof to support the custom or whether the evidence is legally sufficient to support such a custom; 158 IC 109: 1935. The High Court of Rajasthan following the views of the High Court of Madras and differing from that of the High Court of Patna held that the finding in a suit for damages for malicious prosecution that there was malice on the part of the defendant and there was no reasonable and probable cause for the institution of the proceedings are both, finding of fact and cannot be challenged in second appeal (1939 All 554; 1947 Oudh 88 and 1947 Mad 236 foll.; 1932 Pat 91 not foll.) 1951 Raj 160; 1952 San 16, AIR 1952 Sau 9; *Chellu* v. *Municipal Council, Palghat*, AIR 1955 Mad 562: 1955 Mad WN 133: 68 Mad LW 317; *See* also *Sumat Prasad* v. *Ram Sarup*, AIR 1946 All 204: ILR 1945 All 685: 1946 OWN 330. But the High Court of Rajasthan said that the High Court is entitled to examine whether the inference drawn from the facts is legitimate, *i.e.*, whether the facts found did or did not, amount to absence of reasonable and probable cause: 17 L. 190: 1935 L. 765; *Kedarnath* v. *Brahmanand*, AIR 1959 Raj 37: 1958 Raj LW 434. Finding that plaintiff has failed to make out his claim by reliable evidence is purely a question of fact: *Mathai Esthappan* v. *Mathai Anna*, 1952 Ker LT 538: AIR 1953 Trav Co 41. The High Court of Andhra Pradesh said that the inference of the lower appellate court that a particular amount paid to the decree-holder was not taken into account by the Court when decree was scaled down, is one of fact; 1956 Andhra LT 717: 1956 An WR 899. The finding that certain deed is not vitiated by fraud or misrepresentation is one of fact and is binding on the High Court in second appeal; 1956 Andhra WR 771. Whether a transaction was entered into with intent to defeat or delay creditors; 63 IC

169; 38 PLR 577 or whether a transaction was fraudulent 107 IC 490. A finding that certain alterations in a document, were made without the knowledge and consent of the executant of the deed, is one fact, and cannot be challenged in second appeal; ILR 1946 Nag 796: 1946 NLJ 622: *Ramsingh* v. *Babulal*, AIR 1954 Bhopal 3. The High Court of Patna said that the question whether the Nazarat peon who went to serve the notice under section 7 of the Public Demands Recovery Act addressed to the party had or had not used all due and reasonable diligence to find the party sought to be served before affixing or hanging up the notice is not a question of law, nor even a mixed question of law and fact but is really a question of fact and is not open to challenge in second appeal, when there is evidence on which the lower court could come to the conclusion which it did; *Bibi Waziuddinnissa* v. *Janak Singh*, AIR 1952 Pat 65. The Privy Council held that the correct position with regard to rebuttal of statutory presumptions would appear to be this; if the finding arrived at as a result of the rebuttal of a statutory presumption is a finding on a question of fact, such as whether there has been a sale, that finding would be final for purposes of a second appeal, but if, on the other hand, that finding be a finding on a question of law, such as whether a tenancy is permanent or precarious, it would be open to question in a second appeal; (*Dhannamal* v. *Moti Sagar*, AIR 1927 PC 102: ILR 8 Lah 573: 54 IA 178: 52 Mad LJ 663: Ref AIR 930 PC 91: 59 Mad LJ 53, explained) *Abdul Shakur* v. *Kotwaleshwar Prasad*, AIR 1958 All 54.

According to the Patna High Court whether a person has an interest or is interested in a tenure is essentially a question of fact; 1950 Pat. 391. According to a Full Bench of the High Court of Allahabad finding of the lower appellate court that the plaintiff has been in possession of the plot within 12 years before the suit and that defendant had not been in possession of the plot for over 12 years when the suit was instituted is a finding of fact and is binding in second appeal; *Sobha Nath* v. *Ram Baran*, 1954 All LJ 256: 1954 All WR (HC) 02: AIR 1954 All 493 (FB); *Kakarlapudi Janikiramaraju* v. *Gedala Appalaswami*, (1954) 2 MLJ 773: AIR 1954 Mad 772: ILR 1954 Mad 980. Where in rent reduction proceedings tenant represented whole body of representation is a mixed question of fact and law; 26 Pat 592; 1948 Pat 153. A finding in a suit for ejectment on the ground of misuse of the land, that the land had been transformed from agricultural land into a *bhika* at a particular time and that the suit having been brought within two years of that cannot be interfered with in second appeal; *Asrabuddin* v. *Abdul Fazal*, 225 IC 337: AIR 1947 Cal 139. Finding that purpose of tenancy is agricultural is one of fact conclusive in second appeal; *Asrabuddin* v. *Abdul Fazal*, 225 IC 337: AIR 1947 Cal 139. Whether a land held under 'Buta Hak' has been forfeited for mismanagement or not is a question of fact: AIR 1953 San 94. The High Court of Assam relying on the views of the High Court of Madras said that a finding that the defendant had accepted the plaintiff as his landlord by attornment is a pure finding of fact and the High Court in second appeal cannot interfere with it when on the face of it there was no error of law pointed out. (AIR 1934 PC 112; 66 Mad LJ 595, rel. on): *Parameswarlal Agarwalla* v. *Dalu Ram Jalan*, AIR 1957 Assam 188. Question whether time is or is not of the essence of a contract is a question of fact 67 IC 157; but the High Court of

Patna said that such finding can be set aside in second appeal, if it is contrary to the general principles of law; 49 OLR 74: 1946 Pat 298. In a suit for specific performance the contention that the contract had been abandoned is a question of fact. *S. Venkateswara Rao* v. *M. Subbayya*, 1957 Andhra LT 434: AIR 1958 AP 99. The question whether the parties intended to substitute a new contract for the old one is a question of fact in each case depending for its decision in the circumstances of the case; AIR 1956 MB 325: ILR 1956 MB 13.

Ordinarily, a finding of the lower appellate court on the question whether a contract was caused to be made under undue influence is a finding of fact which is binding in second appeal. But where such finding is based on misconception of the evidence on a vital matter and was reached by adopting a procedure which has resulted in an erroneous finding, it is vitiated and is not binding in second appeal; ILR (1950) Nag 105: 1950 Nag. Finding that plaintiff has failed to prove the fraud and misrepresentation alleged by him as a ground for setting aside a consent decree is one of fact binding in second appeal *Motilal Shivnarayan* v. *Vishwanath Waman Thakur*, 48 Bom LR 786: AIR 1947 Bom 133. The question whether the enquiry in respect of a complaint against a Government servant was closed or not is question of fact; *State* v. *Mansinghrao*, AIR 1958 MP 413: 1958 MPC 544: 1958 Cr LJ 1485.

A Full Bench of the High Court of Allahbad held that the finding that the plaintiff had an opportunity of showing cause against the charge which had been leveled against him is a finding on a question of fact: *Mohammed Ahmad Kidwai* v. *Chairman, Improvement Trust, Lucknow*, ILR (1957) 2 All 280: 1958 All LJ 160: AIR 1958 All 353 (FB) Finding of lower appellate court that the defendant had constructive notice of the agreement based on review of evidence, is binding in second appeal. *Sital Chandra Kolley* v. *Heirs of Mihilal Kolley*, 58 Cal WN 1000: ILR (1956) 2 Cal 469: AIR 1955 Cal 21. Whether a clause in an agreement to refer to arbitration or is merely an agreement to refer the matter to a valuer is a question of fact *Governor-General* v. *Simla Banking and Industrial Co.*, AIR 1947 Lah 215: 226 IC 444. The finding on the questions whether the land in suit was proprietor's private land and whether it had been settled with the respondent for purposes of cultivation are finding of facts: 34 Pat 393. A finding as to user of an easement for twenty years is a finding of fact. The fact that the Court has erred in the appreciation of the evidence of one or two witnesses would not entitle the Court of second appeal to go into the finding arrived at by the lower appellate Court: *Natwarlal Gordhandas* v. *Dansinhji Vakhatsinhji*, 3 Sau LR 259: AIR 1951 Sau 35. A finding as to legitimacy is one of fact: 10 Luck 505. But it would not be upheld in second appeal, if the lower appellate court has ignored submission of law in favour of legitimacy: 60 IC 275: 1921 P 611 (1). A factum of marriage 201; re-marriage of Hindu widow is a question of fact: *Harisingh Hiralal Dangi* v. *Ramchandra Takhat Singh Dangi*, AIR 1957 MP 238: 1957 MPC 263: 1957 MPLJ 483. Finding that *A* is not daughter of *B* is a finding of fact: *Ganesh Sahi* v. *Ramdeni Sahi*, AIR 1953 Pat 316. Finding that a woman has taken to a life of immorality is a finding of fact: 31 IC 797; 1926 L 461. Finding that an adopted son was not the son but the step-son of a widow who gave him in adoption is one of fact not open to challenge in second appeal: *Haribhau Ganpatrao* v. *Ajabrao*

Ramji Ingole, ILR (1946) Nag 978: 1947 NLJ 133: 1947 Nag 143. Finding of fact that plaintiff was the adopted son of the defendant even if erroneous is binding in second appeal: AIR 1954 Ajmer 37 (2). The Andhra Pradesh Court said that where the finding that a person is an illatom son-in-law of another person is an interfere of fact, it is not permissible to interference with it in second appeal: 1955 Andhra WR 39. Finding that a lady is not a *pardanashin* lady is a finding of fact: 34 PLR 304: 1933 L. 451. Question whether certain persons were members of a joint Hindu family is a finding of fact: 67 IC 89: 1924 L 267: 97 IC 817 (1): 1926 L 443. A finding by the Court of appeal below that though there was a complete cessor of commensality between the brothers and that they were in separate possession as tenants-in-common is essentially a finding of fact and cannot be re-opened in second appeal; *Amir Mahton* v. *Sheopujan Missir*, AIR 1946 Pat 231: ILR 25 Pat 1. Inference of ouster or exclusion from participation in watan income is a question of fact: *Dhanji Girja Bhailume* v. *Dharma Kanhu*, AIR 1956 Bom 204. According to the Privy Council a question of what constitutes exclusion from a joint estate may be a question of law 21 CWN 1142: 42 IC 258 (PC). Binding nature of family arrangement is a question of fact: 4 LLJ 40: 1921 L 291. Question whether there has been a family settlement among the members of a joint Hindu family is one of fact; 165 IC 217: 1936 N 186; 1941 OA 17: 1941 O. 226. Whether or nor the relations between parties to a suit was such that the consideration was the love and affection of the parties is a question of fact; 154 IC 1043: 1934 P 41; whether a certain sum of money was necessary for personal necessities is a question of fact: 8 L. 340: 1927 L. 605. Question if deed is supported by consideration and necessity is a question of fact; 1958 Ker LJ 396. A finding that the holder of a superior interest acquiring an inferior interest intends to keep the two interests separate and that consequently there is no merger is a question of law and fact: 39 CWN 694. The Court of Madras held that the question whether the sale by the original owner in favour of the plaintiff's father was real and operative or nominal and fraudulent is in root analysis a question of fact and a concurrent finding of the Courts below will not be interfered with in second appeal unless the conclusion is so far vitiated by material error as to merit reversal or re-consideration: *Marneedi Satyam* v. *Venkataswami*, AIR 1949 Mad 689: (1949) MLJ 434. The question whether a road is a public road or a private road is rather question of law than a question of fact, and in any case, it is party to a question of law 1935 OWN 899: 1936 O. 154. The finding of the Courts below that a particular alienation was a gift and not a sale is a finding of fact and is binding in second appeal, holds Patna High Court; 15 Pat IT 596. Whether a mortgage is proved is a question of fact: 96 IC 253: 1926 O. 546. The finding as to record satisfaction is a finding of fact: 152 IC 398: 1934 N. 226. Finding without taking evidence, but based on construction of documents is not binding; 1931 B. 371: 33 Bom LR 663; 1936 B 230: 34 Bom LR 372. Whether a public lane has been so narrowed as to cause damage to the residents is question of fact; 129 A. 504, Whether the judgment-debtor has sufficient property to meet the execution of a decree, after he had parted with some other properties is a question of fact; *Gopichand* v. *Jodhraj Deojit*, AIR 1929 All 458: 116 IC 815. The High Court of Bombay said that a finding that the parties are governed by the customary law of the Punjab in the matter of inheritance being one of fact cannot be challenged in second appeal; *Badrinarayan Gangadhar* v. *Nagarmal Hanumandas,* 60 Bom LR 1022: ILR 1959 Bom 77: AIR 1959 Bom 241. Finding that a custom set up is not existing is a question of fact; 1945 OWN 3: 1946 O. 188; whether a right of privacy exists by custom and the nature and limits of it, are questions of fact: *Tika Ram Joshi* v. *Ram Lal Sah,* AIR 1935 All 754: 1935 All LJ 432. Finding that the right of privacy was in no way diminished: 1929 O. 535. A finding by a lower appellate court that there is a local usage giving the residents a right to transfer their houses is binding on the second appellate court: 223 amount to an accession under T.P. Act, section 63: 113 IC 405: 1929 A 330.

A finding by a lower appellate court that a certain person is not the owner of a site, which belongs to the Municipality is one of fact which cannot be challenged in second appeal and it is not open to the Court in second appeal to go into the question whether the evidence provided by the documents produced has been rightly or wrongly belived by the lower appellate court because on a question of fact the decision of the lower appellate court is final; 1951 A. 634. Finding as to material alteration of instrument; 1929 M. 622; *Rangaswami Reddi* v. *K. Doraiswami Reddi,* (1957) 2 MLJ 196: AIR 1957 Mad 715. A finding that the inhabitants of a particular locality have not in certain circumstances acted in a certain manner; *Municipal Board, Benares* v. *Kanahiya Lal,* 134 IC 21: AIR 1931 All 499. The question as to when arrears of pay became due is a question of fact 1936 C 277.

Finding that a cause of action accrued at particular place: 931 A 556, or particular time and suit is within time is a question of fact: *Asrabuddin* v. *Abdul Fazal,* 225 IC 337: AIR 1947 Cal 139. Where the lower appellate court errs in law in holding on the facts of a case that the dissent has not been from preceptor to disciple, the finding can be interfered with in second appeal: 178 IC 58: 1938 L 182. According to the High Court of Allahabad the question whether the Company did or did not obtain the approval of the Central Government to change its name as provided by sub-section (4) of section 11 of the Companies Act is a question of fact and cannot be raised for the first time in second appeal: *F.S. Abdulqayum* v. *Manindra Land and Building Corpn. Ltd.,* 1955 All LJ 29: AIR 1955 All 192: (1955) 25 Com Cas 143. Question whether property was damaged after the decree for possession - Held, that question was essentially for the first time in appeal: *Shankarlal Narayandas* v. *New Mofussil Co. Ltd.,* AIR 1946 PC 97: 73 Ind App 98: (1946) 2 MLJ 259, foll. *Phool Kuer* v. *Manohar Mal,* 1954 All LJ 730: 1954 All WR (HC) 619: AIR 1955 All 223. The same Court said that that the assessment of damages done by the lower court is wrong is a pure question of fact: *L. Nawal Kishore* v. *Rameshwar Nath,* AIR 1955 All 594, also question about adequacy of damages: 1936 Nag 70. The High Court of Patna held that the question of negligence on the part of a Railway Company in a suit for compensation for loss and non-delivery of goods consigned is not purely one of fact; and the High Court in second appeal can examine the matter to find out whether the conclusion of the lower court is correct; *Phulchand Khandelwal* v. *Governor-General of India in-Council,* 29 PLT 76: 1949 Pat 110.

11. Appreciation of Evidence

The Supreme Court decided that the appellate court in second appeal cannot assume jurisdiction to interfere just because another view is possible on appreciation of evidence; *Veerayee Ammal* v. *Seeni Amal,* AIR 2001 SC 2920: (2002) 1 SCC 134: 2001 AIR SCW 4377: JT 2001 (9) SC 145: 2002 (1) Civ CR 295.

12. Objection as to the Admissibility of Evidence

Objection that the evidence of witnesses of the plaintiff who had deposed to the defendant's admission of his liability and to the negotiations for compromise was not admissible because the negotiations must be deemed to have been without prejudice – The High Court of Nagpur held that this objection to the admissibility of the evidence of the witnesses was not raised in the court below. There was no legal justification for excluding the evidence of those witnesses: ILR (1955) Nag 151: 1955 Nag LJ 487: AIR 1955 Nag 170. Where secondary evidence of contents of a deed is led without objection by the other party, an objection cannot be raised in second appeal: 1935 L. 628: 1923 L. 56; 1929 A. 456, so also an alternative plea not put forth in court below; 7 Pat LT 145: AIR 1926 Pat 156.

13. Case not Set-up in Plaint and not Tried

The High Court of Calcutta held that case not set-up in the plaint and not tried cannot be raised in appellate court in argument. The High Court of Calcutta further said that an appellant cannot raise, for the first time in appeal a so-called constitutional point, namely, that the central legislature or the Central Government acting as a legislature could legislate only with respect to contracts to be performed wholly within India which he had never thought of before and of which he had not given any warning to the respondent at any stage: *Joseph Pyke and Son (Liverpool) Ltd.* v. *Kedarnath Mohanlal,* AIR 1959 Cal 328: ILR (1959) 2 Cal 325. Where no claim for value of improvements was made in the written statement nor was any issue joined in the court below and no reason was alleged for the omission the party cannot raise such a claim for the first time in the High Court; *Narayana Pillai* v. *Raghavan Pillai,* 1953 Ker LT 566: AIR 1953 Trav Co 563. An objection which is taken in the trial court but is not urged in the lower appellate court cannot be raised in second appeal: 43 A. 555; 30 WN 937. Where a point is not taken in the lower appellate court and not argued and not taken even in the ground of second appeal raises questions which would require scrutiny into evidence open up new and unexplored avenue of facts and is not a pure question of law patent on the face of the record, it cannot be allowed to be raised at the stage of arguments in second appeal, 1952 ALJ 177. The High Court of Andhra Pradesh said that it is not possible in second appeal to accede to a new contention whose acceptance depends upon an elucidation of further facts; 1955 Andhra WR 39; *see* also AIR 955 Pat 189. Where neither in the trial court nor in the lower appellate court any case of nuisance has been made on behalf of the plaintiff, he will not be allowed to raise that point for the first time in the second appeal: *Ganga Vishnu Swaika* v. *Machine Manufacturing Co. Ltd.,* AIR 1955 Cal 503: ILR (1956) 2 Cal 679: 60 Cal WN 233; *See* also *Hemendra Lal Roy* v. *Indo-Swiss Trading Co.,* AIR 1955 Pat 375. Where a contention was not advanced in the courts below nor even in the memo of appeal to the High Court, it cannot be allowed to be taken during arguments: *Kothari Revashankar Amulakh* v. *Gauriben Jayashankar Vyas*, 6 Sau LR 198: AIR 1954 Sau 8. The High Court of Hyderabad held that a plaintiff-appellant cannot be allowed to rely on a new ground such as consent for supporting his claim in second appeal when he has not made any such allegation in the plaint: *Gokam Chinna Nagaiah* v. *Nagaram Baliga*, ILR 1956 Hyd 321: AIR 1956 Hyd 170. But an appellant in second appeal is not debarred from raising an objection to the admissibility of a document on the ground of its non-registration although no such objection was taken at any earlier stage of proceedings; 82 CLJ 183. The High Court of Patna distinguished a case relating to question of admissibility of a document and said that the question of inadmissibility of documents is a question of law and can be allowed to be raised in second appeal for the first time *Basanta Kumar* v. *Chota Nagpur Banking Association Ltd.*, AIR 1948 Pat 18: ILR 26 Pat 231.

But according to the Privy Council, a question of admissibility of a document depending on facts will not be allowed to be raised at any stage unless the facts are either admitted or proved beyond controversy (AIR 1932 PC 118; 63 MLJ 131 Ref.) 1958 Ker IJ 1079. The various High Courts like Assam, Hyderabad, Patna insisted that the question whether there has been a failure of justice or not is not pure question of law and cannot be decided without finding fact and if the point was not taken in the lower courts it cannot be raised in second appeal. Omission to raise a question of law does not normally prevent its facts found or on facts admitted or proved. It is almost settled law that a question which is purely one of law and involves no further enquiry into facts, may be taken in second appeal even though it may not have been raised in the Courts below: ILR (1954) 6 Assam 95: AIR 1957 Hyd 120 (constitutional question); *Golap Gadi Goala* v. *Rampariksha Rewani*, AIR 1958 Pat 553; *Thakurai Bhup Narain Singh* v. *Nawab Singh*, AIR 1957 Pat 729: 1957 BLJR 694: ILR 36 Pat 1139.

14. Suit for Redemption

Mortgagee pleading sale of mortgage property in his favour and claiming benefit of doctrine of part-performance, the question that that part of consideration was not paid was raised for the first time in second appeal. Evidence on record was sufficient to be raised in the circumstances of case, the High Court of Rajasthan said that the question could be raised: ILR (1957) 7 Raj 101 1957 Raj LW 73. The High Court of Patna relying on the High Court of Allahabad (AIR 134 All 677, rel. on.) held that objection that no appeal lay to the lower appellate Court under section 96, as there was no decree defined by law, can be raised for the first time in second appeal. It was further said that the legal effect of proved facts is a question of law and may be raised and considered even in second appeal: 30 PLT 388. A question of pure law, however, can be raised in second appeal, especially when the other party knows all the relevant facts which the latter himself has mentioned in his pleading: 1937 ALJ 1252, but not where the pleading necessary to sustain the new plea is inconsistent: (1942) AWR (Rev) 361 (2) 1942: OWN (BR) 496 (2). The High Court of Andhra Pradesh held that new plea inconsistent with, case set-up in plaint cannot be raised. *Bapatla Venkata Subba Rao* v. *Sikharam Ramakrishna Rao*, AIR 1958 AP 322: (1958) 1 Andh WR 331:

30 LW 287: 118 IC 391. Where a suit was resisted in the trial court on the ground that the defendants were the owners of the land and were in possession of it as such for more than 25 years and it was never their case that they had acquired the mortgage-rights by possessing the land adversely to the mortgagor, nor did they resist the suit on the ground that the plaintiffs should have fired a suit for redemption on payment of mortgage money to them, and also the points were not specifically taken in the memorandum of appeal to the High Court. It was held that it was a new case which could not be entertained for the first time in second appeal; *Ram Lal* v. *Chetu*, AIR 1953 Pepsu 101.

15. Proprietary Title by Adverse Possession Claimed by Defendants in a Suit for Ground Rent – Title Found against

Plea of irrevocable license was raised in second appeal, it was held to be not permissible: 126 IC 581: 1933 A. 632. Where a tenant denies the relationship of landlord and tenant in the written statement, it is not open to him in second appeal to repudiate written statement and claim that he is still a tenant and means to retain possession in that character: 39 CWN 882: 1935. The High Court of Mysore said that if the plaintiff had put forward the case of agency, it was possible that there might be other defences open to the defendants: 69 Mad IW 977: (1956) 2 Mad LJ 578. Question regarding applicability of section 53A, T.P. Act not raised by the defendants in his proceedings but gone into at the hearing by the courts below and finding given, the Court held that the High Court will not be justified in refusing to allow defendant to avail himself of provision of section 53A, T.P Act. ILR (1957) Mys 108; *Nanjedevaru* v. *H.V. Rama Rao*, AIR 1959 Mys 173. The High Court of Andhra Pradesh said that question whether appellant was entitled to rely on the explanation not put forward before lower court appellant may be permitted to raise point in second appeal it being purely a legal one; 1955 AIT 22: 1955 Andhra WR 66. As per the High Court of Orissa, whether a person was excluded from enjoyment of joint family property, and if so, whether he had knowledge of such exclusion, are mixed question of law and fact; and when no attempt was made to raise the plea or lead evidence thereon in the Courts below the plea cannot be raised for the first time in second appeal; *Janardan Saraf* v. *Nilkantha Saraf*, AIR 1952 Ori 31: 17 Cut LT 371. The High Court of Calcutta held that the question whether the acts complained of by the plaintiff constituted isolated acts of trespass by the defendant or dispossession of the plaintiff, is a mixed question of law and fact and it cannot be decided without fresh evidence. The appellant cannot, therefore, be allowed to raise this mixed question of law and fact for the first time in second appeal: *Shaikh Mongal* v. *Pure Dishargarh Colliery Co.*, AIR 1950 Cal 328. The Court further said that plea of waiver is a mixed question of law and fact. It has to be specifically pleaded and a specific issue has to be raised otherwise a party cannot be allowed to rely on such a plea: *S. Bhattacharjee* v. *Sentinel Assurance Co. Ltd.*, AIR 1955 Cal 594: (1956) 26 Com Cas 1: ILR (1957) 1 Cal 7. The question whether a person can claim Kudivaram and Malwaran interest is not a pure question of law and cannot, therefore, be allowed to be raised in appeal for the first time, said the High Court of Madras, 68 Mad LW 70: AIR 1935 Mad 369. Whether a person is a necessary party in the suit or not depends upon the decision of mixed question of fact and law which, when not raised and decided either in the trial court or first appellate court will not be permitted to be raised in the second appeal for the first time; *Bhajandas* v. *Nanuram*, 1954 Raj LW 145: AIR 1954 Raj 17: ILR (1953) 3 Raj 720. The High Court of Punjab said that the question whether the heirs of the donor were estopped from getting the gift set aside on the ground of its invalidity is a mixed question of fact and law which when never pleaded before cannot be allowed to be raised at the stage of second appeal; *Parkash Vati* v. *Maya Devi*, 55 Punj LR 381: AIR 1953 Punj 304.

16. Suit for Compensation against Railway

The High Court of Calcutta examined the plea taken by the Railway in a suit for compensation against it and said that in a suit for compensation against the railway administration for damage to the consignments caused by the rain water a plea by the railway administration that its liability commenced only on the dates which appear on the railway receipts is not a pure question of law but a mixed question of law and fact and the Court is not justified in allowing the railway administration to raise the point for the first time in second appeal: *Union of India* v. *Hamirmull Champalal*, AIR 1959 Cal 400. When a plea for giving relief against the penalty clause in a consent decree is not taken in the lower court or in the memo of appeal, it cannot be allowed to be taken for the first time in second appeal as it involves consideration of several relevant facts; *Govind Waman* v. *Murlidhar Shrinivas*, 55 Bom LR 465: ILR (1953) Bom 948: AIR 1953 Bom 412. Objection based on Order VII, rule 14 objection cannot be raised for the first time in second appeal; *Budhe Ram* v. *Hira*, AIR 1953 HP 52.

17. Plea Raised in Second Appeal

The High Court of Punjab examined a case where the tenant-appellant raised a point that lease was not valid as it was not in proper form, but the point was not raised in Courts below. The Court held that the point could not be permitted to be raised for first time in second appeal: *Suraj Bhan* v. *Municipal Committee, Moga*, 55 Punj LR 18: AIR 1953 Punj 38. Where plaintiff's right to get past and future *mesne* profits was not challenged before lower appellate court and even in memorandum of second appeal plaintiff's right to get *mesne* profits was not questioned. It was held that it was not open to appellant at stage of argument to disclaim altogether his liability for *mesne* profits: *Varu* v. *Sankaran Namboodiri*, AIR 1953 Trav Co 360.

When in both the lower courts, the plea that the assignment of decree though requiring registration, was not registered and that the assignee had and so the plea could not be entertained in second appeal: ILR (1938) N 221: 1937 N 237. A question of notice cannot be allowed to be raised for the first time in second appeal: 2 Pat LJ 595: 42 IC 655. Where the question was as to the inalienability of certain property according to custom, and it was found to be so, a party who did not plead in the Court below that the custom was qualified, in the sense of the restraint against alienation, can raise that plea in second appeal: 1936 IWN 260: 1936 O. 235. The High Court will not entertain in second appeal a plea of *res judicata* which was not raised in the grounds of appeal in the appellate court or in the High Court: 13 Luck: 167: 1937 OWN 229: 1937 O. 243; 8 Pat.

18. Case of *Estoppels* cannot be Set-up in Second Appeal

The High Court of Allahabad held that where no case of *estoppel* was set-up in the written statement and no issue was framed, the High Court of Allahabad held that it is too late to set up such a new case in second appeal; 1938 ALJ 1238: 1939 All 194; 1934 All: 151 IC 263; 1940 Pat 480: 186 IC 793; AIR 1957 Tri 11. The High Courts of Bombay and Patna decided that *estoppel* is a mixed question of fact and law, and a plea of *estoppel* cannot be allowed in second appeal, when it would necessitate the taking of further evidence of fact; 40 Bom LR 359: 1938 B 291; 1937 Pat 642.

19. Plea of Custom cannot be Allowed in Second Appeal for the First Time

Objections to maintainability of suit, if raised for the first time in appeal cannot be allowed 3L. 239: 1922 L 363. The contention that the parties did not constitute a joint Hindu family cannot be raised for the first time in second appeal; 66 IC 881. The question as to the validity of an adoption by custom, depending on proof of custom, cannot be permitted to be raised for the first time in second appeal: *Ramachandra Tripathi* v. *Maguni Tripathi*, 1950 Cut 337: 16 Cut LT 233: 1951 Ori 64. Though the general custom was that the widow of a predeceased son was not an heir of her father-in-law but in some tribes a special custom prevailed which made her the heir, and the *onus* of proving the special custom lay on those who asserted it. The Supreme Court said that where the party neither pleaded the special custom, nor proved it nor even made an attempt to do so, no question as to the special custom should be permitted by the High Court to be raised: *Kirpal Kuar* v. *Bachan Singh*, 1958 SCR 948: 1958 SCJ 138: AIR 1958 SC 199. Plaintiff relying on his adoption by defendant for basis of his claim-Defendant merely denying factum of adoption but question as to her authority or capacity to adopt not raised – No issue struck on the point – Question not raised even in memo of appeal – Question of lack of authority or capacity to adopt cannot be allowed to be raised for the first time at the time of hearing of appeal or second appeal AIR 1954 Ajmer 57(2).

20. Where Evidence Required-Pleas must be Rejected

Where a question cannot be decided without taking fresh evidence, the appellate court will generally refuse to entertain the plea. But where the plea of limitation involves a question of law which can be decided on the facts proved or admitted before the Court it can be raised at any stage of the proceedings: *Lal Badri Singh* v. *Mahesh Prasad*, AIR 1955 VP 28. The plea of limitation or *estoppel* involving question of fact which are not admitted or undisputed cannot be taken for the first time in appeal; 27 IC 933; 115 680: 10 Pat LT 53; 56 C 201: 1929 C 437. The High Court of Patna said that a point of limitation taken but not pressed, before the lower appellate court, cannot be raised in second appeal when no materials were placed before the lower court in support of the plea of limitation: *Darshan Singh* v. *Baldeo Das*, ILR 25 Pat 145: AIR 1946 Pat 365. If the case of acquisition of title by adverse possession appears clear from the pleadings and further, if the defendants were never taken by surprise by the plea having been raised for the first time in appeal, relief to the plaintiffs should not be withheld. But on the contrary, if the case of adverse possession does not clearly arise from the pleadings and from the peculiar features of the case, it is considered that such an alternative plea ought to have been specifically raised and further that the parties had not the advantage of adducing evidence at their command on the point, then it will not be permissible in law for the appellate court to allow the party to raise the plea of adverse possession for the first time: (1957) 23 Cut LT 473. Where the authority for a plea is not quoted in the Court below, the Court in second appeal cannot reverse the finding on the strength of the authority: 1930 L. 737. When an appellant confines himself to some of the questions decided by the trial court, if the appellate court judgment proceeds only the questions attacked and dismisses the appeal it will not be open to the appellant to object to the judgment in second appeal on the ground that the judgment was not in accordance with law; *Gajadhar Tewari* v. *Nand Lal*, 150 IC 841: AIR 1934 Pat 55(2). A new plea attacking the validity of a sale deed on the ground of lack of *bona fides* cannot for the first time be allowed in second appeal, the appellant having attacked it in the trial court only on the ground of want of consideration and failed in his contention: 147 IC 952: 10 OWN 1186. Where no objection is taken by a party in the lower court to the competency of the sub-agent to bring a suit, it is not open to him to raise that point in the High Court: 1934 R. 289; 1938 M. 338 (plea of want action under section 91, C.P. Code). Where the case was a surety, and in second appeal the plea was taken that he was co-obligator, held that the new plea could not be allowed to be raised on LW 429: AIR 1934 M 639. The plaintiff's contention that defendant No. 1, had a right of subrogation as against the defendant No. 2 and that instead of passing a decree against the first defendant and driving him to a separate suit against defendant No. 2 all the equities might be worked out in the present suit, cannot be allowed to be raised for the first time in second appeal, when there was no pleading to that effect, no issue framed on it and when there was not even an application for amendment of plaint in the second appeal, the High Court of Andhra Pradesh differing from the views of the High Court of Calcutta held that it could not be allowed in the second appeal. (*Manindra Chandra* v. *Sudir Krishna*, AIR 1932 Cal 182: 59 Cal 216, not followed): *Kattragadda Rathiah* v. *Debineni Santhamma*, (1954) 2 Mad LJ 187: 1954 Mad WN 872: AIR 1954 Andhra 15. The High Court of Allahabad held in a case that where if a plea has been raised in the trial court defences were open to the other party to meet such a plea as in a case where a defendant was all along treated as principal-debtor and was sought to make out he was liable as surety such a new plea cannot be permitted to be raised in second appeal: *Bittan Bibi* v. *Kuntu Lal*, ILR (1952) 2 All 984: AIR 1952 All 996. In a suit for declaration that the plaintiff has title to the Kuti Gaddi Gayawal by virtue of a deed of gift by the last owner of the Gaddi, a plea in second appeal that the business of a Gayawal was no property at all or was a mere religious office which could not be transferred except when a custom was proved cannot be repelled merely on the ground that such a point was not taken in the Court of first instance; *Murari Lal Kuti* v. *Narayan Lal Ahir*, AIR 1956 Pat 345: 1956 BLJR 88.

21. Plaintiff Putting a Lesser Case

The High Court of Madras held that the plaintiff cannot be precluded from putting forward a lesser case in second appeal because be had bargained for a much higher claim in the Court of first appeal. The plaintiff cannot be shut out from putting forward what appears to be a correct and proper construction of a deed which after all is a question of law. *K. Veerankutty* v. *Pathummakutty Umma*, ILR 1956 Mad 1004: AIR 1956 Mad 514: (1956) 1 MLJ 195.

22. Suit by Members of Joint Hindu Family for Possession of their Share in Zamindari Property – Suit Decreed

Pending appeal by the defendant all Zamindaris in the state vested in Government as result of notification under the U.P. Zamindari Abolition and Land Reforms Act thereby disentitling plaintiff to claim possession of the Zamindari property. Appellate court dismissed plaintiffs' suit on this ground- Second appeal was preferred by plaintiff: It was held that while taking note of the changes effected by the Zamindari Abolition and Land Reforms Act and refusing a possessory decree the proper course for the appellate court was to determine the question of the title to compensation in respect of the Zamindari property claimed by the plaintiffs. Held, further, that the failure of the plaintiffs-appellants to raise the question to their right to the compensation in the lower appellate court, though a good ground for depriving them of the costs in the case, was not sufficient to disallow the point to be raised for the first time in second appeal specially when it would avoid multiplicity of proceedings, held the High Court of Allahabad; *Ram Udit* v. *Shyam Kali*, 1954 All LJ 271: AIR 1954 Al 751: 1954 All WR (HC) 208.

23. Evidence

23.1 Admissibility of Evidence

Objections to the admissibility of evidence will not as a general rule be entertained for the first time in second appeal: 104 IC 518: 1927 M 1107; 1934 P 55. The appellant cannot raise objections to the admissibility of documents received in evidence in the lower court if under the circumstances the application is too late; 34 IC 57 (FB); 41 CLJ 374: 1925 C. 1034. Finding of lower appellate court based on inadmissible evidence can be impeached in second appeal; 1923 C 261; 72 IC 985: 1923 C. 378; 148 IC 1158: 35 PLR 360; 1934 P 48: 146 IC 937; When the finding is based really on other evidence, and the inadmissible evidence is only used for the purpose of further support, that does not vitiate the finding or necessitate a review: 39 CWN 311. Where material evidence has been overlooked and the decision is based on wrong assumptions of fact the finding though one of fact, can be set aside in second appeal 142 IC 673 (1): 33 PLR 1013; 1935 M 190: 68 MLJ 648; 39 CWN 277; 108 IC 261; 138 IC 399; 1936 L 1005. Relevancy and proof of document is a question of law and can be raised at any stage, but the question as to the proof of a document is one of procedure and can be waived: 3 Pat LT 149: 1922 P 122; 2 Pat LT 343: 1921 P, 275; 5 Pt. LJ; 410: 1921 P. 61. The High Court of Patna held that where the appellate Court admits additional evidence under Order XLI, rule 27 and the aggrieved party does not ask for any opportunity to produce further evidence, the High Court of Patna said that a finding of fact arrived on such evidence is quite proper: 16 Pat LT 49: 1935 P. 105 (2). Where the appellate court has admitted in evidence certain documents because in its discretion it required that evidence to enable it to pronounce judgment, it is inexpedient for the High Court in second appeal to interfere with the discretion of the lower court: 159 IC 211: 1935 P 470; ILR (1945) Nag 728: 1945 NLJ 235: 1945 N 212.

23.2 Appreciation of Evidence

The Privy Council examined the limitation of powers of the High Courts and said that the High Court will be exceeding its powers under this section if it differs from the view taken by the lower appellate court upon appreciation of oral evidence: 1950 PC 28: (1950) 1 MLJ 294 (PC); 1958 RLW 231: AIR The High Court of Calcutta said that where the plaintiff's evidence has been believed by both the Courts below, even though it was not in conformity with his statement in the plaint, the High Court in a second appeal has no jurisdiction to make a different estimate of that evidence. But it can examine the question whether that evidence, if accepted, would establish the plaintiff's case that the month of the tenancy, as it originally stood, was altered; *Carrara Marble and Terrazo Co. Ltd.* v. *Charu Chandra Guha,* 61 Cal WN 576: AIR 1957 Cal 357. A Court of appeal should hesitate long, before it disturbs the findings of the trial judge, based on verbal testimony and it should satisfy itself that the appellant had discharged the heavy burden of showing that the decision of the trial court was wrong, otherwise it would be assuming a function not warranted by law. Where the High Court differed from the lower courts not only in the estimate of the evidence, but also with regard to the inferences derivable from the document produced in the case and other circumstances the P.C. dealt with the case on its merits; *Jagdeo Narain Singh* v. *Baldeo Singh,* AIR 1922 PC 272: ILR 2 Pat 38: 45 MLJ 460: 49 IA 399 (PC). If a finding of fact is recorded on a misinterpretation of the evidence it can be interfered with in second appeal; 1923 L. 585; 31 IC 695: 19 CWN 1015. It is open to an appellate court to come to its own finding on fact if it finds the evidence produced by any error of law, the second appellate court will not interfere with; it *Teja* v. *Choga,* AIR 1950 Ajmer 50. A finding cannot be contested in a second appeal if it is based on a misreading of first Court's judgment: 1923 L 502 (2); 145 IC 652: 100 WMN 380. Although in second appeal findings of fact cannot be impugned, it is nevertheless open to a party to challenge the correctness of the conclusions drawn from such finding: 1923 L 497 (2); 65 IC 475: 1922 L 140. The credibility of witnesses accepted by the Courts below cannot be considered in second appeal, but the sufficiency of the evidence can be considered in second appeal: 25 IC 869. Omission by the lower court to give effect to an admission by a party to the suit is an error which can be rectified in second appeal: 143 IC 900: 1933 Sind 121; 1933 P. 698. Where the District Judge has not at all discussed the evidence but merely expressed his concurrence in the finding of the lower court on the issue, it cannot be considered a proper finding and the finding though one of fact, is not binding in second appeal; 146 IC 292: 34 PIR 283. Where the lower court misdirects itself in appreciating the evidence and requires a higher standard of proof than the Evidence Act requires, the High Court may interfere: *Venkata Rao* v. *Venkayya,* (1942) 2 MLJ 427: AIR 1943 Mad 38 (2). The High Court of Punjab also said that a finding of fact where the best evidence has not been produced and no explanation is given for its non-production can be re-agitated in second appeal: *Nanak Bakhsh* v. *Rania,* AIR 1952 Punj 233: (1952) 54 Punj LR 40.

23.3 *Consideration of Evidence*

A finding based on inadmissible evidence can be set aside by the High Court: *Saktoo Mal* v. *Gopal Chand*, 66 IC 313: AIR 1922 All 439. If there is no evidence upon which the finding could be supported, then the matter becomes not a question of fact, but a question of law: 167 IC 355: AIR 1937 Sind 36. The High Court of Nagpur said that finding founded on irrelevant evidence is not binding in second appeal: *Sadiq Hussein* v. *Co-operative Central Bank, Yeotmal*, AIR 1952 Nag 106: ILR 1953 Nag 684. The Lucknow Bench held that if from a perusal of the judgment of the lower appellate court, the Chief Court is satisfied that all the relevant material was considered, though specific reference in detail is not made to every piece of evidence on the record it will not be right to interfere with the finding of lower appellate court on a question of fact: 21 Luck 279: 1945 OWN 401: 1946 Uadh 72; *See* also *Boroji Munipurini* v. *State of Assam*, AIR 1958 Assam 34: ILR (1958) 10 Assam 160. An appellate court disposing of an appeal is not bound to repeat in extensor the argument of the entitled to a considered opinion of the appellate Tribunal. It is not the first Court's view but that of the second Court that is final if the question is one of fact: 1938 M. 253: (1937) 2 MLJ 916. Where an appellate court fails to come into close quartets with the evidence, the finding must be held to be vitiated and there must be a re-hearing of the appeal; 103 IC 486: 1927 N 166; 1924 N 91; 1928 L. 737; 1929 P 98: 115; IC 674; 1935 M. 701. A finding of the lower appellate court vitiated by failure to appreciate the true legal effect of recitals of necessity in ancient documents of recent origin consistent with those recitals cannot be supported in second appeal; 42 CWN 387: 1938 C 541. The High Court of Patna made it clear that the mere fact that the Court of first appeal has not made special mention of a document which is a piece of relevant evidence is not sufficient to show that it has not considered it at all; 43 IC 857: 3 Pat LW 213; 42 IC 397; 2 Pat LW 183; 11 LLJ 381. Mere omission to consider a piece of evidence will not alter the character of a finding of fact; 162 IC 21: 1936 Pat 243: 1913 OWN 300: 1943 Oudh 429. The right which is respondent in the lower appellate court has to support the trial court's decree in his favour on any points which were decided against him, if not availed of, cannot be used to ask the Court in second appeal to go into evidence bearing on that issue: *Pannalal* v. *Sumranlal*, AIR (26) 1939 Nag 260: ILR 1939 Nag 624. The lower appellate court is bound, as a matter of law, not to go against the opinion of the trial judge who had an opportunity of seeing and hearing the witnesses before him, in deciding upon the credibility of the witnesses; Unless good reasons are given, any interference with the conclusion of the trial judge on matters of this kind must be deemed to be erroneous in law. A second appeal is competent in such a case under section 100: AIR 1941 M. 393: (1941) 1 MLJ 174. The High Court of Orissa held that where the first appellate court does not take into consideration the evidence on the point, does not discuss the various aspects arising from that evidence and does not give cogent reasons as to why the finding of the trial court which had the advantage of seeing the witnesses should be set aside, its finding cannot be said to be a finding which is binding on the High Court; *Laxmi Narasingha Swami Mahaprabhu* v. *Patta Sahuani*, ILR 1956 Cut 391: AIR 1957 Ori 86. Where the view taken by the trial court approximates never the truth and is more in accord with the probabilities the High Court in second appeal will not disturb the finding of the trial court. Where the lower appellate court has fallen into an error of record and has reversed that finding on a wrong estimate of the oral evidence. It may be interfered with: *Gopi Tihadi* v. *Gokhei Panda*, ILR 1953 Cut 558: AIR 1954 Ori 17. The High Court of Patna has said that the question of representation is question of fact, but if in coming to such a finding of fact, the first Court of appeal has taken into consideration of such a portion of the evidence of the party, after omitting the material portion would not be binding in second appeal on the High Court; *Ishar Singh* v. *Babu Gajadhar Prosad Singh*, 1956 BLJR 745: AIR 1957 Pat 174.

23.4 Inference from Facts

The High Court of Allahabad appreciated the way to draw inference from the facts and said that the proper inference to be drawn from the findings arrived at by the lower appellate court in respect of the disruption of the joint status of a family, is a question of law and can be considered in a second appeal; 1946 AWR (HC) 158 (2): AIR 1946 All 118. If a question refers to the inferences from proved facts, the question is one of law whether such inferences were correct or not. This question is included in what is known as decision being contrary to law under section 100 C.P. Code 1951 HP 49; *Rati Ram* v. *Mam Chand*, AIR 1959 Punj 117: ILR 1959 Punj 626. The High Court of Madras said that when the question of drawing a legal inference from an appraisement of the facts arises, the case involves a question of law on which the High Court in second appeal can finally decide; 1942 Mad 426: (1947) 1 MLJ 79; *See* also *Mcleod and Co.* v. *Sixth Industrial Tribunal, West Bengal*, AIR 1958 Cal 273: ILR (1959) 1 Cal 508. The High Court has no jurisdiction to reverse the finding of fact arrived at by the lower appellate court, however erroneous, unless rule is equally applicable to case in which the findings of the lower appellate court are based on inferences drawn from documents exhibited in evidence; 1934 PC 112: 66 MLJ 595 (PC). While a Court in second appeal will not interfere with findings of fact of the lower appellate court, whether right legal inferences have been drawn from those facts, whether, for instance, the possession is adverse or not, whether a transfer is made with intent to defeat or delay within the meaning of section 53, T.P. Act, are questions of law which can be dealt with in second appeal; AIR 1938 Sind 215; AIR 1938 Sind 206. A second appellate court, though it cannot entertain an appeal upon any question as to the soundness of findings of fact by the lower appellate court, can nevertheless adjudicate as a matter of law upon the soundness of the conclusions which have been derived from those finding AIR 1937 O 47. The question whether a building is a private mosque or a public mosque is not a question of fact but a question of law. That is, a question of interference from proved facts; 1938 OWN 937: AIR 1938 O 238. The question of acquiescence as a matter of legal inference is drawn from the facts proved in the case and can be taken up in second appeals; AIR 1925 C 288. According to the High Courts of Patna and Nagpur, when certain facts are found and an inference is drawn from the facts so found, it is open to the Court in second appeal to consider whether as a matter of law such inference is justified by the facts found; 19 Pat LT 398: 1938 P. 147; 1937 Nag 230.

23.5 Sufficiency of Evidence

It is open to a Court to accept the evidence of one witness in preference to that of others and finding arrived at on such evidence cannot be said to be supported by no evidence; 161 IC 501: 1936 Sind 7. The High Court of Calcutta said that paucity of evidence on particular point is no ground for interference; *Haralal Das* v. *Pasupati Charan Biswas*, 58 CWN 696: AIR 1955 Cal 226. But when the appellate court, on the slenderest of evidence, makes out a case which is not the pleadings, its finding of fact cannot be binding in second appeal; 1938 PWN 741: 1938 P 181. According to the High Court of Allahabad judgment based on opinions of experts is open to challenge in second appeal; 21 ALJ 811: 1924 A. 116. But *see* 157 IC 30: 1935 A 501, where finding based on the relative weight of the opinion of the hand writing experts was held to be one of fact. The mere question of sufficiency of the evidence adduced to establish a custom is not a ground of second appeal 45 C 285; 69 IC 800: 1922 N 52. The sufficiency and insufficiency of evidence as proof of title cannot be debated in second appeal; 1933 M. 163. Where certain convincing evidence has been set aside by the lower appellate court on a ground that can have no legal basis whatever, such a glaring misapplication of the law of evidence is open to correction in second appeal; 1938 N. 385. If an appellate court, while reversing the judgment of the trial court, fails to advert to a material piece of evidence which militates against is its own view, its finding cannot be accepted as final in second appeal; *Maruthamuthu Naicker* v. *Kadir Badsha Rowther*, AIR 1938 Mad 377: ILR (1938) Mad 568: (1938) 1 MLJ 582. A finding as to the existence of an agreement which has not been pleaded and based on no evidence cannot be accepted as binding: 159 IC 96: 18 NLJ 104.

23.6 Misreading of Evidence

The misapprehension of evidence is no ground for a second appeal; 21 IC 393. *See* also *Koklan Devi* v. *Maharaj Kishan*, AIR 1952 Punj 120: (1952) 54 Punj LR 457. But where a finding of fact is arrived at as a result of a complete misreading of a document, a second appeal is competent; 42 IC 218; 1926 P. 725; 1931 A. 499; so also a finding arrived at on as erroneous assumption of an admission by a party who did not make it; 1928 O. 333. The High Court of Nagpur said that there is an error of law when a Court's finding proceeds upon a misconception of the real nature of the issue in the case, when several facts admitted or proved are not considered in their relation to each other and weighed as a whole or when a certain legal consequence which naturally follows from admitted and proved facts is overlooked; ILR (1938) N. 535: 1938 N. 470. The Court further said that if a negative conclusion is reached by the lower appellate court on the mistaken assumption that there is no evidence and the conclusion is based solely on that fact, it is as much an error of law as when a finding is reached with no evidence to support it; ILR (1946) Nag 73: 1946 NLJ 227: 1946 Nag 152.

23.7 Exclusion of Evidence

It was held by the Privy Council that the High Court is not empowered to interfere in second appeal with an order of the lower appellate court rejecting an application made to it for the admission of additional evidence. Where the lower appellate court rejects the oral evidence of possession by applying an erroneous presumption of law; the finding is vitiated 1935 O. 394; 39 CWN 1233.

23.8 Construction of Document

The High Court of Calcutta explained construction of document and said that the expression 'construction' as applied to a document includes two things 'first, the meaning of the words; and secondly, their legal effect.' The meaning of the words is a question of fact in all cases. The effect of the words is a question of law. Hence the interpretation placed upon the words in the deed is a clear question of fact. Even if the document admitted of more than one construction, one of which has been adopted by the lower appellate court, the High Court will not be competent to challenge it; 1937 Sind 51: 1937 Cal 371. Relying on the Privy Council the High Court of Kerala held that when a question of construction in the latter aspect arises not as regards a document which forms merely a plea of evidence in the case but constitutes the cause of action or the root of title of the plaintiff a second appeal for its consideration is competent: (AIR 1930 PC 91 Rel on); *Velu* v. *Lekshmi*, ILR (1953) Trav Co 568: 1953 Ker LT 442: AIR 1953 Trav Co 584. According to the Court of Nagpur where the question to be decided is one of fact, it does not involve an issue of law merely because documents which were not instruments of title or otherwise the direct foundations of right, but were merely historical materials, have to be construed for the propose of deciding that question; and a second appeal would not lie because some portion of the evidence might be contained in a document or documents and the first appellate court has made a mistake as to its meaning. As a question of law a document should be construed if it is a document of title and not merely a piece of evidence in the case is a question of law: 52 IC 119; 1931 Nag 189: 134 IC 673. The High Court of Assam said that the question whether a particular contract is void on ground of particular clause is undoubtedly a question depending upon the interpretation of the terms of a document of title and would, therefore be a question of law open for consideration for the first time in Second Appeal: AIR 1954 Assam 93; unless there has been misconstruction a mistaken inference from documents is an error, not of law but of fact;. 65 MLJ 154 (PC). Where the lower appellate court has come to a conclusion on a construction and perusal of the documents and the proper inference to be drawn from the contents there of, it is a question of law and the High Court, in second appeal, can consider whether the conclusion arrived at by the lower appellate court is correct: 48 Bom LR 185: 1936 Bom. 454. Where the question is what is the proper inference to be drawn from documents whose construction is not open to any controversy the question is one of fact; 42 Bom LR 462: 1940 B. 255. A wrong construction of a document, coupled with a wrong inference from certain facts, constitutes an error of law where there is no other evidence accepted by the Court; 55 IC 366: 18 ALJ 195; 20 NIJ 39. According to the High Court of Bombay although the question covered by an issue is mainly a question of fact a finding given by the Court of first appeal on that issue without taking into consideration documents which have an important bearing on that issue, is not finding on the High Court in second appeal; *Debi Parshad* v. *Jai Ram Dass*, AIR 1952 Punj 284.

MISCELLANEOUS

24. Abandonment of Holding

The question as to whether there has been an abandonment of land by a raiyat is a question of fact. But the inference from the facts found, as to whether there was abandonment or not, is a question of law; 1935 C 80, *see* also 4 Pat 838: 1925 P. 241. The High Court of Allahabad said that whether a raiyat or a tenant has abandoned his holding or not is not a pure question of fact, but a mixed question of fact and law and a finding of the lower Court on such a question is not therefore final in second appeal; [(1936) ALJ 569; 1939 All 392; AIR 1943 All 241, ref.] The High Court of Patna held that where the finding by the lower court as to the abandonment of holding is based on evidence on record in the case the High Court will not in second appeal interfere when the lower court has committed no error of the law in relying upon such evidence; *Sailu Pahan* v. *Poltu Chik*, 1954 BLJR 71: AIR 1954 Pat 368.

25. Abatement

The High Court of Allahabad said that though no second appeal lies from an order of abatement, it may be questioned in a second appeal if it 'affects the decision of the case' *Badri Prasad* v. *Amjid Ali*, 1933 ALJ 561: AIR 1933 All 294. An order that the appeal abates not only with regard to the respondent who has died but with regard to all the respondents comes within the definition of a decree, and as such is appealable; *Sabitribai* v. *Jugal Kishore*, 43 CWN 41: AIR 1938 Cal 639.

26. Acknowledgment

Although a finding as to whether a certain statement amounts to an acknowledgment is not open to second appeal; still when the lower court fails to consider the effect of a statement, the second appellate court can decide whether it amounts to an acknowledgment; 14 L 587: 1933 L 345.

27. Adoption

According to the High Court of Andhra Pradesh adoption is clearly a question of fact; 154 LC 675; 157 IC 865 1955 Andh WR 191. But according to the Rajasthan Court, question whether the facts found make out a valid adoption is a question of law and can be gone into in second appeal; *Gulab* v. *Devilal Gokal Chand*, AIR 1951 Raj 136.

28. Burden of Proof and Presumption

The High Court of Bombay held that the question of *onus* is not necessarily one of law in all cases. How much or what evidence is sufficient to discharge the *onus* is a question which depends upon the weight to be attached to the evidence adduced. 12 IC 691: 18 Bom LR 1021. Where a Court considers the case and the evidence of one side only, and disbelieving the evidence dismisses the claim on the ground that the assertions made have not been proved the case being solely decided on the question of *onus* and so amount of lip service to a rule which is ignored in the letter and in the spirit will serve to turn what is then a question of law into one of fact *Udebhan Zangoji* v. *Vithoba Ukandaji*, AIR 1939 Nag 78: ILR 1939 Nag 160. If the Judge's finding is determined only by the question of burden of proof or on a one-sided examination of the evidence due to the view taken about the burden of proof, then the finding stands in need of revision, but if the evidence and circumstances on both sides are duly considered the question of the burden of proof is of very little importance. *Pandurang* v. *Tukaram*, AIR 1934 Nag 253:152 IC 441. The adjustment of the burden of proof in a case is a question of law. 43 IC 478; 24 ALJ 513. A finding made after throwing the *onus* of proof wrongly and in disregard of the evidence is not binding.

29. Costs

The High Court of Madras held that the trial court has a discretion in the matter of costs and that discretion can be interfered with in appeal only if the trial court has exercised its discretion improperly. Where the lower court does not keep the principal in view but considers the matter of costs as if it had been trying the suit itself, that is not the proper way of approaching the question and the High Court will therefore interfere in second appeal; (1940) 1 MLJ 764.

30. Court Fee

A second appeal lies from an order of an appellate court rejecting a memo of appeal for non-payment of deficit Court-fees, if there is an error in calculating the amount of Court-fees; 51 IC 114.

31. Valuation of Suit

The High Court of Patna said that where the lower courts have held that the valuation for purposes of jurisdiction was not unreasonable; it is not open in second appeal to plead that the valuation was not correct; 22 Pat LT 799: 1942 P 79.

32. Cross-objections

A second appeal lies from the decree of the appellate court, disallowing cross-objection of the respondent; (10 M 292, foll.) 1933 L 400.

33. Findings Based on Custom

The judge first finds what were the things done in alleged pursuance of the custom and then determines whether these facts so found satisfy the requirements of the law; the latter is a question of law and not fact; ILR (1943) Nag 705: (1943) 2 MLJ 173. The High Court of Patna relying on its own earlier decision held that a finding by the lower appellate court that a local custom alleged by a party is ancient, uniform, undoubted and continuous and is proved to exist, is a finding of fact and cannot be interfered with in second appeal; (25 IC 107 rel.) *Keshwar Thakur* v. *Ghulam Hussain*, 30 Pat 606: AIR 1951 Pat 583. It is a question of fact as to whether the acts alleged and proved in each case are sufficient to establish a customary right. The High Court of Andhra Pradesh said that where the Court below have concurrently found that the customary right is made out the High Court has no reason to interfere with that finding. The strict rule of English law governing the establishment of a custom namely that it should be immemorial in its origin, is not applicable to India; 1955. An WR 308. The conclusion arrived at by the lower appellate court that the defendants did not make out the customary right is not a pure question of fact and may be interfered with under section 100. Still a case where the question, whether it is reasonable or not has been gone into by the lower appellate court, the

High Court will not lightly interfere with that finding of fact: *Kommu Venkadu* v. *Candrakota Subbaramaiah,* (1954) 2 MLJ (Andh) 24: AIR 1954 Andh 54. Where the concurrent findings of the lower courts that a certain custom did not exist are based on the rejection of the evidence which should not have been rejected, the findings could be questioned in second appeal; 1941 OWN 623: 1941 O. 468. A finding that a custom has been established is one of fact and cannot be interfered with in second appeal unless vitiated by an error of law; 1937 ALJ 1301: AIR 1938 All 144. The question whether a prevailing practice has the essential attributes of a legally binding custom is a question of law. When the evidence is legally insufficient to prove a custom finding of the existence of custom may be questioned in second appeal but when the finding depends on the weighing of the evidence, it cannot be contested in second appeal; 9 IC 858: 1922 L. 426. *See* also 92 IC 126 (1926) O. 211. The question whether a custom is reasonable or not is a question of law and not of fact 29 IC 312: 19 CWN 1188; ILR (1937) 2. The High Court of Allahabad (Luck) said that existence of a custom has been decided and the decision arrived at is one of fact but whether in arriving at it, the Court has committed an error in law or not for instance, if it was based upon the acceptance of evidence which was inadmissible, it could be questioned in second appeal; 14 Luck 515: 1939 All 500. A decision as to the existence of a custom is a question of fact 134 IC 475: 8 OWN 7979 but an appellant in second appeal is entitled to establish the custom, even if true, does not establish the custom: 14 IC.

34. Damages

The High Court of Nagpur distinguished the status of the principal and the quantum to be awarded and said that the principal on which damages are to be assessed is a matter of law though the quantum to be awarded once the principal is determined is one of fact; 1946 NLJ 684: 1946 Nag 392. Normally, the question of damages is not considered in a second appeal, but the High Court may review the matter so that substantial justice as between the parties may be done: 1934 A: 392. Where on a wrong view, the lower appellate court reduces quantum of damages, High Court will interfere; 1946 M. 147: (1945) 2 MLJ 461.

35. Dedication

The Supreme Court has said that dedication is a mixed question of law and fact *Deoki Nandan* v. *Murlidhar,* 1957 SCR 75: 1956 SCJ 75: AIR 1957 SC 133. The question whether certain property is wakf property is a question of law, at any rate a mixed question of law and fact; 17 IC 303: 33 PLR 288. Whether a dedication is real or nominal is a question of fact; 131 IC 283: 1931 L 170. The High Court of Karnataka held that whether instances of burial in any particular case are adequate in character, number and extent to justify an inference of dedication is a question of fact; ILR 1940 Kar 174: 1940 Sind 43.

36. Defamation

According to the High Court of Madras, the question whether a writing is defamatory of the plaintiff the questions of fair comment, justification, *bona fides* and the quantum of diamantes, awardable to the plaintiff in an action for libel are all questions of fact on which the High Court, in the second appeal, is bound by the findings of the appellate court; 32 MIJ 392.

37. Discretion

The High Court of Patna discussed the position where two Courts exercised discretion and held that where two Courts fully acquainted with the case exercise a discretion, the High Court will not interfere with the exercise of such discretion. Yet if the discretion has not been exercised in a legal manner but in an arbitrary and capricious manner, as the result of an error of law, the High Court will interfere and reverse the decree: 1951 Pat 318. The Supreme Court said that where the lower courts in the exercise of their discretion have refused to grant relief against forfeiture the High Court in second appeal would be justified in refusing to interfere with that discretion exercised in a judicial manner; *Namdeo Lokman Lodhi* v. *Narmadabai*, 1953 SCJ 306: AIR 1953 SC 228: 1953 SCR 1009. Relief against forfeiture incurred by a tenant is an equitable relief in the discretion of the Court; High Court will not in second appeal ordinarily interfere unless the discretion was not Judicially exercised or was exercised without proper materials: ILR (1949) Bom 883: 19580 123: 51 Bom LR 987. The Nagpur High Court said that High Court in second appeal has power to see which of the two Courts exercised discretion properly in accordance with the judicial principles; ILR (1939) Nag 452: 1939 N 110; 1937 Sind 263. Where the lower courts have exercised their discretion on a misapprehension of the legal principles on which the discretion given by a provision of law should be exercised it is competent to the High Court to interfere: 1937 AMLJ 49. An appellate court has a discretion to grant or refuse an adjournment prayed for by the appellant or his pleader; and the exercise for the appellant or his pleader and the exercise of that discretion of a second appeal; 1937 ALJ 174: 1937 All 284. The High Court will always interfere in second appeal where a lower court has wrongly refused to grant an equitable relief: 45 LW 648: 1937 M 520. Where a judge allowing an amendment of the plaint has proceeded on a wrong view of the law, so that he could not have applied his mind into the question whether he should or should not, in his discretion, allow the amendment the High Court would interfere in second appeal; ILR (1936) N 194: 1938 NLJ 198: 1938 N. Where the discretion is exercised arbitrarily on a question of costs, a second appeal will lie; 100 IC 598. The Privy Council said that it is opposed to sound practice for an appellate court to substitute its discretion for that of the Court from which an appeal has been preferred. But where the first appellate court has substituted its discretion for that of trial court in the matter of costs and the High Court finds that the discretion exercised by the first appellate court was more sound, the discretion of the lower appellate court should not be interfered with in second appeal by the High Court [*Rehmat-un-Nissa Begam* v. *Price*, AIR 1917 PC 116: 45 IA 61; 35 MLJ 262 and AIR 1940 PC 20; (1940) 3 FLJ 46: (1940) 1 MLJ (1953) 1 MLJ 715; 1953 SCJ 306 Considered]; *Mahindra Singh* v. *Chander Singh*, AIR 1957 Pat 79. The issue of commission is a matter in the discretion of the Court, and if the discretion is wrongly exercised, the question cannot be agitated for the first time in second appeal; 1933 P. 542. It is admittedly a matter of discretion whether the lower court will or will not grant relief to a lessee against forfeiture under section 114, T.P. Act; and provided the principles on which it acts are not wrong no Court of second appeal will interfere with the exercise of discretion; 48 Bom

LR 608: 1947 utilising Order XLI, rule 33 will not be interfered with in second appeal 130 IC 774: 1931 L. 370. Nor where the lower appellate Court examines on its own motion under Order XLI, rule 27, C.P. Code; a witness who in its opinion, should have been examined by one of the parties; 38 PLR 449: 1937 L 115. The trial judge had not come to any conclusion regarding the admissibility or otherwise of a document 30 years old, but merely doubted the genuineness of it. The appellate court, on the contrary, came to the definite conclusion that the document was not only admissible in evidence, but was entitled to the presumption under section 90. It was held that the discretion once having been exercised by the Court below, the High Court of Orissa relying on a Full Bench decision of the High Court of Allahabad and also secession of the High Courts of Calcutta and Madras said that the High Court ought not to interfere with that discretion without any compelling reason; (AIR 1940 PC 160; (1941) 1 Mad LJ 204 and *Haji Sheikh Bodha* v. *Sukharam Singh*, ILR 47 All 31: AIR 1925 All 1 (FB) and *Shailendranath Mitra* v. *Girijabhushan Mukherji*, ILR 58 Cal 686: AIR 1931 Cal 596, rel. on); *Ramakrushna Mohapatra* v. *Gangadhar Mohapatra*, AIR 1958 Ori 26.

38. Document

Rejection of document not produced at first hearing, not to be interfered with in second appeal; 90 IC 602: 1926 C 106.

39. Dower

A finding to the amount of dower is a mixed question of fact and law 89 IC 672: 1926 O. 128.

40. Easement

Failure to draw inference of easement is a question of law 85 IC. 81: 1925 N 270; 1928 N 168. The High Court of Madras in a case found that question of additional burden was involved. The Court held that a remand was essential. The Court held, "Question of additional burden on the servient heritage of which a remand is essential" 61 MLJ 58: 1931 M 128.

41. Interpretation of Facts Found by Lower Court

Where the lower court has arrived at certain findings of facts and the facts are clear, but the dispute relates not to the facts but to interpretation of facts by the lower court, it can be dealt with in second appeal: 40 PLR 506: 1938 L 180.

42. Issue

Mere failure to frame an issue, if unattended with prejudice is no ground for interference, if there are concurrent findings; 1943 RD 362: 1943 AWR (rev). 312(1).

43. Landlord and Tenant

A finding as to the status of a tenant is a finding of fact and should not be interfered with in second appeal except on the ground of some clear error of law; 46 IC 351: 21 CWN 809. The concurrent findings of the lower court that a particular lease was granted for a justifiable cause cannot be interfered with in second appeal; 1937 MWN 1188. Findings that the tenants are raiyats and have acquired rights of occupancy are findings of fact; 1938 C. 724. The High Court of Bombay said that the question whether a tenancy is one at Will or of permanent nature on certain given facts is a mixed question of law and fact; 31 Bom LR 1279: 1930 B 39. *See* also 35 CWN 1047; 1938 Pat 609; 1938 Pat 333. The nature of a tenancy is a question of law when it turns the construction of certain written instruments: 20 IC 363: 17 CWN 1073. The question whether a legal right, such as the right of a tenant in the land is a question of law 15 IC 857; Division of tenancy under section 88. BT Act 49 CLJ 289: 1929 C 366.

44. Fraud and undue Influence

A finding that an allegation of fraud was not proved is a finding of fact; 35 PLR 578 1941 O. 341. The Patna High Court said that a finding as to the existence of fraud in connection with the service of a sale proclamation or as to non-service of the same, which is not based on evidence, is not binding in second appeal; 19 Pat LT 645: 1938 P 622. According to the Allahabad High Court the question whether there was any fraud or not in transaction is a question of fact: *Kashi Kurmi* v. *Bansraj Kurmi*, 1937 ALJ 1346: AIR 1938 All 150; *Bhusan Chandra Deb* v. *Hiranmay Roy*, AIR 1957 Tripura 1. Concurrent finding that a sale under the Public Demands Recovery Act was not vitiated by fraud is a finding as to undue influence from the facts of the case. The High Court of Oudh dissenting from the High Court of Punjab held that such a finding can be disturbed in second appeal 1937 OWN 277: 1937 Oudh 254 dissented from in AIR 1958 Punj 190. Such a finding is one of the merits, *see* 40 IC 215: 18 NLJ 67. Where in a case fraud is alleged but there is no direct evidence of fraud and only an inference drawn from circumstances such a finding involves a legal question as to whether the circumstances are such that the necessary inference can legally be derived. As the High Court of Patna said that if the lower court proceeds upon a wrong legal view of the nature of the circumstantial evidence from which fraud can be inferred, the finding is based upon a legal error and can be interfered with in second appeal; 20 Pat LT 957 AIR 1950 MP 11 (Excluding from consideration circumstantial evidence altogether).

45. Forfeiture of Tenancy

A finding on the question whether there was forfeiture of tenancy by denial of the title of the landlord is a finding of fact: 34 PLR 881: 1933 L 884: 1993 L. 377. But if the Court failed to take into consideration the effect of a statement made by the tenants, the finding is open to challenge, in second appeal; 149 IC 517: 1934 A. 103.

46. Grant – Nature of

The finding that it was not proved that the Jawa Jama that is to say, the pension money paid by Government-were included in the waten Cr. endowment, and that therefore the plaintiffs could not claim a share in them as such, is a finding of fact; 1993 PC 171: 65 MLJ 154 (PC).

47. Joint Family

The Privy Council discussed the nature of finding regarding disruption of the joint family and held that a finding that there has or has not been a disruption of a joint Hindu family is not a finding of fact and can be questioned in second appeal. It is an inference of the legal effect of the facts found; 144 IC 919: 1934 N 31. The question whether three brothers were joint or separated would ordinarily be a question of fact, but if, in coming to a finding certain documents relied upon by the defendants as evidence of partition are illegally excluded from evidence on the ground that they are not admissible the finding can be challenged in second appeal: 1934 P. 48. The High Court of Patna said that a finding of the Court of first appeal that though there was no partition by *metes* and *bounds* there was a complete cessor of commensality between the brothers and that they were in separate possession as tenants in common is essentially a finding of fact and cannot be reopened in second appeal; *Amir Mahton* v. *Sheopujan Missir*, AIR 1946 Pat 231: ILR 25 Pat 1. A finding by the lower appellate court that a Hindu co-parcener in filing a plaint for partition was under the influence of profligate persons and that the suit for partition was their act rather than his and that, therefore the institution of the suit did not evidence an un-equivocal intention on the part of the member concerned to separate from the other members of the joint family, is one of fact, 17 P 430: 19 Pat LT 281: 1938 P 278.

48. Misjoinder

A finding of fact on a question of misjoinder, arrived at on evidence cannot be disturbed in second appeal; 33 IC 118; (1916) 1 MWN 9. Objection as to misjoinder cannot be taken for first time in second appeal; 1928 M. 635.

49. Non-joinder

The Madras High Court said that an objection as to non-joinder of parties cannot be taken for the first time in second appeal; 44 M. 344: 40 MLJ 282. Non-joinder of the party in second appeal is not permissible: 14 RD 430; 32 Bom JR 1252: 1930 B 554: 54 B 902.

50. Technical Objection

When a Judge in second appeal interferes with the concurrent finding of fact of the Courts below, he exceeds his jurisdiction under section 100, C.P.C., and his decision is liable to be set aside in Letters Patent Appeal; *Manmatha Nath Haldar* v. *Girish Chandra Roy*, 38 CWN 763: AIR 1934 Cal 707.

51. Restoration of Appeal

The Allahabad High Court examined the tenability of the plea of lawyer of the appellant and held that where the appellant's pleader appears when the appeal is called on for hearing and applies for an adjournment of the appeal on the ground that owing to other engagements he could not prepare the appeal, the file of which is very heavy, but the Court rejects his application and dismisses the appeal for want of prosecution the disposal of the appeal clearly amounts to a decree and a second appeal lies under section 100. The dismissal is not a dismissal for default, and the appellant has no right in such a case to apply for restoration of the appeal under Order XLI, rule 19; *Mohammadi Husain* v. *Chandro*, 1937 ALJ 174: AIR 1937 All 284.

52. Review

Where a second appeal is dismissed under section 101 and the decree is sought to be amended, then it has to be obtained by a review application; Order XLVII, rule 1(b) permits a review application, because the second appeal was not one allowed by law; (1941) 1 MLJ 54.

53. Competency One Second Appeal against Several Appeals Preferred against One Decree

Where separate decrees are drawn up in appeals, the High Court of Travancore said that one second appeal from these separate decrees is maintainable; *Velamma Muthamma* v. *Krishnaswamy Naidu Muthu Pillai Naidu,* 1953 Ker LT 75: 1 LR (1952) Trav Co 1027: AIR 1954 Trav Co 28.

54. Propriety of Second Appeal and Revision Petition in the Alternative

The High Court of Madras discussed the propriety of second appeal and revision in the alternative and said that the practice of filing second appeals and civil revision petitions in the alternative by way of adopted caution must be deprecated. The procedure adopted suggests in itself a good deal of debate as to the maintainability of either and a lack of faith in the remedy which is sought to be pursued. The further danger is that these appeals and civil revision petition in the alternative would expose themselves to dismissal with separate sets of costs; *V. Ramaswami Iyengar* v. *Krishnaveni Ammal,* (1952) 2 MLJ 683: AIR 1954 Mad 66.

55. Interference with Concurrent Finding of Fact

The Supreme Court held in *Ranjeet Singh* v. *Jaimal Singh,* (2001) 10 SCC 474 that High Court erred in interfering with the concurrent finding of fact under section 100.

But the Court held in *Deva* v. *Sajjan Kumar* that concurrent finding of fact is liable to be interfered with when a very important piece of evidence in the nature of an admission by defendant has been overlooked by the Courts below. *Deva* v. *Sajjan Kumar,* AIR 2003 SC 3907: 2003 AIR SCW 4501: (2003) 7 SCC 481; *See* also *Janki Narayan Bhoir* v. *Narayan Namdeo Kadam,* AIR 2003 SC 761: 2003 AIR SCW 177: (2003) 2 SCC 91 and *Shah Babu Lal* v. *Melaram,* (2002) 10 SCC 146.

56. Interference with Finding of Fact

Finding reached on the basis of additional evidence which could not have been received by the appellate court.—The second appellate court is entitled to interfere with such finding of fact. Under circumstances of the case the Supreme Court found itself in entire agreement with these observations of the learned Judges. It is no doubt true that a finding of fact, however erroneous, cannot be challenged in a second appeal, but a finding reached on the basis of additional evidence which ought not to have been admitted and without any consideration whatever of the intrinsic and palpable defects in the nature of the entries themselves which raise serious doubts about their genuineness, cannot be accepted as a finding that is conclusive in second appeal. *Arjan Singh* v. *Kartar Singh,* AIR 1951 SC 193: 1951 ALJ SC 78: 1951 (1) MLJ 556: 1951 SCJ 274: 1951 SCR 258.

Finding of fact.—Finding of genuineness of Will is a question of fact.—Interference in second appeal, is not permissible. *Aparsini (dead) through LRs.* v. *Atma Ram,* AIR 1996 SC 1558: (1996) 8 SCC 321: (1996) 2 SCALE 831: JT 1996 (3) SC 645: 1996 (2) Raj LW 82.

Finding of genuineness of Will is a question of fact.—Interference in second appeal, is not permissible. *Aparsini (dead) through LRs.* v. *Atma Ram,* AIR 1996 SC 1558: (1996) 8 SCC 321: 1996 (2) SCALE 831: JT 1996 (3) SC 645: 1996 (2) Raj LW 82.

57. Doctrine of Merger

Doctrine of merger is not applicable to order refusing special leave to appeal under article 136 of the Constitution. An order refusing special leave to appeal may be a non-speaking order or a speaking one. In either case it does not attract the doctrine of merger. An order refusing special leave to appeal does not stand substituted in place of the order under challenge. All that it means is that the Court was not inclined to exercise its discretion so as to allow the appeal being filed. *Kunhayammed* v. *State of Kerala,* AIR 2000 SC 2587: 2000 (3) Ker LT 354: JT 2000 (4) SC 110: (2000) 6 SCC 359: 2000 (2) Cur LJ (CCR) 626 Finding of fact.—Paternity of child born during wedlock.—Finding of first appellate court that husband had no access to wife for more than 280 days before child was begotten.—Cannot be interfered with in second appeal.—No substantial question of law arises from such a finding.—Appeal dismissed; *Kanti Devi* v. *Poshi Ram,* AIR 2001 SC 2226: (2001) 5 SCC 311: JT 2001 (1) (Supp) 87.

58. When Finding of Fact can be Interfered with in an Eviction Petition—*Bona Fide* Requirement

Failure of Courts below to consider requirement of statutory provision regarding availability of reasonable accommodation.—Finding that landlord could easily make arrangements for starting a shop for his son and landlord did not make any offer to tenant for alternate shop room.—High Court justified in setting aside concurrent finding holding that landlord had proved his *bona fide* requirement and was entitled to decree of eviction.

Where the lower court had failed to consider the requirement of the section regarding availability of reasonable accommodation in occupation of the landlord because at the time of filing the suit for eviction one vacant shop room was in occupation of the landlord and in course of the proceedings one more shop room, on being vacated by the tenant, came in his occupation and the Court found that the landlord could easily make arrangements for starting the shop for his son and that the landlord did not make any offer to tenant for alternate shop room for his occupation, the High Court would be justified in setting aside the concurrent judgment of lower court holding that *bona fide* requirement of the landlord was proved and that he was, therefore, entitled to decree of eviction on that ground; *Deena Nath* v. *Pooran Lal,* AIR 2001 SC 2655: (2001) 5 SCC 705: JT 2001 (5) SC 380: 2002 (1) Civ CR 107.

59. Concurrent Finding of Fact License for Construction of Building

License for construction of building granted by Chief Officer of Town Municipal Council and Secretary of Interim Mandal Panchayat under seal of

Chief Officer of Town Municipal Council, but was really a license issued by Mandal Panchayat.—Mandal Panchayat having been newly formed its seals were not available at the time.—Concurrent finding that license was issued by Mandal Panchayat.—High Court finding, without examining this aspect, that license granted to appellant was bad, unjustified. *Padikal Madappa* v. *C.B. Kariapa,* AIR 2001 SC 2695: (2001) 10 SCC 742: JT 2001 (4) SC 367. On question of title of plaintiff.—Based on sale deed executed by Defendant No. 2 in his favour.—Findings that it was valid sale which properly conveyed title of property to plaintiff.—Setting aside by High Court merely on ground that circumstances considered by lower court suggest some other conclusion from proved facts.—Interference by High Court not permissible. *Vidhyadhar* v. *Manikrao,* AIR 1999 SC 1441: 1999 (2) Civil CC 91: 1999 (3) Bom CR 564: 1999 (2) Andh WR 7: (1999) 3 SCC 573: 1999 (3) Mad LW 576: 1999 (3) Andh LT 1.

60. Concurrent Finding of Fact—Subletting—Testimony of Witnesses Rejected

In a suit for ejectment the High Court observed that findings were recorded by courts below on conjectures and surmises during wrong inferences from facts proved ignoring material evidence such as judgments of Consolidation Courts brought on record and status of plaintiff as legally wedded wife of owner in previous proceedings was not taken into consideration.—High Court rightly held that plaintiff was legally wedded wife of owner of suit property. *Vishnu Prakash* and because of lack of detailed pleadings pertaining to period of sub-tenancy.—Mere lack of details in pleading not a ground to set aside concurrent finding of fact.

On the question of sub-letting the finding was based on the deposition of the witnesses to whom the disputed premises was sub-let. Their testimony was rejected by the High Court mainly on the basis that there was no detailed pleading pertaining to the period of sub-tenancy and even the witnesses have not produced any receipt of payment of rent. It is not in dispute that there is pleading that the disputed premises was sublet. The detail, if any, can be supplemented through evidence. Mere lack of details in the pleading cannot be the reason to set aside concurrent finding of facts; *Hari Singh* v. *Kanhaiya Lal,* AIR 1999 SC 3325: 1999 (4) Rec Civ R 107: 1999 (8) ADSC 142: (1999) 7 SCC 288: 1999 (3) Raj LW 415: 1999 (2) Rent LR 613.

On question of title of plaintiff.—Based on sale deed executed by Defendant No. 2 in his favour.—Findings that it was valid sale which properly conveyed title of property to plaintiff.—Setting aside by High Court merely on ground that circumstances considered by lower court suggest some other conclusion from proved facts.—Interference by High Court not permissible; *Vidhyadhar* v. *Manikrao,* AIR 1999 SC 1441: 1999 (2) Civil CC 91: 1999 (3) Bom CR 564: 1999 (2) Andh WR 7: (1999) 3 SCC 573: 1999 (3) Mad LW 576: 1999 (3) Andh LT 1.

Suit for ejectment and possession of suit properties filed by widow of owner.—Concurrent finding of trial court and first appellate court that plaintiff was not legally wedded wife of owner.—High Court observed that findings were recorded by courts below on conjectures and surmises during wrong inferences from facts proved ignoring material evidence such as judgments of Consolidation Courts brought on record and status of plaintiff as legally wedded wife of owner in previous proceedings was not taken into consideration.—High Court rightly held that plaintiff was legally wedded wife of owner of suit property; *Vishnu Prakash* v. *Sheela Devi,* AIR 2001 SC 1862: (2001) 4 SCC 729: JT 2001 (4) SC 396.

61. Finding of fact in Second Appeal.—Allotment of Retail Outlet Dealership by Indian Oil Corporation

Applicant fulfilled age requirement and made application after correction of his date of birth in school register supported by certificate of competent authority.—Allotment made after verification of particulars furnished by appellant, *viz.*, age proof and electoral roll.—Trial court after perusing evidence and report of handwriting expert found that certificate of competent authority was genuine.—Overwhelming evidence to prove that applicant had attained age of 21 years as on date of application.—Order of first appellate court holding that certificate must have been fabricated set aside; *Updesh Kumar* v. *Prithvi Singh,* AIR 2001 SC 703: (2001) 2 SCC 524: JT 2001 (2) SC 308.

62. Finding of Fact in Second Appeal in a Case of Gift Deed

Ancestral property.—Consent by son of deceased in favour of daughter.—Concurrent finding that gift deeds were void lacking consent by coparceners based on evidence.—High Court cannot re-appreciate evidence to arrive at different conclusion.—It could not be held that son had given consent to gift of property; *Thimmaiah* v. *Ningamma,* AIR 2000 SC 3529 (2): 2000 (2) Marri LJ 571: 2000 (4) Rec Civ R 609: (2000) 7 SCC 409: 2000 (C) Cur CC 339.

Finding by first Appellate Court that agreement to sell was not a genuine Document, High Court rightly pointed out that agreement contained reference to plaintiff's name, but where finding was based on rejection of evidence of attestor of agreement and evidence of defendant in relation to agreement, High Court was not entitled to interfere with fact finding of first appellate court; *Taherakhatoon (dead) by LRs.* v. *Salambin Mohammed,* AIR 1999 SC 1104: 1999 (2) Land LR 201: 1999 (3) Mad LW 406: (1999) 2 SCC 635: 1999 (4) Andh LD 1: All Mah LR 404: 1999 (2) Cur CC 1.

Finding recorded by first appellate court neither perverse nor unreasonable nor based on no evidence, cannot be interfered with on mere re-appreciation of evidence, in absence of valid and acceptable reasons, without framing substantial question of law.

The High Court upset the finding of fact recorded by the first appellate Court, taking a different view merely on re-appreciation of evidence in the absence of valid and acceptable reasons to say that the findings recorded by the first appellate court could not be sustained either by being perverse or unreasonable or could not be supported by any evidence. The High Court neither framed a substantial question of law nor any such question was indicated in the impugned judgment as required under section 100 of the Code of Civil Procedure. The approach of the High Court, in view of the Supreme Court was clearly and manifestly erroneous and unsustainable in law; *Hamida* v. *Mohd. Kahlil,* AIR 2001 SC 2282: (2001) 5 SCC 30: JT 2001 (1) (Supp) 173.

Concurrent Findings not only Vitiated Due to Perversity of Reasoning but also Due to Surmises and Misreading of Materials on Record.—Interference with concurrent findings cannot be said to be transgressing the limitations on the jurisdiction under section 100, CPC.

The judgments of the trial and first Appellate Court could be said to be concurrent only in the sense that both the Courts have chosen to reject the suit as well as the First Appeal and on the question as to whether the property in dispute was acquired by Zohra Bibi from out of her income earned as a prostitute. In other respects, namely, the factum of creation of the document of gift, Wakf deed, the conduct of the parties throughout thereafter in acting upon the same and the collusive and void nature of the proceedings before the Court instituted by Haji Mohammed Siddiq and Mubarak Hussain, the conclusions could not be said to be concurrent; *Hafazat Hussain* v. *Abdul Majeed,* AIR 2001 SC 3201: (2001) 7 SCC 189: (2001) 5 SCALE 104: JT 2001 (6) SC 59.

63. Question of Fact

Whether predecessor-in-title were heirs of mortgagor, purely a question of fact.—Concurrent finding was that this fact was not proved.—The High Court appreciated that mere statement in document prepared by interested parties cannot establish facts stated therein, while parties who could establish relationship were available.—They being party defendants had not chosen to step into witness box.—Courts below correctly appreciated evidence. The Supreme Court appreciated that the High Court in re-appreciating evidence and arriving at contrary conclusion erred in law as well as on facts.

The law on the subject is very clear. Even under the unamended section 100 of the Code of Civil Procedure, the Court could only interfere on a question of law. As admitted by High Court, the question whether the predecessors in title were heirs of Lakshamania was purely a question of fact. Both the Courts below had given concurrent findings that it was not proved that the predecessors in title of the 1st respondent were related to Smt. Lakshamania. The justification sought to be given by the judge that there was an error of law in excluding documents from consideration is patently wrong. Both the Courts below had not excluded the documents from consideration. Both the Courts below had considered the documents. Both the Courts below had rightly held that mere statements in documents prepared by concerned/interested parties cannot establish proof of acts stated therein. Parties who could establish the relationship were available. They were party defendants to the suit. Both the Courts below had rightly noted that these parties had chosen not to step into the witness box. In our view both the Courts below had correctly appreciated the evidence and arrived at the correct conclusion. The High Court in re-appreciating evidence and arriving at a contrary conclusion erred not only in law but also on facts; *Dilboo (Smt.) (dead) by LRs.* v. *Dhanraji (Smt.) (dead),* AIR 2000 SC 3146: 2000 (4) Cur CC 184: 2000 (4) Rec Civ R 734: (2000) 7 SCC 702: 2000 All LJ 2481. *Vishnu Prakash* v. *Sheela Devi,* AIR 2001 SC 1862: (2001) 4 SCC 729: JT 2001 (4) SC 396.

64. Interference with Finding of Fact—When Permissible

(1) When material or relevant evidence not considered, or (2) When finding arrived at by appellate court relying upon inadmissible evidence.—Substantial

question of law is necessary to interfere with judgment of first appellate court in both situations. There are two situations in which interference with findings of fact is permissible. The first one is when material or relevant evidence is not considered which, if considered would have led to an opposite conclusion. This principle has been laid down in a series of judgments of this Court in relation to section 100, CPC after the 1976 amendment.

The second situation in which interference with findings of fact is permissible is where a finding has been arrived at by the appellate Court by placing reliance on inadmissible evidence which if it was omitted, an opposite conclusion was possible.

In either of the above situations, a substantial question of law can arise. The substantial question of law that arises for consideration in this appeal is: "whether the Courts below had failed to consider vital pieces of evidence and whether the Courts relied upon inadmissible evidence while arriving at the conclusion that the mortgage was sham and that there was no relationship between the plaintiff and the defendant as mortgagor and mortgagee but the real relationship was as landlord and tenant? *Ishwar Dass Jain (dead) through LRs.* v. *Sohan Lal (dead) by LRs.* AIR 2000 SC 426: 2000 (1) Civ CC 373: 2000 (1) Mad LW 425: 2000 (1) Andh LD 40: (2000) 1 SCC 434: 2000 (1) Raj LW 80: 2000 (125) Pun LR 58: 2000 (1) Cal HN 1.

Suit for permanent injunction restraining defendant from dispossessing plaintiff from suit land.—Decreed.—Question of possession of suit land essentially a question of fact.—Concurrent finding of trial court and first appellate court on plaintiff's possession.—No scope for interference within limited parameters of section 100, C.P.C. The trial court recorded a positive finding based on the revenue records and the oral evidence led by the plaintiff that he had come into possession of the land under the lease deed and continued to possess the same all along. The lower appellate court, which is the final court of fact confirmed the finding of the trial court regarding plaintiff's possession over the suit land and upheld the judgment of the trial court decreeing the suit. Before the High Court the contention that was raised related to the question of possession. There was hardly any scope for the High Court to interfere with the finding of possession concurrently recorded by the Courts below within the limited parameters of section 100 of the Civil Procedure Code. As the second appeal did not involve any substantial question of law the High Court rightly dismissed the same; *Mohan Lal* v. *Nihal Singh,* AIR 2001 SC 2942: (2001) 8 SCC 584: JT 2001 (9) SC 58.

65. Mixed Question of Law and Fact

The High Court of Madras has said that finding as to mixed question of law and fact can be interfered with in second appeal. When the point for determination is one of proper inference of law on the fact found that itself is a question of law. The question of adverse possession is mixed question of fact and law. The findings of the lower appellate court on the factum of possession are binding in second appeal but it is for the High Court to come to its own conclusion whether on the facts found the possession was adverse or not. In this view, the finding of the lower appellate court on a question of adverse possession is not final and conclusive and can be considered in second appeal (1953) 2 MLJ 241. *See* also ILR (1957) Punj 1997. The Patna High Court said that whenever the existence of a custom is in dispute the resulting decision is partly one of fact and partly one of law. Whether a particular piece of evidence is reliable or not is a matter essentially for the Court determining facts. A law point arises when, taking all the facts together, a legal custom has to be inferred. When the custom satisfies the test of reasonableness and the question whether it is exercised as of right are question of law. Also in general case a valid legal custom can be inferred is a question of law. The question whether a family or tribe of non-Hindu origin has been so far Hinduised as to attract the provisions of Hindu Law in matters of inheritance and succession is a mixed question of law and fact; 24 Pat 727: 1946 Pat 218; 1955 BIJR 557: AIR 1956 Pat 123. The Court again referred to the social order of India and said that in view of the social order that is prevalent in our country, the safest rule is to determine whether the money has been advanced, for accommodation or not. No hard and fast rule can be laid down for giving a finding on that point. That will depend on a number of circumstances including the question of frequency and repetition but the most important is the move for which the loan is advanced. It is true that in giving a finding on it the Court will have to be alive to all the essential factors and to that extent only it is a mixed question of fact and law. Therefore a finding on this point in second appeal can be scrutinized only to the extent as to whether in arriving at it the final Court of fact has or has not been alive to all the essential elements that constitute business of money-lending and not to substitute its own finding in place of that even when it has been arrived at after a full weighing of all those elements, for after all the difference between different classes of money-lenders is more a question of degree than of kind; (1957) Pat LR 259. The plea of *res judicata* being a mixed question of fact and law, cannot be entertained for the first time in second appeal; LLR (1957) 9 Assam 109. The question whether a party acted in good faith within the meaning of section 14. Limitation Act, is a mixed question of law and fact and can be questioned in second appeal, provided that the lowers court's findings of fact are not interfered with, (36 LC 702, Foll.): 40 PLR 631: 1938 L 704. Whether in rent reduction proceedings a tenant represented the whole body of tenants is rather a mixed question of fact and law and it cannot be said to be one which is purely of fact; 26 Pat 592: 1948 Pat 153. An issue regarding limitation is a mixed question of fact and law and is liable to reconsideration by the second appellate court, especially where the trial court which had an opportunity of hearing the witness in persons came to conclusions different from that of the lower appellate court 1940 RD 388: 1940 AWR (BR) 229. The question whether certain documents are admissible in evidence is one of law and a finding on that question is not conclusive in second appeal and can therefore be challenged in the High Court 1951 Pat 641. Appeal decided excerpted wrongly by lower appellate court-Second appeal is allowed 117 LC 239 (1). Whether the facts found attract the operation of a provision of law is a mixed question of law and fact. 401 LC 674: 1927 P 256. Also whether reasonable can be taken 99 LC

1: 1922 A 158. Also the question whether a power of authority was effective on the date of transaction by agent; 6 R 113: 1928. The question whether an application is a fresh application within the language of section 48, C.P.C. is a mixed question of fact and law 186 IC 860. The question whether the disputed land is a Sarbasadharan cremation ground is essentially a mixed question of law and fact. The conclusion of the Court that there had been a dedication or lost grant of the disputed area for the purpose claimed, most properly be regarded as proposition of law derived from fact found than as finding of fact itself: 1950 PC 56: (1950), 1 MLJ 100 (PC). The High Court of Patna said that the question of *vis major* is a mixed question of fact and law, *District Board of Manbhum* v. *Shyamapada Sarkar*, 1955 BLJR 492: 34 Pat 661: AIR 1955 Pat 432. The question whether the parties by their agreement and conduct contemplated to observe the Samwat calendar or the English calendar: *Banarsilal* v. *Shri Bhagwan*, 1955 RLW 129: AIR 1955 Raj 167. Question whether a piece of land is cantonal 1931 M. 213: 59 MLJ 844. Whether a new tenancy has been created is a mixed question of fact and law, 163 IC 538: 1936 P 411. The said Court further said that where in considering the question whether a Hindu family is joint or separate the appellate court has fallen into an error in the proper appreciation of some of the material documentary evidence in the case as well as in regard to the legal effect of certain important piece of evidence its finding is open to reconsideration in second appeal as these are mixed questions of fact and law: 1946 Pat 278. The question of necessity or benefit in relation to an alienation by a guardian is one of mixed law and fact; 147 IC 1144 (1): 1934 I. 329. The question of latches is a mixed question of law and fact as the inference of latches; based upon finding or fact is an inference of law: *Babu Rameshwar Prasad* v. *Anandi Devi*, AIR 1956 Pat 53. The question whether information given to the police is directed against a particular person, 1934 P. 14. Question as to the vicarious liability of master originally sued as principal 1933 N 209. Whether the interpretation of a particular order is a question of fact, or a question of law, mixed question of fact and law depends on the circumstances of each particular case. The general rule is quite clear. Where intention is to be inferred from the terms of a document the question is that of law or mixed question of fact and law; where the intention is to be inferred from the other facts circumstance tending to show what was the real intention the question may be either a question of pure fact or may be a mixed question of fact and law 1941 I. 62. A finding by the lower appellate court that the land on suit is rent-free fakirana grant, is an inference of law from the facts found, and it can therefore be challenged in second appeal: *Ashfaque Ali Khan* v. *Asharfi Mahaseth*, AIR 1951 Pat 641. The question whether the status of the defendant is that of a lessee or a licensee is a mixed question of law and fact, resting as it does on the agreement between the parties and the surrounding facts and circumstances. The inference arising on the findings is an inference of law, and the finding arrived at on the concession of parties is not conclusive in second appeal; *Jai Narain* v. *Syed Ali Murtaza*, AIR 1951 Pat 190.

66. Per Shah, J. (in order of reference)

Justice Shah examined the question of inference as to permanent tenancy and said that it is a mixed question of facts. He says—An inference as to permanent tenancy is a mixed question of law and fact and can be raised in second appeal. But the facts found from which the inference in favor of a party claiming to be a permanent tenant is sought to be raised must be regarded as binding in second appeal, though the question as to what inference should be raised from those facts must be regarded as a question of law: *Dhondi Tukaram* v. *Dadoo Piraji*, 55 Bom LR 663: ILR (1953) Bom 969: AIR 1954 Bom 100. The question whether a person is a partner or an agent of a firm, is a mixed question of law and fact. That being so in second appeal the High Court is competent to examine the correctness of the finding of the Court of first appeal on that question: *Debi Parshad* v. *Jai Ram Dass*, AIR 1952 Punj 284. The question whether there is a partnership and whether other persons besides the plaintiff are his partners is a mixed question of law and fact; AIR 1956 Hyd 477.

Question of law as contemplated by section 100(5) not framed.—Reversal of finding on question of readiness and willingness to perform contract being mixed question of law and fact without discussion on evidence recording basic finding of fact improper. The Supreme Court appreciated that under section 100 of the C.P.C. (as amended in 1976) the jurisdiction of the High Court to interfere with the judgment of the courts below is confined to hearing on substantial question of law. Interference with finding of fact by the High Court is not warranted if it involves re-appreciation of evidence. The High Court did not frame any substantial question of law as contemplated by sub-section (5) of section 100 of the C.P.C. It has not even discussed any evidence. No basic finding of fact recorded by the Courts below has been reversed much less any reason assigned for taking a view to the contrary still the finding on the question of readiness and willingness to perform the contract which is a mixed question of law and fact has been upset; *Ram Kumar Agarwal* v. *Thawar Das (dead) through LRs.*, AIR 1999 SC 3248: 1999 (4) Cur CC 97: (1999) 7 SCC 303: 1999 (7) AD SC 670: 1999 (2) All Rent Cas 546: 1999 All LJ 2088.

67. Judgment Based on a Question not Framed at Admission Stage

Where neither law was discussed nor any reasons assigned for taking a view different from the one concurrently taken by the two courts below, the Supreme Court held that the second appeal was not satisfactorily disposed off by High Court; *Mahadeva* v. *Tanabai*, AIR 2004 SC 3854: 2004 AIR SCW 3927: (2004) 5 SCC 88.

68. Existence of Substantial Question of Law in Second Appeal

Sine qua non.—Hearing without formulating question of law illegal and without jurisdiction. The High Court cannot proceed to hear a second appeal without formulating the substantial question of law involved in the appeal and if it does so it acts illegally and in abnegation or abdication of the duty cast on the Court. The existence of substantial question of law is the *sine qua non* for the exercise of the jurisdiction under the amended section 100 of the Code; *Santosh Hazari* v. *Purushottam Tiwari (dead) by LRs.*, AIR 2001 SC 965: (2001) 2 SCC 179: JT 2001 (2) SC 407.

Substantial question of law.—Meaning of.—Where a point of law has not been pleaded or is found to be arising between the parties in the absence of any factual format, a litigant should not be allowed to raise that question as substantial question of law in second appeal. The mere appreciation of the facts, the documentary evidence or the meaning of entries and the contents of the document cannot be held to be raising a substantial question of law. But where it is found that the first appellate court has assumed jurisdiction which did not vest in it, the same can be adjudicated in the second appeal, treating it as substantial question of law. Where the first appellate court is shown to have exercised its discretion in a judicial manner, it cannot be termed to be an error either of law or of procedure requiring interference in second appeal; *Kondiba Dagadu Kadam* v. *Savitribai Sopan Gujar,* AIR 1999 SC 2213: 1999 (2) Mad LJ 105: 1999 (2) Cur CC 36: 1999 (4) Andh LD 57: 1999 (3) All Mah LR 467: (1999) 3 SCC 732: 1999 (3) Bom LCR 532.

Meaning of the phrase "substantial question of law".—The Supreme Court said in the case of *Santosh Hazari* that paramount consideration is to strike a judicious balance between indispensable obligation to do justice at all stages and impelling necessity of avoiding prolongation of *lis.*

A point of law which admits of no two opinions may be a proposition of law but cannot be a substantial question of law. To be substantial, a question of law must be debatable, not previously settled by law of the land or a binding precedent, and must have a material bearing on the decision of the case, if answered either way, insofar as the rights of the parties before it are concerned. To be a question of law involving in the case there must be first a foundation for it laid in the pleadings and the question should emerge from the sustainable findings of fact arrived at by Court of facts and of law for a just and proper decision of the case. An entirely new point raised for the first time before the High Court is not a question involved in the case unless it goes to the root of the matter. It will, therefore, depend on the facts and circumstances of each case whether a question of law is a substantial one and involved in the case, or not, the paramount overall consideration being the need for striking a judicious balance between the indispensable obligation to do justice at all stages and impelling necessity of avoiding prolongation of the life of any *lis*; *Santosh Hazari* v. *Purushottam Tiwari (dead) by LRs.,* AIR 2001 SC 965: (2001) 2 SCC 179: JT 2001 (2) SC 407.

The Supreme Court again examined the meaning and scope of the term 'a recently' in many cases and has been of the view that a question of law which affects right of the party to suit will be substantial, if it is not covered by any specific provision of law, or settled legal principle emerging from binding precedence of High Court concerned, Privy Council or Supreme Court – *Hero Vinoth* v. *Seshammal,* AIR 2006 SC 2234: 2006 AIR SCW 2833: (2006) 5 SCC 545 (Supra), *Madan Lal* v. *Balkrishan,* AIR 2006 SC 645: 2005 AIR SCW 6525: (2005) 13 SCC 555; *Jwala Singh* v. *Jagat Singh,* (2006) 10 SCC 148; *Lankeshwar Malakar* v. *R. Deka,* (2006) 13 SCC 574; *Gurdev Kaur* v. *Kaki,* (2007) 1 SCC 546: AIR 2006 SC 1975: 2006 AIR SCW 2404; *Patrick JJ. Saldanha* v. *Antony M. Saldanha,* AIR 2007 SC 2620: 2007 AIR SCW 4682: (2007) 6 SCALE 676; *Boodireddy Chandraiah* v. *Arigela Laxmi,* 2007 AIR SCW 7062: AIR 2008 SC 380: (2007) 8 SCC 155.

69. Substantial Question of Law in Concurrent Finding on Subletting and Nuisance

Setting aside without formulating substantial question of law.—Not permissible; *Hari Singh* v. *Kanhaiya Lal*, AIR 1999 SC 3325: 1999 (4) Rec Civ R 107: 1999 (8) ADSC 142: (1999) 7 SCC 288: 1999 (3) Raj LW 415: 1999 (2) Rent LR 613.

Substantial question of law in a mortgage by conditional sale.—The Supreme Court held that in a case of mortgage by conditional sale or sale with a condition of re-purchase, the nature of transaction is a substantial question of law; *Ramlal* v. *Phagua*, (2006) 1 SCC 168: AIR 2006 SC 623: 2005 AIR SCW 6348: 2005 (7) SCJ 688.

Non-mention of substantial question of law in memo of appeal, serious infirmity.—The apex Court stressed that power of High Court to hear on any other substantial question of law not earlier formulated not taken away if the case involves such question and records reasons for its satisfaction; *Santosh Hazari* v. *Purushottam Tiwari (dead) by LRs.*, AIR 2001 SC 965: (2001) 2 SCC 179: JT 2001 (2) SC 407.

70. Substantial Question of Law in Eviction Suit

Main issue whether tenant is entitled to protection of Land Reforms Act.—Cannot be treated as substantial question of law.—Substantial question of law is to be resolved for deciding main issue involved in the suit.—Impugned judgment in second appeal decreeing eviction suit set aside.—There was no scope for entertaining second appeal. The prime question involved in this appeal is whether the first respondent (tenant) is entitled to protection under section 106 of the Kerala Land Reforms Act. Learned counsel pleaded that the said question was treated by the High Court as substantial question of law. That question appears to be too *omnibus* in nature as that was the main issue of the suit. Substantial questions of law, if any, shall be resolved for deciding the main issue involved in the suit. At any rate, the Court said, we cannot treat the above as a substantial question of law to be determined by the High Court in the second appeal; *K.C. Mathew and Sons* v. *A. Sulaikha Beevi*, AIR 2000 SC 3408: 2000 (4) Cur CC 50: 2000 (2) ICC 651: 2000 (40) All CJ 990.

Substantial question of law in reversal of judgment of first appellate court not permissible without formulating substantial question of law.—The Supreme Court said in the case of *Ishwar Das* that under section 100, C.P.C., after the 1976 amendment, it is essential for the High Court to formulate a substantial question of law and it is not permissible to reverse the judgment of the first appellate court without doing so; *Ishwar Dass Jain (dead) through LRs.* v. *Sohan Lal (dead) by LRs.*, AIR 2000 SC 426: 2000 (1) Civil Court C 373: 2000 (1) Mad LW 425: 2000 (1) Andh LD 40: (2000) 1 SCC 434: 2000 (1) Raj LW 80: 2000 (125) Pun LR 58: 2000 (1) Cal HN 1.

71. Substantial Question of Law not Framed

High Court deciding second appeal without keeping in view limited jurisdiction conferred on it.—Impugned order set aside.—Second appeal restored to file of High Court for redeciding following procedure laid down in section 100.

The Supreme Court observed: "A mere look at the impugned order shows that the High Court has allowed the second appeal and remanded the proceedings without strictly following the procedure laid down under section 100 of the Code of Civil Procedure, only on this short ground and without expressing any opinion on the merits of the controversy between the parties, this appeal is allowed. The impugned judgment and order of the High Court are set aside. Second Appeal No. 7 of 1998-A is restored to the file of the High Court with a request to re decide the same in accordance with the limited jurisdiction conferred under section 100 of the Code of Civil Procedure after following the procedure laid down therein"; *Manorama Thampuratti* v. *C.K. Sujatha Thampuratti,* AIR 2000 SC 3400: 2000 (3) Cur CC 31: 2000 (38) All LR 821: 2000 (1) All CJ 481.

Substantial question of law or fact.—Suit for specific performance of agreement to sell.—Issue framed by trial court "whether the plaintiff was ready and willing to perform his part of contract" was of issue of fact held in favour of plaintiff by concurrent finding.—High Court cannot take a different view in second appeal by re-appreciation of evidence treating the issue as substantial question of law; *Veerayee Ammal* v. *Seeni Ammal,* AIR 2001 SC 2920: JT 2001 (9) SC 145: 2002 (1) Civ CR 295.

72. Substantial Questions of Law in Claim to Property.—Construction of Document Raises Substantial Question of Law

The second appellate court has categorically stated that there is a substantial question of law between the parties in as much as the construction of the documents under which the claim to property is made is a substantial question of law. That construction of documents would be a substantial question of law is now a well settled proposition. This proposition has been settled as far back as the judgment of the Privy Council in the case of *Guran Ditta* v. *T. Ram Ditta,* reported in *Guran Ditta* v. *T. Ram Ditta,* AIR 1928 PC 172: 55 IA 235: ILR 55 Cal 944. It has since been reaffirmed by this Court in the case of *Kochukakkada Aboobacker* v. *Attah Kasim,* AIR 1996 SC 3111: 1996 AIR SCW 1606: (1996) 7 SCC 389 and the case of *Neelu Narayani* v. *Lakshmanan,* (1999) 9 SCC 237: 2000 AIR SCW 1949. *Santakumari* v. *Lakshmi Amma Janaki Amma (dead) by LRs.,* AIR 2000 SC 3009: 2000 (3) Mad LJ 188: 2000 (4) All Mah LR 702: (2000) 7 SCC 60: 2000 (41) All LR 36: 2000 (4) Rec Civ R 281.

73. Second Appeal.—Necessity of Framing Substantial Question of Law under Section 100 cannot be Excluded by Section 41 of Punjab Courts Act

Section 41 of Punjab Courts Act in conflict with amended provisions of section 100.—Stands repealed in view of section 97(1), C.P.C.

Section 100(1), C.P.C. even though after amendment saves local law, it has to be read with section 97(1). Language of section 97(1) of the Amendment Act of 1976 clearly spells out that any local law inconsistent goes but what is not inconsistent, it could be said the local law would still continue to occupy its field. But so far the present case, section 41 of the Punjab Act, it is expressly in conflict with the amending law, *viz.,* section 100 amended which would be deemed to have been repealed. Therefore, section 41 of the Punjab Courts Act is not saved on subject of second appeal. More so by reason of the clarification rendered by the legislature in section 101 of the Code which provides that no second appeal shall lie except on the ground mentioned in section 100 indicating thereby the further reinforcement to the legislative intent to be obtained from section 100 as regards the issue of substantial question of law. This refers to substantial question of law having regard to the language of section 103 it cannot however be said to even imply a contra note apart from what is stated herein before. This is so, however, by reason of the provisions of section 97 of the Amending Act; *Kulwant Kaur* v. *Gurdial Singh Mann (dead) by LRs.,* AIR 2001 SC 1273: (2001) 4 SCC 262: JT 2001 (4) SC 158.

The Supreme Court said in the case of *K. Raj*: that it is mandatory to formulate a substantial question of law while entertaining the appeal in absence of which the judgment is to be set aside and the High Court cannot proceed to hear a second appeal without formulating the substantial question of law; *K. Raj* v. *Muthamma,* AIR 2001 SC 1720: (2001) 6 SCC 279: 2001 AIR SCW 1736.

74. Dismissal of Letters Patent Appeal

Interference with record.—Objection raised by registry that memo of appeal did not contain for condonation of delay.—Prayer for condonation of delay added afterwards.—High Court accepting unconditional apology but dismissing appeal on ground of interference with record.—Appellant cannot be made to suffer due to fault of Advocate.

When this fact was brought to the notice of a Division Bench of the High Court, the Court felt that this course of action was not permissible since the correction had been made in the memo of appeal after it had been filed without obtaining permission of the Court. An unconditional apology was tendered by the Advocate-on-record of the appellant before the learned Judges. The said unconditional apology had been accepted by the court in the impugned judgment. But at the same time the appeal had been dismissed on the ground of interference of record. The Supreme Court said, "We are of the opinion that the High Court should not have dismissed the appeal. As a result of the dismissal of the appeal, the appellant who had no role, had been made to suffer on account of a fault on the part of the Advocate in respect of which the Court has accepted the unconditional apology of the Advocate"; *Prakash Seshmal Jain* v. *Sykhmal & Sons,* AIR 1999 SC 2630: JT 1999 (8) SC 536: (1998) 9 SCC 718: 1999 (35) All LR 294.

75. New Plea or Case in Second Appeal

A plea not raised in either of the Courts below cannot be entertained for the first time in second appeal: 29 IC 761: 29 IC 895; 45 IC 101; 2 LL. The question whether the legal representatives of a dead party were joined within time, is a question of fact and cannot be raised for the first time in second appeal: *Saligram Rai Chunilal Bahadur and Co.* v. *Abdul Gani,* ILR (1952) 4 Assam 357: AIR 1953 Assam 206. Correctness of facts admitted by respondent in Court of first appeal—he cannot be allowed to challenge their correctness in second appeal: *State* v. *Jamna Das,* AIR 1955 Punj 117: 56 Punj LR 380: ILR 1955 Punj 365. A judge sitting in second appeal is not justified in deciding the second appeal on a point which has not been raised at any stage by the parties and which is taken by him *suo motu;* 1947 Mad 360 (1): (1947) 1 MIJ 248.

76. New Plea in a Suit Based on Contract

Plea regarding novation of contract cannot be raised for first time in second appeal when neither any issue framed by trial court nor any evidence led. The Supreme Court said that novation under section 62 of the Contract Act requires a clear plea, issue and evidence. Such a question cannot be raised or accepted under section 100, C.P.C. for the first time in Second Appeal. There was no such issue in the Courts below and the defendant's evidence was contrary to such a theory. *Babu Ram* alias *Durga Prasad* v. *Indra Pal Singh (dead) by LRs.,* AIR 1998 SC 3021: 1998 (2) Guj LH 686: 1998 (3) Cur CC 145: (1998) 6 SCC 358: 1998 (5) Andh LT 13.

77. Disposal of Second Appeal

The Supreme Court directed that the High Court has to frame substantial questions of law and then dispose of second appeal. *Taherakhatoon (dead) by LRs* v. *Salambin Mohammed,* AIR 1999 SC 1104: 1999 (2) Land LR 201: 1999 (3) Mad LW 406: (1999) 2 SCC 635: 1999 (4) Andh LD 1: All Mah LR 404: 1999 (2) Cur CC 1.

78. Second Appeal in Eviction Petition.—*Bona Fide* Requirement

Where there was concurrent finding of fact that landlord required ground floor for his growing children and for private coaching to students, High Court was justified in not interfering in second appeal. The case of the respondent that he needs the room on the ground floor for use by himself and his four growing children (sons) has been accepted by the Courts below. The Courts have also accepted the case that the respondent who is an assistant teacher in a government middle school is often approached by students for giving private coaching for the purpose of which he needs the room on the ground floor. In view of the concurrent findings recorded by the Courts below the High Court was justified in not interfering with the finding in the second appeal; *Har Narain Daga* v. *Heeralal,* AIR 2001 SC 341: (2001) 1 SCC 41: JT (2000) Supp (3) 464.

The Supreme Court stressed that existence of question of law is *sine qua non.* Concurrent finding recorded by Courts below that need of landlord was not *bona fide* based on proper appreciation of evidence, reversal of finding without reference to question of law was to be set aside.

The Court said that existence of a 'substantial question of law' is the *sine qua non* for the exercise of jurisdiction by the High Court under the amended provisions of section 100, C.P.C. It appears that the learned Single Judge overlooked the change brought about to section 100, C.P.C. by the Amendment made in 1976. The High Court unjustifiably interfered with pure question of fact while exercising jurisdiction under section 100, C.P.C. It was not proper for the learned Single Judge to have reversed the concurrent findings of fact while exercising jurisdiction under section 100, C.P.C.; *Sheel Chand* v. *Prakash Chand,* AIR 1998 SC 3063: 1998 HRR 657: (1998) 6 SCC 683: 1998 (2) Rent Cr 410: 1998 (3) Cur CC 230.

In a suit for ejectment personal use and occupation is a question of fact, lower appellate court after extensively discussing evidence on record opined that property not required for personal use and occupation.—High Court rightly refused to interfere with finding of fact. The Supreme Court found that the lower appellate court extensively discussed the evidence on record and has come to the finding that the property in question was not required for the use and occupation of the landlord in as much as she has got sufficient accommodation. We hold that the High Court rightly refused to interfere with the findings on this point of the lower appellate court. The Court observed, "we may state here that learned counsel for the appellant has drawn our attention to the judgment of the High Court wherein it has been recorded that nine rooms were in occupation of the landlady which was not a fact and therefore, High Court has misdirected itself. This contention has no force as High Court dismissed the appeal on the ground that there was no substantial question of law involved"; *Labanya Neogi (through LRs.)* v. *W.B. Engineering Co.,* AIR 1999 SC 3331: 1999 (8) ADSC 181: (1999) 7 SCC 431: 1999 (2) Rent LR 628: (1999) 5 SCALE 378.

79. Execution of Gift Deed

Objection as to its validity is a mixed question of fact and law.—The Supreme Court held that such objection cannot be raised in appeal; *Brij Raj Singh (dead) by LRs.* v. *Sewak Ram,* AIR 1999 SC 2203: 1999 (3) Mad LJ 117: 1999 (2) Land LR 379: 1999 (122) Pun LR 594: 1999 (2) Rec Civ R 654: (1999) 4 SCC 331: 1999 (3) Raj LW 434: 1999 (2) All CJ 1452.

80. Fact-Finding that Property in Question was Wakf Property

Concurrent finding of Courts below cannot be interfered within a routine and casual manner by substituting subjective satisfaction.—Judgment and decree of High Court liable to be set aside; *Karnataka Board of Wakf* v. *Anjuman-E-Ismail Madris-Un-Niswan,* AIR 1999 SC 3067: 1999 (3) Land LR 617: 1999 (2) Hindu LR 398: 1999 (4) All Mah LR 281: (1999) 6 SCC 343: 1999 (3) BLJ 866.

Interference with judgment of first appellate court.—No ground to interfere that first appellate court had not come to grips with reasoning of trial court.

The Supreme Court in the case of Arumugham discussed the jurisdiction of the two appellate courts and held that second appellate court cannot interfere with the judgment of the first appellate court. It is open to the first appellate court to consider the evidence adduced by the parties and give its own reasons for accepting the evidence on other side. It is not permissible for the second appellate court to interfere with such findings of the first appellate court only on the ground that the first appellate had not come to grips with the reasoning given by the trial court; *Arumugham (dead) by LRs.* v. *Sundarambal,* AIR 1999 SC 2216: 1999 (36) All LR 751: 1999 (3) Mad LJ 127: 1999 (3) All Mah LR 471: (1999) 4 SCC 350: 1999 (4) Civ LJ 460.

81. Jurisdiction of High Court Confined to Appeals Involving Substantial Question of Law Only

The Supreme Court in the case of *Roop Singh* reiterated that under section 100 of the C.P.C. jurisdiction of the High Court to entertain a second appeal is confined only to such appeals which involve substantial question of law and it does not confer any jurisdiction on the High Court to interfere with pure questions of fact while exercising its jurisdiction under section 100, C.P.C. *Roop Singh (dead) through LRs.* v. *Ram Singh (dead) through LRs.*, AIR 2000 SC 1485: 2000 (2) Land LR 4: 2000 (1) Jab LJ 368: (2000) 3 SCC 708: 2000 (3) Andh LD 18: 2000 (2) Cur CC 71.

Jurisdiction of High Court to be exercised only on the basis of substantial questions of law framed at the time of admission of second appeal.—Judgment delivered without following procedure liable to be set aside.

The High Court can exercise its jurisdiction under section 100, C.P.C. only on the basis of substantial questions of law which are to be framed at the time of admission of the second appeal and the second appeal has to be heard and decided only on the basis of such duly framed substantial questions of law. The impugned judgment shows that no such procedure was followed by the High Court. Thus the judgment rendered by the High Court under section 100, C.P.C. without following the aforesaid procedure cannot be sustained; *Dnyanoba Bhaurao Shemade* v. *Maroti Bhaurao Marnor,* AIR 1999 SC 864: 1999 (3) Land LR 307: ILR (1999) Kant 1705: 1999 (2) Bom LR 436: 1999 (2) SCC 471: 1999 (1) Cur CC 65: 1999 (2) Cr LJ 525.

82. Matter Remanded Back Calling Further Finding after Giving Opportunity to all Parties

Only a tentative conclusion—Only a tentative ground is not a ground to reject finding recorded earlier by trial court. The Supreme Court in the case of *Subramaniam Reddi* discussed the effect and import of an order of remand by the appellate court asking for further findings. The Court said that the High Court while calling for further findings after giving opportunity to all parties made it clear that it was only a tentative conclusion to call for findings and would not mean that a finding recorded earlier cannot be accepted. It was in the context of the parties desire for an opportunity to scrutinise the additional records which were sought to be produced in the High Court in the appeal which were sent back to the courts below to submit its findings. Therefore, the entire matter had to be examined again and thus it could not be said that no reliance could have been placed on the findings of the trial court before calling for further findings; *Subramaniam Reddi (dead)* v. *Venkatasubba Reddi (dead),* AIR 1999 SC 1116: 1999 (1) Cur CC 122: (1999) 3 SCC 240: 1999 (2) All Mah LR 447: 1999 (4) Andh LD 10: 1999 (3) Civ LJ 598.

The Madras High Court in *S. Madasamy Thevar* v. *A.M. Arjuna Raja,* AIR 2000 Mad 465: 2000 (3) Mad LW 793 examined whether question of title may be examined in a second appeal. In the said case The following substantial questions of law are framed in the Second Appeal:—

(1) Whether the judgment and decree of the lower appellate court is in accordance with Order XLI, rule 31, C.P.C.?

(2) in a suit for declaration of title and for consequential injunction does not the initial burden of proof lie on the plaintiff?

(3) in keeping with the initial burden. Is not the plaintiff bound to prove his case by positive evidence on his side, rather than by reliance on the loopholes, if any. on the side of the defendant?

(4) is not secondary evidence as provided under section 65 of the Indian Evidence Act worthy of credence and entitled to be acted upon and in the absence of the original in any way detract from the merits of a case?

(5) in the absence of a clear and specific finding as to actual possession and enjoyment, is the plaintiff entitled to a consequential relief of permanent injunction on mere proof of title alone?

(6) Should a Court be swayed by the volume of evidence in a case without testing its quality?"

On 7-1-2000, both the parties requested this Court to frame an additional substantial question of law which is as follows:—

"Whether the High Court can determine issue regarding title, which has not been determined by appellate court properly, in exercise of its powers under section 103 of Code of Civil Procedure?

The Court said "While considering the additional issue, we have given substantial reasons in the foregoing paragraphs basing on the decisions of Their Lordships of the Supreme Court and any such question of law which is necessary for deciding the right of the parties on the basis of documents can be considered by the High Court in the Second Appeal. The various reasons pointed out by the Supreme Court are also stated in the foregoing paragraphs and in accordance with such decisions, the case of the parties herein are considered to arrive at a conclusion on the basis of the questions of law".

The substantial questions of law framed in the Second Appeal are answered and accordingly, the judgment and decree passed by the first appellate court was held liable to be set aside.

In the result, the judgment and decree in A.S. No. 91 or 1989 on the file of the Subordinate Judge, Srivilliputhur were set aside and that of the trial court are restored and the Second Appeal was allowed, accordingly.

83. New Case in a Suit for Partition

Will executed by ancestor of plaintiff and defendant and sale made thereunder.—Sale deeds neither challenged nor any issues framed by trial court.—No pleadings in plaint about Will also.—High Court fell in error in deciding legality of sale deeds and validity of Will for first time in appeal.—Prayer for partition in conflict with partition already made.— The Supreme Court held that impugned judgment of High Court set aside and that of trial court that suit was barred by previous partition upheld; *Gangajal Kunwar* v. *Sarju Pandey*, AIR 2001 SC 2693: 2001 AIR SCW 2611: (2002) 9 SCC 735.

84. New Plea Regarding Part Performance of Contract.—Mixed Question of Law and Fact

New plea regarding part performance cannot be urged first time at stage of second appeal. The Supreme Court in the case of *Ram Kumar Agrawal* discussed the provisions of section 53A of T.P. Act. The Court said that plea under section 53A of the Transfer of Property Act raises a mixed question of law and fact and therefore cannot be permitted to be urged for the first time at the stage of second appeal. That apart, performance or willingness to perform his part of the contract is one of the essential ingredients of the plea of part performance. Thawar Das having failed in proving such willingness protection to his possession could not have been claimed by reference to section 53A of the Transfer of Property Act; *Ram Kumar Agarwal* v. *Thawar Das (dead) through LRs.*, AIR 1999 SC 3248: 1999 (4) Cur CC 97: (1999) 7 SCC 303: 1999 (7) AD SC 670: 1999 (2) All Rent Cas 546: 1999 All LJ 2088.

High Court in a title suit granting relief based on easementary rights which was not pleaded – Sustainability of – It was held that in the absence of pleadings and no opportunity to the first defendant to deny such claim, the High Court could not have granted the relief of injunction by assuming that plaintiffs had an easementary right to use the schedule property as a passage; *Bachhaj Nahar* v. *Nilima Mandal*, AIR 2009 SC 1103: 2009 AIR SCW 287: (2008) 15 SCALE 158: (2009) 1 SCC 220.

85. Power of Court

Finding on issue not pressed in trial court is without jurisdiction and liable to be set aside. In Second Appeal under section 100 the High Court has no jurisdiction to give a finding on an issue which was not pressed in the trial court. So far as the finding as to a new contract is concerned, there was no issue or evidence. The evidence was to the contrary. Accordingly the findings could be liable to be set aside; *Babu Ram* alias *Durga Prasad* v. *Indra Pal Singh (dead) by LRs.*, AIR 1998 SC 3021: 1998 (2) Guj LH 686: 1998 (3) Cur CC 145: (1998) 6 SCC 358: 1998 (5) Andh LT 13.

86. Power of Court where Issue not Framed by Trial Court as well as First Appellate Court

Plaintiff's Claim for Adverse Possession.—Second appellate court cannot give finding for first time that title of defendant stood extinguished; *Tirumala Tirupati Devasthanam* v. *K.M. Krishnaiah*, AIR 1998 SC 1132: 1998 (2) Andh LT 22: (1998) 3 SCC 331: JT 1998 (2) SC 231.

87. Powers of High Court.—Suit for Eviction Dismissed

Finding reversed by first appellate court on basis of material on record that defendant was in unauthorised occupation of land.—High Court without considering relevant pleadings and findings of lower courts, after appreciation of evidence set aside the order of first appellate court, which was based on material on record, cannot be interfered with in second appeal.

The Supreme Court examined the subject-matter in the case of *Shashikant* and was of the view that a bare perusal of the impugned judgment of the High Court would indicate that the Court has not considered the relevant pleadings and the findings arrived thereon after appreciation of the evidence by the lower appellate court and on the other hand, the High Court has straightway by surmises and conjectures, interfered with the conclusions on the question of facts arrived at by the lower appellate court. The Court said, "we really fail to understand as to how the High Court would record a finding that the tenancy of the plaintiff was in respect of the structure and not the land and further the lease in favour of the plaintiff was in respect of the land other than the land on which the defendants had the possession. Having considered the judgment of the lower appellate court in both these cases, the Court came to the conclusion that the said lower appellate court recorded findings on the materials on record and the conclusions arrived thereunder cannot be said to be erroneous in any manner. In this view of the matter, we see no justification for remitting the second appeals to the High Court again for re-disposal". The Court held that the High Court committed serious error in interfering with the judgment and decree of the lower appellate court in exercise of its jurisdiction under section 100 of the Code of Civil Procedure, accordingly the Court set aside the impugned judgment of the High Court in the second appeals and affirmed the judgments and decrees of the lower appellate court and decreed the suits. *Sashi Kanta Ruia* v. *Indo Minerals*, AIR 2000 SC 2745: 2000 (3) Land LR 6: 2000 (2) Ori LR 442: (2000) 6 SCC 604: 2000 (3) Cur CC 226: 2000 (2) All Rent Cas 413.

88. Purchase of Land in Adjacent Survey Numbers

Clause in sale deed that parties had right of ingress and egress over open passage.—Suit for declaration that respondent encroached upon land and for possession.—Report of Local Commissioner showed that plaintiff was in possession of land more than what was purchased by him.—Trial court finding upheld by first appellate court that any short fall in land occupied by plaintiff than extent stated in sale deed must necessarily be encroachments.—High Court held that trial court had proceeded in most summary fashion and over-simplified complex question of law and fact and such an approach was unsustainable in law.—Appeal dismissed; *Saraswathi* v. *S. Ganapathi,* AIR 2001 SC 1844: 2001 AIR SCW 1625: (2001) 4 SCC 694.

89. Question of Law

Question whether fact-finding reached by Courts below is against the weight of evidence or not, remains in the realm of appreciation of evidence.—If it does not project any question of law, much less any substantial question of law, decision reached by Single Judge in second appeal merely on re-appreciation of evidence unsustainable. Whether a finding of fact reached by Courts below is against the weight of evidence or not is a question which will remain in the realm of appreciation of evidence and does not project any question of law, much less, any substantial question of law, which can enable the High Court in second appeal to upset such a finding of fact. On relevant evidence, both the Courts below had come to the conclusion that the original sale deed (Exhibit 59) dated 29th January, 1973 was a nominal one and was executed by way of security for the loan taken by the appellant from the defendant and similarly the latter two sale deeds Exhibit 52 dated 31-10-1975 and Exhibit 53 of even date were exchange transaction. These findings were well-sustained on record and could not have been interfered with by the High Court in second appeal. Hence, even on merits of the controversy between the parties, the decision rendered by the learned Single Judge and the conclusion of facts to which he reached on re-appreciation of evidence cannot be sustained. The appellant had made out his case on merits and equities were also in his favour. The respondent cannot take advantage of such a nominal sale transaction to defeat plaintiff's claim; *Dnyanoba Bhaurao Shemade* v. *Maroti Bhaurao Marnor,* AIR 1999 SC 864: 1999 (3) Land LR 307: ILR (1999) Kant 1705: 1999 (2) Bom LR 436: (1999) 2 SCC 471: 1999 (1) Cur CC 65: 1999 (2) Cr LJ 525.

90. Illustrative Cases of Question of Law

In revision, the High Court may decline interference if substantial justice has been done, but in deciding questions of law in second appeal, there is no room for such a consideration: 47 PLR 130: 1945 L 175. Points involving questions of law can be raised for the first time in second appeal; 1923 All 343. But their decision should not depend on the determination of questions of fact. The question whether a point is one of fact or of law is itself a question of law; 109 IC 253; 1941 Pat 228. Where the lower court Judge states the law correctly and does not misdirect himself and comes to a particular conclusion, he decides the point as a question of law and not as a question of fact: *Bibi Zainab* v. *Mohammad Ayub,* 17 Pat LT 366: AIR 1936 Pat 136. Questions of law and of fact are sometimes difficult to be separated. The proper legal effect of a proved fact is essentially a question of law. An erroneous inference drawn from a proved fact justifies interference in second appeal; *Thirai Doloi* v. *Singheswar Chutia,* ILR (1950) 2 Assam 137: 1950 Assam 216; *Rishab Kumar* v. *Singai Motilal,* ILR 1948 Nag 299: AIR 1949 Nag 21: 1948 NIJ 316. So also is the question of admissibility of evidence, and the question whether any evidence has been offered on one side or the other; but the question whether the fact has been proved, when evidence for and against has been properly admitted, is necessarily a pure question of fact 16 C 189: 51 IC 760. A Full Bench of the High Court of Assam held that a provisional finding upsetting a very close and elaborate judgment of the trial courts, without any discussions of evidence whatever or without giving any reason except the general reason that the evidence is not satisfactory, is contrary to law and will be set aside in second appeal; 1937 M. 282 *Biswanath Rajanikanta Roy Choudhury* v. *Chunilal Kanailal Firm,* ILR (1952) 4 Assam 89: AIR 1952 Assam 69 (FB). The term contrary to law has not been defined in the Code but in certain circumstances an erroneous finding of fact can amount to a decision contrary to the law; For example if a decision is based upon no legal evidence or available evidence was not considered or if the decision is perverse in the sense that no normal person could have arrived at that opinion it will amount to an error of law and is not binding on the High Court in second appeal. Similarly, if first appellate court failed to draw the only inference possible (Not one of the possible inferences) from the proved facts, the High Court can interfere with the finding in second appeal: *Rajmal* v. *Moti,* AIR 1956 Bhopal 22. It is a question of law whether the alleged expulsion of a member, effected by means of a communication operates by itself as a dissolution of this partnership which is not for a fixed term: 1935 L. 132. The question whether the inference about the dissolution or non-dissolution of a particular partnership, drawn by the lower appellate court from the facts found by it, is or is not correct, is a question of law; 1935 A. 1008. Inferences drawn from documentary evidence are not question of law and cannot be challenged in second appeal; 74I.C. 811: 1924 O. 185. The rules against interference in second appeal with the findings of fact of the lower appellate court apply equally to the case of finding of fact based on inferences of fact drawn wholly or in part from documents: 15 Luck 418: 1940 OWN 193: 1940 O. 217. The statement that the proper legal effect of a proved fact essentially a question of law does not mean that it is a question of law whether a certain inference should be drawn from proved facts. It only means that the legal effect of a finding of fact is question of law: 1941 OWN 1027: 17 Luck 158 *Muhammad Zeyauddin* v. *Shaikh Dargahan,* 18 Pat 571: AIR 1939 Pat 448. As an abstract principle of law it is correct to say that where the decision as to the nature and character of a tenancy depends upon inference to be drawn from entries in a record of rights, the inferences are inferences of fact with which the High Court cannot interfere under section 100, C.P.C. upon a second appeal: However, the question whether the defendants, as being settlers from the usufructuary mortgagee can acquire in the record of right, but is to be determined on the interpretation of the provisions of the Tenancy Act, which is purely a question of law. The presumption of correctness of the entry in the record of right is thus rebutted simply on the interpretation of the law itself; *Kanhaiya Singh* v. *Bhagwat Singh,* 1954 BLJR 170: AIR 1954 Pat 326. Validity of notice to quit is one of law; *Bejoy Chand* v. *Kali Prasanna Seal,* 29 CWN 620: 87 IC 708: AIR 1925 Cal 752.

91. Re-appreciation of Evidence

Submission that evidence of witnesses unworthy of reliance.—Neither a case of no evidence nor perverse finding.—All such submissions within realm of appreciation of evidence.—Neither Supreme Court nor High Court can interfere in such case.

The finding recorded on subletting and nuisance by both the Courts below being based on evidence on record, its setting aside by reappraisal of evidence, and in any case without framing any substantial question of law by the High Court cannot be sustained and further we also do not find any substantial question of law arising therein. Learned counsel for the respondent tried to submit with force by attempting to take us to the evidence of the witnesses to show their unworthiness for reliance. It is neither a case of no evidence nor perverse finding. All these submissions are within the realm of appreciation of evidence which should not have been interfered by the High Court far less for us to examine; *Hari Singh* v. *Kanhaiya Lal,* AIR 1999 SC 3325: 1999 (4) Rec Civ R 107: 1999 (8) ADSC 142: (1999) 7 SCC 288: 1999 (3) Raj LW 415: 1999 (2) Rent LR 613.

92. Suit for Permanent Injunction.—Against Forcible Dispossession

Suit partially decreed.—Single Judge overlooking earlier order of remand travelled outside scope of suit went on to record findings based on alleged title of plaintiffs to suit property and dismissed suit.—Judgment of Single Judge of High Court falls within scope of clause 15 of Letters Patent.—Letters Patent appeal maintainable.—However, second appeal is not maintainable.

The learned counsel contended that the remedy of the respondent was to file a second appeal under section 100, C.P.C. against the judgment of the learned Single Judge. However, he realised his folly when he read out section 100, C.P.C. and found that it applied only to decrees passed in appeal by a Court subordinate to the High Court. There can be no doubt whatever that the judgment of the learned Single Judge of the High Court fell within the scope of clause 15 of the Letters Patent and the appeal was maintainable; *Prataprai N. Kothari* v. *John Braganza*, AIR 1999 SC 1666: 1999 (2) Land LR 585: 1999 (2) Cur CC 138: 1999 (3) Pun LR 55: 1999 (2) Raj LW 292: 1999 (2) All Mah LR 566: (1999) 4 SCC 403.

93. Suit for Permanent Injunction

Restraining defendants from interfering in suit land.—The Supreme Court held in the case of *Banarsi Das* that finding by first appellate court that sale deed was invalid without any issue and without impleading vendees in whose favour sale deed was executed.—No finding that plaintiff was in possession of land or jamabandi was forged without any evidence or plea raised by plaintiff.—Whole approach of first appellate court based on mere suspicion and bias against second defendant.—Case based on substantial error or defect in procedure.—High Court justified in entertaining second appeal; *Banarsi Dass* v. *Brig. Maharaja Sukhjit Singh*, AIR 1998 SC 179: 1998 (4) Andh LT 1: 1998 (1) Rec Civ R 84: (1998) 2 SCC 81.

94. Suit for Recovery of Excess Demurrage Charged by Railways

Suit Decreed.—Absence of pleading that Rule relied upon was *ultra vires* Railways Act, 1890.—No issue framed by trial court.—High Court on its own considered validity of rule holding the rule was *ultra vires* Railways Act.—Pleadings comprising of averments and defence put up in written statement relating to validity of rule did not relate to validity of rule.—High Court travelled beyond pleadings in declaring rule to be *ultra vires*.—Judgment of High Court cannot be sustained.

There was no pleading that the Rule upon which the reliance was placed by the respondent was *ultra vires* the Railways Act, 1890. In the absence of the pleading to that effect, the trial court did not frame any issue on that question. The High Court of its own proceeded to consider the validity of the Rule and ultimately held that it was not in consonance with the relevant provisions of the Railways Act, 1890 and consequently held that it was *ultra vires*. This view is contrary to the settled law that a question, which did not form part of the pleadings or in respect of which the parties were not at variance and which was not the subject-matter of any issue, could not be decided by the Court. The scope of the suit was limited. The pleading comprising of the averments set out in the plaint and the defence put up by the present appellant in their written statement did not relate to the validity of the Rule struck down by the High Court. The High Court, therefore, travelled beyond the pleadings in declaring the Rule to be *ultra vires*. The judgment of the High Court, therefore, on this question cannot be sustained; *Union of India* v. *E.I.D. Parry (India) Ltd.*, AIR 2000 SC 831: 2000 (1) Andh WR 137: 2000 (2) Mad LJ 39: 2000 (125) Pun LR 64: 2000 (2) SCC 223: 2000 (1) Cur CC 210: 2000 (2) BLJ 366.

95. Suit for Redemption of Mortgage

Property vested in State by *escheat*.—Trial court dismissed suit holding that remaining land could not be redeemed.—High Court reversed finding of courts below holding that mortgage deed was not admissible and application moved by State did not conform to requirements of section 65 of Evidence Act.—Dispute before High Court was not about admissibility of document, but mode of proof only.—High Court ignored cumulative effect of material produced and fact that none of plaintiffs chose to go to witness box to substantiate their claims, nor challenged admissibility of document before lower courts.—Matter remanded back granting opportunity to both sides to lead evidence in the light of evidence on record.

The High Court appears to have done what is not permissible for it in a second appeal, be it one even filed under the amendment section 100, C.P.C., by re-appreciating the evidence, adopting a process of elimination by being merely critical of the materials produced on behalf of the State without taking into account the cumulative effect of those materials and completely ignoring the fact that none of the plaintiffs have chosen to go into the box to substantiate their claims. The overwhelming materials of which due notice has been taken and consideration made by the Courts below seem to have escaped the attention of the High Court in upsetting the concurrent findings of fact, recorded by the Courts below.

All the more so, when there was no challenge or dispute with reference to the admissibility of the said document by the plaintiffs at the appropriate stage before the trial court or the first appellate court. Even the grievance before the High Court seems to be not that the document is *per se* an admissible one but about the mode or method of proof only; *State of Himachal Pradesh* v. *Akshara Nand (dead) by LRs.*, AIR 2000 SC 1828: 2000 (2) Mad LJ 87: 2000 (3) Land LR 24: (2000) 3 SCC 661: 2000 (2) All Mah LR 694: 2000 (2) Cur CC 1: 2000 (2) All CJ 899.

Suit for specific performance of agreement to repurchase property.—Concurrent finding that appellant was ready and willing to buy-back.—Purchaser merely claiming credit for certain amount does not mean that he was seeking variation in sale consideration.

The Supreme Court found that the appellant proved the agreement made and the parties were not at issue as to its existence. The appellant had expressed his readiness and willingness to perform the agreement by paying the consideration fixed not once but repeatedly in several paragraphs of the plaint. The Supreme Court held that the High Court erred in overlooking the fact that the appellant had never said that the consideration for re-conveyance under the agreement was less than what was stated. Conceding that the appellant had merely claimed credit for certain amounts, this could not mean that he was seeking a variation in the agreement itself; *V. Pechimuthu* v. *Gowrammal*, AIR 2001 SC 2446: 2002 (1) Civ CR 9: (2001) 7 SCC 617: JT 2001 (6) SC 162.

Trial court finding that ownership of suit property vested in plaintiff and negatived plea of adverse possession holding that he forcibly occupied disputed area, reversed by first appellate court.—High Court dismissed second appeal *in limine* holding that no substantial question of law arose for determination.—Defendant's plea of adverse possession raised substantial question of law as plaintiff's suit was barred by limitation under article 65 of Limitation Act.—High Court order suffered from legal infirmity.—Case remanded back for fresh decision uninfluenced by observations made; *Santosh Hazari* v. *Purushottam Tiwari (dead) by LRs.*, AIR 2001 SC 965: (2001) 2 SCC 179: JT 2001 (2) SC 407.

Specific Relief Act, 1963, section 16(c) specific performance of contract.—Fact-finding by lower court binding on plaintiff in second appeal.

The Supreme Court said that in the present case before us there is no proof that any attitude of the defendant towards the plaintiff was the cause for the plaintiff not being able to pay the amount to the defendant. As already stated, the finding of fact arrived at by the Courts below that no effort has been made by the plaintiff to pay the sale consideration to the defendant are findings of fact, binding in second appeal; *Bismillah Begum (dead) by LRs.* v. *Rahmatullah Khan (dead) by LRs.*, AIR 1998 SC 970: 1998 (1) Andh LT 24: 1998 (1) Mad LW 825: (1998) 2 SCC 226.

Whether a second appeal can be decided merely on equitable grounds.—No ground to interfere with concurrent finding of facts, though erroneous, in second appeal.—The right of appeal is neither a natural nor an inherent right attached to the litigation. The Supreme Court said that being a substantive statutory right, it has to be regulated in accordance with law in force at the relevant time. The conditions mentioned in the section must be strictly fulfilled before a second appeal can be maintained and no court has the power to add to or enlarge those grounds. The second appeal cannot be disturbed by the High Court in exercise of the powers under this section. The substantial question of law has to be distinguished from a substantial question of fact; *Kondiba Dagadu Kadam* v. *Savitribai Sopan Gujar*, AIR 1999 SC 2213: 1999 (2) Mad LJ 105: 1999 (2) Cur CC 36: 1999 (4) Andh LD 57: 1999 (3) All Mah LR 467: 1999 (3) SCC 732: 1999 (3) Bom LCR 532.

Section 100 (as amended by Act of 1976).—Second appeal.—Perversity itself a substantial question of law.—Worth adjudication.—Interference with finding on perversity permissible.

While it is true that in a second appeal a finding of fact even if erroneous will generally not be disturbed but where it is found that the findings stand vitiated on wrong test and on the basis of assumption and conjectures and resultantly there is an element of perversity involved therein, the High Court will be within its jurisdiction to deal with the issue. This is, however, only in the event such a fact is brought to light by the High Court explicitly and the judgment should also be categorical as to the issue of perversity *vis-à-vis* the concept of justice. Needless to say, however, that perversity itself is a substantial question worth adjudication.—What is required is a categorical finding on the part of the High Court as to perversity. The requirements stand specified in section 103 and nothing short of it will bring it within the ambit of section 100 since the issue of perversity will also come within the ambit of substantial question of law as noticed above. The legality of finding of fact cannot but be termed to be a question of law; *Kulwant Kaur* v. *Gurdial Singh Mann (dead) by LRs.*, AIR 2001 SC 1273: (2001) 4 SCC 262: JT 2001 (4) SC 158.

96. General Principal of Findings of Fact – Interference with

Unless the factual finding is perverse, contrary to material on record, held, there is practically no scope for interference; *Sugani* v. *Rameshwar Das*, AIR 2006 SC 2172: 2006 AIR SCW 2606: 2006 (4) Supreme 684; *See* also *H.P. Pyarejan* v. *Dasappa*, AIR 2006 SC 1144: 2006 AIR SCW 715: (2006) 2 SCC 496; *Hero Vinoth* v. *Seshammal*, AIR 2006 SC 2234: 2006 AIR SCW 2833: (2006) 5 SCC 545; *Town Planning Municipal Council* v. *Rajappa*, (2008) 2 SCC 593; *Bakhtiyar Hussain* v. *Hafiz Khan*, (2007) 12 SCC 420: AIR 2007 SC (Supp) 947.

Joint Hindu Family Property – Suit by widowed daughter-in-law against her mother-in-law for partition and separate possession – Substantial question of Law to be determined – High Court calculating development of shares from shares of son and father, it was held that High Court ought to have calculated also the shares of daughter-in-law and of her mother-in-law in joint family properties. *Lehaja Bai* v. *Saraswati Bari*, (2009) 6 SCC 800.

97. Concurrent Findings of Fact – Consideration of and Interference with – Scope

The Supreme Court re-affirmed the previous views regarding interference with the concurrent findings of facts and held that second appeal against decree for specific performance passed by the lower appellate court – both the courts below, after dealing with the facts and circumstances of the case, concluding that the plaintiff was ready and willing to perform his part of the contact, held, High Court erred in concluding otherwise; *Saraswati Devi Gupta* v. *Harnarayan Johri*, (2006) 1 SCC 729; *See* also *Ramlal* v. *Phagua*, (2006) 1 SCC 168: AIR 2006 SC 623: 2005 AIR SCW 6348: 2005 (7) SCJ 688; *Haryana State Industrial Development Corpn.* v. *Corp. Mfg. Co.*, (2007) 8 SCC 120; *Shakuntala* v. *Lt. Col. Mukhtiya Singh*, (2008) 11 SCC 42 and *Madan Kishore* v. *Major Sudhir Sewal*, (2008) 8 SCC 744: AIR 2009 SC (Supp) 978.

In a case where both trial court and appellate court found that there was valid execution of Will and that it was not forged – High Court's non-interference with these pure questions of fact, held, justified; *Shyam Lal* v. *Sanjeev Kumar*, (2009) 12 SCC 454: AIR 2009 SC 3115: 2009 AIR SCW 5006; *See* also *Waheed Baig* v. *Bangi Lakshmamma*, (2008) 14 SCC 435: AIR 2009 SC (Supp) 391 and *United Church of Northern India* v. *Jibhral Narjinary*, (2008) 15 SCC 728.

98. Perversity of the Factual Findings as Substantial Question of Law – Permissibility of Scrutiny of Evidence in Second Appeal

The Supreme Court explained the perversity of factual findings and said in the case of *Maria Colaco* that normally in second appeal the High Court should not interfere on the questions of fact, but if on the scrutiny of the evidence it is found that the finding recorded by the first appellate court is totally perverse then certainly the High Court can interfere in the matter as it constitutes a question of law; *Maria Colaco* v. *Alba Flora Herminda D'Souza,* AIR 2008 SC 1965: 2008 AIR SCW 2275: (2008) 5 SCC 268.

Similar view was expressed by the Supreme Court in the case of *Dr. Ramnath Murti* also and it was held that the High Court can interfere with findings of facts only when the findings of facts recorded by the trial court appears to be perverse; *Dr. Ram Nath Murti* v. *Ramappa,* (2011) 1 SCC 158.

99. Second Appeal Non-compliance with Mandatory Provisions

The Supreme Court directed High Court to formulate substantial questions of law if any arising then dispose of the same in accordance with law. *Ragulavalasa Chiranjivi Rao* v. *State of Andhra Pradesh,* (2009) 13 SCC 33. The Supreme Court again said in the case of *Jaskaran Singh* that the second appellate court can not decide the second appeal without formulating substantial question of law. The Supreme Court examined the issue in detail and held that formulation of substantial question of law in second appeal is mandatory; *Jaskaran Singh* v. *Punjab State, Ministry of Home Affairs,* (2009) 9 SCC 59: AIR 2009 SC (Supp) 1417, *Kamla* v. *Gaurav Kumar Gupta,* (2009) 13 SCC 253: 2009 AIR SCW 5844.

100. Section 100(5) Proviso – Scope and Application of

The Supreme Court explained that the proviso is applicable only when any substantial question of law has already been formulated *Gyan Das* v. *Gram Panchayat,* (2006) 6 SCC 271, *B.C. Shivshankara* v. *B.R. Nagraj,* (2007) 3 SCR 389; *Mahant Dooj Das* v. *Udasin Panchayati Bara Akhara,* (2008) 7 SCR 470: AIR 2008 SC (Supp) 1867: (2008) 12 SCC 181; *Kappi Shetti* v. *Venkat Ratnam,* (2009) 3 SCR 574; *K.K. Kannam* v. *Koolivathukkal Karkhan Mandi,* (2010) 2 SCC 239: AIR 2010 SC (Supp) 194 *and Municipal Committee* v. *Punjab Electricity Board,* (2010) 11 SCALE 69.

101. Section 100 – Is Such an Appeal Automatically Admitted

In *D. Venkatalakshmamma* v. *Veluru Rajeswaramma,* 2014 1 ALT 564 (AP) the High Court said, learned counsel for the respondent/plaintiff contended that neither father of appellant Nos.2 to 5 nor the appellants have filed any suit for Specific Performance of Contract based on agreement of sale; that as the appellants dispossessed the respondent from the plaint schedule property, she filed a suit and basing on the evidence available on record, the trial Court decreed the suit; that even the said agreement of sale, dated 15.04.1972 has not been filed into the Court so as give a finding and hence, he prays to dismiss the appeal.

In view of amendment to Section 100 C.P.C, admitting of Second Appeal is not automatic or routine. It must be shown that the findings are perverse or that findings are not based upon admissible evidence or inadmissible evidence has been taken into consideration in arriving such findings.

Learned counsel for the appellants, relied on EX.A.4-judgment in A.S.No.14 of 1995, in earlier round of litigation. It is not in dispute that originally, the respondent herein filed a suit O.S.No.383 of 1987 for permanent injunction and the said suit was decreed. Father of appellant Nos.2 to 5 filed an appeal A.S.No.14 of 1995, where under certain observations are made by the first appellate Court that father of appellant Nos.2 to 5 has got right, title and interest over the schedule property. It is a perverse finding. That finding ought not have been given because such a finding is not warranted in a suit for permanent injunction. Therefore, any observation made in A.S.No.14 of 1995, does not confer any title to the appellants because the Original Suit therein is filed for declaration of title. On the other hand, in view of the fact that the respondent filed the suit for declaration of title and recovery of possession, the initial burden is on her to establish her title. To prove the title, the respondent filed Photostat copy of sale deed, dated 17.12.1970, which is not disputed. By virtue of said sale deed, the respondent has got right, title and interest. As seen from the record, the respondent has not transferred title in respect of immovable property to anybody. But, appellant Nos.2 to 5 are claiming that their father entered into an agreement of sale, dated 15.04.1972, and by virtue of the same, entire amount has been paid to the Vendee and Vendor inducted the Vendee into possession of the property. The said agreement of sale has not been marked so as to establish that father of appellant Nos.2 to 5 inducted into possession. Except filing Exs.B1 and B.2, which are revenue records, no title deed was filed by the appellants in the trial Court. There cannot be any dispute that the revenue records like Exs.B.1 and B.2, do not confer any title to the parties. In the absence of any title to the appellants, they cannot claim that they got right, title and interest by virtue of finding given by the competent Court in A.S.No.14 of 1995. When father of appellant Nos. 2 to 5 claims that they are in possession and enjoyment of the property by virtue of the sale letter, dated 15.04.1972, the defendants cannot turn round and say that they have perfected their title by adverse possession. Therefore, the findings, if any, observed by the learned judge in A.S.No.14 of 1995, do not confer any title to the appellants. In the absence of any title to the appellants, both the Courts below rightly decreed the suit. None of the findings is shown to be perverse or contrary to law. In the absence of any perverse finding, admitting the Second Appeal does not arise.

102. Section 100 – Second Appeal Challenging the Judgment and Decree

In *Emam Jagan Reddy* v. *Keesari Padma,* 2014 (3) ALT 217 (AP) the High Court said, -it appears from the materials on record that defendant remained silent for about 22 years and woke up after the plaintiff secured a temporary injunction against him clearly indicates negligence of defendant-Defendant was duty bound to verify the boundaries of the plot which he has purchased-Since the title of the suit plot is with the plaintiff and since possession follows title, plaintiff to be deemed in possession of the suit plot on the date of filing suit.

103. Section 100 – Findings not Proper – Boundaries to Prevail

In *Rukmini Bai Alias Laxmi Bai* v. *K. Mohanlal,* 2011 (4) ALD 537: 2011 (4) ALT 219: 2011 8 RCR (Civ) 1193 (AP) the High Court held, where there is inconsistency between the boundaries and survey numbers, boundaries shall prevail. Where the earlier judgment is with reference to another property but not the property now in question, but separate property, the earlier judgment will not operate as *res judicata*.

104. Section 100 – Findings of Trial Court not Based on Evidence – High Court in Second Appeal can Interfere

In *Rukmini Bai Alias Laxmi Bai* v. *K. Mohanlal,* 2011 4 ALD 537: 2011 4 ALT 219: 2011 (8) RCR (Civ) 1193 (AP) the learned first appellate Court being led away by certain misconceived notions and ignoring the well settled principles relating to proof of certain facts in civil cases, unjustly reversed the judgment rendered by the learned trial Court. It is true that insofar as the finding relating to facts, the conclusion reached by the first appellate Court is final, but such finality will be attached to the conclusions reached by the first appellate Court, if they are based on proper reappraisal of the evidence on record and only when the findings are in accordance with the evidence on record and not being perverse. Though, the essential requirement for entertaining the second appeal is involvement of substantial question of law, this Court while exercising its jurisdiction under Section 100 C.P.C can interfere with the findings of fact, if such findings recorded by the trial Court are either not based on evidence on record or based on no evidence or perverse. The reasons assigned by the first appellate Court for reversing the judgment of the trial Court must be adequate and they should be in accordance with the settled principles of law. If such findings are totally misconceived and not in accordance with law, they can be said to be perverse and require interference of this Court in the second appeal.

The Andhra Pradesh High Court in second appeal said, in proof of their title, the plaintiffs filed Ex.A.1 registered sale deed dated 14.06.1966 under which the deceased first plaintiff purchased the property from Dasarath Kumar. They also filed their vendor's sale deed dated 11.01.1960 which is marked as Ex.A.2 and according to the said sale deed, their vendor Dasarath purchased the schedule mentioned site from Mohd. Ulfat Ali Khan. The recitals of Ex.A.1 reveal that the deceased first plaintiff purchased 1500 sq. yards of site in Jangummet, Falaknuma, Hyderabad in Ward No.18. The Northern boundary of Ex.A.1 is the land of Makkaji, who is no other than the father of the defendant. In Ex.A.2, which is the link document of the plaintiffs also, the northern boundary is shown as the land of Makkaji. In Exs.A.1 and A.2 sale deeds only municipal Ward No.18 is mentioned, but either the survey number or town survey number are not mentioned. Ex.B1. is the sale deed dated 06.02.1961 under which the defendant is claiming rights. In the said document southern boundary is mentioned as Mohd. Ulfat Ali Khan and northern boundary is shown as Balabai W/o Makkaji Saheb. Ex.B.1 is an extent of 32000 sq. yards of non-agricultural land of Ward No. 18. As already noticed, Mohd. Ulfat Ali Khan is no other than the plaintiffs' vendor. It is significant to note that in Ex.B.1 sale deed also only Ward No.18 is mentioned and that there is no mention of survey number or town survey number.

One more important aspect requires consideration is that DW1 had specifically admitted in the cross examination that the schedule mentioned site does not cover any lands under Exs.B1 and B.2 sale deeds. DW.1 also admitted in the cross-examination that it is so mentioned in Ex.B.1 sale deed. As per

Ex.B.1 sale deed the southern boundary is the land of Mohd. Ulfat Ali Khan. He also further admitted that Mohd. Ulfat Ali Khan is one of the attestors of Ex.B.1 and that his vendor's property is situated on the northern side of the property covered under Exs.A.1 and A.2.

In the light of the evidence above referred, the learned trial Court rightly arrived at the conclusion that absolutely there is no dispute about the identity of the suit schedule site. Ex.A.4 is another important document. It is a receipt dated 11.10.1999 relating to nonagricultural land assessment tax which shows that the plaintiffs paid the Nala tax for the suit property from 1966-1999. Though tax was collected under nala from the plaintiffs under Ex.A.4 for several years, its genuineness cannot be doubted on the said ground alone in the absence of any other evidence or circumstances showing that it was a brought up document.

The appellate court examined further materials on record and said, the learned trial Court considering the evidence of DW1 in the cross-examination which is to the effect that the property forming part of O.S.No.60 of 1968 is the western part of Survey No.5 and the property in Ex.B.7 is a different one to that of the schedule mentioned property in the present case and there being no proof that Dattari Kumar and Dasarath Kumar are one and the same persons, rightly held that the decision in O.S.No.60 of 1968 does not operate as res judicata against the plaintiffs.

Thus, in the instant case, there is highly reliable and convincing evidence adduced by the plaintiffs in proof of their title in respect of the schedule mentioned site. The defendant had admitted specifically in his evidence that the property belonging to him under Exs.B.1 and B.2 sale deeds is different to that of the property under Exs.A.1 and A.2 sale deeds. The law is well settled that if there is any inconsistency between the boundaries on one side and survey numbers or extent on the other, the boundaries will prevail. The learned first appellate Court reversed the well-considered judgment of the learned trial Court in utter disregard of the above said principle and took an erroneous view that the plaintiffs could not be able to establish the identity of the subject matter of the suit.

As I have already said, if the first appellate Court failed to assign any convincing reasons for reversing the judgment of the trial Court and when such reversal of findings is based on misconceived notions and contrary to the well-established principles, the said findings arrived at by the first appellate Court therefore, can be considered as perverse and this Court can interfere with the said findings in the second appeal even though some of the findings relate to fact.

105. Section 100 – Findings of Trial Court if Perverse

In *Meenugu Mallaiah* v. *Ananthula Rajaiah,* 2017 (1) ALD 457 the question before the learned trial Court was as to whether the plaintiff proved that he purchased the property under unregistered sale deed from Bhadraiah and took possession of the same under the unregistered sale deed about 20 years back from the date of filing of the suit?

It is pertinent to note that the plaintiff did not file the said unregistered sale deed on the ground that it was lost. None of the witnesses were examined on behalf of the plaintiff stated about the purchase by the plaintiff of the schedule mentioned land under unregistered sale deed from late Sri Samudrala Bhadraiah. However, he filed Ex.A-2 pattedar passbook and Exs.A-1 to A-16 pahanies. There is some oral evidence adduced by the plaintiff to the effect that he is in possession of the schedule mentioned land. The learned trial Court after considering the fact that for several years the name of the plaintiff was not incorporated in the pahanies and other revenue records after the alleged purchase and also taking into account that Ex.A-20 pattedar passbook and Exs.A-1 to A-16 pahanies for some latter years held that they are not reliable and are not sufficient enough to establish the title of the plaintiff over the schedule mentioned property and accordingly dismissed the suit filed by the plaintiff. The learned trial Court also declined to grant injunction and cancellation of registered sale deed dated 29-07-1993 executed by the first defendant in favour of the second defendant. The trial Court was of the view that the documents produced by the defendants such as land revenue receipts which are marked as Ex.B-8 reveal that the defendants paid land revenue in respect of Ac:2-27 guntas of land in the same survey No.187 and that the registered sale deed, which is marked as Ex.A17 indicated Acs:4-36 guntas of land was purchased by D2. The learned trial Court took into consideration the evidence of PWs 2 and 3 examined for the plaintiff and held that the defendants are in possession of the land in dispute. Keeping in mind that the plaintiff claimed title to the property of an extent of Ac:3-09 guntas and whereas the defendants claimed title in respect of the land of an extent of Acs:4-36guntas and the evidence adduced on either side is conflicting and following the principles that the plaintiff has to succeed on the strength of his own case and shall not have recourse to the weakness of the case of the defendants, dismissed the suit filed by the plaintiff.

The learned trial Court took into consideration Ex.B-1 certified copy of pahani for the year 1974-75 relating to survey No.187, which is an extent of Acs:19-07 guntas. Ex.B-2 certified copy of pahani for the year 1976-77. Ex.B-3 is the pahani pertaining to the year 1978-79. Ex.B-4 the pahani for the year 1979-80. Ex.B-5 the pahani showing the name of the defendant as purchaser of Acs:3-08 guntas. Ex.B6 is the pahani for the year 1983-84. Ex.B7 is the pahani for the year 1993-94 and also Exs.B11, B12, 13 showing the name of the plaintiff as well as the defendants in the pahanies column.

The learned first appellate court though agreed that the finding of the learned trial Court that the plaintiff failed to prove the unregistered sale deed allegedly executed by late Samudrala Bhadraiah in his favour, under which he became entitled to the plaint schedule mentioned land. Considering the pattedar passbook and the pahani patriks filed by the plaintiff expressed the view that the said documents would show that the plaintiff is in possession of the schedule mentioned land and therefore, the plea of adverse possession taken by the plaintiff has to be upheld. The learned first appellate Court also took an erroneous view that under the registered sale deed dated 29-07-1993, the defendant No.2 did not acquire any title to the schedule mentioned land on the premise that the land was long back sold to the plaintiff by the first defendant's father late Sri Samudrala Bhadraiah. The learned first appellate Court lost sight of the fact that the plaintiff miserably failed to prove that he purchased the schedule mentioned land from late Sri Bhadraiah under unregistered sale deed. In the absence of any such proof, it cannot be said that the title in fact passed on to the plaintiff. The learned first appellate Court also failed to understand the effect of conflicting versions taken by the plaintiff in respect of his title to the schedule mentioned land. On one hand the plaintiff asserted his title to the schedule mentioned land under unregistered sale deed said to have been executed by late Sri Bhadraiah. On the other hand, he took an inconsistent plea that he perfected his title to the property by adverse possession. These two pleas are wholly inconsistent. There is no averment in the plaint that the first defendant, who is no other than the son of late Bhadraiah is aware of the unregistered sale deed executed by his father in favour of the plaintiff and that by asserting hostile against the defendant and remaining in possession of the schedule mentioned land with the said hostile unanimous for more than statutory period he perfected the title to the property by adverse possession and that the defendant No.1 never objected to any such hostile assertion made. Although the plaintiff stated that he perfected his title to the suit property by adverse possession, he did not assert either in his plaint or in his evidence as to how he acquired the adverse title to the schedule mentioned property against the defendants. If he purchased the property under an unregistered sale deed from the first defendant's father, the question of his asserting any hostile title against the first defendant does not arise. Further the evidence adduced by the plaintiff at best shows that during some years the plaintiff was in possession of the schedule mentioned property. The witnesses examined on either side stated that both the parties are in possession of the schedule mentioned property, consequently the question of exclusive possession of the plaintiff by asserting hostile title does not arise. In fact there is no such averment. There being no evidence in proof of assertion of hostile title by the plaintiff, the learned first appellate court misdirected itself to the factual and legal position and decreed the suit upholding the plea of perfecting title by adverse possession set-up by the plaintiff. The finding is not merely erroneous but is not legal.

The learned counsel appearing for the plaintiff would submit that the finding in relation to the fact given by the first appellate court is final and this Court in exercise of its jurisdiction under section 100 of CPC while dealing the second appeal shall not interfere with such finding of fact recorded by the first appellate Court. It is not possible to accede to the contention of the learned counsel. This Court in dealing with the second appeal can certainly interfere with the findings of fact recorded by the courts below if they are perverse or not based on evidence or based on no evidence. Here is a case, absolutely where there is no evidence indicating that the plaintiff had perfected his title to the schedule mentioned land by adverse possession. The version of the witnesses examined on behalf of the plaintiff is at variance in regard to the possession of the plaintiff. The witnesses examined on either side have stated that both the parties are in possession of the schedule mentioned land. Therefore, it is impermissible for the trial Court in view of the lack of evidence in support of the plea of adverse possession pleaded by the plaintiff to give a finding that the plaintiff had perfected his title by adverse possession. Since the finding is based on no evidence and contrary to the settled principles of law relating to the concept of adverse possession is liable to be set aside and the second appeal deserves to be allowed.

The Court in second appeal concluded, for the reasons afore-mentioned, the judgment and decree passed by the learned first appellate Court is set aside and the judgment and decree passed by the learned trial Court in dismissing the suit filed by the plaintiff in toto is confirmed. The second appeal therefore succeeds and is allowed. There shall be no order as to costs.

106. Section 100 – Filing of a Separate Suit for Cancellation of an Exparte Decree – Whether Permissible

In *Nannuri Sathi Reddy* v. *Nannuri Narsi Reddy*, 2012 (2) ALD 563: 2012 (2) ALT 113: 2012 2 CivCC 181 (AP) Sri K.Narasimhachari, learned counsel for the appellant, submits that the very institution of O.S. No. 205 of 1991 was opposed to law. He contends that, in case respondents 1 to 4, 7 and 8 were of the view that the summons were not served in accordance with law, they could have filed an application under Rule 13 of Order IX C.P.C. or preferred an appeal. He submits that even on merits, the trial Court recorded a finding to the effect that the summons were properly served. Learned counsel further submits that during the pendency of O.S. No. 205 of 1991, the 9th respondent herein filed O.S.No.61 of 1998, against the appellant and respondents 1 to 8 and certain others, for partition.

The second appellate court said, this Court is of the view that a substantial question of law, viz., Whether a separate suit can be instituted for cancellation of a decree in another suit, by the persons, who figured as parties to such decree?, arises for consideration in this second appeal.

It is not uncommon that the suits are dismissed for default or decreed ex parte, depending on the non-appearance of the plaintiff or defendants, as the case may be. Order IX C.P.C. prescribes the nature of steps to be taken in this regard. While the plaintiffs are entitled to file applications for restoration of the suits, the defendants are conferred with the right to file applications to set aside the ex parte decrees. Further remedies in the form of appeals, or revisions, as the case may be, are provided against the orders allowing, or rejecting the applications filed under the said provisions. Alternatively, a defendant, who suffered an ex parte decree can prefer an appeal, without exhausting the remedy under Order IX C.P.C. Filing of a separate suit, for cancellation of an ex parte decree, by persons, who are parties to that very decree, is unknown to law. It is not only opposed to the provisions of C.P.C., but also to the public policy. Once persons, who figure as parties to the suit, or proceedings are conferred with the rights of filing applications, revisions, appeals or further appeals, they cannot be permitted to file a suit in respect of those very proceedings. If such a course is permitted, an independent suit can be filed for setting aside the decree, which acquired finality after the exhaustion of remedies of appeals, simply by raising the plea of fraud. Assuming that one of the parties played fraud in obtaining a decree, the same can be urged in the further remedies.

107. Section 100 – Suit for Declaration of Management Right on the Basis of a Will – The First Appellate Court Allowing the Suit on the Basis of Properietory Right – Can be Interfered

In *Matha Sunandananda Theertha* v. *Ch. Someswara Rao,* 2012 1 ALD 531: 2012 2 ALT 280 (AP) On a close reading of the judgment rendered by the lower appellate Court, disclosed that it was of the view that The Maharshi would have entertained the idea of executing a Will, if only he enjoyed the proprietary rights over the Ashram and its property. Neither the appellant nor the respondents expressed any doubt about the total control of the Ashram by The Maharshi. The lower appellate Court has totally misdirected itself in the very framing of the question, which does not at all arise for consideration. The assumption that The Maharshi could have entertained the idea of executing the Will, if only he felt that the Ashram is his exclusive property, is fallacious. Even while answering these points, the lower appellate Court was not consistent. For instance, while answering Point No.1, the lower appellate Court observed as under:

> "So Satyananda Masharshi treating a particular Ashramam as his exclusive property is not comprehensible. At the same time it can be said that Swamiji was certainly interested in effectively running of the Ashramams including the suit Ashramam even after his lifetime. Then Swamiji nominating some person to be at the helm of the affair of a particular Ashramam after the lifetime of Swamiji is neither unnatural nor violating the ascetic feelings of Swamiji. In fact D.W.2 was named by Swamiji as his successor and to be the president of Satyananda Ashramam after the lifetime of Swamiji by writing down that portion of the resolution in his own hand in the resolution dated 08.09.1985 contained pages at 134 and 135 of Ex.X1. In the same way Swamiji might have decided to name some person who is capable of managing the Ashramam as his successor for Visakhapatnam Ashramam also."

The High Court replied, "I therefore hold on this point that Satyananda Maharshi did not appear to have treated the Ashramam properties as his own property subject to transfer and passing on the legacy to anyone. At the same time, I hold that Swamiji was interested in effective running of the Ashramam and there is nothing to show that he did not think of choosing some one as his successor for effective management of the Ashramam though he was not directly involved in management of the suit Ashramam. His word of advice must have been considered by the managing committee as a command."

108. Appeal is Continuation of the Suit

The Court further said, An appeal is treated as continuation of a suit. No limits or fetters exist as to the scope of adjudication by an appellate Court. It can function as though it is a Court of first instance. It can scrutinize the pleadings, re-appreciate the evidence and arrive at its own conclusions without feeling any restrictions as to the scope of its power. However, it cannot widen or restrict the scope of the suit. The contours of adjudication, be it by the trial Court or by the lower appellate Court are determined by the pleadings of the parties. Once the parties have delivered the pleadings, the adjudication must be strictly with reference to them. Even where the arguments are advanced outside the scope of the pleadings, the adjudication must be restricted to the pleadings. In case any necessity arises to add to the pleadings, it is the look out of the parties and not that of the Court. Therefore, the first question framed by this Court is answered in favour of the appellant.

109. Where the Trial Court Raising Suspicious Circumstances

The lower appellate Court has indicated some other suspicious circumstances. One of it is that Ex.A1 is silent as to the activities undertaken by the Sangam. The relevant portion reads as under:

> "It is not under dispute that all the persons who are connected with the functioning of the Ashramam were not after any self-enriching activities and their intention is to serve the devotees and to offer prayers to the devotees. They have all long been exhibiting due respect to Swamiji. The words of Swamiji were taken as binding commands. In such case Swamiji would have mention the activities of the governing body and the part to be played by the plaintiff in connection with the affairs of the governing body in running the Ashram if he actually intended to bequeath the stewardship to the plaintiff. Ex.A1 is conspicuously silent as to the executive body or Viswa Viganana Sangam which was to carry on the activities of the suit Ashramam".

After this, the lower appellate Court pointed out one more circumstance, which according to it, would tell upon the un-naturality of Ex.A1. It reads as under:

> "Another glaring circumstance throwing doubt is the absence of succession after the lifetime of the plaintiff and the rights of the plaintiff as a legatee to nominate any other person to look after the Ashramam."

While dealing with the truth and legality of a Will, the Court not only has to insist that the document be proved as required under law, but also must be satisfied that there do not exist any suspicious circumstance. The first aspect is mostly dealt with by the provisions of the Evidence Act and hardly there would be any element of discretion. If a document is required to be proved in a particular manner and if such a proof is forthcoming, the Court has to take it as proved. The other aspect, however, is virtually unregulated. Hardly any objective guidelines exist to decide as to which factors can be treated as suspicious circumstances and which not, in respect of a Will. Much depends upon the nature and subject matter of disposition, the affinity between the testator on the one hand and the beneficiary under the Will, on the other.

One of the well-recognized suspicious circumstances is where the natural and legal descendants are excluded from the bequest. The others include the frail health condition of the testator or the probability of his not being in a position to take decisions on his own accord. If such grounds do not exist, it is not at all advisable for any Court to enter the area of speculation and multiply the grounds by letting its mind free to suspect and imagine every possible aspect. Human mind and intelligence is such that if it is given freedom to imagine as it likes, it may sometimes drift into a path, which has no destination at all. Such a tendency can be controlled if only the process of thinking is controlled by the factors such as objectivity, reason, logic and law.

The suspicion that was expressed by the lower appellate Court in the instant case vis-à-vis Ex.A1 was totally unguided, uncontrolled and meaningless. On the one hand, it did not doubt the control which The Maharshi had upon the Ashrams and his intention to nominate his successors and on the other hand, it suspected the genuinity of Ex.A1 on the ground that the Will did not reflect the prevailing state of affairs in the Ashram and that it did not provide for the succession after the appellant. In other words, it assumed to itself, that a Will must be comprehensive enough narrating the every possible detail prevailing as on the date of its execution and that it must provide for a scheme, for eternity. Such results emerge only when the Court deviates from the subject matter of the proceedings and the contours of adjudication thereof. This Court is of the view that the judgment rendered by the lower appellate Court cannot be sustained in law.

While parting with the judgment, the lower appellate Court expressed its concern over the administration of the Ashram. The concern may be genuine. However, it cannot be said that the management of the Ashram by the appellant would hamper its activities. Even when The Maharshi was alive, the Sangam played its own role and there is no reason why the role of the Sangam would in any way be restricted or confined on account of the appellant being in management. The effect of Ex.A1 would be that the appellant would act as a representative of The Maharshi and the activities would go on, as they used to be earlier.

Hence, the second appeal is allowed and the judgment and the decree passed by the lower appellate Court is set aside. The decree passed by the trial Court declaring that the appellant shall be entitled to manage the Ashram by virtue of Ex.A1 is upheld. So far as the relief of perpetual injunction is concerned, it is directed that the Sangam shall be entitled to undertake the same activities and discharge same functions as it did during the life time of The Maharshi. There shall be no order as to cost

110. Section 100 – Both the Courts Below Failing to Look into the Substantial Question of Law

In *Shri Raghuram Cut Pieces Cloth Shop* v. *Adilakshmi Textiles,* 2012 (2) ALD 12: 2012 (2) ALT 251 (AP) the High Court said, where both the courts below failed to consider the substantial question of law the second appellate court can interfere.

In the case under reference, the declaration prayed for by the plaintiff was that he is a statutory tenant. He did not mention the statute under which he is entitled to be declared as tenant. Assuming that he was referring to the A.P. Buildings (Lease, Rent and Eviction) Control Act, 1960 (for short 'the Act'), he did not state as to how he is entitled to be inducted into possession.

The Act regulates the rights of the tenants, on the one hand, and the owner of the property, on the other hand, in respect of certain category of buildings, depending on their location and the extent of land. Even if it is to be assumed that the suit schedule property is covered by the provisions of the Act, the plaintiff could have claimed any rights vis-à-vis the property, if only he was in possession thereof. Admittedly, he was not in possession of the property. The Act does not contain any provision, which directs that a tenant covered by its provisions is entitled to be re-inducted into possession, in case he was wrongfully evicted. Unless such a provision exists, the question of the plaintiff being re-inducted into possession, does not arise.

Here, it is necessary to take note of provisions of certain enactments, which provide for such facility. For instance, the A.P. (Telangana Area) Tenancy and Agricultural Lands Act, 1950 (for short 'the Tenancy Act), mandates that if a protected tenant is dispossessed from the land in question, he is entitled to be put back in possession in case proceedings under Section 32 of the Tenancy Act are initiated. No such provision is contained in the Act. Therefore, the whole basis on which the suit was instituted, was untenable and there was no justification on the part of the trial Court to decree the suit or for the lower Appellate Court in dismissing the appeal. This important aspect was not taken into account.

Therefore, the Second Appeal is allowed by answering the substantial question of law mentioned above, viz., "Whether in the absence of any specific provision of law, a plaintiff in a suit can seek the relief of re-induction into possession of a property, as regards which, he has no title?", in the negative. When the relief of even perpetual injunction cannot be granted against a true owner, the question of passing a decree to dispossess him, does not arise. The decree passed by the trial Court and the one passed by the lower Appellate Court upholding the decree of the trial Court, are set aside.

111. Section 100 – Suit for Specific Performance of Contract – Escalation in Price cannot be a Defence

In *Smt. Chama Radamma* v. *Sri Chama Venu Gopal Reddy*, 2012 (3) ALD 690: 2012 (4) ALT 384: 2012 (3) CivCC 751 (AP) the plaintiff prayed for specific performance of a contract. Considering the evidence of PW.1 coupled with Exs.A.1 to A.11 and also considering the evidence of DW.1 coupled with Exs.B.1 toB.3, the trial Court dismissed the suit holding that the plaintiffs are not entitled to claim specific performance of an agreement of sale dated 2.10.1997 and that the said agreement is not binding on defendant Nos. 2 to 5. The unsuccessful plaintiffs, carried the matter in appeal in A.S. No. 215/2006 on the file of the Court of IV Additional District Judge, Ranga Reddy District and the said first appellate Court after hearing both sides and after re-appreciating the evidence, answered two points framed by it against the plaintiffs and thereby dismissed the appeal suit. Aggrieved thereby, the plaintiffs filed this Second Appeal.

It was contended that the plaintiffs are not entitled to the relief of specific performance which is discretionary owing to the conduct of Sri Chama Narsimha Reddy during his life time and the conduct of the plaintiffs thereafter. However, it is the plea of the plaintiffs all along that their final performance depended on the terms of the Ex.A1 particularly Clauses 3 and 8 of Ex.A.1 which are to the effect that the Vendor had to obtain encumbrance certificate for 13 years preceding the date of sale at his costs and also paying property tax etc and to execute sale deed within one year from the date of recording the names of the vendors in revenue records. Defendants submit that it is not known for what reasons and why the term in Ex.A.1 is included that the vendor had to get his name recorded in the revenue records before execution of sale deed, when the contention of the defendants is that the suit schedule property is their ancestral property and their names already recorded in the revenue records.

In reply to the contentions of the defendants, the plaintiffs would submit that since in Ex.A5 reply notice, the name of perspective buyer Sri K Prabhakar Reddy was not mentioned, therefore, his name was not included in the array of defendants. That non-mentioning the name of the buyer in Ex.A.5 reply notice as well as the date of the agreement alleged to have been executed in favour of the prospective buyer K. Prabhakar Reddy and mentioning his name for the first time in the written statement creates a doubt about the conduct of the defendants. It is possible that it was a sort of manipulation to see that the rights arising out of Ex.A.1 are frustrated. DW.1 has admitted in his cross examination that the dates of Exs.B.1 to B.3 (notice from prospective buyer, reply thereto and postal receipt) are not mentioned in the written statement filed by them. Therefore, it is contended that had Exs.B.1 to B.3 were in their possession, they would have disclosed the same in the written statement. These documents appear to have been brought in to existence to frustrate the plaintiffs' claim. A perusal of Ex.B.1 discloses that it is undated and it does not disclose that through which channel it has reached the defendants either by hand delivery or through postal delivery. DW.1 has admitted in his cross examination that they received Ex.B.1 in the year 2004 and gave reply under Ex.B.1. However, in Ex.B.2, the date is mentioned as 20.12.2000. It appears that the defendants were bent upon manufacturing false documents with aid and help of the prospective buyer in order to frustrate the claim of the plaintiffs. Therefore, it is contended on behalf of the plaintiffs that the conduct of the defendants is at stake. As such, they are not entitled to question the right of the plaintiffs to claim the specific relief which is a discretionary relief in law. So far as the alleged incapacity of the plaintiffs is concerned, the defendants never questioned their capacity in the proceedings before the courts below. It is a fact that they are residents of same village and that too own substantial properties, both landed and otherwise and they have abundant capacity to pay the balance amount of consideration under Ex.A.1. Moreover, their capacity cannot be questioned in view of their depositing the balance consideration of Rs.3,00,000/-into the Court when they were directed to do so by the trial Court. It also goes to show that they were solvent enough to meet the situation. So far as Clauses 3 and 8, as contained in Ex.A1 are concerned, it is for the parties to incorporate such covenants and honour the same. Once they are incorporated they are binding on the parties thereto and the validity thereof cannot be questioned now. The question of time being the essence of the contract is concerned, once it is admitted that agreement was orally cancelled, in the absence of reference to any particular date, it is to be inferred that the time stipulated becomes unconfined, whereupon the onus lies on the defendants to show that they terminated Ex.A.1 lawfully. That it is the case of the plaintiffs throughout that they were ready and willing to perform their part of contract and as such, they are protected by the provisions of Section 16 (c) of the Act as well as the explanation thereto. From the above facts and circumstances, what emerge is that both the Courts below appears to have committed error in coming to the conclusion that the plaintiffs are not entitled for specific performance of Ex.A1-agreement of sale.

It is the contention of the defendants that their father-defendant No.1 cancelled Ex.A-1 agreement of sale orally. But the same was not corroborated by examining an independent witness. Further, no prescribed procedure is followed and/or steps were taken to cancel Ex.A.1. The defendants nowhere in the proceedings have stated the date of cancellation of Ex.A.1 by defendant No.1. It appears, the trial Court as well as the first appellate Court considering the relationship between the parties and hospitalisation and death of Sri Chama Narsimha Reddy, believed that the said agreement of sale could be cancelled. The termination of Ex.A.1 is not in accordance with law. The material on record does not disclose that Sri Chama Narsimha Reddy failed to perform his contract and that he had requested to cancel the agreement, except self-serving statement of defendant No.1 in reply notice as well as in the written statement. It is more so in the light of nothing being said in Ex.A.5 about the advance payment of sale consideration of Rs.1,00,000 paid to defendant No.1 by deceased Sri Chama Narsimha Reddy under the agreement of sale. It is settled proposition of law that escalation of real estate price is not a ground to deny the specific relief.

So far as readiness, willingness and capacity of the plaintiffs are concerned, this Court, having regard to the facts and circumstances of the case, is of the view that the plaintiffs are ever ready and willing to perform their part of contract and that they have capacity to pay the balance sale consideration particularly having regard to the fact that they have deposited balance sale consideration of Rs.3,00,000/-into the Court.

The defendants relied on the following decisions of the Supreme Court:

J.P. Builders v. *A.Ramadas Rao,* (2011) 1 SCC 429: 2010 (12) SCALE 400, *Coromandel Indag Products Private Limited* v. *Garuda Chit, Trading Company Private Limited,* (2011) 8 SCC 601: (2011) 8 MLJ 112 (SC) and *Janak Dulari Devi* v. *Kapildeo Rai,* (2011) 6 SCC 555: AIR 2011 SC 2521, in support of their contention that the plaintiffs are not ready and willing to perform their part of contract. *Parakunnan Veetill Joseph's Son Mathew* v. *Nedumbara Kuruvila's Son,* AIR 1987 SC 2328: 1987 (13) ALR 676, wherein it was held while exercising discretion the Court should meticulously consider the facts and circumstances of the case. *Dinesh Kumar* v. *Yusuf Ali,* (2010) 12 SCC 740: AIR 2010 SC 2679, wherein it was held that Second Appeal is maintainable on a substantial question of law and not on facts. *Municipal Committee Hoshiarpur* v. *Punjab State Board,* (2010) 13 SCC 216: 2010 (4) RCR (Civil) 859, wherein it was held that Second Appeal cannot be decided merely on equitable grounds.

In view of the above reasons, having regard to the material available on record, the questions raised by the plaintiffs are substantial questions of law and they are proved and that this Court is of the view that the Courts below have committed error in deciding the suit and the first appeal in favour of the defendants. Therefore, the judgment and decree dated 26.09.2011 in A.S.No.215 of 2006 and the judgment and decree dated 31.07.2006 in O.S.No.196 of 2000 of the first appellate Court and the trail Court respectively are set-aside and thereby O.S.No.196 of 2000 stands decreed.

Accordingly, the Second Appeal was admitted and the same is allowed. There shall be no order as to costs.

112. Section 100 – Plea of *bonafide* Purchase for Value without Knowledge of Earlier Contract

In *A.S. Pachhapure* v. *Venkataswamya Reddy*, 2013 3 CivCC 664: 2012 6 KarLJ 174: 2012 (3) KCCR 2429 (Kar) The 1st respondent herein instituted the suit for specific performance of the contract of Sale Agreement, dated 21.12.2000, executed by respondent Nos.2 and 3 herein [defendant Nos.1 and 2 before the trial Court], agreeing to sell the suit property bearing Sy. No. 36/3, measuring 1 acre 61/2 guntas out of 2 acres and 13 guntas, fully described in the schedule to the plaint for a consideration of Rs. 2,23,200-00. Though the plaintiff was ready and willing to perform his part of the contract, defendant Nos.1 and 2 did not execute the Sale Deed and therefore, the plaintiff instituted the suit seeking specific performance.

Though defendant No.1 admitted the Agreement of Sale, the 2nd defendant denied the same and filed a written statement. During pendency of the suit, the 3rd defendant i.e., the appellant herein was impleaded and it is his contention that defendant Nos.1 and 2 executed a Sale Deed in respect of the suit property in his favour on 23.06.2001. Therefore, he contended that he is the bona fide purchaser of the suit property, being unaware of any transaction of Agreement of Sale in between the plaintiff and defendant Nos.1 and 2. The suit came to be decreed by the trial Court granting the relief of specific performance of the contract.

Admittedly, the suit came to be instituted by the plaintiff on 16.06.2001. The Sale Deed executed in favour of the appellant by defendant Nos. 1 and 2 was on 23.06.2001. To mean, the said Sale Deed was executed after institution of the suit. As could be seen from the provisions of Section 52 of the Transfer of Property Act, 1882 [hereinafter called as "the T.P. Act" for short] during pendency of a suit or proceeding, which is not collusive and in which any right to movable property is directly and specifically in question, the property cannot be transferred or otherwise dealt with by any party to the suit or proceeding so as to affect the right of any other party thereto under the decree or order, which may be made therein, except under the authority of the Court and on such terms as it may impose. Admittedly, the permission of the Court was not obtained by the 3rd defendant to get a Sale Deed executed in his favour from defendant Nos. 1 and 2. Further, the suit is not collusive. Therefore, the Sale Deed executed would hit by principle of *lis-pendens*. Whatever transfer that is made during pendency of the suit is subject to result of the suit. So, when the plaintiff succeeded in getting a decree for specific performance of the contract against defendant Nos. 1 and 2, the 3rd defendant had no right, authority or competency to get a Sale Deed executed in his favour, as the said property was subject matter of the suit. Therefore, there is no necessity for the plaintiff to seek any relief for setting aside the Sale Deed or any direction to the 3rd defendant to execute the Sale Deed as the said Sale Deed is invalid, unenforceable, in view of Section 52 of the T.P. Act. In such circumstances, I am of the opinion that there is no error or illegality in the Orders of the Courts below, granting a decree for specific performance and it is also not necessity for the plaintiff to seek any relief either a declaration or an order to set aside the Sale Deed executed by defendant Nos.1 and 2 in favour of defendant No.3. The appellant at the most may take action against defendant Nos.1 and 2 for refund of sale consideration or compensation and the remedy for him is elsewhere. In that view of the matter, I answer the substantial question of law in negative and proceed to pass the the order that the appeal is dismissed.

113. Section 100 – Scope of Interference with Findings of Fact under Section 100 CPC is Limited

In *Bommanayaka* v. *Bommanayaka,* 2013 (3) AIR (Kar) (R) 299: 2013 (2) Kar LJ 114: 2012 (3) KCCR 2175 (Kar) the High Court said, scope of interference with findings of fact while exercising jurisdiction under Section 100 CPC is limited. Re-appreciation of evidence is not permissible, except where the Courts below misdirected themselves in appreciating the question of law or placed the onus on the wrong party. Where the facts required for a point of law have not been pleaded, a litigant cannot be allowed to raise that question as substantial question of law in a second appeal. Appreciation of record of the case in a judicial manner is well within the jurisdiction of the Trial and the First Appellate Courts. Interference with the findings is permissible in cases where the Courts have, (i) ignored material evidence or acted on no evidence; (ii) drawn wrong inferences from proved facts by applying the law erroneously; or (iii) wrongly cast the burden of proof.

Ex.D1 is the sale deed of the suit property executed by the plaintiff in favour of Smt. Lingamma, mother of defendants 1 to 4. Said document has been marked in the cross-examination of the plaintiff – PW1. PW1 has admitted that Ex.D1 was executed by him in favour of the mother of defendants 1 to 4 in respect of the suit vacant site. He has identified the signatures of the scribe and the attestors to the said document. That apart, he has admitted that he gave the instructions to draft the said document. In view of Ex.D1, the sale deed of the suit property, executed by the appellant/plaintiff in favour of Smt. Lingamma, mother of defendants 1 to 4, the sale of suit property by the plaintiff has stood proved.

The plaint does not contain any plea relating to adverse possession. The contention that the plaintiff being in continuous possession and enjoyment of the suit property, even after the execution of Ex.D1, there is perfection of right by way of adverse possession is not well founded. Having sold the property under Ex.D1, the plaintiff, if had remained in the possession of the property, ought to have pleaded and proved, assertion of his independent hostile adverse possession to the knowledge of the purchaser or her successors in title or interest and they having acquiesced to his illegal possession during the entire period of 12 years. To establish a claim of title by prescription, the possession of the claimant must be actual, exclusive, open, uninterrupted, notorious and hostile to the true owner for a period exceeding 12 years. Continuous possession by itself would not constitute adverse possession, if it was without *animus possidendi*. Unless the person possessing the property has the requisite animus to possess a property hostile to the true owner, the period for prescription will not commence, as has been held, in catena of decisions of the Apex Court. As already noticed, there is neither pleading nor any proof with regard to the claim of acquisition of title by prescription. Therefore, the contention of Sri Patel D. Karegowda, that plea of adverse possession is not available to the plaintiff is well founded.

The defendants 1 and 2 have made out a clear and absolute title to the property in view of its sale by the plaintiff in favour of their mother. The suit property being a vacant site, in view of Ex.D1, the sale deed executed by the plaintiff in favour of Smt. Lingamma, the legal doctrine 'possession follows title' applies. The plaintiff has not been able to make out title by adverse possession for more than 12 years. Since the plaintiff has failed to plead and prove adverse possession, the First Appellate Court is justified in allowing the counter-claim of the defendants 1 and 2 and dismissing the suit filed by the plaintiff.

There is correct appreciation of record of the case by the First Appellate Court. The findings recorded by the First Appellate Court on the material aspects of the matter are neither perverse nor illegal. The material evidence has been appreciated in the correct perspective. The First Appellate Court has neither omitted from consideration any material evidence nor is there any misreading of the evidence, much less wrong placing of the burden of proof. The findings recorded are pure finding on facts, with which, there cannot be interference in exercise of the jurisdiction under Section 100 CPC.

In the circumstances, the impugned Judgment has not given rise to any substantial question of law. Consequently, the second appeals being not maintainable, shall stand rejected with no order as to cost

114. Section 100 – The Appellant Intended to Place Substantial Question of Law in Place of the Questions Already Framed at the Time of Placing the Memorandum

In *Saraswati Bhagat* v. *Khurdula Sivakoti (Died) per L.Rs.*, 2016 (4) ALT 110 (AP) at the time of admission of this appeal, the grounds nos.4 to 11 mentioned in the memorandum of grounds of appeal were taken note of. However, the learned counsel for the appellant had stated at the time of hearing that the questions already formulated need not be considered and that they may be eschewed from consideration and that in the place of the said questions, the substantial questions, which are involved, may be reframed. Accordingly and as desired, the questions earlier framed are deleted. After hearing the learned counsel for both the sides, the following substantial questions of law were formulated by this Court.

The learned counsel for the appellant had contended as follows:

> The evidence brought on record shows that Eswaramma and Salamma are the wives of Sivalingam. The suit property was purchased in the name of K. Salamma in the year 1955. Even if it is admitted that the

said transaction is a benami transaction, Eswaramma and Salamma are co-sharers of the property. Hence, Eswaramma cannot claim adverse possession against a co-sharer. She was in permissive possession. If the transaction under the sale deed in favour of Salamma is to be treated as a benami transaction, after the death of Sivalingam the property stood devolved upon Salamma and Eswaramma being his two wives and hence, Eswaramma alone cannot be declared to be the owner of the property by adverse possession. DW1 deposed that elders decided to provide a house to his mother for residence. His statement goes to show that his possession is permissive possession. Permissive possession can never become adverse to the rightful owners. The Courts below had ignored the findings given in the maintenance proceedings filed by the sole defendant (since died) and his mother-Eswaramma against Sivalingam. The suit schedule property, according to the version of the sole defendant, was given towards maintenance of Eswaramma for her life time. The Courts gave much importance to status quo orders ignoring the fact that the status quo orders were granted in the other suit which is a mere suit for injunction. There was no order passed prohibiting Salamma from alienating the property. The Courts below had failed to see that entries in revenue records do not confer title. Exhibit A15- assessment register of the Municipal Corporation would show that the property was mutated in the name of the plaintiff/appellant herein. The courts below ought to have seen that in the suit-OS.2070 of 1987 it was admitted that the suit schedule property was purchased by Salamma in the year 1955 and that she is the second wife of Sivalingam. The courts below ought to have seen that earlier the suit-OS.2068 of 1989 (old 3413 of 1986) was filed and that therefore the later suit-OS.2070 of 1987 is not maintainable on the same cause of action. It is not imperative for a landlord to rush to a court and seek declaration of title to the property when the tenant denies title. Proof of ownership is sufficient. The title of Salamma, the original owner is not disputed. The sale deed executed by Salamma in favour of Sharada and the sale deed executed by Sharada in favour of the plaintiff herein are valid. The courts below ought to have seen that mere payment of property tax does not confer title. The courts below had failed to appreciate that even assuming that Sivalingam had purchased the property in the name of his wife Salamma, she became absolute owner and such a transaction cannot be said to be benami transaction as there is a contribution of the wife to the earnings of the husband. The courts below had erroneously considered the title deed of the plaintiff as invalid as it was obtained in spite of the existence of a prohibitory order.

On the other hand, the learned senior counsel for the respondents/plaintiffs having supported the concurrent findings in the judgments of the courts below had stated as follows:

None of the questions raised are pure questions of law; and they are only a blend of facts and law; and no substantial questions of law are involved. Hence, there is no necessity to interfere with the decrees and judgments of the courts below which are rendered after recording concurrent findings supported by cogent and valid reasons. The findings in the maintenance order of the criminal court are not binding on the civil court as rightly held by the Courts below.

It is relevant to refer to the decision in *Gurudwara Sahib* v. *Gram Panchayat Village Sirthala*, (2014) 1 SCC 669: 2014 (2) ALD 3. In this cited decision the facts are as follows:

> "The Appellant is the original Plaintiff. It had filed the suit for decree of declaration to the effect that it had become owner of the suit property by adverse possession. Declaration was also sought to the effect that the Revenue record showing ownership of Respondent No. 1 herein i.e. Gram Panchayat (Defendant in the suit) is liable to be corrected in the name of the Appellant and the auction already held by the Gram Panchayat of the land in dispute is null and void. Consequential relief of permanent injunction restraining Gram Panchayat from dispossessing the Appellant from the disputed land was also prayed for. This suit was partly decreed by the trial court granting relief of injunction. First Appeal against that part of the judgment whereby relief of declaration was denied was dismissed by the learned Additional District Judge and the Second Appeal preferred by the Appellant has also been dismissed by the High Court of Punjab and Haryana vide judgment dated 22nd September 2011. The Appellant had, therefore, filed a civil appeal before the Supreme Court with the plea that its suit be decreed in entirety and had claimed ownership by adverse possession on the ground that it is in possession of the land in dispute for sufficiently long period which fact has been established and, therefore, its suit could not be dismissed."

In the above factual back drop, the Supreme Court held as follows:

> "There cannot be any quarrel to this extent that the judgments of the courts below are correct and without any blemish. Even if the Plaintiff is found to be in adverse possession, it cannot seek a declaration to the effect that such adverse possession has matured into ownership. Only if proceedings are filed against the Appellant and the Appellant is arrayed as Defendant that it can use this adverse possession as a shield/ defence."

In view of this settled legal position and since it was found that the 1st defendant-Sivakoti and his mother-Eswaramma had perfected title by adverse possession and as this suit is filed by the plaintiff against the 1st defendant-Sivakoti (since died) and his legal representatives, the claim of adverse possession can be used by them as a shield or defence to successfully contend that the plaintiff herein is not entitled to evict them from the suit schedule property, since the plaintiff herein had not acquired any title to the property, she being a purchaser from Sharada, who in her turn had not acquired valid title while obtaining a sale deed in the year 1986 from Salamma.

I have carefully gone through the pleadings and analytically examined the evidence in this case. Having regard to the facts and the evidence and the reasons assigned, this Court finds that the plaintiff herein is not entitled to seek either declaration of title or recovery of possession of the schedule house property from the defendants as they had perfected title by adverse possession being the legal heirs of deceased 1st defendant-Sivakoti.

115. Section 100 – Second Appeal – Trial Court and First Appellate Court Returning Concurrent Finding of Fact

In *Laxmidevamma* v. *Ranganath,* 2015 Supp AIR (SC) 602: 2015 1 BBCJ (SC) 534: 2015 (2) CivCC 793: 2015 2 JT 228, the Apex Court held, High Court, in second appeal, cannot reverse concurrent finding of fact by trial court and first appellate court.

Based upon oral and documentary evidences, the courts below recorded concurrent findings that the plaintiffs are the owners of 'A' schedule property. While so, the High Court ignoring the material evidence, erred in interfering with the concurrent findings of fact. While holding that 'A' schedule property has been left for the road and that plaintiffs cannot seek declaration of title, in our considered view, the High Court brushed aside the oral and documentary evidence based on which the courts below recorded concurrent findings of fact that 'A' schedule property though earmarked for road, the same was not formed and that plaintiffs established their right in the 'A' schedule property.

Based on oral and documentary evidence, both the courts below have recorded concurrent findings of fact that plaintiffs have established their right in 'A' schedule property. In the light of concurrent findings of fact, no substantial questions of law arose in the High Court and there was no substantial ground for re-appreciation of evidence. While so, the High Court proceeded to observe that the first plaintiff has earmarked the 'A' schedule property for road and that she could not have full-fledged right and on that premise proceeded to hold that declaration to plaintiffs' right cannot be granted. In exercise of jurisdiction under Section 100 C.P.C., concurrent findings of fact cannot be upset by the High Court unless the findings so recorded are shown to be perverse. In our considered view, the High Court did not keep in view that the concurrent findings recorded by the courts below, are based on oral and documentary evidence and the judgment of the High Court cannot be sustained.

In the result, the appeal is allowed, impugned judgment in R.S.A. No. 297/2007 dated 27.9.2012 passed by the High Court of Karnataka is set aside and the judgment passed by the Addl. Civil Judge (Jr. Divn.), Chikmagalur as confirmed by the lower appellate court is restored. Parties are left to bear their own costs.

116. Section 100 – Civil Procedure Code, Order XLI, Rule 5 (3) – Second Appeal

In *Raghavendra Swamy Mutt* v. *Uttaradi Mutt,* 2016 (161) AIC 265: 2016 AIR (SCW) 1589: 2016 (3) JT 420: 2016 (3) SCALE 514 (SC) the Apex Court examined the scope of second appeal under section 100 CPC before the High Court. The Apex Court said, a plain reading of Section 100 CPC makes it explicit that the High Court can entertain a second appeal if it is satisfied that the appeal involves a substantial question of law. More than a decade and a half back, in *Ishwar Dass Jain* v. *Sohan Lal,* 1999 (2) RCR (Rent) 714: 2000 (1) RCR (Civil) 168: (2000) 1

SCC 434, it has been ruled that after the 1976 Amendment, it is essential for the High Court to formulate a substantial question of law and it is not permissible to reverse the judgment of the first appellate court without doing so.

In *Roop Singh* v. *Ram Singh*, 2000 (1) RCR (Rent) 427: 2000 (2) RCR (Civil) 592: (2000) 3 SCC 708 the Court had to say thus:—

> "It is to be reiterated that under Section 100 CPC jurisdiction of the High Court to entertain a second appeal is confined only to such appeals which involve a substantial question of law and it does not confer any jurisdiction on the High Court to interfere with pure questions of fact while exercising its jurisdiction under Section 100 CPC."

In *Municipal Committee, Hoshiarpur* v. *Punjab SEB*, 2010 (4) RCR (Civil) 859: 2010 (6) Recent Apex Judgments (RAJ) 175: (2010) 13 SCC 216 it has been categorically laid down that the existence of a substantial question of law is a condition precedent for entertaining the second appeal and on failure to do so, the judgment rendered by the High Court is unsustainable. It has been clearly stated that existence of a substantial question of law is the sine qua non for the exercise of jurisdiction under the provisions of Section 100 CPC.

In *Umerkhan* v. *Bismillabi alias Babulal Shaikh*, 2011 (3) RCR (Civil) 872: 2011 (4) Recent Apex Judgments (RAJ) 312: (2011) 9 SCC 684 a two-Judge Bench was constrained to ingeminate the legal position thus:—

> "In our view, the very jurisdiction of the High Court in hearing a second appeal is founded on the formulation of a substantial question of law. The judgment of the High Court is rendered patently illegal, if a second appeal is heard and judgment and decree appealed against is reversed without formulating a substantial question of law. The second appellate jurisdiction of the High Court under Section 100 is not akin to the appellate jurisdiction under Section 96 of the Code; it is restricted to such substantial question or questions of law that may arise from the judgment and decree appealed against. As a matter of law, a second appeal is entertain able by the High Court only upon its satisfaction that a substantial question of law is involved in the matter and its formulation thereof. Section 100 of the Code provides that the second appeal shall be heard on the question so formulated. It is, however, open to the High Court to reframe substantial question of law or frame substantial question of law afresh or hold that no substantial question of law is involved at the time of hearing the second appeal but reversal of the judgment and decree passed in appeal by a court subordinate to it in exercise of jurisdiction under Section 100 of the Code is impermissible without formulating substantial question of law and a decision on such question."

The Court pointed out that The High Court can entertain a second appeal if it is satisfied that the appeal involves a substantial question of law:

1. After the 1976 Amendment, it is essential for the High Court to formulate a substantial question of law and it is not permissible to reverse the judgment of the first appellate court without doing so - 2000 (1) SCC 434 Relied.

2. High Court has no jurisdiction to interfere with pure questions of fact while exercising its jurisdiction under Section 100 CPC - 2000 (2) RCR (Civil) 592: 2000 (1) RCR (Rent) 427 Relied.

3. When appeal is admitted on substantial question of law and question of law is framed it is open to the High Court to reframe substantial question of law or frame substantial question of law afresh or hold that no substantial question of law is involved at the time of hearing the second appeal

In the instant case, the High Court has not yet admitted the matter. It is not in dispute that no substantial question of law has been formulated as it could not have been when the appeal has not been admitted. We say so, as appeal under Section 100 CPC is required to be admitted only on substantial question/ questions of law. It cannot be formal admission like an appeal under Section 96 CPC. That is the fundamental imperative. It is peremptory in character, and that makes the principle absolutely cardinal. The issue that arises for consideration is; whether the High Court without admitting the second appeal could have entertained IA No. 1/2015 which was filed seeking interim relief. In Ram Phal (supra), from which Mr. Nariman, learned senior counsel has drawn immense inspiration, the two-Judge Bench was dealing with a case where the High Court had granted an interim order by staying the execution of the decree but had not framed the substantial question of law. In that context, the Court held:

> "... However, the High Court granted interim order by staying the execution of the decree. It is against the said order granting interim relief the respondent in the second appeal has preferred this appeal. This Court, on a number of occasions, has repeatedly held that the High Court acquires jurisdiction to decide the second appeal or deal with the second appeal on merits only when it frames a substantial question of law as required to be framed under Section 100 of the Civil Procedure Code. In the present case, what we find is that the High Court granted interim order and thereafter fixed the matter for framing of question of law on a subsequent date. This was not the way to deal with the matter as contemplated under Section 100 CPC. The High Court is required to frame the question of law first and thereafter deal with the matter. Since the High Court dealt with the matter contrary to the mandate enshrined under Section 100 CPC, the impugned order deserves to be set aside."

Submission of the learned senior counsel for the appellant is that Order XLI, Rule 5 confers jurisdiction on the High Court while dealing with an appeal under Section 100 CPC to pass an ex parte order and such an order can be passed deferring formulation of question of law in grave situations. Be it stated, for passing an ex parte order the Court has to keep in mind the postulates provided under sub-rule (3) of Rule 5 Order XLI. It has to be made clear that the Court for the purpose of passing an ex parte order is obligated to keep in view the language employed under Section 100 CPC. It is because formulation of substantial question of law enables the High Court to entertain an appeal and thereafter proceed to pass an order and at that juncture, needless to say, the Court has the jurisdiction to pass an interim order subject to the language employed in Order XLI, Rule 5 (3). It is clear as day that the High Court cannot admit a second appeal without examining whether it raises any substantial question of law for admission and thereafter, it is obliged to formulate the substantial question of law. Solely because the Court has the jurisdiction to pass an ex parte order, it does not empower it not to formulate the substantial question of law for the purpose of admission, defer the date of admission and pass an order of stay or grant an interim relief. That is not the scheme of CPC after its amendment in 1976 and that is not the tenor of precedents of this Court and it has been clearly so stated in *Ram Phal (supra)*. Therefore, the High Court has rectified its mistake by vacating the order passed in IA No. 1/2015 and it is the correct approach adopted by the High Court. Thus, the impugned order is absolutely impregnable

117. Section 100 – Specific Relief Act, 1963 Section 34 – Suit for Declaration on Basis of Lay Out Plan

In *Girdhari Lal* v. *Gurbhachan Singh*, 2017 (2) AD Del 34 (Del) the first Appellate Court re-appreciated the entire evidence as well the lay out plan and held that the opening of door and window towards Southern side appears to be at the time when there was open space in Southern direction of the property of the plaintiff. This does not prove existence of any road towards South of his property. Learned First Appellate Court has also examined the directions recorded in the Sale Deeds when the two plots were purchased by the appellant/ plaintiff from two different persons. There was no mention of existence of any 4 mtr. wide road on the South side of the said property. The First Appellate Court has affirmed the finding of the learned Trial Court that there was no road towards the South side of the property of the appellant/plaintiff.

14. Before this Court the grievance of the appellant/plaintiff is based only on the lay out plan and submit that the lay out plan could not have been contrary to the existing situation. However, he does not dispute that Virender Nagar was unauthorised colony which was regularized subsequently. The fact that even the plaintiff has given one number i.e. 79E to his property which in fact consists of two separate plots purchased from two different persons. The manner in which part of the plot has been sold by Smt.Surinder Kaur to two separate persons Sh.Gurpreet and Sh.Inder Mohan Singh is an example in which the properties are sold and assigned numbers.

Reliance placed by learned counsel for the appellant on the decision of this Court in *East Pakistan D.P. Association* v. *Municipal Corporation of Delhi,* 1995 RLR 505, has absolutely no applicability to this case for the reason the issue involved in that writ petition was alleged misuse of the zonal park in the colony known as Chitranjan Park. But the MCD was proposing to use for teh bazari business and the proposal was contrary to the zonal plan. Herein the instant case no such issue is involved.

The High Court held, the general rule is that the Second Appeal cannot be entertained on the issues of facts. High Court cannot disturb the finding of fact given by the Courts below, nor an appeal can be admitted unless a case is made out under Section 100 CPC and a substantial question of law is raised in the memorandum of appeal. The settled position in this regard is that the High Court should not interfere with the concurrent findings of the facts. After the amendment in the year 1976, scope of Section 100 CPC has been further curtailed. The Second Appellant Court has the jurisdiction to interfere under Section 100 CPC only where substantial question of law is involved.

In my considered opinion the arguments raised by the learned counsel for the appellant are misconceived inasmuch as if there was a 4 mtr. wide road on the South side of the property of the appellant/plaintiff, it should have been clearly so depicted not only in the two sale deeds vide which he purchased the property but MCD in the written statement would have taken this plea.

118. Section 100 – Second Appeal – Transfer of Property Act, 1882 Section 107 Registration Act, 1908 Section 17(i)(d) – Order II, Rule 2 – Pleadings

In *International Institute of Neuro Sciences & Oncology Ltd.* v. *Sahibjit Singh Sandhu*, 2017 (1) PCR (Rent) 632: 2017 (3) PCR (Civil) 554: 2017 (3) PCR 51 (P&H) the Punjab High Court said, as per provisions of Section 100 CPC, in the second appeal, it is not permissible for the High Court to interfere with the concurrent findings of fact recorded by the learned Court below except in two situations. The first is that when material or relevant evidence is not considered which if considered would have led to an opposite conclusion. The second situation is where a findings has been arrived at by the learned Lower Appellate Court by placing reliance on inadmissible evidence which if it was omitted, would have led to the opposite conclusion. The second appeal is also maintainable where the findings recorded by the learned Courts below are perverse or that the factual findings are based on no evidence. Keeping in view the aforesaid principles of law, we have to examine the case in hand.

As per the case of the plaintiffs-respondents, the demised premises were let out to the appellants-defendants vide lease deed dated 20.09.1996 for a period of four and half years commencing from 01.08.1996 to 31.01.2001. It was also the case of the plaintiffs-respondents that the initial rate of rent was L 1,95,000/- per month w.e.f. 01.08.1996 to 31.07.1997 and thereafter, the rate of rent was to be enhanced every year on 1st August by 7 = % of the monthly rent payable during the immediate preceeding year. The plaintiffs-respondents have alleged that the tenancy of the appellants was terminated vide notice dated 17.11.2000 Ex.PW6/33.

However, in the written statement, appellants-defendants have pleaded that they were never inducted as tenants on the terms and conditions mentioned in the alleged lease deed dated 20.09.1996. The possession of the demised premises was handed over to them on 01.09.1996 when the terms and conditions of tenancy were settled orally by the parties and the rate of rent was settled to be L 1,95,000/- without any enhancement.

There is absolutely no dispute with the proposition of law that as per Section 107 of the T.P. Act, a lease of immovable property from year to year or for any term exceeding one year can be made only by a registered instrument. Same is the requirement of Section 17 (1)(d) of the Indian Registration Act. Admittedly, in the present case, the lease deed dated 20.09.1996 is unregistered document. So, the said unregistered lease deed cannot be taken into consideration with respect to the terms and conditions of the lease. It can only be used for the collateral purposes. The terms and conditions of the lease are the main purpose of the contract of lease. Thus, as the lease deed dated 20.09.1996 is unregistered document, which cannot be taken into consideration so, the lease of the demised premises shall be the lease from month to month.

Considering the question of eviction the Court said, in order the ascertain the reasons for termination of tenancy, we have to take into consideration the notice of termination of tenancy Ex.PW6/33 in addition to the averments of the plaint. It has been repeatedly mentioned in the plaint that the tenancy of the appellants has been terminated vide notice dated 17.11.2000 (copy Ex.PW6/33). The perusal of the notice dated 17.11.2000 depicts that the tenancy has been terminated not only on the ground that the appellants were in arrears of rent, but it is also mentioned that the appellants have not proved to be good tenants. If, the tenants do not prove to be good tenants that can also be a valid ground for termination of tenancy. As per the direction given in the notice dated 17.11.2000, tenancy of the appellants stood terminated after the expiry of period of three months. The period of three months will complete on 17.02.2001. As per the case of the plaintiffs, the period of tenancy was w.e.f. 01.08.1996 to 31.01.2001. The present suit has been filed on 09.04.2001 when the period of tenancy had already expired. As already discussed in detail in the upper portion of the judgment, the appellants have not been able to establish the extension of the period of tenancy. So, when the present suit was filed the tenancy of the appellants had already come to an end. In that situation, even the filing of the suit itself is a notice regarding the termination of tenancy. The Hon'ble Apex Court in case *Nopany Investiments (P) Ltd. Santokh Singh (HUF) (supra)* has laid down as under:-

> "In any view of the matter, it is well settled that filing of an eviction suit under the general law itself is a notice to quit on the tenant. Therefore, we have no hesitation to hold that no notice to quit was necessary under Section 106 of the Transfer of Property Act in order to enable the respondent to get a decree of eviction against the appellant. This view has also been expressed in the decision of this Court in *V. Dhanappal Chettiar* v. *Yesodai Ammal*, 1979 (2) RCR (Rent) 352: AIR 1979 SC 1745"

The same proposition of law has been laid down by this Court in cases *Neelam* v. *Sanjay Pahwa* (supra), *Hazari* v. *Vinod Kumar (now deceased) through Lrs.* (supra) and *Harikesh* v. *Smt. Narain Devi (widow) (supra)*. Thus, there is no escape from the conclusion that the tenancy of the appellants was validly terminated by the plaintiffs-respondents.

There is no dispute with the proposition of law that the pleadings is the foundation in the civil litigation. All the grounds of attack and defence have to be pleaded and then to prove the same by leading cogent and convincing evidence. At the same time, it is settled legal position that a pure question of law can be even raised for the first time in the second appeal. But, where the plea is a mixed question of law and facts, the same cannot be raised for the first time in the second appeal. In the instant case, learned counsel for the appellants has raised the plea that the suit of the plaintiffs-respondents were barred under the provisions of Order II, Rule 2 CPC due to the filing of the previous recovery suit and that the appellants-defendants were entitled for protection of provisions of Section 53A of T.P. Act. Both these grounds were not pleaded by the appellants-defendants in their written statement.

Appellants-defendants have projected that the period of lease was extended voluntarily by the appellants-defendants vide letter dated 04.09.1998 (copy Ex.DW2/3). As per the contents of the said letter, the period of lease was extended up to 01.08.2006. As already mentioned, as per the provisions of Section 107 of the T.P. Act, the lease of immovable property from year to year or for any term exceeding one year can only be by a registered instrument. If the lease deed dated 20.09.1996 is inadmissible in evidence except for collateral purposes being unregistered, the same principle of law will apply to the letter Ex.DW2/3 and will not be admissible in evidence to show the extension of the period of tenancy, which cannot be stated to be a collateral purpose by any stretch of imagination.

119. Section 100 – Specific Relief Act, 1963 Section 34 Tamil Nadu District Municipalities Act, 1920, Rule 9, Schedule IV

In the case of *Kottar Elankadai Musliem Samudhaya Trust* v. *The Commissioner (Madras),* 2017 (1) MLJ 48: 2016 (5) LW 694, the learned Senior Counsel for the appellant/plaintiff further relied upon another judgment of this Court in the case of *Shanmuga Nadar* v. *The Corporation of Madurai by its Commissioner* reported in 1980 (2) MLJ 140 wherein it has been held that a suit to set aside the assessment cannot be dismissed merely on the ground that alternative remedy is available, if the assessment of property tax does not in substance and in effect comply with the provisions of the Act. The learned Senior Counsel then relied upon another judgment of this Court in the case of *Sanjai Gupta* v. *The Commissioner, Corporation of Chennai,* reported in 2009 (2) CTC 465 wherein a Division Bench of this Court has held that the assessment without considering the objection of the assessee before revision of tax is illegal. A learned Single Judge of this Court in the judgment in *Mangayarkarasi* v. *The Kumbakonam Municipality, rep. by its Executive Authority, The Commissioner, Dr. Murthy Salai, Kumbakonam Munsif, Kumbakonam Town* reported in 2009 (5) CTC 220 has followed the judgment cited above and held as follows:

> "14. In the instant case the following vital points have been raised on the side of the appellant/plaintiff. The first and foremost vital point is that the revised tax has not been made in accordance with the provision of Section 4 of the Tamil Nadu Buildings (Lease and Rent Control) Act, 1960. It was an everlasting principle of law that tax has to be revised only as per the provision of Section 4 of the said Act and further as per D.O. Lr. No. 60572/R1/98, dated 3.9.1998, the Government of Tamil Nadu has categorically stated that working sheet contain details of property and calculation should also be sent along with special notice. In the instant case as rightly pointed out on the side of the appellant/plaintiff, no

working sheet has been annexed with Exs.A4 to A6. In fact this Court has closely perused Exs.A4 to A6, wherein it has been simply stated that the plaintiff should pay the revised tax. Therefore, the mode of calculation of revised tax has not at all been stated in Exs.A4 to A6 and in short working sheet as per the said D.O. letter, has not been annexed with. Therefore, the first contention urged on the side of the appellant/plaintiff is really tenable."

The High Court said, when we consider the facts of the present case in the light of the relevant rules found in Schedule IV of the Tamil Nadu District Municipalities Act, 1920 and the precedents above referred to, the demand notice under Ex.A4 is illegal. The demand notice was issued under Ex.A4 even before an assessment and this fact is admitted. From the reading of the relevant rules, I am of the view that whenever the Municipality wants to enhance the tax either on account of the general revision or on account of alteration of existing building, a show cause notice is required to be issued informing the assessee without any ambiguity about the basic facts and figures which are proposed to be taken for the proposed revision or enhancement. Only thereafter, there can be an assessment of property tax. It is only after an assessment of property tax following the principles of natural justice, a demand notice can be issued. In the present case, the demand notice under Ex.A4 has been issued even before an assessment or a show cause notice to the appellant. In such circumstances, I have no hesitation to hold that the demand notice under Ex.A4 is liable to be set aside. Hence, I have no hesitation to answer the first question of law framed in this second appeal in favour of the appellant by stating that revision of assessment of property tax involving enhancement of tax cannot be valid, in the absence of any show cause notice to the assessee, as per proviso to Rule 9 of Schedule IV of Taxation and Finance Rules framed under the Tamil Nadu District Municipalities Act, 1920. Before considering the second question of law, it is necessary to refer to the document filed by the respondent municipality as Ex.B1 before the trial Court. Ex.B1 is the register containing the list of property by which the tax requires revision. On the defendant side, this document was marked to show that the working sheet attached to this document gives the particulars and details which form the basis for revision of tax. Even this working sheet was not served on the assessee. The working sheet found in Ex.B1 shows that the municipality has fixed the cost of construction at Rs.11,38,655.20. Apart from the cost of building, a sum of Rs. 24,04,900/- has been added towards the value of the land for an extent of 2 acre 49 cents. It is to be seen that the total constructed area is less than ?th of the vacant land. However, for the entire vacant land, the value for the land is taken. It is conceded that for the purpose of arriving at the annual rental value, the municipality is required to follow Section 4 of the Tamil Nadu Buildings (Lease and Rent Control) Act, 1960. Under Section 4 of Tamil Nadu Buildings (Lease and Rent Control) Act, 1960, a procedure and a formula is prescribed for the purpose of calculating the annual rental value and fair rent for any building. Depending upon the nature of enjoyment whether a building is commercial or residential, 12% or 9% of the cost of the land and building is taken as annual rental value. In addition to the total cost of the actual building and cost of land in which the building is constructed, a further extent of land upto 50% of the constructed area is also taken into account for the purpose of arriving at total value of the building. However, in the present case, the plinth area of construction is only 1421.92 square meter. However, the value of land has been arrived at by taking into account an extent of 9730.52 square meter approximately 2.40 acres. Hence, this calculation for arriving at the total cost of land and building is unacceptable, having regard to the specific formula that is prescribed. Hence, the second substantial question of law is answered to the effect that the demand notice for the property tax issued under Ex.A4 is not in conformity with the procedure contemplated under Section 4 of the Tamil Nadu Buildings (Lease and Rent Control) Act, 1960.

120. Section 100 – Specific Relief Act, 1963 Sections 16 and 20 Specific Performance of Contract

In *Gurdev Singh* v. *Manjinder Singh,* 2016 (1) LAR 599 (P&H) the High Court said, I have heard counsel for the appellants and perused the records.

RSA NO. 2301 of 2015

Before adverting to the submissions made by counsel representing two sets of appellants, it is appropriate to recapitulate the enunciation of law laid down by Hon'ble the Supreme Court of India in *M.M.S. Investments, Madurai* v. *V.V. Veerappan,* 2007 (2) RCR (Civil) 816: AIR 2007 SC 2663, wherein the Court has held in para 06, quoted thus:—

> "Questioning the plea of readiness and willingness is a concept relatable to an agreement. After conveyance the question of readiness and willingness is really not relevant. Therefore, the provision of the Specific Relief Act, 1963 (in short the "Act") is not applicable. It is to be noted that the decision in Ram Awadh's case (supra) relates to a case where there was only an agreement. After the conveyance, the only question to be adjudicated is whether the purchaser was a bona fide purchaser for value without notice. In the present case the only issue that can be adjudicated is whether the appellants were bona fide purchasers for value without notice. The question whether the appellants were ready and willing is really of no consequence. In Ram Awadh's case (supra) the question of the effect of a completed sale was not there. Therefore, that decision cannot have any application so far as the present case is concerned. Once there is a conveyance the concept would be different and the primary relief could be only cancellation."

In view of the above, contention raised by appellant Gurdev Singh that the plaintiffs/respondents were not ready and willing to perform their part of the agreement loses its relevance for the reason that the suit property stands alienated in favour of Jaswant Singh and another vide sale deed dated 8.1.2008.

This brings the Court to the two fold submissions made by counsel for appellant to assail the judgments and decrees impugned. The plea with regard to the agreement being the result of fraud or forgery does not get substantiated from the materials on record. The mere fact that the FIR was got registered by the appellant or challan has been presented in the Court is not at all sufficient to hold in favour of the appellant that the agreement is the result of fraud or forgery. I would hasten to add that what to talk of registration of an FIR or presentation of challan in the Court, even judgment passed by a criminal court accepting plea of the appellants would not be binding upon the civil court as the civil court has to record its independent finding on the plea of fraud or forgery in the light of materials on record. Counsel is not in a position to point out any such evidence which has either been ignored or misinterpreted by the court much less the evidence being sufficient to substantiate the plea of fraud, required to be proved beyond shadow of doubt. One thing more to be added here is that plea of the appellant that the respondents prepared the agreement as he demanded loan obtained by Palwinder Singh, father of plaintiff No. 1, it is an undisputed position that the appellant filed a suit for recovery of the amount against Palwinder Singh but later withdrew the same for the reasons best known. The very fact that the appellant withdrew the suit for recovery goes a long way to reject his contention that the agreement in question was prepared by the plaintiffs to put pressure upon the appellant in regard to his claim against Palwinder Singh. In this view of the matter, I do not find any merit in the contention of the appellants that consistent findings recorded by the courts below rejecting plea of the appellant in regard to fraud and forgery, warrant intervention.

Ordinarily, in contract for sale of immovable property, time is not essence of the contract. There is nothing on record suggestive of the fact that there was increase in price of the property with effect from 13.10.2005 to January 2008 in order to doubt plea of the contesting respondents that they always remained ready and willing to perform their part of the contract. On the contrary, it is an admitted case of the appellant that the suit land has been sold to respondents for a sale consideration of Rs. 10,00,000/- whereas in the agreement executed in favour of the contesting respondents, the price was settled at Rs. 10,62,187.50. The respondents had already paid a substantial amount of Rs. 9,00,000 towards earnest money, therefore, there can be no reason for them to be not willing and ready to perform their part of the agreement. Taken from any angle, contention of the appellant that filing of suit after two years of the agreement negatives claim of the respondents with regard to readiness and willingness is devoid of merit and is accordingly rejected.

121. Section 100 – Second Appeal – Maintainability

There must be a decree passed by first appellate court –In *Chandrakant Somnath Melge* v. *Balasaheb Somnath Melge*, 2017 (2) All MR 624: 2017 (3) Mh LJ 668 (Bom) in the first appeal ex parte order was challenged on the ground of non-service of notice. There was delay of 11 years, 4 months and 16 days in filling appeal.

There must be a decree—The High Court said that for maintaining an appeal what is relevant for the purposes of Section 100 of the Code of Civil Procedure is that, there must be a decree passed by the first appellate court. A decree means a formal expression of adjudication which, so far as regards the court expressing it, conclusively determines the rights of the parties with regard to all or any of the matters in controversy. The matter in controversy in the appeal between the parties was as to the entitlement of the Appellant herein to challenge the *ex parte* decree passed against him by the trial court. That matter is conclusively determined and the right of the Appellant with regard to the same is conclusively denied, when in the appeal an order was passed on the application for condonation of delay, rejecting the same, and thereby dismissing the appeal. Just because there is no formal merger between the appellate order and the decree passed by the trial court in the sense of the doctrine of merger implied by law, it cannot be said that there is no decree of the appellate court. Since in this case, the appeal is dismissed on the ground that delay is not condoned, the order passed by the appellate court is nevertheless a decree and a second appeal from such decree would certainly lie under Section 100 of the Code if it does give rise to a substantial question of law.

Coming now to the questions of law raised in the present appeal, namely, whether or not the first appellate court could have dismissed the appeal on the ground of limitation by holding that the suit summons was admittedly served on the Applicant/Defendant and whether, the first appellate court could have disposed of the matter merely on pleadings and without allowing the Applicant/Defendant to lead evidence or without the Applicant/Defendant having filed any pursis of closure of evidence, the following needs to be noted. The Appellant herein had expressly approached the First Appellate Court on a plea of nonservice of the notice of the suit. In the face of such plea, the Appellate Court could not have proceeded on the basis that the suit summons was admittedly served on the Applicant/Defendant. This is plainly contrary to the pleadings and there is no possible justification for the same.

122. Condonation of Delay

As held by this Court in the case of *Holya Lasha Mahale* v. *Raghunath Holya Mahale*, 2006 (5) Mh LJ 80: 2007 (1) Bom CR 506, whenever an application for condonation of delay is made and there are contested facts, the court must allow the applicant to lead oral evidence on the ground of condonation applied for. This is all the more so, when there is an ex parte decree and there is a delay in filing an appeal. In the absence of a pursis of the parties that they do not intend to lead evidence and/or that they have closed their evidence, it was inappropriate on the part of the First Appellate Court to dispose of the matter merely on the basis of the pleadings of the parties. The first appellate court, in the present case, has not only disposed of the matter contrary to this mandate on the basis of pleadings of the parties, but it has actually decided the Appeal in the face of such pleadings. That is clearly impermissible.

The second appeal, in the premises, deserves to be allowed. The impugned order of the first appellate court dated 26 March 2014 is accordingly set aside and the matter is remanded to the District Court for a fresh hearing in accordance with law. The learned District Judge 1, Solapur is directed to hear the application for condonation of delay after allowing the parties to lead such evidence, as they may desire to lead.

123. Section 100 Second Appeal – Substantial Question of Law is *sine qua non* for Maintaining Regular Second Appeal

In the case of *Bhuru* v. *Chandgi Ram,* 2016 (Law Herald) 2827: 2016 (4) ICC 504: 2017 (1) PCr (Civil) 470 (P&H). Before the lower Appellate Court, Matadeen-defendant also moved an application for leading additional evidence to the effect that copy of decree-sheet was very material piece of evidence in order to know whether decretal amount was paid or not. A copy of decree-sheet of aforesaid Civil Suit No. 104 of 1980 dated 25.08.1981 sought to be tendered by way of additional evidence. A copy of judgment in Civil Suit No. 104 of 1980 titled as Matadeen and Chadgi Ram and others decided on 25.08.1981 was already on record as PW9/2A. Matadeen claimed that there was mistake in the decree-sheet and therefore, he wanted to file the same on record as additional evidence and the document was very material for just decision of the case. The prayer of Matadeen for leading additional evidence was rejected by the lower Appellate Court. The lower Appellate Court dismissed the appeal by relying upon the copy of judgment Ex.PW9/2A only.

In view of Full Bench judgment of this Court in *Ganpat* v. *Smt. Ram Devi,* 1977 PLR 1: AIR 1978 P&H 137, framing of question of law was having no effect on the maintainability of the appeal. However, in view of amendment of Section 100 CPC, framing of substantial question of law is sine qua non for maintaining regular second appeal in this Court. Prior to amendment, the appeal could have been filed on the ground set out in clauses (a) to (c) of Section 100(1) CPC. Now second appeal requires substantial question of law to be framed. The interference cannot be made only because the order is contrary to law, but when the disputed issues raised a substantial question of law. Limiting such a power in the Appellate Authority is based on public policy having roots in the maxim *"interest reipublicae ut sit finis litium"*.

Though no substantial questions of law have been framed, however, this Court proceeded to consider:—

> "Whether decree dated 25.08.1981 sought to be adduced as additional evidence before the lower Appellate Court was liable to be allowed in additional evidence being essential and material document for just and substantial justice between the parties?"

The Court said,, only decree was to be complied with in the context of depositing or non-depositing of the amount within the time specified. In the instant case, a specific amount was mentioned in the decree and in the opinion of this Court, decree was to be complied with. It was not the case of the respondents that amount was not deposited within the time as specified in the decree. It was an amount itself which was claimed to be not requisite amount. In any case the amount mentioned in the decree was legally required to be ascertain for which an application under Order XLI, Rule 27 CPC was moved before the lower Appellate Court. In consider opinion of this Court, application should have been allowed and thereafter, the lower Appellate Court should have decided the appeal on merits.

124. Section 100 – Specific Relief Act, 1963 and Section 20 Specific Performance of Contract

In the case of *Dr. D.C. Khosla (Deceased) Through Lrs* v. *Vinod Kumar Jain*, 2016 (7) AD (Del) 352: 2016 (232) DLT 354 (Del), the High Court said, I completely agree with the discussions and conclusions of the first appellate court inasmuch as once the respondent/defendant himself applied for the permission to the competent authority under the Urban Land (Ceiling and Regulation) Act, 1976 in July, 1980, then, the respondent/defendant could not contend that time of performance was of the essence and the transaction had to be completed by March, 1979. Even assuming for the sake of completion of arguments that if time was of the essence of the contract the respondent/defendant by his conduct proceeded that time of performance should not be treated as essence of the contract. The first appellate court has dealt with the same in paras which are reproduced above and there is no perversity of any manner in the same for this Court to interfere as contended on behalf of the respondent/defendant.

7. The next issue is as to whether plaintiff was ready and willing to perform his part of the contract i.e whether the plaintiff had financial capacity to complete the sale transaction. It is argued on behalf of the respondent/defendant that no documents have been filed on record by the plaintiff to establish his financial capacity to pay the balance sale consideration of Rs. 18,500/-. It is therefore argued that once the plaintiff failed to prove his readiness and willingness, this issue should be decided in favour of the respondent/defendant and consequently, the present appeal had to be dismissed.

8. In my opinion, the arguments urged on behalf of the respondent/defendant that plaintiff has failed to prove his readiness and willingness are arguments which completely lack substance inasmuch as the first appellate court has very exhaustively dealt with this aspect in para 13 of the impugned judgment wherein the first appellate court notes that merely not placing on record the deposit receipt or the copy of the pass book was not material in the facts of the present case wherein the plaintiff had brought the original pass book to the court and had made a statement on the basis of that pass book and in spite of the same the respondent/defendant did not contest the content of the pass book including by asking the pass book to be filed on record. The first appellate court rightly notes that things had been different if plaintiff had not brought the receipt of deposit of the amount or the pass book, and in which case court could have come to a conclusion that there is no production of material documents and thus raising of adverse inference against the plaintiff, but that cannot be once the plaintiff has brought the original pass book and receipt during his deposition. The mere fact that these copies were not placed on record cannot lead to any presumption against the plaintiff with respect to his lack of financial capacity in the facts of this case. Learned first appellate court also rightly notes that if really the case of the plaintiff of lack of financial capacity was doubted by the respondent/defendant, then since the plaintiff had given the number of his account, name of the bank, the date of deposit, as also the amount, the respondent/defendant could have well rebutted the testimony of the plaintiff by summoning the relevant record from the bank but the respondent/defendant failed to do so. In my opinion,

therefore, there is no perversity in the findings of the first appellate court for this Court to interfere under Section 100 CPC by holding that appellants/plaintiff should be held not to have necessary financial capacity. Learned counsel for the appellants/plaintiff is also justified in arguing that the cross-examination of the plaintiff as PW1 was only on the aspect that plaintiff did not have the financial capacity and there was no cross-examination that the plaintiff did not have the deposit receipt and the pass book showing the actual deposit of the amount of Rs. 18,500/- in his bank account and which deposit was done by the plaintiff on account of the defendant/respondent having refused to receive this balance amount of sale consideration.

> Reliance placed by the counsel for the respondent on the judgment of the learned Single Judge of this Court (Hon'ble Mr. Justice R.C. Lahoti, as he then was) in the case of *Sudhir Engineering Company* v. *Nitco Roadways Ltd* 1995 (34) DRJ 86: 1995 RLR 286 is misconceived because the said judgment deals with the admitting or denying documents at the stage of admission/denial of documents before the issues are framed and not with respect to proving of documents during the course of recording of testimonies of the witnesses and deposing on the basis of the same and the failure of the opposite party i.e respondent/defendant to cross-examine on the same. The judgment therefore relied in the case of *Sudhir Engineering Company* (supra) does not help the respondent/defendant.

***100A. No further appeal in certain cases.*—Notwithstanding anything contained in any Letters Patent for any High Court or in any other instrument having the force of law or in any other law for the time being in force, where any appeal from an original or appellate decree or order is heard and decided by a Single Judge of a High Court, no further appeal shall lie from the judgment and decree of such Single Judge.**

Comments

Effect of Section 100A – Whether Prospective

The provisions have been introduced by the Amendment Act of 1999 w.e.f. from 1-7-2002. By introducing the provision, right to second appeal has been made a vested right. Section 100A has taken away the letter patent power of the High Court The Supreme Court has held that there are several relevant factors calling for consideration for exercise of discretion by the Court for and against decreeing a suit *Dulara Devi* v. *Mahdei,* (2005) 1 SCC 432, *Sanjay Z. Rane* v. *Saibai S. Dubaxi,* (2004) 130 SCC 439.

The Supreme Court examined the subject in *Salem Advocate Bar Association* v. *Union of India,* (2003) 1 SCC 49: AIR 2003 SC 189: 2002 AIR SCW 4627 and held that a letter patent appeal filed prior to coming into force of the provision (1.7.2002) is maintainable. The provision is prospective and not retrospective. (2003) 1 SCC 49; *see* also *Kamla Devi* v. *Khushal Kanwar,* AIR 2007 SC 663: 2007 AIR SCW 268: (2006) 13 SCALE 645 and *Geeta Devi* v. *Puran Ram Raigar,* (2010) 9 SCC 84: 2010 AIR SCW 5824 wherein similar view was expressed.

***101. Second appeal on no other grounds.*—No second appeal shall lie except on the ground mentioned in section 100.**

SYNOPSIS

Comments

1. Section 100, Section 101 – For Hearing under Order XLI Rule 11 of the Code

In *Parmanand Prasad Singh* v.*Jai Kishore Prasad Singh*, 2013 2 PLJR 116 (Pat) the plaintiff/Respondent No.1 filed the suit for declaration of title over the suit land as described in the schedule attached to the foot of the plaint, for confirmation of his possession over the suit land as also for declaration that Panchnama Batwara was binding upon the parties. The plaintiff also sought for a declaration that the survey entry in respect of the suit land in the name of defendant No. 1/appellant was wrong and illegal. 5. Plaintiff's case before the trial court was that plaintiff's and defendants were full brothers and sons of Late Debilal Singh. Their father had purchased four Kathas and 17 dhurs of land of old Khata No. 154, 155, plot No. 1351, 1352 in Mohalla- Gangjala, Ward No. 12, Saharsa in the name of defendant No. 1/appellant in the state of jointness and they came in possession over the suit land. There was a partition in the family after death of Debilal Singh and each of four brothers got one Katha and ¼ dhur of land. The plaintiff came in possession over his share as other brothers did. Further case of the plaintiff before the trial court was that a Khista Panchanama was also prepared over which all the four brothers put their signature along with panches. After the partition, names of all brothers were mutated in the Sirista of the State of Bihar and since then the plaintiff came in the possession over the suit property.

This is to be noted that there is concurrent finding of facts by the courts below on all counts, that is, the title of the plaintiffs over the suit property, plea of adverse possession as raised by the defendant No.1 as also possession of the plaintiffs over the suit property. Learned counsel for the Appellant has not been able to satisfy this court, with reference to any specified finding recorded by the court below that the same are either without evidence or contrary to evidence. Learned first appellate court has assigned reasons for not accepting the story of exchange of property which reason cannot be termed as perverse so as to warrant interference under section 100 of the Code. 13. Section 100 of the Code of Civil Procedure envisages that a Second Appeal would lie to the High Court from a decree passed in appeal by any court sub-ordinate to the High Court if the High Court is satisfied that the case involves a substantial question of law. In order to re-assert the mandatory requirement of involvement of substantial question of law for a second appeal to be maintained under Section 100 of the Code, Section 101 of the Code provides that no second appeal shall lie "except on the ground mentioned in Section 100 of the Code". Such being the legislative mandate, the superior courts have on several occasions laid down law as to what would constitute and what would not, a "substantial question of law" within the meaning of Section 100 of the Code while scrutinizing scope of the Section. By now, it is settled position of law that the High Court cannot interfere with the concurrent finding of fact unless the same is found to be perverse being based on no evidence or contrary to material available on record or that on the evidence on record no reasonable person could have come to that conclusion. Reference may be made in this regard to the Supreme Court judgments in the cases of *Vidyadhar Manik Rao,* (1999) 3 SCC 573: AIR 1999 SC 1441; *Sugani (Mst.)* v. *Rameshwar Das,* (2006) 11 SCC 87: AIR 2006 SC 2172; *Gurudev Kaur* v. *Kaki,* (2007) 1 SCC 546; *Prakash Kumar* v. *State of Gujarat* (2007) 4 SCC 266: 2007 CriLJ 2731; *Thingarajan* v. *Venugopalaswamy B. Koil,* (2004) 5 SCC 762: AIR 2004 SC 1913l and *Narayanan Rajendran* v. *Lakshmi Sarojini,* (2004) 5 SCC 762.

From reading of the judgments of the courts below, I am of the view that the same cannot be said to be perverse or without any evidence. Taking note of the judicial pronouncement mentioned above, in my opinion, the appeal does not involve any substantial question of law so as to be entertained under section 100 of the Code. It, accordingly, does not merit admission and is, therefore, dismissed.

2. Sections 100 and 101 – Second Appeal

In *Madan Kumari (Smt.)* v. *Udaipur University, Udaipur,* 2012 (2) RLW 1889 (Raj the Court referred to a case of Supreme Court and said that the the Hon'ble Supreme Court in *Bhim Singh* v. *Kan Singh,* AIR 1980 SC 727: (1980) 3 SCC 72, has held that if a plea is not specifically made and yet it is covered by an issue by implication and the parties knew that the said plea was involved in the trial, then the mere fact that the plea was not expressly taken in the pleadings would not necessarily disentitle a party from relying upon it if it is satisfactorily proved by the evidence.

The Court said, thus, from the above discussion, it can be concluded:—

(1) That the reason for the general rule that a party is bound by his pleadings is that if he is allowed to substantiate a case different from that pleaded, his opponent will be seriously prejudiced. But the Court may depart from the strict enforcement of the general rule, if it is satisfied that rigid compliance of the rule will lead to injustice.

(2) That where no prejudice was caused by the variation between the pleading and the proof to the opposite party, even no objection was raised about it when evidence was being led, such variance would not be fatal to defence of party who has made variation.

(3) That generally the parties should not be allowed to travel beyond their pleadings. However, pleadings should be construed liberally and the Court should not adopt a pedantic approach. If the substance of the essential material facts for grant of relief is stated in the pleading, the Court should not throw away the same on the ground of defective form or the deficiency in the pleading. Even if the plea is not raised in the pleading even then a claim of the party cannot be defeated, if the parties know the respective cases of each other on the said plea and led evidence in support of their cases.

(4) That if the alternative case is admitted by the defendant in his written statement and not only that, thereafter, both parties have led evidence, in such a situation, decree can be granted on such alternative case.

(5) That if the parties have led evidence considering the pleas taken either in pleadings or in evidence, in such circumstances, it is not proper to say that such type of evidence should not be looked into.

(6) That if a plea is not specifically made and yet it is covered by an issue by implication and the parties knew that the said plea was involved in the trial, then the mere fact that the plea was not expressly taken in the pleadings would not necessarily disentitle a party from relying upon it if it is satisfactorily proved by evidence.

(7) That if the parties led evidence knowing what they are going to allege and prove, then in such case general rule would not be applicable and the case would be covered by an issue by implication that though the matter has not been specifically pleaded, yet it is implied in the pleadings of the parties. It is not desirable to place undue emphasis on form, instead substance of pleadings should be considered.

In view of the discussion made above, the findings of the learned trial court on the issue No. 1 and 1A appears to be correct and the same do not suffer from any infirmity or illegality, therefore, in this second appeal, the findings on the issue No. 1 and 1A should not be disturbed. For the reasons stated above, the substantial question No. 1 and 2 framed by this Court are answered in the manner that in this particular case, the parties were not allowed to travel beyond the pleadings and the evidence adduced by the respondent-defendant about the proportionate deduction of marks cannot be said to have been allowed without there being any pleadings.

3. Order I Rule 10, Order 21 Rule 97, Section 101

In *S.A. Babu Reddy* v. *Munireddy*, 2016 2 CivCC 152: 2016 2 KCCR 971 (Kar) the facts to be stated in brief are that the petitioner filed suit O.S No. 1748/2004 on the file of the City Civil Judge, Bangalore CCH-8 for the reliefs of specific performance against respondents 1 to 9 directing them to execute sale deed as per the agreement of sale dated 5.12.1993 in respect of the land bearing Sy. Nos. 15 & 68/1 measuring 2 acres 4 guntas and 34 guntas respectively situated at Parappana Agrahara Village, Begur Hobli, Bangalore South Taluk.

In the above suit, the impleading applicants (obstructers/applicants) filed application under Order I Rule 10 of Code of Civil Procedure to implead themselves as additional defendants. The petitioner filed objections to the said application. After contest the court below has rejected the applications by the order dated 1.4.2010. The impleading applicants (obstructers) accepted the order rejecting their application for impleading and they have not agitated the said order any further.

The High Court after hearing the parties said, admitted facts are that the petitioner has filed the suit for the reliefs of specific performance and the said suit came to be decreed in favour of the petitioner. During pendency of the suit, the obstructers made impleading application on the ground that they have purchased residential sites formed in the suit schedule lands from the defendants and they are in occupation of the respective sites as absolute owners, they are the bona fide purchasers for valuable consideration under respective sale deeds. The plaintiff and defendants colluded with each other in order to defraud the impleading applicants, filed the suit. The applicants are proper and necessary parties to the suit. If the applications are not allowed, they would be put to greater hardship and irreparable loss and there will be multiplicity of proceedings.

The plaintiff/petitioner filed objections to the impleading application that the suit schedule property belonged to the defendants and it was their ancestral property. The plaintiff is the agreement holder executed by the defendants in respect of the suit schedule properties, they have paid substantial amount towards sale consideration, the properties alleged to have been purchased by the impleading applicants is the residential sites situate in gramthana and bear khata number and assessment number. The suit schedule property has not at all been converted for non agricultural purpose and it is not vested with the Village Panchayat. Hence it is contended that the impleading applicants are nothing to do with the suit schedule property. Therefore, it is contended that applicants are neither proper nor necessary parties to the suit.

The court below while passing the order rejecting the impleading application has held that the impleading applicants are claiming their sites said to have situated in gramatana, whereas the suit schedule lands are still agricultural lands and not converted for non agricultural purposes. Thus the suit schedule lands are distinct from that of the properties said to have been purchased by the impleading applicants from the defendants. Apart from that the impleading applicants are claiming independent title and possession over the sites which they alleged to have purchased from their vendors and that being the case, they can very well protect their properties on the basis of the title deeds and also on the basis of the necessary municipal documents. So, the judgment and decree in case if it is passed in favour of the plaintiff in the suit, it does not in any manner affect the right and title of the impleading applicants in respect of their respective properties. Thus relying upon the decision reported in ILR 2005 KAR 2475 to the effect that for specific performance of contract, the person having independent title and possession over contracted property is neither necessary nor proper party and therefore, not entitled to join as party defendant in suit, court below held that the impleading applicants (Obstructors) are neither necessary nor proper parties and accordingly rejected the impleading application.

***102. No second appeal in certain cases.*—No second appeal shall lie in any suit of the nature cognizable by Courts of Small Causes, when the amount or value of the subject-matter of the original suit does not exceed three thousand rupees.**

SYNOPSIS

Comments

1. Scope and Application

The principle that where an appellate court entertains an appeal which does not lie to it, a second appeal would be competant, would not be applicable where there is a definite prohibition against the second appeal as in section 102. AIR 1952 MB 122. The provision of section 42 are controlled by those of this section when a Court of Small Causes transfers decree for execution to another Court, 25 C 872. A Full Bench of the High Court of Madras said that the words of a nature cognizable seem to have reference to the subject-matter of the suit as distinguished from the amount of the claim 23 M 547 (FB) overruling 22 M 229. The fact that a question of title is raised does not prevent the suit from being one of a small cause nature. AIR 967; 1935 OWN 503: 1935 O 410. Section 102, C.P.C., does no apply to a suit *bona fide* framed as a mortgage suit, although the only claim which could be established by the plaintiff is a money claim; ILR (1933) 2 C 81: 42 OWN 381: 1938 C 336. Section 102 contemplates a suit of the nature cognizable by Courts of Small Cause irrespective of when defence is put up in the case; 1935 OWN 503: 1935 O 413. The value of the subject-matter of the suit must be determined by the reference to the value put by the plaintiff not only for fiscal purposes but also for purpose of jurisdiction 27 A 200; 13 IC 403. The High Court of Andhra Pradesh decided how to determine question involved under section 102 and held that it is the nature of the suit and not of appeal that is material for purpose of section 102; *Bokka Sreeramulu* v. *Kalipatnapu Venkateswar Rao*, AIR 1959 AP 92: (1959) 1 Andh WR 148: ILR 1958 AP 836. The section assumes the original character of the suit rather than the character it may assume by reason of the finding of the Courts: 6 Bom. Where the Munsif or the trial court possessed both jurisdictions, ordinary as well as Small Cause, when hearing a Small Cause suit the Judge must be taken to have if he was not quite alive to it at the time. A suit taken cognizance of in this way does not cease to be a suit tried under the Small Cause Court Act because of some divergence from its summary procedure; *Abdeali Alimohamad* v. *Fidahussain Abdulkarim*, 1956 MBLR 778 (Civil): AIR 1957 MB 122. Plaint returned by small Cause Court under section 23 in suit for money due and occupation on the ground of permissive possession. According to the High Court of Madras, no second appeal lies. 1929 M 781 (1); (Small cause suit tried as regular suit). 251: 1931 ALJ 967. Section is not restricted to cases where the Court trying the suit on the original side was also empowered to try the suit on the Small Cause Court side. The toss in deciding whether a second appeal lies or not the Court which tried the suit 7 OWH 1112: 1931 O 49. What is to be considered is whether the suit is of the nature cognizable by Court of Small Cause and not whether it was or could have been so taken cognizance of in this way does not cease to be a suit under the Small Cause Court Act, because of some divergence from its summary procedure; *Abdeali Alimohamad* v. *Fidahussain Abdulkarim*, MBLR 1956 Civil 778: AIR 1957 MB 122. Plaint returned by Small Cause Court under section 23 in suit money due for use and occupation on the ground of permissive possession. No second appeal lies. 1929 M 781 (1). Session is not restricted to cases where the Court trying the suit on the original side also empowered to try the suit on the Small Cause Court side. The test in deciding whether a second appeal lies or not is to be found in the suit and not in the powers of the Court which tried the suit; 7 OWN 1112: 1931 O 49. What is to be considered is whether the suit is of the nature cognizable by Court of Small Cause and not whether it was or could have been so taken cognizance of. There may not be a Judge invested with the jurisdiction of the Court of Small Cause. Nevertheless the suit will be of the nature cognizable by the Court of small causes it does not fall under the exceptions specified; *Rajbai* v. *Meghji Manshi*, AIR 1954 Kutch 28; *Santosh Singh Makund Singh Thakur* v. *Jageshwar Ghapole*, AIR 1954 VP 16, test as to competency of second appeal is whether the suit is excluded by the second schedule to the Small Cases Courts Act, 1954. OWN [HC] 264. A suit for the recovery of rent other than house rent is a suit of the nature cognizable in Courts of small causes; 56 LC 845 but *see* 1922 p. 184; 1928 C 709. A suit to recover the rent of agricultural land is not a suit of the nature cognizable by Court of small Cause: (J.R. 300, overruled.) 13 R 633: 1935 R 386 (FB). No second appeal lies from a decision in a suit for *mesne* profits when the value of the suit is less than Rs. 500: 24 MLS. But *see* contra 158 IC 1119: 18 NLJ 26. A claim for profits by a person who has obtained a decree for septic performance of an agreement of sale of land, against the defendant in possession, is a suit for *mesne* profits and for damages; 158 IC 1119: 18 NLJ 76. The High Court of Allahabad said that a *mala fide* prayer for injunction does not alter the nature of a small cause suit for money; 1930 ALJ 1043. The High Court of Madras said that section 102 bars a second appeal in suits for small sums of money, if the claim is merely to recover money. But if, in addition, the suits are also and perhaps mainly, for an injunction a second appeal would lie and would not be barred; 1938 M. 941: (1938) 2 MIJ 589. According to the High Court of Nagpur where a suit cognizable by a small cause Court has been tried against the provisions of A-16 in an ordinary suit by a Judge who is not invested with Small cause powers the parties should not be considered as a small cause suit and an appeal would lie from the decision 30 NLR 252: 1934 N 121. The section does not apply to appeals from orders. An order on appeal from a decree in an original suit of the nature cognizable in a Court of Small Cause, the suit for re-trial is appealable 3 A 18 (FB) (a case under section 588, of the old Code). In the case of a suit of the nature of Small Cause no second appeal lies. A Full Bench of the High Court of Allahabad held that a second appeal against an order passed in execution proceedings arising out of a suit of the nature of small cause is not entertainable, though one appeal against such an order is permissible: (31 All 1: 1938 Bom 534 rel. on); *Janki Sahu Trust* v. *Ram Palat*, 1950 ALJ 833: ILR (1951) 2 All 375: AIR 1950 All 580 (FB). This section debars second appeal against a decree for recovery of money where the value does not exceed Rs. 25,000 formerly, this amount was Rs. 500 which was subsequently replaced by figure of Rs. 1000 Thereafter this figure was again replaced by Rs. 3000 by the Amendment Act, 1976. Now by the Amendment Act of 2002, it has been settled at Rs. 25,000. It means no second appeal will lie in the matter of a suit for recovery where the amount to be recovered is Rs. 25,000 or less.

It is a disabling provision. Section 100 provides for filing of second appeal. Therefore, even if an appeal is provided by section 100, it may not lie by virtue of bar of section 102, where the value of the suit does not exceed Rs. 25,000. Thus, the enabling provision of section 100 and the disabling provision of section 102 should be examined together so as to give a coherence between the two.

For the purpose of this section, the expression 'suit' includes an execution proceeding. Therefore, in the matter of recovery of money, no second appeal will lie from an order made in the proceeding of execution of the decree, unless the value of the suit is above Rs. 25,000.

2. Section 102-Scope and Application

The Allahabad High Court also in *Pooran Singh* v. *Jai Singh*, 17 Ind Cas 522 had examined the scope of section 102 of the Code of Civil Procedure. In the present case, The plaintiffs sought to enforce an illegal contract. The High Court observed that the present case seemed to be covered by the authorities and it must hold that the suit should have been dismissed.

In the suit under reference the claim was for a simple money decree for Rs. 400 and the question arose whether a second appeal is not barred by section 102 of the Code of Civil Procedure. *Prima facie* the suit is of a nature cognizable by Courts of Small Causes and the learned Counsel for the defendant-appellant is unable to show that the suit falls within any of the articles of the second schedule to the Provincial Small Cause Courts Act. He referred to article 6, but that article applies only to suits for foreclosure for sale or for redemption of a mortgage. The present suit is clearly not a suit of the kinds contemplated by article 6. It is merely a case of an erroneous decision of a question of law and this Court cannot interfere in revision. Therefore, the appeal was dismissed as barred by the provisions of section 102 of the Code of Civil Procedure.

3. Section 102 of CPC and 16 of Provincial Small Cause Court Act

Madhya Pradesh High Court examined the legality of the decision of suit of small cause nature tried as a regular suit. The question which has been referred to the Full Bench for decision is whether the decisions of a Division Bench of this Court reported in *Jagannath Bheraji* v. *Harisingh Kishanji*, 1968 Jab LJ 566: 1668 MPLJ 693: AIR 1969 MP 56 and *Poonamchand Bansidhar* v. *Ramprasad Gopilal Sarda*, 1968 Jab LJ 583: AIR 1969 MP 44: 1668 MPLJ 698, laid down the correct law. According to the aforesaid decisions, where a suit of a small cause nature is instituted and tried as a regular suit in contravention of the provisions of Section 16 of the Provincial Small Cause Courts Act, the judgment so rendered in it is one which is without jurisdiction and nullity.

The short facts of the case are that the plaintiff decree-holder, on 20-1-1967, started proceedings for the execution of the decree aforesaid. On 26-4-1967 the defendant judgment-debtor raised an objection that the suit as framed, being for payment of money, was exclusively triable by a Court of Small Causes and that as it had been tried as a regular civil suit by a Court of Civil Judge, Class II, in contravention of the provisions of section 16 of the Provincial Small Cause Courts Act, its decree, being one without jurisdiction, was a nullity. The objection was overruled by the executing Court; but, on appeal, the objection was upheld by the learned Additional District Judge, Narsimhapur. The plaintiff decree-holder, therefore, came up in miscellaneous second appeal.

It appears that before the learned Single Judge the question that was canvassed was that where a Civil Court tries a suit of a Small Cause nature as a regular civil suit, *i.e.,* as a long cause, MB judgment and decree are not nullities, and that the two judgments of this Court reported in *Jagannath Bheraji* v. *Harisingh Kishanji,* 1968 Jab LJ 566: 1668 MPLJ 693: AIR 1969 MP 56, and *Poonamchand Bansidhar* v. *Ramprasad Gopilal Sarda,* 1968 Jab LJ 583: AIR 1969 MP 44: 1668 MPLJ 698 required reconsideration.

Examining the reasons for the decision, the Court held that the decision mainly rests on an interpretation of section 16 of the Provincial Small Cause Courts Acts and in the opinion of the learned Judges:

(i) that section was 'imperative in its terms';

(ii) it 'takes away jurisdiction of the regular Court to try a suit of small cause nature as an ordinary suit if there is at the time of the institution a Court of small Causes having jurisdiction to try the suit as a Small Cause Suit';

(iii) the words "shall not be tried by any other Court having jurisdiction within the local limits ...."..'' mean that a regular Court is incompetent to try a suit cognizable by a Court of Small Causes having jurisdiction to try it;

(iv) the expression "Save as expressly provided by this Act or by any other enactment for the time being In force", with which section 16 of the Provincial Small Cause Courts Act begins, only emphasizes the fact that if a regular Court by error tries a suit, which is of small cause nature and is cognizable by a Small Cause Court exercising jurisdiction within the same local limits, then the proceedings of such Court are without jurisdiction and a nullity; and

(v) the observations in *Jodha* v. *Maganlal,* AIR 1930 Bom 80 that failure to comply with section 16 was merely a defect in procedure were *obiter*".

The Court further held as "Order XLVI, rule 6, C.P.C. provides for a reference by a regular Court or by a Small Cause Court to the High Court, where that

Court is in doubt whether the suit is cognizable by a Court of Small Causes or is not so cognizable. Such a reference has undoubtedly to be made before the delivery of judgment. In that event the High Court can resolve the doubt and can order the trial of the case by a particular Court. A similar reference is provided for by rule 7, Order XLVI, C.P.C, by subordinate Court. The District Court can make a reference to the High Court and on such reference, the High Court can pass an appropriate order. As has been pointed out by Shiv Dayal, J., the decree passed by the subordinate Court cannot be treated to be a nullity, because the High Court has not been given the power to validate a nullity, but only to pass an appropriate order as in the circumstances of a case may appear to the High Court to be just and proper. All these instances which come within the ambit of the saving clause of section 16 of the Provincial Small Cause Courts Act, would make the decree valid. These are the eventualities in which the trial of a case would be saved by the saving clause and the trial in such cases, at least, cannot be said to be a nullity. If the matter comes to the High Court either on appeal or in revision, the matter can be set right in exercise of appellate or revisional powers. There is no bar to that course being adopted. It would be a matter relating to procedure only, as has been suggested by Naik, J. Under section 9 of the Code of Civil Procedure, a Civil Court has the jurisdiction to try all causes of civil nature and as such it would have jurisdiction to try even a small cause suit or a suit of a small cause nature, but for the provisions of section 16 of the Provincial Small Cause Courts Act, which, however, has provided for a very comprehensive saving clause so as to include many categories of cases, and moreover, section 15 of the M.P. Civil Courts Act, 1958 having an overriding effect over the provisions of the Code of Civil Procedure and the Provincial Small Cause Courts Act, the trial of a case in contravention of section 16 of the Provincial Small Cause Courts Act, cannot be said to be vitiated so as to be treated as trial without jurisdiction and to render the decree passed in such a trial an utter nullity. For this reason, the Court agree with the view expressed by Naik, J. and disagreed with Shiv Dayal, J. with respect to conclusion No. 1 and conclusion No. 4 (partly) as mentioned in the concluding portion of its opinion.

Therefore, the Court answered the reference by agreeing with the view expressed by Naik, J. on the question referred to this Full Bench and therefore, the Court ordered:

> In accordance with the opinion of the majority, it was held that the decisions of the Division Bench of this Court in *Jagannath Bheraji* v. *Harisingh Kishanji*, 1968 Jab LJ 566: 1668 MPLJ 693: AIR 1969 MP 56 and *Poonamchand Bansidhar* v. *Ramprasad Gopilal Sarda*, 1968 Jab LJ 583: AIR 1969 MP 44: 1668 MPLJ 698 did not lay down the correct law and are therefore, hereby overruled. In their opinion, where a suit of a small cause nature is instituted and tried as a regular suit in contravention of the provisions of section 16 of the Provincial Small Cause Courts Act, the judgment so rendered in it is one which is not without jurisdiction and, therefore, not a nullity". *Bhaiyalal Girdharilal Shrivastava* v. *Tikaram Udaichand Jain*, 1970 MPWR 522: 1970 MPLJ 622: AIR 1970 MP 237 (FB).

Madhya Pradesh High Court in *Food Corporation of India* v. *Munnilal Singh*, 2003 (2) MPLJ 290: AIR 2003 MP 66: 2003 (4) JCR 320 MP, examined the scope of section 102 of CPC. Short facts of the case are that plaintiff entered into an agreement with appellants for transportation of goods from Itarsi Railway station to the godowns of appellants. For this purpose respondent No. 1 submitted a guarantee through respondent No. 2, New Bank of India. Contention of the plaintiff was that he has completed the work as per conditions of the agreement and was entitled for refund of bank guarantee and in spite of several requests, appellants have not refunded the guarantee amount. On these grounds suit was filed for recovery of Rs. 16,900.

Appellants denied the claim contending that plaintiff has committed breach of the agreement. He has not transported 120 bags of sugar in time to godown of defendant at Pipariya and there was delay in transporting the aforesaid sugar. He has misused stock of sugar resulting loss to the appellants and, in consequence, the bank guarantee was forfeited. Respondent bank contended that it was unnecessarily made party. There is defect of misjoinder of party. Apart from this, as per condition of bank guarantee, plaintiff is not entitled for refund of amount of bank guarantee and plaintiff is under obligation to return the bank guarantee after due discharge from appellants.

In the circumstances, the newly substituted section 102 by Code of Civil Procedure (Amendment) Act, 2002 came into force with effect from 1st July, 2002 and the second appeal from any decree, when the subject-matter of the original suit was for recovery of money not exceeding twenty-five thousand rupees, will be barred. The Court further pointed out that aforesaid section 102 of the Code of Civil Procedure. Code of Civil Procedure (Amendment) Act, 2002, under section 16 provides for repeal and savings. The relevant provision is section 16(2)(a), which reads as under: "16(2) Notwithstanding that the provisions of this Act have come into force or repeal under sub-section (1) has taken effect, and without prejudice to the generality of the provisions of section 6 of the General Clauses Act, 1887, (a) the provisions of section 102 of the principal Act as substituted by section 5 of this Act, shall not apply to or affect any appeal which had been admitted before the commencement of section 5; and every such appeal shall be disposed of as if section 5 had not come into force;" The aforesaid clause provides that the appeals which are pending on 1-7-2002 and already admitted before commencement of section 5 (substitution of section 102) are to be disposed of as if section 5 has not come into force. The word 'admitted' is not used in the Code of Civil Procedure.

Regarding section 102, newly amended, the Court said that it can reasonably be held that until and unless substantial question of law is formulated, an appeal cannot, be deemed to have passed through the stage of Order XLI, rule 11, Code of Civil Procedure. In the circumstances, intention of legislature in section 102 is that when the substantial question of law is formulated as required under section 100, and Order XLII, rule 2 of the Code, appeal shall be deemed to be admitted. If before this. Court has issued notice to the other side, it is in the stage of determining whether in the appeal any substantial question of law is involved or not. Thereafter, the Court will either formulate such substantial question of law and the appeal will proceed further, otherwise appeal shall be dismissed. Only after admission of appeal, provision of rule 16 of Order XLI will apply. In the circumstances, the word 'admitted' used in section 16(2)(a) of the Code of Civil Procedure (Amendment) Act, 2002 will mean that Court after hearing the appeal on formation of substantial question of law and is satisfied that the substantial question of law is involved and formulates such substantial question of law then; *Food Corporation of India* v. *Munnilal Singh*, 2003 (2) MPLJ 290: AIR 2003 MP 66: 2003 (4) JCR 320 MP.

4. Section 102, CPC and Article 227 of the Constitution

Andhra High Court also considered the scope of section 102 of the Code of Civil Procedure and maintainability of a writ petition filed under article 227 of the constitution of India. This civil revision petition filed under article 227 of the Constitution of India was directed against the judgment and decree, dated 31-5-2004, passed by the IV Additional District Judge, Kurnool, partly allowing the appeal in A.S. No. 23 of 2003, setting aside the judgment and decree, dated 12-9-2002, passed by the II Additional Junior Civil Judge at Kurnool, in O.S. No. 1376 of 2001 and decreeing the suit with proportionate costs of Rs. 13,237.

The only question that fell for consideration in the present civil revision petition filed under article 227 of the Constitution of India was - as to whether a civil revision filed under article 227 of the Constitution of India was maintainable against the judgment and decree passed by the first appellate court despite the specific bar contained in section 102 of the Code Civil Procedure which ordains that no second appeals would lay if the value of the subject-matter does not exceed Rs. 25,000?

In the instant case, the Court observed that it is to be seen that the value of the subject-matter of appeal, after passing of partial decree by the lower appellate court, is less than Rs. 25,000. Therefore, the present civil revision petition is attracted by section 102 of the Code of Civil Procedure, which created a clear bar postulating that no second appeal would lay from any decree, when the subject-matter of the original suit is for recovery of money not exceeding twenty-five thousand rupees. The Legislature enacted section 102 CPC with the clear and obvious object of reducing the scope of the litigation and to give quietus to the same.

Furthermore, if the present civil revision petition is entertained under article 227 of the Constitution of India, it amounts to exercising the appellate jurisdiction, which was prohibited by the apex court by way of guidelines in the judgments referred to supra.

The Court further held, that apart, the judgment under challenge is not an interlocutory order. Further, the judgment under challenge, as already noticed, is final and rendered by the lower appellate court.

For the foregoing reasons, without going into the merits of the case, and in view of the specific and unambiguous language contained in section 102 of the Civil Procedure Code, the Court held that the remedy available to the petitioner is to file a second appeal, if so advised, and the present civil revision petition filed under article 227 of the Constitution of India is not maintainable. Therefore, this civil revision is liable to be dismissed.

Subject to the above observation, the civil revision petition was dismissed, at the stage of admission without any order as to costs; *Shaik Abdul Haq* v. *Aiswarya Nilaya Chit Fund Pvt. Ltd.*, 2005 (3) ALD 513: 2005 (3) ALT 676: IV (2005) BC 70.

5. Section 102 and Second Appeal

The Allahabad High Court examined maintainability of a second appeal in view of the provision of section 102 of CPC . In the case under reference, at the hearing of the second appeal a preliminary objection was taken on behalf of the respondent that no second appeal lay in view of section 102 of the Code of Civil Procedure. The Single Judge, however, heard the appeal on the question that the decree passed by the trial court was without jurisdiction and a nullity. He found that conflicting inferences could be drawn from different Full Bench decisions of this Court, and in view of the importance of the question involved in the context of the new Civil Laws Amendment Act, 1972, it was a fit case in which the appeal should be heard by a larger Full Bench, the Judge referred the appeal itself to a larger Bench. That is how the appeal has come up before the Full Bench.

At the commencement of the hearing the question arose whether the second appeal was competent. The Court said that it cannot be gainsaid that the present suit became small causes in nature after the coming into force of the Civil Laws Amendment Act, 1972, It is true that under section 9 of the Amending Act such suit was, triable by the Small Cause Court and was liable to be transferred to it from the regular side, but nonetheless, it continued to retain its nature, namely, small causes. In that event section 102 which applies to suits of the nature of small causes but which are tried on the regular side, is fully applicable. Under it no second appeal lies. The present second appeal was clearly incompetent.

At this stage learned counsel for the appellant prayed that the memorandum of appeal be permitted to be converted into a civil revision. The Court held that this is a discretionary matter, we find that the defendant-appellant did not inform the trial court that it has lost jurisdiction to continue to try the suit because of the coming into force of section 9 of the Civil Laws Amendment Act, 1972, otherwise the trial court would have immediately transferred the case to the relevant Small Cause Court. There is no evidence to show that the defendant was not aware of the coming into force of the Amending Act. Under the circumstances the position is that the defendant voluntarily had a trial on the merits before a, regular Court. The procedure before a regular Court is more detailed. Further, the defendant has had another innings on the merits before the lower appellate court. Under the circumstances a Full Bench of the High Court of Allahabad held it to be a fit case where the prayer for conversion of the appeal into a revision should be sustained. The appeal was accordingly dismissed as incompetent; *Bisheshwar Prasad Gautam* v. *R.K. Agarwal*, AIR 1977 All 103: (1976) 2 All LR 324: 1976 All WC 603 (FB).

The Punjab-Haryana High Court also examined the maintainability of a second appeal. Counsel for the respondent basing himself on the decision in *Hari Kishan* v. *Amar Nath*, 52 Punj LR 13: AIR (38) 1951 Punj 346, urges a preliminary objection that E.S.A. No. 337 of 1949 is not competent. In *Hari Kishan* v. *Amar Nath*, 52 Punj LR 13, the judgment-debtor raised an objection in the execution proceedings that he could not be evicted in execution of a decree passed before or after the commencement of the Punjab Urban Rent Restriction Act, 1947, except in accordance with the provisions of section 13 of that Act. The plea did not find favour either with the Executing Court or with the Court of the District Judge. From the order passed by the District Judge in appeal, Hari Kishan judgment-debtor preferred an appeal in this Court and in the appellate proceedings a preliminary objection was taken by the learned counsel for Amar Nath landlord that the appeal was not competent.

In allowing the objection, Kapiir, J., said:

> "I am of the opinion that in this case if no second appeal lay from the original matter under section 13 of Act IV of 1947 no second appeal would lie in execution of the order passed under that section"; *Hans Raj Salig Ram* v. *L. Niranjan Lal,* AIR 1952 Punj 159: (1952) 54 Punj LR 31.

The Andhra High Court also decided maintainability of a second appeal in the case of *Tummala Tirumala Rao* v. *Pemmasani Laxmaiah*, 2004 (3) ALT 522: I (2005) BC 125. Here, this Second Appeal was admitted on 29-6-1993. The value of the Second Appeal for the purpose of Court-fee and jurisdiction is Rs. 8404.

Tummala Tirumalarao, appellant/plaintiff filed O.S. No. 532/79 on the file of I Additional Munsif Magistrate, Tenali for recovery of Rs. 6400 against the respondent-defendant, Pemmasani Laxmaiah. The suit was partly decreed by the Court of first instance on 16-1-1986 and aggrieved by the same, the plaintiff carried the matter by way of Appeal A.S. No. 7/86 on the file of Principal Subordinate Judge, Tenali and the same was dismissed on 19-11-1992. The plaintiff being aggrieved by the said Judgment and decree had preferred the present Second Appeal.

6. Section 102 – Second Appeal – Recovery Suit

In *Food Corporation of India* v. *Walaiti Ram Amar Nath, Commission Agent,* 2017 1 Law Herald 359: 2017 1 Law Herald 359 (P&H) the dispute that arose between the parties was whether there was any shortage at the time when the paddy was purchased. It would be relevant to refer to para no. 7 of the judgment of the appellate Court which reads as under:—

> "After hearing the learned counsel for the parties and going through the evidence on record, I am of the considered opinion that no exception can be taken to the finding recorded by the trial Court. The letter mark X has not been proved according to the law. So the letter mark X cannot be read into evidence. Further more, one of the partner has appeared as PW1. This letter was not got confronted from him. So no reliance can be placed on this letter. Admittedly, the appellant has purchased the paddy worth Rs. 1,32,14,871/- on 15.11.1982 and Rs. 77,837-00 on 20.11.1982 when this purchase was made by the appellant, it has not been shown that there was

any shortage of the paddy. There is no evidence on the record that when the bags of the paddy were handed over to the officials of the appellant, then there was shortage. DW8 Purana Chand Assistant General Manager admitted the signatures on forms ST-XXII Ex.P2 and Ex.P3. These were signed by the Assistant Manager Mr. Bhatia. He also admitted that as per these forms the paddy worth amount mentioned in the same was purchased by them from the plaintiff/respondent and the same reached in their custody and the entries regarding the same was made in their account books. So the sole controversy has been cleared by DW8 that the paddy worth Rs.299086-34 were purchased from the plaintiff vide Ex.P2 and Ex.P3 and there was no shortage when the appellant had purchased it. If any shortage occurred in the godown of the appellant plaintiff/ respondent is not liable for that. Admittedly the appellant has not made payments claimed by the plaintiff/respondent. Therefore, the appellants are liable to pay that amount to the plaintiff."

The High Court said, the provisions of Section 102 CPC are clear. No second appeal lies against any decree when the subject matter of the original suit is for recovery of money not exceeding Rs. 25,000/-. Reference can also be made to *Haryana Dairy Development Cooperative Federation Ltd.* v. *Jagdish Lal,* (2014) 3 SCC 156: 2014 LLR 225 and *Gurudawara Singh Sabha* v. *Uttar Haryana Bijli Vitran Nigram Ltd.,* RSA No. 4972 of 2012 (O&M), decided on 21.05.2014, wherein such law as laid down. Therefore, the appeal was not maintainable. There is no substantial question of law involved. No ground for interference in the concurrent finding is made out.

7. Section 102 – Amount Including Total Mediclaim Amounting to Rs. 8,724

In *Haryana Dairy Development Cooperative Federation Limited* v. *Jagdish Lal,* 2014 (2) JCR (SC) 166: 2014 3 SCC 156: 2014 2 SCC (Civ) 265: 2014 2 SCC (Cri) 134, the Supreme Court examined the scope of section 102.The Apex Court said, in spite of the fact that the Parliament has amended the Code of Civil Procedure, 1908 altering the provisions of Section 102 CPC providing that money recovery suit involving less than Rs. 25,000/- shall not be entertained in Second Appeal, we are being burdened with cases where the litigation cost may be hundred times more than the amount involved. It has become the definite attitude of the officials not to take any responsibility even for petty issues and would waste public money approaching this Court. Government departments would spend any amount on litigation instead of paying petty amount to the other party. In the instant case, an amount of Rs. 8,724/- is to be paid to the respondent employee as reimbursement of his medical claim and the petitioner Haryana Dairy Development Cooperative Federation Limited treating the litigation as luxury must have spent the amount already by filing this petition more than the total amount involved herein.

Many a time this Court has felt unhappy about the time of the Court being taken for days together by petty matters. (*The Constitution Bench judgment Sukhdev Singh, Oil & Natural Gas Commission, Life Insurance Corporation, Industrial Finance Corporation Employees Associations* v. *Bhagat Ram, Association of Class II, Officers, Shyam Lal, Industrial Finance Corporation,* AIR 1975 SC 1331: 1975 Lab IC 881).

In *Kadra Pahadiya* v. *State of Bihar*, AIR 1997 SC 3750: 1997 (2) PLJR 71, this Court observed that if the load of such petty cases is taken out of the regular Courts, those Courts would have time to deal with more serious crimes rather than have their time consumed by such petty cases.

The Law Commission of India in its 155th report has observed that what further agitates is the number of pending litigations relating to trivial matters or petty claims, some of which has been hanging for more than fifteen years. It hardly needs mention that in many such cases money spent on litigation is far in excess of the stakes involved, besides wasting valuable time and energy of the concerned parties as well as the Court.

We direct that the expenses of the litigation shall be incurred by the Managing Director personally who has signed affidavit in support of the petition and it shall not be taken from the Federation. A copy of the order be sent to the learned Chief Secretary of the State of Haryana as well as to the Managing Director. The special leave petition is dismissed. In view of the above, question of law, if any is kept open.

In *Dr. Rajesh* v. *Bharat Lal Bhargava*, 2016 2 Law Herald 1846: (2016) 182 PLR 323, the High Court of Punjab & Haryana said, there is a complete bar for second appeal in a suit for recovery of amount involving less than Rs. 25,000.

In *Shriram General Insurance Company Limited* v. *Arvind Kumar*, 2017 2 ADJ (NOC) 38 The High Court of Punjab & Haryana said, It is settled law that courts of justice generally do not take trifling and immaterial matters into account in view of the maxim de minimis non curat lex which means that the law does not concern itself with trifles.

There may be some injuries of so little consideration that in law no action lies for them. It is in such cases of small injuries of immaterial nature that the above maxim has been frequently applied. A familiar instance of application of the above maxim are cases of assessment with more rigorous application in financial matters.

It is important to refer to Section 102 C.P.C. which prohibits filing of second appeal in certain cases where the subject matter of the original suit is for recovery of money not exceeding Rs. 25,000/-. The said provision is supposed to be based upon the above legal maxim.

8. Section 115, 102 – Revision Petition – Maintainability – Revision if Allowed to Come would Amount to Eclipsing Section 102, C.P.C.

In *Uttam Chand* v. *Gulab Chand Narendra Kumar*, 2013 (2) RLW (Raj) 1298 this revision petition had been filed under Section 115, C.P.C. against the judgment and decree passed by the trial Court and affirmed by the first appellate Court for recovery of Rs. 10,000/-. Section 102, C.P.C. provides that no second appeal lies from any decree, when the subject-matter of the original suit is for recovery of money not exceeding Rs. 25,000/-; meaning thereby, although second appeal is permissible but the legislature with open eyes put a restriction under Section 102, C.P.C. so that matter should come to an end, therefore, it is specifically provided that notwithstanding there being appeal provision under Section 100,

C.P.C., when the subject-matter of the original suit is for recovery of money not exceeding Rs. 10,000/-, then, such second appeal shall not lie. In the opinion of this Court, the legislature in its wisdom has curtailed the right of filing second appeal by way of putting above restriction on the point of pecuniary limit of the cause. Therefore, even if any substantial question of law is involved, no second appeal shall lie against the judgment and decree if the initial suit was filed for recovery of money less than Rs. 25,000/-. If it is the intention of the legislature, then, of course, it can be said that petitioner cannot invoke jurisdiction of this Court under Section 115, C.P.C. because such invocation of the revisional jurisdiction will render the specific provision of Section 102 to nullity which is not permissible. Under Section 115, C.P.C. the legality and propriety as well as perversity can be seen, so also, while exercising jurisdiction of second appeal the appeal can be admitted upon substantial question of law. Both are peri materia, therefore, a revision petition filed under Section 115, C.P.C. is not maintainable. Here, in this case, recovery of suit was filed by the petitioner for Rs. 10,000/- and second appeal is prohibited or specifically barred under Section 102, C.P.C. Therefore, it cannot be said that no appeal is provided against the judgment thereby invoke jurisdiction under Section 115, C.P.C. because if cases of this nature are allowed to be entertained it would amount to eclipsing Section 102, C.P.C. which specifically aims at ending the litigation in view of the pecuniary quantum involved in the cause. In this view of the matter, this revision petition under Section 115, C.P.C. is not maintainable.

9. Section 102, Section 102(1), Section 102(3) – Kerala Protection of River Banks and Regulation of Removal of Sand Act, 2001

In *Rajeev* v. *District Collector, Thrissur,* 2012 2 KLT 547 (Ker) the High Court said, Section 20 of the Act provides the penalty for contravention of the provisions of the Act or the rules made thereunder. Section 21 provides the penalty for abetment of any offence punishable under the Act. Taking cognizance of any offence punishable under the Act stands governed by sections 24 and 25. Statutory provisions authorizing various actions in terms of the provisions of the Act, either by the revenue authorities or by the criminal courts, have been dealt with, quite elaborately, in different decisions; *Abdul Samad* v. *State of Kerala,* 2007 (4) KLT 473; *Moosakoya* v. *State of Kerala,* 2008 (1) KLT 538: 2008 Cri LJ 2388; *Ahammed Kutty* v. *State of Kerala,* 2008 (1) KLT 1068: 2008 (1) KLJ 809; *Shoukathali* v. *Tahsildar,* 2009 (1) KLT 640: ILR 2009 (1) Ker 699, and few others as well. Examining them, we do not find any conflict among those precedents on any issue relating to Sections 20, 21, 22, 24 or 25 of the Act.

We also need to note that section 22 of the Act provides that nothing in the Act shall prevent any person from being prosecuted under any other law, for the time being in force, for any act or omission made punishable under the Act. This means that if the act or omission resulting in the violation of sections 20, 21 or 22 of the Act also amounts to an offence punishable under any other law, including the Indian Penal Code, the law will take its due course and the provisions as to the taking of cognizance would not then be controlled by sections 24 and 25 of the Act in so far as the criminal proceedings are relatable to the allegation as to commission of such other offences, as may be made out. Ignoring section

22, while construing sections 20, 21, 24 and 25, would be counterproductive to the objects sought to be achieved by the Act.

The Court then took under consideration the provisions of section 102 and said. section 102(1) of Crl.P.C. empowers any police officer to seize any property which may be alleged or suspected to have been stolen, or which may be found under circumstances which create suspicion of the commission of any offence. Under subsection (3) of Section 102, the police officer shall forthwith report the seizure to the Magistrate having jurisdiction. The provision in Section 102 undoubtedly would apply when any police officer finds any property under circumstances which create suspicion of the commission of any offence which would be punishable under any law. In its application to sand or vehicle which is subjected to proceedings under section 23 of the Act, even if the seizure is done by a revenue official, a police officer may effect seizure of the self same goods, in terms of Section 102(1) of Crl.P.C. and the revenue official shall then hand over the seized goods to that police officer. This is because the authority, power and the corollary duty of the police officer under section 102(1) of Crl.P.C. is not abridged in any manner by the provisions in the Act. The legislative authorization in section 23 of the Act, though a clumsily worded provision, is only to seize for the purpose of confiscation and not to effect seizure for purposes intended by section 102(1) of Crl.P.C., which include detection, containment, investigation, prosecution and trial in terms of the penal laws. Remember, the offences under the Act are cognizable, meaning that a police officer may arrest without warrant; though, section 25 of the Act interdicts cognizance by Court, except on a complaint by a person authorized in terms of that section of the Act. Following such seizure, police officer shall report such seizure to the Magistrate concerned, in terms of section 102(3) Crl.P.C.

The directions, 12 in number, contained in *Moosakoya* v. *State of Kerala,* 2008 (1) KLT 538: 2008 Cri LJ 2388 deal exclusively with the domain of the confiscation or appropriation of the value of the vehicle. They do not, in any manner, deal with the prosecution of the offenders in terms of the Act. However, coming to *Shoukathali* v. *Tahsildar,* [2009 (1) KLT 640], the three further directions issued in paragraph 27 may give an impression that they are intended to govern also cases where prosecution has to be initiated. Though advertence is made to section 102 Crl.P.C. in *Moosakoya (supra)* and *Shoukathali (supra),* the focus by the learned Judges deciding those cases was only on the aspect of seizure under section 23 of the Act for confiscation of vehicles. We read those decisions only in that manner because, as already noted, the confiscation provided thereby is, as noted in *Moosakoya(supra),* a power that rests with the District Collector or such revenue authority, as the case may be. Now, looking at section 23, we see that the Legislature has clearly envisaged the requirement to punish the offenders apart from confiscation of vehicles. This means that the requirement to initiate action by filing complaint in terms of section 25 has necessarily to be followed in all cases where situation calls for such action. The purport of the Act and the clear provision in section 23 that whoever transports sand without complying with the provisions of the Act "shall be liable to be punished" categorically shows that under such circumstances, the person effecting the seizure, be it a police official or a revenue official, has the bounden duty to have the culprit brought to face the consequence of the penal laws governing the situation. That duty is also on the person authorized in terms of section 25 of the Act. This duty can never be disregarded. Therefore, the directions in *Shoukathali(supra)* apply only to seizure for confiscation and appropriation by the State as noticed in Moosakoya(supra). Those directions do not regulate seizures for and in connection with prosecution; which matter falls under section 102 Crl.P.C.

10. Section 102 – Suit for Possession – Suit Seeking Possessing Allowed by trial Court – Order set aside by Appellate Court while Relying upon Section 102

In the case of *Sohan Lal* v. *Ved Kumari*, 2016 (4) Law Herald 3324: 2017 (1) PCR (Civil) 1027 (P&H) the case set out in the plaint was that owing to the succession/legal heir of Sewa Ram, appellant-plaintiff had become the owner of the property and defendants No.1 to 4 who were related to each other closely in conspiracy and with other persons of the society got the name of the plaintiff struck off which was referred to the Arbitrator and ultimately came in his favour but they had raised the construction to let out the same to defendant no.5. It is in this background of the matter, the suit for possession was filed.

He submitted that the nature of the suit does not fall in any of the category in view of the provisions of Section 102 of 1984 Act and thus, urged this Court for setting aside the findings under challenge.

Per contra, Mr. Shakti Bhardwaj, Advocate for Mr. Vinod S. Bhardwaj, learned counsel appearing on behalf of the respondents submitted that the jurisdiction of the Civil Court was expressly barred as the claim of the plaintiff had been on the basis of withdrawal of the membership and thus, until and unless the same could not be settled, he could not have sought the possession. He could not have join two cause of action regarding removal of membership and possession, for, first relief jurisdiction of the Civil Court barred and thus, urged this Court for affirming the findings under challenge.

I have heard learned counsel for the parties and appraised the judgments and decrees of both the Courts below and of the view that findings rendered by the Lower Appellate Court are not only fallacious but perverse. On perusal of the provisions of Section 102 of 1984 Act (supra) supported the jurisdiction of the Civil Court is barred in case, any of the aforementioned situation arises as stated above. The nature of the suit is for possession of the property and the membership of the appellant had already been decided as per the awards noticed above, i.e., Ex.P2 and Ex.P3.

It is conceded position on record that the defendants are in illegal occupation of the aforementioned shop. Once the appellant has been held to be member and legal heir of Sewa Ram, the Lower Appellate Court ought to have upheld the findings of the trial Court. The defendants have chosen not to file the cross objection disputing the fact that possession was not based upon the title.

The Court said, no doubt, this Court, on earlier occasions had been framing the substantial questions of law while deciding the appeals but in view of the ratio decidendi culled out by five learned Judges of the Hon'ble Supreme Court in *Pankajakshi (dead) through LRs* v. *Chandrika,* 2016 (2) RCR (Civil) 245: 2016 (2) Recent Apex Judgments (RAJ) 124: AIR 2016 SC 1213, wherein the proposition arose as to whether in view of the provisions of Section 97(1) CPC, provisions of Section 41 of the Punjab Courts Act, 1918 would apply or the appeal i.e. RSA would be filed under Section 100 of Code of Civil Procedure, so there is need to frame the substantial questions of law or not. The Constitutional Bench of Hon'ble Supreme Court held that the decision in *Kulwant Kaur* v. *Gurdial Singh Mann (dead) by LRs,* 2001 (4) SCC 262 on applicability of Section 97(1) of CPC is not a correct law, in essence, the provisions of Section 41 of the Punjab Courts Act, 1918 had been restored back.

For the sake of brevity, the relevant portion of the judgment of five learned Judges of the Hon'ble Supreme Court in *Pankajakshi 's case (supra)* reads thus:-

> "Since Section 41 of the Punjab Act is expressly in conflict with the amending law, viz., Section 100 as amended, it would be deemed to have been repealed. Thus we have no hesitation to hold that the law declared by the Full Bench of the High Court in the case of *Ganpat* [AIR 1978 P&H 137: 80 Punj LR 1 (FB)] cannot be sustained and is thus overruled." [at paras 27 - 29]"
>
> "27. Even the reference to Article 254 of the Constitution was not correctly made by this Court in the said decision. Section 41 of the Punjab Courts Act is of 1918 vintage. Obviously, therefore, it is not a law made by the Legislature of a State after the Constitution of India has come into force. It is a law made by a Provincial Legislature under Section 80A of the Government of India Act, 1915, which law was continued, being a law in force in British India, immediately before the commencement of the Government of India Act, 1935, by Section 292 thereof. In turn, after the Constitution of India came into force and, by Article 395, repealed the Government of India Act, 1935, the Punjab Courts Act was continued being a law in force in the territory of India immediately before the commencement of the Constitution of India by virtue of Article 372(1) of the Constitution of India. This being the case, Article 254 of the Constitution of India would have no application to such a law for the simple reason that it is not a law made by the Legislature of a State but is an existing law continued by virtue of Article 372 of the Constitution of India. If at all, it is Article 372(1) alone that would apply to such law which is to continue in force until altered or repealed or amended by a competent Legislature or other competent authority. We have already found that since Section 97(1) of the Code of Civil Procedure (Amendment) Act, 1976 has no application to Section 41 of the Punjab Courts Act, it would necessarily continue as a law in force."

11. Section 102 – Suit for Recovery of Amount less than L 25,000

In *Dr. Rajesh* v. *Bharat Lal Bhargava,* 2016 (2) PLR 323: 2016 (2) Law Herald 1846: 2016 (162) AIC 624 (P&H) respondent/plaintiff had filed suit for recovery of L 18,897/- and the Court of learned Civil Judge (Junior Division), Rewari decreed the said suit. Present petitioner filed first appeal against the said judgment &

decree and the same was dismissed by the Court below on 28.1.2014. Learned counsel for the petitioner submitted that the said findings of both the Courts below are erroneous and are liable to be set aside.

Learned counsel for the respondent raised objection that as per Section 102 CPC, present petition, being second appeal in a suit for recovery of an amount not exceeding L 25,000/-, is not maintainable. While arguing on this point, learned counsel for the petitioner submitted that present case is a petition under Article 227 of the Constitution of India and not the second appeal and the same is not maintainable. In support of his arguments, learned counsel for the petitioner placed reliance upon the view taken by co-ordinate Bench of this Court in case *Om Parkash* v. *Sardha Ram,* (Civil Revision No. 2793 of 2012, decided on 31.8.2012). On the same point, reliance was placed upon the judgment from Madras High Court in case *K. Chockalingam* v. *K.R. Ramasamy Iyer and Jenbagam,* 2004 (4) LW 586 (Mad).

The Court said, this Court has considered the submissions made by learned counsel for the parties and also gone through the view taken by the coordinate Bench of this Court in Om Parkash's case (supra) and also by the Madras High Court in K.Chockalingam's case (supra) and of the view that as per amended provisions of Section 102 CPC, there is a complete bar for second appeal in a suit for recovery of amount involving less than L 25,000/-. Merely filing of revision petition in lieu of filing second appeal does not make out a case for maintainability of the matter before this Court. The very object of incorporating such an amendment in the Code of Civil Procedure is to bring an end to litigation involving petty matter and there being no dispute that the matter in controversy is based on a suit for recovery of money not exceeding L 25,000/- and legislature has already enacted the provisions while being conscious that there should be no second appeal in such like suits for recovery of money not exceeding L25,000/-. Filing of petition under Article 227 of the Constitution is just to frustrate the very object of such a legislation which is not permissible.

12. Sections 102 and 115 – Constitution of India, 1950 Article 227 Recovery Suit

In *Sarwan Singh* v. *Mohar Singh,* 2017 (2) Himachal LR 687 (HP) recovery suit was allowed by the trial court but was partly modified in appeal. The Court held, the main object of Article 227 is to keep strict and judicial control by the High Court on the administration of justice within its territory and to ensure that the wheels of justice do not come to a halt and the foundation of justice remain pure and pristine in order to maintain public confidence in the functioning of the Courts subordinate to the High Court.

Thus, this Court has no difficulty in concurring with the view expressed by a Co-ordinate Bench of this Court in Subhadra Devi, Mohan Lal's cases (supra) whereby it has been held that the provisions under Article 227 of the Constitution of India cannot be used as a means to circumvent the bar to filing of an appeal, yet the powers under Article 227 of the Constitution of India can always be exercised where the judgment or order challenged is totally illegal or perverse. However, while exercising such powers under Article 227 of the

Constitution, the High Court shall have to bear in mind the principles as laid down in *Surya Dev Rai* and *Chhabi Nath* cases (supra). However, this Court expresses its inability to concur with the ratio as laid down by a Co-ordinate Bench of this Court in Managing Director's case (supra) wherein it was observed that in exercise of revisional jurisdiction, this Court can look into the question as to the correctness, legality or propriety of any decision or order impugned.

A second appeal is not maintainable in the present case in view of Section 102 of the Code which has already been quoted above.

Section 102 was substituted by the Code of Civil Procedure (Amendment) Act 1999 (Act 46 of 1999) wherein the amendment sought to be introduced was as follows:—

> "102. No second appeal in certain cases:- No second appeal shall lie from any decree, when the amount or value of the subject matter of the original suit does not exceed twenty-five thousand rupees."

Subsequently, by the Code of Civil Procedure (Amendment) Act 2002 (Act 22 of 2002) which came into force on 01.07.2002, the amendment proposed to be effected by Act 46 of 1999 was substituted with the present Section 102. As per the amendment of Act 1999, irrespective of the nature of the suit, no Second Appeal would lie against the decision in a suit where the value of the subject matter is below Rs. 25,000/-. By the amendment introduced by Act 22 of 2002, the bar under Section 102 is limited to suits where the subject matter is for recovery of money not exceeding twenty five thousand rupees. It was pursuant to the Law Commission 145th report that the amendment was carried out in Section 102 of the Code in order to ensure that trivial matters or petty claims where the money spent on litigation is far excess of the stakes involved do not enter the Courts which besides wasting the valuable time and energy of the parties, but also of the Court."

26. This was so observed by the Hon'ble Supreme Court in *Nagarpalika Thakurdwara* v. *Khalil Ahmed,* JT 2016 (9) SC 425: AIR 2016 SC 4477, the relevant observations read thus:—

> "14. The purpose behind enactment of Section 102 of the CPC is to reduce the quantum of litigation so that courts may not have to waste time where the stakes are very meagre and not of much consequence. In the instant case, though apparently the amount which was sought to be recovered was Rs.11,006.07, looking at the prayer made in the plaint, the consequences of the final outcome of the litigation would be farreaching."

A Second Appeal is maintainable only on a substantial question of law as provided under Section 100 of the Code of Civil Procedure. A Revision under Section 115 of the Code of Civil Procedure lies where the subordinate court appears to have exercised jurisdiction not vested in it by law; or to have failed to exercise jurisdiction so vested; or to have acted in the exercise of its jurisdiction illegally or with material irregularity. The question is whether the High Court would be entitled to entertain a Civil Revision Petition, in a case where a Second Appeal is barred under section 102 of the Code of Civil Procedure, on any ground which is less rigorous than that provided in Section 100 of the Code of Civil Procedure.

28. Even in matters where the valuation exceed Rs. 25,000/-, a second appeal could be entertained only on a substantial question of law. When Section 102 provides that no second appeal would lie in respect of a suit where the subject matter is for recovery of money not exceeding Rs. 25,000/-, it cannot be assumed the Parliament thought it fit to take such category of cases out of the rigour of Section 100 and to provide a less rigorous remedy in such cases. If so, it is to be taken that a revision under Section 115 cannot be entertained on a ground which is less rigorous than that provided in Section 100 of the Code of Civil Procedure.

29. The purpose of substituting Section 102 C.P.C. was to restrict entertaining Second Appeals in cases where the subject matter of the suit is for recovery of money not exceeding Rs. 25,000/-. The purpose sought to be achieved cannot be defeated by entertaining a revision under section 115 of the Code of Civil Procedure on a less rigorous test than that provided in Section 100 C.P.C.

The Court referred to the provisions of section 115 and said, in addition to the aforesaid, it would be noticed that Section 115 of the Code does not refer to a decree and further provides that revision can be invoked where no appeal lies against the impugned order/judgment. There is a marked difference as regards an order or judgment against which no appeal lies and the judgment or order against which an appeal is prohibited or restricted by the Code.

Under Section 115 CPC, the legality and propriety as well as perversity can be seen, so also, while exercising jurisdiction of second appeal, appeal can be admitted only on substantial questions of law. The scope of both these provisions is quite similar and, therefore, the petitioners cannot invoke jurisdiction of this Court under Section 115 CPC because such invocation of revisional jurisdiction will render the specific provision of Section 102 of the Code to be otiose which is not permissible.

Accordingly, with all humility at my command, I regret my inability to concur with the view expressed by a Co-ordinate Bench of this Court in Managing Director's case (supra). In view of this difference, it is necessary for me to refer the matter to a larger Bench. Even otherwise, the issue is of great importance and the views expressed by the different High Courts on the question are otherwise not consistent and it is desirable that an authoritative pronouncement be made by a larger Bench.

***103. Power of High Court to determine issues of fact.*—In any second appeal, the High Court may, if the evidence on the record is sufficient, determine any issue necessary for the disposal of the appeal,**

(a) which has not been determined by the lower appellate court or both by the Court of first instance and the lower appellate court, or

(b) which has been wrongly determined by such Court or Courts reason of a decision on such question of law as is referred to in section 100.

SYNOPSIS

Comments

1. Section 103 – Scope and Application

This section supersedes the ruling given by a Full Bench of Allahabad High Court in 9 A 147 (FB) and 9 A 26 [30] although no second appeal can be preferred, no question of fact can be raised, but when such an appeal is already before the High Court, it may determine issues of fact when such issues (1) have not been determined by the lower appellate court, and (2) have been wrongly determined by reason of any illegality, mission error or defect such as referred to in sub-section (1) of section 100, C.P.C. provided the evidence on record is sufficient for such determination; *Buddha* v. *Balwanta*, AIR 1958 All 699. Where both the courts below did not consider the admissible evidence on the record and the first court decided the case merely on probabilities and the second court on the basis of inadmissible evidence the result is that the findings are vitiated and the second appeal lies, though the question involved is one of fact and in the circumstances, the High Court must examine the admissible evidence and come to its own conclusion on such question of fact; *Thongam Yaimabi Singh* v. *Thounaojam Kali Singh*, AIR 1959 Manipur 32. Where the lower court has decided a question of which one is one of facts on inadmissible evidence and other evidence, the High Court can remand the case to the lower appellate court directing it to record a fresh finding after eliminating the inadmissible evidence or may proceed under section 103, C.P.C. and arrive at its own finding on perusal of the relevant and admissible evidence: 1936 L. 788. Where the evidence on the record is sufficient within the purview of section 103, C.P.C. and section 167 of the Evidence Act. It is open to the High Court in second appeal itself to determine as issue of fact if it finds that it has been wrongly determined by reason of any illegality and there would be no question of a remand for a new trial: *Abdul Shakur* v. *Kotwaleshwar Prasad*, AIR 1958 All 54. Where the lower appellate court has improperly admitted any evidence the High Court has no right to look at the evidence to decide whether the remaining evidence in a case other than that which has been improperly admitted is sufficient to warrant the finding of the Court below the only cases which can with propriety be disposed of under such circumstances without remand are those where independently of the evidence improperly admitted, the lower court has apparently arrived at its conclusions upon other grounds; 1987 C 537: ILR (1937) 2 C 661. When the lower court has not framed the appropriate issue the second appellate court may raise and decide it itself if there is sufficient evidence on record for deciding it; 47 C. 107: 1919 PC 219: 37 MLJ 36 (PC). The High Court of Patna said that where a final court of fact has come to a finding of fact without considering material evidence on the record, the High Court is competent in second appeal to decide the question of fact on consideration of such evidence under section 103; *Kanhaiya Singh* v. *Bhagwat Singh*, 1954 BLJR 170: AIR 1954 Pat 326.

When the lower court has not given any finding on a question of fact the High Court can under section 103, arrive at a finding on the evidence on record; 28 IC 673: 1 LW 249; ILR (1945) Kar 301, or may remit the case to the lower court for a finding on that issue with liberty to the parties to adduce additional evidence 49 IA 286: 45 M 586: 1922 PC 292: 43 MLJ 640 (PC). The Madras High Court said that where the judgment of a Court of appeal is reversed on a question of customs or usage on a preliminary point, the High Court should not take on itself to examine the evidences as to usage but should remand the case for disposal on the merits by the lower appellate court; 40 M 1108: 32 MLJ 237. The Supreme Court examined the scope of the provision envisaged by section 103 and held that object of the provision is to avoid remand of the case; *Municipal Committee, Hoshiarpur* v. *Punjab State Electricity Board,* JT 2010 (11) SC 615: (2010) 11 SCALE 69: 2010 (7) SLT 451.

2. Section 103 and Order XLI, Rule 25

Order XLI, rule 25 refers primarily to first appeals, though the rule, so far as possible, can be applied to second appeals. The rule as it stands allows reference only to the Court from whose decree the appeal is preferred, which in the case of second appeals would be the lower appellate court. Therefore, it does not follow in the case of second appeal that a finding from a first Court is to be treated on the same footing as finding from an appellate court. Where an issue has not been determined by the a High Court and the issue is remitted on remand to the trial court the evidence having been found to be insufficient, and the trial court after recording such evidence and giving its finding on that issue returns the case to the High Court, the issue cannot be said to have been determined by the lower appellate court. Therefore, High Court has jurisdiction to determine such issue of fact under section 103; 1939 NLJ 315: ILR (1940) N 643; *Kuseshwar Jha* v. *Uma Kant Jha,* 22 Pat LT 1001: AIR 1942 Pat 188.

3. Section 103 and Order XLI, Rule 27

The provisions contained under section 103 should be considered along with the provisions of Order XLI and Order XLII of the Code. The High Court of Andhra Pradesh made it clear that there is nothing either in section 103 or in Order XLI, rule 27. C.P.C. excludes the applicability of the latter provision to second appeals. The terms of rule 27 are general in application and in an appropriate case it is open to the High Court in second appeal to admit additional evidence. (*P.V. Subba Raja* v. *S.S. Narayana Raja,* AIR 1954 Mad 1074: 1954 Mad WN 677, dissented from); *Venku Reddi* v. *Pichi Reddi,* 1956 Andh WR 824: AIR 1956 Andh 250.

The power of the High Court to determine issues depends on three things. *First,* it is necessary that there must be sufficient evidence on record to determine such an issue. *Secondly,* the Court may proceed to determine such issue where the lower appellate court or both the lower courts had either not determined the said issue, or thirdly, had wrongly determined it.

Where the compromise decree was alleged to have been obtained by practising fraud on the Court, and the plea was raised, but the lower courts did not address themselves to it, the Supreme Court held that the High Court is in second appeal entitled to determine the question *Jadu Gopal Chakravarty* v. *Pannalal Bhowmick,* AIR 1978 SC 1329: (1978) 3 SCC 215. Obviously, this issue was taken as one having not been determined by the High Court. As already stated the jurisdiction of the High Court to decide such a question of facts not determined by the lower court depends on existence of sufficient evidence on record *i.e.,* the evidence which is sufficient to determine the question; *Balai Chandra Hazra* v. *Shewdhari Jadav,* AIR 1978 SC 1062: (1978) 3 SCR 147: (1978) 2 SCC 559.

4. Section 103—Power of High Court to Determine Issue of Facts

The Court has held that vital issues important to the entire controversies may be determined by the High Court; *Haryana State Electronics Development Corporation Ltd.* v. *Seema Sharma,* AIR 2009 SC 2592: 2009 Lab IC 3031: 2009 AIR SCW 4511.

5. Scope of Additional Evidence

The High Court of Karnataka in *Munivenkatappa* v. *Chikkapapamma,* ILR 1991 Kar 3014: 1991 (4) Kar LJ 6 examined the plea of adducing additional evidence. The question was raised during second appeal and the question was whether in a Second Appeal presented before this Court under section 100 of the C.P.C. this Court has no power to allow a party to produce additional evidence even if the conditions specified in Clause (aa) of Order XLI, rule 27 are satisfied?

In support of the contention that no additional evidence can be received in a Second Appeal, the learned Counsel relied on the judgment of a learned Judge of this Court in the case of *Balbant Yadneshwar* v. *Srinivas Appaji Kulkarni,* 1959 Mys LJ 581, in which the learned Judge after referring to various decisions cited at the Bar, held that no additional evidence could be received in a Second Appeal. The relevant portion of the judgment reads:—

> "If we look to the scheme of the Civil Procedure Code, we find that Part VII which relates to appeals is sub-divided into five divisions *viz.,*
>
> 1. appeals from original decrees (sections 96 to 99);
> 2. appeals from appellate decrees (sections 100 to 103);
> 3. appeals from orders (sections 104 to 106);
> 4. general provisions relating to appeals (sections 107 & 108);
> 5. appeals to the Supreme Court (sections 109 to 112).

It will be found that the scope of the provisions relating to second appeals is very narrow. Whereas section 96 provides that an appeal shall lie from every decree, except one passed by consent of parties, section 100 lays down that a second appeal shall lie only on one of the three grounds, *viz.,*

a. When the decision is contrary to law or to some usage having the force of law;
b. When it has failed to determine some material issues of law or usage having the force of law; and
c. When there is a substantial error or defect in procedure which may have produced some error or defect in the decision of the case upon the merits.

Section 101 lays down emphatically that no second appeal shall lie except on the said grounds. From these provisions, it is clear that no second appeal can lie on a question of fact. In other words, the High Court, in second appeal, is bound to accept the finding of the first appellate court as final and it cannot enter into questions of fact. An exception to this Rule is provided by section 103. It provides that the High Court in second appeal may determine any issue of fact where it is necessary for the disposal of the appeal under two circumstances *viz.*,

1. Where such an issue has not been determined by the lower appellate court; or
2. Where it has been wrongly determined by that Court by reason of any illegality, omission or error or defect such as is referred to in section 100(1). Except under such circumstances, it is not open for the High Court in second appeal to enter into questions of fact. It was thus observed:

   "On a careful consideration of the foregoing, I reach the conclusion that the provisions of rule 27 of Order XLI, C.P.C. are not applicable to second appeals and no document can be allowed to be produced in second appeal."

Now the next question for consideration was whether there is any justification to permit the appellant to adduce additional evidence. The documents sought to be produced by the appellant are certified copies of the two documents registered in the office of the Sub-Registrar, Kolar, and the third document sought to be produced is the correct certified copy of the Record of Rights in which there is reference to the two registered documents. *Prima facie*, the Court had to proceed on the basis that the two Sale Deeds being documents registered in the office of the Sub-Registrar more than 35 years ago are genuine.

The next point for consideration was what is the type of order that should be passed so that no prejudice should be caused to the respondent in the event of a finding by the Court below that even on the basis of the additional evidence no case is made out for the appellant. For that purpose, the Court considerd it expedient to make it clear that if only on the basis of additional documents received by us a finding were to be recorded by the Court below in favour of the appellant, the Judgment and Decree should go in his favour and if not the finding already recorded on the basis of evidence by the trial Court and the First Appellate Court should remain undisturbed and consequently judgment should be rendered once again on that basis.

The Bombay High Court also examined the issue in the case of *Laxminarayan Deepchand* v. *Bhiku Punjaji Lewa*, (1974) 76 Bom LR 83. In the said case two questions were raised by Shri Mandlekar appearing on behalf of the appellants in this appeal. The first question was that Exh. D-29 should not have been permitted to be brought on record and the second question, which was the only substantial question, which had been argued, was that additional evidence could not be admitted in a second appeal since, according to the learned counsel, the provisions of Order XLI, rule 27, Code of Civil Procedure, are not applicable to second appeals. In support of the argument that there is no jurisdiction in a second appeal Court to admit additional evidence, the learned counsel for the appellants have relied on two decisions, (1) *Balvant Yadneshwar* v. *Srinivas Appaji*, AIR 1959 Mys 244, and (2) *Subba Raja* v. *Narayana Raja*, AIR 1954 Mad 1047. In the Mysore case a learned Single Judge of that Court has held that provisions of Order XLI, rule 27, Code of Civil Procedure, do not apply to second appeals and that no document can be allowed to be produced in a second appeal. The learned Judge has based this view on a construction of section 103 of the Code of Civil Procedure and for that construction has relied on certain authorities cited by him.

As mentioned above, the only occasion when in a second appeal the High Court can go into a question of fact is circumscribed by the provisions of section 103, Civil P.C. One of the conditions for such going into the questions of fact under that section is when the evidence on record is sufficient to determine any issue of fact necessary for the disposal of the appeal.

This necessarily implies that even if the evidence on record is insufficient, the High Court cannot allow the evidence to be supplemented for the purpose of going into a question of fact. If so, it follows that the provisions of rule 27 of Order XLI, C.P.C. cannot apply to second appeals. To allow fresh evidence in second appeals would amount to going into a question of fact even where the evidence on record is insufficient. This would be contrary to the provisions of section 103, C.P.C. The Court referred to a decision of the supreme Court and said that it has been held by the Supreme Court in *K. Venkatwramiah* v. *Seetharama Reddy*, AIR 1963 SC 1526 that under rule 27(1) of Order XLI the appellate Court has the power to allow additional evidence not only if it requires such evidence "to enable it to pronounce judgment", but also for "any other substantial cause," and there may well be cases where even though the Court finds that it is able to pronounce judgment on the state of record as it is and so it cannot strictly say that it requires additional evidence to enable it to pronounce judgment, it still considers that in the interest of justice something which remains: obscure should be filled-up so that it can pronounce its judgment in a more satisfactory manner, such a case will be one for allowing additional evidence for any other substantial cause under rule 27(1)(b) of the Code. The sufficiency of evidence contemplated by section 103 of the Code is sufficiency for the purpose of passing or pronouncing a proper judgment. If in a given case the High Court comes to the conclusion that a finding of fact is vitiated and that for the purpose of pronouncing a proper judgment the evidence on record is not sufficient and the evidence sought to be made available by a party under Order XLI, rule 27, of the Code of Civil Procedure, fills up that lacuna so that if that is taken into consideration a proper judgment can be pronounced, we fail to see anything in the provisions of section 103 which would restrict the powers of the High Court to admit such additional evidence.

6. Section 103 – Whether Finding of Fact is Open to Challenge in Second Appeal

The High Court of Rajasthan examined whether finding of fact is open to challenge in the second appeal. In the case of *Chatar Lal* the question was "Whether the finding recorded by the first appellate court on the issue relating to comparative hardship remitted by this Court, being a finding of fact, is not open to challenge in the second appeal?"

The material facts leading to the present reference may be briefly stated as follows:—Mahant Ramdas, plaintiff-respondent, instituted a suit for arrears of rent and ejectment from the disputed premises on the ground of personal necessity and default in the Court of Munsif, Udaipur, who by his judgment dated 30-11-1966 decreed the suit for eviction having found Issue No. 2 regarding personal necessity in favour of the plaintiff. The defendant went in appeal, but his appeal was dismissed by the learned Additional District Judge, *vide* his judgment dated 10th of July, 1968. The defendant then preferred the second appeal. During the pendency of the second appeal the Rajasthan Premises (Control of Rent and Eviction) (Amendment) Act, 1976, came into force and in view of the amended section 14(2) the following issue of comparative hardship was remitted for trial by this Court to the first appellate court *vide* order dated 31-3-1976:—

> "Whether having regard to all the circumstances of the case including the question whether any other reasonable accommodation is available to the landlord or the tenant, greater hardship would be caused by passing a decree than by refusing to pass it?"

"Having considered the case-law which was brought to our notice we find ourselves in respectful agreement with the view that when an issue is remitted under Order XLI, rule 25, C.P.C., in second appeal to the first appellate court, the finding of fact sent back by the first appellate court is not open to attack, except on the grounds stated in section 100, C.P.C. This view appears to be in consonance and harmony with the provisions contained in Order XLII, rule 1 and sections 100, 101 and 103, C.P.C. Even in the amended section 103, C.P.C., we find as to when the High Court can determine the issue of facts. The High Court is empowered to determine any issue necessary for the disposal of the appeal, if the evidence on the record is sufficient, when the same has not been determined by the lower appellate court or by the court of first instance and the lower appellate court, or which have been wrongly determined by such court or courts by reason of a decision on such question of law, as is referred to in section 100. The power to determine the issues on facts, is limited to the situations mentioned in section 103, In case the issue of fact has been determined by the lower appellate court, whether on being remitted in second appeal or otherwise, such a finding of fact given by the lower appellate court cannot be determined by the High Court and the reason appeals to be that as a senior and experienced Judge presides over the first appellate court, it will be taken that the findings of facts arrived at by him, are correct. If this would not have been the intention, an exception would have been provided that even in second appeal when issue of fact is remitted to the first appellate court, the findings on that issue can be assailed in second appeal. Rather we find a contrary intention expressed in the language of Order XLII, rule 1, C.P.C,, coupled with the legal bar provided in sections 100 and 101, C.P.C, and if these provisions are further read with the provisions of section 103, the intention in our opinion becomes abundantly clear. The only way out appears to be that in order to obviate such an eventuality or result, the issues of fact should be remitted to the first court in second appeal; *Chatar Lal* v. *Ramdas,* AIR 1979 Raj 87: (1979) Rent LR 821: (1979) 1 Ren CR 754.

The Andhra High Court in the case of *Chapala Chinnabbayi* v. *Naralasetti Anusuyama,* AIR 2006 AP 142: 2006 (1) ALD 669: 2006 (1) ALT 293 decided the advisability of an additional evidence in a second appeal. This is a reference made by a learned Single Judge of this Court to answer the following questions by a Division Bench:

(1) Whether additional documents throwing light by way of subsequent events can be brought on record in a Second Appeal, and if so, what is the scope and ambit and the applicability of Order XLI, rule 27 read with section 151 of the Code of Civil Procedure in such a case?

(2) Whether the view expressed by the Division Bench of this Court in *Anisetti Bhagyavathi* v. *Andaluri Satyanarayana,* AIR 1992 AP 304 (DB) can be extended to cases of bringing subsequent events to the notice of the High Court in Second Appeals?

After making a combined reading of sections 100, 103, Order XLI, rule 27, 28 and Order XLII, C.P.C. and in view of the latest legal position, the Court came to a different conclusion from the conclusion in *Anisetti Bhagyavathi's* case (1 supra).

The Court held that the High Court may interfere with the findings of fact when material or relevant evidence is not considered by the Courts below which, if considered, would have led to an opposite conclusion and when a finding has been arrived at by the appellate court by placing reliance on inadmissible evidence which, if omitted, an opposite conclusion was possible. Though the High Court should not interfere in pure findings of fact reached by the Courts below, without coming to the conclusion that the findings of fact are either perverse or are not based on material on record, it may interfere with the findings of fact also if it finds that those findings are perverse or that they were made on imaginary basis without any material available on record. If the High Court considers necessary and appropriate to receive further evidence at the stage of second appeal and in the interest of justice and both parties, it may permit the additional evidence to be adduced by invoking Order XLII, C.P.C. and by taking the aid of Order XLI, rule 27, C.P.C. Though the parties to the proceedings in a second appeal are not entitled as a matter of right to adduce additional evidence, in exceptional and compelling circumstances, the High Court may take the aid of Order XLII, C.P.C. and permit adducing of additional evidence in the second appeal in the interest of justice.

In the light of the above discussion, the Court held that the High Court may permit a party to adduce additional evidence in Second Appeal under the following circumstances:—

(1) Adducing additional evidence is in the interest of justice;

(2) Evidence relating to the subsequent happenings or events, which are relevant for disposal of the Second Appeal. The reference was accordingly answered.

APPEALS FROM ORDERS

***104. Orders from which appeal lies.*—An appeal shall lie from the following orders, and save as otherwise expressly provided in the body of this Code or by any law for the time being in force, from no other orders:**

(a) to (f) omitted;

(ff) an order under section 35A;

(ffa) an order under section 91 or section 92 refusing leave to institute a suit of the nature referred to in section 91 or section 92, as the case may be;

(g) an order under section 95;

(h) an order under any of the provisions of this Code imposing a fine or directing the arrest or detention in the civil prison of an person except where such arrest or detention is in execution of a decree;

(i) any order made under rules from which an appeal is expressly allowed by rules:

Provided that not appeal shall lie against any order specified in clause (ff) save on the ground that no order, or an order for the payment of a less amount, ought to have been made.

No appeal shall lie from any order passed in appeal under this section.

SYNOPSIS

Comments

1. Scope and Applicability

There are two parts of this Order. In the first part, it provides for appeal against the orders enumerated in clauses (ff) to (i), and in the second place, it also provides for appeal against those orders as are permitted by the Code. Therefore, this provision is in agreement with the list of appealable orders as mentioned in Order LIII. The orders mentioned in clauses (a) to (f) are now not appealable, having been omitted by the Arbitration Act X of 1940. The orders mentioned in clauses (ff) to (i) are appelable because of the specific provision of section 104(1) which is in addition to and independent of the provisions of Order XLIII, rule 1, and not in its derogation; *Joshi Girjadharji* v. *Rao Sanwal Das Shahpuri,* AIR 1958 All 639: ILR (1957) 2 All 240; *Suresh Dutta* v. *Randhir Singh,* AIR 1958 All 641: 1958 All LJ 232: 1958 All WR (HC) 302.

The provision restricts the scope of appeal to the orders specified in it, and from 'no other orders'. No appeal lies against an order which does not amount to a decree as defined by section 2(2), in which case it is opened to appeal either under section 96 or within Order XLIII, rule 1. Accordingly, various orders have been held to be not appealable. The High Court of Patna held that order under Order I, rule 3 holding that the suit is bad for multifariousness and asking the plaintiff to elect is not appealable; *Shri Ram Krishan Das* v. *Bindeshwari Prasad,* AIR 1951 Pat 364.

An order holding that the Court has jurisdiction to try the suit is not appealable – *Manash Ranjan Chakravarty* v. *Tropical Accumulators Ltd.,* AIR 1957 Cal 135: 60 Cal WN 591. An order appointing a commission to ascertain *mesne* profits is not appealable – *Re: Badrajalu Naidu,* (1958) 1 MLJ 9. An Order XXXVII Rule 3 granting or refusing leave to defend is not appealable; *Bunwar Lal Roy* v. *Sohen Lal Daga,* (1955) ILR 1 Cal 299.

Where first appellate court passed an order under section 104, no appeal will lie against it because of the restrictions put by sub-section (2) of section 104. In a case in which the trial court rejected an application for interim injunction and an appeal against such refusal, the first appellate court also rejected it, it was held that only revision would lie; *Murari Kumar Saraf* v. *Jagannath,* AIR 1994 Cal 205.

Section 102 does not bar an appeal from the decision of a Single Judge of the High Court to a Division Bench under the letters patent – *Shri Chand* v. *Tejinder Singh,* AIR 1979 MP 76: 1979 MPLJ 170: 1979 Jab LJ 180. The accepted view is now that section 104 adds to, but does not detract from; *Shah Babulal Khimji* v. *Jayaben D. Kania,* AIR 1981 SC 1786: 1981 Rajdhani LR 624 (SC): (1981) 4 SCC 8.

Section 104 applies to appeals to High Court from Courts subordinate to it. It does not deal with appeals from a Single Judge of the High Court to a Bench under the Code for a right of appeal from the decision of a Single Judge to a Bench. Such appeals are provided by Clause 10 of Allahabad and Clause 15 of the Calcutta, Madras and Bombay High Courts. They cannot be said to be barred by section 104 in the absence of an express provision. On the other hand, such appeals are recognized by section 104 of the Code *Ganpati Wadgoo* v. *Pilaji Kothuji*, ILR 1926 Nag 226: 1956 Nag LJ 179: AIR 1956 Nag 211 The appeal provided under the High Court Ordinance from a decision of a Single Judge to the Bench is a special jurisdiction and cannot be affected by the provisions of section 104, which deal only with appeals under the Code, that is appeals to the High Court from the decisions of Courts subordinate to it. A judge of the High Court sitting singly is not a Court subordinate to the High Court and section 104 does not bar an appeal from his decision to the Bench. An appeal under certificate from an order of remand passed by the Single Judge of the High Court is, therefore, competent under the High Court Ordinance; 7 Sind LR 123: AIR 1954 San 152.

2. Section 104, Clause (f)

An order refusing compensatory costs under section 35. A.C.P. Code, is not appealable in view of the provision to section 104(ff); 18 NLJ 309. *See* also AIR 1954 Nag 272.

3. Clause (g)

Clause (g) of section 104 supersedes the decisions passed by the High Courts of Allahabad and Bombay on sections 28A, 31 and 24 M. 62. According to this clause an appeal lies under section 104(g) from an order refusing relief under section 93 as well as from one granting such relief; 49 IC 86: 9 LW 69. An appeal lies against an order awarding compensation for improper attachment; 11 IC 349: 21 MIJ 460.

4. Other Cases Where No Appeal Lies

The High Court of Madras said that no appeal lies against an order under section 95 passed by a Judge of Small Cause Court; 36 MLJ 435. An order passed in execution of a decree under section 9 of the Specific Relief Act is not appealable. Also an order passed in execution of such a decree directing the arrest of a judgment-debtor; 39 IC 379: 18 PLR 1917; 39 IC 375. No appeal lies against the order of a Court holding that a suit as framed is bad for multi-fariousness as contravening Order I, rule 3, C.P.C. and directing the plaintiff to elect against which defendant or set of defendants he proposed to go on with the suit, and also directing that in the event of not exercising the election before a specified date, the plaint will stand rejected. Such an order, may however be revised under section 115, C.P.C. If a question of jurisdiction is involved; 1951 Pat 364. No appeal lies from an order passed in appeal remanding for trial and merits a case in which the plaint had been returned for presentation 33A, 479. There is appeal from the order of an appellate Court restoring a suit dismissed for want of process 9 IC 484.

5. Section 104 and Order XLIII

Section 104(1) read with Order XLIII, rule 1 confers additional powers of appeal to a larger Bench within the High Court. Section 104 (2) only bars appeals against orders passed in appeal under section 104(1). Thus, section 104(2) does not bar appeals permitted by any law; *P.S. Sathappan* v. *Andhra Bank Ltd.*, AIR 2004 SC 5152: 2004 AIR SCW 5934: (2004) 11 SCC 672.

6. Section 104.—Effect of Letters Patent Appeal

Trial of suit by the Single Judge of the High Court.—Appeal to Larger Bench of High Court against such order is not affected by the provision of the Code.—The Bench said, "Our conclusions are: (1) That there is no inconsistency between section 104 read with Order XLIII, rule 1 and the appeals under the Letters Patent and there is nothing to show that the Letters Patent in any way excludes or overrides the application of section 104 read with Order XLIII, rule 1 or to show that these provisions would not apply to internal appeals within the High Court. (2) That even if it be assumed that Order XLIII, rule 1 does not apply to Letters Patent Appeals, the principles governing these provisions would apply by process of analogy. (3) That having regard to the nature of the orders contemplated in the various clauses of Order XLIII, rule 1, there can be no doubt that these orders purport to decide valuable rights of the parties in ancillary proceedings even though the suit is kept alive and that these orders do possess the attributes or character of finality so as to be judgments within the meaning of clause 15 of the Letters Patent and hence, appealable to a larger Bench. (4) The concept of the Letters Patent governing only the internal appeals in the High Court and the Code of Civil Procedure having no application to such appeals is based on a serious misconception of the legal position". *Shah Babulal Khimji* v. *Jayaben D. Kania,* AIR 1981 SC 1786: (1981) 4 SCC 8: (1982) 1 SCR 187: (1981) 3 SCALE 1169: 1981 Rajdhani LR 624.

7. Whether an Order Passed by the Single Judge is Governed by Section 104 and Order XLIII, Rule 1

The Supreme Court examined the maintainability of an appeal filed before the Division Bench against an order passed by the Single Judge. In a suit for specific performance of an agreement to sell filed on the original side of the Bombay High Court the plaintiff (appellant) prayed for certain interim reliefs. A Single Judge of the High Court dismissed the application. A Division Bench of the High Court, on appeal by the plaintiff, held that the appeal was not maintainable on the ground that the impugned order of the Single Judge was not a 'judgment' within the meaning of clause 15 of the Letters Patent of the High Court. In appeal to this Court, it was contended on behalf of the appellant that since the trial judge is governed by the procedure prescribed by the Code of Civil Procedure, by virtue of the provisions of section 104 read with Order XLIII, rule (1) the impugned order is appealable to a larger Bench; (2) assuming that the Letters Patent was a special law, section 104 read with Order XLIII is in no way inconsistent with clause 15 of the Letters Patent; (3) even if section 104 read with Order XLIII, rule 1 does not apply an order refusing to appoint a receiver or to grant injunction has the attributes of finality and, therefore, amounts to a judgment' within the meaning of Letters Patent. Allowing the appeal the Court said:

> "Since the Order of the trial judge was one refusing appointment of a receiver and grant of ad-interim injunction, it is a 'judgment' within the meaning of the Letters Patent both because Order XLIII, rule 1 applies to internal appeals in the High Court, and such an order even on merits contains the quality of finality and would be a judgment within the

meaning of clause 15 of Letters Patent. Hence an appeal is maintainable to the Division Bench. The Division Bench was in error in dismissing the appeal without deciding it on merits".

The Court further held that there is no inconsistency between section 104 read with Order XLIII, rule 1, C.P.C. and appeals under Letters Patent. There is nothing to show that Letters Patent in any way excludes or overrides the application of section 104 read with Order XLIII, rule 1 or that these provisions do not apply to internal appeals within the High Court. It was held that the Code of Civil Procedure 1877, by sections 588 and 589, did not make any distinction between appeals to the High Court from the District Court and internal appeals to the High Court under Letters Patent. Notwithstanding the clear enunciation of law by the Privy Council that section 588 did not affect nor was it inconsistent with the provisions of Letters Patent and that, therefore, orders of a trial Judge which fall beyond section 588 could be appealable to a larger Bench under the Letters Patent if its orders amounted to a 'judgment' within the meaning of clause 15 of the Letters Patent, there was a serious controversy among the High Courts on this question. Section 104 of the C.P.C., 1908 made it clear that appeals against orders mentioned in Order XLIII, rule 1 were not in any way inconsistent with the Letters Patent but merely provide additional remedy by allowing appeals against miscellaneous orders passed by the trial Judge to a larger Bench.

In dealing with a suit, the Supreme Court directed that the trial judge has to follow the procedure prescribed by the Code. It is indisputable that any final judgment passed by the trial judge amounts to a decree and under the provisions of the Letters Patent an appeal lies to a larger Bench. Letters Patent itself does not define the term 'judgment' and has advisedly not used the word 'decree' in respect of a judgment given by the trial Judge; *Shah Babulal Khimji* v. *Jayaben D. Kania,* AIR 1981 SC 1786: (1981) 4 SCC 8: (1982) 1 SCR 187.

Supreme Court of India in *Subal Paul* v. *Malina Paul,* also examined the issue whether an appeal lies before the Division Bench against an order passed by the Single Judge. In the said case the facts giving rise to this appeal were that on 8.12.1986 one Srish Chandra Paul executed his last Will. On 17.3.1988 he died. The appellant herein who is a son of Srish Chandra Paul applied for probate before the Additional District Judge, Agartala. The learned Additional District Judge rejected the prayer for issue of probate. Aggrieved the appellant preferred an appeal under section 299 of the Act before the Gauhati High Court. A learned Single Judge of the High Court allowed the appeal and granted letters of administration with a copy of the Will annexed thereto. Aggrieved, the respondents preferred a Letters Patent Appeal before a Bench of the High Court. Before the said Bench, the appellant herein raised a preliminary objection that no such appeal is maintainable being barred by section 104 of the Code of Civil Procedure, 1908. The Bench overruled the objection and directed for hearing of the appeal. It is at this stage the appellant herein filed the present appeal by special leave and by virtue of the interim order passed by this Court the hearing in the letters patent appeal way stayed.

The short question that arose for consideration in this appeal was as to whether a Letters Patent Appeal would lie against the judgment of a learned Single Judge of the High Court filed under section 299 of the Indian Succession Act, 1925.

The Court noticed that even in *Municipal Corporation of Brihanmumbai* v. *State Bank of India,* this Court while interpreting the provisions of section 218D and 217(1) of the Bombay Municipal Corporation Act, 1888, held that when an appeal is in the form of second appeal having regard to the bar contained in section 100A of the Code of Civil Procedure, no further appeal shall lie. It was observed:

> "This section has been introduced to minimize the delay in the finality of a decision. Prior to the enactment of the above provision, under the letters patent, an appeal against the decision of a Single Judge in a second appeal was in certain cases, held competent, though under section 100 of the Code of Civil Procedure, there was some inhibition against interference with the findings of fact. The right of taking recourse to such an appeal has now been taken away by section 100A of the Code of Civil Procedure (*supra*). Since an appeal under section 217(1) of the Act is a first appeal in a second forum/court and an appeal under section 218D of the Act is the second appeal in the third forum/court no further appeal would be competent before the fourth forum/court in view of Section 100A of the Code of Civil Procedure (*supra*)."

In *Prataprai N. Kothari* v. *John Braganza,* AIR 1999 SC 1666: 1999 (2) Land LR 585: 1999 (2) Cur CC 138: 1999 (3) Pun LR 55: 1999 (2) Raj LW 292: 1999 (2) All Mah LR 566: (1999) 4 SCC 403 even in a suit for possession only not based on title, a Letters Patent Appeal was held to be maintainable. The decision of this Court in *Sharda Devi* v. *State of Bihar,* AIR 2002 SC 1357 is also to the same effect, wherein in para 9 it was held:

> "A Letters Patent is the charter under which the High Court is established. The powers given to a High Court under the Letters Patent are akin to the constitutional powers of a High Court. Thus when a Letters Patent grants to the High Court a power of appeal, against a judgment of a Single Judge, the right to entertain the appeal would not get excluded unless the statutory enactment concerned excludes an appeal under the Letters Patent."

Section 54 of the Land Acquisition Act, 1894 provides for an appeal before the High Court and thereafter to the Supreme Court and despite the same it was held that a Letters Patent appeal under clause 15 would be maintainable. For the aforesaid reasons, the Court took the view that the order passed by the Single Judge was appealable to Letters Patent Bench and the objection in regard to maintainability of appeal was rightly overruled by the High Court. Consequently, this appeal falls and is, accordingly, dismissed. We direct the High Court to decide the Letters Patent appeal expeditiously; *Subal Paul* v. *Malina Paul,* AIR 2003 SC 1928: 2003 (1) CTC 627: JT 2003 (5) SC 193.

Jharkhand High Court also decided the question of maintainability of the appeal. In the case under reference the State Bank of India, the respondent No. 1 in the present appeal, filed Money Suit No. 12 of 1983 against the appellant and proforma respondents for recovery of its dues amounting to Rs. 6,43,663,84 P. The defendants appeared and contested the suit by filing their written statement and taking the plea that there was no cause of action for the suit, which was, therefore, not maintainable. As many as 11 Issues were framed. While Issues Nos. 4, 5, 6, 7 and 8 were decided against the plaintiff and in favour of the contesting defendants No. 1 to 6, issues No. 9 and 8 were partly allowed. Issue No. 3 was decided in favour of the plaintiff and so were the Issues No. 1, 2 and 11. In the result, the suit was decreed in part. Aggrieved by the judgment and decree passed in the suit, the State Bank of India, filed an appeal in this Court, being FA No. 766 of 1992 R. The said appeal ultimately succeeded and by judgment dated 20th August, 2004, the findings of the trial court relating to interest payable were set aside and the suit was decreed.

Aggrieved by the judgment and decree passed in appeal the defendants No. 3 and 6 in the suit, *Sri Satya Narayan Agiwal* and *Sri Bishwanath Agiwal* filed the instant appeal under clause 10 of the Letters Patent. When the matter was placed for admission before the Division Bench on 17th March, 2005, certain questions of law relating to the maintainability of the appeal were raised having regard to the provisions of clause 10 of the Letters Patent, read with section 100A and section 104 of the Code of Civil Procedure. The matter was, therefore, referred to a Full Bench of 3 Judges to consider and decide the said issues, which had been raised. The matter was thereafter taken up for consideration by the Full Bench in terms of the said reference.

The Bench held that reading together the provisions of sections 96, 100, 100A, 104 and Order XLIII, rule 1A of the Code of Civil Procedure, it created a very anomalous situation in as much as a Letters Patent Appeal will lie to the Division Bench of this Court as against the judgment and order passed by the learned Single Judge exercising appellate jurisdiction under section 104 of the Code of Civil Procedure but a Letters Patent Appeal will not lie against the judgment and order passed by the learned Single Judge exercising appellate jurisdiction against the judgment and decree passed by the subordinate Court exercising original jurisdiction. The bar created under section 100A, CPC is in direct conflict with the right of appeal provided under the Letters Patent of the High Court. The matter would have been otherwise, if First Appeal is placed for final hearing before the Division Bench of the High Court. The bar created under section 100A, CPC taking away a vested right of appeal under the Letters Patent of the High Court will cause serious prejudice to a party particularly when such right of Letters Patent Appeal has been provided in respect of cases arising out of special statute. In my opinion, therefore, unless High Court Rules is properly amended, the right conferred under Letters Patent of the High Court cannot be taken away by a bar created under section 100A, CPC. This Letters Patent Appeal was, therefore, held maintainable against the decree passed by the learned Single Judge. *Satya Narayan Agiwal* v. *State Bank of India,* 2005 (2) BLJR 1580: 2005 (3) JCR 1 Jhr.

Bombay High Court also decided the issue in the case of *Robert Punaji Salvi* v. *The Bombay, Diocesan Trust*. In the said case the learned Counsel, for the respondents-plaintiff has raised a preliminary objection regarding the maintainability of the appeal. His objection is that in view of the provisions of section 104(2) of the Code of Civil Procedure, no appeal can lie from any order passed in an appeal under section 104 read with Order XLIII, rule 1(r) of the Code of Civil Procedure. Counsel contended that the Order dated 7th Feb., 1995 that was passed in C.A. No. 349 of 1995 and which was confirmed on 23rd March, 1995 is undoubtedly an order in the pending A.O. No. 93 of 1995, which appeal is under section 104 read with Order XLIII, rule 1(r), C.P.C. Since the plaintiffs failed to get any interim order in their Motion in the pending suit, they have filed A.O. No. 93 of 1995 in this Court. The said appeal is clearly under the provisions of section 104 read with Order XLIII, rule 1(r), C.P.C

Having considered all the submissions above, the Court took the view that the preliminary objection raised by Shri Thorat to the maintainability of the Letters Patent Appeal must be upheld. As indicated earlier, the order passed by the learned Single Judge is an order on the Civil Application in the pending A.O. No. 93 of 1995. Such an order was clearly under section 104, C.P.C. The appeal from Order is squarely under section 104 read with Order XLIII, rule 1(r) of the C.P.C. In view of the clear pronouncement of the Supreme Court in *Shah Babulal Khimji's* case and the four decisions of this Court referred to above, we are of the view that a further appeal even under clause 15 of the Letters Patent is clearly barred, having regard to the mandate of sub-section (2) of section 104, C.P.C. We accordingly hold that the L.P.A. is not maintainable. Appeal is, therefore, dismissed. However, in the circumstances of the case, there will be no order as to costs; *Robert Punaji Salvi* v. *The Bombay Diocesan Trust*, AIR 1996 Bom 39: 1996 (2) Bom CR 15: (1995) 97 Bom LR 109.

The High Court of Calcutta also examined the similar issue in *Tanusree Art Printers* v. *Rabindra Nath Pal*, 2000 (2) Cal HN 213: (1999) 3 Cal LT 232 HC. In the said case the objection to the maintainability of such appeal is founded on the ground that under section 104 read with Order XLIII, rule I and the Clauses thereunder, no appeal has been provided against an order passed by a learned single Judge under Order XXXVII, rule 5. In other words, the contention against maintainability of such appeal is that section 104 of the Code creates a bar to entertaining such appeals. Sustenance for the said argument is sought from the words "no other orders" appearing in section 104 of the Code. The Court said that section 104 of the Code, provides for appeals against certain orders. Under clause (1) thereof, appeal shall lie from the orders specified therein and save as otherwise expressly provided in the body of the Code or by any law for the time being in force and from no other orders. Under this Clause [(section 104(1)], it is only these orders which are specified therein are appealable under the provisions of that section. If there are orders under other Acts and appealable under such provisions they are to be considered under such provisions. Sub-section (2) of section 104 contains an express provision that no appeal shall lie from any order passed in appeal under this section 104(1). That, as I understand it, means that if an order is passed in an appeal arising under section 104(1), then there shall not be a further appeal against such order. Patent and sub-section (2) of section 104 of the Code was attracted in that case. The question before the Supreme Court was whether a further appeal would lie under clause 10 of the Letters Patent of the Punjab High Court (corresponding to clause 15 of the Letters Patent of this High Court) against an order passed by a learned Single Judge in an appeal under section 39(1) of the Arbitration Act, 1940. Section 39(2) of the Arbitration Act prohibits a second appeal from an order passed in appeal under section 39(1), except an appeal to the Supreme Court. The contention before the Supreme Court was that a Letters Patent Appeal would not be treated as a second appeal within the meaning of clause 10 of the Letters Patent. That contention was negatived. The Supreme Court held that the expression 'second appeal' used in section 39 of the Arbitration Act did not mean an appeal under section 100 of the Code and it meant only a further appeal from an order passed in an appeal under section 39(1) of the Arbitration Act. Considering the provisions of section 39 of the Arbitration Act, the Supreme took into consideration the provision of section 4 and section 104 of the Code of Civil Procedure, *inter alia*, held as under; ".....Section 4(1) of the Code of 1908 which is a saving provision clearly provides that in the absence of any specific provision to the contrary the provisions of the Code do not limit or affect any special or local law. Thus, the test contained in section 4 is not applicable in the instant case because even if the Letters Patent of the High Court be deemed to be a special law as contemplated by section 4, the provisions of section 104 do not seek to limit or affect the provisions of the Letters Patent." It is evident from the above that the provisions of section 104 of the Code do not limit or affect the provisions of the Letters Patent. In other words, the right to file appeal and the power of Court to entertain the same under clause 15 of the Letters Patent is not curtailed by the provisions of section 104(1) of the Code. This was further clarified when the Supreme Court agreed with the contentions put-forth.

The Patna High Court also dealt with an appeal by the plaintiff against the judgment of a Single Judge of this Court reversing the judgment of the third Subordinate Judge, Patna, and dismissing the plaintiff's suit for recovery of a certain sum said to have been due to her from the defendant in full payment of the price of goods (grains) supplied together with interest and other charges The defendant's plea was one of complete denial of the so-called purchase of grains from the plaintiff. There was no documentary evidence, such as voucher signed by the defendant, to prove the plaintiff's claim and the plaintiff relied solely on the oral evidence of her brother. P.W. 2. corroborated by the evidence of two other witnesses, namely, P.Ws. 1 and 3 The trial court was inclined to believe these witnesses, but the learned single Judge on appeal held that the plaintiff's version was highly improbable specially in view of the serious discrepancies in the evidence of the witnesses and the absence of any documentary evidence in support of the supply of grains by the plaintiff to the defendant. He was also inclined to accept the defendant's claim that there was a transaction of sale between the parties and that a sale deed was executed and registered by the defendant, though the entire consideration money was not paid.

The Court observed that apparently, the suggestion seemed to have been that the plaintiff brought the suit with a view to escape liability for payment of the balance of the consideration money due on the sale deed.

The Court referred to the provisions of Letters Patent and said that clause 10 of the Patna Letters Patent (omitting immaterial portions) refers to three classes of appeals that may be heard by a Division Bench: (1) appeals from the judgment of a Single Judge in exercise of his original jurisdiction; (2) appeals from the judgment of a Single Judge in first appeals; and (3) appeals from the judgment of a Single Judge in second appeals. The said clause does not give an indication as to whether the scope of an appeal in respect of the aforesaid three classes will be the same, the only restriction being that an appeal from a second appellate judgment of a Single Judge will not lie unless he certifies that it is a fit case for appeal. It is true that ordinarily the same words occurring in a statute, specially in the same clause or section, must be given the same meaning unless there is repugnancy in the subject or context, but it is also well-settled that however wide the language of a statutory provision may be, some restricted meaning may have to be given to the statutory expression in the light of the context. To quote the classic words of Viscount Simonds in the House of Lords case in *Attorney-General* v. *Prince Ernest Augustus of Hanover*, 1957 AC 486 (461):

> "For words, and particularly general words, cannot be read in isolation: their colour and content are derived from their context. So it is that I conceive it to be my right and duty to examine every word of a statute in its context, and I use 'context' in its widest sense, which I have already indicated as including not only other enacting provisions of the same statute, but its preamble, the existing state of the law, other statutes in *pari materia*, and the mischief which I can by those and other legitimate means, discern the statute was intended to remedy".

Thus, both the textual context and what may be compendiously called historical context will have to be taken into consideration in arriving at a correct conclusion regarding the true scope of the expression "appeal" (its colour and content) occurring in clause 10 of the Letters Patent. Ultimately, the Court held that the opinion of the majority is that a Letters Patent Appeal from the first appellate judgment of a Single Judge is controlled by the provisions of section 100 of the Code of Civil Procedure. Unanimously it was decided that the appeal should be dismissed with costs; *Asho Devi* v. *Dukhi Sao*, AIR 1965 Pat 472: 1965 BLJR 300: ILR 44 Pat 360.

8. Sections 104 and 2(9), Order XXXIX, Rule 1 and Order XLIII, Rule 1(r).—Letter Patent.—Clause 10

LPA against order of Single Judge.—Maintainability.—Appellant filed a suit for injunction under Order XXXIX, rule 1. In a case the trial court granted *status quo* of the suit premises. On appeal filed by the respondents, the learned Single Judge vacated the injunction. Thereafter Appellant filed Letters Patent Appeal.—The Supreme Court held that it was not valid. LPA would not lie against an order of the learned Single Judge. *M/s. New Kenilworth Hotel (P) Ltd.* v. *Orissa State Finance Corporation*, AIR 1997 SC 978: (1997) 3 SCC 462: (1997) 1 SCALE 472: JT 1997 (1) SC 712: 1997 (2) Mad LJ 52: 1997 (2) Rec Civ R 294.

9. Section 104 – Appeal for Setting aside Judgment and Decree

In *Urmila (Smt.)* v. *Amit Kumar Agrawal & Anothers*, 2012 95 All LR 290: 2012 3 ARC 99 (All) the appellant has sought relief in this appeal for setting aside the judgment and order dated 26.3.2012 passed by Additional Civil Judge (Senior Division), Court No. 4, Meerut in Original Suit No. 1266 of 2007 and reject the application 8Ga for temporary injunction.

The High Court in similar facts and circumstances in FAFO No. 271 of 2011: *Jitendra Verma* v. *Amit Kumar Agrawal*, on 1.2.2011 has passed the following order. The operative portion of the said order reads thus:

> "We have given our thoughtful consideration to the various plea raised by the learned counsel for the parties. We are not inclined to go into the merits of the case as to whether the interim award has been obtained by collusion or not as the objections are pending before the learned District Judge, we cannot pre empt the decision in the arbitration case herein. We, therefore, decline to go into this issue. According to appellant, as he has purchased the property in question for valuable consideration but the fact remains that the said property is subject matter of suit giving rise to the present appeal against the impugned order granting temporary injunction the principle of lis pendense would be applicable and, therefore, it would be in the interest of justice that the appellant be restrained to alienate, transfer and encumber the said property during the pendency of the suit. So far as the order regarding maintenance of status quo is concerned, we are of the opinion that it was not necessary in the facts and circumstances of the case.
>
> In view of the foregoing discussion, the order dated 27th October, 2010 passed by the learned Civil Judge (Senior Division), Meerut is modified and it is directed that the appellant shall not transfer, alienate and encumber the property in question during the pendency of the suit."

10. Section 104 – Appeal against the Order to Maintain Status Quo

In *Rizwan Khan* v. *Gaurav Jaiswal*, 2013 96 AllLR 195: 2012 3 ARC 132: 2013 2 CivCC 143: 2013 118 RD 603 (All) the appellant challenged the order dated 13.4.2012 passed by Civil Judge (Senior Division), Allahabad in O.S. No. 428 of 2011, whereby while disposing of the respondent's application (paper no. 6-ga), the court below has directed the parties to maintain status quo in respect of the house in dispute.

The High Court said, it is not in dispute that earlier the suit property belongs to Rajesh Kumar Jaiswal. The case of the defendant/appellant is that he purchased the entire suit property from Rajesh Kumar Jaiswal through registered sale-deed dated 14.3.2011 and his name was also mutated in the record of Nagar Nigam on 18.4.2011. The appellant has incorrectly described himself as plaintiff in the memo of appeal, while he is defendant in the suit. On behalf of the respondents, it was contended that the appellant is not in possession over the suit property, as it is evident from the written statement filed by him in the suit, whereby he has preferred counter claim seeking relief of possession over the entire house. These facts clearly show that the defendant is not in possession of the suit property.

Learned counsel for the respondents further submitted that the defendant/ appellant got the sale-deed surreptitiously executed from their father and they have filed suit for cancellation of suit being O.S. No. 305 of 2011, wherein the appellant has not filed written statement so far.

In view of the above facts, it is apparently clear that the defendant is not in possession over the suit property. The learned trial court has simply directed the parties to maintain status qua the house in dispute

11. Civil Procedure Code: Section 104 Portuguese Civil Code: Article 1414, Article 1435

In *Lourdes Gregorio Gomindes* v. *Milagres Santana Gomindes,* 2016 2 All MR 806: 2016 3 Mh LJ 673 (Bom) the learned District Judge relied upon Articles 1414 and 1435 of the Portuguese Civil Code which was applicable in respect of inventory proceedings. The learned District Judge has come to the conclusion that the orders challenged in appeal are only directing how the partition should be effected and there is no final order in respect of the partition and, therefore, appeals are not maintainable.

The learned Counsel for the parties agree that in the inventory proceedings by any order if assets are included or are excluded, then such order is appealable under section 104 of Civil Procedure Code. The question that arises is whether an order directing that effect of the transaction of the properties which are earlier disposed, is to be considered for determining the shares would amount to inclusion of those properties in the inventory, and whether from such order, an appeal would lie.

Mr. Usgaonkar, the learned Counsel for the petitioners relying on the various provisions of Portuguese Civil Code pointed out that the scheme of the Code indicates that only that estate which is definitely listed before the Court can be considered, and that would also include notional inclusion. He submitted that it is not permissible for the Court to even notionally consider the properties which are not part of the proceedings, without formally including the same. Mr. Usgaonkar further submitted that having failed to get the said properties included in inventory proceedings, an attempt is made to notionally include them. He submitted that such order will have the same effect as actual inclusion, for the purpose of maintainability of the appeal. Mr. M. P. Almeida, the learned Counsel for the respondents on the other hand submitted that under the provisions of Portuguese Civil Code itself it is a mandate of law to consider the effect of such transactions.

The question therefore arises, and which is missed by the Appellate Court while dismissing the appeals as not maintainable, is what is the effect of considering a property notionally for the purpose of determining the share in an inventory proceedings. If the inventory proceedings must take place only in respect of the estate described, then question would arise as to what is the effect of notional inclusion thereof. It appears from the impugned order that learned District Judge has not gone into those aspects at all and has simply held that the order directs how the partition should be effected and therefore it is not appealable at this stage. The various questions which are indicated above have not been addressed by the learned District Judge.

The learned Counsel for the parties state that there is no decision of this Court in that regard. Since the learned District Judge has not addressed itself to this issue it would be appropriate that the learned District Judge considers this aspect while deciding whether the appeal is maintainable or not. Therefore, the matter needs to be remanded back to the District Court for reconsideration.

12. CPC Section 104 – Constitution of India – Article 227 and Specific Relief Act – Section 38

In *Jennifer Mascarenhas* v. *Jose Antonio Domnic Dias*, 2015 5 All MR 745: 2015 6 MhLJ 680 (Bom); the respondent no. 1 filed Regular Civil Suit No. 161 of 2011 in the Court of the Civil Judge, Junior Division, at Panaji, against the Petitioner and the respondent no. 2, inter alia, seeks for a permanent and mandatory injunction and other consequential reliefs. An application for temporary injunction was filed therein, inter alia, to restrain the petitioners from doing any construction activity in the suit property and/or from changing the nature thereof in any manner. A reply and written statement was filed in the suit by the petitioners and the respondent no.2. The Petitioner also filed a counter claim in the said suit. The learned Civil Judge by an Order dated 31.10.2012, dismissed the application for temporary injunction.

Being aggrieved by the said Order, the respondent no.1 filed an appeal before the Lower Appellate Court, which came to be disposed of on 19.11.2012 thereby allowing the Appeal and quashing and setting aside the Order of the learned Trial Judge dated 31.10.2012.

The High Court said, The pleadings of the petitioners disclose that the petitioners contend that the respondent no.1 has misrepresented the material facts and the suit is bad for non joinder of necessary parties. It is further their case that pursuant to the deed of sale dated 07.01.1998 along with deed of rectification dated 06.05.1999, the petitioners have become the owners of the property surveyed under no. 416/6 of Village Calapur. The said sale deed was never challenged by the father of the respondent no.1 at any point of time despite of his knowledge in the year 2001 in Regular Civil Suit No. 82/2001. It is further their case that the property of the respondent no.1 and the suit property are separated by an access road of 1.50 metres which road is available in the property surveyed under no. 416/2 of village Calapur and that the petitioners have already filed an application for restoration of the said suit. It is also their case that the construction undertaken by the petitioners is carried on the already existing structure surveyed under no. 416/6 and as such there is no question of conversion. It is further their case that stop order issued by respondent no.2 is without any authority of law and is totally contrary to the provisions of Panchayat Raj Act, which the petitioners have independently challenged by preferring Panchayat Appeal No. 134/2011 and the same is pending adjudication. It is further their case that as far as the deviation are concerned such aspect would have to be examined under the provisions of the Goa Land Development and Building Construction Regulation Act, 2010 and in particular sub clause (b) to clause 3.8 whereby such revision can be obtained even at the time of applying for occupancy certificate.

The respondent no.2 has also filed the written statement inter-alia contending that the said respondent has already issued a construction licence dated 10.08.2011 to the petitioners and there is no new construction licence issued. It is also stated that no prejudice or irreparable injury would be caused to the respondent no.1 in case an injunction is not granted.

13. Sections 24, 104 and 105 – Application – Family Dispute

In *Mahendra Pratap Bhatt* v. *Smt. Saroj Mahana,* 2016 5 ADJ 282(All): (76 (Clmc) 2015) the aggrieved party assailed the aforesaid judgment of the Division Bench, to which one of us [Justice A.P. Sahi] was a member, before the Apex Court and the same was upheld with remarks which judgment is in *Raja Khan* v. *Uttar Pradesh Sunni Central Waqf Board,* 2011 (2) SCC 741: 2011 (1) ADJ 193. The said judgment was subjected to review for expunging of such remarks which was disposed of and the same is in *Raja Khan* v. *Uttar Pradesh Sunni Central Waqf Board,* 2010 (15) SCC 228: 2011 (1) ADJ 193.

The above propositions therefore as applied on the facts of the present case leave no room for doubt that neither the application under Section 24 was maintainable before this Court nor was the order passed by the learned Single Judge related to a subject-matter within the territorial jurisdiction of this Court. This inherent lack therefore has to be co-related to the nature of the order passed.

The High Court said, in our opinion, at the best, the impugned order of the learned Single Judge would be, if at all, in the purported exercise of power under Article 226 of the Constitution of India. That being so, such purported exercise of power under Article 226 of the Constitution of India would be amenable to an intra-Court Special Appeal under Chapter VIII Rule 5 of the Allahabad High Court Rules, 1952 which is extracted hereunder:

14. Special Appeal

An appeal shall lie to the Court from a Judgment (not being a judgment passed in the exercise of appellate jurisdiction) in respect of a decree or order made by a Court subject to the superintendence of the Court and not being an order made in the exercise of revisional jurisdiction or in the exercise of its power of superintendence or in the exercise of criminal Jurisdiction or in the exercise of jurisdiction conferred by Article 226 or Article 227 of the Constitution in respect of any judgment, order or award (a) of a Tribunal, Court or statutory arbitrator made or purported to be made in the exercise or purported exercise of jurisdiction under any Uttar Pradesh Act or under any Central Act, with respect to any of the matters enumerated in the State List or the Concurrent List in the Seventh Schedule to the Constitution, or (b) of the Government or any officer or authority, made or purported to be made in the exercise or purported exercise of appellate or revisional jurisdiction under any such act of one Judge."

15. Order XLI, Rule 23, Order XLIII, Rule 1, Section 104 – Appeal against an Order

In *Parvat Singh* v. *Gram Pancahyat, Makad Seema, Udaipur,* 2016 3 DNJ 1039; 2016 1 WLC (UC) 626: 2016 4 WLN 39 (Raj), the instant civil misc. appeal was filed by the appellant under Order XLIII, Rule 1 read with Section 104 CPC against the judgment and decree dated 11.9.2015 passed by the learned Addl. District Judge, Salumber, District Udaipur in Appeal No. 26/2012 whereby the learned appellate court though allowed the appeal filed by the appellant, but while observing that judgment and decree of the learned trial court is liable to be dismissed, yet instead of decreeing the suit, remanded the matter to the learned trial court for rehearing and re-deciding the matter while setting aside the judgment and decree of the learned trial court dated 12.10.2011 passed in Civil Suit No. 59/2014.

The learned counsel for the appellant submits that the learned lower appellate court committed an error of law in remaining the matter to the learned trial court because as per Order XLI, Rule 23 and 23A of CPC the remand order can be made where the appellate court considers that retrial of the case is necessary, but from perusal of the impugned judgment of appellate court it is clear that neither any direction has been given nor any observation has been made for retrial of the case is necessary, therefore, the appellate court was under obligation to decide the appeal on its merit.

Learned counsel for the appellant submits that as per the law laid down by the Hon'ble Supreme Court if there are already evidence on record than the appellate court should decide the matter on merit in stead of re d of remanding the matter to the learned trial court for deciding the matter afresh as the appellate court itself is having jurisdiction to decide the case on merit. In support of his contention, the learned counsel for the appellant invited my attention towards the judgment of the Hon'ble Supreme Court in the case of *Ashwin Kumar K. Patel* v. *Upendra J. Patel,* reported in 1999 DNJ (SC) 207: AIR 1999 SC 1125 and submits that the judgment impugned may kindly be quashed.

> In our view, the High Court should not ordinarily remand a cause under Order XLI, Rule 23 CPC to the lower Court merely because it considered that the reasoning of the lower court in some respects was wrong. Such remand orders lead to unnecessary delays and cause prejudice to the 5 parties to the case. When the material was available before the High Court, it should have itself decided the appeal one way or other. It could have considered the various aspects of the case mentioned in the order of the trial Court and considered whether the order of the trial Court ought to be confirmed or reversed or modified. It could have easily considered the documents and affidavits and decided about the prima facie case on the material available. In mattes involving agreements of 1980 (and 1996) on the one hand and an agreement of 1991 on the other, as in this case, such remand orders would lead to further delay and uncertainty. We are, therefore, of the view that the remand by the High Court was not necessary.

16. Section 104 Companies Act: Section 454(5) – Appeal Challenging the Order on a Review Petition Filed by the Appellant

In *Tata Teleservices Limited represented by its Legal Manager Bobby Joseph* v. *Tngicube Technology Resources India Pvt Ltd.,* 2014 1 KLT 734 (Ker) the learned counsel for the appellant submitted that Section 104 of the Code of Civil

Procedure leaves room for appeals from applications of other kinds as well where appeal is provided under any other law. He referred to Section 483 of the Companies Act and submitted that against the dismissal of the review petition as well, appeal would be maintainable.

The learned counsel for the respondents relied on the judgment of the Supreme Court reported in *Municipal Corporation* v . *Yashwant Singh Negi*, 2013 (136) DRJ 1: 2013 3 AWC 2978 SC, where the Supreme Court held that once the High Court has refused to entertain the review petition and the same was dismissed confirming the main order, there is no question of any merger and the aggrieved person has to challenge the main order and not the order dismissing the review petition because on the dismissal of the review petition the principle of merger does not apply. In *DSR Steel (Private) Ltd* v. *State of Rajasthan*, (2012) 6 SCC 782: AIR 2012 SC 1602, the Supreme held as follows:

> "25.3. The third situation with which we are concerned in the instant case is where the revision petition is filed before the Tribunal but the Tribunal refuses to interfere with the decree or order earlier made. It simply dismisses the review petition. The decree in such a case suffers neither any reversal nor an alteration or modification. It is an order by which the review petition is dismissed thereby affirming the decree or order. In such a contingency there is no question of any merger and anyone aggrieved by the decree or order of the Tribunal or court shall have to challenge within the time stipulated by law, the original decree and not the order dismissing the review petition. Time taken by a party in diligently pursing the remedy by way of review may in appropriate cases be excluded from consideration while condoning the delay in the filing of the appeal, but such exclusion or condonation would not imply that there is a merger of the original decree and the order dismissing the review petition."

17. Sections 104 (ffa), 92 and Order I, Rule 8 – Private Trust

In *L.D. Kaushik* v. *Devendra Kumar Modi,* 2013 1 ADJ 635: 2013 2 AllLJ 651: 2013 97 All LR 786: 2013 3 CivCC 263 (All) this First Appeal From Order under Section 104 (ffa) of the Code of Civil Procedure arose out of an order passed by the District Judge, Mathura dated 3.10.2012 in Misc. Case No. 21 of 2010 (*L.D. Kaushik* v. *Devendra Kumar Modi*) by which the application filed by the applicants-appellants for leave of the Court to file a suit under Section 92 of the Code of Civil Procedure, has been rejected.

The District Judge refused the leave of the Court to file the suit on the grounds that there is no evidence on record to show that the applicants have any interest in the Trust, or that they have filed the suit as representatives of general public. They have not produced any receipts of staying in the Dharmsala maintained by the Trust nor they have published any advertisement in the newspapers to file the Suit under Order I Rule 8 CPC. It is thus clear that they have filed the suit at the instance of opposite party Nos. 8 and 9 and for their benefit, which cannot be the object of the filing of the suit under Section 92 of the Code of Civil Procedure.

So far as the appointment of the Chairman is concerned, the District Judge has referred to an arrangement by a Memorandum of Understanding between the two groups in Modi family, which was accepted by Hon'ble Supreme Court in *K.K. Modi* v. *K.N. Modi*, 1998 (3) SCC 573: AIR 1998 SC 1297 and under which the management of the Trust was given to K.N. Modi group. The District Judge has also referred to Suit No. 152 of 2007 *K.K. Modi* v. *Modi Charitable Trust* which has been transferred to the Court of Additional District Judge (Court No. 4) Ghaziabad, in which the Memorandum of Understanding dated 24.1.1989 has been acknowledged and it has also been accepted that the trust is being managed by the K.N. Modi group, which also shows that the members of K.K. Modi group, even if they were trustees, stopped attending the meeting of the Trust, could not have carried out the objects of the trust.

18. Order XXXIX Rule 11, Order XXXIX Rule 2(a), Order XLIII Rule 1, Section 104 – The Petitioners Challenge the Order Passed by the District Judge, Goa dated 9 July 2014 Dismissing the Preliminary Objection Taken by the Petitioner

In *Gajanan Bala Gawas* v. *Sagun Narayan Morjkar*, 2016 2 All MR 277: 2015 5 BomCR 66: 2016 2 Mh LJ 862 (Bom) the petitioners had filed a Civil Suit praying for an injunction against the respondents. On 24 October 2009, an order was passed by the learned Civil Judge Junior Division, granting injunction in favour of the petitioners. This order was confirmed by the District Judge in Misc. Civil Appeal. It is the case of the petitioners that thereafter the respondent obstructed the suit pathway. The petitioners accordingly filed an application under Order XXXIX Rule 2-A and 11 of Civil Procedure Code. The learned Civil Judge heard both sides in the application and by detailed order came to the conclusion that the respondent has obstructed the suit pathway and, accordingly, issued show cause notice to the respondent under Order XXXIX Rule 11 of the Civil Procedure Code. Thereafter, the respondent filed a Misc. Civil Appeal, in this Civil Appeal, the learned District Judge stayed the order passed by the learned Civil Judge dated 21 February 2013. The petitioners took an objection to the maintainability of the appeal which the learned District Judge which was negatived by the impugned order.

The learned Civil Judge by order dated 21 February 2013 had issued a show cause notice to the respondents under Order XXXIX Rule 11. There is no final order passed by the learned Civil Judge. Neither section 104 of the Civil Procedure Code nor Order XXXXIII

Rule1 contemplate any Misc. Appeal from issuance of show cause notice under Order XXXIX Rule 11. The final order is yet to be passed by the learned Civil Judge. In the circumstances, an appeal to the District Court was clearly not maintainable.

The High Court said, the learned District Judge has erred in entertaining the appeal and granting stay to the proceedings before the Civil Judge. It is also not clear from the impugned order whether the learned District Judge has held appeal to be maintainable or has postponed the decision till the disposal of the appeal. Either course of action are not correct in law. First the appeal was not maintainable. Secondly, the learned District Judge ought to have considered the nature of the proceedings and what was at stake was allegation of disobedience of the order of the Court. By grant of stay in an appeal, which is not maintainable, the proceedings taken out in respect of breach of judicial order have been scuttled. The appropriate course of action would be to permit the learned Civil Judge to pass the final order in the matter and then entertain the appeal from such final order. In view of the above position, the petition succeeds. Rule is made absolute in terms of prayer clause (a). The interim relief granted by the learned District Judge stands vacated. The proceedings before the learned Civil Judge will continue as per law and the learned Civil Judge will pass final order in the proceedings. It will be open to the respondent to challenge the same as per law. All contentions of both the parties on merits are kept open

19. Order XXXIX Rule 1(r), Order XLIII Rule 1, Order XLIII Rule 1, Section 104, Section 104(2), Section 108, Section 35(a), Section 91, Section 92 and Section 95

In *Sadasivam* v. *Kasilingam,* 015 2 LW 478 (Mad) the civil revision petition arose out of a judgment of the learned Subordinate, Panruti dated 29.08.2011 made in C.M.A.No.6 of 2011, which was in turn filed against the order of the learned District Munsif, Panruti dated 27.4.2011 made in I.A.No.20 of 2011 in O.S.No.8 of 2011 on the file of the District Munsif Court, Panruti. The above said suit was filed for declaration that they have easementary right over the passage to reach their property. The passage admittedly runs through the property of the respondent herein/defendant. Along with the suit, they filed an application in I.A.No.20 of 2011 for an interim injunction pending disposal of the suit not to prevent them from using the passage.

The learned trial Judge, by order dated 27.04.2011 allowed the said petition and granted interim injunction pending disposal of the suit. The said order was challenged before the lower appellate Court, namely the Sub-Court, Panruti in C.M.A.No.611 of 2011. The learned Subordinate Judge, panruti, after hearing, allowed the said appeal, set aside the order of the trial Court dated 27.04.2011 by his judgment dated 29.08.2011. Impugning the said judgment, the present civil revision petition has been filed under Article 227 of the Constitution of India by the revision petitioners, who are the plaintiffs in the original suit.

The Court said, the contention of the learned counsel for the respondent, if accepted, shall have the drastic effect of unsettling the settled positions of law, besides the same being totally untenable as one raised without properly understanding the scope of Section 108 of CPC which is concerned with Second Appeal allowed by any other provisions of the Civil procedure Code or by a special enactment. Hence, this Court does have no hesitation to come to a conclusion that the contention raised by the counsel for the respondent regarding the maintainability of the Civil Revision Petition is bound to be discountenanced.

As pointed out supra, regarding merits, the learned counsel for the respondent does not have anything to submit. In addition, when the petitioners claim easementary right to use the passage to reach their land pending disposal of the suit, refusing injunction will result in irrepairable loss and hardship to the petitioners. The learned trial Judge, properly appreciating the existence or otherwise of a prima facie case and also balance of convenience, decided the interlocutory application in favour of the revision petitioners, whereas the learned lower appellate Judge committed an error in setting aside the well considered order of the learned trial Judge. It is also brought to the notice of the Court that right from the date of filing of the suit, the petitioners had the benefit of ad-interim injunction and after the disposal of the interlocutory application by the trial Court and during the pendency of the Civil Miscellaneous Appeal before the lower appellate Court, the interim injunction granted in the trial Court had not been suspended and that this Court also granted interim stay pending disposal of the Civil Revision petition. Hence, this Court comes to the conclusion that the revision shall succeed. The decree of the lower appellate Court shall be set aside and the order of the learned trial Judge dated 27.04.2011 made in I.A.No.20 of 2011 in O.S.No. 8 of 2011 has to be restored.

20. Section 104 – Appeal Against Interlocutory Order XLIII Rule 1

In *Sri Madhava Prabhu* v. *Sri Subhas Shetty,* 2016 ILR (Karn) 2086: 2016 (4) KCCR 3761 (Karn) the appellant in Regular Appeal No. 43/2015, pending before the Court of the Principal Senior Civil Judge, Udupi, has presented this appeal. This appeal is directed against an interlocutory order dated 05.12.2015 passed by the aforesaid Court rejecting I.A. No. 5 filed by him under Order XXXIX Rules 1 & 2 of CPC in the appeal in R.A. No. 43/2015.

The High Court said, in my opinion, Section 104 (2) of CPC will not bar an appeal under Order XLIII, Rule 1 (r) of CPC against an order passed in exercise of the power under Order XXXIX Rules 1 & 2 of CPC, if it is not passed in an appeal presented under Section 104 of CPC.

It is relevant to state that the interlocutory order impugned in this appeal is an order passed in exercise of the power under Order XXXIX Rules 1 & 2 of CPC in a Regular appeal presented under Section 96 of CPC and not in an appeal presented under Section 104 of CPC. Hence, this appeal is not barred under Section 104(2) of CPC.

21. Section 104 (1)(h) – Order XXXIX, Rule 2A and Order XLIII, Rule 2A

In *Shankar Jadhav* v. *Sainath Jadhav,* 2016 (3) All MR 575: 2016 (4) Mh LJ 430: 2017 MCR 719 (Bombay) (Aurangabad Bench) the proceeding was filed under provision of Order XXXIX, Rule 2A of the Code of Civil Procedure by the plaintiff. The trial Court has held the present petitioner guilty of breach of order of temporary injunction and the trial Court has ordered to send the present petitioner to civil prison for 15 days. Both the sides are heard.

The provision of Order XLIII, Rule 1 (r) of the CPC was not made applicable to this State in view of the Bombay Amendment of 1st October 1983. It appears that there are conflicting decisions on the tenability of the revision against the order made under aforesaid provision. It appears that in cases reported as *Dry Chillies Brokers Association* v. *Dnyaneshwar Chamat,* 1993 (1) Bom CR 131: 1992 Mh LJ 1503 (Nagpur Bench); *Vitthal Shriram Kharbadkar* v. *Pandurang Irbhanji Kadu* and 2002 (3) Bom CR 593: 2002 (2) All MR 757 (Nagpur Bench) it was held by this Court that as the provision of Order XLIII, Rule 1 (2) of the CPC as amended for this State does not provide for filing of appeal, the appeal is not tenable and so revision needs to be filed. As against these two decisions there are three decisions of this Court like *Harivilas Madhavprasad Ruia* v. *Viraf Ardeshir Udwadia* 1994 (1) Bom CR 366; *Bansidhar Ramratan Upadhyay* v. *Ramchandra Ramnarayan Totla*, 2005 (2) Bom CR 43; and *Vasant Raghobaji Talekar* v. *Natwarlal Rantansi Thakkar,* 2010 (Supp) Bom CR 940. In these 3 cases this Court considered other provision of the CPC like provision of section 104(1)(h) of the CPC which runs as under:

> "***104. Orders from which appeal lies.***—(1) An appeal shall lie from the following orders, and save as otherwise expressly provided in the body of this Code or by any law for the time being in force, from no other orders:—
>
> (h) an order under any of the provisions of this Code imposing a fine or directing the arrest or detention in the civil prison of any person except where such arrest or detention is in execution of a decree."

In a case it was held that the revision is not tenable as the order would not put to an end the suit itself.

Learned counsel for the petitioner submitted that there is one more portion in section 104 of the CPC like 104(1)(i). that portion reads as under:

> "(i) any order made under rules from which an appeal is expressly allowed by rules."

Learned counsel submitted that in view of this provision and when in Maharashtra, provision of Order XLIII, Rule 1 (r) of the CPC is not applicable the appeal cannot lie and only revision can lie. This proposition is not acceptable. In section 104 of the CPC categories of the cases in which appeal is available are given and section 104(1)(i) is one of those categories. Due to State amendment of some portions of Order XLIII, Rule 1 of the CPC, the scope of other provision of section 104, the part like 1(h) cannot be reduced. In the present matter it can be said that provision of section 104(1)(h) is applicable. The provision of remaining portion like (i) of this section was also applicable in the past. By the State amendment care is taken to remove the relevant portion of section 104(1)(i) but due to that it cannot be said that appeal cannot be filed as specifically provided under section 104(1)(h) of the CPC.

22. Section 104 – Order of Injunction – Order XXXIX Rules 1 and 2, Order XLIII, Rule 1(r)

In along with the plaint, the respondents/plaintiffs also filed an interlocutory application in I.A.No. 683 of 2015 to grant an order of temporary injunction as against the revision petitioner/first defendant and other defendants in the suit. The revision petitioner/first defendant has contested the suit by filing his written statement. No contest is made on behalf of the fourth respondent/second defendant as he had passed away. After hearing both sides and on appreciation of the evidences adduced on both sides, the learned Additional District Munsif,

Karur has proceeded to allow the petition granting an order of interim injunction. This order dated 09.09.2015 has been challenged in this revision.

The High Court said, learned counsel appearing for the respondents 1 to 3.

> 5. Before, we go into the merits of the case, the question of maintainability of this revision is arisen for the consideration of this Court. It is obvious to note that the impugned order seems to have been passed by the trial Court under Order XXXIX, Rule 1 and 2 of the Code of Civil Procedure. As contemplated under Order XLIII, Rule 1(r) as well as Section 104 of the Code of Civil Procedure, the order passed under Section XXXIX Rule 1 and 2 CPC is an appealable order and not revisable order.

However, a revision under Article 227 of the Constitution of India can also be maintained before this Court to exercise its power of superintendence to stretch its hand over the Subordinate Courts to set their wrong at right. Article 227 of the Constitution of India confers on the High Court, the power of superintendence over the Courts and Tribunals within the State or within its jurisdiction. It is significant to note here that the power of superintendence conferred by Article 227 of the Constitution of India is in addition to the power conferred upon this Court to control inferior Courts or Tribunals through Writs under Article 226 of the Constitution of India. The supervisory jurisdiction extends to keeping the subordinate Tribunals within the limits of that authority and ensuring that they obey the law. As observed by the Apex Court in *Baby* v. *Travancore Devaswom Board* reported in (1998) 9 SCC 310: AIR 1999 SC 519, this power of superintendence is also in addition to the powers of revision under any legislation. However, since it being a supervisory power, it has to be exercised as such, distinct from appellate power. This principle is also laid down by the Apex Court in *Mohan Amba Prasad Agnihotri* v. *Bhaskar Balwant Aher* reported in (2000) 3 SCC 190: AIR 2000 SC 931. It is to be noted that the power of superintendence under Article 227 of the Constitution of India is of an administrative as well as judicial nature. If necessary, the High Court can interfere with the administrative orders of the inferior courts.

It may also be relevant to note here that as laid down by the Apex Court in *Jagir Singh* v. *Ranbir Singh* reported in (1979) 1 SCC 560: AIR 1979 SC 381, the supervisory power under this Article can be exercised even in those cases in which no appeal or revision lies to the High Court. In *M.G. Burjarji* v. *S.N. Misra* reported in (1977) 1 SCC 227: AIR 1976 SC 2446, it is held by the Apex Court that this power should not ordinarily be exercised if any other remedy is available to the aggrieved party, even though the pursuing of that remedy may involve some inconvenience or delay.

23. Section 104, Order XLIII, Rule 1 – Decree of District Judge Remanding case to Trial Court for Rehearing and Re-deciding the Matter

In *Parvat Singh* v. *Gram Pancahyat, Makad Seema, Udaipur,* 2016 WLC (Raj) (UC) 626: 2016 (3) DNJ 1039 (Raj) (Jodhpur Bench) the High Court said upon perusal of the order, I am of the opinion that the judgment cited by the learned counsel for the appellant in the case of *Ashwin Kumar K. Patel* (supra) is not applicable in the present case because as per the finding given by the learned lower appellate court there is no finding in the judgment of the learned trial court with regard to presumption of the document under Section 90 of the Evidence Act, 1972. Therefore, obviously if no finding was given by the learned trial court then, there was no material to reverse the any erroneous finding given by the learned trial court. In view of the above fact, I have perused the para no.8 of the judgment in the case of *Ashwin Kumar K. Patel* (supra), which reads as under:

> "8. In our view, the High Court should not ordinarily remand a cause under Order XLI, Rule 23 CPC to the lower Court merely because it considered that the reasoning of the lower court in some respects was wrong. Such remand orders lead to unnecessary delays and cause prejudice to the 5 parties to the case. When the material was available before the High Court, it should have itself decided the appeal one way or other. It could have considered the various aspects of the case mentioned in the order of the trial Court and considered whether the order of the trial Court ought to be confirmed or reversed or modified. It could have easily considered the documents and affidavits and decided about the prima facie case on the material available. In mattes involving agreements of 1980 (and 1996) on the one hand and an agreement of 1991 on the other, as in this case, such remand orders would lead to further delay and uncertainty. We are, therefore, of the view that the remand by the High Court was not necessary.

Upon perusal of the above adjudication made by the Hon'ble Supreme Court it is obvious that as per above verdict ordinarily the matter should not be remanded under Order XLI, Rule 23 CPC to the lower court because reasoning of the lower court in some respect may be wrong but here in this case, there is no finding with regard to presumption, therefore, the first appellate court has rightly remanded the case to the trial court to decide the case afresh.

In view of the above, without interfering in the judgment dated 11.9.2015 the instant appeal is disposed of with direction to the learned trial court to decide the suit within a period of three months from the date of receiving certified copy of this order.

24. Sections 96 and 104 Succession Special Notaries and Inventory Proceeding Act, 2012

In *Mrs. Ida Barreto* v. *Mr. Maxmiano Guilherme Furtado*, 2017 (4) BCR 717, the High Court said, In terms of Section 451 of the new Act, an appeal from the final order made in the inventory proceeding shall lie to the competent Court depending upon the value of the assets and such appeal shall be deemed to be appeal under Section 96 of the Code of Civil Procedure,1908. However, in terms of sub-section 2, an appeal from an order shall lie from every order, other than a merely administrative order, made in the inventory proceedings to the competent Court depending upon the value given to the assets at the time the order is made and appeal shall be deemed to be an appeal under Section 104 of the Code of Civil Procedure, 1908. In other words an appeal from a final order which is deemed to be an appeal under Section 96 i.e. an appeal from an original decree shall lie to the Court depending on the value of the assets while an appeal from order which is akin to that under Section 104 of Code of Civil Procedure, 1908 shall lie to the competent Court depending on the value given to the assets at the time order is made. A reading of Section 451 of the new Act clearly makes a distinction between an appeal to the competent Court from a final order in terms of sub-section 1 and an appeal in terms of sub-section 2 being an appeal from order to the competent court based on the value at the time of the order. Therefore there is no basis in the contention of Shri M.P. Almeida, learned Advocate that these two situations are not synonymous. A reference to this section also does not substantiate his contention that the appeal would lie to the High Court considering the judgment in *Vero Nunes, Lourdes Gregorio Gomindes and Renoir I.B. Cota* (supra). In the ultimate , it is apparent as contended by Shri S. M. Usgaonkar, learned Senior Counsel for the respondent in A.O. No. 50 of 2016 that these three judgments hold the field and in view thereof the appeals are required to be returned to be filed before the District Court considering the valuation of the assets. In view of the above discussion, the appeal memos along with the annexures are ordered to be returned to the appellants to be tendered before the competent Court having jurisdiction within two weeks from the receipt thereof. It goes without say that the learned District Judge will consider the aspect of delay in preferring the appeal. In the event the issue of limitation arises, the appellants would be at liberty to urge that they were prosecuting the above appeals in this Court and which shall be taken into consideration while deciding the issue of limitation.

25. Sections 100 and 104, Order XLIII, Rule 1 – Second Appeal from Order

In *Swapan Kumar Paul* v. *State of Assam*, 2017 (1) Gau LT 422: 2017 (2) Gau LT 158 (Gau), the High Court examined the maintainability of second appeal against an order under section 104.In the case under refrence on a query to Mr. Roy, learned counsel appearing on behalf of the appellants with regard to the maintainability of the present second appeal, he submits before this court that as the order impugned arises from an order passed under Order VII, Rule 10 as such the present second appeal is maintainable.

Mr. Ghosh, learned counsel, appearing on behalf of the respondents aforesaid, submits that the Order XLIII emanates from Section 104 of the CPC and as per the provision of Section 104 (2) of the CPC, no appeal lie from any order passed in appeal under Section 104. Thus, the finality of the order passed in the appeal has been prescribed by Section 104(2) of the CPC. The appeal preferred before the learned Civil Judge, (Senior Division), Karimganj was an appeal under Section 104 CPC and the same having attained finality, so Mr. Gosh submits that this second appeal that too under Section 100 of the CPC is not at all maintainable.

This court after hearing the learned counsel appearing on behalf of the parties to this appeal, finds force in the submission of Mr. Ghosh and accordingly dismissed the second appeal without entering into any merit of the present second appeal. However, the appellants shall be at liberty to file proper petition if so advised, in the proper forum of law.

105. *Other orders.*—(1) Save as otherwise expressly provided, no appeal shall lie from any order made by a Court in the exercise of its original or appellate jurisdiction; but, where a decree is appealed from, any error, defect or irregularity in any order, affecting the decision of the case, may be set forth as ground of objection in the memorandum of appeal.

Notwithstanding anything contained in sub-section (1), where any party aggrieved by an order of remand from which an appeal lies does not appeal therefrom, he shall thereafter be precluded from disputing its correctness.

SYNOPSIS

Comments

1. Scope and Application

Whereas section 104 and Order XLIII lay down which orders are appealable, section 105 prohibits appeal against any other order, unless specifically provided. At the same time, it lays down that if the decree is appealed from, any error defect or irregularity in any order may be set forth as a ground of objection, if such error defect or irregularity affects decision of the case.

Sub-section (2) is an exception to sub-section (1) insofar as the order of remand is concerned. If the aggrieved party does not prefer appeal against an order of the appellate court remanding a case to the original court, he may not dispute its correctness subsequently.

The present section makes it quite clear that an order appealable under section 104 may be questioned under section 105 in an appeal from the decree in the suit although no appeal from the order has been preferred under section 104; *Narayan Nambissan* v. *Krishna Nair,* 1943 Mad; *Marjnaba Dasi* v. *Kumar Surjendu,* (1956) ILR 1 Cal 197.

2. Section 105, 11—Applicability – *Res Judicata*

Where matter coming before High Court in second appeal after matter had been remanded to trial court for a fresh decision, views expressed by High Court in earlier second appeal seriously doubted by the High Court in later second appeal, but the same not having been challenged, the Supreme Court held that later High Court rightly felt bound and helpless in respect of said observation; *Krishna Pillai Rajasekharan Nair* v. *Padmanabha Pillai*, AIR 2004 SC 1206: 2004 AIR SCW 106: (2004) 12 SCC 754.

3. Error, Defect or Irregularity – Nature & Meaning of

The High Court of Allahabad made it clear that the error, defect or irregularity referred to in this section must be an error defect or irregularity in law or procedure and not in matters of fact; *Sankali* v. *Murlidhar*, (1890) ILR 12 All 200.

4. Meaning of – 'Affecting Decision'

It has been settled that the words affecting the decision of the case mean affecting the decision of the case on its merits which is a condition for raising the question of such error, defect or irregularity as a ground in appeal; *Radha Mohan Datt* v. *Abbas Ali Biswas*, AIR 1931 All 294: ILR 53 All 612: 1931 All LJ 377 (FB).

5. Section 105(2)—Appeal against the Order of Remand—Effect of Failure to File Appeal

The aggrieved party cannot, subsequently file appeal against such order, after disposal of the suit remanded for re-consideration. The Supreme Court made it clear that under Order XLIII, rule 1 clause (u) C.P.C. an appeal lies against an order remanding a case where an appeal would lie from the decree of the appellate court. From the fact that the respondent has filed Second Appeal, which is the subject of attack before us against the decision in an appeal to the District Court in the same proceedings, it is clear that the respondent should have filed an appeal against the order of remand. The consequence of an omission to file an appeal against the order of remand, under such circumstances, is indicated in section 105, sub-section (2), C.P.C. *Sita Ram Goel* v. *Sukhnandi Dayal*, AIR 1972 SC 1612: (1972) 1 SCR 836: (1971) 3 SCC 488; *Nainsingh* v. *Koonwarjee*, AIR 1970 SC 997: 1970 Jab LJ 544: 1970 MPLJ 568: (1971) 1 SCR 207: (1970) 1 SCC 732.

The Rajasthan High Court examined whether a remand can be challenged in a revision under section 115 of CPC. This was a reference by a learned Single Judge of this Court, and the point referred has been formulated as follows:—

> "Whether an order of remand passed under section 151, C.P.C. or otherwise and from which no appeal lies can he challenged by way of revision under section 115, C.P.C. in view of the decision of this Court in *Prohit Swarup Narain* v. *Gopi Nath*, ILR (1953) 3 Raj 483: AIR 1953 Raj 137 (FB) (A) and whether the revision against the order of remand in the present case is competent?"

The Court considered the law laid down in *Prohit Swarupnarain* v. *Gopinath*, ILR (1953) 3 Raj 483: AIR 1953 Raj 137 (FB) (A) which was in these terms—

> "Where it is open to a party to raise a ground of appeal in High Court under section 105, C.P.C. from the final decree or order with respect to any order which has been passed during the pendency of the case, it should be held that an appeal in that case lies to the High Court within

the meaning of the term "in which no appeal lies thereto" appearing in section 115 of C.P.C."

The Court discussed the types of remand order and said that an order of remand can be of two kinds. It may be an order under Order XLI, rule 23 in which case an appeal lies under Order XLI, rule 1(u). The question before the Court was not concerned with this kind of remand order. The other kind of remand order by an Appellate Court is one which is not covered by Order XLI, rule 23. Such orders have generally been held to be under the inherent powers of the Court under section 151, C.P.C., and the question that we have to reply is whether a revision is entertainable from such an order of remand in view of the decision in *Prohit Swarup Narain's* case (A) for no appeal is provided against it. The Court after examining the issue held that where an order of remand is passed under section 151, C.P.C., or where the order is not covered by the express terms of Order XLI, rule 23, and if no appeal lies from such an order of remand, it cannot be challenged by way of revision under section 115, C.P.C. in view of the decision of this Court in *Swarup Narain's* case (A), as the order of remand can be challenged on an appeal from the final decree under section 105, C.P.C. (assuming always that the decree can be brought in appeal to the High Court).

In the present case, the suit was for the recovery of possession of a house and second appeal would lie to this Court. As such, the order of remand passed in this case by the first appellate court could be challenged under section 105, C.P.C. in the second appeal which would finally lie to this Court, and, therefore, the present revision against the order of remand is incompetent. The answer was returned to the Bench concerned; *Chandmal* v. *Ramakishan,* AIR 1957 Raj 71: 1957 Raj LW 54: ILR (1957) 7 Raj 496.

6. Sections 115 and 151 of CPC

The High Court of Madras in the case of *M. Ponnupandian* v. *Selvabakiyam,* AIR 2004 Mad 272: 2003 (4) CTC 225: 2003 (3) Mad LJ 590 examined the provisions of sections 115 and 151. In that case the plaintiff Selvabakiyam filed Execution Petition in E.P. No. 178 of 2001 on 19.10.2001. In the Execution Petition, respondents 2 to 4, namely defendants 2 to 4 remained absent and were set *ex parte*. The first defendant, namely, the revision petitioner entered appearance on 2.4.2002 and took time to file counter till 10.12.2002 and on that date, since no counter was filed, delivery was ordered by 31.12.2002.

The revision petitioner filed E.A. No. 72 of 2003 to set aside the *ex parte* order dated 10.12.2002 in E.P. No. 178 of 2001 and E.A. No. 71 of 2003 to condone the delay of 23 days in filing such petition by stating in the affidavit of petitions that he was doing business in Kerala and only on 20.1.2003 he came to know about the *ex parte* order and on contact his advocate informed that since he did not file counter, he was set *ex parte*. After obtaining copy of necessary papers relating to O.S. No. 6 of 1992 from Tirunelveli District Court, a counter has been prepared in which there has been delay of 23 days in filing the petition to set aside *ex parte* order dated 10.12.2002. Therefore, the revision petitioner filed both the petitions. The point for determination in the case was as to whether there is any ground to interfere with the common order passed by the Court below.

The question of invoking inherent powers under section 151, Civil Procedure Code does not arise in this case. That is because of the specific provisions contained under Rule 106 of Order XXI, Civil Procedure Code. If, therefore, there is repugnancy between the Central Code under rule 106 and the Madras Amendment under sub-rule (4) of rule 105 of Order XXI it is section 97 of the Civil Procedure Code in relation to repeal and savings that would apply. That says that any amendment made or any provision inserted in the principal Act by a State Legislature or a High Court before the commencement of this Act shall except insofar as such amendment of provision is consistent with the provisions of the principal Act as amended by this Act, shall stand repealed.

It was held that the principal Act, namely Central Code, does not make section 5 of the Limitation Act applicable, while the Madras Amendment does make it applicable. Therefore to that extent there is repugnancy.

There is yet another way of looking at the matter. Sub-rule (4) of rule 105 of Order XXI, Civil Procedure Code (Madras Amendment) makes a reference only to the Indian Limitation Act, 1908. After it is repealed there is no possibility of applying the same."

The above judgment had been approved by a Division Bench of this Court in *S.M. Natarajan* v. *Devayanai Ammal*, 1989 (1) LW 178.

Therefore, in any view of the matter, it is clear that E.A. No. 71 of 2003 filed to condone the delay of 23 days in filing E.A. No. 72 of 2002 to set aside the *ex parte* Order dated 10.12.2002 in E.P. No. 178 of 2001 is not maintainable. In that, Order XXI, rule 106 and section 151, C.P.C. have no application and consequently E.A. No. 72 of 2002 to set aside the *ex parte* order dated 10-12-2002 cannot also be allowed and taking all these aspects, rightly the executing Court has dismissed both the applications. Such finding does not call for any interference by this Court.

The Civil Revision Petitions were dismissed with costs. Consequently, the petition in C.M.P. No. 4073 of 2003 was also dismissed.

7. Section 105 and Order XXI, Rule 90

The Madras High Court in the case of *Saradambal* v. *A.M.P. Arunachalam*, (1968) 2 MLJ 266: AIR 1969 Mad 324: 81 Mad LW 387 examined the two provisions together. In that case the appellant herein who was the judgment-debtor in O.S. No. 5 of 1953, filed an application under Order XXI, rule 90, Civil Procedure Code on 30th September, 1963 for setting aside the sale of the property that took place in execution of the decree in the suit and purchased by the respondent herein, and also filed an application for dispensing with the furnishing of security contemplated by the proviso to Order XXI, rule 90, Civil Procedure Code. The Court said that the suit itself was based on a mortgage and the respondent herein who was the decree-holder purchased the property in auction for a sum of Rs. 2,005. The application filed by the appellant for dispensing with the furnishing of security was numbered as E.A. No. 525 of 1963, the same was dismissed and the appellant herein was directed to furnish security for a sum of Rs. 2,000 within one month from the date of the order, dated 14th November, 1963. The learned Subordinate Judge of Chingleput who disposed of that application stated that the point for determination before him was whether it was a fit case for dispensing with security to be furnished under Order XXI, rule 90, Civil Procedure Code and then answered the point as follows:

> On behalf of the petitioner, an affidavit filed by Valliammal in C.M.P. No. 2194 of 1953 in C.M.A. No. 127 of 1953, High Court, Madras, has been marked as Exhibit A-1 and in paragraph 5 of the said affidavit, it is alleged that the building was fetching a rent of Rs. 500 per month. Exhibit A-2 gives the value of the property at Rs. 60,600 while according to Exhibit A-1, the four mortgage debts amounted to Rs. 35,000. It is contended that all the mortgages are old and have ripened to decrees and that no amount was paid, whether towards principal or interest, and that the property has deteriorated, in value, and therefore security cannot be dispensed with. On the materials placed before me, I find that it is a fit case to call upon the applicant to furnish security to the extent of Rs. 2,000 and therefore the petition for dispensing with the security to be furnished under Order XXI, rule 90 of the Civil Procedure Code, is dismissed with costs.

Thereafter the appellant furnished an extent of 72 cents of punja in S. No. 88/6 in Aviyur village, Gingee Taluk, South Arcot District as security. The respondent herein opposed it on the ground that the same was insufficient. Thereafter, by an order dated 10th December, 1964 the learned Subordinate Judge of Chingleput held that the security offered by the appellant was not sufficient, that the same could not be accepted as security furnished in terms of the order in E.A. No. 525 of 1963 and that once the security was not furnished as called for, the application could not be maintained; and he consequently dismissed with costs the application E.A. No. 15 of 1964 filed by the appellant for setting aside the sale. The present appeal has been filed against that order.

The Court referred to the observations of this Court in *Venkata Lingamma* v. *Rajagopala Venkata Narasimha,* C.M.A. Nos. 86 and 92 of 1959, to the following effect:

> "It is clear, therefore, the Court held, that in issuing notice the Court did not intend to deprive itself of the power of deciding whether the security to be eventually furnished by the petitioner was adequate or not, and when it was found that the security was not adequate, the Court was entitled under rule 90 as now amended to dismiss the application without any further consideration on its merits."

Therefore, the Court took the view that on the facts of this case the contention of Mr. Ramanathan that by virtue of the order, dated 16th January, 1964 the learned Subordinate Judge had denied to himself the right to insist on the compliance with his order, dated 14th November, 1963 is not tenable. However, in view of my conclusion that the order dated 14th November, 1963 dismissing the application of the appellant to dispense with security is erroneous, this appeal succeeds and has to be allowed, with the result that the learned Subordinate Judge will have to dispose of the application of the appellant for setting aside the sale on merits.

8. Section 105 – Jurisdiction of the Rent Control Tribunal

The High Court of Delhi examined the question of jurisdiction of a Rent Control Tribunal. In the case under reference, the only question for decision was whether the Rent Control Tribunal was right in disregarding the decision of Gurdev Singh, J., as being wrong on a question of law in view of the Supreme Court decision in *Mathura Prasad* v. *Dossibai,* AIR 1971 SC 2355: (1970) 3 SCR 830. The proposition established by the Supreme Court in *Mathura Prasad's* case was summarised by Shah, J., speaking for the Court at the end of paragraph 5 of the decision as follows:—

> "A decision on an issue of law will be as *res judicata* in a subsequent proceeding between the same parties, if the cause of action of the subsequent proceeding be the same as in the previous proceeding, but not when the cause of action is different, nor when the law has since the earlier decision been altered by a competent authority, nor when the decision relates to the jurisdiction of the Court to try the earlier proceeding, nor when the earlier decision declares valid a transaction which is prohibited by law."

The applicability of this Supreme Court decision to the case may be considered under the following headings:—

(A) Whether the decision, of Gurdev Singh, J., is not binding between the parties as being a wrong decision on a pure question of law?

(B) Whether it is not the general principle of *res judicata* but the specific rule of statutory finality embodied in section 105(2), Civil Procedure Code which applies to the present case ?

(C) Whether the order of Gurdev Singh, J., was without jurisdiction and can, therefore, be challenged as being void.

(D) Whether the correctness of the order of Gurdev Singh, J., can be challenged on the ground that subsequently the Supreme Court took a different view and disapproved the view taken by Gurdev Singh, J., in *M.M. Chawla* v. *J.S. Sethi,* 1969 Ren CR 861: (1970) 2 SCR 390.

(E) Whether the decision of Gurdev Singh, J." had the effect of declaring valid a transaction which is prohibited by law, and

(F) An initial distinction must be made between the same proceeding and a subsequent proceeding. A finding arrived at by the competent Court between parties which has become final by not being.

The Court appreciated that the Rent Control Tribunal while deciding the two appeals was really considering one subject-matter, namely, the application for fixation of standard rent. There was, therefore, no need for the tenant to file two separate appeals against the two separate orders of the Tribunal. The law on this point has been considered fully under question No. 2 in *Jawahar Singh* v. *Jai Gopal Grover,* 1972 Ren CR 224 (Del) referred to above. For the reasons stated therein this contention is untenable. *R. Dhiren Kiri* v. *Suraj Balaram Sahni & Sons,* ILR 1974 Del 210: 1975 RLR 73.

9. Section 105 – Appeal against Interim Order

In *Janeshwar Kumar Jain* v. *Aadeshwar Kumar Jain s/o Shri Walaiti Ram Jain*, 2014 (2) Law Herald 1577 (P&H) Punjab High Court examined the appellibility of an interim order. The High Court said, an interim order which will have a direct bearing to the disposal of the suit could be a subject of ground of appeal under Section 105 CPC.

In all matters relating to joint possession or partition, it is the plaint averment that shall decide the issue of court fee. If the plaintiff has contended that he is a joint owner of the property for 1/6th share of a property that belonged to the mother unless the plaintiff was excluded from possession by a hostile assertion, the plaintiff's averment must stand, to allow for the valuation to be made as in joint possession. If the plaintiff has also contended that the Will propounded by the defendant was not true, it did not require to be set aside, for, the fundamental precept in law is that the person that propounds the document has to prove it. The plaintiff was not required to make any valuation for the claim that the Will was not true. If there had been a direction by the trial Court that the suit had not been properly valued, I would find that this Court did not have an occasion to adjudicate on the same and, therefore, it cannot be said to be conclusive as regards the plaintiff. The counsel for the respondents points out that there is not even a ground of appeal against the direction given at the interim stage. An interim order which will have a direct bearing to the disposal of the suit could be a subject of ground of appeal under Section 105 CPC. If the interim order relating to the frame of suit had not been reaffirmed, then it should only be taken that the Court has not adjudicated on the valuation in suit.

The Court was in error in directing the petitioner to pay ad valorem court fee on the objection taken by the respondents. I have already observed that the person that propounds the Will alone has to prove the Will and there is no need to set aside the Will or value the relief, if such a relief is sought. The plaintiff may ignore the Will as invalid and he is not required to value the same and the valuation as made, on the basis of the averment in plaint must be taken as appropriate. The direction given by the court below is set aside. The revision petition is allowed.

10. Section 105(2) – Order of Remand should not be Made Mechanically

In *Periyanayagasamy* v. *Jesudoss*, 2012 2 MLJ 81 (Mad) learned counsel appearing on behalf of the appellant/defendant would submit that the order of remand should not be made mechanically. In the instant case, there is no dispute with regard to the title of Chinnappan to the suit property. When there is no dispute with regard to the title of Chinnappan with regard to the suit property, there is no need for impleading Chinnappan and amending the prayer and the appellate Court itself can decide the suit on merits. In support of his contentions, the learned counsel has relied on the judgments in *Somasundaram Chettiar* v. *Balasubramanian* (1998) 2 MLJ 562: (1998) 1 CTC 626, *Kannathal* v. *Arulmighu Kanniammal Karuppasamy Thirukoil*, (2007) 1 MLJ 725: 2007 (2) CTC 49 and *Parimal* v. *Veena Alias Bharti*, (2011) 3 SCC 545: (2011) 4 MLJ 540.

Per contra, the learned counsel for the 4th and 5th respondents submitted that it is the main defence of the appellant before the trial Court that the suit property belonged to Chinnappan, the 5th respondent and he purchased 0.33 cents situated on the northern side of the suit property from the same from Chinnappan, but Chinnappan was not impleaded as a party to the suit before the trial Court. But, before the lower appellate Court, the respondents have taken two applications, one to implead the Chinnappan as one of the parties to the suits and also to amend the plaint to add the prayer for declaration declaring the right of Chinnappan in the suit property. The said applications were allowed by the Court on 13.8.2004 and 22.7.1997 respectively. Since the declaration prayer is added, the nature of the suit has totally changed. Under such circumstances, the order of remand passed by the lower appellate Court to record the evidence of Chinnappan cannot be found fault with. The learned counsel further submitted that the appellant having failed to challenge the orders passed in LA. Nos. 18 of 2004 and 35 of 1997, now cannot challenge the order of remand. In support of the said submissions, the learned counsel has relied on the decisions in *Md. Najibuzzaman* v. *Sheo Shankar,* AIR (30) 1943 OUDH 288 and *Purushottam Reddy* v. *Pratap Steels Limited,* (2002) 2 MLJ 99 (SC): AIR 2002 SC 771.

The High Court said, it is, no doubt, the interim order could be challenged in the appeal filed as against the order of remand. But at the same time, the appellant ought to have raised the grounds with regard to the correctness of the interim order in the grounds of appeal filed against the order of remand. In the instant case, the appellant has raised the grounds with regard to the order passed by the lower appellate Court in I.A. 18 of 2004 in impleading Chinnappan as one of the parties and the appellant has not chosen to raise the ground, with regard to the amendment of the prayer in the plaint. Moreover, as per Section 105(2) C.P.C., any error, defect or irregularity in any order, affecting the decision of the case, may be set forth as a ground of objection in the memorandum of appeal. Therefore, only if an error, defect or irregularity is found in the interim order passed by the Court below, the correctness of the same could be challenged while challenging the order of remand. So far as in the instant case, it is the specific defence of the appellant himself that he had purchased the property from the father of plaintiffs 1 to 4 and from the date of purchase, he was put in possession in the suit property. But in spite of this defence, the plaintiffs have not chosen to implead the said Chinnappan before the trial Court; but, during pendency of the appeal, they filed the applications and the same were allowed by the lower appellate Court. It is to be noted that the appellant has also kept quiet without challenging the interim orders independently. Under such circumstances, I do not find any error or defect or irregularity in the order passed by the lower appellate Court in impleading Chinnappan as one of the parties and consequential amendment made in the prayer, which is necessary for effective adjudication of the issue involved in the suit.

11. Section 105, Section 105(1)

In *Hindustan Petroleum Corporation Ltd.* v. *Sau. Nivedita wife of Pritamsingh Jain,* 2014 5 All MR 270: 2014 (4) CivCC 273: 2014 (4) Mh LJ 874: 2014 (16) RCR (Civ) 1042.

The High Court said, it appears from the record that the plaintiff-landlady, after institution of the suit in 1979, commenced her evidence and examined four witnesses for the period from 7th September, 1985 till 15th January, 1987, and on the last date, namely 15th January, 1987, by the Pursis [Exh.101], she closed her case. On the same date, the counsel for the appellant-HPCL filed an application [Exh.142] praying for adjournment of a month and the counsel for the plaintiff gave reply to that application, stating that the defendant no.1 should have kept its evidence ready, as if the plaintiff had already informed that she would close her case on 15th January, 1987 and the defendant no.1 should bring the witnesses on that date. Court granted adjournment till 3rd February, 1987, on which date Presiding Officer of the Court was on leave. The case was then posted to 25th February, 1987, on which date the counsel for the appellant stated that he wanted to examine a witness on the next date, and prayed for a months time. The counsel for the plaintiff opposed the application, stating there was no sufficient cause. The Court granted the application by imposing cost of Rs. 25/-. On the next date, namely 20th March, 1987, an application for adjournment was filed on the ground that the counsel for the appellant was suffering from blood pressure and was unable to attend the court, while the witness Mr. Pillai, who was to come from Coimbatore, was unable to come and in support of the same, a copy of the telegram was placed on record about Mr. Pillai, in which it was stated that next date, namely 19th should be taken. The counsel for the plaintiff opposed the application and the learned Trial Judge referring to earlier adjournment applications [Exhs.142 and 143], stated that from January, 1987, sufficient time was given and even no summons was taken from the Court and hence rejected the application, thus, closing the case of defendant and then proceeded further.

12. Section 105 (1) – When an Order may Fall under Section 105

In *Nilamadhab Deo* v. *Major Balakrushna Sharma,* 2015 Sup 2 OLR 774 (Ori) the High Court said, it has been specifically provided in sub-section (1) of Section 105 of the Code that save as otherwise expressly provided, no appeal shall lie from any order made by a Court in the exercise of its original or appellate jurisdiction where a decree is appealed from any error, defect or irregularity in any order affecting the decision of the case may be set forth as a ground of objection in the memorandum of appeal. Thus, a careful reading goes to show that an order so as to fall within the ambit of sub-Section (1) of Section 105 of the Code, first of all, there must be an error, defect or irregularity therein. Secondly, the order must be such that it would be found to have affected the decision of the case. When these above conditions are satisfied, the same can be a ground of objection and it may be so set-forth as a ground in the memorandum of appeal filed challenging the final judgment and decree.

Adverting to the submission of the learned counsel for the appellants, it is seen that the error, defect or irregularity in the said order as has been pointed out to be one on account of non-service of notice to the parties prior to striking off the defence basing on which the next limb of submission stands that the appeal has to be allowed with an order of remand of the suit to the trial Court for adjudication a:fresh affording due opportunity to the defendant no. 1. It is the provision of law that an order of striking out the defence may be made on such application after notice to the parties and giving them reasonable opportunity of being heard. In the present case, such order has been passed by the trial Court on 17.09.1986 where the trial Court has rejected the affidavit by the defendant no. 1 having made a detail discussion as regards each of the questions required to be answered and finally on facts it has been stated that the interrogatories have not been properly answered as directed. With the above the petition dated 17.01.1987 came for consideration when the plaintiff made a prayer to strike out the defence filed by the defendant no. 1. Objection was invited. It was so filed and then after hearing finally order has been passed on 19.08.1987 striking out the defence. It is no doubt correct to say that the parties were not issued with any notice. However, the undeniable fact remains that the defendants were represented by their counsel in the suit who received the copy of the petition. He also filed objection and took part in the hearing of that petition. So, it cannot at all be said that such matter had been taken up behind the back of the parties and they had no knowledge about that, when the relationship between the party and the lawyer was subsisting and no such assertion is made throwing any light as regards something in detrimental to such relationship or for any other reason to have deliberately acted against the interest.

13. Sections 24, 104 and 105 – Application – Family Dispute

In *Mahendra Pratap Bhatt* v. *Smt. Saroj Mahana,* 2016 (5) ADJ 282 (All): 76 (CLMC) 2015, the High Court said, In our opinion, at the best, the impugned order of the learned Single Judge would be, if at all, in the purported exercise of power under Article 226 of the Constitution of India. That being so, such purported exercise of power under Article 226 of the Constitution of India would be amenable to an intra-Court Special Appeal under Chapter VIII Rule 5 of the Allahabad High Court Rules, 1952 which is extracted hereunder:

14. Order 43 Rule 1, Order 9 Rule 13, Order 9 Rule 7, Order 9 Rule 9, Section 100, Section 105, Section 105(1), Section 105(2), Section 108, Section 2(2), Section 99

In *Raj Mohan Dewangan* v. *State of C.G.,* 2015 1 CGLJ 107: 2014 (4) MPHT 24 (Chh) the High Court held, a close reading of Section 105(1) of the CPC would show that any error, defect of Irregularity in the order, affecting the decision of the case, may be set forth as a ground of objection in memo of appeal, while preferring appeal against the decree provided no appeal lies against that order. Thus, in order to attract Section 105(1) of the CPC, the abovestated two conditions must be satisfied.

In *Banda Pulla Reddy* v. *Banda Lakshmamma,* 2014 (6) ALT 251: 2014 (5) ALD 442, the High Court of Andhra Pradesh said, entire judicial system has been created only to discover and find real truth .About an eviction suit the Court said, In a suit for ejectment once plaintiff has been able to create a high degree of probability so as to shift onus on the defendant, it is for defendant to discharge his onus and in absence thereof, the burden of proof lies on plaintiff shall be held to have been discharged so as to prove plaintiff's title.

15. Section 105 and Order XLI, Rule 27

In *Kaliya Perumal* v. *Kelannji Ammal @ Kelannji,* 2017 (1) Mad WN (Civil) 273 (Mad) on a consideration of the oral and documentary evidence adduced by the parties, the trial Court was pleased to decree the suit. The first appeal filed before the first appellate Court against the judgment and decree of the trial Court had come to be dismissed. Aggrieved over the judgment and decree of the Courts below, the present second appeal has been preferred by the defendants.

The second appeal came to be admitted on the following substantial questions of law:

(i) When the assignment in favour of the plaintiff had been cancelled by the revenue officials, are the courts below justified in overlooking the cancellation and decreeing the suit as prayed for?

(ii) In the absence of any proof to show the possession and enjoyment over the suit property, are the plaintiff entitled for any relief?

The defendants took a plea that the assignment given to the plaintiff had been obtained based on misrepresentation and wrong measurements and that, the suit property has been in possession and enjoyment of the defendants along with their patta lands. Further, according to the defendants, at the most, the plaintiff would be entitled to get only ?rd share in respect of the patta lands and the suit property and therefore, the plaintiff should be non suited.

The trial court decreed the suit as prayed for. The defendants preferred the first appeal. At that point of time, it is admitted by the parties concerned that the assignment granted to the plaintiff has been cancelled by RDO (Revenue Divisional Officer), Thirukovilur. So, while preferring the first appeal, the defendants have also preferred an application under Order XLI, Rule 27 CPC to admit the cancellation order of the assignment as an Additional document in support of their case. However, their application has come to be rejected by the trial Court.

No doubt, the defendants have not preferred any separate appeal against the order of the first appellate court rejecting their application filed under Order XLI, Rule 27CPC. However, it is argued by the learned counsel for the appellants that as per Section 105 of the Code of Civil Procedure, the appellants while appealing against a decree, any error, defect or irregularity in any order passed by a Court in the exercise of its original or appellate jurisdiction, which affects the decision of the case, are entitled to set forth the same as a ground of objection in the memorandum of appeal. The above contention of the learned counsel for the appellants deserves acceptance. Even though they have not preferred any appeal against the order, rejecting the application filed under Order XLI, Rule 27 CPC, but still, as rightly argued, they are entitled to canvass the said order in the second appeal, which has been preferred against the decree passed by the first appellate court. It could be seen that the order of the first appellate court rejecting the application filed under Order XLI, Rule 27 CPC has affected the decision of the case materially and went against the defendants. On account of the same, it could be seen that the defendants have also taken grounds with reference to the same in the memorandum of appeal, particularly, in ground Nos.6 and 7.

A perusal of the Judgment of the first appellate court would go to show that it has been in a state of confusion, as to whether it should admit or reject the additional evidence projected by the defendants/appellants, while disposing of the first appeal. This could be seen from the judgment of the first appellate court, while disposing of the application filed under Order XLI, Rule 27 CPC in I.A. No.22 of 2008, though the first appellate Court has discussed and found that it is just and necessary to receive the document of cancellation of assignment Order as Additional document, thereafter, proceeded to hold that it is not necessary to invoke Order XLI, Rule 27 CPC to receive the additional evidence and resultantly, dismissed the petition.

In such view of the matter, the first appellate Court should not have endeavoured to discuss about the merits or demerits of the additional evidence, while disposing of the main appeal. On the other hand, a perusal of the judgment of the first appellate court would go to disclose that even though it had rejected the application filed under Order XLI, Rule 27 CPC taken out by the defendants, still it has proceeded to dwell upon the merits and demerits of the additional evidence sought to be projected by the appellants/defendants and the same could be gathered from reading para Nos. 15,17,20,21,and 22 of the first appellate Court's judgment. Therefore, it could be seen that on the one hand, the first appellate court had rejected the application filed under Order XLI, Rule 27 CPC and in contradiction, it has also discussed the merits and demerits of the cancellation of the assignment order, while disposing of the main appeal, which, as rightly argued by the learned counsel for the appellants, is perverse and also erroneous. It could be seen that the appellants were denied the opportunity of projecting the facts vis-a-vis the additional evidence in the right perspective in the first appellate court. They were led to the impression that their application having been rejected by the appellate court, therefore, would not have been in a position to canvass about the merits of the additional evidence projected by them, before the first appellate court, at the time of the arguments. Therefore, it could be seen that the appellants had been seriously prejudiced in projecting the case before the first appellate court. In such view of the matter, it could be seen that inasmuch as the rejection of application under Order XLI, Rule 27 CPC has seriously affected the decision of the case rendered by the first appellate Court, the appellants are entitled to canvass the same in the memorandum of appeal before this Court. Accordingly, as found earlier, they have taken such a plea and put-forth their grounds with reference to the same in this appeal.

16. Sections 24, 104 and 105 – Appeal Arising Out of An Application under Section 24

In *Mahendra Pratap Bhatt* v. *Saroj Mahana*, 2016 (5) ADJ 282: 2016 (2) ARC 203: 2016 (3) All WC 4881 (All) (DB) (Lucknow Bench) the aggrieved party assailed the aforesaid judgment of the Division Bench, to which one of us [Justice A.P. Sahi] was a member, before the Apex Court and the same was upheld with remarks which judgment is reported in, *Raja Khan* v. *Uttar Pradesh Sunni Central Waqf Board*, 2010 (15) SCC 228: 2011 (2) SCC 741. The said judgment was subjected to review for expunging of such remarks which was disposed of and the same is reported in, *Raja Khan* v. *Uttar Pradesh Sunni Central Waqf Board*, 2010 (15) SCC 228: 2011 (2) SCC 741

The above propositions therefore as applied on the facts of the present case leave no room for doubt that neither the application under Section 24 was maintainable before this Court nor was the order passed by the learned Single Judge related to a subject matter within the territorial jurisdiction of this Court. This inherent lack therefore has to be co-related to the nature of the order passed.

In our opinion, at the best, the impugned order of the learned Single Judge would be, if at all, in the purported exercise of power under Article 226 of the Constitution of India. That being so, such purported exercise of power under Article 226 of the Constitution of India would be amenable to an intra-Court Special Appeal under Chapter VIII Rule 5 of the Allahabad High Court Rules, 1952 which is extracted hereunder:

> "5. ***Special Appeal***.—An appeal shall lie to the Court from a Judgment (not being a judgment passed in the exercise of appellate jurisdiction) in respect of a decree or order made by a Court subject to the superintendence of the Court and not being an order made in the exercise of revisional jurisdiction or in the exercise of its power of superintendence or in the exercise of criminal Jurisdiction or in the exercise of jurisdiction conferred by Article 226 or Article 227 of the Constitution in respect of any judgment, order or award (a) of a Tribunal, Court or statutory arbitrator made or purported to be made in the exercise or purported exercise of jurisdiction under any Uttar Pradesh Act or under any Central Act, with respect to any of the matters enumerated in the State List or the Concurrent List in the Seventh Schedule to the Constitution, or (b) of the Government or any officer or authority, made or purported to be made in the exercise or purported exercise of appellate or revisional jurisdiction under any such act of one Judge."

Consequently, for all the reasons above, the special appeal would be maintainable.

In the instant case, the learned Single Judge has assumed jurisdiction to send the matter for mediation at Lucknow on a stated submission which according to the learned Single Judge was a concession.

We are of the considered opinion that a jurisdiction cannot be assumed on the concession of the counsel for the parties or even otherwise, in a matter that squarely relates to the dispute at Allahabad.

Merely because the opposite party had lodged an F.I.R. at Lucknow and instituted a criminal case, the same would not make the application under Section 24 CPC maintainable in relation to the dispute pending before the Family Court at Allahabad. This assumption, therefore, by the learned Single Judge in our considered view is not the correct view for assuming jurisdiction that is totally lacking.

Learned Counsel for the opposite party Sri Tiwari submits that he does not propose to file any counter affidavit in the matter.

17. Sections 105 and 106 – Bar of Jurisdiction of Civil Court – In the matter of Property in Dispute not Falling within the Purview of the Rent Act

In *Gurbax Singh* v. *Harminderjit Singh alias Bobby Choudhry*, 2017 (2) RCR (Rent) 120: 2017 (3) RCR (Civil) 1005 (P&H) the High Court of Punjab said, having considered the aforesaid arguments as also the judgments of the learned Civil Judge and the learned Ist appellate Court, as regards the right of the plaintiff to seek possession of the suit property, he admittedly being the owner thereof and having terminated the lease, in the opinion of this Court in accordance with the provisions of the Transfer of Property Act, 1882, I find no ground to interfere with the said judgments and decrees.

This is so because even if the lease deed, Ex.D1, (shown to be dated 30.05.1994), is to be ignored as contended by the learned counsel for the respondent-plaintiff (though in the context of the plaintiff having to pay L 60,000/- with bank interest to the appellant, upon vacation of the suit property), however the factum of a lease having existed, has not been denied even in the written statement of the appellant-defendant.

Though the word "lease" is not written anywhere, either in the plaint or in the written statement, however, in terms of Section 105 of the Act of 1882, the transaction of the transfer of the right to enjoy the suit property, for a certain time, in consideration of a price paid or promised, is a lease as per the definition contained in the said provision.

Similarly, the transferor of the property is the lessor and the transferee is the lessee, and the money to be rendered as the price/premium for such transfer, for enjoyment of the property for the time that it is so enjoyed by the transferee/ lessee, is defined as rent, in Section 105 itself.

Hence, with the property eventually having been admitted to be not within the purview of the East Punjab Urban (Rent Restriction) Act 1949, it is to be treated to be leased out by the respondent to the appellant, in terms of the Transfer of Property Act itself.

That being so, the plaintiff was within his right to terminate the lease, either in terms of any contract pertaining to the lease, or, in the absence of any written contract, then at any time after giving a notice of 15 days to the defendant-lessee, i.e. the appellant herein.

However, before going on to discuss the validity of the notice, Ex. P-3, it would need to be seen as to whether the lease was one deemed to be from month to month, or would be governed by the agreement Ex.D1, and whether the agreement was compulsorily registrable or not.

This would be more so for the reason that the said document (Ex. D-1), does not fix any specific time period of the lease, but envisages two situations; (a) that if the lease is to be terminated by the lessee (present appellant), he would do so by giving an advance notice of two months to the owner (lessor), and (b) whenever the premises is vacated (with no stipulation that it could only be at the instance of the lessee), the amount of L 60,000/- paid by the lessee to the lessor by way of security, would be returned with bank interest thereupon.

However, the instrument also speaks of an increase in the rent by 3%, after a period of 15 years. Therefore, in the opinion of this Court, even with no specific period of the lease given in the instrument, the recital of an increase in rent after 15 years would have to be interpreted to imply that the lease was definitely intended to continue for more than one year, unless it was terminated earlier by the lessee.

36. Thus it is first necessary to examine as to whether the said instrument, propounded by the appellant-defendant, was admissible in evidence at all or not, the lease created thereby, being for a period of more than one year.

Section 107 of the T.P. Act already having been reproduced earlier in this judgment, a perusal thereof shows that any instrument by which a lease of immovable property is created, either from year to year, or for any term exceeding one year, or by which a yearly rent is reserved, must only be a registered instrument.

Any other lease may either be by way of a registered instrument or even by oral agreement accompanied by delivery of possession. The proviso to Section 107 does stipulate that the State Government may by notification in the official gazette direct that leases of immovable property other than leases from year to year or even for any term exceeding one year or reserving an yearly rent, may be made by unregistered instrument, or orally, even without delivery of possession. However, no notification issued by the Government of Punjab has been brought to the notice of this Court by learned counsel for the appellant, by which any lease as is required to be registered under Section 107, is exempted from being so registered.

Admittedly, Ex.D1 is not a registered instrument though the language thereof, stipulating an increase in rent of 3% after 15 years, would, in the opinion of this Court, make the lease in question to be one executed for a term exceeding one year, as already held.

Therefore, once it is accepted that the lease between the parties is a lease which is either from year to year, or for any term exceeding one year, the document, Ex. D-1, was to be compulsorily registered.

Though this Court may otherwise have no doubt that the said instrument was actually executed between the appellant and Joginder Singh, i.e. the grand father of the plaintiff, Harminderjit Singh, with even one of the witnesses thereto (Nirmal Chand) having testified to that effect as DW2, yet, the instrument being compulsorily registrable as per Section 107 aforesaid and it not having been registered, it cannot be held to be admissible in evidence, in view of Section 49 of the Registration Act 1908, which reads as follows:-

> "**49. Effect of non-registration of documents required to be registered.**—No document required by section 17 [or by any provision of the Transfer of Property Act, 1882], to be registered shall—
>
> (a) affect any immovable property comprised therein, or
>
> (b) confer any power to adopt, or
>
> (c) be received as evidence of any transaction affecting such property or conferring such power, unless it has been registered:

Provided that an unregistered document affecting immovable property and required by this Act or the Transfer of Property Act, 1882, to be registered may be received as evidence of a contract in a suit for specific performance under Chapter II of the Specific Relief Act, 1877, or as evidence of any collateral transaction not required to be effected by registered instrument."

Hence, once an instrument is compulsorily required to be registered under the provisions of the Transfer of Property Act and it is not so registered, it cannot be received as evidence of any transaction affecting such property, except in relation to a suit seeking specific performance.

38. As regards the judgment of the Supreme Court in Satish Kumars' case (supra), cited by Mr. Sharma in that context, the said judgment holds to the effect that a lease deed executed from month to month, reduced into writing, with possession delivered to a tenant, need not be registered, but would still be admissible in evidence, it not being a compulsorily registrable instrument.

***106. What Courts to Hear Appeals.*—Where an appeal from any order is allowed it shall lie to the Court to which an appeal would lie from the decree in the suit in which such order was made, or where such order is made by a Court (not being a High Court) in the exercise of appellate jurisdiction, then to the High Court.**

SYNOPSIS

Comments

1. Section 106 and Section 69.—Mortgagor's Right

The Madras High Court examined a case involving right of a mortgagor. In the said case the appellant-purchaser filed E.A. No. 5287 of 1973 on the file of the X, Assistant Judge, City Civil Court, Madras, claiming to be the absolute owner of the property and praying:

(a) That the attachment of the half share of the property No. 57, Sir Thiagaraya Road, T. Nagar, Madras and more fully described in the schedule hereto and made in E.P. No. 2573 of 1973 in O.S. No. 4650 of 1970 may be set aside and the property released from the attachment;

(b) The E.P. filed for bringing the half share in the property may be dismissed;

(c) That the sale of the said property may be postponed, pending the hearing of this petition;

(d) That the first respondent-plaintiff may be ordered to pay the costs of this petition;

(e) That such further or other reliefs as this Hon'ble Court may deem fit and necessary in the circumstances of the case may be passed.

This petition was filed on 19th October, 1973. The learned X Assistant Judge, City Civil Court, Madras was of the view that the mortgage cannot prevail over the attachment before judgment and that, therefore, the attachment could not be raised in respect of the half share of the judgment-debtor. In that view he dismissed the application. The purchaser filed C.M.A. No. 230 of 1977 on the file of this Court quoting the provision of law under which the appeal was filed as Order XXI, rule 58(4), Civil Procedure Code, section 106, Civil Procedure Code, and section 15 of the City Civil Court Act. This appeal was disposed of by a Single Judge. Before the Single Judge the first respondent decree-holder took a preliminary objection that the appeal was not maintainable on the ground that the claim application should have been dealt with under rule 58 of Order XXI as it stood prior to its amendment by Act CIV of 1976, which came into force on 1st February, 1977, and under the provisions then existing, the order made in respect of a petition under rule 58 is final and can be questioned only by way of a claim suit and not an appeal against that order. Though the judgment is not very clear about the reasonings on which this preliminary objection was disposed of, the ultimate finding of the learned Judge is that the appeal was maintainable. However, the learned Judge held that it is not possible or permissible to a mortgagee to nullify the order of attachment by selling the property attached is exercise of his powers under section 69 of the Transfer of Property Act and that, therefore, the sale is not binding and the interest of the judgment-debtor could be proceeded against in execution of the decree against him. In that view, he dismissed the appeal. It is against this order the present appeal has been filed under clause 15 of the Letters Patent.

The appellate court said that it is erroneous to suggest that the mortgagee is acting as the agent of the mortgagor in selling the property. The mortgagor exercises his right under a different claim. The mortgagee's right is different from the mortgagor's. The mortgagee exercises his right under a totally superior claim which is not under the mortgagor, but against him.

In other words, the sale is against the mortgagor's wishes. Rights and interests of the mortgagor and the mortgagee in regard to sale are conflicting.

In fact, section 69 is one of those rare instances where a person, who is not the owner of the property, could convey the right, title and interest of a third party mortgagor. The mortgagee gets a power to sell the mortgagor's interest in the property alongwith his interest and while exercising such power of sale, as observed by the Supreme Court he is not acting under the mortgagor or as an agent of the mortgagor. The attachment order will have, therefore, no effect on the power of sale exercised by the mortgagee. The Privy Council in the decision reported in *Raja Kishendatt Ram* v. *Rajah Mumtaz Ali Khan,* (1880) ILR 5 Cal 198 (211): 6 IA 145 held with reference to a sale under section 69 of the Transfer of Property Act thus:

> "The effect of a sale under a power of sale is to destroy the equity of redemption in the land and to constitute the mortgagee exercising the power of a trustee of the surplus proceeds, after satisfying his own charge first, for the subsequent incumbrances, and ultimately for the mortgagor.

The estate, if purchased by a stranger passes into his hands free of all the incumbrances."

Thus, the purchaser, though did not derive title under or through the mortgagee acquires a larger estate free from all incumbrances. In the suit filed by the first respondent he could have dealt with only the mortgagor's right and he could not have dealt with the mortgagee's right who is neither a party to the suit nor is he in any way indebted to the plaintiff. We are, therefore, of the view that the sale held in exercise of the power under section 69 of the Transfer of Property Act is not affected by the attachment made and the purchaser in such an auction held by the mortgagee gets absolute title free from all incumbrances. The execution, therefore, could not be proceeded against even to the extent of the interest of the judgment-debtor in the property, which is mentioned above. Accordingly this appeal was allowed, the judgments and decrees of the Court below and the learned Single Judge were set aside and the execution application E.A. No. 5287 of 1973 was allowed.

With reference to article 134(A) of the Constitution of India, learned Counsel for the first respondent decree-holder made an oral application for leave to appeal to the Supreme Court. We are not satisfied that the proposed appeal to the Supreme Court involves any substantial question of law of general importance which, in our opinion, needs to be decided by the Supreme Court. Accordingly this request was rejected; *S.U.S. Davey and Sons* v. *P.M. Narayanaswami*, (1983) 2 MLJ 534.

2. Sections 106 and 80, CPC

In the case under reference, the relevant facts, in brief, were that the plaintiff/ respondent R.B. Narain Singh Sugar Mills Ltd. was a Company incorporated under the Indian Companies Act, 1913 now 1956, which was established in the year 1932-33 at Baraut, District Meerut (hereinafter referred as 'the Mill'). The Mill worked there till 1938-39 and it was shifted to and established at its present site at Laksar, District Haridwar in 1939. The Mill purchased land at the site and is in exclusive possession over there. In the year 1989 Laksar was notified a Town Area and the limits of Town Area were expanded covering the area of some adjoining villages including Simli and Khera. It was also alleged that Lord Krishna Sugar Mill also sold properties to the plaintiffs. Before the declaration of Town Area the disputed land had already vested in plaintiffs on the date of vesting by virtue of provisions of section 9 of U.P.Z.A. & L.R. Act. Due to the ignorance of plaintiffs the Courts could not be moved for mutation in the year 1939.

Thereafter, there were certain disputes with some persons about the properties and survey and inspections were made and it was detected that the name of plaintiff was not in the revenue records properly therefore in 1958 application for correction of records was moved. The application was allowed and the name of the plaintiff was entered in the register Malikan and Khasra Khautanis. In 1987 the Town Area filed Suit No. 50 of 1987 in the Court of Assistant Collector, 1st Class, Haridwar on wrong allegations with regard to the disputed property. The said suit was still pending in revision No. 5 of 1988-89 before the Board of Revenue and the proceedings of Court below were stayed. Thereafter, Haridwar was declared as District and Laksar was declared as one of the Tehsils. S.D.O. Laksar passed order dated 21-8-1990 expunging the name of the plaintiff from the revenue record about the disputed property without issuing any notice to the plaintiffs and the said order was mutated in the name of Gram Sabha, Simli. Against this order revision was preferred before the Additional Commissioner, Meerut who stayed the operation of the order dated 21-8-1990 and the knowledge of the same was to the defendants.

After hearing the parties the Court found that the disputed land was in the exclusive possession of the Sugar Factory, some of the land has been purchased/transferred/handed over to the Mill and the land appurtenant to the Factory land had already vested in the mill on the date of vesting.

The next argument of the learned Standing Counsel was that the suits were barred by the provisions of section 331 of the U.P.Z.A. & L.R. Act and sections 34, 38 and 41 of Specific Relief Act and the finding of the Courts below on the point is erroneous. Learned Standing Counsel has submitted that some part of the disputed land was used for agricultural purpose, therefore, the best way for the plaintiff was to file suit before Revenue Court under the provision of section 229B of U.P.Z.A. & L.R. Act. He further argued that the plaintiff was not in possession of the disputed land and wanted to declare its possession over the land in suit. Therefore, the suits were barred by the provisions of Specific Relief Act.

The Court did not find substance in the argument advanced by the learned counsel for the appellant, *firstly* on the ground that the disputed land is an Abadi land and it is not being used as the agricultural land and *secondly* the plaintiff has not sought relief of declaration, rather it has sought the relief of permanent injunction not to interfere in its peaceful possession over the, disputed land. It was held that the trial courts were well within their jurisdiction to decide the above issues in favour of the plaintiff/Mill.

The learned Standing Counsel lastly submitted that the suits instituted before the Courts below were not maintainable as Notice 80 C.P.C. and 106 Panchayat Raj Act were not served on the defendants and the trial courts have committed error of law in deciding the points in favour of the plaintiff/Mill.

Perusal of the record revealed that the above pleas were taken by the defendant-State and the burden to prove the same was on the defendant-State. The defendant-State did not adduce any evidence about the above allegation. The defence witness Shravan Kumar has not deposed even a single word about the factum of non-receipt of notice. On the other hand the plaintiff has asserted that the notice was sent to the defendant-State. In support it filed postal receipts paper Nos. 10-C, 11-C and 12-C showing therein that notices were sent to Gram Pradhan, Officer I/C, Town Area and Collector, Haridwar respectively. The receipts show that the envelopes were got served on 10-8-1991. The notices were proved by P.W. 1, Prakat Singh in O.S. No. 3/1992 and in O.S. No. 4/1992 the receipts paper Nos. 167-C/1 to 167-C/3 and 168-C have been proved by the same witness Prakat Singh produced in this case also. In the aforesaid circumstances, it cannot be said that no notice under section 80, C.P.C. and section 106 Panchayat Raj Act was served upon the defendants/appellants before filing the petition.

In view of foregoing discussion, the Court held that both the appeals had no merit and the same were liable to be dismissed; *State of Uttar Pradesh* v. *R.B. Narain Singh Sugar Mills Ltd.*, AIR 2007 Utr 87.

3. Section 106 and Section 111(a) – After the Initial Expiry of 11 Months Period of Tenancy there was no Tenancy at All

In *Aravindharaj Adhithan* v. *R. Perumal*, 2011 (3) CTC 31: 2011 2 LW 50 (Mad) this second appeal was filed by the defendant, inveighing the judgment and decree dated 29.11.2008 passed by the Principal Subordinate Court, Chengalpattu, in A.S. No. 71 of 2008 confirming the judgment and decree dated 31.10.2007 passed by the District Munsif, Chebngalpattu, in O.S. No. 64 of 2006, which was filed for delivery of possession and damages.

Ultimately, the trial Court ordered eviction, as against which, the appeal was filed for nothing but to be dismissed by the appellate Court, confirming the judgment and decree of the trial Court.

Challenging and impugning the judgments and decrees of the Courts below, this second appeal has been filed on various grounds inter alia to the effect that the Courts below were wrong in holding as though after the initial expiry of 11 months period of tenancy there was no tenancy at all and there was no necessity at all for issuance of notice etc, which was totally wrong.

The High Court referred to the following decisions:

At the outset itself I recollect and call up the following decisions of the Honourable Apex Court:

(i) *Hero Vinoth (Minor)* v. *Seshammal*, (2006) 5 SCC 545.

(ii) *Kashmir Singh* v. *Harnam Singh*, 2008 (4) SCALE 300.

(iii) *State Bank of India* v. *S.N. Goya*, 2009 (1) LW 1.

A bare and plain reading of those precedents would reveal and demonstrate that in second appeal, this Court could not interfere relating to the concurrent finding of facts by the Courts below, unless there is any perversity or illegality or any substantial question of law is involved.

The contention on the side of the appellant/defendant that there was holding over of tenancy even after the initial period of 11 months even if accepted, at the most under the Transfer of Property Act, the tenant, namely, the defendant is entitled to statutory notice under Section 106 of the Act.

The learned counsel for the respondent/plaintiff, at this juncture, appropriately and appositely, correctly and convincingly would place reliance on the amended Section 106 of the Transfer of Property Act and submit that even though in the termination notice only 10 days' time was granted for the defendant to vacate the premises, in fact, the suit was filed long after the statutory period of 15 days, so to say, the notice was admittedly received on 3.2.2006 and the plaint was presented only on 21.2.2006 and in such a case, only after a lapse of statutory 15 days' time as contemplated under Section 106 of the Transfer of Property

Act, the suit was instituted and even if the notice was treated as a defective one, it got cured by virtue of the suit itself having been filed after 15 days as contemplated under Section 106 of the T.P.Act.

Indubitably and indisputably, unarguably and unassailably, the tenancy itself was for running a hardware shop and it was not one for agricultural or manufacturing purpose and in such a case only 15 days' statutory notice was contemplated and in view of the suit itself having been filed after the receipt of the notice by the plaintiff, the question of setting aside the judgments of the Courts below does not arise and in my opinion, no question of law much less substantial question of law is involved in this case.

GENERAL PROVISIONS RELATING TO APPEALS

***107. Powers of Appellate Court.*—(1) Subject to such conditions and limitations as may be prescribed, an appellate court shall have power:**

(a) to determine a case finally;

(b) to remand a case;

(c) to frame issues and refer them for trial;

(d) to take additional evidence or to require such evidence to be taken.

(2) Subject as aforesaid, the appellate court shall have the same powers and shall perform as nearly as may be the same duties as are conferred and imposed by this Code on Courts of original jurisdiction in respect of suits instituted therein.

SYNOPSIS

Comments

1. Scope and Application

The Supreme Court in the case of *State of Punjab* said that the appellate court or the Supreme Court has the power to take *suo moto* judicial notice and exercise power conferred under section 105 of the Code; *State of Punjab* v. *Bakshish Singh,* AIR 1999 SC 2626: 1999 (1) Lab LJ 1208: 1998 (8) AD SC 73: (1998) 8 SCC 222: 1999 (1) All WC 245: 1999 AIR SCW 1704; *Nani Gopal Paul* v. *T.P. Prasad Singh,* (1995) 3 SCC 579: AIR 1995 SC 1971: 1995 AIR SCW 3078.

The Court said that the term 'appellate court' includes Tribunals while exercising judicial function in civil proceedings, such as a Labour Appellate Tribunal; *Upper Ganges Electric Employee's Union* v. *Upper Gange Valley Electric Supply Co.,* AIR 1956 All 491.

The powers referred to in clauses (a) to (d) are limited by the Rules; *Money Mohan* v. *Ram Rattan,* (1916) ILR 43 Cal 48.

Thus, the Supreme Court held that according to section 107, an appellate court has the same powers as are exercisable by the trial court. The appellate court could determine the case finally by virtue of clause (a) of sub-section (1) of section 107; *State of Punjab* v. *Bakshish Singh,* AIR 1999 SC 2626: 1999 (1) Lab LJ 1208: 1998 (8) AD SC 73: (1998) 8 SCC 222: 1999 (1) All WC 245: 1999 AIR SCW 1704.

Punjab-Haryana High Court examined whether a party to the original suit who has not been impleaded in appeal within the period of limitation prescribed for filing the same can be added as a party to the appeal either under the provisions of Order XLI, rule 20, Civil Procedure Code, or those of Order I, rule 10, Civil Procedure Code, read with section 107, Civil Procedure Code, or under the inherent powers of the Court saved by section 151, Civil Procedure Code?

In order to appreciate the true nature and import of the question of law raised in this case, it is necessary to state the relevant facts. Six persons: Gobind Ram, Babu Sumer Chand, Gajinder Parshad, Miri Mal, Prakash Chand and Raghunath Das brought the present suit under the provisions of Order I, rule 8, Civil Procedure Code, for perpetual injunction restraining the Notified Area Committee, Buria, from imposing and levying house-tax on the plaintiffs and other inhabitants of Buria Town in the District of Ambala. On an application made to the trial court the aforesaid six persons were allowed to represent the inhabitants of the whole town. In their plaint they alleged that the imposition of the house-tax by the Notified Area Committee, Buria was illegal, *ultra vires* and arbitrary, and prayed for a permanent injunction restraining the Committee from imposing and realising the said house-tax.

The learned counsel for the appellant contended that the mistake in the present case occurred due to the error in the certified copy of the judgment supplied to his client and that in the circumstances of this case it was necessary that the mistake should be allowed to be rectified. Reliance was placed on a case; *Rodger* v. *Comptoir D'Escompte de Paris'* (1871) 3 PC 465 (475): 17 ER 120, Where it was observed by Carlas, L.J.:

> "One of the first and highest duties of all the Courts is to take care that the act of the Court does no injury to any of the suitors, and when the expression 'the act of the Court' is used, it does not mean merely the act of the primary, or of any intermediate Court, but the act of the Court as a whole from the lower court which entertains the jurisdiction over the matter up to the highest Court which finally disposes of the case."

> In *Bishna* v. *Sucha Singh*, 154 Ind Cas 914: AIR 1934 Lah 402 (2), it was observed:

> "Litigants and members of the legal profession have the right to expect that the headings of attested copies of the judgments would show the names of the parties correctly. The omission was through a mere oversight and that he should be made a respondent."

In *Keshorao* v. *Yeshwantrao*, AIR 1957 MB 17: 1956 MBLR Civil 188: 1956 MBLJ 774, an appeal was preferred by the plaintiff against certain persons. The name of one of the defendants was not mentioned in the memorandum of appeal on account of the fact that the certified copies of the judgment and decree supplied to the appellant in that case did not include the name of the said defendant. A Division Bench of the Madhya Bharat High Court allowed the name to be added under the inherent powers of the Court and for this purpose relied on the Privy Council case referred to above as also on the observations made by a Division Bench of the Lahore High Court: AIR 1934 Lah 402 (2).

In *Alabhai Vajsurbhai* v. *Bhura Bhaya*, ILR 1937 Bom 602: AIR 1937 Bom 401: 39 Bom LR 444, and in *Kunhanna Rai* v. *Manakke*, AIR 1929 Mad 343: 117 IC 796, the same proposition of law was laid down.

For the reasons given above, no inflexible rule of interpretation of the words "interested in the result of the appeal" as given in Order XLI, rule 20, Civil Procedure Code, has been given by their Lordships of the Privy Council in ILR 6 Rang 29: AIR 1927 PC 2521 and that the view taken of this case by the Full Bench in *Labhu Ram* v. *Ram Partap*, ILR 1945 Lah 18: AIR 1944 Lah 76, as also in the other cases referred to above is not correct, and that it must be decided on the facts and circumstances of each particular case whether the person sought to be added in that case is one interested in the result of the appeal. The Privy Council case cannot at any rate, be taken to be an authority for the proposition that a party left out or not impleaded in appeal on account of a *bona fide* mistake cannot be so impleaded under the inherent powers Of the Court, more especially when the error is on the part of the Court or its officials in supplying an erroneous copy either of the decree or of the judgment.

The Court, therefore, answered the question referred to as follows:

1. that if a party to the original proceedings is not impleaded in appeal on account of a *bona fide* and honest mistake on the part of the appellant, the appellate court has ample powers under Order XLI, rule 20, Civil

Procedure Code, to allow the mistake, to be rectified and the party to be added;

2. that section 107(2) read with Order I, rule 10, Civil Procedure Code, enables the appellate court to add parties in appeals in suitable cases, but this power must be exercised within the period of limitation; and
3. that apart from the provisions of Order XLI, rule 20, Civil Procedure Code, the appellate court has inherent powers to permit parties to be added to appeals in suitable cases and the language of rule 20 of Order XLI is not exclusive or exhaustive so as to deprive the appellate court of the Inherent powers in this respect; *Notified Area Committee Buria* v. *Gobind Ram Lachhman Dass,* AIR 1959 Punj 277: 61 Pun LR 326: ILR 1959 Punj 1066.

2. Section 107 and the Order of the Board of Revenue

Madras High Court examined in a reference whether the High Court can interfere with a decision of the Board of Revenue under the Madras Estates Land Act.

The questions referred were:

(1) whether the High Court has power to interfere with a decision of the Board of Revenue under Chapter XI of the Madras Estates Land Act,

(2) whether the Board of Revenue has in this particular case exceeded the jurisdiction conferred upon it, and

(3) what should be "the final order to be passed in this case," *i.e.*, on this revision petition.

The Court said that it is true that the Revenue Officer, constituted as a Tribunal for the settlement of fair and equitable rents, is given, in the matter of arriving at his decisions, wider powers, larger discretion, and greater scope for making alterations in the existing rates of rent, by way of enhancement or reduction, than the Revenue Officers who have to decide suits or applications under sections 25, 30, 38 and 40 of the Act. The Revenue Officer settling fair and equitable rents should by virtue of section 168(2) have regard to the provisions of the Act, for determining the rates of rent payable by the ryot. This means that he should apply the principles laid down in other sections, for enhancing or reducing the existing rents in force as lawful rents, but he is not restricted to those considerations alone in deciding what is the fair and equitable rent. If by means of special legislation in Chapter XI of the Act, a Revenue Officer is invested with larger powers than the Revenue Officers exercising functions under some other sections of the Act, and has more freedom in making inquiries and investigations, and is less bound by the restrictions observed by ordinary Civil and Revenue Courts, in matters of procedure, is such an officer to be regarded as acting not in a judicial capacity, but only as an executive or administrative officer? The Legislature may exempt some Courts dealing with a particular kind of litigation, from the observance of the ordinary procedure prescribed for Courts, and invest them with some extraordinary and even summary powers of disposal. They do not, for that reason, cease to be Courts. There are, no doubt, some peculiar features in the exercise of the functions by the Revenue Officer appointed under Chapter XI of the Act for the settlement of rents. Are they really repugnant to the idea of his being a Court exercising judicial power (as defined in the Privy Council decision above referred to)? It seems that though an application is made under section 168(1) by the ryots owning not less than one-fourth of the total extent of the holdings in the village, the Revenue Officer, if appointed by the Government, for the purpose of settlement of rent, may settle fair and equitable rents for the whole village. There is provision even in the Code of Civil Procedure, enabling one or more persons to sue on behalf of numerous persons having the same interest, with the Court's permission. In such a suit, if a decision is given, it affects even persons who are not actually 'parties to the suit or who take no part in the conduct of the suit. Section 170(3) of the Act provides for the incorporation of the rates settled, after sanction by the confirming authority, in the record-of-rights published under sub-section (2) of section 166 (which may be deemed to be a document prepared by an executive officer). But even all orders or decrees of Civil Courts passed in suits under section 173 should be similarly incorporated in the said record-of-rights (*vide* section 174). The Judge felt constrained to observe that the decisions of the Revenue, Officer, in the matter of settlement of rents, which seem to be not open to question as regards the correctness of the rates finally fixed, by means of a civil suit under section 173 of the Act, and which have, therefore, the force of *res judicata* in any subsequent proceeding between the landholder and the ryots in a Civil or Revenue Court, cannot be easily distinguished from those given by Courts, as between parties seeking their civil rights.

On a due consideration of the provisions in Chapter XI relating to the settlement of rent as compared with other provisions in the Act and also of certain fundamental principles which serve as indicia for determining the character of the Tribunal, the Court was of the opinion that the Revenue Officer settling fair and equitable rents on an application under section 168 of the Act cannot be deemed to be an executive or administrative functionary. I am inclined to hold, the Court said that such an Officer as also the appellate or revisional authority in the same matter must be deemed to be a Revenue Court and in the sense in which their Lordships of the Privy Council have defined a Civil Court in *Nilmoni Singh Deo* v. *Taranath Mukerjee*, (1882) LR 9 IA 174: ILR 9 C 295 (PC), it should be viewed also as a Civil Court.

It appears that under section 164 of the Estates Land Act the Local Government ordered that a survey should be made and a record-of-rights should be prepared for 21 villages in the Mandasa Zamindari in the Ganjam District, which was done. On an application made by the ryots of the villages the Local Government afterwards ordered under section 168 of the Act that a settlement of rent should be made for the villages. The Revenue Officer appointed for the purpose of settling the rents for the villages. The ryots being dissatisfied, appealed against his orders to the Board of Revenue, which had been appointed by the Local Government to be the appellate authority for the purpose under section 171 of the Act. Their appeal was dismissed as time-barred. Later on however the Board of Revenue in consequence of representations made on behalf of the ryots to His Excellency the Governor took the matter up in revision, purporting to proceed under section 172 of the Act, and ordered a general reduction of the rents settled by approximately 3 annas in the rupee. The Zamindar has presented this petition to this Court for the exercise of revisional powers under section 115 of the Code of Civil Procedure or section 107 of the Government of India Act in respect of that order of the Board of Revenue; *Lieutenant Srinivasa Rajamani* v. *Senapathi Jagannayakulu,* 140 Ind Cas 331: (1932) 63 MLJ 450.

3. Section 107 – Power of the Appellate Court to Consider Question of Court Fees

The Supreme Court of India examined the provisions of the Code of Civil Procedure, 1908—Sections 107(2), 149, Order VII—Proper court-fees not paid on the memorandum of appeal—Duty of appellate court indicated—Costs to respondents for appellants negligence. In the case under reference, the plaintiff—Wakf Board's suit for declaration of the right to the passage and possession thereof having been dismissed by the trial court, a title appeal was filed before the District Judge. A Court-fee of Rs. 15 was paid on the plaint by the Wakf Board by an exemption notification. On its memorandum of appeal, the plaintiff had paid the same amount of Court-fee. Respondents asked for dismissal of the memorandum of appeal as it had not been sufficiently stamped. The Additional District Judge dismissed the memorandum of appeal.

The High Court did not interfere, when plaintiff took the matter before it. Hence, this appeal by special leave by the plaintiff was filed contending that the learned Additional District Judge instead of dismissing the memorandum of appeal, an opportunity should have been given and the appellant should have been called upon to make good the deficiency. Allowing the appeal, this Court held that when the lower appellate court came to hold that the memorandum of appeal had not been sufficiently stamped, an opportunity should have been given by the Court to the appellant to make good the balance court-fee within a time to be indicated and if there was failure to comply with the direction of the Court, the memorandum of appeal could have been dismissed. This opportunity having not been given, the dismissal of the appeal was not appropriate.

It was further held that this is a case of negligence on the part of the appellants and, therefore, the respondents who have been dragged in these proceedings for about 10 years should be compensated, by way of costs of Rs. 1,000.

From the Judgment and Order dated 16.8.1977 of the Punjab and Haryana High Court in Regular Second Appeal No. 1001 of 1966, this appeal by special leave was brought in which the following Order of the Court was delivered:

This is an appeal by special leave by the plaintiff- Wakf Board. Its suit for declaration of the right to the passage and possession thereof having been dismissed by the trial court, a title appeal was filed before the District Judge of Karnal. By an exemption notification on the plaint in a suit of this type filed by the Wakf Board, Court-fee of Rs. 15 is payable. On its memorandum of appeal, the plaintiff had paid the same amount of Court-fee also. Objection was raised to sufficiency of Court-fee and respondents asked for dismissal of the memorandum of appeal as it had not been sufficiently stamped. As a fact, while Court-fee of Rs. 638 was payable, Court-fee of Rs. 15 had been paid. This matter was preliminarily considered by the appellate court and by the order dated 5.5.1966 the Additional District Judge sustained the objection and directed the memorandum of appeal to be dismissed. The High Court did not interfere when plaintiff took the matter before it. Ultimately, special leave had been granted by this Court and at the time of grant of leave, the following order was made: "As the petitioner is willing to pay deficit Court-fee on the memo of appeal before the District Judge without prejudice, we direct the issue of show cause notice to the other side"?

The plea raised by the appellant before the learned Additional District Judge that the appeal was a continuation of the suit and the same Court-fee as was payable on the plaint was appropriate in appeal had been rightly negatived. At the trial stage, there was an exemption and since it was specifically confined to the trial stage there was no ground to claim the benefit at the appellate stage also. But when the learned Additional District Judge came to hold that the memorandum of appeal had not been sufficiently stamped, instead of outrightly dismissing the memorandum of appeal, an opportunity should have been given and the appellant should have been called upon to make good the deficiency. Under the provisions of Order VII of the Code of Civil Procedure which applies to suits, when the plaint does not bear appropriate Court-fee this is the requirement of the law. Section 107(2) of the Code of Civil Procedure provides:

> "(2) Subject as aforesaid, the appellate court shall have the same powers and shall perform as nearly as may be the same duties as are conferred and imposed by this Code on Courts of original jurisdiction in respect of suits instituted therein."

The Court referred to the provisions of section 149 of the Code of Civil Procedure which provides:

> "Where the whole or any part of any fee prescribed for any document by the law for the time being in force relating to Court-fees has not been paid, the Court may, in its discretion, at any stage, allow the person, by whom such fee is payable, to pay the whole or part, as the case may be; of such Court-fee; and upon such payment the document, in respect of which such fee is payable shall have the same force and effect as if such fee had been paid in the first instance."

The Court said that reading these two provisions together and keeping fairness of procedure in view, we are inclined to agree with the counsel for the appellant that when the lower appellate court came to hold that the memorandum of appeal had not been sufficiently stamped, an opportunity should have been given by the Court to the appellant to make good the balance Court-fee within a time to be indicated and if there was failure to comply with the direction of the Court the memorandum of appeal could have been dismissed. This opportunity having not been given, we are of the view that the dismissal of the appeal was not appropriate.

The Court agreed with counsel for the respondents that this is a case of negligence on the part of the appellants and, therefore, the respondents who have been dragged in these proceedings for about 10 years should be compensated. We direct that the restoration of the appeal in the appellate court on payment of appropriate Court-fee shall be subject to the further condition of payment by way of costs of Rs. 1,000. The appeal was disposed of accordingly; *Mohammad Mahibulla* v. *Seth Chaman Lal,* AIR 1993 SC 1241: 1992 AIR SCW 3275: 1991 SCR Supp (1) 179.

4. Finding of Facts – Principle and Scope

The Supreme Court has deprecated the practice of recording a finding on a vital question which was not raised in issue. *Gomathinayagam Pillai* v. *Palaniswami Nadar,* AIR 1967 SC 868: (1967) 2 SCWR 147: (1967) 1 SCR 227. Where a decree is appealed from, the appellate court should see that the findings of fact of the trial court prevail, unless it clearly appears that some special feature about the evidence of a particular witness has escaped the notice of the Court or there is a sufficient balance of improbability to displace the opinion of the trial court as to where the creditability lies; *Madhusudan Das* v. *Narayani Bai* AIR 1983 SC 114: (1983) 1 SCC 35: (1983) 1 SCR 851; *Aras Khan* v. *Ali Mian* AIR 1985 Pat 126.

5. Considerations For – Interference with Finding of Fact

The rule of practice is that where the evidence is conflicting and decision hinges upon the credibility of witnesses, the appellate court should not interfere with finding of Civil Court on question of fact.

In such cases, the appellate court has got to bear in mind that it has not the advantage which the trial judge had in having the witnesses before him and of observing the manner in which they deposed in Court. This certainly does not mean that when an appeal lies on facts, the appellate court is not competent to reverse a finding of fact arrived at by the trial judge. The rule is and it is nothing more than a rule of practice that when there is conflict of oral evidence of the parties on any matter in issue and the decision hinges upon the credibility of the witnesses, then unless there is some special feature about the evidence of a particular witness which has escaped the trial judge's notice or there is a sufficient balance of improbability to displace his opinion as to where the credibility lies, the appellate court should not interfere with the finding of the trial judge on a question of fact. The High Court was wrong in thinking that it would detract from the value to be attached to a trial judge's finding of fact if the judge does not expressly base his conclusion upon the impressions he gathers from the demeanour of witnesses. The duty of the appellate court in such cases is to see whether the evidence taken as a whole can reasonably justify the conclusion which the trial court arrived at or whether there is an element of improbability arising from proved circumstances which in the opinion of the Court, outweighs such finding. Applying this principle to the present case, we do not think that the High Court was justified in reversing the finding of the trial judge on the question of attestation of the document; *Sarju Pershad Ramdeo Sahu* v. *Jwaleshwari Pratap Narain Singh,* AIR 1951 SC 120: 1951 ALJ 1: 64 MLW 373: 1950 SCJ 583: 1950 SCR 781.

6. Categorical Finding of Fact that Proper Opportunity of Hearing was not Afforded in Departmental Proceedings

In the case under reference, Lower Appellate Court confirmed finding that period of unauthorised absence from duty was regularised. The Charge did not survive. There was no finding about opportunity of hearing to delinquent.—The Supreme court held that it was not open to lower appellate court to remand case for fresh order of punishment. Judgment and decree passed by trial court setting aside dismissal was upheld. The appellate court cannot, in the garb of exercising power under Order XLI, rule 33, enlarge the scope of the appeal. Whether this power would be exercised or not would depend upon the nature and facts of each case.

The apex Court said that the powers of the appellate court are also indicated in section 107 of the Code of Civil Procedure which provides that the appellate court shall have the same powers as are conferred on the original Court. If the trial Court could dispose of a case finally, the appellate court could also, by virtue of clause (a) of sub-section (1) of section 107, determine a case finally. *State of Punjab* v. *Bakshish Singh,* AIR 1999 SC 2626: 1999 (1) Lab LJ 1208: 1998 (8) AD SC 73: (1998) 8 SCC 222: 1999 (1) All WC 245: 1999 AIR SCW 1704.

7. Decision of Appellate Court not to be Based on Facts not Pleaded

The Supreme Court has said that the decision of the case cannot be based on grounds outside the plea of the parties; *Siddavenkappa Devadiga* v. *Rangu S. Devadiga,* AIR 1977 SC 890: 1977 (2) SCJ 52: (1977) 3 SCC 532; *Govind Prasad Chaturvedi* v. *Hari Dutt Shastri,* AIR 1977 SC 1005: (1978) 1 SCWR 473.

8. Desirability of a Remand Order

Allahabad High Court also examined a remand order in the case of *Anwar Hussain* v. *S.L. Franklin,* AIR 1958 All 562: 1958 All LJ 299: 1958 All WR (HC) 441. This was an application in revision against an order of remand dated the 22nd of December, 1952, made by the Civil Judge of Farrukhabad.

The matter came up before a learned Single Judge of this Court and in view of certain important questions of law which arose in the case he has referred it to a Bench for decision. The facts may be briefly stated. A suit was filed for an injunction and for recovery of Rs. 500 as damages. The trial court gave the plaintiff a decree for injunction and for damages to the extent of Rs. 200 only. One of the defendants preferred an appeal. The plaintiffs filed a cross-objection in respect of that part of the damages which had been disallowed by the trial court. The lower appellate court went into the questions that were raised by the parties and came to the conclusion that the trial of the case by the Munsif had been unsatisfactorily conducted and that there had been no clarification of pleadings of the parties; nor had proper issues in the case been struck. The lower appellate court therefore remanded the case, acting apparently under its inherent jurisdiction and not under any specific provision of the Code of Civil Procedure. The operative portion of the order of the Court below is in these words:

> "The result is that the appeal is allowed. The judgment and decree of the trial court are set aside. The suit is remanded for retrial with the directions that after clearance of pleadings where necessary the trial court

will frame specific issues on all the points, 1 to 7, set out in this judgment and will give parties an opportunity to produce evidence on them. It will then proceed to decide the suit according to law."

The Court said that the contention of Mr. Saksena may conveniently be considered in two parts. *First*, whether the power of the appellate court with regard to a remand under section 107 of the Code of Civil Procedure of 1908 is restricted to the case specified in Order XLI, rule 23; and, *second*, whether it was competent to the appellate court to remand a case in which in the opinion of the Court there has been no proper trial.

The Court referred to the Oudh decision in AIR 1941 Oudh 561 (F), that the power of remand is not circumscribed within Order XLI, rules 23 and 25 and that the appellate court has ample power to remand a case apart from the aforesaid provisions. Where, therefore, some of the most material propositions of fact and law arising from the pleadings of the parties were not properly considered by the trial court and proper issues had not been framed, the Court was perfectly justified in remanding the case for a re-trial as it was necessary for the ends of justice. In such a case the Court could not have prevented the parties from adducing additional evidence on the matter.

Therefore, the Court did not find force in this revision and dismissed it with costs.

9. Payment of Court-fees – Power to Extend Time – Question of Remand

The High Court of Orissa also examined a remand order in the case of *Smt. Nirmala Ben Patel* v. *Indersingh Bagi*, In the writ under reference, an order of remand was under challenge which was passed by the appellate authority under the Orissa House Rent Control Act, 1967.

The petitioner filed an application under section 7(4) of the Orissa House Rent Control Act for eviction of opposite party No. 1 from a house alleging that she required the same for her personal occupation. Opposite party No. 1 admitted that he was a monthly tenant under the petitioner in respect of the house in question, but contended that the petitioner did not require the house *bona fide* for her personal occupation. The case was posted to 19-10-1974 for hearing. On that day opposite party No. 1 applied for adjournment which was rejected by the learned House Rent Controller and an order of eviction was passed *ex parte*. Opposite party No. 1 preferred an appeal before the Chief Judicial Magistrate (opposite party No. 2) and prayed for remanding the case to the House Rent Controller for giving him an opportunity to put forth his case. After hearing the parties the learned Chief Judicial Magistrate, Sambalpur came to the findings that though the case was not covered by the provisions of Order XLI, rule 23, Civil Procedure Code yet in exercise of his inherent powers he could remand the case for fresh disposal. Upon such finding he remanded the case to the House Rent Controller for fresh disposal.

It was urged on behalf of the petitioner that section 13 of the Orissa House Rent Control Act does not confer on the appellate authority all the powers under the Civil Procedure Code and that the order of remand is outside the scope of the jurisdiction of the appellate authority. The learned counsel appearing for the opposite parties contended that though there is no specific provision in the Act enabling the appellate authority to remand the case for fresh disposal yet the appellate authority has inherent power to remand a case for fresh disposal in cases not falling strictly within the provisions of the Act.

The Court said that on a careful analysis of the relevant provisions of the Act and from a conspectus of the principles laid down in the decisions referred to above we come to the conclusion that the appellate authority under the Orissa House Rent Control Act, 1967 has jurisdiction only to make such further enquiries as it thinks fit and decide the appeal but has no power to remand the case to the Controller for a fresh decision. The order of the appellate authority in the instant case is in excess of his jurisdiction and is vitiated accordingly. The writ petition is allowed and the order of remand is set aside. In view of the law set out above, the appellate authority shall now proceed with the further enquiry itself and decide the appeal according to law.

While disposing off the case the Court also made certain remarks and said that our learned and noble Brother T.L. Viswanatha Iyer felt some doubt as to the semantics, the drift tenor and impact of section 52 and its provisos of the Kerala Court-fees and Suits Valuation Act (hereinafter referred to as 'the Act'). Section 52 of the Act provides for payment of Court-fee for appeals.

It was further said that there is a catena of decisions taking a purposive interpretation consistent with the intention of the legislature and the mischief sought to be redressed by the enactment and the other relevant context and circumstances where even though a provision is couched in a language apparently mandatory in character or prohibiting certain things; not as a rule; on a pedagogic approach that word indicating a prohibition or indicating a mandatory provision shall never be construed as directory; See (*Lila Gupta* v. *Laxmi Narain*, AIR 1978 SC 1351: (1978) 3 SCR 922: 1978 (2) SCJ 428).

Considering all these aspects of the matter, the Court expressed the opinion that the Courts have got adequate powers to enlarge the time beyond the period of 30 days mentioned in the third proviso to section 52 of the Court-fees Act. Ofcourse, it is a discretionary power and the discretion has to be exercised judicially on sound and legal reasons; *Nirmala Ben Patel* v. *Inder Singh Bagi*, AIR 1977 Ori 211: (1977) 1 Cut WR 369: ILR 1977 Cut 390.

10. Order of Appellate Court must be Reasoned and Speaking

Where rival interpretations are possible, the High Court ought to give a brief statement of reasons while dismissing the appeal summarily – *Shankar Gopinath Apte* v. *Gangabai Hariharrao Patwardhan*, AIR 1976 SC 2506: (1976) 4 SCC 112: (1977) 1 SCR 411. Where the finding of facts was brushed aside by the High Court without any reason, without any appreciation of documents and without any appreciation of contentions of the parties, held, the judgment was perfunctory; *State of Tamil Nadu* v. *S. Kumaraswami*, AIR 1977 SC 2026: (1977) 4 SCC 602.

11. Sections 107 – Clubbing all Issues at a Time

In *Munga Lal Gupta* v. *Hussaini Mahto*, 2011 3 JLJR 149 (Jhk) the High Court said, the appellate court has power under Section 107 (b) C.P.C. to remand the case and not necessarily determine it himself or to frame issue and refer only the said issue for retrial. It is further stated that in the instant case since the lower appellate court considered that question of facts requires re-adjudication and, therefore, instead of remitting a single issue, it has clearly stated that separate issue should have been framed regarding the fact that the chain of title of the plaintiffs is complete from its initial stage i.e. from the stage of settlement till the date the sale deed was executed. Unless the chain of title is complete, the suit could not be decreed declaring title of the plaintiff. The plaintiff was liable to substantiate its claim and, therefore, the appeal was rightly remanded and the judgment of trial court set at naught. The learned counsel has further stated that since the settlement in favour of Tilak Dhari Mahto is specifically disputed; therefore, the question of inheritance does not arise. In absence of inheritance Jagan Mahto, Biren Mahto and Sita Mahto-nephew of Tilak Dhari Mahto had no title and Tilak Dhari Mahto could not have gifted the disputed property and, therefore, the chain was incomplete. Besides it is also argued that the instant case remand order is in fact one under Order XLI Rule 23A C.P.C. In the present case, the appellate court has not disposed of the appeal on a preliminary point. In fact the learned District Judge has reversed the decree in appeal and directed the trial court for a retrial and the appellate court has exercised the same powers as under Rule 23 of Order XLI C.P.C.

While replying the arguments of the respondents counsel, the appellants counsel reiterated his argument and disputed that it is a remand under Order XLI Rule 23 or 23A C.P.C.

After hearing the respective counsel for the parties at length and going through the judgment of the lower appellate court, it is evident that the trial court recorded its judgment by clubbing all the issues and the final conclusion was arrived without analysing individual questions. The facts of the case, the legal questions that emerges and thereafter the entitlement of relief of the plaintiff is all taken together without taking into consideration that the questions framed in separate issues are independent in nature. The relief of declaration of title and possession were to be decided separately while going into the question of title, the court should have traced the right of settlement and consequent sale deed and the initial title separately and thereafter the question of possession since the relief was for a declaration of title as well as a declaration of possession. In case the settlement as alleged by the plaintiffs was a question of dispute between the two persons between Aliyar Mahto and Tilak Dhari Mahto, the court was liable to give a specific and separate decision regarding the gift deed by Tilak Dhari Mahto in favour of Jagan Mahto, Biren Mahto and Sita Mahto who had also executed the sale deed, the vendor of the plaintiffs. I am not inclined to give any finding on the merits of the case, but while examining the judgment of the lower appellate court, I am in agreement with the conclusions arrived at that the issues framed are liable to be decided separately as well as the question whether the settlement was made by the ex-landlord in the joint name of Aliyar Mahto and Tilak Dhari Mahto and whether Tilak Dhari Mahto executed the gift deed in favour of Jagan Mahto, Biren Mahto and Sita Mahto was valid and thereafter the question of right to execute the sale deed and the consequent title of Bansi Prasad Gupta, the vendor of the plaintiffs should have been decided as an individual issue. The judgment cited by the counsel appearing on behalf of the appellants in *Gaya Mahto* v. *Lila Devi,* 2004 (3) JCR 624 (Jhr): 2004 (2) BLJR 1536 is a case which deals with the remand of a case without recording any finding that the retrial of the suit was necessary and, therefore, it was held the mandate of Rule 24 C.P.C. was not valid and further said that ordinarily remand of a case under Rule 23A is not correct. This finding is based only because the appellate court considered that the reasonings given by the trial court in some respect was wrong or inconsistent with the evidence. This is not the circumstance in the instant case. The lower appellate court has gone through the entire record and evidence, thereafter recorded specific reasons that since all the issues have been inter-linked resulting in an improper adjudication and a declaration without tracing out chain of title. This is admittedly required to be done after taking evidence and recording a specific and a separate conclusion. Finding has been recorded that the trial court did not critically examine the issue involved in the case and joined multifarious issue; whereas each of the issue required independent adjudication on the basis of evidence. Evidence recorded to prove one issue could not be taken to be sufficient to arrive at a conclusion in respect of all the issues and, therefore, the order of remand is not under Rule 24 or 25 of Order XLI C.P.C. as asserted by the learned counsel and, in my view, the remand order does not call for any interference in the instant appeal.

12. Sections 107 and 96 – Judgment of Reversal by the Appellate Court

In *Brij Vallabh* v. *Baijnath Singh,* 2013 (3) MPWN 124 (MP) the High Court said, "When there is a conflict of oral evidence on any matter in issue and its a resolution turns upon the credibility of the witnesses , the general rule is that the appellate Court should permit the findings of fact rendered by the trial Court to prevail unless it clearly appears that some special feature about the evidence of particular witness has escaped the notice of the trial Court or there is a sufficient balance of improbability to displace its opinion as to where the credibility lies".

The suit was merely for permanent injunction, without seeking declaration of title. The suit land is disputed to be that of owner ship of the plaintiff and for want of relief of declaration over the suit land, the suit could not have been decreed by the first appellate Court holding the plaintiff is owner of the suit land and entitled for permanent injunction, moreover, when there was no documentary evidence as regards title of the suit land. For the proposition where any matter at issue conclusions are to be drawn on the basis of the oral evidence, for want of documentary evidence the credibility to the witnesses as assessed by the trial Court should not normally be interfered with by the first appellate Court until and unless there is perversity of approach by the trial Court and the conclusions are drawn are based wholly irrelevant consideration. I may profitably place the reliance on the judgment of the Supreme Court in *Madhusudan Das* v. *Smt Narayani Bai,* 1983 JLJ 131 (SC): AIR 1983 SC 114.

13. Section 107(1)(d) and Order XLI, Rule 27 – Powers of Appellate Court

In *Shiv Karan* v. *Special Judge E.C. Act, Lko.,* 2016 11 ADJ 65 (All) the High Court said, as a general rule, the Appellate Court should not admit additional evidence for the purpose of the disposal of an appeal, and the parties are not entitled to produce additional evidence, whether oral or documentary in the appellate Court. The Code, however under this rule empowers an appellate Court to take additional evidence subject to certain conditions. The power is discretionary and must be exercised on sound judicial principles and in the interest of justice. Additional evidence does not mean evidence over and above the evidence led by the party in the lower Court. The basic principles for the admission of the additional evidence are:.

i. The party seeking the admission of additional evidence should be able to establish that such additional evidence could not have been adduced at the first instance with the best efforts;

ii. The party affected by the admission of additional evidence should have an opportunity to rebut it;

iii. The additional evidence must be relevant for the determination of the issue.

For entertaining an application for the production of additional evidence in an appeal, any one or more of the conditions as enumerated in Rule 27 of the Code have to be fulfilled. Under the scheme of Code, whether oral or documentary, it is the trial Court before whom parties are required to adduce their evidence. But in three exceptional circumstances, additional evidence can be adduced before the appellate Court, as provided under S. 107(1)(d) read with Rule 27 of the Code of Civil Procedure. Order XLI, Rule 27 reads as follows:

> "27. Production of additional evidence in Appellate Court.—(1) The parties to an appeal shall not be entitled to produce additional evidence, whether oral or documentary, in the Appellate Court. But if - (a) The Court from whose decree the appeal is preferred has refused to admit evidence which ought to have been admitted, or (aa) the party seeking to produce additional evidence, establishes that notwithstanding the exercise of due diligence, such evidence was not within his knowledge or could not, after the exercise of due diligence, be produced by him at the time when the decree appealed against was passed, or (b) The Appellate Court requires any document to be produced or any witness to be examined to enable it to pronounce judgment, or for any other substantial cause, The Appellate Court may allow such evidence or document to be produced, or witness to be examined. (2) Wherever additional evidence is allowed to be produced by an Appellate Court, the Court shall record the reason for its admission."

The Court further said, having considered the material on record and keeping in mind the settled position of law on the issue, I am of considered opinion that a party cannot be allowed to fill the lacunae in their evidence at the appellate stage. It is against the spirit of the Code to allow a party to adduce additional evidence without fulfillment of either of the three conditions mentioned in Rule 27. In *R. Mohan Reddy* v. *Net Work Inc.*, (2007) 14 SCC 257: AIR 2008 SC 579 the Apex Court has held that appellate Court should not pass an order so as to patch up the weakness of the evidence of the unsuccessful party before the trial

Court, but it will be different if the Court itself requires the evidence to do justice between the parties. The ability to pronounce judgment is to be understood as the ability to pronounce judgment satisfactorily to the mind of the Court. But mere difficulty is not sufficient to issue such direction to the appellate Court.

14. Order XLI Rule 27, Order XLI Rule 27(1)(b), Section 107, Section 107(d) and Section 115

In *Medidhi Chakra Veni* v. *Kamisetti Venkata Ramanam,* 2016 (2) ALD 155: 2016 (1) ALT 677 (AP) the High Court said, "whenever additional evidence is allowed to the produced, by an Appellate Court, the court shall record the reason for its admission."

What the lower Appellate Court should have seen is whether the appellants were diligent in prosecuting their case or making an attempt to cover up the latches in their case. Without going into such relevant aspect of the matter, the lower Appellate Court passed the above orders. The learned counsel for the respondents/appellants relied on *Mahavir Singh* v. *Naresh Chandra,* (2001) 1 SCC 309: AIR 2001 SC 134; *K. Venkataramaiah* v. *A. Seetharama Reddy,* AIR 1963 SC 1526: 1964 (1) An WR 13 and *North Eastern Railway Administration, Gorakhpur* v. *Bhagwan Das (D) by Lrs.,* AIR 2008 SC 139: 2009 (74) ALR 370. The decisions cited by the learned counsel for the respondents do not help their case.

In *K. Venkataramaiah* v. *A. Seetharama Reddy (supra),* the Supreme Court considered the case of receiving evidence in an election petition by the High Court when additional evidence was sought to be produced before the Court. A Constitution Bench of the Supreme Court held that the Court has to allow the additional evidence on the examination of the evidence that is available before it. The Court observed with approval that the distinction pointed out by the Privy Council in *Parsotim* v. *Lal Mohar,* (1931) 0 Supreme (SC) 36: (1931) 0 AIR (PC) 143 that the legitimate occasion for the exercise of discretion to receive additional evidence is not whenever before the appeal is heard a party applies to adduce fresh evidence, but "when on examining the evidence as it stands, some inherent lacuna or defect becomes apparent".

In the present case, it is not the case of either party that the first situation is attracted. So far as the second circumstance noticed above is concerned, question of exercise of due diligence would not arise because the concerned scientific laboratory from which examination is sought to be made itself was not in existence at the time of trial and so that clause is also not attracted. In the third circumstance the appellate court may require any document to be produced or any witness to be examined to enable it to pronounce judgment, or for any other substantial cause. The expression to enable it to pronounce judgment has been subject of several decisions including *Syed Abdul Khader* v. *Rami Reddy,* AIR 1979 SC 553: (1979) 2 SCC 60 wherein it was held that when the appellate court finds itself unable to pronounce judgment owing to a lacuna or defect in the evidence as it stands, it may admit additional evidence. The ability to pronounce a judgment is to be understood as the ability to pronounce a judgment satisfactory to the mind of court delivering it. It is only a lacuna in the evidence that will empower the court to admit additional evidence See: *The*

Municipal Corporation of Greater Bombay v. *Lala Pancham*, AIR 1965 SC 1008. But a mere difficulty in coming to a decision is not sufficient for admission of evidence under this rule. The words or for any other substantial cause must be read with the word requires, which is set out at the commencement of the provision, so that it is only where, for any other substantial cause, the appellate court requires additional evidence, that this rule would apply as noticed by the Privy Council in *Kesowji Issur* v. *G.I.P. Railway [supra]*. It is under these circumstances such a power could be exercised. Therefore, when the first appellate court did not find the necessity to allow the application, we fail to understand as to how the High Court could, in exercise of its power under Section 115 CPC, could have interfered with such an order, particularly when the whole appeal is not before the court. It is only in the circumstances when the appellate court requires such evidence to pronounce the judgment the necessity to adduce additional evidence would arise and not in any other circumstances. When the first appellate court passed the order on the application filed under Order XLI, Rule 27 CPC, the whole appeal was before it and if the first appellate court is satisfied that additional evidence was not required, we fail to understand as to how the High Court could interfere with such an order under Section 115 CPC. In this regard, we may notice the decision of this Court in *Gurdev Singh* v. *Mehnga Ram*, 1997 (6) SCC 507: AIR 1997 SC 3572, in which the scope of exercise of power under Section 115 CPC on an order passed in an application filed under Order XLI, Rule 27 CPC was considered. When this decision was cited before the High Court, the same was brushed aside by stating that the principle stated therein is not applicable to the facts of this case. We do not think so. The High Court ought not to have interfered with such an order….."

15. Section 107(1)(d) r/w Order XLI, Rule 27 and Section 115

In *A. Andisamy Chettiar* v. *A. Subburaj Chettiar*, 2015 4 BBCJ (SC) 464: 2016 1 CivCC 731: 2016 (1) JCR (SC) 276: 2016 1 JLJR (SC) 256: the Apex Court held, High Court, in its revisional jurisdiction, will not be entitled to interfere with the order passed by the first appellate court as regards adducing additional evidence.

16. Section 107(1)(d), C.P.C. – Sections Enable the Appellate Court to Admit Additional Evidence, Whereas Order XLI, Rule 27, C.P.C. Furnishes Grounds on which Additional Evidence may be Taken

In *Sankar Pradhan* v. *Premananda Pradhan (dead)*, 2015 2 OLR 607 (Ori): 2016 (I) ILR CUT 1151 the High Court held, Section 107 (1) (d) C.P.C. enables the appellate court to admit additional evidence, whereas Order XLI Rule 27 C.P.C. furnishes grounds on which additional evidence may be taken. It confers discretionary power on the appellate court to allow additional evidence in appeal. The said power is circumscribed by limitations prescribed in Clauses (a), (aa) or (b) of Rule 27(1) of C.P.C.

In *Persotim Thakur* v. *Lal Mohar Thakur*, AIR 1931 Privy Council 143, it is held that under Cl. (1) (b) of Rule 27 it is only where the appellate Court "requires" it, (i.e., finds it needful) that additional evidence can be admitted. It may be required to enable the Court to pronounce judgment or for any other substantial cause, but in either case it must be the Court that requires it. This is the plain grammatical reading of the sub-clause. The legitimate occasion for the exercise of this discretion is not whenever before the appeal is heard a party applies to adduce fresh evidence, but "when on examining the evidence as it stands some inherent lacuna or defect becomes apparent." It may well be that the defect may be pointed out by a party, or that a party may move the Court to supply the defect, but the requirement must be the requirement of the Court upon its appreciation of the evidence as it stands. Wherever the Court adopts this procedure it is bound by Rule 27(2) to record its reasons for so doing (emphasis laid). The same view was taken by this Court in the cases of *Banchhanidhi Behera* v. *Ananta Upadhaya*, AIR 1962 Ori 9: 27 (1961) CLT 141 and *State Bank of India* v. *Ashok Stores*, 53 (1982) CLT 552: AIR 1982 Ori 34.

17. Order XXXIX, Rule 3, Order VI, Rule 17, Section 107(2) and Section 151

In *Puttamaramma* v. *Giriyappa*, 2016 1 KCCR 73 (Kar) the Court said, application I.A. No. 4 filed by plaintiff as could be seen from the Appellate Court records would indicate that appellant/plaintiff had sought leave of Appellate Court to amend the plaint by answering Clauses (a) to (h) and also for additional prayer. At this stage itself it would be appropriate to notice that while considering the application for amendment Courts would not go into the correctness or falsity of case for amendment. Likewise, Courts would not record a finding on the merits of amendment sought for. Such adjudication at the stage of considering the prayer for allowing the application or dismissing the same would be alien. The Hon'ble Apex Court in *Rajesh Kumar Aggarwal* v. *K.K. Modi* reported in AIR 2006 SC 1647 has held that while considering an application for amendment of pleadings, Court should not go into the correctness or falsity of case proposed in the amendment. It has been held by the Hon'ble Apex Court as under:

> "20. While considering whether an application for amendment should or should not be allowed, the Court should not go into the correctness or falsity of the case in the amendment. Likewise, it should not record a finding on the merits of the amendment and the merits of the amendment sought to be incorporated by way of amendment are not to be adjudged at the stage of allowing the prayer for amendment. This cardinal principle has not been followed by the High Court in the instant case."

In that view of the matter, Appellate Court was not justified in entering into the merits of the claim, by examining the contents of proposed amendment and as such, on this short ground the judgment of the Appellate Court cannot be sustained

18. Section 107, Order XLI, Rules 23 to 25 and 27 – Where Trial Court did not Frame Issues

In the case of *Fatik Routh* v. *Thakur Routh*, 2016 (3) JCR 276: 2016 (166) AIC 490 (Jhar) the High Court of Jharkhand examined whether judgement delivered without framing issues which ought to have been framed can be set aside by the appellate court.

The Court discussed the argument advanced by the parties and said, Mr. Atanu Banerjee, the learned counsel for the appellant submits that the factum of adoption of Thakur Routh was under challenge and the trial court has disbelieved the story of adoption of Thakur Routh by Maga Routh and therefore, the order of the lower Appellate Court interfering with the judgment and decree in Title (Partition) Suit No. 18 of 1999 on the ground that no issue was framed on the question of adoption is erroneous. Alternatively, it has been argued that while exercising powers under Order XLI, Rule 25 C.P.C., the lower Appellate Court could have remanded the matter to the trial court for taking additional evidence on an issue framed by it however, a mere lapse in framing an issue would not render the whole of the judgment unsustainable.

Per contra, Mr. Kaushik Sarkhel, the learned counsel for the respondents submits that the whole case of the defendants is based on the adoption of defendant no. 1 namely, Thakur Routh, a fact which was disputed by the plaintiff and therefore, the trial court was under a duty to frame an issue on the question of adoption. The learned counsel submits that failure of the trial court to frame an issue on the question of adoption would definitely vitiate the judgment of the trial court.

No doubt, the Appellate Court has power under Section 107 of the Code of Civil Procedure to frame an issue and remand the same for trial. However, the exercise of such power is regulated by the provisions under Order XLI, Rule XXIII to 25 and Rule 27 of the Code of Civil Procedure. In the present case, Rule 25 Order XLI C.P.C. is attracted. The power of the Appellate Court under Rule 25 is circumscribed and one of the limitations is, whether the trial court has omitted to frame an issue which the Appellate Court considers essential for arriving at a right decision in the case. The object of framing of an issue is to identify the questions from the pleadings which is required to be decided by the court and to enable the parties to lead evidence thereon. It is well settled that for a valid adoption it must be proved that there was an intention to give the child and the same was reciprocated by adoptee by expressing an intention to adopt the child. There are certain other rituals also which a party claiming adoption may be required to prove. Undoubtedly, one of the questions contested by the parties before the trial court was the question of adoption. The parties led some evidence on the said question however, that does not satisfy the requirement of law.

However, in Title (Partition) Suit No. 18 of 1999, the question of adoption is not the only question which would conclusively decide the fate of the case. May be, it was one of the issues which should have been framed and the Lower Appellate Court has rightly held that it was one of the issues arising in the suit and therefore, it should have been decided by framing an issue. But, the Lower Appellate Court just went tangent and instead of exercising powers under Order XLI, Rule 25 C.P.C., set aside the entire judgment and order dated 28.06.2010 in Title (Partition) Suit No. 18 of 1999. The procedure adopted by the lower Appellate Court was completely erroneous. A judgment cannot be set aside on the ground that the trial court has failed to frame one of the issues which may arise in the case.

As a sequel to the aforesaid discussion, order dated 09.05.2012 in Title Appeal No. 06 of 2010 is hereby set aside and the Title Appeal No. 06 of 2010 is restored to its original file. However, the issue framed by the lower Appellate Court would be treated as one under Order XLI, Rule 25 C.P.C. The trial court shall adjudicate the said issue and, if necessary, permit the parties to lead additional evidence. Let this exercise be done within a period of 9 months and after the trial court records its finding on the issue so framed, the lower Appellate Court shall proceed to decide the Title Appeal No. 06 of 2010, in accordance with law.

19. Section 107(2), Order XLI, Rule 5, Order XXXIX, Rules 1 and 2 – Appellate Court has Same Powers as are Vested in the Trial Court

In *Jyotika Gogoi* v. *Nupur Kumar Gogoi*, 2017 (1) Gau LT 8: 2017 (3) Gau LR 11: 2017 10 Gau LJ 388 (Gau) the High Court examined the nature of power to grant an ad interim injunction and said, power to grant ad-interim injunction is a discretionary power. The Court said, Mr. Mozumdar has placed reliance upon the case of *Wander Ltd.* v. *Antox Indoa (P) Ltd.*, as reported in 1990 (Supp) SCC 77 (para-9 & 14), *Gujarat Bottling Co. Ltd.* v. *Coca Cola Co.*, as reported in 1995 (5) SCC 545 (para-47), and states that the ratio laid down in those cases is squarely covers the issues raised by the respondent Nos. 3 & 4, for which, the order of status quo dated 05.10.2016 passed in RFA 67/2016 is liable to be vacated. He further submits that as on today, the appellant have made no prayer for staying of the operation of the judgment and order dated 23.08.2016, passed by the Civil Judge (Sr. Division), Lakhimpur, dismissing Title Suit No. 17/2015 as not maintainable and, as such, the said suit continues to be dismissed. In the said context, he submits that the prayer for injunction, as mandated under the provisions of Order XXXIX, Rule 1 and Rule 2 CPC, can be entertained only in a suit, and therefore, in the present case in hand, as the present appeal has merely been admitted, it would not amount to continuation of the suit. Hence, Mr. Mozumdar submits that even on this legal ground, the order of status quo granted on 05.10.2016 by this Court is liable to be vacated. On the principles for granting an order of injunction, the learned Senior Counsel has relied on the case of *M. Gurudas* v. *Rasaranjan*, as reported in (2006) 8 SCC 367 and submits that the court would, apart from finding out a prima facie case, balance of convenience and also irreparable injury that the plaintiff might suffer if injunction is refused, must also see that the contention of the petitioner must be bona fide.

Mr. P.P. Dutta, learned counsel appearing for the respondents No. 1 & 2 in RFA No. 67/2016 submits that he is adopting the arguments pressed by Mr. D. Mozumdar, learned senior counsel for the respondent Nos. 3 & 4 and further submits that the order dated 05.10.2016 passed by this Court in RFA No. 67/2016, is liable to be recalled on the ground of suppression of material facts because the appellants in IA(C) No. 1652/2016 as well as in the RFA No. 67/2016 did not disclose that the respondents No. 1 & 2 i.e. Essar Oil Limited had contested Misc.(J) Case No. 26/2015 by submitting their written objection, wherein they had disclosed that the construction of the retail outlet is almost completed and was on the verge of commissioning and ready to be made open for service to public. He further submits that in the said objection, they had also disclosed before the trial court that the Deputy Commissioner, Lakhimpur had already issued a no objection certificate and by now the requisite explosive license has also been issued in respect of the proposed retail outlet. He further submits that as the appellants had remained silent from 18.11.2014, which was the date of execution of the lease deed till 17.8.2015, when the present suit was filed, a valuable right has been created in favour of the respondents and on the principle that "delay defeats equity", this is a fit and proper case for refusing injunction because of lack of the 3 golden principles of granting injunction, i.e. (i) lack of prima facie case, (ii) lack of balance of convenience, and (iii) lack of injury or loss to the appellants, which is apparent on the face of record.

Mr. A.K. Purkayastha, learned counsel for the respondents Nos. 1 & 2, while replying in the matter, has meticulously read each and every paragraph of the plaint and had pointed out that he was on the verge of reading each and every material on record to establish that there was no suppression of facts by the appellants. Thus, at the commencement of the argument, it is perceived by this Court that if such a detailed reading is permitted at the bar, it would consume almost two to three days of full length hearing and therefore, this Court, after his reading of the plaint was over, inquired from the learned counsel for the respondent whether he was proposing to argue the entire matter i.e. RFA No.67 of 2016 as well as the two connected IA's, i.e. I.A (C) No. 1652/16 and I.A. (C) No. 1930/16 and if so, he could continue reading materials on record to his fullest satisfaction, but if he is satisfied only on the disposal of both the IA's, then he must make a pointed reply to the aforementioned issues raised by the respondents. Thereupon, Mr. Purkayastha, with his all his usual fairness, restricted his reply only on the issues raised by the learned Senior counsel for the applicants in both the Interlocutory applications.

The points of determination, which arises in this case is as follows:—

i. Whether there is any suppression of material facts before this court, which could have influenced this court to issue ad-interim order dated 05.10.2016 directing the parties to maintain status-quo? And whether the said ad-interim order is liable to be discharged/ varied on ground of suppression of material facts?

ii. Whether the jurisdiction of Order XXXIX Rule 1 and 2 CPC read with section 151 CPC can be exercised in the case in hand?

The second point of determination is taken up first for decision. It is stated that although the argument put forward by Mr. Mozumdar, ld. Senior Counsel for the defendants No.3 and 4 appear to be appealing, but I have come across the judgment dated 22.02.2006 of this court rendered in W.P.(C) No. 989/06- *Reboti Ray* v. *Sashi Kanta Budhia @ Agarwal*, as reported in (2006) 3 GLR 42: 2006 (2) GLT 311, this court was pleased to reject the prayer, similar to the one made by Mr. Mozumdar. As per the ratio of the said case, I have no hesitation to hold that the present appeal i.e. RFA No. 67/2016 is an extension of the suit and therefore, by operation of the provisions of section 107(2) CPC, this appellate court has the same powers and may perform as nearly as the same duties as are conferred and imposed by the Code of Civil Procedure on courts of original jurisdiction in respect of suits instituted therein. I am of the opinion that once the appeal has been admitted, then notwithstanding that no application under Order XLI, Rule 5 CPC has been filed, the appellate court has the power to grant ad-interim injunction, not only under the provisions of Order XXXIX Rules 1 and 2 CPC but also by invoking the provisions of section 151 CPC. Therefore, I hold that this court does have the power to issue injunction. Hence, this point is determined in favour of the plaintiff/appellant and against the defendants/ Respondents.

Having considered the rival arguments and materials on record, it is well known that as a general rule, the power to grant ad-interim injunction is a discretionary power, because the litigant must demonstrate that not only it had approached the court with clean hands, but the three golden principles, required to be present for issuing ad-interim injunction were present in the case. Also, as a general rule, suppression of material facts by a litigant, disqualifies such litigant from obtaining any relief. In this regard, the decision of the Hon'ble Supreme Court of India, rendered in the case of *S.J.S. Business Enterprises Pvt. Ltd.* v. *State of Bihar*, reported in (2004) 3 CCC 1: (2004) 7 SCC 166 may be referred to. In the present case in hand, we find that not only the plaintiff had suppressed material facts before the learned trial court, but material facts had been suppressed in the present appeal. The plaintiffs could have, after the injunction was rejected by the trial court on grounds of suppression of material facts, presented true and fair picture. However, this court finds that the plaintiffs had not only deliberately chose to suppress the order of dismissal of injunction, but in para 4 of the IA(C) No. 1652/16, stated as follows—

> "That the Appellants/Plaintiffs as petitioners also preferred a Misc. Case which was registered as Misc. (J) Case No. 23/15 under Order XXXIX, Rule 1 C.P.C. for injunction against the Opposite Parties restraining them not to enter into the RCC Building and land in Schedule A till disposal of the Title Suit and the Respondent/Defendant has also filed their written objection. A copy of the written objection filed by the defendant Nos. 3 and 4 is annexed as Annexure-I."

Thus, there is no statement that the said injunction petition was rejected by the learned trial court by order dated 04.06.2016. It is seen on the perusal of the order dated 04.06.2016 that the learned trial court by orders passed in Misc. (J) Case No. 1/2016, had appointed a Commissioner to inspect the suit premises and it is, inter-alia, held in the order dated 04.06.2016 that:

> "after perusing Commissioner's report in the title suit it appears from commissioner's report in Misc. (J) Case No. 1/2016 prima facie that there is a Assam Type House situated over the suit land......".

It appears that the mis-description of the Schedule-A premises is aimed to project before this court that the purported RCC house is a big structure covering an area of 9 lechas (1 lecha is equivalent to 144 square feet, as such, 9 lechas would be about 1,296 sq. feet), whereas, the Assam Type House is covering only an area of 38'X18' sq. ft (equivalent to about 684 sq. feet or 4.75 lechas). Having seen the above referred photographs at Annexure-K of IA, the plinth does not appear to be covering 9 lechas land, but the land beneath the house does not exceed 38X18 ft., which is equivalent to 684 square feet (or 4.75 lechas). The learned trial court further disbelieved at that stage that the plaintiff No.2, being an advocate and attesting witness of the deed was ignorant of the said lease. Thus, the learned trial court did not find any prima facie case against Defendant No. 3. The balance of convenience was found in favour of defendant No. 4, as continuance of injunction would cause loss to defendant No. 4, who had already incurred expenses for developing retail outlet over the suit land as per the lease deed executed by defendant No. 3. The learned trial court further held that irreparable loss would be caused to the Defendant No. 4 and not to plaintiffs, who have no prima facie case at that stage and, as such, this court finds that the material so far suppressed by the plaintiff has occasioned this court to be prevented from appreciating the fact that the learned trial court had already rejecting the prayer for injunction. Referring to the two case law citations canvassed by Mr. Purkayastha, this court finds that in the said two cases, the Hon'ble Supreme Court of India has made strong observations on misrepresentations made before the court and, as such, the said two citations cannot be of any assistance to the appellant, who have indulged in suppression of material facts, as held above.

20. Section 107 and Order XLIII, Rule 1(u) – Remand of Case to Trial Court

In *Smt. Chennamma* v. *Sheenappa Gowda*, 2016 (4) KCCR 3284: 2016 (ILR) (Karn) 5163, the High Court said, the remand of the case leads to delay and causes prejudice to the parties to the *lis*, as an unwarranted order of remand gives the litigation an undeserved lease of life and therefore must be avoided. When the evidence is available, the Court should decide the appeal one way or the other. If necessary issue has not been raised, issues can be re-casted or additional issue raised and the appeal should be decided. The lower Appellate Court being headed by the Senior and experienced Judicial Officer should keep in view the powers of Appellate Court under Section 107 of CPC and the guidelines provided as per Order XLI, Rules 24 to 31 of CPC and decide the appeal(s).

13. The Court below, instead of considering the evidence brought on record and deciding the controversy between the parties finally, has passed the Judgment of remand which is wholly arbitrary.

If necessary issue not raised, issues can be re-casted or additional issue raised and appeal should be decided - Lower Appellate Court being headed by Senior and experienced Judicial Officer should keep in view powers of Appellate Court under *Section 107* of *Civil Procedure Code* and guidelines provided as per Order XLI, Rules 24 to 31 of *Civil Procedure Code* and decide appeal(s).

21. Section 107(1)(d) and Order XLI, Rule 27 – Powers of Appellate Court under Section 107 (1)(d) to Take Additional Evidence

In *Shiv Karan* v. *Special Judge E.C. Act, Lko*, 2016 (11) ADJ 65: 2016 (6) All WC 6441: 2017 (1) ICC 612 (All) (Luck Bench) plaintiffs-petitioners moved application before appellate Court for permission to produce at least a marginal witness of Will – This attempt cannot be said to the condition that "plaintiff even with due diligence could not have moved such application before trial Court" –The High Court said, As a general rule, the Appellate Court should not admit additional evidence for the purpose of the disposal of an appeal, and the parties are not entitled to produce additional evidence, whether oral or documentary in the appellate court. The Code, however under this rule empowers an appellate court to take additional evidence subject to certain conditions. The power is discretionary and must be exercised on sound judicial principles and in the interest of justice. Additional evidence does not mean evidence over and above the evidence led by the party in the lower court. The basic principles for the admission of the additional evidence are:

(i) The party seeking the admission of additional evidence should be able to establish that such additional evidence could not have been adduced at the first instance with the best efforts;

(ii) The party affected by the admission of additional evidence should have an opportunity to rebut it;

(iii) The additional evidence must be relevant for the determination of the issue.

For entertaining an application for the production of additional evidence in an appeal, any one or more of the conditions as enumerated in Rule 27 of the Code have to be fulfilled. Under the scheme of Code, whether oral or documentary, it is the trial court before whom parties are required to adduce their evidence. But in three exceptional circumstances, additional evidence can be adduced before the appellate court, as provided under Section 107(1)(d) read with Rule 27 of the Code of Civil Procedure. Order XLI, Rule 27 reads as follows:—

> "27. *Production of additional evidence in Appellate Court.*—(1) The parties to an appeal shall not be entitled to produce additional evidence, whether oral or documentary, in the Appellate Court. But if - (a) The Court from whose decree the appeal is preferred has refused to admit evidence which ought to have been admitted, or (aa) the party seeking to produce additional evidence, establishes that notwithstanding the exercise of due diligence, such evidence was not within his knowledge or could not, after the exercise of due diligence, be produced by him at the time when the decree appealed against was passed, or (b) The Appellate Court requires any document to be produced or any witness to be examined to enable it to pronounce judgment, or for any other substantial cause, The Appellate Court may allow such evidence or document to be produced, or witness to be examined. (2) Wherever additional evidence is allowed to be produced by an Appellate Court, the Court shall record the reason for its admission."

A party cannot be allowed to fill the lacunae in their evidence at the appellate stage. It is against the spirit of the Code to allow a party to adduce additional evidence without fulfilment of either of the three conditions mentioned in Rule 27. In *K.R. Mohan Reddy* v. *Net Work Inc.*, (2007) 14 SCC 257: AIR 2008 SC 579 the Apex Court has held that appellate court should not pass an order so as to patch up the weakness of the evidence of the unsuccessful party before the trial court, but it will be different if the court itself requires the evidence to do justice between the parties. The ability to pronounce judgment is to be understood as the ability to pronounce judgment satisfactorily to the mind of the court. But mere difficulty is not sufficient to issue such direction to the appellate court.

In the case at hand, undisputedly, no application was moved before the trial court seeking examination of marginal witness nor can it be said that the plaintiff with due diligence could not have moved such an application to get examine the marginal witnesses.

The court below rightly observed after relying upon the law as laid down in *Ramchandra* v. *Brijlal*, 2008 (105) RD 219 that the suit was filed in the year 1997 whereas the appeal was filed against the order of the Trial Court in the year 2009, but no application at any stage was moved and now after considerable long lapse of time, the said application has been moved, which is not justified as giving an opportunity at this stage would mean to allow for filling the lacunae.

For the reasons aforesaid, I do not find any perversity or illegality in the impugned order. Accordingly, the writ petition is dismissed at the admission itself. However, it is provided that as the Appeal is pending since the year 2009, the Appellate Court shall make an earnest endeavour to decide the appeals preferred by the petitioners expeditiously, say within six months, if possible.

22. CPC Sections 96 and 107 – Specific Relief Act, 1963 Section 20 – Dismissal of Suit for Specific Performance

In *Rajesh Kumar Sood* v. *Parvej Nowrojee*, 2016 (3) Shim LC 1673 (HP) (DB), the High Court said, Section 96 of the Code of Civil Procedure (for short, CPC) mandates as to who is competent to file an appeal and also contains the mechanism how an appeal is to be filed. Section 107 of the CPC provides that the Appellate Court has the same powers as the court of original jurisdiction, with some fetters contained in Order XLI of the CPC. It is apt to reproduce Section 107 of the CPC hereunder:

> "107. Powers of appellate court.—(1) Subject to such conditions and limitations as may be prescribed, an appellate Court shall have power-
>
> (a) to determine a case finally,
>
> (b) to remand a case;
>
> (c) to frame issues and refer them for trial;
>
> (d) to take additional evidence or to require such evidence to be taken.
>
> (2) Subject as aforesaid, the appellate court shall have the same powers and shall perform as nearly as may be the same duties as are conferred and imposed by this Code on courts of original jurisdiction in respect of suits instituted therein."

Thus, from the perusal of the above provision of law, it is clear that the first appeal is continuation of the suit and is to be decided on merits after discussing pleadings, facts and the evidence led by the parties. While hearing the first appeal, the Appellate Court is within its powers and competence to uphold the judgment, set aside or reverse it, or remand the case. The Appellate Court has to discuss the case from all angles, like the court of original jurisdiction.

The Apex Court in *Ishwar Dutt* v. *Land Acquisition Collector*, 2005 AIR SCW 3578: AIR 2005 SC 3165, held that the High Court has wide power in terms of Section 107 of the CPC. However, it has also been observed that the High

Court, while exercising power in terms of Section 107 of the CPC, cannot travel beyond pleadings. It is apt to reproduce paragraph 34 of the said judgment hereunder:

> "34. The High Court, in our opinion, although has a wide power in terms of Section 107 of the Code of Civil Procedure but it could not have gone outside the pleadings and make out a new case."

The Apex Court in *Shiv Kumar Sharma* v. *Santosh Kumari*, 2007 AIR SCW 6384: AIR 2008 SC 171, while interpreting the scope of the jurisdiction of the High Court in appellate proceedings under Section 96 of the CPC, held that the High Court must act within the four corners of statute. It is apt to reproduce paragraph 18 of the said judgment as under:

> "18. Scope and ambit of jurisdiction of the High Court in determining an issue in an appeal filed in terms of Section 96 of the Code of Civil Procedure (which would be in continuation of the original suit) and exercising the power of judicial review under Articles 226 and 227 of the Constitution of India would be different. While in the former, the court, subject to the procedural flexibility has laid down under the statute is bound to act within the four corners thereof, in adjudicating a lis in exercise of its power of judicial review, the High Court exercises a wider jurisdiction. No doubt, the court in an appropriate case, even in a civil suit may mould a relief but its jurisdiction in this behalf would be confined to Order VII, Rule 7 of the Code of Civil Procedure. (See *Bay Berry Apartments Pvt. Ltd.* v. *Shobha*, 2006 (10) SCALE 596 and *U.P. State Brassware Corpn. Ltd.* v. *Udai Narain Pandey*, (2006) 1 SCC 479)"

23. Specific Relief Act, 1963 Section 20 – Specific Performance Agreement to Sell

The plaintiff has admitted that he had reduced the terms and conditions of the document into writing, thus, the possibility of interposing conditions No.6 to 9 (overleaf page 1) and a note (overleaf page 2), being afterthought, also cannot be ruled out.

36. Another aspect of the case is that the plaintiff, for the reasons best known to him, has not examined the stamp vendor from whom two non-judicial papers were purchased on 13th July, 2000. The stamp vendor would have been the best witness to depose as to who had purchased the said papers. Thus, adverse inference has to be drawn against the plaintiff.

24. Sections 100A, 104 and 107 – Constitution of India, 1950 Article 227

In *S. Umapathy* v. *V. Ezhilarasi*, 2016 (3) Mad WN (Civil) 321: 2016 (4) CTC 662 (Mad) (DB), the High Court examined the maintainability of appeal against Review order. In the case under reference the revision was filed by seeking to invoke the power of superintendence available to the High Court over an inferior Court under Article 227 of the Constitution of India. Thus, no intra-Court appeal against the said decision passed in the revision is available before the Bench. When such is the position, certainly, an appeal would not lie against the order passed in the review application in the revision petition. Furthermore, it is trite that an appeal against the order made in a review application, even in a case when it is otherwise maintainable, cannot be entertained without challenging the main order when a subsequent order merely confirms the earlier order. Useful reference can be had to the decision of the Supreme Court in *D.S.R. Steel* v. *State of Rajasthan*, (2012) 6 SCC 782: AIR 2012 SC 1602. Therefore, even on that account, the appeal is not maintainable. The reliance made on the provisions of the Civil Procedure Code does not merit acceptance as they do not apply to the facts of the case.

Section 100A of the Civil Procedure Code merely places an embargo on further appeal. Similarly, Section 104 deals with the availability of appeal against certain orders. Section 107 of the Code prescribes the availability of the power to the appellate Court while hearing the appeals. Thus, these provisions do not have any application to the case on hand, which involves dismissal of a review application in a revision petition.

The learned counsel made a submission that if a Civil Miscellaneous Appeal is not maintainable then a Letters Patent Appeal would lie. This submission also cannot be countenanced as Clause 15 of the Letters Patent once again does not deal with an order made in exercise of the revisional jurisdiction under the power of superintendence available to the High Court. The decisions relied upon by the learned counsel for appellant do not have any application, as we are not concerned with Order XLVII, Rule 7 and Clause 15 of the Letters Patent in this case.

***108. Procedure in Appeals from Appellate Decrees and Orders.*—The provisions of this Part relating to appeals from original decree shall, so far as may be, apply to appeals.**

(a) from appellate decrees, and

(b) from orders made under this Code or under any special or local law in which a different procedure is not provided.

APPEALS TO THE SUPREME COURT

***109. When appeals lie to the Supreme Court.*—Subject to the provisions in Chapter IV of Part V of the Constitution and such rules as may, from time-to time, be made by the Supreme Court regarding appeals from the Courts of India, and to the provisions hereinafter contained, an appeal shall lie to the Supreme Court from any judgment, decree or final order in a civil proceeding of a High Court, if the High Court certifies:**

(i) that the case involves a substantial question of law of general importance; and

(ii) that in the opinion of the High Court the said question needs to be decided by the Supreme Court.

SYNOPSIS

Comments

1. Historical Background

The provisions contained in section 109 and under article 133(1) of the Constitution of India are identical in nature and its application. It may further be examined along with the provisions contained in Order XLV of the Code also which provides for appeal to the Supreme Court. The jurisdiction under section 109 is subjected to the Rules regarding appeals framed by the Supreme Court under the provisions contained in Chapter IV of Part V of the Constitution of India. By the Code of Civil Procedure (Amendment) Act (49 of 1973), section 109 has been put in line with that of amended article 133. Now the provisions contained under article 133 and under section 109 are identical.

The jurisdiction under section 109 further depends on two things, *viz.*, if the High Court certifies (i) that the case involves a substantial question of law of general importance; and (ii) that in the opinion of the High Court, the said question needs to be decided by the Supreme Court. Hence, these two conditions must be there, to invoke jurisdiction under this section.

The jurisdiction conferred by article 133 is in addition to and independent of the provisions of article 136. If no appeal lies under article 133, there is no bar to approach the Supreme Court under article 136 even without applying to the High Court for a certificate as required by section 109 of CPC and by article 133 of the Constitution; *Collector* v. *Mishra,* (1968) 1 SCR 372 (379).

Section 109 provides for an appeal to the Supreme Court from any judgment, decree or final order in a civil proceeding of a High Court.

Thus, prior to the amendment, there were three alternative grounds for appeal to the Supreme Court from a High Court in a Civil proceeding, The grounds were (i) Value of appeal being 20,000 and above, (ii) The matter on appeal indirectly involving same value. The case being otherwise fit for appeal, those grounds have been substituted by a single ground that the case involves a substantial question of law which needs to be decided by the Supreme Court.

Clause (2) of article 133 ignores the existence of the provisions under article 132 for deciding a case being fit for appeal to the Supreme Court. It may be noted that said article 132 is confined to constitutional question, but comprises appeals from civil, criminal and other cases, while article 133 is confined to civil appeals only.

Under the old provisions "substantial question of law" did not come for consideration where the value test was satisfied. Now no such value test is a ground and the "substantial question of law" is the objective condition.

2. Section 109, Article 133

Prior to 1973, there were certain discrepancies between the two provisions. The Code of Civil Procedure (Amendment) Act of 1973 removed the discrepancies and brought the provisions contained in section 109 in the line of article 133 and now the two provisions, as said earlier also, are identical in nature.

3. The Provisions for Appeal – Whether Confined to Suits

The two provisions contemplate appeal against judgment, decree and final order passed in any civil proceeding and is not limited to suits only.

The Privy Council had said that the word 'judgment' indicates a judicial decision given on the merits of the dispute before the Court, *Kuppu Swami* v. *The King,* AIR 1949 PC 1. The Privy Council said in the case of *Amin Bros.* that "the judgment" does not include an interlocutory judgment; *Amin Bros.* v. *Dominion of India* AIR 1950 PC 77: 1949 FCR 842: 1950 SCJ 139.

The Supreme Court said that there is no "Judgment" or "Order" where the function of the Court was mere to dissolve; *Premchand* v. *State of Bihar,* AIR 1950 SCR 799: AIR 1951 SC 14: 1951 SCJ 5.

4. Meaning of Judgment

It is clear that the jurisdiction under section 109 is dependent upon the Rules framed by the Supreme Court regarding the appeals as has been mandated by article 133 also. Therefore, the term judgment has to be examined within the scope of article 133. The term has been used in the sense of a decision finally determining the rights of the parties in the proceedings and not as defined strictly in CPC; *S. Kuppusami Rao* v. *King,* AIR 1949 FC 1: 1947 FCR 180: 49 Cr LJ 625; *Syedna Taher Saifuddin Saheb* v. *State of Bombay,* AIR 1958 SC 253: 1958 SCR 1007: 1958 SCJ 403. The decision of a vital issue which may ultimately affect the fate of the proceeding is not enough. *Amin Bros.* v. *Dominion of India,* AIR 1950 FC 77: 1949 FCR 842. Therefore, an order which is not final is not a judgment. To be a judgment, it must be a decision pronounced by a Court in a cause which it hears on the merits; *Hanskumar Kishan Chand* v. *Union of India,* AIR 1958 SC 947: 1959 SCJ 603: 1959 SCR 1177. Hence, the following were held not to be judgments – (i) The order of the Court for filing of an arbitration award, (ii) An order of the High Court in appeal from an award in an arbitration proceeding, (iii) The decision of the High Court in its consultative or advisory jurisdiction; *Commissioner of Income-tax, Bombay North, Kutch and Saurashtra* v. *Patel and Co., Jamnagar,* AIR 1960 SC 278 (280): (1959) 37 ITR 412.

5. Meaning of Decree

This word includes both preliminary and final decrees. Hence, appeal lies to the Supreme Court from both – *C.F. Rahimbhai* v. *Turner,* (1891) 15 Bom 155 PC;

See also *Sanyasi Charan Mandal* v. *Krishnadhan Banerji,* AIR 1922 PC 237: ILR 49 Cal 560: (1922) 49 IA 108. It may be noted that section 2(2) also defines decree as including preliminary decree.

6. Meaning and Scope of Final Order

The meaning and scope of 'final order' was examined by the Supreme Court in the case of *Tarapur & Co.* It laid down the following tests to be satisfied for an order to be final within the meaning under the present context – (a) it is not interlocutory, (b) it should not leave the original proceeding alive, (c) there should be a final determination of the rights of the parties See *Tarapore and Co., Madras* v. *V/O. Tractors Export, Moscow,* AIR 1970 SC 1168: (1969) 2 SCR 699: 1970 (1) SCJ 514; *Prem Chand* v. *State of Bihar,* 1960 SCR 199; *Jethanand & Sons* v. *State of Uttar Pradesh,* AIR 1961 SC 794: 1962 (1) SCJ 713: (1962) 3 SCR 751. Hence, in order to be final, the controversy raised in the suit or proceeding must be finally over; *Ramesh* v. *Gendalal Motilal Patni,* AIR 1966 SC 1445: 1966 (2) SCJ 152: (1966) 3 SCR 198.

Hence, no certificate under article 133(1) is available against the following orders.

(i) An order remanding a suit – *Abdul Rahman* v. *Cassim and Sons,* AIR 1933 PC 58: 60 IA 76.

(ii) An order in an execution petition for further proceeding holding that it is not barred by limitation or *res judicata* without deciding the case on merits – *Sindhuram Chaudhury* v. *Krishna Dutta,* AIR 1951 Assam 73: 55 C W N 219; *Daulat Ram Singh* v. *Swami Dayal,* AIR 1955 All 252: 1955 All LJ 59; *Basudevanand* v. *Raghubir Saran Rastogi,* AIR 1954 Pat 241: 1953 BLJR 623: 32 Pat 880; *Leelavati* v. *Ravi,* (1971) 3 SCC 790 (para 4).

But if the appellate court remands a suit after finally determining all the material issues directing the lower court to draw up a decree in terms of the order of remand, the order is final.

(iii) An order deciding a preliminary issue – *Syedna Taher Saifuddin Saheb* v. *State of Bombay,* AIR 1958 SC 253: 1958 SCJ 403: 1958 SCR 1007.

(iv) An order directing the lower court to entertain an application – *Velchata Rajeswara Rao* v. *Kalvakota Venkataramarao,* AIR 1961 AP 310: 1960 Andh LT 901: ILR (1961) 2 AP 449.

(v) An order setting aside an interim injunction in the suit *Tarapore and Co., Madras* v. *V/O. Tractors Export, Moscow,* AIR 1970 SC 1168: (1969) 2 SCR 699: 1970 (1) SCJ 514.

(vi) An order rejecting an application under section 5 of the Limitation Act; *State of Bihar* v. *Birla Gwalior P. Ltd.,* AIR 1974 Cal 202: 78 Cal WN 884.

(vii) An order allowing an application under Order IX, rule 13 of CPC; *Prakash Chand Agarwal* v. *Hindustan Steel Ltd.,* AIR 1971 SC 2319: (1971) 2 SCR 405: 1971 (2) SCJ 122.

(viii) An appellate order directing a scheme for management of the property in the suit under section 92 of CPC; *Haji Saleh Mohammed Ahmed Sait* v. *M. Enayatulla Mekhra,* AIR 1961 Mys 104: ILR 1959 Mys 1129.

(ix) An order rejecting an application for leave to appeal in *forma pauperis Jagat Ram* v. *Ganga,* AIR 1951 Punj 30: 53 PLR 19: 1951 Punj 185.

(x) An order setting aside a compromise decree and directing disposal of the suit on merit; *Yasin* v. *Himmat,* AIR 1952 Ajmer 15.

(xi) An order refusing to grant an interim injunction; *See* also *Union of India* v. *Gopal Singh,* (1967) 2 SCWR 639: (1967) SC (CA) 1635/66 dated 27-7-1967; *Gaya Electric Supply Co. Ltd.* v. *State of Bihar,* AIR 1951 Pat 619: ILR 30 Pat 853.

7. Article 134 of Constitution and Section 109 of CPC.—Definition of Judgment and Final Order

Calcutta High Court also examined the meaning and nature of the terms 'judgment', 'decree' and 'final order'. In the present case the petitioner who asks for a certificate under article 134(1)(c) of the Constitution was placed on his trial on a charge under section 366 of the Indian Penal Code and tried by the Assistant Sessions Judge of 24-Parganas with the help of a jury. As a result of the trial the jury brought in unanimous verdict of not guilty in favour of the petitioner and the learned Judge accepting the said verdict acquitted him. Against the order of acquittal one Indu Bhusan Roy Choudhury who describes himself as the father of the girl alleged to have been abducted filed a petition under section 430 of the Code of Criminal Procedure in this Court for setting aside the order of acquittal and obtained a Rule. The Rule was heard by a Division Bench which by a judgment dated January 25, 1961, has set aside the order of acquittal and directed that the petitioner be retried by an Additional Sessions Judge to be selected by the Sessions Judge of 24-Parganas. Against this order of the Division Bench the petitioner now intends to take a further appeal to the Supreme Court.

The words "judgment and final order" which occur in article 134(1) also occur in article 133(1) of the Constitution and section 109 of the Code of Civil Procedure and they also occurred in section 205 of the Government of India Act, 1935. In the case of *Firm Ramchand Manjimal* v. *Firm Goverdhandas Vishandas Ratanchand,* 47 Ind App 124: AIR 1920 PC 86: ILR 47 Cal 918, the Privy Council had to consider whether an order refusing to stay a suit under the Arbitration Act was a judgment or final order within the meaning of Section 109 of the Code of Civil Procedure, and answered that question in the negative. That decision was followed by Sir George Lowndes in the case of *Abdul Rahman* v *D.K. Cassim and Sons,* where the Privy Council had to consider the question whether an order of remand was a judgment or final order within the meaning of section 109 of the Code of Civil Procedure and again answered that question in the negative. These two decisions of the Privy Council were followed by Sulaiman, J., in the case of *Dr. Hari Ram Singh* v. *Emperor,* AIR 1939 FC 43: 40 Cr LJ 468. In this case the appellant before the Federal Court was placed on his trial under section 477A of the Indian Penal Code, and the appellant took the plea in the trial court that the prosecution was not maintainable in the absence of the sanction of the Governor under section 270 of the Government of India Act, 1935. The trial court upheld that plea and dismissed the prosecution case.

Against that order of the trial court the Crown filed an appeal before the Lahore High Court which held that no sanction of the Governor was necessary and directed a re-trial. The High Court, however, granted a certificate under section 205 of the Government of India Act. The point as to whether an appeal lay to the Federal Court against an order or re-trial was not raised by the respondent to the appeal but Sulaiman, J., raised the point for himself and considered the question whether the order appealed from was a judgment or final order within the meaning of section 205 of the Government of India Act After referring to the Privy Council Judgments and certain other English Authorities His Lordship made the following observations at page 48:

> "Thus, neither under the English nor the Indian Law the term 'judgment' in a criminal case includes an interlocutory order. In section 205(1) of the Act, the word 'judgment' does not occur by itself, but is used in conjunction with the final order. When both the terms judgment and final order are used together in one expression, they undoubtedly connote different and distinct meanings and judgment cannot be interpreted as embracing even interlocutory orders, which would make the category 'final order' wholly superfluous and unnecessary ...... I am of the opinion that the order of the High Court directing a rehearing of the criminal appeal by the Sessions Court is not a judgment within the meaning of section 205, Government of India Act".

The Court held that with great respect to the learned Judges who decided that case I am bound to say that this passage in no way supports the conclusion that an order directing retrial is a judgment within the meaning of article 134(1) of the Constitution. The passage clearly indicates that in order to be a judgment the order must terminate either in conviction or in acquittal and an order of re-trial does not certainly conform to that test if it had been necessary for us we would have referred this question to a Full Bench, because we are dissenting from the view taken by another Division Bench, but it is unnecessary, because, in our view, the decision in that case is contrary to the decisions of the Privy Council and also to the several decisions of the Federal Court and also of the Supreme Court.

The order sought to be appealed from in the present case does not terminate the case started against the petitioner as a result of the setting aside of the order of acquittal. The case against the petitioner revives and the trial will proceed in accordance with law. Such an order keeps alive the case and cannot be said to be a judgment or final order within the meaning of article 134(1) of the Constitution.

For the reasons given above, the Court refused to grant the certificate asked for by the petitioner and I dismiss this application; *Dilip Kumar Ghosh* v. *State*, AIR 1962 Cal 417: 1962 (2) Cr LJ 321.

The Punjab-Haryana High Court in the case of *State of Punjab* v. *Sodhi Sukhdev Singh*, AIR 1960 Punj 487: 62 Pun LR 514 also examined the meaning and nature of the terms, judgment and final order. This was an application under article 133 of the Constitution of India read with sections 109 and 110 and Order XLV, Code of Civil Procedure, for leave to appeal to the Supreme Court.

In a suit brought by *Sodhi Sukhdev Singh* against the State of Punjab the plaintiff summoned a number of documents from the defendant in respect of which privilege was claimed. The trial court upheld the privilege, but on revision we varied the order of the trial court with respect to some of the documents. With respect to those documents also it was expressly mentioned in the order passed by us that the question of their relevancy, if permissible under the law, was open to be raised by the Department in the trial court.

It was conceded by Dewan Chetan Das, Assistant Advocate-General that the order against which certificate of fitness for leave to appeal to the Supreme Court is sought is not a 'final order' within the contemplation of article 133 of the Constitution. He has, however, contended that our decision would certainly be a judgment and, therefore, it is competent for the Court to certify it to be a fit case for appeal to the Supreme Court under article 133. In support of his contention he has drawn our attention to *Central Brokers* v. *Ramnarayanan Poddar and Co.*, AIR 1954 Mad 1057: (1954) 2 Mad LJ 525: ILR 1954 Mad 1052. This case dealt with the meaning of the word "judgment" as used in clause 15 of the Letters Patent of the Madras High Court, but even in this case it has been held that an order made under section 10, Code of Civil Procedure, or any other provision of law, for the stay of trial of a suit, does not amount to a judgment so as to be appealable under clause 15 of the Letters Patent. The words "judgment, decree or final order" as used in article 133 appear to me to connote that the expression "judgment" must be taken in the same sense as the word "decree" in the Code of Civil Procedure and must be construed as meaning the declaration of final determination of the rights of the parties.

It was held that this reasoning fully applies to the construction to be placed on the words "judgment, decree or final order" occurring in article 133 of the Constitution.

The respondent has also drawn our attention to the fact that even with respect to the admission of these documents as evidence in the suit, the impugned order of this Court can obviously not be considered to be final, because their relevancy is yet to be determined by the trial court. I do not find it necessary to express any opinion on this contention, because independently of it, the order in question was neither a judgment nor a final order.

8. Meaning of Civil Proceeding

A Full Bench of the High Court of Kerala said that any proceeding involving the adjudication of a right to property or any other civil right would be a civil proceeding; *Dhanalakshmi Vilas Cashew Co.* v. *President, Cashew Industries Staff Association,* AIR 1962 Ker 1: 1961 Ker LJ 360: 1961 Ker LT 427 (FB).

A proceeding is a civil proceeding if it relates to a civil right, whether resting on, common law or created by statute; *S.A.L. Narayan Row* v. *Ishwarlal Bhagwandas,* AIR 1965 SC 1818 (1821): (1966) 1 SCR 190: 1965 (2) SCJ 359. The expression covers all proceedings which directly affect civil right; *Arbind Kumar Singh* v. *Nand Kishore Prasad,* AIR 1968 SC 1227: (1968) 3 SCR 322.

In *Ramesh* v. *Genda Lal,* it was held that a proceeding under article 226 of the constitution is a civil proceeding; *Ramesh* v. *Gendalal,* AIR 1966 SC 1445 (Supra).

Allahabad High Court in *Bhagwan Dass and Co. Private Ltd.* v. *Income-tax Officer, Dehradun*, AIR 1958 All 800: ILR (1958) 2 All 740 also examined the meaning and nature of the term 'civil proceeding'

This was an application for a certificate under articles 132 and 133 of the Constitution and sections 109 and 110 of the Code of Civil Procedure in respect of an order passed by this Court on 28th February, 1958, on a petition for issue of writs under article 226 of the Constitution. So far as article 132 of the Constitution is concerned, learned counsel for the applicant has not advanced any arguments at all to show that the case, which came up before this Court, or the appeal which is sought to be taken before the Supreme Court raises any substantial question of law as to the interpretation of the Constitution. Article 132 of the Constitution is, therefore, clearly not applicable.

There was another preliminary objection that this order was passed in proceedings which could not be held to be civil proceedings and this was an additional ground on account of which no certificate could be granted under article 133 of the Constitution or sections 109 and 110 of the Code of Civil Procedure but, because of the view we are taking on the first point, we have not considered it necessary to enter into this second point.

Under the Constitution, discretion was vested in the High Court to exercise its powers under article 226 of the Constitution and the procedure for exercising the powers was laid down in the Rules of Court. The Rules of Court required that an application should be made to this Court for exercising that discretionary power only by persons who were interested.

It was in this sense that the Court held that the petitioner in that case was entitled to move the Court for relief under article 226 of the Constitution. What the Court did was merely to say that, being a person interested, he was the appropriate person for moving the Court to exercise its discretion under article 226 of the Constitution and not to lay down that such a person had any legal right to move the Court and to claim issue of a writ, direction or order under article 226 of the Constitution, as of right, provided the merits of his claim justified it. In the circumstances, this decision does not go against the view which was taken by the Full Bench of this Court in the case of AIR 1951 All 746 (G), cited above.

In these circumstances, the Court held the view that the order, against which this application was moved, was not a judgment or a final order as it did not decide any right of the applicant in this Court, nor did it affect any right of the applicant which might have been the subject-matter of dispute before other authorities or Tribunals, in respect of which the applicant has been left to seek his remedy in accordance with the appropriate procedure provided by law. This application, therefore, was dismissed with costs which we fix at Rs. 150.

9. Certificate

The procedure for granting or refusing certificate by the High Court obtained for appeal to the Supreme Court is laid down in article 134A of the Constitution.

10. Nature of Certificate – Whether Conclusive

In the case of *Venkatramana* it was held that by article 133, the Supreme Court may entertain a preliminary objection that appeal does not lie before the Supreme Court. *Venkatramana* v. *State of Mysore,* AIR 1958 SC 258. Hence, the certificate is not conclusive in nature. The Supreme Court can examine imperative of the certificate granted by the High Court, whether the case fulfils the requirements of article 133 or not. The Court may refuse to entertain an appeal in spite of the certificate *Manehar* v. *Charanchandra,* AIR 1955 SC 258. In the case of *Nirod,* the Supreme Court examined the criteria for granting or refusing a certificate as stated by article 133 and section 109. The word "certifies" carries its normal dictionary meaning, but the criteria for granting or refusing a certificate has been subject of judicial scrutiny. In the case of *Nirod,* the Supreme Court said that the High Court, in determining whether certificate should be granted or should be refused, should be confined to two questions, namely whether the case involves a substantial question of law of general importance, and whether the question need to be decided by the Supreme Court. Thus, the Supreme Court stressed on strict compliance of the statutory requirements for entertaining a question of certificate; *Nirod* v. *Deputy Commissioner,* AIR 1980 SC 1109: 1980 BLJR 238: (1980) 3 SCC 5.

It may be noted here that the law requires the High Court to simplify, but at the same time, expressly state, while granting a certificate that the case involves a substantial question of law of general importance and that it needs to be decided by the Supreme Court. The High Court is not required to record reasons for arriving at the said conclusion. The law does not say that the High Court will grant certificate for reasons to be recorded.

However, in *Express Newspaper* v. *State of Madras,* AIR 1981 SC 968: (1981) 2 SCC 479: 1981 UJ (SC) 312, the Supreme Court held that the certificate must give reasons.

Substantial question of law is such a question of law which materially influences decision of a particular issue. If a particular view of the law is taken, it may turn the decision one way or the other. Then, all questions of law are not substantial question of law; See *Raghunath* v. *Deputy Commissioner,* AIR 1927 PC 101.

11. Power to Grant Certificate – Whether Mandatory

A Division Bench of the High Court of Calcutta held that even if all the tests are satisfied, the High Court may refuse certificate on the ground that the error may be corrected in a similar case in future by a special Bench. *State of West Bengal* v. *Somendra Kumar Mitra,* AIR 1975 Cal 335. The Shorter Construction of India Twelfth condition, the foot note of page 383 said that this decision seems to go to the other extreme and deserves a reconsideration.

12. The Case 'Involves'

Meaning of the term "involve" suggests that the question has been raised and decided, though not raised.

13. What is a Question of Law

The Supreme Court explained the meaning of the term 'law' and said that it is not restricted to statutory law. The term in the present context means the general law. The Supreme Court asked some case for example also. In the case of *Nafar*, the Court said that the legal effect of a proved fact is a question of law, *Nafar Chandra Pal* v. *Shankar*, AIR 1918 PC 92: 45 IC 183. In *Deshmukh* v. *Kothari*, 1951 (6) DLR SC 73 the Supreme Court said that application of section 18 of Limitation Act upon proved fact is a question of law. Whether a property is secular or debettar, or whether the defendant had accepted the mortgage deed, as a binding obligation upon himself are the cases of "question of law". See *Midnapur Zamindari Co. Ltd.* v. *Uma Charan Mandal*, AIR 1923 PC 187: 29 Cal WN 131, *Secretary of State* v. *Rameshwaram*, 1934 (61) IA 163.

14. A Substantial Question of Law

So that a question of law may be a "substantial question of law" it is necessary that there must be some doubt or difference of opinion. Then, if a law is well-settled by a Court of appeal or by an overwhelming consensus of judicial opinion, mere question of application of it to a particular set of facts is not a substantial question of law; *Chunnilal* v. *Century Spinning Co.*, AIR 1962 SC 1314: 65 Bom LR 267: 1963 Mah LJ 457. The scheme of the provisions in sections 100 and 109 are quite distinct. A second appeal lies under section 100, CPC if there involves a substantial question of law, whereas section 109 in agreement with article 133 of the constitution provides that an appeal shall lie before the Supreme Court only when there is not only a substantial question of law but such a question must also be of general importance. The Supreme Court has also said that Legislature has chosen not to qualify the scope of "substantial question of law" by suffering the words "of general importance"; *Boodireddy Chandraiah* v. *Arigela Laxami*, 2007 (9) SCR 1061: AIR 2008 SC 380: (2007) 1 SCALE 188.

15. "Of General Importance" – When it is

A question of law may be a substantial question for the parties to the litigation, but it may not be important for general public. Prior to 1973, the term occurred in connection with an affirmance of the decree. Hence, necessarily, it referred to the interest of the parties to litigation. But the Constitution (Thirtieth Amendment) Act, 1972 substituted the previous provisions with effect from 27.2 1973 and the term general importance was inserted. Now for grant of a certificate, the question of law not only should be substantial but it must also be of general importance which means that the question should not only be in the interest of the parties to litigation but also in the interest of general public; *State Bank of India* v. *N. Sundera Mani*, AIR 1976 SC 1111: (1976) 1 SCC 822: (1976) 3 SCR 160.

A Full Bench of the High Court of Rajasthan and also the High Court of Patna made it clear that in order to be of general importance, it must affect a large number of persons or a number of pending proceedings, involving the same question. See *Cf. Gulab Bai* v. *Mst. Manphool Bai*, AIR 1953 Raj 42: ILR (1952) 2 Raj 755 (FB); *Lachhman Prasad Bhagat* v. *Government of Bihar*, AIR 1952 Pat 386: ILR 30 Pat 1252: 1952 Cr LJ 1639.

16. Question Needs to be Decided by the Supreme Court – Meaning and Scope of

Prior to the amendment (Thirtieth Amendment) of 1972 the expression was "The case is a fit one for appeal to the Supreme Court", but such a condition was required where value test was satisfied. Thus, the condition operated only when the value test was not satisfied. If these tests were satisfied then a certificate could be issued on a question of fact also. Now, See *Kutoor Vengayil Rayarappen Nayanar Karnavan of Kullon Vengayil Tarwad* v. *Kutoor Vengayil Valiyu Madhavi Amma,* AIR 1950 Mad 215: (1949) 2 Mad LJ 601.

The word 'need' suggests that there must be some imperative necessity arising from the facts and circumstances of the case that there should be decision of the question by the Supreme Court. *Mathur* v. *Commissioner,* 1973 (2) Del 266.

A Full Bench of the High Court of Delhi also examined the nature and meaning of the term 'needs to be' in the case of Union of India and held that where two views are possible regarding the question and the High Court whose certificate is sought for has taken one of said two views, the matter is one which 'needs to be decided by the Supreme Court; *Union of India* v. *Hafiz Mohd. Said, Delhi,* AIR 1975 Del 77: 1975 Pun LR (D) 275: ILR (1973) 2 Del 673 (FB).

The said Bench also brought into the purview, a case where two High Courts held different views.

17. Appeal Direct to the Supreme Court – Whether Permissible

The Supreme Court has made it clear that rights of appeal before it refers to appeals under articles 132 and 133 against any judgment, decree or final order of the High Court, other conditions being satisfied. The appellant could not directly approach the Supreme Court against orders of the District Court; *Shin-Etsu Chemical Co. Ltd.* v. *Vindhya Telelinks Ltd.,* AIR 2009 SC 3284: 2009 AIR SCW 3433: (2009) 5 SCALE 273.

18. Articles 133 & 137 – Expunging of Adverse Remarks

The Supreme Court held that the remark based on pleadings and necessity to decide this controversy in issue may not be expressed; *State of Madhya Pradesh* v. *Narmada Bachao Andolan,* AIR 2012 SC 260: 2011 AIR SCW 6175: (2011) 11 SCALE 260.

19. Articles 133, 136, 226 and Section 109, CPC – New Plea in Appeal before Supreme Court

A recovery proceeding was launched by the Bank. The property was sold in auction. An appeal filed before the Board of Revenue was allowed. A petition was filed against the Sales Officer. The auction purchaser did not question the findings of facts before the Board of Revenue. The question arose whether he could raise the question of fact for the first time before the Supreme Court. The Court held that the auction purchaser could not do; *Kishorilal* v. *Sales Officer,* (2006) 7 SCC 796: JT 2006 (8) SC 200.

20. Sections 109 and 112—Permissibility Interference in Concurrent Finding of Fact

The question relating to proper inference of law to be deducted on the basis of the facts of the case.—Interference by Supreme Court is permissible.

Bejoy Gopal Mukherji v. *Pratul Chandra Ghose,* AIR 1953 SC 153: 1953 SCJ 195: 1953 SCR 930.

21. Right of Appeal to the Supreme Court

The High Court of Punjab-Haryana in *Gulzari Lal* v. *The Swadeshi Mills Ltd., Bombay,* AIR 1952 P&H 379 examined the right of appeal to the Supreme Court. Two applications were filed for the similar purpose. The points also involved in both the applications were the same and, therefore, they were disposed of by one judgment. It is submitted by the learned counsel for the petitioner that the petitioner firm, Gopal Rai Gulzari Mal, have got some cases pending in the Subordinate Judge's Court and if we add the amounts involved in those cases to the amounts involved in the present applications the subject-matter of appeal will be more than Rs. 10,000 and he, therefore, submitted that as the judgments of this Court are judgments of variance he is, under section 110 of the Code of Civil Procedure, entitled, as a matter of right, to go in appeal to the Supreme Court, because the decree indirectly involves claim or question to or respecting property of more than Rs. 10,000. But, according to section 110, Civil Procedure Code, before the Constitution a person could go, as a matter of right, in appeal to the Federal Court if the subject-matter of the suit in the Court of the first instance was Rs. 10,000 or over and the amount of the subject-matter in dispute on appeal was also the same. In the present cases, there is no doubt that the subject-matter of suit was in the one suit about Rs. 5,000 and in the other about Rs. 9,800. So, the first condition is not fulfilled even if the petitioner is entitled to rely on section 110, Civil Procedure Code, as it was before the coming into operation of the Constitution.

It may here be pointed put that in the appeal against which Civil Miscellaneous No. 291C of 1950 was directed, this Court found on a question of fact that Note No. 2 in the Textile Commissioner's order of the 31st of October, 1943, does not apply to the 15 bales (which were in dispute) which were to be delivered in July and the maximum prices mentioned in the order of the Textile Commissioner therefore did not apply to these 15 bales. It was further held by this Court that there was a contract to make delivery in July to which the Textile Commissioner's order does not apply. After giving this finding, the question was further discussed whether the word 'dealer' also included the word 'manufacturer'. The judgment of this Court therefore proceeded not merely on the interpretation of a section but also on facts as to whether delivery was to be made before or after July.

The Court said that in regard to the appeal which was dealt with in Civil Miscellaneous No. 292C of 1950, again the case was primarily decided on its peculiar facts. At page 6 of the judgment my learned brother Soni, J., said that as the price was fixed in December 1943 the section would not be applicable and no refund was allowable. Here again the question of a manufacturer not being included in the word 'dealer' was subsequently discussed. This case also therefore was decided on the peculiar facts of this case and no question of law really arose. In my opinion, the petitions do not fall under section 109(c) or second clause of section 110 of the Code of Civil Procedure and are therefore dismissed with costs.

22. Section 109 and article 133—Nature of 'Award'

The Madras High Court examined the nature of the term 'award' in the case of *T.S. Krishnamoorti.*

The Court said, "The discussion of the above cases has resulted in a number of very nice points being argued, and we are much obliged to the learned Counsel for the help they have given us in the consideration of those cases, which we should have deemed it our duty very carefully to have analysed, had it not appeared that this preliminary objection can be upheld on a much shorter and simpler point. In *Mahant Bagavathi Das* v. *Sarangaraja Iyengar,* 33 LW 528: 135 Ind Cas 460; *Bagavathi Das Bavaji* v. *Sarangaraja Iyengar*, AIR 1931 Mad 586: 61 MLJ 312: 54 M 722: (1931) MWN 290: Ind Rul (1932) Mad 140, it was decided by a Bench of this High Court that the Court, at least when it was constituted by the appointment of a Special Judicial Officer under the provisions of section 3(d), was a special Court, that is to say it was not an ordinary Civil Court but a Court established under the provisions of the Act. From which it follows, and it was there so decided, that no appeal lies from such a Court unless by statute the right to appeal is given. In this statute a right of appeal is given in one class of cases, and in one class of cases only, that is to say, where the Court arrives at the decision that amounts to an award. As was pointed out by the Privy Council in *Ramchandra Rao* v. *Ramchandra Rao,* AIR 1922 PC 80: 49 IA 129: 23 ALJ 684: 43 MLJ 78: 24 Bom LR 963 (PC) (329) Page of 45 M.—[Ed.]:"

There are two perfectly separate and distinct forms of procedure contemplated by the Land Acquisition Act. The first is that necessary for fixing the amount of the compensation and this is described as being an award.

The Court held that the present decision is clearly not an award and it appears to us that whatever you call it, it is a decision of a Court specially constituted under statutory authority and unless from that decision the right to appeal is given, no right to appeal lies. It might well be that it would be otherwise if the Court in question were an ordinary Civil Court to which this matter, the matter in dispute had been under powers conferred by the statute, referred for decision by the proper authority. That, however, is not the scheme of the Act. The scheme of the Act contemplates that sometimes the Court shall be an ordinary Civil Court and sometimes a special Court specially constituted. In the latter case, except where the Court makes an award, the Act does not make any statutory provision for appeals from that Court. And on this short ground we are of the opinion that the objection succeeds. We desire, however, to observe that the result is unsatisfactory in our opinion. Although it might well be in the contemplation of the Legislature that preliminary points, such as those falling under section 49, that is to say, those that are the subject-matter of this present appeal, should not be appealable, it is difficult to believe that it was the intention of the Legislature to prevent persons disputing as to the right property, as might well be the case where an award having been made and money due under that award paid into Court, various claimants come forward claiming that money as their and endeavouring to establish, in support of that claim, title to the subject-matter in respect of which the compensation was paid into Court, it is difficult to imagine that it was intended to shut out all such claimants from all rights of appeal, where the Court in question was a Court specially constituted and not an ordinary Court though this result appears to follow when the Court is a special Court from which no appeal lies unless there be a statutory provision to that effect. This, however, as was pointed out in *Mahant Bagavthi Das* v. *Sarangaraja Iyenger,* AIR 1931 Mad 586: 61 MLJ 312: 54 M 722: (1932) Mad 140, may result in an anomaly, but one that can only be put right by the legislature if the legislature thinks fit so to do.

Thus, the preliminary objection succeeded and the appeal was accordingly dismissed with costs. *T.S. Krishnamoorthi Ayyar* v. *Special Deputy Collector of Land,* 165 Ind Cas 405.

23. Section 109 Appeal – Entry in the Mutation Records

In *Atin Kundu Chowdhury* v. *State of West Bengal,* (SC) Civil Appeal No. 3 of 2016. D/d. 4.1.2016. the present appeal, by special leave, was directed against the order dated 05.12.2012 passed by the High Court at Calcutta in W.P.L.R.T. No.279 of 2012 whereby the High Court has concurred with the view recorded by the West Bengal Land Reforms Tenancy Tribunal in O.A. No.1783 of 2009 whereby it has upheld the order passed by the appellate authority who has affirmed the recording of the mutation entry in favour of the 5th respondent herein.

The Supreme Court said, we have been apprised by Mr. Soumitra Ghosh Chaudhury, learned counsel appearing for the State that the judgment and decree passed in the civil suit is under assail in an appeal. At this juncture, we have also been told that the appellants who have entered into an agreement for sale have instituted a civil suit for specific performance of contract in the year 2005.

In these circumstances, the question that arises for consideration is whether the Revenue Tribunal as well as the High Court is justified in upholding the entry in the mutation records.

6. Having heard, learned counsel for the parties, in our considered opinion the cause of justice would be best sub-served if the mutation entry is maintained subject to the final decision in the suit which has been instituted by the plaintiff for specific performance of the contract. If eventually the suit is decreed, the appellants can claim for mutation of the suit land in their favour. Needless to say, their right to remain in possession has been protected by the judgment and decree passed in Title Suit No.40 of 2005. In case, the verdict in the Title Suit is reversed in the appeal which is stated to have been filed, it will affect only the possessory rights of the appellants. The possession shall be governed by the result of the suit filed by the plaintiff's.

Cause of justice would be best sub served if the mutation entry is maintained subject to final decision in the suit which has been instituted by plaintiff for specific performance of contract - If eventually the suit is decreed, the appellants can be claim for mutation of the suit land in their favour Their right to remain in possession has been protected by the judgment and decree passed in Title suit. Thus, the appeal was modified.

ARTICLE 133 OF CONSTITUTION OF INDIA

The provisions of section 109 and article 133 being identical to each other, a short study of the provisions of article 133 must complement to the views of section 109.

Article 133.—**Appellate jurisdiction of Supreme Court in appeals from High Courts in regard to civil matters**

(1) An appeal shall lie to the Supreme Court from any judgment, decree or final order in a civil proceeding of a High Court in the territory of India if the High Court certifies under article 134A

(a) that the case involves a substantial question of law of general importance; and

(b) that in the opinion of the High Court the said question needs to be decided by the Supreme Court

(2) Notwithstanding anything in article 132, any party appealing to the Supreme Court under clause (1) may urge as one of the grounds in such appeal that a substantial question of law as to the interpretation of this Constitution has been wrongly decided

(3) Notwithstanding anything in this article, no appeal shall, unless Parliament by law otherwise provides, lie to the Supreme Court from the judgment, decree or final order of one Judge of a High Court.

SYNOPSIS

Comments

1. Appellate Jurisdiction of Supreme Court of India

Certain aspects of the provision have already been studied earlier along with the provisions of section 109 of CPC. The appellate jurisdiction of the Supreme Court can be invoked by a certificate granted by the High Court concerned under article 132(1), 133(1) or 134 of the Constitution in respect of any judgement, decree or final order of a High Court in both civil and criminal cases, involving substantial questions of law as to the interpretation of the Constitution. Appeals also lie to the Supreme Court in civil matters if the High Court concerned certifies: (a) that the case involves a substantial question of law of general importance, and

(b) that, in the opinion of the High Court, the said question needs to be decided by the Supreme Court. In criminal cases, an appeal lies to the Supreme Court if the High Court (a) has on appeal reversed an order of acquittal of an accused person and sentenced him to death or to imprisonment for life or for a period of not less than 10 years, or (b) has withdrawn for trial before itself any case from any Court subordinate to its authority and has in such trial convicted the accused and sentenced him to death or to imprisonment for life or for a period of not less than 10 years, or (c) certifies that the case is a fit one for appeal to the Supreme Court. Parliament is authorised to confer on the Supreme Court any further powers to entertain and hear appeals from any judgment, final order or sentence in a criminal proceeding of a High Court.

The Supreme Court has also a very wide appellate jurisdiction over all Courts and Tribunals in India in as much as it may, in its discretion, grant special leave to appeal under article 136 of the Constitution from any judgment, decree, determination, sentence or order in any cause or matter passed or made by any Court or Tribunal in the territory of India.

2. Appeals Permitted under the Constitution

Article 132 of the Constitution of India, 1950 provides for an appeal to the Supreme Court from any judgment, decree or final order of a High Court, whether in civil, criminal or other proceedings, if the High Court certifies that the case involves a substantial question of law as to the interpretation of the Constitution.

Article 133 of the Constitution of India, 1950 provides for an appeal to the Supreme Court from any judgment, decree or final order in a civil proceeding of a High Court if the High Court certifies that the case involves a substantial question of law of general importance and in its opinion the said question needs to be decided by the Supreme Court.

The appellate jurisdiction of the Supreme Court can be invoked by a certificate granted by the High Court concerned under articles 132(1), 133(1) or 134 of the Constitution in respect of any judgement, decree or final order of a High Court in both civil and criminal cases, involving substantial questions of law as to the interpretation of the Constitution.

Appeals also lie to the Supreme Court in civil matters if the High Court concerned certifies: (a) that the case involves a substantial question of law of general importance, and (b) that, in the opinion of the High Court, the said question needs to be decided by the Supreme Court. In criminal cases, an appeal lies to the Supreme Court if the High Court (a) has on appeal reversed an order of acquittal of an accused person and sentenced him to death or to imprisonment for life or for a period of not less than 10 years, or (b) has withdrawn for trial before itself any case from any Court subordinate to its authority and has in such trial convicted the accused and sentenced him to death or to imprisonment for life or for a period of not less than 10 years, or (c) certifies that the case is a fit one for appeal to the Supreme Court. Parliament is authorised to confer on the Supreme Court any further powers to entertain and hear appeals from any judgement, final order or sentence in a criminal proceeding of a High Court. The Supreme Court has also a very wide appellate jurisdiction over all Courts and Tribunals in India in as much as it may, in its discretion, grant special leave to appeal under article 136 of the Constitution from any judgment, decree, determination, sentence or order in any cause or matter passed or made by any Court or Tribunal in the territory of India.

3. Article 133—Scope

The Supreme Court examined a case on the issue being *Puran Lal Sah* v. *State of Uttar Pradesh,* AIR 1971 SC 712: (1971) 3 SCR 468: 1971 Civ App J (SC) 88. Appeal was preferreed from the judgment and decree dated March 8, 1965 of the Allahabad High Court in First Appeal No. 84 of 1954. The Judgment of the Court was delivered by P. Jaganmohan Reddy, J. This appeal is by a certificate under article 133(1)(a) of the Constitution against the judgment and decree of the Allahabad High Court dated 8th March, 1965 setting aside the decree of the trial court and dismissing the suit of the, plaintiff-appellant. The appellant had submitted a tender to construct mile 3 of Nainital-Bhowali Road at 13 per cent below the rates given in Schedule B to the notice issued by the Government of the United Provinces on the 30th September, 1946. This tender was accepted and a contract was signed on 20th November, 1946. It is alleged by the appellant that the rates given in Schedule B were based, on the calculation that stone required for the road construction work would be available at a distance of 26 chains while as a matter of fact no stone was available within that distance. The appellant had in fact to get stone from Gadhera and Bhumadar from a distance of 79 and 110 chains respectively. It is his contention that by reason of the non-availability of the stone and the definite understanding and assurance given by the local authorities of the P.W.D. that higher rates would be given for the extra work done, over and above the work provided in the contract he carried on the work. It was also alleged that during the construction work, on the road very hard shale rock came in the way most originally provided for in the contract, as such he was entitled to get the costs for the work so done at the current rates from the P.W.D. which was not paid to him. In respect of these items of work done as also due to his having done the work by bringing stone from a longer distance than was given in the estimates the appellant claimed Rs. 48,840 due as balance together with interest by way of damages at 12% amounting to Rs. 17,582, making a total of Rs. 66,422.

The Public Works Department of the respondent-State had issued a tender notice for the construction of a road. The appellant inspected the site, went to the place where stone for the construction was said to be available, and after satisfying himself submitted a tender below the estimates in the tender notice. It was accepted and a contract was signed. The estimates in the tender notice were prepared by the P.W.D. on the basis that stone was available at a distance of 26 chains from the work spot. In fact, stone was available at that distance in the Cantonment area but for its removal permission of the Cantonment authorities had to be taken. The appellant was not able to obtain the necessary permission and so, he bad to get the stone from a Much longer distance. He requested for a higher rate but his request was rejected. Thereafter, he commenced work, and after the work was completed the Executive Engineer recommended his case for a higher rate.

By a subsidiary contract the appellant undertook to execute some additional work for the department. The quantity of work which the appellant actually performed was far in excess of what was mentioned in the contract. He claimed a higher rate of payment for such extra work also. Since he did not get the higher rates he claimed, he filed a suit which was dismissed by the High Court in appeal. Hence, the appeal was filed before the Supreme Court. After examining the scope of appeal it was held:

(1) (a) In none of the clauses of the tender notice or conditions of contract or in any other document was there any assurance that if stone was not available at the distance of 26 chains the appellant would be paid higher rates. It was for the appellant to have satisfied himself before entering into the contract that the Cantonment authorities would permit him to take the stone. Since be commenced work after his request for higher rate was rejected, it could not be said that the appellant was in any way induced by any assurance. The Executive Engineer's letter was only recommendatory and did not establish any right to obtain a higher rate. [472 G-H; 473 G-H; 475 C.] (b) It could not be said that once stone was not available at a distance, of 26 chains, the contract was at an end and that because the appellant had done the work, he should be paid on the basis of quantum meruit. That remedy would be available only when the original contract had been discharged by the defendant in such a way as to entitle the plaintiff to regard himself as discharged from any further performance, and be elects to do so; but, where work is done under a contract pursuant to its terms no amount can be claimed by way of quantum meruit; *Alopi Parshad and Sons Ltd.* v. *Union of India*, AIR 1960 SC 588: (1960) 2 SCR 793: 1960 SCJ 763, followed.

(2) On the second item also the appellant could not succeed, because of clause 12 of the contract. Under the clause the appellant was bound to perform all additional work which was required of him on the same terms and conditions in which be undertook to do the main work. Further, paragraph 5 of the special instructions which formed part and parcel of the original contract provided that unless he gave notice that he was not prepared to do any extra work in excess of the quantity of the work mentioned in the contract plus 30 per cent of that quantity of work, and settled fresh rates for such extra work over 30 per cent, the appellant could not claim anything other than the rates mentioned in the contract.

4. Article 133 read with Article 134A – Grant of Certificate of Leave

In *Muniyamma* v. *Anitha Vaz*, 2017 (6) SCALE 502 (SC) the Supreme Court examined the question of grant of leave for appeal to it. In the case under reference the learned counsel appearing for the respondent stated that the sale deed has been executed and registered before the Trial Court pursuant to impugned judgment in respondent's favour in relation to suit property and, therefore, the appeal has been rendered as infructuous.

The Apex Court said, even otherwise, we find that this Court, vide order dated 21.08.2008 had issued Show Cause Notice to the respondent confining it to examine the question as to why the order granting leave by the High Court be not revoked.

We find that the learned Single Judge, in the present case, had granted certificate of leave under Articles 133 read with Article 134-A of the Constitution of India to the appellant to file this appeal. The said article , in our view, specifically prohibits learned Single Judge of the High Court to grant leave as has been held by this Court in *State Bank of India* v. *S.B.I. Employees' Union*, 1987 (4) SCC 370: AIR 1987 SC 2203 and followed by this Court in Civil Appeal No. 5817 of 2012 entitled *Agnigundala Venkata Ranga Rao* v. *Indukuru Ramchandra Reddy (Dead)* by L.Rs. (dated 13.04.2017).

Since this Court has confined the issue of notice of this appeal only for limited purpose to examine the issue of grant of leave by the High Court and the same having been decided against the appellant supra, we are not inclined to examine the merits of the case by invoking our powers under ***Article*** 136 of the Constitution once we revoke the grant of leave by the High Court.

5. Articles 133, 134A and 136 – Grant of Leave to Appeal to Supreme Court

In *Agnigundala Venkata Ranga Rao* v. *Indukuru Ramachandra Reddy (Dead) by Lrs.*, AIR 2017 SC 2042: 2017 (6) JT 11: 2017 (3) JLJR 61 (SC), the this appeal was filed on a certificate granted by the High Court (Single Judge) on the oral application made by the appellant immediately after the pronouncement of the impugned judgment as provided under Article 134A of the Constitution. The order granting certificate is a part of the impugned judgment in its concluding Para which reads thus:

> *"Learned counsel for the respondent seeks leave of this Court to prefer an appeal against this judgment.*
>
> *Accordingly, leave is granted."*

What is the true interpretation of Articles 133 and 134-A of the Constitution and who can grant the certificate of fitness to appeal to the Supreme Court remains no more *res integra*. It is settled by the decision of this Court in *State Bank of India* v. *S.B.I. Employees' Union*, 1987 (4) SCC 370: AIR 1987 SC 2203.

19. The facts of this case and the one involved in the *SBI case (supra)* are somewhat similar wherein Their Lordships examined the issue as to whether the certificate granted by the High Court (Single Judge) satisfied the requirements contained in Articles 133 and 134-A. Justice Venkataramiah (as His Lordship then was and later became CJI) speaking for the Bench held thus:

> "2. The certificate contemplated under Article 134-A of the Constitution can only be a certificate which is referred to in clause (1) of Article 132 or in clause (1) of Article 133 or in sub-clause (c) of clause (1) of Article 134 of the Constitution. This is quite obvious from the language of Article 134-A of the Constitution. This case does not fall either under Article 132(1) or under sub-clause (c) of Article 134(1) as it neither involves a substantial question of law as to the interpretation of the Constitution nor it is a criminal proceeding. It can only fall, if at all, under Article 133 (1) of the Constitution. Article 133 of the Constitution reads thus:
>
> "***133*** . (1) An appeal shall lie to the Supreme Court from any judgment, decree or final order in a civil proceeding of a High Court in the territory of India if the High Court certifies under Article 134-A-(a) that the case involves a substantial question of law of general importance; and

(b) that in the opinion of the High Court the said question needs to be decided by the Supreme Court.

(2) Notwithstanding anything in Article 132, any party appealing to the Supreme Court under clause (1) may urge as one of the grounds in such appeal that a substantial question of law as to the interpretation of this Constitution has been wrongly decided.

(3) Notwithstanding anything in this article , no appeal shall, unless Parliament by law otherwise provides, lie to the Supreme Court from the judgment, decree or final order of one judge of a High Court."

3. Clause (3) of Article 133 says that notwithstanding anything in that article no appeal shall, unless Parliament by law otherwise provides, lie to the Supreme Court from the judgment, decree or final order of one judge of the High Court. Before the introduction of Article 134-A of the Constitution by the Forty-fourth Amendment of the Constitution there was no express provision in Articles 132, 133 and 134 of the Constitution regarding the time and manner in which an application for a certificate under any of those articles could be made before the High Court. There was also a doubt as to the power of the High Court to issue a certificate suo motu under any of those articles. Article 134A was enacted to make good the said deficiencies. Article 134-A does not constitute an independent provision under which a certificate can be issued. It is ancillary to Article 132(1), Article 133 (1) and Article 134(1)(c) of the Constitution. That is the reason for the use of words "if the High Court certifies under Article 134-A" in Article 132(1) and Article 133 (1) and for the use of the words certifies under Article 134-A in Article 134(1)(c). The High Court can issue a certificate only when it is satisfied that the conditions in Article 132 or Article 133 or Article 134 of the Constitution as the case may be are satisfied. In the instant case such a certificate could not have been issued by reason of clause (3) of Article 133 of the Constitution by the learned Single Judge.

4. The fact that in a similar case a certificate had been issued by a Division Bench of the High Court consisting of two judges in a case decided by the Division Bench did not empower the Single Judge to issue the certificate under Article 133 (1) of the Constitution in a case decided by him. The restriction placed by clause (3) of Article 133 of the Constitution could not be got over by relying upon the order of the Division Bench.

5. We, therefore, revoke the certificate. This petition of appeal may, however, be treated as a special leave petition under Article 136 of the Constitution and posted for preliminary hearing."

The Court held, in our considered opinion, the law laid down in *S.B.I case (supra)* would squarely apply to the case at hand because in the instant case also, the impugned judgment and the certificate of fitness to file an appeal was passed by the Single Judge of the High Court.

21. As held in S.B.I. case, such certificate/leave could not have been issued/granted by the Single Judge by reason of clause (3) of Article 133 of

the Constitution. In other words, the Single Judge of the High Court had no jurisdiction to grant certificate in the light of restrictions contained in clause (3) of Article 133 of the Constitution.

6. Article 136 – Question of Facts

In this case (*supra*) the Court held, One cannot dispute the legal proposition being well settled that the question as to who is in possession of the suit property is essentially a question of fact. Such question is required to be decided on appreciation of evidence adduced by the parties in support of their respective contentions. Once the Trial Court renders a finding either way and the same is then appreciated by the first appellate Court in exercise of its appellate jurisdiction, such finding is usually held binding on the second appellate Court and this Court.

It is only when such finding of fact is found to be against the pleading or evidence or any provision of law or when it is found to be so perverse or/ and arbitrary to the extent that no judicial person of an average capacity can ever record, the same would not be binding on the higher Courts and may in appropriate case call for interference.

Coming to the facts of the case, we are of the considered opinion, that the appellant (plaintiff) simply abused the process of law in filing the suit for permanent injunction in relation to the suit land against the respondents. The suit, in our opinion, was misconceived and deserved dismissal on facts and in law on the grounds, which are indeed apparent on the face of the record of the case as mentioned below.

7. Article 133 Counter-claim Regarding Ownership – Legality of Remand of Matter to Trial Court

In *Nirmala Devi* v. *Gurgaon Scheduled Caste Vimukta Agricutlure Thrift and Credit Society Limited,* (SC) (Civil Appeal Nos. 8716-8717 of 2017 (Arising out of S.L.P (C) Nos.27029-27030 of 2016). D/d. 7.7.2017.) Mr. S.R. Singh, learned senior counsel for the appellant has drawn our attention to paragraph 10 of a two-Judge Bench decision in *P. Purushottam Reddy* v. *Pratap Steels Ltd.,* 2002 (2) RCR (Civil) 70: (2002) 2 SCC 686. The said paragraph reads as follows:—

> "The next question to be examined is the legality and propriety of the order of remand made by the High Court. Prior to the insertion of Rule 23A in Order XLI of the Code of Civil Procedure by CPC Amendment Act 1976, there were only two provisions contemplating remand by a court of appeal in Order XLI of CPC. Rule 23 applies when the trial court disposes of the entire suit by recording its findings on a preliminary issue without deciding other issues and the finding on preliminary issue is reversed in appeal. Rule 25 applies when the appellate court notices an omission on the part of the trial court to frame or try any issue or to determine any question of fact which in the opinion of the appellate court was essential to the right decision of the suit upon the merits. However, the remand contemplated by Rule 25 is a limited remand in as much as the subordinate court can try only such issues as are referred to it for trial and having done so, the evidence recorded, together with findings

and reasons therefore of the trial court, are required to be returned to the appellate court. However, still it was a settled position of law before 1976 Amendment that the court, in an appropriate case could exercise its inherent jurisdiction under Section 151 of the CPC to order a remand if such a remand was considered pre-eminently necessary *ex debito justitiate,* though not covered by any specific provision of Order XLI of the CPC. In cases where additional evidence is required to be taken in the event of any one of the clauses of sub-rule (1) of Rule 27 being attracted, such additional evidence oral or documentary, is allowed to be produced either before the appellate court itself or by directing any court subordinate to the appellate court to receive such evidence and send it to the appellate court. In 1976, Rule 23 A has been inserted in Order XLI which provides for a remand by an appellate court hearing an appeal against a decree if (i) the trial court disposed of the case otherwise than on a preliminary point, and (ii) the decree is reversed in appeal and a retrial is considered necessary. On twin conditions being satisfied, the appellate court can exercise the same power of remand under Rule 23A as it is under Rule 23. After the amendment, all the cases of wholesale remand are covered by Rule 23 and 23 A. In view of the express provision of these rules, the High Court cannot have recourse to its inherent powers to make a remand because, as held in *Mahendra* v. *Sushila,* AIR 1965 SC 365 (399), it is well settled that inherent powers can be availed of *ex debito justiatiate* only in the absence of express provisions in the Code. It is only in exceptional cases where the court may now exercise the power of remand de hors the Rules 23 and 23A. To wit, the superior court, if it finds that the judgment under appeal has not disposed of the case satisfactorily in the manner required by Order XX Rule 3 or Order XLI Rule 31 of the CPC and hence it is no judgment in the eye of law, it may set aside the same and send the matter back for re-writing the judgment so as to protect valuable rights of the parties. An appellate court should be circumspect in ordering a remand when the case is not covered either by Rule 23 or Rule 23A or Rule 25 of the CPC. An unwarranted order of remand gives the litigation an undeserved lease of life and, therefore, must be avoided."

The Supreme Court said, in this context, we may also refer to a decision in *Nedunuri Kameswaramma* v. *Sampati Subba Rao* AIR 1963 SC 884: 1963 (2) AnWR 49, wherein it has been held that 'where the parties were fully aware about the rival case and led the evidence not only in support of their contentions but in refutation of those of the other side, it cannot be said that the absence of an issue was fatal to the case, or that there was that mis-trial which vitiates proceedings.' We have referred to this judgment solely for the purpose of the counter claim. As we have noted earlier, the issue pertained to denial of the ownership of the plaintiff and assertion of the same by the defendants and, therefore, the plaintiff was well aware that there was refutation of the claim. The counter claim was not, in that way, an independent claim.

In view of the aforesaid, the High Court should have been well advised to dwell upon the merits of the case and should not have remanded the matter to the trial court.

Resultantly, the appeals are allowed, the judgment and order passed by the High Court is set aside and the High Court is requested to adjudicate the Second Appeal in accordance with law. As we are remanding the matter, the parties shall maintain status quo, existing as on today, till the Second Appeal is decided by the High Court. There shall be no order as to costs.

8. Constitution Article 133 – Civil Procedure Code, Order XXXIX, Rules 1 and 2

In *Dev Prakash* v. *Indra*, 2017 (6) SCALE 450: AIR 2017 SC 3808 the Court considered the recorded facts to the extent necessary at this stage as well as the rival contentions. The order indeed presents certain discomfiting features. To reiterate, the property involved is the subject matter, amongst others of the aforementioned suit and the appeals before the High Court, all of which are presently pending. There is a dispute inter alia, as to whether this property is an asset of the partnership firm in question. Prayer for declaration of the title thereto and rendition of accounts, as made by the respondents/plaintiffs is pending scrutiny of the Trial Court. Not only an order of injunction has been passed by the Trial Court, noticing the nature and extent of the lingering controversy revolving around the suit property, it has also construed it to be expedient to appoint a receiver to keep the same in its custody, pending final resolution of the *lis* in accordance with law.

The impugned order, to start with, has been passed at an interim stage pending the disposal of the appeals assailing the order of injunction and appointment of receiver. It does not record any convincing reason for electing the course of disposal of the suit property in this overwhelming background, by public auction. Not only, this initiative has the potential of possible annihilation of the suit property, the purported justification cited that such an auction would facilitate determination and realisation of the current fair market value and that appointment of receiver would unnecessarily put the suit property in disuse, is wholly indefensible. Noticeably, the High Court not only had estimated the value of the suit property at Rs. 2 crores, it had directed amongst others, that the said amount be quoted as the minimum reserve price in the auction notice to be issued. It has directed as well that a committee, as suggested by it, be constituted to conduct the court auction and also to submit a report with regard thereto, to it. Direction thereby has also been issued to the appellants/defendants to hand over the peaceful and vacant possession of the suit premises to the highest bidder/auction purchaser on the completion of the exercise.

In the preponderant factual backdrop, as outlined herein above, we are of the view that not only the reasons endeavoured to be cited in the impugned order in justification of the direction for public auction of the suit property lack in persuasion, those are apparently speculative and illogical, to say the least. The direction for disposal of the suit property by public auction, in the facts and circumstances of the case, clearly militates against the fundamental precept of preservation of subject matter of any dispute pending adjudication in a court of law, more particularly relatable to a civil litigation, to appropriately decide on the rights of the parties for administering the reliefs to which they would be entitled eventually on the culmination of the adjudication. As it is, the very essence of the concept of temporary injunction and receivership during the pendency of a civil litigation involving any property is to prevent its threatened wastage, damage and alienation by any party thereto, to the immeasurable prejudice to the other side or to render the situation irreversible not only to impact upon the ultimate decision but also to render the relief granted, illusory. We do not wish to burden this order by the decisions of this Court on the issue except referring to the one in *Maharwal Khewaji Trust (Regd.) Faridkot* v. *Baldev Dass,* AIR 2005 SC 104: 2005 (1) MhLJ 1043 wherein it has been underlined that unless and until a case of irreparable loss or damage is made out by a party to the suit, the court should not permit the nature of the property to be changed, which may include alienation or transfer thereof leading to loss or damage been cause to the party who may ultimately succeed and which would as well lead to multiplicity of proceedings. Judicial discretion has to be disciplined by jurisprudential ethics and can by no means conduct itself as an unruly horse.

The course adopted by the High Court in this perspective is in a way unprecedented and rather unknown in law. The impugned order seems to be the yield of an unfathomable urge divorced from the bearing of the consequences thereof on the pending adjudication of the proceedings between the parties and is noticeably unusual and unexpected at the level of High Court. The follow up steps to execute the order also display a cavalier and committed approach so much so that it goes to the extent of fixing the estimated price of the property to be mentioned in the notice for sale. As it is, none of the parties did suggest the disposal of the suit property by public auction. Neither any exceptional circumstance nor any compelling necessity in the interest of adjudication exists as on date to compel the disposal of the property as directed. This assumes great significance as well in view of the dispute as to whether the same belongs to the partnership firm or not. The impugned order thus not only is per se illegal, being violative of the basic tenets of law, but also seems to be informed with an overzealous disposition rendering the same unmistakably unsustainable. The same is thus set-aside. The High Court would decide the appeals on their own merits as expeditiously as possible. We make it clear that the observations made herein above are wholly in the context of the issue that arose in the present proceedings before this Court and the High Court would answer the appeals without being in any way influenced thereby.

APPEAL UNDER ARTICLE 136

Article 136 also vests in the apex Court appellate jurisdiction. To have a complete look over the appellate jurisdiction of the Supreme Court, it is essential to study the various aspects of the provisions contained in article 136. The article reads as follows:

(1) Notwithstanding anything in this Chapter, the Supreme Court may, in its discretion, grant special leave to appeal from any judgment, decree, determination, sentence or order in any cause or matter passed or made by any court or Tribunal in the territory of India

(2) Nothing in clause (1) shall apply to any judgment, determination, sentence or order passed or made by any court or Tribunal constituted by or under any law relating to the Armed Forces.

SYNOPSIS

Comments

1. Scope of SLP

In the case of *Bal Niketan,* the Court said that section 2(1)(b) of the U.P. Urban Building Regulation of Letting, Rent and Eviction Act, 1972 lays down that "nothing in this Act shall apply to any building belonging to or vested in a recognised institution, the whole of the income from which is utilised for the purpose of such institution." The manager of the appellant school, a recognised institution under the U.P. Basic Education Act, 1972, run and managed by a Registered Society issued notice of termination of tenancy to the four tenants of the super-structures (Khaprails) purchased by it, under section 106 of the Transfer of Property Act and demanded surrender of possession. As the tenants failed to surrender possession, he filed separate suits against the four tenants for ejectment and payment of arrears of rent. The respondent and the other tenants contended that the school was not a recognised educational institution entitled to the benefit of section 2(1)(b) of the U.P. Urban Building Regulation of Letting, Rent and Eviction Act, 1972 and that the notice of termination of tenancy was not valid. The trial court rejected the contentions of the tenants and decreed the suits in favour of the school. The revisional court confirmed the judgment and decree of the trial court and dismissed all the revision petitions.

In the writ petitions before the High Court, it was contended for the first time that the appellant school was not a juristic person and was not, therefore, entitled to file the suits through its Manager. It was submitted on behalf of the school that as a recognised institution under the U.P. Basic Education Act, 1972, it has juristic status, that the suit had been instituted by a person who was not only the Manager of the school but also the Secretary of the Registered

Society and as such the suits were fully maintainable under law. The appellant school, also filed a petition under Order I, rule 10 of Code of Civil Procedure for amending the plaint by correcting the name of the plaintiff into the name of the Society by its Secretary in place of the name of the school by its Manager. The High Court held that in view of the specific provision in clause (14) of the Constitution of the Registered Society to the effect that "all the legal proceedings by the Society and against the Society will be done either by the Manager or by the Secretary or by a person authorised by them", the appellant school was not a juristic person and only the Registered Society had the authority and competence to file the suits and that the suits filed by the appellant school were not maintainable. It quashed the judgments and decrees passed by the courts below in three suits since the fourth suit had been compromised after the filing of the writ petition.

Insofar as the application under Order I, rule 10 was concerned the High Court held that the proper course for the appellant school was to move the trial court for getting the description of the appellant corrected and then pursue the proceedings for eviction.

Allowing the appeal by special leave, this Court, held:

1. It is well-settled that if the Court is satisfied that a *bona fide* mistake has occurred in the filing of the suits in the name of the wrong person, then the court should set right matters in exercise of its powers under Order I, rule 10 and promote the cause of justice. The Courts have also held that even if the suit had been instituted in the name of a person who had no competence to file the suit, the Courts should set right matters by ordering the addition or substitution of the proper plaintiff for ensuring the due dispensation of justice. *Bal Niketan Nursery School* v. *Kesari Prasad*, AIR 1987 SC 1970: (1987) 3 SCC 587: (1987) 3 SCR 510.

The Supreme Court of India is the highest judicial forum and final court of appeal as established by Part V, Chapter IV of the Constitution of India. According to the Constitution, the role of the Supreme Court is that of the guardian of Constitution and that of a federal court. The Supreme Court is the highest appellate court which takes up appeals against the verdicts of the High Courts and other Courts of the states and territories. The Supreme Court has the power of Constitutional review. It replaced both the federal court of India and the Judicial Committee of the Privy Council which were at the apex of the Indian Court system. The Supreme Court of India held its inaugural sitting on 28 January, 1950.

Article 136 of the Constitution of India, 1950 provides that the Supreme Court may in its discretion grant special leave to appeal from any judgment, decree, determination, sentence or order in any case or matter passed or made by any Court or Tribunal in the territory of India except the Court or Tribunal constituted by or under any law relating to armed forces.

2. Whether the Powers of the Supreme Court and High Courts are Concurrent

Right and duty of the apex Court is not abrogated merely because the High Court also has this right and duty of protection of the subordinate courts. The jurisdictions are concurrent and not exclusive or antagonistic. [967G-H] 2.2 article 136 vests the Supreme Court with wide powers to grant special leave to appeal from any judgment, decree determination sentence or order in any cause or matter passed or made by any Court or Tribunal in the territory of India except a Court or Tribunal constituted by or under any law relating to the Armed Forces. The Court's appellate power under article 136 is plenary, it may entertain any appeal by granting special leave against any order made by any Magistrate, Tribunal or any other subordinate court. The width and amplitude of the power is not affected.

The difference between article 136 and articles 132-135 of the Constitution is:

(1) under article 132 to 135 appeal can be entertained by the Supreme Court only against the final order. But under article 136, the word order is not qualified by the adjective final and hence the Court can grant special leave to appeal even from interlocutory order.
(2) under article 132 to 134 appeal lies only against the final order of the High Court; while under article 136 the Supreme Court can grant special leave for appeal from any Court or Tribunal *viz*. from any subordinate court below the High Court, even without following the usual procedure of filing appeal in the High Court or even where the law applicable to the dispute does not make provision for such an appeal.
(3) under article 132 to 134 an appeal can lie in the Supreme Court only against any judgment, decree, determination sentence or order of any Court or Tribunal, but under article 136 an appeal may lie against any case or matter.

Scope of article 136 referred to Constitution Bench.—Scope of article 136 was examined in the case of *Mathai* v. *George*, (2010) 4 SCC 358: 2010 AIR SCW 2161. In this case the Supreme Court has referred the question of the interpretation of article 136 to a Constitution Bench. The Court (Katju and Lodha, JJ.) observed, after referring to the leading cases on the scope of article 136, "...we feel it incumbent on us to reiterate that article 136 was never meant to be an ordinary forum of appeal at all like section 96 or even section 100, CPC. Under the constitutional scheme, ordinarily the last court in the country in ordinary cases was meant to be the High Court. The Supreme Court as the apex court in the country was meant to deal with important issues like constitutional questions, questions of law of general importance or where grave injustice had been done... After all, the Supreme Court has limited time at its disposal and it cannot be expected to hear every kind of dispute." The Court also refers to the lack of uniformity in grant of leave to appeal under article 136.

The author of the article observed, I remain doubtful whether another Constitution Bench decision on the point will serve any purpose. As far back as in 1950, a Constitution Bench had already observed in *Pritam Singh* v. *State*, AIR 1950 SC 169:

> *"On a careful examination of article 136 alongwith the preceding article, it seems clear that the wide discretionary power with which this Court is invested under it is to be exercised sparingly and in exceptional cases only, and as far as*

possible a more or less uniform standard should be adopted in granting special leave in the wide range of matters which can come up before it under this article. By virtue of this article, we can grant special leave in civil cases, in criminal cases, in income-tax cases, in cases which come up before different kinds of Tribunals and in a variety of other cases. The only uniform standard which in our opinion can be laid down in the circumstances is that Court should grant special leave to appeal only in those cases where special circumstances are shown to exist..."

Evidently, this Constitution Bench decision has done little or nothing to curb the widespread (ab) use of article 136. Will another Constitution Bench decision really help, then? A more fundamental change – for instance, such as the one recently proposed by Mr. K.K. Venugopal involving the creation of separate Regional Courts of Appeal – might perhaps be a better solution. Reference-Posted by Mihir Naniwadekar E-mail This Blog This! Share to Twitter.

Re-examining the scope of article 136.—A Bench was constituted to re-examine the scope of article 136, as desired by the Supreme Court while hearing the *Mathai* case. The Supreme Court in *Mathai* v. *George,* (2010) had sought for constitution of a Constitution Bench to issue guidelines and decide on the scope and qualifications on entertaining Special Leave Petitions under article 136 of the Constitution. This reference was long awaited, and much needed in the present judicial scenario where the apex court of the country is being crushed under an overwhelming backlog of cases majority of them being Special Leave Petitions under article 136. Consequently, the apex Court is increasingly being treated as a court of appeal. Article 136 today has become a hit and trial method for obtaining relief with dissatisfied litigants seeking to challenge each and every order all the way up to the Supreme Court.

Though in catena of earlier judicial pronouncements the Supreme Court has opined time and again that due diligence of the case must be exercised to determine if it is fit for warranting the apex court's interference. However, in the last decade, the exercise of this power by the Supreme Court has been far from moderate.

This state of affairs stem from the fact that whilst the inherent discretionary power under article 136 is wide and article 136 does not expressly define the limitations on the exercise of this power or mention the circumstances under which special leave to appeal can be granted.

The predicament is inherent in the power conferred to the Supreme Court under article 136, which is of a plenary nature as there are no words in article 136 itself qualifying this power. In the absence of any conclusive pronouncement (statutory or judicial) on how this discretion is to be exercised, there has been no uniform standard followed by the Supreme Court in admitting special leave appeals.

In *Mathai* (Katju and Lodha, JJ.), the Supreme Court has noted that while seeking a reference of this issue to a Constitution Bench, article 136 does not expressly define the limitations or fetters on the exercise of the discretionary power conferred on Supreme Court under this article and the increased indulgence of the Judiciary has converted the Supreme Court into an ordinary appellate court even though this power was only envisaged to be a residual in nature. This was never the intention of the Constitution. While discussing the scope of article 136, the Supreme Court had observed that it has been vested with wide powers to grant special leave to appeal from any judgment, decree, determination, sentence or order, in any cause or matter, passed or made by any Court or Tribunal, in the territory of India. This power of the Supreme Court, though discretionary and clearly wide in its ambit, was intended by the framers to be used sparingly in exceptional cases. It held further that "*The Supreme Court as the apex Court in the country was meant to deal with important issues like constitutional questions, questions of law of general importance or where grave injustice had been done... After all, the Supreme Court has limited time at its disposal and it cannot be expected to hear every kind of dispute*".

In order to bring about a conclusive regime under article 136 and attempting to resolve the state of affairs, the Supreme Court in the matter of *Mathai* also quoted lecture delivered by K.K. Venugopal, wherein he had enlisted a category of cases that may be allowed to be heard in a Special Leave Petition: *(i) All matters involving substantial questions of law relating to the interpretation of the Constitution of India; (ii) All matters of national or public importance; (iii) Validity of laws, Central and State; (iv) After* Kesavananda Bharati *v.* State of Kerala, *[(1973) 4 SCC 225: AIR 1973 SC 1461], the judicial review of Constitutional Amendments; (v) To settle differences of opinion of important issues of law between High Courts; (vi) where the Court is satisfied that there has been a grave miscarriage of justice and (vii) where a fundamental right of a person has* prima facie *been violated (the last two grounds have been added by the Bench).*

Undoubtedly, the decision on scope of article 136, as and when passed will be a much needed respite in view of the mounting arrears, however, how far this decision will ultimately aid in providing a practical solution, would be hard to predict. The present is not the first case where the Supreme Court has attempted to harness the ambit of article 136. As far back as in 1950, an attempt was made by the Constitutional Bench in *Pritam Singh* v. *State,* AIR 1950 SC 169 to define and limit the scope of article 136. The Court held that "*The only uniform standard that can be laid down in the circumstances is that Court should grant special leave to appeal only in those cases where special circumstances are shown to exist...*". Evidently, this Constitution Bench decision has done little or nothing to curb the widespread use of article 136 as it did not really set out clear and defined limits of article 136. Therefore, the need of the hour is to formulate a holistic, carefully analyzed and precise set of guidelines indicating the scope of cases in which special leave to appeal, may be entertained.

A well drafted Constitutional Bench decision will not only go a long way in bringing about uniformity in standards of admitting Special Leave Petition and checking litigation which need not be contested all the way to the Supreme Court, but will also relieve the Supreme Court from being further choked with cases that do not merit the Supreme Court's consideration under article 136. Needless to say, the judges themselves will have to refrain from being seduced by the quixotic temptation to right every fancied wrong which may parade before them.

Although, the reference is a step in the direction, it remains to be seen if the Constitution Bench, successfully manages the tight rope task of setting guidelines for entertaining Special Leave appeals, which while retaining the plenary nature of the power under article 136, would encapsulate the intent of the Constitution makers that article 136 is to come into play only in exceptional cases. The moot point still remains whether another Constitution Bench decision will help in bringing about this balance. But till such time as this decision comes, one can only hope that guidelines as and when issued will be exhaustive and not be treated as mere pious wishes as has been the case with the earlier Constitutional Bench decisions on the scope of article 136. (From Hindu, Friday dated May, 27, 2011).

3. Appellate Jurisdiction of Supreme Court of India

The Supreme Court, while deciding to examine the scope of article 136 of the Constitution, said it was like article 226 (Writ Jurisdiction of High Courts) a discretionary remedy and the Supreme Court was not bound to interfere even if there was an error of law or fact in the order under challenge.

A Bench consisting of Justices Markandey Katju and R.M. Lodha, quoting various judgments, pointed out that article 136 was never meant to be an ordinary forum of appeal at all. "It has become a practice of filing SLPs against all kinds of orders of the High Court or other authorities without realising the scope of article 136."

4. Exceptional Circumstances

The Bench said: "The very conferment of the discretionary power defies any attempt at exhaustive definition of such power. The power is permitted to be invoked not in a routine fashion but in very exceptional circumstances as [and] when a question of law of general public importance arises or a decision sought to be impugned before the Supreme Court shocks the conscience. The Supreme Court would not under article 136 constitute itself into a Tribunal or Court just settling disputes and reduce itself to a mere court of error."

5. Limited Time

The judges said: "After all, the Supreme Court has limited time at its disposal and it cannot be expected to hear every kind of dispute. The apex court lays down the law for the whole country and it should have more time to deliberate upon the cases it hears before rendering judgment as Mr. Justice Frankfurter observed. However, sadly the position today is that it is under such pressure because of the immense volume of cases in the Court that judges do not get sufficient time to deliberate over the cases, which they deserve, and this is bound to affect the quality of our judgments." Let notice be issued to the respondents, they said.

6. Alarming Situation

The Bench noted the concern expressed by senior advocate K.K. Venugopal in a lecture pointing out that an alarming state of affairs "has developed in this Court because this Court has gradually converted itself into a mere Court of Appeal which has sought to correct every error which it finds in the judgments of the High Courts of the country as well as the vast number of Tribunals. Mr. Venugopal has further observed that this Court has strayed from its original character as a Constitutional Court and the apex Court of the country. According to him, this is a self-inflicted injury, which is the cause of the malaise which has gradually eroded the confidence of the litigants in the apex Court of the country, mainly because of its failure to hear and dispose of cases within a reasonable period of time."

Mr. Venugopal, the Bench said, "has pointed out that in the year 1997 there were only 19,000 pending cases in this Court, but now, there are over 55,000 pending cases and in a few years' time the pendency will cross one lakh cases. In 2009, almost 70,000 cases were filed in this Court, of which an overwhelming number were SLPs under article 136. At present, all these cases have to be heard orally, whereas the U.S. Supreme Court hears only about 100 to 120 cases every year and the Canadian Supreme Court hears only 60 cases per year."

The Bench, therefore, wanted the issue to be settled by a Constitution Bench. It issued notice to the Supreme Court Bar Association, the Bar Council of India and the Supreme Court-Advocates-on-Record Association. The Constitution Bench may also consider appointing some senior advocates of this court as *amicus curiae* to assist in the matter so that it can be settled after considering the views of all the parties concerned. BY J. VENKATESAN IN THE HINDU

7. Matters to be Brought before the Supreme Court

Mr. Venugopal has suggested the following categories of cases which alone should be entertained under article 136 of the Constitution.

(i) All matters involving substantial questions of law relating to the interpretation of the Constitution of India;

(ii) All matters of national or public importance;

(iii) Validity of laws, Central and State;

(iv) After *Kesavananda Bharati* v. *State of Kerala,* (1973) 4 SCC 225: AIR 1973 SC 1461, the judicial review of Constitutional Amendments; and

(v) To settle differences of opinion of important issues of law between High Courts.

The Judges constituting the Bench said, "We are of the opinion that two additional categories of cases can be added to the above list, namely (i) where the Court is satisfied that there has been a grave miscarriage of justice, and (ii) where a fundamental right of a person has prima facie been violated. However, it is for the Constitution Bench to which we are referring this matter to decide what are the kinds of cases in which discretion under article 136 should be exercised".

8. Categories of Cases which should be Entertained under Article 136 of the Constitution of India

The Two-Judge Bench opined that only the following categories of cases should be entertained by the Supreme Court under article 136 of the Constitution of India:—

(i) All matters involving substantial questions of law relating to the interpretation of the Constitution of India;

(ii) All matters of national or public importance;

(iii) Validity of laws, Central and State;

(iv) After *Kesavananda Bharati* v. *State of Kerala*, (1973) 4 SCC 225: AIR 1973 SC 1461, the judicial review of Constitutional Amendments; and

(v) To settle differences of opinion of important issues of law between High Courts.

We are of the opinion that two additional categories of cases can be added to the above list, namely:

(i) Where the Court is satisfied that there has been a grave miscarriage of justice; and

(ii) Where a fundamental right of a person has *prima facie* been violated. However, it is for the Constitution Bench, to which we are referring this matter, to decide what are the kinds of cases in which discretion under article 136 should be exercised.

In our opinion, the time has now come when an authoritative decision by a Constitution Bench should lay down some broad guidelines as to when the discretion under article 136 of the Constitution should be exercised, *i.e.*, in what kind of cases a petition under article 136 should be entertained. If special leave petitions are entertained against all and sundry kinds of orders passed by any Court or Tribunal, then this Court after some time will collapse under its own burden; *Mathai @ Joby* v. *George*, JT 2010 (3) SC 160: (2010) 2 SCALE 172.

9. Restoring the Supreme Court's Exclusivity

The country's highest judicial institution has lost its original character by a vast self-enlargement of its jurisdiction that has virtually turned it into a general court of appeal. The Supreme Court of India is perceived by the lay public as the most potent institution in the Constitution by its appellate authority over all Courts and Tribunals and by its striking orders correcting and supervising government actions. In the public euphoria over this functioning of the Supreme Court, there is no awareness that the Supreme Court has radically changed its character and stature which was prescribed by the makers of the Constitution.

When the Supreme Court was established in 1950, the Constitution conferred on it limited but important functions of deciding cases involving fundamental rights, cases of Constitutional importance and substantial questions of law of general importance. The Supreme Court was given a residuary power to grant special leave to appeal, in its discretion from any judgment of any Court or Tribunal (article 136 of the Constitution) sparingly and in exceptional cases. The Supreme Court was not to be the apex court to decide ordinary disputes between litigants. Only exceptionally, such disputes between litigants would be decided by the Court. The lower courts and the High Courts were considered as generally competent and adequate for the dispensation of justice between litigants.

9.1 Small and Compact

Consistently with this restricted jurisdiction of the Supreme Court, the Constitution provided that the Supreme Court, like Supreme Courts in other jurisdictions, would be a small, compact court of the Chief Justice and not more than seven Judges unless Parliament otherwise provided. Further, as substantial questions relating to the interpretation of the Constitution were of the utmost importance, the Constitution provided that such questions should be decided by large Benches of Judges and the minimum number of judges who were to sit for deciding such questions should be five.

From 1950 to about 1990, the Supreme Court generally retained this character comparable to the character of Supreme Courts in other jurisdictions. Special leave to appeal from a decision of a High Court or Tribunal was sparingly given in the discretion of the Court. The composition of the Court was of Benches of three Judges, and five Judges and, exceptionally, Benches of seven Judges and even 13 judges, as in the famous case of *Kesavananda Bharati*, deciding important cases.

9.2 Progressive Dilution

Today, all this has changed. The Supreme Court of India has lost its original character by a vast self-enlargement of its jurisdiction making itself a general court of appeal by routinely entertaining special leave petitions between litigants which do not involve important constitutional issues or issues of law of general importance. Up to June 2013, 35,439 Special Leave Petitions which do not involve such issues are pending in the Court. Public Interest Litigation (PIL), which was laudably innovated by the Supreme Court in 1970 to redress the rights of disadvantaged sections of the society, has been converted into litigation for correcting Government actions from corruption scams to banning tinted glasses on automobiles. Writ petitions to enforce fundamental rights under article 32 of the Constitution are less than one per cent of the petitions annually admitted by the Court.

Cases of constitutional and national importance have been sidelined and not heard for years. The last major Constitutional case with a Bench of nine judges was decided in 2007 in *I.R. Coelho* v. *State of Tamil Nadu,* AIR 2007 SC 861, which considered Parliament's power to amend the Constitution by including statutes in the Ninth Schedule of the Constitution. Important Constitutional cases referred to nine judges such as the scope of Inter-State Trade, Commerce & Intercourse, the right of States to tax minerals have not been heard for several years. Atleast five cases for consideration by seven Judges, and 36 cases for consideration by a Bench of five Judges are pending for several years. Only 15 cases were decided by five Judges between 2011 to 2013.

9.3 Bench Strength

With the increasing load of appeals from High Court decisions the number of Judges have had to be increased periodically from eight Judges in 1950 when the Constitution came into force to 31 in 2008. Presently, the Supreme Court is composed of one Bench of the Chief Justice's Court of three Judges and 13 or 14 Benches of two Judges in 13 or 14 courtrooms sitting regularly day after day.

In no Supreme Court of other jurisdictions are there Benches of 13 to 14 courts of two Judges each as the Indian Supreme Court now has. Supreme Courts of other jurisdictions such as the United States, the United Kingdom, Canada, Australia and South Africa sit either *en banc*, i.e. of its full strength, or in large Benches of five or more Judges considering the importance of the case, as such a large composition of Judges is considered fitting for deciding important cases in the Highest Court.

By contrast, the Supreme Court of India today decides cases of major importance by Benches of two Judges. Recently, the Supreme Court nullified section 8(4) of the Representation of the People Act, 1951. This important decision on the interpretation of Parliament's legislative powers on members of legislatures convicted of offences was delivered by a Bench of two Judges of the Court despite the Constitutional requirement that substantial questions of interpretation of the Constitution should be decided by not less than five Judges. Important policy matters are decided by a Bench of two Judges of the Court. In the *2G Spectrum* case, a Bench of two Judges prescribed a national policy for disposing of all public resources by public auctioning. A Bench of two Judges has laid down the law in the vexing cases of inordinate delay in the disposing of petitions for clemency by the President in death penalty cases. The important question of decriminalising homosexuality under the Indian Penal Code has been heard, and the judgment which is reserved will be given by a Bench of two Judges.

When Sir B.N. Rau, the Constitutional Advisor at the time of the framing of the Constitution met Justice Frankfurter of the U.S. Supreme Court, he was told by Justice Frankfurter that the jurisdiction exercisable by the Supreme Court should be exercised by the full court and the Highest Court of appeal in the land should not sit in divisions. The Drafting Committee of the Indian Constitution also drew attention to the practice in the U.S. Supreme Court of not sitting in divisions and how the judges of the Supreme Court of the U.S. attached the greatest importance to this practice.

9.4 Separate Court

In most of the other Supreme Courts, the cases decided by them are few and are of constitutional and national importance leaving the lower courts to decide finally the cases which the Supreme Courts do not consider deciding to overload themselves with. The Supreme Court of the U.S. selects from among 7,000 petitions for *certiorari* (admission) around 100 cases in which *certiorari* is granted. On an average per year about 80 cases are decided by the Supreme Court of the U.K., the Supreme Court of Canada and the High Court of Australia. The Constitutional Court of South Africa – which has been ably functioning since 1994 deciding major constitutional cases and cases of national importance – decides on an average 38 cases per year. In contrast in 2012, the Supreme Court of India decided 898 cases, with few cases of constitutional or national importance.

The Supreme Court of India understandably is compelled to take up cases from 24 High Courts whose judgments increasingly require correction, and litigants have no forum for their correction except the Supreme Court. In this situation, the only solution to preserve the exclusivity and standing of the Supreme Court is to create a separate national court of appeals distinct from the Supreme Court in which appeals from High Courts and Tribunals can be entertained. Such a provision for a Supreme Appellate Court at the highest level distinct from a Constitutional Court is provided by the Constitution of South Africa. Simultaneously, the number of judges of the Supreme Court can be reduced from 31 to a smaller strength and the Court can function with Benches of three and five Judges as it functioned earlier. Above all, it is imperative to create awareness by lawyers, judges and informed public opinion of the necessity for restoring the character and standing of our Supreme Court comparable to the Supreme Courts in other jurisdictions.

(T.R. Andhyarujina is a senior advocate of the Supreme Court and former Solicitor-General of India.) Keywords: Supreme Court, Indian constitution, Indian legal system,

10. Constitution Article 136 – Indian Penal Code, 1860 Section 302 – Criminal Procedure Code, 1973 Section 378

In the case of *Amanullah* v. *State of Bihar,* 2016 (2) Law Herald 1349: 2017 AIR SCW 1871 (SC), examining the meaning of the term *'Locus standi'* the Supreme Court said, the term `*locus standi'* is a latin term, the general meaning of which is `place of standing'. The Concise Oxford English Dictionary, 10th Edn., at page 834, defines the term `*locus standi'* as the right or capacity to bring an action or to appear in a court. The traditional view of `*locus standi'* has been that the person who is aggrieved or affected has the standing before the court, i.e., to say he only has a right to move the court for seeking justice. Later, this Court, with justice-oriented approach, relaxed the strict rule with regard to `*locus standi'*, allowing any person from the society not related to the cause of action to approach the court seeking justice for those who could not approach themselves. Now turning our attention towards the criminal trial, which is conducted, largely, by following the procedure laid down in the CrPC. Since, offence is considered to be a wrong committed against the society, the prosecution against the accused person is launched by the State. It is the duty of the State to get the culprit booked for the offence committed by him. The focal point, here, is that if the State fails in this regard and the party having *bonafide* connection with the cause of action, who is aggrieved by the order of the court cannot be left at the mercy of the State and without any option to approach the appellate court for seeking justice. In this regard, the Constitution Bench of this Court in the case of *P.S.R. Sadhanantham's case (supra)* has elaborately dealt with the aforesaid fact situation. The relevant paras 13, 14 and 25 of which read thus:

> "13. It is true that the strictest vigilance over abuse of the process of the court, especially at the expensively exalted level of the Supreme Court, should be maintained and ordinarily meddlesome bystanders should not be granted "visa". It is also true that in the criminal jurisdiction this strictness applies a fortiori since an adverse verdict from this Court may result in irretrievable injury to life or liberty.

> 14. Having said this, we must emphasise that we are living in times when many societal pollutants create new problems of unredressed grievance when the State becomes the sole repository for initiation of criminal action. Sometimes, pachydermic indifference of bureaucratic officials, at other times politicisation of higher functionaries may result in refusal to take a case to this Court under Article 136 even though the justice of the lis may well justify it. While "the criminal law should not be used as a weapon in personal vendettas between private individuals", as Lord Shawcross once wrote, in the absence of an independent prosecution authority easily accessible to every citizen, a wider connotation of the expression "standing" is necessary for Article 136 to further its mission. There are jurisdictions in which private individuals - not the State alone - may it statute criminal proceedings".

The Law Reforms Commission (Australia) in its Discussion Paper No. 4 on "Access to Courts - I Standing: Public Interest Suits" wrote:

> "The general rule, at the present time, is that anyone may commence proceedings and prosecute in the Magistrate court. The argument for retention of that right arises at either end of the spectrum - the great cases and the frequent petty cases. The great cases are those touching Government itself - a Watergate or a Poulson. However independent they may legally be any public official, police or prosecuting authority, must be subject to some government supervision and be dependent on Government funds; its officers will inevitably have personal links with government. They will be part of the 'establishment'. There may be cases where a decision not to prosecute a case having political ramifications will be seen, rightly or wrongly, as politically motivated. Accepting the possibility of occasional abuse the Commission sees merit in retaining some right of a citizen to ventilate such a matter in the courts."

Even the English System, as pointed by the Discussion Paper permits a private citizen to file an indictment. In our view the narrow limits set in vintage English Law, into the concept of person aggrieved and "standing" needs liberalisation in our democratic situation. In *Dabholkar case* this Court imparted such a wider meaning. The American Supreme Court relaxed the restrictive attitude towards "standing" in the famous case of *Baker* v. *Carr*. *Lord Denning*, in the notable case of the *Attorney-General of the Gambia* v. *Pierra Sarr N'jie*, spoke thus:

> "... the words "person aggrieved" are of wide import and should not be subjected to a restrictive interpretation. They do not include, of course, a mere busybody who is interfering in things which do not concern him;"

In India also, the criminal law envisages the State as a prosecutor. Under the Code of Criminal Procedure, the machinery of the State is set in motion on information received by the police or on a complaint filed by a private person before a Magistrate. If the case proceeds to trial and the accused is acquitted, the right to appeal against the acquittal is closely circumscribed. Under the Code of

Criminal Procedure, 1898, the State was entitled to appeal to the High Court, and the complainant could do so only if granted special leave to appeal by the High Court. The right of appeal was not given to other interested persons. Under the Code of Criminal Procedure 1973, the right of appeal vested in the States has now been made subject to leave being granted to the State by the High Court. The complainant continues to be subject to the prerequisite condition that he must obtain special leave to appeal. The fetters so imposed on the right to appeal are prompted by the reluctance to expose a person, who has been acquitted by a competent court of a criminal charge, to the anxiety and tension of a further examination of the case, even though it is held by a superior court. The Law Commission of India gave anxious thought to this matter, and while noting that the Code recognised a few exceptions by way of permitting a person aggrieved to initiate proceedings in certain cases and permitting the complainant to appeal against an acquittal with special leave of the High Court, expressed itself against the general desirability to encourage appeals against acquittal. It referred to the common law jurisprudence obtaining in England and other countries where a limited right of appeal against acquittal was vested in the State and where the emphasis rested on the need to decide a point of law of general importance in the interests of the general administration and proper development of the criminal law. But simultaneously the Law Commission also noted that if the right to appeal against acquittal was retained and extended to a complainant the law should logically cover also cases not instituted on complaint. It observed:

> "Extreme cases of manifest injustice, where the Government fails to act, and the party aggrieved has a strong feeling that the matter requires further consideration, should not, in our view, be left to the mercy of the Government. To inspire and maintain confidence in the administration of justice, the limited right of appeal with leave given to a private party should be retained, and should embrace cases initiated on private complaint or otherwise at the instance of an aggrieved person."

However, when the Criminal Procedure Code, 1973 was enacted the statute, as we have seen, confined the right to appeal, in the case of private parties to a complainant. This is, as it were, a material indication of the policy of the law.

Further, this Court in the case of *Ramakant Rai's* case (supra) has held thus:

> "12. A doubt has been raised about the competence of a private party as distinguished from the State, to invoke the jurisdiction of this Court under Article 136 of the Constitution of India, 1950 (in short "the Constitution") against a judgment of acquittal by the High Court. We do not see any substance in the doubt. The appellate power vested in this Court under Article 136 of the Constitution is not to be confused with the ordinary appellate power exercised by appellate courts and Appellate Tribunals under specific statutes. It is a plenary power, "exercisable outside the purview of ordinary law" to meet the pressing demands of justice (see *Durga Shankar Mehta* v. *Raghuraj Singh,* [1955] 1 SCR 267). Article 136 of the Constitution neither confers on anyone the right to

invoke the jurisdiction of this Court nor inhibits anyone from invoking the Court's jurisdiction. The power is vested in this Court but the right to invoke the Court's jurisdiction is vested in no one. The exercise of the power of this Court is not circumscribed by any limitation as to who may invoke it. Where a judgment of acquittal by the High Court has led to a serious miscarriage of justice, this Court cannot refrain from doing its duty and abstain from interfering on the ground that a private party and not the State has invoked the Court's jurisdiction. We do not have slightest doubt that we can entertain appeals against judgments of acquittal by the High Court at the instance of interested private parties also. The circumstance that the Criminal Procedure Code, 1973 (in short "the Code") does not provide for an appeal to the High Court against an order of acquittal by a subordinate court, at the instance of a private party, has no relevance to the question of the power of this Court under Article 136. We may mention that in *Mohan Lal* v. *Ajit Singh,* AIR 1978 SC 1183: 1978 Cri LJ 1107 this Court interfered with a judgment of acquittal by the High Court at the instance of a private party. An apprehension was expressed that if appeals against judgments of acquittal at the instance of private parties are permitted there may be a flood of appeals. We do not share the apprehension. Appeals under Article 136 of the Constitution are entertained by special leave granted by this Court, whether it is the State or a private party that invokes the jurisdiction of this Court, and special leave is not granted as a matter of course but only for good and sufficient reasons, on well-established practice of this Court."

The Court further said, after considering the case law relied upon by the learned counsel for the appellants as well as the respondents, in the light of the material placed on record, we are of the view that the appellants have *locus standi* to maintain this appeal. From the material placed on record, it is clear that the appellants have precise connection with the matter at hand and thus, have locus to maintain this appeal. The learned counsel for the appellants has rightly placed reliance upon the Constitution Bench judgment of this Court, namely, *P.S.R Sadhanantham (supra)* and other decisions of this Court in *Ramakant Rai, Esher Singh, Ramakant Verma (supra)*. Further, it is pertinent here to observe that it may not be possible to strictly enumerate as to who all will have locus to maintain an appeal before this Court invoking Article 136 of the Constitution of India, it depends upon the factual matrix of each case, as each case has its unique set of facts. It is clear from the aforementioned case law that the Court should be liberal in allowing any third party, having *bonafide* connection with the matter, to maintain the appeal with a view to advance substantial justice. However, this power of allowing a third party to maintain an appeal should be exercised with due care and caution. Persons, unconnected with the matter under consideration or having personal grievance against the accused should be checked. A strict vigilance is required to be maintained in this regard.

11. Constitution Article 136 – Exercise of power by Supreme Court

In *Mathai @ Joby* v. *George,* 2010 (6) AWC 6243 (SC): (2010) 4 SCC 358 (Constitution Bench) the Supreme Court referred another decision and said, in

Penu Balakrishna Iyer v. *Ariya M. Ramaswami Iyer*, (1964) 7 SCR 49 (53) this Court held as under:

> "... Even so, we do not think it would be possible to lay down an unqualified rule that leave should not be granted if the party has not moved for leave under the Letters Patent and it cannot be so granted, nor is it possible to lay down an inflexible rule that if in such a case leave has been granted it must always and necessarily be revoked. Having regard to the wide scope of the powers conferred on this Court under Article 136 , it is not possible and, indeed, it would not be expedient, to lay down any general rule which would govern all cases. The question as to whether the jurisdiction of this Court under Article 136 should be exercised or not, and if yes, on what terms and conditions, is a matter which this Court has to decide on the facts of each case."

Once again in *Union Carbide Corporation* v. *Union of India, (*1991) 4 SCC 584, this Court in para 58 held as under:

> "This Court had occasion to point out that Article 136 is worded in the widest terms possible. It vests in the Supreme Court a plenary jurisdiction in the matter of entertaining and hearing of appeals by granting special leave against any kind of judgment or order made by a Court or Tribunal in any cause of matter and the powers can be exercised in spite of the limitations under the specific provisions for appeal contained in the Constitution or other laws. The powers given by Article 136 are, however, in the nature of special or residuary powers which are exercisable outside the purview of the ordinary laws in cases where the needs of justice demand interference by the Supreme Court. [See *Durga Shankar Mehta* v. *Thakur Raghuraj Singh,* (1955) 1 SCR 267]".

Upon perusal of the law laid down by this Court in the aforesaid judgments, in our opinion, no effort should be made to restrict the powers of this Court under Article 136 because while exercising its powers under Article 136 of the Constitution of India, this Court can, after considering facts of the case to be decided, very well use its discretion. In the interest of justice, in our view, it would be better to use the said power with circumspection, rather than to limit the power forever. In the circumstances, we do not see any reason to answer the issue which has already been answered in the aforesaid judgments. We are of the opinion that no further elaboration is required on the issue involved in this case.

12. Article 136 – Scope of Interference in Criminal Appeal

In *Devraj* v. *State of Chhattisgarh*, 2016 AIR SCW 3498: 2016 (3) Crmes 339 (SC): AIR 2016 SC 3498, the Apex Court examined scope of interference in criminal appeal.

Status of a hostile witness—

In a three-Judge bench judgment of this Court in *Bhagwan Singh* v. *State of Haryana*, (1976) 1 SCC 389, the witness Jagat Singh was declared hostile. The appellant was convicted under Section 165A IPC. It was contended that the whole case is destroyed since the witness was declared as hostile. In the aforesaid decision the Court held that there is no legal bar to base a conviction upon his testimony if corroborated by other reliable evidence. Following was stated in paragraph 8:

> "8. We have carefully perused the evidence of Jagat Singh, who was examined in the trial after more than a year of detection of the case. The prosecution could have even avoided requesting for permission to cross-examine the witness under Section 154 of the Evidence Act. But the fact that the court gave permission to the prosecutor to cross-examine his own witness, thus characterising him as, what is described as a hostile witness, does not completely efface his evidence. The evidence remains admissible in the trial and there is no legal bar to base a conviction upon his testimony if corroborated by other reliable evidence. We are satisfied in this case that the evidence of Jagat Singh, but for whose prompt assistance the case would not have seen the light of day and whose statement had immediately been recorded by the D.S.P., is amply corroborated by other evidence mentioned above to inspire confidence in his testimony. Apart from that the fact of recovery of the gold coins in the pocket of the appellant gave a seal of finality to the truth of the charge against the appellant. If Jagat Singh had accepted the bribe he would have been guilty under Section 161 IPC. There is, therefore, clear abetment by the appellant of the offence under Section 161 IPC and the ingredients of Section 165-A IPC are established against him."

Another judgment which needs to be noted is *Khujji* v. *State of M.P.*, 1992 (3) RCR (Criminal) 158: (1991) 3 SCC 627. This Court in the above case held that merely because a witness was declared hostile, his entire evidence cannot be treated as effaced from the record,his testimony, to the extent found reliable, can be acted upon. In paragraph 6 following was observed:

> "6......The evidence of PW 3 Kishan Lal and PW 4 Ramesh came to be rejected by the trial court because they were declared hostile to the prosecution by the learned Public Prosecutor as they refused to identify the appellant and his companions in the dock as the assailants of the deceased. But counsel for the State is right when he submits that the evidence of a witness, declared hostile, is not wholly effaced from the record and that part of the evidence which is otherwise acceptable can be acted upon. It seems to be well settled by the decisions of this Court - *Bhagwan Singh* v. *State of Haryana*, (1976) 1 SCC 389; *Rabindra Kumar Dey* v. *State of Orissa*, (1976) 4 SCC 233 and *Syad Akbar* v. *State of Karnataka*, (1980) 1 SCC 30, that the evidence of a prosecution witness cannot be rejected in to merely because the prosecution chose to treat him as hostile and cross-examined him. The evidence of such witnesses cannot be treated as effaced or washed off the record altogether but the same can be accepted to the extent their version is found to be dependable on a careful scrutiny thereof....."

Refering the above decisions the Apex Court said, The above propositions have again been reiterated by this Court in *Vinod Kumar* v. *State of Punjab*, 2015 (1) RCR (Criminal) 647: 2015 (1) Recent Apex Judgments (RAJ) 689: (2015) 3 SCC 220, where in paragraph 31 following has been stated:

> "31. The next aspect which requires to be adverted to is whether testimony of a hostile evidence that has come on record should be relied upon or not. Mr. Jain, learned senior counsel for the appellant would contend that as PW-7 has totally resiled in his cross-examination, his evidence is to be discarded in to. On a perusal of the testimony of the said witness, it is evincible that in examination-in-chief, he has supported the prosecution story in entirety and in the cross-examination he has taken the path of prevarication. In *Bhagwan Singh* v. *State of Haryana*, (1976) 1 SCC 389, it has been laid down that even if a witness is characterised has a hostile witness, his evidence is not completely effaced. The said evidence remains admissible in the trial and there is no legal bar to base a conviction upon his testimony, if corroborated by other reliable evidence. In *Khuji @ Surendra Tiwari* v. *State of Madhya Pradesh*, 1992 (3) RCR (Criminal) 158: (1991) 3 SCC 627, the Court after referring to the authorities in Bhagwan Singh (supra), *Rabindra Kumar Dey* v. *State of Orissa*, (1976) 4 SCC 233 and *Syad Akbar* v. *State of Karnataka*, (1980) 1 SCC 30, opined that the evidence of such a witness cannot be effaced or washed off the record altogether, but the same can be accepted to the extent it is found to be dependable on a careful scrutiny thereof."
>
> 19. The evidence of a witness who has been declared hostile can be relied if there are some other material on the basis of which said evidence can be corroborated. More so, that part of evidence of a witness as contained in examination-in-chief, which remains unshaken even after cross-examination, is fully reliable even though the witness has been declared hostile.

There being clear evidence of stopping of the motorcycle near pakkar tree and ensuing quarrel and assault on Devraj the theory of accident as sought to be suggested by the learned counsel for the appellant is wholly unreliable. The details in the Panchnama of the dead body and position of the dead body as stated by Anup Shai Rajwade, Inspector of Police-PW.11, in his statement completely bely the theory of accident. In the examination-in- chief he stated about the injuries, further stated that in between both the legs, between the thigh one white bottle of one litre having half bottle of liquor was kept and at a distance of 4 ft. the motorcycle was there key of which was put on a stone. He further stated that motorcycle was not damaged since only back light was damaged which indicates that motorcycle was brought and thrown in the water. The manner in which liquor bottle was kept between the thigh of dead body and glass of back light of the motorcycle alone being damaged does not support the theory of accident. Thus, there are more than one reasons for rejecting the theory of accident and there was evidence to prove that the deceased was assaulted and murdered and thereafter body and the motorcycle was brought and put below the Pulia. Both Trial Court and the High Court have referred to and relied on sufficient evidence for convicting the accused. We, ourselves after going through the evidence relied on by the courts below for convicting the accused, are of the opinion that the prosecution has successfully proved beyond reasonable doubt that it was accused who had caused homicidal death of the deceased.

We are also conscious that the jurisdiction which this Court exercises under Article 136 has its own self-imposed restrictions. It is sufficient to refer to this Court's decision reported in *Ganga Kumar Srivastava* v. *State of Bihar,* 2005 (3) RCR (Cri) 707: (2005) 6 SCC 211, where this Court after referring to various decisions has laid down certain principles for exercising the power of this Court under Article 136 . It is useful to refer to paragraph 10 of the judgment, which is

> "**10.** From the aforesaid series of decisions of this Court on the exercise of power of the Supreme Court under Article 136 of the Constitution following principles emerge:
>
> (i) The powers of this Court under Article 136 of the Constitution are very wide but in criminal appeals this Court does not interfere with the concurrent findings of fact save in exceptional circumstances.
>
> (ii) It is open to this Court to interfere with the findings of fact given by the High Court, if the High Court has acted perversely or otherwise improperly.
>
> (iii) It is open to this Court to invoke the power under ***Article 136*** only in very exceptional circumstances as and when a question of law of general public importance arises or a decision shocks the conscience of the Court.
>
> (iv) When the evidence adduced by the prosecution fell short of the test of reliability and acceptability and as such it is highly unsafe to act upon it.
>
> (v) Where the appreciation of evidence and finding is vitiated by any error of law of procedure or found contrary to the principles of natural justice, errors of record and misreading of the evidence, or where the conclusions of the High Court are manifestly perverse and unsupportable from the evidence on record."

To the similar effect, another judgment of this Court reported in *Alamelu* v. *State*, 2011 (1) RCR (Criminal) 498: 20111) Recent Apex Judgments (RAJ) 227: (2011) 2 SCC 385, where this Court held that even though the powers of this Court under Article 136 are very wide, but in criminal appeals, this Court would not interfere with the concurrent findings of facts, save in very exceptional cases. Following was laid down in paragraph 19:

> "**19.** We have considered the submissions made by the learned counsel for the parties. Before we embark upon an examination of the evidence, we may point out that even though the powers of this Court under Article 136 of the Constitution are very wide, but in criminal appeals, this Court would not interfere with the concurrent findings of facts, save in very exceptional cases. In an appeal under Article 136 of the Constitution, this

Court does not normally appreciate the evidence by itself and go into the question of credibility of witnesses. The assessment of the evidence by the High Court is accepted as final except where the conclusions recorded by the High Court are manifestly perverse and unsupportable by the evidence on record. Keeping in view the aforesaid principles, we have examined the findings recorded by the courts below."

13. Article 136 – Long Delay in Disposal of Cases

In *V. Vasanthakumar* v. *H.C. Bhatia,* 2016 All SCR 1477: 2016 (7) SCC 686 (SC), the S C said, we have given our anxious consideration to the submissions made at the Bar. Certain facts are beyond dispute. It is not in dispute that the Supreme Court was never meant to be a regular court of appeal. It was meant to exercise its powers under Article ***136*** of the Constitution only in cases which raised important questions involving interpretation of the Constitution or questions of general public importance or questions of constitutionality of State or Central legislations or those raising important issues touching Centre-State relationship etc. The jurisdiction may also have been available to the Court where it found gross miscarriage of justice or an error so outrageous as no reasonable person would countenance. The power to interfere was not meant to be exercisable just because prolonged argument would eventually reveal some error or irregularity or a possible alternative view on a subject that did not cause any miscarriage of justice of a kind that would shock the conscience of the court on the subject. The long line of decisions of the Court to which we have made reference earlier supports that view. The fact, however remains that the filing of cases in the Supreme Court over the past six decades has grown so sharply that the Judge strength in the Supreme Court is proving inadequate to deal with the same. Statistics show that more than 3/4th of the total number of cases filed are dismissed in limine. Even so, the dismissal is only after the court has applied its mind and heard arguments which consume considerable time of the Judges. Dismissal of an overwhelming number of cases has not and does not discourage the litigants or the member of the Bar from filing cases. That is why the number of cases filed is on the rise every year.

It is common knowledge that the huge backlog of cases in the Supreme Court not only attracts criticism from the litigant public but also from independent observers of the judicial systems. To add to the woes of the Court there are a number of new legislations which provide for a first appeal to the Supreme Court, a role which the Supreme Court was never intended to play in the Constitutional scheme. Suffice it to say that the pronouncement of this Court sounding notes of caution against liberal grant of special leave to appeal or exercise of restraint in the matter of entertaining cases have led to no meaningful improvement in the situation.

What then is the way forward?. Venugopal and Andhyarujina argue that the way forward is setting up of Regional Courts of Appeal, firstly, because the same would take justice closer to the doorsteps of the litigants, especially those living at distant places and secondly, because an intermediary court would reduce the burden of the Supreme Court without denying to the litigants an opportunity to agitate his case before a court higher than the High Court. The only difference in that situation will be that in place of the Supreme Court the Court of Appeal would look into the matter and correct whatever needs to be corrected in the judgment impugned before it. It is in that backdrop that following questions arise for our consideration.

14. Article 136 Indian Penal Code, 1860 Sections 452, 324, 326, 341 read with 34

In *R. Bhagirathi Reddy* v. *State of Odisha*, 2017 (68) Ori Criminal R 245 (Ori) the High Court of Orrisa said, once the criminal case signs its judgment disposing of a case, it shall not alter or review the same except to correct a clerical or arithmetical error.

The Court after and considering various decisions said, the decisions placed by the learned counsel for the petitioners are distinguishable in the context of the present facts of the case. Section 362 of Cr.P.C. clearly stipulates that once the criminal Court signs its judgment or final order disposing of a case; it shall not alter or review the same except to correct a clerical or arithmetical error. Even though there is no such things as the principle of constructive res judicata in a criminal case but there is no scope for any review of the judgment by a Court after it signs its judgment or final order disposing of the case either at the instance of any party or even suo motu by exercising its inherent power under section 482 of Cr.P.C. The power of recall is different than the power of altering or reviewing the judgment. A criminal revision petition, once admitted, cannot be dismissed for default but has to be adjudicated on merits. The Code of Criminal Procedure does not contemplate of making an order of dismissal of revision for default. Once the records of the Courts below are called for, the High Court can exercise its powers under section 401 read with section 397 of Cr.P.C. to examine the correctness, legality or propriety of the order, recorded or passed irrespective of the fact whether the counsel for the petitioner is present or not at the time of call of the matter for final hearing. However, if on a petition filed by the petitioner, the Court is satisfied that due to some unavoidable reason, the learned counsel for the petitioner could not appear when the matter was taken up for hearing, it may recall the order passed in rare cases for the ends of justice and to prevent miscarriage of justice. As soon as the judgment or final order disposing of the case is signed, it becomes final and the Court is functus officio. The only remedy available to the aggrieved party is to challenge the order in the higher Court. Unlike the statutory provision under Order XLVII of Civil Procedure Code of, there is no provision in the Cr.P.C. for review of the judgment or final order disposing of a case once it is signed.

It cannot be lost sight of that the Hon'ble Supreme Court has passed the following order:—

> "Heard learned counsel for the petitioners.
>
> No proper explanation has been given out by the petitioners to condone the delay of 1114 days in filing the SLP. The application for condonation of delay is accordingly dismissed.

Even on merits, we find no ground to interfere with the impugned order in exercise of our jurisdiction under ***Article 136*** of the Constitution of India.

This special leave petition is accordingly dismissed on the ground of delay as also on merit."

Even though the order passed by the Hon'ble Supreme Court is a non-speaking one and no reasonings have been assigned thereon for dismissal of the special leave petition but it is clear that the Hon'ble Court not only considered the matter on the ground of delay but also on merit. Such order refusing special leave to appeal may not stand substituted in place of the judgment of this Court under challenge and may not attract the doctrine of merger and may not be a declaration of law by the Supreme Court under Article 141 of the Constitution of India but it is apparent that the Hon'ble Court was not inclined to exercise its discretion so as to allow the petitioners to file an appeal. After dismissal of the special leave petition, when there is no statutory right of review available for the petitioners under Cr.P.C., this Court cannot assume such a jurisdiction to decide the case on merits when there is no apparent error noticed in the earlier judgment.

15. Article 136 –Nature of Remedy under this Article

In *Reena Suresh Alhat* v. *State of Maharashtra,* 2017 AIR (SC) 967: 2017 (1) BBCJ 366 (SC) the Apex Court held, it was passionately urged by the learned senior counsel appearing in both the matters that this Court ought to examine the questions of law involved in the petitions because these elections at the grass root level are of great importance in the civic administration of Pune. By the impugned orders, the High Court deprived the petitioners of their valuable electoral rights. Though the petitioners have an alternative remedy to challenge the election of returned candidates, such a remedy is time consuming and in the process a substantial (if not the entire) portion of the term of the office would expire and, therefore, this Court is bound to examine the cases on merits.

The remedy under ***Article 136*** is a discretionary remedy though it does not mean that the discretion should be exercised whimsically. Learned counsel for the petitioners relied upon a judgment of the Constitution Bench in the case of *Mohinder Singh Gill* v. *The Chief Election Commissioner, New Delhi,* AIR 1978 SC 851: (1978) 1 SCC 405, in support of the submission that in appropriate cases, this Court ought to interfere in certain specified circumstances in the election process notwithstanding the fact that the aggrieved candidate would have an opportunity to question the election at a later point of time by filing an election petition.

16. Articles 136 and 226 Special Leave Petition Dismissed in limine by Non-speaking Order

In *Dr. Virendra Singh* v. *Banaras Hindu University,* 2017 (6) ADJ 1: 2017 (4) All WC 3612 (All) (DB) the Supreme Court held, in case review petition has been filed before High Court prior to date SLP is dismissed by Hon'ble Supreme Court, same may be entertained - However, a party cannot file review petition before High Court after approaching Supreme Court as it would amount to abuse of process of Court - Review dismissed.

17. Articles 136 and 141 Special Leave Petition – Dismissed in limine

In *Bholanath Hansda @ Bhola Hansda* v. *State of Jharkhand*, 2017 (3) AJR 280: 2017 (3) LLN 661 (Jhar) (FB) a Full Bench of the High Court of Jharkhand held, that when the S.L.P is dismissed by a non-speaking order, in limine, where no reason has been assigned and no law has been declared by the Supreme Court, neither the Doctrine of Merger nor Article 141 of the Constitution of India is attracted to such an order. Where the order rejecting the S.L.P is speaking order i.e. where reason has been assigned by the Apex Court for rejecting the petition for Special Leave and are stated in the order, still the order remains the one rejecting prayer for the grant of leave to appeal. Petitioner has been turned away at the threshold without having been allowed to enter in the appellate jurisdiction of the Apex Court. Here also the Doctrine of Merger would not apply. But the law stated or declaration by the Hon'ble Supreme Court in its order shall attract applicability of Article 141 of the Constitution. The reasons assigned by the Apex court in its order expressing its adjudication (expressly or by necessary implication) on the point of fact or law shall take away jurisdiction of any other Court, Tribunal or Authority to express any opinion in conflict with or departure from the view taken by the Apex Court because permitting to do so would be subversive of judicial discipline. However, this should not be so by reference to the Doctrine of Merger. Once the S.L.P is granted, the order impugned before the Supreme Court becomes an order appealed against. Any order passed thereafter would be an appellate order and would attract the applicability of Doctrine of Merger. It would also not make any difference if the order is speaking or non-speaking one. As has been further elucidated in the passage quoted above, the Hon'ble Supreme Court cannot and does not reverse or modify the decree/order appealed against while deciding the petition of Special Leave.

MAY 2013

SUPREME COURT GUIDELINES

18. Article 136 and Section 100 of the People Representation Act – Scope

Constitution of India, articles 136, 173, 329 – Supreme Court – Power to grant special leave to appeal – Decision of Election Tribunal – Representation of the People Act (XLIII of; 1951), sections 36, 100(1)(c) and (2)(c), 105-Non-compliance with the provisions of article 173 – Constitutional disability – Election void – Whether under section 100(1)(c) or section 100 (2) (c) of the Act – Non-compliance with the provisions of Constitution in section 100(2) (c) – Scope of.

The Supreme Court of India in *Durga Shankar Mehta* v. *Thakur Raghuraj Singh*, AIR 1954 SC 520: 1954 SCJ 728: 1955 SCR 267 examined the scope of article 135 and section 100 of the Representation of the Peoples Act, 1950. This civil appeal was filed before the Supreme Court with special leave within the civil appellate jurisdiction from the judgment and order dated 30th, 1953, of the Election Tribunal Jabalpur.

The Court said that article 136 of the Constitution is worded in the widest terms possible. It vests in the Supreme Court a plenary jurisdiction in the matter of entertaining and hearing appeals by granting special leave against any kind of judgment or order made by a Court or Tribunal in any cause or matter and the powers can be exercised in spite of the specific provisions for appeal contained in the Constitution' or other laws. The powers given by the article are, however, in the nature of special or residuary powers which are exercisable outside the purview of ordinary law, in cases where the needs of justice demand interference by the Supreme Court.

The *non-obstante* clause in article 329 of the Constitution which debars the Supreme Court as well as any other Court in India from entertaining a suit or a proceeding calling in question any election to Parliament or the State Legislature and section 105 of the Representation of the People Act which gives finality to the decision of the Election Tribunal so far as that Act is concerned and does not provide for any further appeal, do not cut down or affect the overriding powers which the Supreme Court can exercise in the matter of granting special leave under article 136 of the Constitution. The overriding power vested in the Supreme Court under article 136 of the Constitution is wider than the prerogative right of entertaining an appeal exercised by the Judicial Committee of the Privy Council in England because the prerogative right of the Grown can be taken away or curtailed by express legislation but the Constitutional provision in article 136 cannot be limited or taken away by any Parliamentary legislation and this Constitutional provision overrides ordinary laws and no presumption can arise from words and expressions declaring an adjudication of a particular Tribunal to be final and conclusive that there was an intention to exclude the exercise of the special power.

Where on the finding of the Tribunal there has been a violation of or non-compliance with the provision of article 173 of the Constitution because the candidate suffers from a Constitutional disability by reason of his under-age the case falls under sub-section (2)(c) of section 100 of the Representation of the People Act and not under sub-section (1)(c) of section 100 of the Act and election should be held to be void on the ground of the Constitutional disqualification of the candidate and not on the ground that his nomination was improperly accepted by the Returning Officer and therefore the 'election of that candidate only should be declared void and not the whole election. The expression "non-compliance with the provisions of the Constitution" in clause (c) of sub-section (2) of section 100 of the Act is sufficiently wide to cover such cases where the question is not one of improper acceptance or rejection of the nomination by the Returning Officer but there is a fundamental disability in the candidate to stand for election at all.

The Court held that when a person is incapable of being chosen as a member of a State Assembly under the provisions of the Constitution itself but has nevertheless been returned as such at an election, it can be said without impropriety that there has been non-compliance with the provisions of the Constitution materially affecting the result of the election. There is no material difference between "non-compliance" and "non-observance" or "breach" and this item in clause (c) of sub-section (2) may be taken as a residuary provision contemplating cases where there has been infraction of the provisions of the Constitution or of the Act but which have not been specifically enumerated in the other portions of the clause. When a person is not qualified to be elected a member, there can be no doubt that the Election Tribunal has got to declare his election to be void. Under section 98 of the Act this is one of the orders which the Election Tribunal is competent to make. If it is said that section 100 of the Act enumerates exhaustively the grounds on which an election could be held void either as a whole or with regard to the returned candidate, it would be a correct view to take that in the case of a candidate who is constitutionally incapable of being returned as a member there is non-compliance with the provisions of the Constitution in the holding of the election and as such sub-section (2)(c) of section 100 of the Act applies. The result therefore was that the contention of the appellant succeeded and the Court allowed the appeal in part and modified the order of the Election Tribunal to this extent that the election of respondent No. 2 Vasant Rao only was declared to be void; the election of the appellant however will stand. We make no order as to costs of this appeal.

19. Award of Industrial Tribunal – Whether Appealable

Application for special leave – Maintainability – Nature of functions of Industrial Tribunal-Industrial Disputes Act, 1947, Appeal by special leave was filed from an Award of the All-India Industrial Tribunal (Bank Disputes) Bombay, dated 1st January, 1950. The facts of the case are set out in the judgment.

The Supreme Court of India in the case of The *Bharat Bank Ltd., Delhi* v. *Employees of the Bharat Bank* examined the scope of appeal to it against an order passed under the Industrial Disputes Act, 1947.

The apex Court said that the functions and duties of the Industrial Tribunal constituted under Industrial Disputes Act, 1947, are very much like those of a body discharging judicial functions although it is not a Court, and under article 136 of the Constitution of India the Supreme Court's jurisdiction to entertain an application for leave to appeal from decision of the Tribunal, even though it will be very unlikely to entertain such an application. *Per* Mukerjea, J. (Patanjali Sastri, J. concurring).—An Industrial Tribunal functioning under the Industrial Disputes Act is not a judicial Tribunal. The nature of the determinations made and the materials and considerations on which it has to decide a dispute are also such that the powers of an appellate court cannot be exercised fully and effectively in respect of them and such determinations are therefore outside the purview of article 136 of the Constitution. Even assuming that the Court had jurisdiction to entertain appeal, the present case was not a fit one for entertaining an appeal from the determination of the Tribunal.

The next question was whether under article 136 the Court has jurisdiction to entertain an application for leave to appeal against the decision of such a body. It is not disputed that the Court has power to issue writs of *certiorari* and *prohibition* in respect of the work of the Tribunal. The only question is whether there is a right of appeal also. In my opinion the wording of article 136 is wide enough to give jurisdiction to the Court to entertain an application for leave to appeal, although it is obvious that having regard to the nature of the functions of the Tribunal, this Court will be very reluctant to entertain such an application.

As regards the merits, I do not think this is a case in which I would admit the appeal. The aggrieved parties may apply for redress by adopting other appropriate proceedings. The appeal therefore should be dismissed with costs. Fazal Ali, J.—The important question to be decided in this case is whether the present appeal lies at all to this Court. The question is not free from difficulty, but on the whole I am inclined to think that the appeal does lie. It is fully recognized that the scope of article 136 of the Constitution is very wide, but the significance of the language used in the section can be appreciated only by comparing it with the articles which precede it. Article 132 deals with the appellate jurisdiction of the Supreme Court in cases involving a substantial question of law as to the interpretation of the Constitution, and the words used in that article are: "appeal...... from any judgment, decree or final order." Article 133 deals with appeals in civil matters and the same words are used here also. Article 134 deals with appeals in criminal matters, and the words used in it are: "appeal...... from any judgment, final order or sentence." In article 136, the words "judgment" and "decree," which are used in articles 132 and 133 are retained. Similarly, the words "judgment" and "sentence" occurring in article 134 are also retained. But the expression "final order" becomes "order," and, instead of the High Court, reference is made to "any court." Certain other words are also used in the article which seem to me to have a special significance, these being "determination," "cause or matter" and "Tribunal." It is obvious that these words greatly widen the scope of article 136. They show that an appeal will lie also from a determination or order of "any Tribunal" in any cause or matter. Can we then say that an Industrial Tribunal does not fall within the scope of article 136? If we go by a mere label, the answer must be in the affirmative.: *Bharat Bank Ltd., Delhi* v. *Employees of the Bharat Bank Ltd.*, AIR 1950 SC 188: 1950 SCR 459: 86 CLJ 230.

20. Revocation of Special Leave – Principles for Granting it

In the case of Udaichand the Supreme Court examined the principles of granting and revoking a special leave. In the said case ultimately, upon the decree of eviction by the trial court and affirmed by the First Appellate Court, the defendant-petitioner again challenged the view that he was estopped from questioning the title of Bhurdas, by way of second appeal before the High Court. The High Court dismissed the appeal quoting a recital in Exhibit 10 wherein the petitioner has admitted the ownership of the shop by Bhurdas to whom he would pay rent. The petitioner thereafter filed special leave petition and obtained *ex-parte ad-interim* stay of eviction by alleging in Ground No. 7 that the rent note, Exhibit 10, no where stated that Bhurdas was the owner of the shop and, therefore, there was no proper appreciation of the said Exhibit.

The respondent filed an application for revocation of the special leave petition. Revoking the special leave and dismissing it the Court held that in dealing with application for special leave, the Court naturally takes statements of facts and grounds of fact contained in the petitions at their face value and it would be unfair to betray the confidence of the Court by making statements, which are untrue and misleading. Supreme Court cannot permit abuse of the process of law and of law courts. *Hari Narain* v. *Badri Das*, AIR 1963 SC 1558:

1964 (1) SCJ 51: (1964) 2 SCR 203 (209) and *Rajabhai Abdul Rehman Munshi* v. *Vasudev Dhanjibhai Mody*, AIR 1964 SC 345: 1964 (2) SCJ 196: (1964) 3 SCR 480 (488 & 493) followed and reiterated *King* v. *Williams*, (1914) 1 KB 608: 110 LT 372, *The King* v. *The General Commissioners for the purposes of the Income Tax Act, for the District of Kensington*, (1917) 1 KB 486: 86 LJ KB 257; *Rex* v. *Kensington Income-tax Commrs.*, (1917) 1 KB 486: 86 LJ KB 257: 116 LT 136 and *Asiatic Engineering Co.* v. *Achhru Ram*, AIR 1951 All 746: 1951 ALJ 576: ILR (1952) 2 All 838 referred to.

The Court also observed:

> "Supreme Court cannot mitigate possible rigours of any law by permitting defaulting tenants to hold up their evictions indefinitely or for inordinately long periods on flimsy or unsustainable grounds"; *Udai Chand* v. *Shankar Lal*, AIR 1978 SC 765: (1978) 2 SCC 209: (1978) 2 SCR 809.

In the case of *Mange Ram* v. *Brij Mohan*, the Court while examining a special leave said that sub-rule (1) of rule 1 of Order XVI, Code of Civil Procedure, 1908 casts an obligation on every party to a proceeding to present a list of witnesses whom it proposes to call and to obtain summons to such persons for their attendance in court; sub-rule (2) requires that the party seeking such assistance from the court must make an application stating the purpose for which the witness is proposed to be summoned; and sub-rule (3) confers a discretion on the Court to permit a party to summon through Court or otherwise any witness other than those whose names appear in the list submitted under sub-rule (1), if such party shows sufficient cause for the omission to mention the name of such witness in the said list. Rule 1A of Order XVI enables a party to bring in any witness without applying for summons under rule 1 but this enabling provision is subject to sub-rule (3) of rule 1. Rule 22 of the "Rules of Procedure and Guidance in the matter of trial of Election Petition under Part Vl of the Representation of the People Act, 1951" of the Punjab and Haryana High Court merely re-enacts sub-rules (1) and (2) of rule 1 of Order XVI, C.P.C.

Sub-section (1) of section 87 of the Representation of the People Act, 1951 makes Order XVI, C.P.C. applicable to the trial of election petitions and the proviso thereto gives the High Court the discretion to refuse to examine any witness if it is of the opinion that the evidence of such witness is not material or that the party tendering such witness is doing so on frivolous grounds or with a view to delay the proceedings.

The appellant, who was the petitioner in an election petition, had filed an application seeking permission to produce and examine witnesses whose names were set out in the application and the Court had passed appropriate orders thereon. When the Court was recording the evidence of the appellant he submitted another list of witnesses whom he had kept present in the Court for being examined, but the court rejected the same for two reasons. (i) that the appellant had not mentioned their names in the application made by him earlier; and (ii) that there was no mention of the purpose for which they were being offered for examination. The appellant challenged the validity of the Court's order. The Court allowed the appeal; *Mange Ram* v. *Brij Mohan*, AIR 1983 SC 925: (1983) 4 SCC 36: (1983) 3 SCR 525.

21. Condonation of Delay *Ex Parte*

In the case of *V. Kameshwari* delay was condoned *ex parte* by the order dated November 5, 1990 without notice to the respondent. It appears that proviso to rule 10(1) of Order XVI of the Rules of this Court was not brought to the notice of the Bench. The condonation is being opposed by respondent No. 3. In these circumstances it is directed that the matter may be placed before a Bench presided over by Hon'ble Mr. Justice M.N. Venkatachaliah for considering the question of condonation.

The petition for condonation of delay thereafter came up for consideration and the said petition has been considered afresh.

Respondent No. 3 opposed the condonation of delay and relied upon the objections filed in that behalf. After hearing learned Counsel for the parties at length and considering the entire material on record and the circumstances of the case, the Court said, "we are satisfied that the delay in the filing of the special leave petition was not wanton. We are satisfied with the explanation furnished by the petitioner as regards the cause of the delay, as projected in the affidavit and elaborated at the time of hearing. We, accordingly, allow I.A. No. 1 of 1989 and condone the delay in the filing of the special leave petition. Having heard learned Counsel for the parties, we hereby grant special leave to appeal against 15 the order dated September 19, 1988, passed by the Tribunal, in Review Petition No. 39 of 1987 and proceed to dispose of the appeal". *V. Kameshwari (Smt.)* v. *Union of India,* JT 1993 (1) SC 108: (1993) II LLJ 992 SC 1993.

Code of Civil Procedure, 1908.—Section 104 Order XLIII, rule 1.—Scope of.—Letters Patent.—Clause 15.—Right of Appeal under clause 15.—If affected by section 104, Order XLIII, rule 1.—The Supreme Court in the case of *Shah Babulal Khimji* examined whether right to appeal under clause 15 is affected by sections 104 and Order XLIII, rule 1.—In a suit for specific performance of an agreement to sell filed on the original side of the Bombay High Court the plaintiff (appellant) prayed for certain interim reliefs. A Single Judge of the High Court dismissed the application. A Division Bench of the High Court, on appeal by the plaintiff, held that the appeal was not maintainable on the ground that the impugned order of the Single Judge was not a 'judgment' within the meaning of clause 15 of the Letters Patent of the High Court.

In appeal to this Court, it was contended on behalf of the appellant that since the trial judge is governed by the procedure prescribed by the Code of Civil Procedure, by virtue of the provisions of section 104 read with Order XLIII, rule (1) the impugned order is appealable to a larger Bench; (2) assuming that the Letters Patent was a special law, section 104 read with Order XLIII is in no way inconsistent with clause 15 of the Letters Patent; (3) even if section 104 read with Order XLIII, rule 1 does not apply an order refusing to appoint a receiver or to grant injunction has the attributes of finality and, therefore, amounts to a judgment within the meaning of Letters Patent.

HELD: (*Per* Fazal Ali and A. Varadarajan, JJ.)

(Amarendra Nath Sen, J. concurring.)

Since the Order of the trial judge was one refusing appointment of a receiver and grant of *ad-interim* injunction, it is a 'judgment' within the meaning of the Letters Patent both because Order XLIII, rule 1 applies to internal appeals in the High Court, and such an order even on merits contains the quality of finality and would be a judgment within the meaning of clause 15 of Letters Patent. Hence an appeal is maintainable to the Division Bench. The Division Bench was in error in dismissing the appeal without deciding it on merits. [259 F-G] *Shah Babulal Khimji* v. *Jayaben D. Kania,* AIR 1981 SC 1786: (1981) 4 SCC 8: 1981 Rajdhani LR 624 (SC).

PART II

RULES OF PROCEDURE

ORDER XLI

APPEALS FROM ORIGINAL DECREE

1. Form of appeal.—What to accompany memorandum.—(1) Every appeal shall be preferred in the form of a memorandum signed by the appellant or his pleader and presented to the Court or to such officer as it appoints in this behalf. The memorandum shall be accompanied by a copy of the judgment:

Provided that where two or more suits have been tried together and a common judgment has been delivered therefor and two or more appeals are filed against any decree covered by that judgment, whether by the same appellant or by different appellants, the appellate court dispense with the filing of more than one copy of the judgment.

(2) **Contents of memorandum.**—The memorandum shall set forth, concisely and under distinct heads, the grounds of objection to the decree appealed from without any argument or narrative; and such grounds shall be numbered consecutively.

(3) Where the appeal is against a decree for payment of money, the appellant shall, within such time as the appellate court may allow, deposit the amount disputed in the appeal or furnish such security in respect thereof as the Court may think fit.

HIGH COURT AMENDMENT

Allahabad.—In Order XLI, in rule 1,—

(1) in sub-rule (1), after the proviso, insert the following *Explanation*, namely:—

> "*Explanation*.—The copy of the decree referred to in sub-rule (1) of rule 1 above shall include a deemed decree as provided in Order XX in clause (b) in sub-rule (2) of rule 6A."

[*Vide* Notification. No. 345-VIId-134, dated 8th August, 1994 (w.e.f. 22-10-1994).]

(2) in sub-rule (2), insert the following proviso, namely;—

> "Provided that the Court may, for sufficient reasons, accept a memorandum of appeal without a copy of the decree appealed from if the counsel for the appellant certifies that the copy has been applied for and has not yet been issued, subject to the copy being filed subsequently within the time granted by the Court." (w.e.f. 13-12-1969)

(3) Omit sub-rule (3),

[*Vide* Notification. No. 552/VII d-184 dated 30th October, 1993 published in Uttar Pradesh Gazette. Pt.2, pp. 1-2, dated 1st January, 1994.]

Andhra Pradesh.—In Order XLI, for rule 1, substitute the following rule, namely:—

> "(1) Every appeal shall be preferred in the form of memorandum signed by the appellant or his pleader and presented to the Court or to such officer as it appoints in this behalf. The memorandum shall be accompanied by such number of copies of judgment as may be required by the Rules or Notifications issued by the High Court and (unless the appellate court dispenses with the filing of the decree or judgment or both for the time being) the decree drawn pursuant to the said judgment," (w.e.f. 2-8-1988).

Bombay.—In Order XLI, for rule 1, substitute the following rule, namely:—

> "1. Form of appeal, what to accompany memorandum.—(1) Every appeal shall be preferred in the form of a memorandum signed by the appellant or his pleader and presented to the Court or to such officer as it appoints in this behalf. The memorandum shall be accompanied by a copy of the decree appealed from – and (unless the appellate court dispenses therewith) of the judgment on which it is founded: Provided that where two or more suits have been tried together and a common judgment has been delivered, therefor and two or more appeals are filed against any decree covered by that judgment, whether by the same appellant or by different appellants, the appellate Court may dispense with the filing of more than one copy of the judgment. *[*Explanation*.—The copy of the decree-referred to in sub-rule (1) of rule 1 above shall include a deemed decree as provided in Order XX in clause (b) in sub-rule (2) of rule 6A], (2) Contents of memorandum.—The memorandum shall set forth, concisely and under distinct heads, the grounds of objection to the decree appealed from without any argument or narrative; and such grounds shall be numbered consecutively. (3) Where the appeal is against a decree for payment of money, the appellant shall, within such time as the appellate court may allow, deposit the amount disputed in the appeal or furnish such security in respect thereof as the Court may think fit: Provided that the Court may dispense with the deposit or security where it deems fit to do so for sufficient cause. (4) The appellant shall file along with the memorandum of appeal as many copies thereof on plain paper as there are respondents for being served on the respondents along with the notice of appeal: Provided that the Court in its discretion may permit the appellant to file the necessary number of copies of the memorandum of appeal after the appeal is admitted, within such time as the Court may grant in this behalf." (w.e.f. 1-10-1983) and *(w.e.f. 9-12-1987)

Delhi.—Same as in Punjab, (w.e.f. 31-10-1966)

Haryana.—Same as in Punjab.

Himachal Pradesh.—Same as in Punjab, (w.e.f. 25-1-1971)

Karnataka.—(i) In Order XLI, in rule 1, in sub-rule (1), at the end, insert the proviso as in Madras, item (iii);

(ii) in sub-rule (2) at the end, insert the following, namely:—

"The memorandum shall also contain a statement of the amount or value of the subject-matter in dispute in the Court of first instance and in the appeal and a statement of the amount of Court-fee paid or payable on the appeal together with the provisions of law under which it is calculated".

[*Vide* Notification No. ROC 2296/59, dated 5th November, 1959.]

(iii) insert the following sub-rule, namely:—

(3) "When an appeal is presented after the period of limitation prescribed therefor it shall be accompanied by an application supported by affidavit setting forth the facts on which the appellant relies to satisfy the Court that he had sufficient cause for not preferring the appeal within such period, and the Court shall not proceed to deal with the appeal in any way (otherwise than by dismissing it either under rule 11 of this Order or on the ground that it is not satisfied as to the sufficiency of the reason for the delay) until notice has been given to the respondent and his objections, if any, are heard."

Kerala.—Same as in Madras items (ii), (iii) and (v) with the following modifications:—

(i) in item (ii), insert the following marginal note:—

"Copy of Judgment to be printed for appeal";

(ii) in item (iii), insert the following marginal note:—

"Power to admit appeal subject to production of copy of decree or order under special or local Act."

[*Vide* Notification No. Bl-3312/58, dated 7th April, 1959.]

Madras.—In Order XLI, in rule 1,—

(i) in sub-rule (1), before the word "copy", insert the word "certified", (w.e.f, 25-12-1963) (ii) to sub-rule (1), insert the following words, namely:—

"The copy of the judgment shall be printed copy in every case in which the High Court has prescribed that the judgment shall be printed when a copy is applied for, for the purpose of appeal."

[*Vide* GO No. 933, Home (Judl.), dated 3rd May, 1917.]

(iii) in sub-rule (1), insert the following proviso, namely:—

"Provided that, in appeals from decrees or order under any special or local Act to which the provisions of Parts II and III of the Limitation Act IX of 1908, do not apply and in which certified copies of such decrees or orders have not been granted within the time prescribed for preferring an appeal, the appellate court may admit the memorandum of appeal subject to the production of the copy of the decree or order appealed from within such time as may be fixed by the Court."

[*Vide* Dis. No. 2135 of 1918.]

(iv) in sub-rule (1), insert the following further proviso and *Explanation*, namely:—

"Provided further that when the decree appealed from is a final decree in partition suit with schedules attached thereto, the appellate court may dispense with the production of the copy of the decree, if the appellant filed a certified copy of the judgment appealed against and produces also a certificate from the Lower Court as to the value of the subject-matter of the proposed appeal."

[*Vide* Dis. No. 97 of 1963, dated 20th March, 1963.]

"*Explanation*.—The words 'appellate court' in sub-rule (1) be deemed to include the Registrar of the High Court, where the appeal is preferred to the High Court." (w.e.f. 25-12-1963) (v) in sub-rule (2), at the end, insert the following words, namely:—

The memorandum shall also contain a statement of the valuation of the appeal for the purposes of the Court-fees Act."

[*Vide* Dis. No. 2057 of 1917.]

Orissa.—Same as in Patna.

Patna.—(i) In Order XLI, in rule 1, in sub-rule (1), insert the following proviso, namely:—

"Provided that when the decree appealed from is a final decree in a partition suit and embodies the allotment papers, the appellate court may accept a copy of the decree containing only a portion of the allotment papers, provided further that the appellate court may, subsequently, on the application of the respondent require a copy of the remaining or any further portion of the allotment papers to be filed by the appellant."

(ii) insert the following as second proviso, namely:—

"Provided further that, in appeals from decrees or orders under any special or local Act to which the provisions of Parts II and III of the Limitation Act, 1908, do not apply and in which certified copies of such decrees or orders have not been granted within the time prescribed for preferring an appeal, the appellate court may admit the memorandum of appeal subject to the production of the copy of the decree or order appealed from within such time as may be fixed by the Court" (w.e.f. 5-4-1961).

Punjab.—In Order XLI, in rule (1), in sub-rule (1), after the proviso, insert the following further proviso, namely:—

"Provided further that the Court may permit the appeal to be filed with true copies duly authenticated by an advocate as correct."

Rajasthan.—In Order XLI, in rule 1, insert the following proviso, namely:—

"Provided that when the decree appealed from is a final decree in a partition suit, the appellate court may dispense with the production of the copy of the decree if the appellant filed a certified copy of the judgment appealed against."

2. Grounds which may be taken in appeal.—The appellant shall not except by leave of the Court, urge or be heard in support of any ground of objection not set forth in the memorandum of appeal, but the appellate court in deciding the appeal, shall not be confined to the grounds of objections set forth in the memorandum of appeal or taken by leave of the Court under this rule:

Provided that the Court shall not rest its decision on any other ground unless the party who may be affected thereby has had a sufficient opportunity of contesting the case on that ground.

3. Rejection or amendment of memorandum.—(1) Where the memorandum of appeal is not drawn up in the manner hereinbefore prescribed, it may be rejected, or be returned to the appellant for the purpose of being amended within a time to be fixed by the Court or be amended then and there.

(2) Where the Court rejects any memorandum, it shall record the reasons for such rejection.

(3) Where a memorandum of appeal is amended, the Judge, or such officer as he appoints in this behalf, shall sign or initial the amendment.

HIGH COURT AMENDMENT

Allahabad.—In Order XLI, in rule 3, for sub-rule (1), substitute the following sub-rule, namely:—

> "(1) Where the memorandum of appeal is not drawn up in the manner hereinbefore prescribed, or accompanied by the copies mentioned in rule 1(1), it may be rejected, or where the memorandum of appeal is not drawn up in the manner prescribed, it may be returned to the appellant for the purpose of being amended within a time to be fixed by the Court or be amendment then and there."

[*Vide* Notification No. 2058/35{a), dated 17th June, 1916.]

3A. Application for condonation of delay.—(1) When an appeal is presented after the expiry of the period of limitation specified therefor, it shall be accompanied by an application supported by affidavit setting forth the facts on which the appellant relies to satisfy the Court that he had sufficient cause for not preferring the appeal within such period.

(2) If the Court sees no reason to reject the application without the issue of a notice to the respondent, notice hereof shall be issued to the respondent and the matter shall be finally decided by the Court before it proceeds to deal with the appeal under rule 11 or rule 13, as the case may be.

(3) Where an application has been made under sub-rule (1), the Court shall not make an order for the stay of execution of the decree against which the appeal is proposed to be filed so long as the Court does not, after hearing under rule 11, decide to hear the appeal.

4. One of several plaintiffs or defendants may obtain reversal of whole decree where it proceeds on ground common to all.—Where there are more plaintiff or more defendants than one in a suit, and the decree appealed from proceeds on any ground common to all the plaintiffs or to all the defendants, any one of the plaintiffs or of the defendants may appeal from the whole decree, and thereupon the appellate court may reverse or vary the decree in favour of all the plaintiffs or defendants, as the case may be.

Stay of proceedings and of execution

5. Stay by Appellate Court.—(1) An appeal shall not operate as a stay of proceedings under a decree or order appealed from except so far as the appellate court may order, nor shall execution of a decree be stayed by reason only of an appeal having been preferred from the decree; but the appellate court may for sufficient cause order stay of execution of such decree.

Explanation —An order by the appellate court for the stay of execution of the decree shall be effective from the date of the communication of such order to the Court of first instance, but an affidavit sworn by the appellant, based on his personal knowledge, stating that an order for the stay of execution of the decree has been made by the appellate court shall, pending the receipt from the appellate court of the order for the stay of execution or any order to the contrary, be acted upon by the Court of first instance.

(2) Stay by Court which passed the decree—Where an application is made for stay of execution of an appealable decree before the expiration of the time allowed for appealing therefrom, the Court which passed the decree may on sufficient cause being shown order the execution to be stayed.

(3) No order for stay of execution shall be made under sub-rule (1) or sub-rule (2) unless the Court making it is satisfied—

(a) that substantial loss may result to the party applying for stay of execution unless the order is made;

(b) that the application has been made without unreasonable delay; and

(c) that security has been given by the applicant for the due performance of such decree or order as may ultimately be binding upon him.

(4) Subject to the provisions of sub-rule (3)], the Court may make an *ex parte* order for stay of execution pending the hearing of the application.

(5) Notwithstanding anything contained in the foregoing sub-rules, where the appellant fails to make the deposit or furnish the security specified in sub-rule (3) of rule 1, the Court shall not make an order staying the execution of the decree.]

HIGH COURT AMENDMENT

Allahabad.—In Order XLI, in rule 5, for sub-rule (5), substitute the following sub-rule, namely:—

"(5) Notwithstanding anything contained in the foregoing sub-rules where the appeal is against a decree for payment of money, the appellate court shall not make an order staying the execution of the decree, unless the appellant shall, within such time as the appellate court may allow, deposit the amount disputed in the appeal or furnish such security in respect thereof as the appellate court may think fit."

[*Vide* Notification No. 552/VII-d-134 dated 3rd October, 1993, published in Uttar Pradesh Gazette Pt. II, pp. 1-2, dated 1st January, 1994.]

Andhra Pradesh.—Same as in Madras.

Calcutta.—In Order XLI, in rule 5, in sub-rule (2), for the words "but the appellate court may for sufficient cause order stay of execution of such decree", substitute the words "but the appellate court may subject to sub-rule (3) of rule 6 of this Order, for sufficient cause order stay of execution of such decree".

[*Vide* Notification No. 6874-G, dated 5th October, 1948.]

Karnataka.—In Order XLI, in rule 5, in sub-rule (1), at the end, insert the following words, namely:—

"and may, when the appeal is against a preliminary decree, stay the making of a final decree in pursuance of the said preliminary decree or the execution of any such final decree if already made or when made or stay all or any of the further proceedings to be taken pursuant to such preliminary decree.

Nothing herein contained shall affect or limit the inherent power of the Court to stay other proceedings either before it or any Court subordinate to it in appropriate cases."

[*Vide* Notification No. ROC 2296/59, dated 5th November, 1959.]

Kerala.—(a) Same as in Madras.

(b) in sub-rule (3), insert the following proviso, namely:—

"Provided that in the case of decree charging immovable properties the appellate court may in its discretion dispense with such security in whole or in part."

[*Vide* Notification No. Bl-312/58, dated 9th June, 1959.]

Madras.—In Order XLI, in rule 5,—

(a) in sub-rule (1), after the words "but the appellate court may for sufficient cause order stay of execution of such decree", insert the words "on such terms and conditions as the Court may deem fit".

(b) in sub-rule (1), at the end, delete full stop and insert the following words, namely:- "and may, when the appeal is against a preliminary decree stay the making of a final decree in pursuance of the preliminary decree or the execution of any such final decree, if already made."

[*Vide* P. Dis. No. 164 of 1932.]

6. Security in case of order for execution of decree appealed from.—(1) Where an order is made for the execution of a decree from which an appeal is pending, the Court which passed the decree shall, on sufficient cause being shown by the appellant, require security to be taken for the restitution of any property which may be or has been taken in execution of the decree or for the payment of the value of such property and for the due performance of the decree or order of the appellate court, or the appellate court may for like cause direct the Court which passed the decree to take such security.

(2) Where an order has been made for the sale of immovable property in execution of a decree, and an appeal is pending from such decree, the sale shall, on the application of the judgment-debtor to the Court which made the order, be stayed on such terms as to giving security or otherwise as the Court thinks fit until the appeal is disposed of.

HIGH COURT AMENDMENT

Calcutta.—In Order XLI, in rule 6, after sub-rule (2), insert the following sub-rule, namely:—

> "(3) Where no such application has been presented to the Court which made the order an application for stay of the sale shall not be entertained by the appellate court." (w.e.f. 5-10-1948)

7. No security to be required from the Government or a public officer in certain cases.—*Rep. by the A.O. 1937.*

8. Exercise of powers in appeal from order made in execution of decree.—The powers conferred by rules 5 and 6 shall be exercisable where an appeal may be or has been preferred not from the decree but from an order made in execution of such decree.

Procedure on Admission of Appeal

9. Registry of memorandum of appeal.—(1) The Court from whose decree an appeal lies shall entertain the memorandum of appeal and shall endorse thereon the date of presentation and shall register the appeal in a book of appeal kept for that purpose.

(2) Such book shall be called the register of appeal.

10. Appellate Court may require appellant to furnish security for costs.—(1) The appellate court may in its discretion, either before the respondent is called upon to appear and answer or afterwards on the application of the respondent, demand from the appellant security for the costs of the appeal, or of the original suit, or of both:

Where appellant resides out of India—Provided that the Court shall demand such security in all cases in which the appellant is residing out of India, and is not possessed of any sufficient immovable property within India other than the property (if any) to which the appeal relates.

(2) Where such security is not furnished within such time as the Court orders, the Court shall reject the appeal.

HIGH COURT AMENDMENT.

Allahabad.—In Order XLI, in rule 10, in sub-rule (1), in the proviso, for the word "India" occurring for the second time substitute the words "the State".

[*Vide* Notification No. 43/vii-d-29, dated 1st June, 1957.]

11. Power to dismiss appeal without sending notice to Lower Court.—(1) The appellate court after fixing a day for hearing the appellant or his pleader and hearing him accordingly if he appears on that day, may dismiss the appeal.

(2) If on the day fixed or any other day to which the hearing may be adjourned the appellant does not appear when the appeal is called on for hearing, the Court may make an order that the appeal be dismissed.

(3) The dismissal of an appeal under this rule shall be notified to the Court from whose decree the appeal is preferred.

(4) Where an appellate court, not being the High Court, dismisses an appeal under sub-rule (1), it shall deliver a judgment, recording in brief its grounds for doing so, and a decree shall be drawn up in accordance with the judgment.

11A. Time within which hearing under rule 11 should be concluded.—Every appeal shall be heard under rule 11 as expeditiously as possible and endeavour shall be made to conclude such hearing within sixty days from the date on which the memorandum of appeal is filed.

12. Day for hearing appeal.—(1) Unless the appellate court dismisses the appeal under rule 11, it should fix a day for hearing the appeal.

(2) Such day shall be fixed with reference to the current business of the Court.

[**13.** Omitted.]

14. Publication and service of notice of day for hearing appeal.—(1) Notice of the day fixed under rule 12 shall be affixed in the appellate court house, and a like notice shall be sent by the appellate court to the Court from whose decree the appeal is preferred, and shall be served on the respondent or on his pleader in the appellate court in the manner provided for the service on a defendant of a summons to appear and answer; and all the provisions applicable to such summons, and to proceedings with reference to the service thereof, shall apply to the service of such notice.

(2) Appellate court may itself cause notice to be served – Instead of sending the notice to the Court from whose decree the appeal is preferred, the appellate court may itself cause the notice to be served on the respondent or his pleader under the provisions above referred to.

(3) The notice to be served on the respondent shall be accompanied by a copy of the memorandum of appeal.

(4) Notwithstanding anything to the contrary contained in sub-rule (1), it shall not be necessary to serve notice of any proceeding incidental to an appeal on any respondent other than a person impleaded for the first time in the appellate court, unless he has appeared and filed an address for the service in the Court of first instance or has appeared in the appeal.

(5) Nothing in sub-rule (4) shall bar the respondent referred to in the appeal from defending it.

HIGH COURT AMENDMENTS

Allahabad.—In Order XLI, in rule 14, in sub-rule (1), for the words "or on his pleader in appellate court", substitute the following words, namely:—

"or on his pleader competent to service the notice on his behalf".

[*Vide* Notification No. 714-IVH-36A, dated 21st March, 1981.]

Andhra Pradesh.—In Order XLI, rule 14, in sub-rule (1), insert the following proviso, namely:—

> "Provided that the appellate court may dispense with service of notice on respondents who have remained absent, against whom the suit has proceeded *ex parte* in the Court from whose decree the appeal is preferred or who have been declared absent by the said Court."

Calcutta.—In Order XLI, in rule 14, after sub-rule. (2), insert the following sub-rule, namely:—

> "(3) It shall be in the discretion of the appellate court to make an order, at any stage of the appeal whether on its own motion, or *ex parte*, dispensing with service of such notice on any respondent who did not appear, either at the hearing in the Court whose decree is complained of or at any proceeding subsequent to the decree of that Court or on the legal representatives of any such respondent: Provided that—
>
> (a) The Court may require notice of the appeal to be published in any newspaper or newspapers as it may direct.
>
> (b) No such order shall percolate any such respondent or legal representative from appearing to contest the appeal."

Delhi.—Same as in Punjab.

Guahati.—Same as in Calcutta.

Haryana.—Same as in Punjab.

Himachal Pradesh.—Same as in Punjab.

Kerala.—In Order XLI, after rule 14, insert the following rule, namely:—

> "14A. Substitution of letter for notice.—(i) The Court may, notwithstanding anything hereinbefore contained, substitute for notice a letter signed by the Judge or such officer as he may appoint in this behalf, where the respondent is the Presiding Officer of a House of Parliament or of a State Legislature or the Chairman of a Committee thereof or, in the opinion of the Court of a rank entitling him to such mark of consideration."

Karnataka.—Same as in Andhra Pradesh.

Madras.—In Order XLI, in rule 14, in sub-rule (1), insert the following proviso, namely:—

"Provided that the appellate court may dispense with service of notice on respondent who have remained absent, against whom the suit has proceeded *ex parte* in the Court from whose decree the appeal is preferred or who have been declared absent by the said Court."

[*Vide* Notification No. 221 of 1976, published in Tamil Nadu Gazette, Pt. III, section 2, dated 17th November, 1976.]

Orissa.—In Order XLI, in rule 14, after sub-rule (2), insert the following sub-rule, namely:—

"(2A) Where the passing of an *ex parte* interlocutory order has, in the opinion of the Court, the effect of causing delay in any proceeding pending in a subordinate Court, notice shall issue simultaneously both to the respondent and to his pleader in the said proceeding in the subordinate Court, fixing a short date for return of the service. If the pleader has been served with the notice but the notice to the respondent is returned unserved and no appearance is made on his behalf the appellate court may in its discretion declare the service on the pleader to be sufficient service on the respondent and shall intimate the same to the respondent by registered post at the cost of the appellant." (w.e.f. 14-5-4984)

Punjab.—In Order XIL, in rule 14,—

(i) in sub-rule (2), insert the following proviso, namely:—

"Provided that the notice shall be served on the Advocate of the party who appeared in the subordinate Court where the matter is still pending."

[*Vide* Notification. No. G.S.R.39C.A.5/1908/S.12257 (w.e.f. 11-4-1975).]

(ii) after sub-rule (2), insert the following sub-rule, namely:—

"(3) it shall be in the discretion of the appellate court to make an order, at any stage of the appeal whether on the application of any party or on its own motion, dispensing with service of such notice on any respondent who did not appear, either at the hearing in the Court whose decree is complained of, or at any proceedings subsequent to the decree of that Court, or on the legal representatives of any such respondent:

Provided that—

(a) that Court may require notice of the appeal to be published in any newspaper or in such other manner as it may direct;

(b) no such order shall preclude any such respondent or legal representative from appearing to contest the appeal."

(iii) after sub-rule (3), insert the following sub-rules, namely:—

"(4) Where the respondent or any respondents has migrated to Pakistan and he cannot be served in the ordinary way, if the appeal has arisen out of a suit to obtain relief respecting, or compensation for wrong to immovable property, the notice shall be served on the Custodian of Evacuee Property, Punjab or Delhi, as the case may be. In all other cases, the notice shall be served on such Custodian and a copy of the notice shall be sent, by registered post, to the Secretary-General to the Pakistan Government.

(5) The provisions of sub-rule (4) shall *mutatis mutandis* apply to appellants, who have migrated to Pakistan and who cannot be served in the ordinary way."

(iv) after sub-rule (5) insert the following sub-rule, namely:—

"(6) Every notice of appeal to a respondent other than a respondent stated to be *pro forma* shall be accompanied by a copy of the memorandum of appeal or, if so permitted, by a concise statement."

Kerala.—In Order XLI, after rule 14, insert the following rule, namely:—

"14A. Substitution of letter for notice.—(1) The Court may, notwithstanding anything hereinbefore contained, substitute for notice a letter signed by the Judge or such officer as he may appoint in this behalf, where the respondent is the Presiding Officer of a House of Parliament or of a State Legislature or the Chairman of a Committee thereof or, in the opinion of the Court, of a rank entitling him to such mark of consideration.

(2) A letter substituted under sub-rule (1) shall contain all the particulars required to be stated in a notice and subject to the provisions of sub-rule (3), shall be treated in all respects as a notice.

(3) A letter so substituted may be sent to the respondent by post or by a special messenger selected by the Court, or in any other manner which the Court thinks fit; and where the respondent has an agent empowered to accept service, the letter may be delivered or sent to such agent." (w.e.f. 16-7-1963).

Orissa.—Same as in Patna.

Patna.—In Order XLI, after rule 14, insert the following rule, namely:—

"14A. The appellate court may, in its discretion, dispense with the service of notice herein before required on a respondent, or on the legal representatives of a deceased respondent, in a case where such respondent did not appear, either at any stage of the proceedings in the Court whose decree is appealed from or in any proceedings subsequent to the decree of that Court and no relief is claimed against such opposite party or respondent or his legal representative either in the original case or appeal."

15. Contents of Notice.

HIGH COURT AMENDMENTS

Bombay.—In Order XLI, after rule 15, insert the following rule, namely:—

"15A. Dismissal for want of prosecution.—Where after the admission of an appeal the rules or the special directions of the Court require the appellant to take any steps in the prosecution of the appeal before a fixed date, and where after due notice intimating the steps to be taken the appellant fails to take such steps within the time prescribed by the rules or allowed by the Court, the Court may direct the appeal to be dismissed for want of prosecution or may pass such other order as it thinks fit."

Madhya Pradesh.—In Order XLI, after rule 15, insert the following rule, namely:—

"15A.—Failure to take necessary steps after admission of an appeal in the High Court.—Where on the admission of an appeal in the High Court, the Rules of the High Court require the appellant to take any steps in

the prosecution of the appeal before a fixed date, and where, after due service of a notice intimating the steps to be taken and the date before which they must be taken, the appellant fails to take such steps within the prescribed time, the Court may direct the appeal to be dismissed for want of prosecution or may pass such other order, as it thinks fit." (w.e.f. 16-9-1960).

Procedure on Hearing

16. Right to begin.—(1) On the day fixed, or on any other day to which the hearing may be adjourned, the appellant shall he heard in support of the appeal.

(2) The Court shall then, if it does not dismiss the appeal at once, hear the respondent against the appeal and in such case the appellant shall be entitled to reply.

HIGH COURT AMENDMENT

Allahabad.—In Order XLI, in rule 16, in sub-rule (1), for the words "On the day fixed, or on any other day to which the hearing may be adjourned", substitute the words "When the appeal is called on for hearing".

[*Vide* Notification No. 14186/VII-d-147, dated 22nd December, 1951.]

17. Dismissal of appeal for appellants' default.—(1) Where on the day fixed, or on any other day to which the hearing may be adjourned, the appellant does not appear when the appeal is called on for hearing, the Court may make an order that the appeal be dismissed.

Explanation—Nothing in this sub-rule shall be construed as empowering the Court to dismiss the appeal on the merits.

(2) Hearing appeal *ex parte*—Where the appellant appears and the respondent does not appear the appeal shall be heard *ex parte*.

HIGH COURT AMENDMENT

Allahabad.—In Order XLI, in rule 17, in sub-rule (1), omit the words "on the day fixed, or on any other day to which the hearing may be adjourned".

[*Vide* Notification No. 14186/VII-d-147, dated 22nd December, 1951.]

18. Dismissal of appeal where notice served in consequence of appellant's failure to deposit cost.—[*Repealed*]

HIGH COURT AMENDMENT

Bombay.—In Order XLI, after rule 18, insert the following rule, namely:—

"18A. Dismissal for want of prosecution.—Where after the admission of an appeal the rules or the special directions of the Court require the appellant to take any steps in the prosecution of the appeal before a fixed date, and where after due notice intimating the steps to be taken the appellant fails to take such steps within the time prescribed by the rule or allowed by the Court, the Court may direct the appeal to be dismissed for want of prosecution or may pass such other order as it thinks fit." (w.e.f. 1-10-1983)

19. Re-admission of appeal dismissed for default.—Where an appeal is dismissed under rule 11, sub-rule (2) or rule 17, the appellant may apply to the appellate court for the re-admission of the appeal; and, where it is proved that he was prevented by any sufficient cause from appearing when the appeal was called on for hearing or from depositing the sum so required, the Court shall re-admit the appeal on such terms as to costs or otherwise as it thinks fit.

HIGH COURT AMENDMENTS

Andhra Pradesh.—Same as in Madras.

Bombay.—In Order XLI, for rule 19, substitute the following rule, namely:—

> "19. Re-admission of appeal dismissed for default.—Where an appeal is dismissed under rule 11, sub-rule (2), or rule 15A or rule 17 or rule 18, the appellant may apply to the Appellate Court for re admission of the appeal and where it is proved that he was prevented by any sufficient cause from appearing when the appeal was called on for hearing or in taking the necessary steps in the prosecution of the appeal or from depositing the sum so required the Court shall re-admit the appeal on such terms as to costs or otherwise as it thinks fit." (w.e.f. 1-10-1983)

Delhi.—Same as in Madras.

Gujarat.—Same as in Madras.

Himachal Pradesh.—Same as in Madras.

Karnataka.—Same as in Madras.

Kerala.—Same as in Madras.

Madras.—In Order XLI,—

(a) renumber rule 19, as sub-rule (1) thereof, and

(b) after sub-rule (1) as so renumbered, insert the following sub-rule, namely:—

> "(2) The provisions of section 5, Limitation Act, 1908, shall apply to applications under sub-rule (1)."

Madhya Pradesh.—After the words and figures "sub-rule (2)", insert the words and figures "or rule 15A", (w.e.f. 16-9-1960)

Punjab.—Same as that of Madras.

20. Power to adjourn hearing and direct persons appearing interested to be made respondents.—(1) Where it appears to the Court at the hearing that any person who was a party to the suit in the Court from whose decree the appeal is preferred, but who has not been made a party to the appeal, is interested in the result of the appeal, the Court may adjourn the hearing to a future day to be fixed by the Court and direct that such person be made a respondent.

(2) No respondent shall be added under this rule, after the expiry of the period of limitation for appeal, unless the Court, for reasons to be recorded, allows that to be done, on such terms as to costs as it thinks fit.

21. Re-hearing on application of respondent against whom *ex parte* decree made.—Where an appeal is heard *ex parte* and judgment is pronounced against the respondent, he may apply to the appellate court to re-hear the appeal; and, if he satisfies the Court that the notice was not duly served or that he was prevented by sufficient cause from appearing when the appeal was called on for hearing, the Court shall re-hear the appeal on such terms as to costs or otherwise as it thinks fit to impose upon him.

HIGII COURT AMENDMENTS

Andhra Pradesh.—Same as in Madhya Pradesh

Gujarat.—Same as in Madhya Pradesh. (w.e.f. 17-8-1961)

Karnataka.—Same as in Madhya Pradesh. (w.e.f. 5-11-1959)

Kerala.—Same as in Madhya Pradesh. {w.e.f. 9-4-1959)

Madhya Pradesh.—In Order XLI,—

(a) re-number rule 21 as sub-rule (1) thereof; and

(b) after sub-rule (1), as so renumbered, insert the following sub-rule, namely:—

"(2) The provision of section 5 of the Indian Limitation Act, IX of 1908 (now section 5 of Limitation Act, 1963) shall apply to applications under sub-rule (1)." (w.e.f. 16-9-1960)

Madras.—Same as in Madhya Pradesh.

22. Upon hearing respondent may object to decree as if he had preferred a separate appeal.—Any respondent, though he may not have appealed from any part of the decree, may not only support the decree but may also state that the finding against him in the Court below in respect of any issue ought to have been in his favour; and may also take any cross-objection to the decree which he could have taken by way of appeal provided he has filed such objection in the appellate court within one month from the date of service on him or his pleader of notice of the day fixed for hearing the appeal, or within such further time as the appellate court may see fit to allow.

Explanation.—A respondent aggrieved by a finding of the Court in the judgment on which the decree appealed against is based may, under this rule, file cross-objection in respect of the decree insofar as it is based on that finding, notwithstanding that by reason of the decision of the Court on any other finding which is sufficient for the decision of the suit, the decree, is, wholly or in part, in favour of that respondent.

(2) Form of objection and provisions applicable thereto—Such cross-objection shall be in the form of a memorandum, and the provisions of rule 1, so far as they relate to the form and contents of the memorandum of appeal, shall apply thereto.

[(3) Omitted]

(4) Where, in any case in which any respondent has under this rule filed a memorandum of objection, the original appeal is withdrawn or is dismissed for default, the objection so filed may nevertheless be heard and determined after such notice to the other parties as the Court thinks fit.

(5) The provisions relating to appeal by indigent persons shall, so far as they can be made applicable apply to an objection under this rule.

HIGH COURT AMENDMENT

Allahabad.—In Order XLI, in rule 22, in sub-rule (1), after the word "hearing" and before the word "the" insert the words "or appearance".

[*Vide* Notification No. 348/VII-d.168, dated 8th August, 1999 (w.e.f. 22-10-1994).]

23. Remand of case by appellate court.—Where the Court from whose decree an appeal is preferred has disposed of the suit upon a preliminary point and the decree is reversed in appeal, the appellate court may, if it thinks fit, by order remand the case, and may further direct what issue or issues shall be tried in the case so remanded, and shall send a copy of its judgment and order to the Court from whose decree the appeal is preferred, with directions to re-admit the suit under its original number in the register of civil suits, and proceed to determine the suit; and the evidence (if any) recorded during the original trial shall, subject to all just exceptions, be evidence during the trial after remand.

HIGH COURT AMENDMENTS

Allahabad.—In Order XLI, in rule 23,—

(a) after the words "and the decree is reversed in appeal", insert the words "or where the appellate court while reversing or setting aside the decree under appeal considers it necessary in the interest of justice to remand the case, it".

(b) omit the words "the appellate court" occurring thereafter and omit also the words "if it thinks fit", occurring after the word "may", (w.e.f. 1-6-1957)

Andhra Pradesh.—Same as in Madras.

Karnataka.—In Order XLI, for rule 23, substitute the following rule, namely:—

"23. Where the Court from whose decree an appeal is preferred has disposed of the suit upon a preliminary point and the decree is reversed in appeal, or where the appellate court in reversing or setting aside the decree under appeal considers it necessary in the interests of justice to remand the case, the appellate court may by order remand the case, and may further direct what issue or issues shall be tried in the case so remanded and whether any further evidence shall or shall not be taken after remand, and shall send a copy of its judgment or order to the Court from whose decree the appeal is preferred, with directions to re-admit the suit under its original number in the register of 'civil suits, and proceed to determine the suit; the evidence, if any, recorded during the original trial shall subject to all just exceptions, be evidence during the trial after remand." (w.e.f. 5-11-1959)

Kerala.—Same as in Madras, (w.e.f. 9-6-1959)

Madras.—In Order XLI, in rule 23,—

(a) after the words "the decree is reversed in appeal", insert the words "or where the appellate court, in reversing or setting aside the decree under appeal considers it necessary in the interests of justice to remand the case"; and

(b) omit the words "if it thinks fit," occurring after the words "the appellate court may".

Rajasthan.—In Order XLI, for rule 23, substitute the following rule, namely:—

"23. Remand of case by appellate court.—Where the Court from whose decree an appeal is preferred has disposed of the suit on a preliminary point and the decree is reversed in appeal, or where the appellate court while reversing or setting aside the decree under appeal, considers it necessary in the interests of justice to remand the case, it may by order remand the case, and may further direct what issue or issues shall be tried in the case so remanded, and shall send a copy of its judgment and order to the Court from whose decree the appeal is preferred, with direction to re-admit the suit under its original number in the register of civil suits, and proceed to determine the suit; and the evidence, if any, recorded during the original trial shall, subject to all just exceptions, be evidence during the trial after remand." (w.e.f. 11-3-1965)

23A. Remand in other cases.—Where the Court from whose decree an appeal is preferred has disposed of the case otherwise than on a preliminary point, and the decree is reversed in appeal and a re-trial is considered necessary, the appellate court shall have the same powers as it has under rule 23.]

24. Where evidence on record sufficient, appellate court may determine case finally.—Where the evidence upon the record is sufficient to enable the appellate court to pronounce judgment, the appellate court may, after resettling the issues, if necessary, finally determine the suit, notwithstanding that the judgment of the Court from whose decree the appeal is preferred has proceeded wholly upon some ground other than that on which appellate court proceeds.

25. Where appellate court may frame issues and refer them for trial to Court whose decree appealed from.—Where the Court from whose decree the appeal is preferred has omitted to frame or try any issue, or to determine any question of fact, which appears to the appellate court essential to the right decision of the suit upon the merits the appellate court may, if necessary, frame issues, and refer the same for trial to the Court from whose decree the appeal is preferred, and in such case shall direct such Court to take the additional evidence required; and such Court shall proceed to try such issues, and shall return the evidence to the appellate court together with its findings thereon and the reasons therefor within such time as may be fixed by the appellate court or extended by it from time to time.

26. Finding an evidence to be put on record.—Objections to finding.—(1) Such evidence and findings shall form part of the record in the suit; and either party may within a time to be fixed by the appellate court, present a memorandum of objections to any finding.

(2) **Determination of appeal**—After the expiration of the period so fixed for presenting such memorandum the appellate court shall proceed to determine the appeal.

26A. Order of remand to mention date of next hearing.—Where the appellate court remands a case under rule 23 or rule 23A, or frames issues and refers them for trial under rule 25, it shall fix a date for the appearance of the parties before the Court from whose decree the appeal was preferred for the purpose of receiving the directions of that Court as to further proceedings in the suit.

27. Production of additional evidence in appellate court.—(1) The parties to an appeal shall not be entitled to produce additional evidence, whether oral or documentary, in the appellate court, But if—

(a) the Court from whose decree the appeal is preferred has refused to admit evidence which ought to have been admitted, or

(aa) the party seeking to produce additional evidence, establishes that notwithstanding the exercise of due diligence, such evidence was not within his knowledge or could not, after the exercise of due diligence, be produced by him at the time when the decree appealed against was passed, or

(b) the appellate court requires any document to be produced or any witness to be examined to enable it to pronounce judgment, or for any other substantial cause, the appellate court may allow such evidence or document to be produced, or witness to be examined.

(2) Wherever additional evidence is allowed to be produced by an appellate court, the Court shall record the reason for its admission.

28. Mode of taking additional evidence.—Wherever additional evidence is allowed to be produced, the appellate court may either take such evidence or direct the Court from whose decree the appeal is preferred, or any other subordinate Court, to take such evidence and to send it when taken to the appellate court.

29. Points to be defined and recorded.—Where additional evidence is directed or allowed to be taken, the appellate court shall specify the points to which the evidence is to be confined and record on its proceedings the points so specified.

Judgment in Appeal

30. Judgment when and where pronounced.—(1) The appellate court, after hearing the parties or their pleaders and referring to any part of the proceedings, whether on appeal or in the Court from whose decree the appeal is preferred, to which reference may be considered necessary, shall pronounce judgment in open Court, either at once or on some future day of which notice shall be given to the parties or their pleaders.

(2) Where a written judgment is to be pronounced, it shall be sufficient if the points for determination, the decision thereon and the final order passed in the appeal are read out and it shall not be necessary for the Court to read out

the whole judgment, but a copy of the whole judgment shall be made available for the perusal of the parties or their pleaders immediately after the judgment is pronounced.

31. Contents, date and signature of judgment.—The judgment of the appellate court shall be in writing and shall state—

(a) the points for determination;

(b) the decision thereon;

(c) the reasons for the decision; and

(d) where the decree appealed from is reversed or varied, the relief to which the appellant is entitled, and shall at the time that it is pronounced be signed and dated by the Judge or by the Judges concurring therein.

HIGH COURT AMENDMENTS

Allahabad.—In Order XLI, in rule 31, at the end, substitute a colon for the full stop and insert the following proviso, namely:—

"Provided that where the Presiding Judge pronounces his judgment by dictation to a shorthand writer in open Court, the transcript of the judgment so pronounced shall, after such revision as may be deemed necessary, be signed by the Judge and shall bear the date of its pronouncement."

[*Vide* Notification No. 8799, dated 13th January, 1939]

Andhra Pradesh.—Same as in Madras.

Bombay.—In Order XLI, in rule 31, at the end, substitute a colon for the full stop and insert the following proviso, namely:—

"Provided that where the judgment is pronounced by dictation to a shorthand writer in open Court the transcript of the judgment so pronounced shall, after making such corrections therein as may be necessary, be signed by the Judge or the Judges concerned and shall bear the date of its pronouncement." (w.e.f. 1-10-1983)

Gujarat.—Same as in Allahabad.

Karnataka.—In Order XLI, in rule 31, insert the following proviso, namely:—

"Provided that where the Presiding Judge is specially empowered by the High Court to pronounce his judgments by dictation to a shorthand writer in open Court, the transcript of the judgment so pronounced shall after such revision as may be deemed necessary be signed by the Judge."

[*Vide* Notification No. ROC 2296/59, dated 5th November, 1959].

Kerala.—In Order XLI,—

(a) re-number rule 31 as sub-rule (1) thereof, and

(b) after sub-rule (1) as so renumbered, insert the following sub-rules, namely:—

"(2) In cases where a judgment is not written by the Judge in his own hand, but dictated and taken down *verbatim* by another person, each page of the judgment shall be initialled by him.

(3) Where the judgment is pronounced by dictation to a shorthand writer in open Court, the transcript of the judgment so pronounced shall, after such revision as may be deemed necessary, be signed by the Judge."

[*Vide* Notification No. Bl-3312/58, dated 7th April, 1959.]

Madras.—In Order XLI, for rule 31, substitute the following rule, namely:—

"31. The judgment of the appellate court shall be in writing and shall state (a) the points for determination; (b) the decision thereon; (c) the reasons for the decision; and (d) where the decree appealed from is reversed or varied, the relief to which the appellant is entitled; and shall bear the date on which it is pronounced and shall be signed by the Judge or the Judges concurring therein:

Provided that, where the presiding Judge is specially empowered by the High Court, to pronounce his judgment by dictation to a shorthand-writer in open Court, the transcript of the judgment so pronounced shall, after such revision as may be deemed necessary, be signed by the Judge."

Orissa.—Same as in Allahabad, (w.e.f. 21-9-1960)

Patna.—Same as in Allahabad inserting after the words "signed by the Judge" the words "or by Judges concurring therein".

Rajasthan.—In Order XLI,—

(a) renumber rule 31 as sub-rule (1) thereof; and

(b) after sub-rule (1) as so renumbered, insert the following sub-rules, namely:—

"(2) Where the judgment is pronounced by dictation to a shorthand-writer in open Court, the transcript of the judgment so pronounced shall, after such revision as may be deemed necessary, be signed by the Judge and shall bear the date of its pronouncement.

(3) In cases where a judgment is not written by the Judge in his own hand, but dictated and taken down verbatim by another person, each page of the judgment shall be initialled by him." (w.e.f. 11-3-1965).

32. What judgment may direct.—The judgment may be for confirming, varying or reversing the decree from which the appeal is preferred, or, if the parties to the appeal agree as to the form which the decree in appeal shall take, or as to the order to be made in appeal, the appellate court may pass a decree or make an order accordingly.

33. Power of Court of Appeal.—The appellate court shall have power to pass any decree and make any order which ought to have been passed or made and to pass or make such further or other decree or order as the case may require, and this power may be exercised by the Court notwithstanding that the appeal is as to part only of the decree and may be exercised in favour of all or any of the respondents or parties, although such respondents or parties may not have filed any appeal or objection and may, where there have been decrees in cross-suits or where two or more decrees are passed in one suit, be exercised in respect of all or any of the decrees, although an appeal may not have been filed against such decrees:

Provided that the appellate court shall not make any order under section 35A, in pursuance of any objection on which the Court from whose decree the appeal is preferred has omitted or refused to make such order.

Illustration

A claims a sum of money as due to him from *X* or *Y*, and in a suit against both obtains a decree against *X*. *X*, appeals, and *A* and *Y* are respondents. The appellate court decides in favour of *X*. It has power to pass a decree against *Y*.

34. Dissent to be recorded.—Where the appeal is heard by more Judges than one, any Judge dissenting from the judgment of the Court shall state in writing the decision or order which he thinks should be passed on the appeal, and he may state his reasons for the same.

Decree in appeal

35. Date and contents of decree.—(1) The decree of the appellate court shall bear date of the day on which the judgment was pronounced.

(2) The decree shall contain the number of the appeal, the names and descriptions of the appellant and respondent, and a clear specification of the relief granted or other adjudication made.

(3) The decree shall also state the amount of costs incurred in the appeal, and by whom, or out of what property, and in what proportions such costs and the costs in the suit are to be paid.

(4) The decree shall be signed and dated by the Judge or Judges who passed it:

Judge dissenting from judgment need not sign decree.—Provided that where there are more Judges than one and there is a difference of opinion among them, it shall not be necessary for any Judge dissenting from the judgment of the Court to sign the decree.

HIGH COURT AMENDMENTS

Andhra Pradesh.—Same as in Madras.

Bombay.—In Order XLI, in rule 35, in sub-rule (2), after the word "respondent", insert the words "their registered addresses", (w.e.f. 1-10-1983)

Delhi.—Same as in Punjab.

Haryana.—Same as in Punjab.

Himachal Pradesh.—Same as in Punjab.

Kerala.—In Order XLI, in rule 35,—

(a) in sub-rule (2), at the end, omit the full stop and insert the words "in appeal as also in the decree appealed from."

(b) in sub-rule (4), insert the following proviso, namely:—

"Provided that the provisions of the sub-rule shall not apply to decrees passed by the High Court."

[*Vide* Notification No. Bl-3312/58, dated 9th June, 1959.]

Madras.—In Order XLI, in rule 35, in sub-rule (2), after the word "respondent," insert the words "their addresses for service,",

[*Vide* ROC No. 3299 B-I, dated 29th January, 1930.]

Punjab.—In Order XLI, in rule 35, insert the following further proviso, namely:—

> "Provided also in the case of the High Court that the Registrar, or such other officer as may be in charge of the Judicial Department from time to time, shall sign the decree on behalf of the Judge or Judges who passed it; but that such Registrar, or such officer, shall not sign such decree on behalf of a dissenting Judge."

Vide Notification No. 20-R-XI-Y-I, dated 29th January, 1937.

36. Copies of judgment and decree to be furnished to parties.—Certified copies of the judgment and decree in appeal shall be furnished to the parties on application to the appellate court and at their expense.

37. Certified copy of decree to be sent to Court whose decree appealed from.—A copy of the judgment and of the decree, certified by the appellate court or such officer as it appoints in this behalf, shall be sent to the Court which passed the decree appealed from and shall be filed with the original proceedings in the suit, and an entry of the judgment of the appellate court shall be made in the register of civil suits.

HIGH COURT AMENDMENTS

Allahabad.—In Order XLI, in rule 37,—

(a) omit the words "and shall be filed with the original proceedings in the suit";

(b) insert the following para, namely:—

"Where the appellate court is the High Court the copies aforesaid shall be filed with the original proceedings in the Court."

(c) after rule 37, insert the following rule, namely:—

"38. (1) An address for service filed under Order VII, rule 19, or Order VIII, rule 11, or subsequently altered under Order VII, rule 24, or Order VIII, rule 12, shall hold good during all appellate proceedings arising out of the original suit or petition.

(2) Every memorandum of appeal shall state the addresses for service given by the opposite parties in the Court below, and notices and processes shall issue from the appellate court to such address.

(3) Rules 21, 22, 23 and 24 or Order VII shall apply, so far as may be, to appellate proceedings."

Bombay.—In Order XLI, after rule 37, insert the following rule, namely:—

"38. Registered address to hold good during appellate proceedings.—(1) The registered address filed under Order VI, rule 14A shall hold good during all appellate proceedings arising out of the original suit for petition, subject to any alteration under sub-rule (3) hereof.

(2) Every memorandum of appeal shall state the registered address given by the opposite parties in the Court below, and notices and processes shall issue from the appellate court to such addresses.

(3) Sub-rules (2) and (4) (i) and (ii) of rule 14A of Order VI shall apply, so far as may be, to appellate proceedings." (w.e.f. 1-10-1983)"

Delhi.—Same as in Punjab.

Gujarat.—In Order XLI, after rule 37, insert the following rule, namely:—

"38. Every memorandum of appeal shall state the addresses for service given by the opposite parties in the Court below, and notices and processes shall issue from the appellate court to such addresses." (w.e.f. 17-8-1961).

Orissa.—Same as in Patna.

Patna.—In Order XLI, after rule 37, insert the following rule, namely:—

"38. (1) An address for service filed under Order VII, rule 19, or Order VIII, rule 11, or subsequently altered under Order VII, rule 22 or Order VIII, rule 12, shall hold good for all notices of appeals and all appellate proceedings of the original suit or petition.

(2) Every memorandum of appeal shall state the addresses for service given by the opposite parties in the Court below, and notices and processes shall issue from the appellate court for such addresses.

(3) Rules 21 and 22 of Order VII, shall apply, so far as may be, to appellate proceedings."

Punjab and Haryana.—In Order XLI, after rule 37, insert the following rule, namely:—

"38. (1) An address for service filed under Order VII, rule 19 or Order VIII, rule 11, or subsequently altered under Order VII, rule 24, or Order VIII, rule 12, shall hold good during all appellate proceedings arising out of the original suit or petition.

(2) The notice of appeal and other processes connected with proceedings therein, shall issue to the addresses mentioned in clause (1), above, and service effected at such addresses shall be as effective as if it had been made personally on the appellant or respondent, as the case may be.

(3) Rules 21, 22, 23, 24 and 25 of Order VII shall apply, so far as may be, to appellate proceedings." (w.e.f. 24-11-1927)

Allahabad.—After Order XLI insert the following Order XLIA, namely:—

"ORDER XLIA

APPEALS FROM ORIGINAL DECREES IN THE HIGH COURT

1. Extent.—The rules contained in this Order shall apply to appeals in the High Court notwithstanding anything to the contrary contained in Order XLI or any other Order and the rules contained in Order XLI shall be deemed to have been modified or repealed in their application to such appeals to the extent of their inconsistency or repugnancy or as indicated herein.

2. Service of notice on pleader.—If a party appears by a pleader all notices to him shall be served upon such pleader, unless the Court directs otherwise.

3. Hearing appeal under rule 11 of Order XLI on date of presentation.—Where a memorandum of appeal is admitted on presentation the Court may, if it deems fit, proceed to hear the appeal under rule 11 or Order XLI on the date at which it is presented.

4. Day for appearance of respondent.—Unless the appeal is dismissed under rule 11 of Order XLI a day shall be fixed for the appearance of the respondent and notice thereof shall be given to him. The notice shall call upon him to enter appearance on or before the day so fixed and answer the appeal and inform him that the appeal shall be heard on such day thereafter as may be subsequently notified.

5. Mode of entering appearance.—The respondent shall enter appearance by filing a memorandum of appearance in such form as may be prescribed by the Court.

6. Notice of day for hearing appeal.—Notice of the day fixed for the hearing of the appeal shall be given by making an entry thereof in the day's cause list of the Court for that day and no other notice to the parties shall be necessary.

7. Application of rules 14 and 15 of Order XLI.—Rules 14 and 15 of Order XLI shall not apply insofar as they may be inconsistent with the rules of the Court regarding the nature, service or publication of notices.

8. Amendment of rules 16, 17 and 18 of Order XLI.—The following amendments shall be deemed to have been made in Order XLI, namely:—[The Amendments to the rules have been incorporated in the rules themselves (*see* ante)].

9. Dismissal of appeal for default.—Where default is made is compliance with any rules of the Court which provide for the dismissal of an appeal for such default, the Court may dismiss the appeal.

10. Upon hearing, respondent may object to decree as if he had preferred separate appeal.—Any respondent, though he may not have appealed from any part of the decree, may not only support the decree on any of the grounds decided against him in the Court below, but take any cross-objection to the decree which he could have taken by way of appeal, provided he has filed such objection within one month from the day fixed for his appearance in the notice served upon him in accordance with rule 4 or within such further time as the Court may deem fit to allow.

11. Application of rule 31 of Order XLI.—Rule 31 of Order XLI shall not apply when the Court dismisses an appeal under rule 11 of that Order."

[*Vide* Notification No. 14186/VII-d-147, dated 22nd December, 1951.]

Andhra Pradesh.—After Order XLI, insert Order XLIA, rules 1 to 14 which are same as in Madras except rule 11 which is as follows:—

> "11. Cost of application and of adjournment.—When costs are awarded, unless the Court otherwise orders, the costs of a party appearing upon any application before the Registrar of the Court shall be Rs. 15, and the costs of appearing when the appeal is in the daily cause list for final hearing and is adjourned shall be Rs. 30. At the request of any party the Registrar shall cause the order to be drawn up and the costs to be inserted therein."

Karnataka.—After Order XLI, insert the following Order, namely:—

"ORDER XLIA

APPEALS TO THE HIGH COURT FROM ORIGINAL DECREES OF SUBORDINATE COURTS

1. Rules contained in Order XLI shall apply to appeals in the High Court of Mysore with the modifications contained in this Order.

2. Where the memorandum of appeal is presented through an Advocate the memorandum shall state his address for service within the City of Bangalore and such address shall be the address for service of the appellant for all notices and processes issued in or in connection with the appeal or any Interlocutory Application in the appeal.

3. When any notice issued in an appeal preferred to the High Court fixes a date on which or a period within which the parties served with the notice shall enter appearance in the appeal such notice shall be deemed to be a notice fixing a day for hearing the appeal within the meaning of rule 12 of Order XLI.

4. The Court may direct that service of a notice of appeal or other notice of process shall be made by sending the same in a post registered cover prepaid for acknowledgment and addressed to the address for service of the party to be served which has been filed by him in the lower Court or in the High Court. A notice sent in accordance with this rule shall be deemed to be served on the day on which it would in ordinary course of post be delivered to him if the postal cover is not returned within a period of 15 days. When the cover is actually delivered to the party the postal acknowledgment purporting to contain the signature of the party may be deemed to be proof of sufficient service of the notice on the party on the day on which it is actually delivered to him. If the postal cover is returned unserved, any endorsement purporting to have been made thereon by delivery peon or other employee or officer of the postal department shall be *prima facie* evidence of the statements made therein.

5. If any party or his Advocate to whom a memorandum of cross-objections has been tendered has refused or neglected for three days from the date of such tender to give the acknowledgement mentioned in rule 22(3) of Order XLI the

respondent preferring such memorandum of cross-objections may file into Court an affidavit stating the facts and the Registrar may dispense with service of the copies of the memorandum.

6. (1) Rule 31 of Order XLI shall not apply to the High Court. If judgment is given orally, a shorthand note thereof shall be taken by a shorthand writer appointed for the purpose and a transcript made by him shall be signed or initialled by the Judge or Judges concurring therein after making such corrections as may be considered necessary.

(2) Sub-rule (4) of rule 35 of Order XLI shall not apply to the High Court. Decrees of the High Court shall be signed by the Registrar, Deputy Registrar or Assistant Registrar, as indicated by the Chief Justice.

7. (1) If an appellant or petitioner fails to show due diligence in making all deposits or payments or in taking all necessary steps as required by the Rules of the High Court in the matter of the preparation of the paper book of any appeal or petition, the Registrar may in his discretion, and shall, if the maximum period of extension of the time permissible under sub-rule (9) of rule 1, Chapter IV has expired, post the appeal or petition before the appropriate Bench for orders. The Bench may either grant further time for rectifying the default or omission, or if it thinks fit dismiss the appeal or petition.

(2) Any appeal or petition dismissed under sub-rule (1) may be re-admitted by Court if an application for readmission is made accompanied by a certificate signed by the Registrar certifying that the default or omission for which the order of dismissal was passed has been rectified".

[*Vide* Notification No. ROC 2296/59, dated 5th November, 1959.]

Kerala.—After Order XLI, insert the following Orders namely:—

"ORDER XLIA

APPEAL TO THE HIGH COURT FROM ORIGINAL DECREES OF SUBORDINATE COURTS

1. Modification in first appeals to High Court.—The rules contained in Order XLI shall apply to appeals in the High Court of Kerala with modifications contained in this order.

2. Notice fee, etc. to accompany appeal memo.—(1) The memorandum of appeal shall be accompanied by twelve printed copies of the judgment, one of such copies being a certified copy, the prescribed fees for service of notice of appeal and the receipt of the accountant of the Court of the sum prescribed by rules of Court.

(2) Time for respondent's appearance.—Notwithstanding anything contained in rule 22 of Order XLI the period prescribed for entry of appearance by the respondent and filing by him of memorandum of cross-objections, if any, shall unless otherwise ordered, by thirty days from the service of notice upon him.

3. Appearance to be filed by respondent.—(1) If the respondent intends to appear and defend the appeal he shall within the period specified in the notice of appeal enter an appearance by filing in Court a memorandum of appearance.

(2) Penalty for default.-If a respondent fails to enter an appearance within the time and in the manner provided by the sub-rule above, he shall not be allowed to translate or print any part of the record.

(3) Petition for enlargement of time and procedure thereon.-Provided that a respondent may apply by petition for further time; and the Court may thereupon make such order as it thinks fit. The application shall be supported by evidence to be given on affidavit as to the reason for the applicant's default and notice thereof shall be given to the appellant and all parties who have entered an appearance. Unless otherwise ordered the applicant shall pay the costs of all parties appearing upon the application.

4. (1) Address for service.—(1) The memorandum of appeal and the memorandum of appearance shall state an address for service within the town of Ernakulam at which service of any notice, order or process may be made on the party filing such memorandum.

(2) When party appears in person or by pleader.—If a party appears in person, the address for service may be within the local limits of the jurisdiction of the Court from whose decree the appeal is preferred:

Provided that if such party subsequently appears by a pleader, he shall state in the Vakalat an address for service within the town of Ernakulam and shall give notice thereof to each party who has appeared.

(3) Service at pleader's address.—If a party appears by a pleader, his address for service shall be that of his pleader, and all notice to the party shall be served on his pleader at that address.

5. Service by registered post.—The Court may direct that the service of a notice of appeal or other notice or process shall be made by sending the same in a registered cover prepaid for acknowledgment and addressed to the addressee for service of the party to be served, which has been filed by him in the lower Court:

Provided that, after a party has given notice of an address for service in accordance with rule 4, service of any notice or process shall be made at such address.

6. Notice to respondents appearing separately.—If there are several respondents and all do not appear by the same pleader, they shall give notice of appearance to such of the other respondents as appear separately.

7. Procedure where record not translated and printed before hearing.—(1) If, upon a case being called on for hearing, by the Court, it appears that the record has not been translated or printed in accordance with the rules of Court, the Court may dismiss the appeal or may adjourn the hearing and direct the party in default to pay costs, or may make such order as it thinks fit.

(2) If the Court proceeds to hear the appeal, it may refuse to read or refer to any part of the record which is not included in the printed papers.

(3) When an appeal is dismissed under sub-rule (1), the appellant may apply to the Court for re-admission of the appeal; and when the Court is satisfied that

there was sufficient cause for the default, it shall re-admit the appeal on such terms as to costs or otherwise as it thinks fit. (w.e.f. 20-1-1970).

8. Costs of application and of adjournment.—When costs are awarded, unless the Court otherwise orders, the costs of a party appearing upon any application before the Registrar or the Court shall be Rs. 15, and the costs of appearing when the appeal is in the daily cause list for final hearing and is adjourned shall be Rs. 30. At the request of any party the Registrar shall cause the order to be drawn up and said to be inserted therein.

Memorandum of Objections

9. (1) Copies of memorandum of objections when to be filed.-If the acknowledgment mentioned in rule 22(3) of Order XLI is not filed, the respondent shall together with the memorandum of objections file so many copies thereof as there are parties affected thereby.

(2) Prescribed fees for service.—The prescribed fees for service shall be presented together with the memorandum to the Registrar." (w.e.f. 9-6-1959)

Madras.—After Order XLI, insert the following Orders, namely:—

ORDER XLIA

APPEALS TO THE HIGH COURT FROM ORIGINAL DECREES OF SUBORDINATE COURTS

The rules contained in Order XLI shall apply to appeals in the High Court of Judicature at Madras with the modification contained in this Order.

2. (1) The memorandum of appeal shall be accompanied by twelve printed copies of the judgment, one of such copies being a certified copy, the prescribed fees for service of notice of appeal and the receipt of the accountant of the Court for the sum prescribed by the Rules of Court.

(2) Notwithstanding anything contained in rule 22 of Order XLI the period prescribed for entry of appearance by the respondent and filing by him of Memorandum of Cross-Objections, if any, unless otherwise ordered, be thirty days from the service of notice upon him.

3. (1) If the respondent intends to appear and defend the appeal he shall within the period specified in the notice of appeal enter an appearance by filing in Court a memorandum of appearance.

(2) If a respondent fails to enter an appearance within the time and in the manner provided by the sub-rule above, he shall not be allowed to translate or print any part of the record:

Provided that a respondent may apply the petition for further time, and the Court may thereupon make such order as it thinks fit. The application shall be supported by evidence to be given on affidavit as to the reason for the applicant's default, and notice thereof shall be given to the appellant and all parties who have entered an appearance. Unless otherwise ordered the applicant shall pay the costs of all parties appearing upon the application.

4. (1) The memorandum of appeal and the memorandum of appearance shall state an address for service within the City of Madras at which service of any notice, order or process may be made on the party filling such memorandum.

(2) If a party appears in person, the address for service may be within the local limits of the jurisdiction of the Court from whose decree the appeal is preferred:

Provided that if such party subsequently appears by a pleader he shall state in the Vakalatnama an address for service within the City of Madras, and shall give notice thereof to each party who has appeared.

(3) If a party appears by a pleader, his address for service shall be that of his pleader, and all notices to the party shall be served on his pleader at that address.

5. The Court may direct that service of a notice of appeal or other notice or process shall be made by sending the same in a registered cover prepaid for acknowledgement and addressed to the addressee for service of the party to be served which has been filed by him in the lower court:

Provided that, after a party has given notice of an address for service in accordance with rule 4, service of any notice or process shall be made at such address.

6. All notices and processes, other than a notice of appeal, shall be sufficiently served if left by a party or his pleader, or by a person employed by the pleader, or by an officer of the Court, between the hours of 11 a.m. and 5 p.m. at the address for service of the party to be served.

7. Notices which may be served by a party or his pleader under rule 6, or which are sent from the office of the Registrar, may, unless the Court otherwise directs, be sent by registered post; and the time at which the notice so posted would be delivered in the ordinary course of post shall be considered as the time of service thereof and posting thereof shall be a sufficient service.

8. If there are several respondents, and all do not appear by the same pleader, they shall give notice of appearance to such of the other respondents as appear separately.

9. A list of all cases in which notice is to be issued to the respondent shall be affixed to the Court notice board after the case has been registered.

10. (1) If upon a case being called on for hearing by the Court, it appears that the record has not been translated and printed in accordance with the rules of Court, the Court may hear the appeal or dismiss it, or may adjourn the hearing and direct the party in default to pay costs, or may make such order as it thinks fit.

(2) If the Court proceeds to hear the appeal, it may refuse to read or refer to any part of the record which is not included in the printed papers.

11. When costs are awarded, the costs of a party appearing upon any application before the Registrar shall be Rs. 25. At the request of any party the Registrar shall cause the order to be drawn up and the said costs to be inserted therein. (Amended on 14-11-1963)

Memorandum of Objections

12. (1) If the acknowledgment mentioned in rule 22(3) of Order XLI is not filed, the respondent shall together with the memorandum of objections file so many copies thereof as there are parties affected thereby.

(2) The prescribed fees for service shall be presented together with the memorandum to the Registrar.

13. If any party or the pleader of any party to whom a memorandum of objections has been tendered has refused or neglected for three days from the date of tender to give the acknowledgement mentioned in rule 22(3) of Order XLI, the respondent may file an affidavit stating the facts and the Registrar may dispense with service of the copies mentioned in rule 12(1).

14. Rule 31 of Order XLI shall not apply to the High Court. If judgment is given orally a shorthand note thereof shall be taken by an officer of the Court and a transcript made by him shall be signed or initialedss by the Judge or by the Judges concurring therein after making such corrections as may be considered necessary.

Comments

1. Order XLI – Scope and Application

Supreme Court of India examined the scope and application of rule 41 in the case of *Kiran Singh* and also explained the term 'prejudice'. In that case the Subordinate Judge, relying on certain receipts marked as Exhibits A to A-114 which were in the handwriting of the Patwaris of the second party and which ranged over the period from fasli 1336 to 1347, held that defendant Nos. I to II had been in possession for over 12 years as cultivating tenants and had acquired occupancy rights, and that the settlement dated 12th April, 1943, conferred no rights on the plaintiffs. He accordingly dismissed the suit. The plaintiffs preferred an appeal against this decision to the Court of the District Judge. Monghyr, who agreed with the trial Court that the receipts, Exhibits A to A-114 were genuine, and that defendants Nos. I to 11 had acquired occupancy rights, and accordingly dismissed the appeal.

The plaintiffs took up the matter in second appeal to the High Court, Patna, S.A. No. 1152 of 1946, and there, for the first time; an objection was taken by the Stamp Reporter to the valuation in the plaint and after enquiry, the Court determined that the correct valuation of the suit was Rs. 9,980. The plaintiffs paid the additional Court-fees required of them, and then raised the contention that on the revised valuation, the appeal from the decree of the Subordinate Judge would lie not to the District Court but to the High Court, and that accordingly S.A. No. 1152 of 1946 should be heard as a first appeal, ignoring the judgment of the District Court. The learned Judges held following the decision of a Full Bench of that Court in *Ramdeo Singh* v. *Raj Narain*, AIR 1949 Pat 278, that the appeal to the District Court was competent, and that its decision could be reversed only if the appellants could establish prejudice on the merits, and holding that on a consideration of the evidence no such prejudice had been shown, they dismissed the second appeal. The matter now comes before us on special leave. It will be noticed that the proper Court to try the present action would be the Subordinate Court, Monghyr, whether the valuation of the suit was Rs. 2,950 as given in the plaint, or Rs. 9,880 as determined by the High Court; but it will make a difference in the forum to which the appeal from its judgment would lie, whether the one valuation or the other is to be accepted as the deciding factor. On the plaint valuation, the appeal would lie to the District Court; on the valuation as determined by the High Court, it is that Court that would be competent to entertain the appeal. The contention of the appellants is that as on the valuation of the suit as ultimately determined, the District Court was not competent to entertain the appeal, the decree and judgment passed by that Court must be treated as a nullity, that the High Court should have accordingly heard S.A. No. 1152 of 1946 not as a second appeal with its limitations under section 100 of the Civil Procedure Code but as a first appeal against the judgment and decree of the Subordinate Judge, Monghyr, and that the appellants were entitled to a full hearing as well on questions of fact as of law. And alternatively, it is contended that even if the decree and judgment of the District Court on appeal are not to be treated as a nullity and the matter is to be dealt with under section 11 of the Suits Valuation Act, the appellants had suffered "Prejudice" within the meaning of that section, in that their appeal against the judgment of the Subordinate Judge was heard not by the High Court but by a Court of inferior jurisdiction, *viz.*, the District Court of Monghyr, and that its decree was therefore liable to be set aside, and the appeal heard by the High Court on the merits, as a first appeal. (1) ILR 27 Pat 109; AIR 1949 Pat 278, 121.

The answer to these contentions, the Court said, must depend on what the position in law is when a Court entertains a suit or an appeal over which it has no jurisdiction, and what the effect of section II of the Suits Valuation Act is on that position. It is a fundamental principle well established that a decree passed by a Court without jurisdiction is a nullity, and that its invalidity could be set up whenever and wherever it is sought to be enforced or relied upon, even at the stage of execution and even in collateral proceedings. A defect of jurisdiction, whether it is pecuniary or territorial, or whether it is in respect of the subject-matter of the action, strikes at the very authority of the Court to pass any decree, and such a defect cannot be cured even by consent of parties. If the question now under consideration fell to be' determined only on the application of general principles governing the matter, there can be no doubt that the District Court of Monghyr was coram non-judice, and that its judgment and decree would be nullities. The question is what is the effect of section 11 of the Suits Valuation Act on this position.

When the plaintiffs lost the suit after an elaborate trial, it is they who appealed to the District Court as they were bound to, on their valuation. Even there, the defendants took no objection to the jurisdiction of the District Court to hear the appeal. When the decision went on the merits against the plaintiffs, they preferred S.A. No. 1152 of 1946 to the High Court of Patna, and if the Stamp Reporter had not raised the objection to the valuation and to the Court-fee paid, the plaintiffs would not have challenged the jurisdiction of the District Court to hear the appeal. It would be an unfortunate state of the law, if the plaintiffs who initiated proceedings in a Court of their own choice could subsequently turn round and question its jurisdiction on the ground of an error in valuation which was their own. If the law were that the decree of a Court which would have had no jurisdiction over the suit or appeal but for the over-valuation or undervaluation should be treated as a nullity, then of course, they would not be estopped from setting-up want of jurisdiction in the Court by the fact of their having themselves invoked it. That, however, is not the position under section 11 of the Suits Valuation Act. Why then should the plaintiffs be allowed to resile from the position taken up by them to the prejudice of their opponents, who had acquiesced therein? There is considerable authority in the Indian Courts that clauses (a) and (b) of section 11 of the Suits Valuation Act should be read conjunctively, notwithstanding the use of the word "or." If that is the correct interpretation, the plaintiffs would be precluded from raising the objection about jurisdiction in an appellate court. But even if the two provisions are to be construed disjunctively, and the parties held entitled under section 11(1)(b) to raise the objection for the first time in the appellate Court, even then, the requirement as to prejudice has to be satisfied, and the party who has resorted to a forum of his own choice on his own valuation cannot himself be heard to complain of any prejudice. Prejudice can be a ground for relief only when it is due to the action of another party and not when it results from one's own act. Courts cannot recognise that as prejudice which flows from the action of the very party who complains about it. Even apart from this, we are satisfied that no prejudice was caused to the appellants by their appeal having been heard by the District Court. There was a fair and full hearing of the appeal by that Court;' it gave its decision on the merits on a consideration of the entire evidence in the case, and no injustice is shown to have resulted in its disposal of the matter. The decision of the learned Judges that there were no grounds for interference under section 11 of the Suits Valuation Act is correct.

In the result, the appeal was dismissed with costs; *Kiran Singh* v. *Chaman Paswan,* 1955 SCR 117: 1954 SCJ 514: AIR 1954 SC 340.

2. Rules of Supreme Court – Scope of Additional Evidence

Supreme Court of India in the case of *Chitturi Subbanna* also examined the scope of second appeal and Order XLI specially with reference to 'additional evidence'.

In a suit for possession and *mesne* profits the High Court gave a direction in the preliminary decree that the trial court should make an enquiry into the *mesne* profits payable by the appellant (judgment-debtor), from the date of the institution of the suit, and pass a final decree for payment of the amount found due up to the date of delivery of possession of the properties to the respondent (decree-holder). The trial court appointed a Commissioner for making the enquiry, and after considering his report, passed a final decree for a certain amount. No objection was taken by the appellant, either before the Commissioner or the trial court that accounts could be taken under Order XX, rule 12, Civil Procedure Code, only for 3 years from the date of the preliminary decree and not till the later date when possession was delivered to the respondent. In his appeal to the High Court also, the appellant did not raise the ground in the memorandum of appeal, but when the appeal was argued he sought to raise the contention. The High Court did not allow him to do so and dismissed the appeal. Along with the appeal the High Court dealt with the cross-objections preferred by the respondent in which he claimed enhancement of the amount of *mesne* profits and partially allowed the cross-objections. In the appeal to the Supreme Court it was contended that (i) the High Court was in error in not allowing the appellant to raise the objection based on Order XX, rule 12 of the Code, (ii) the respondent was not entitled to be granted *mesne* profits for a period beyond three years from the date of the preliminary decree, and (iii) the High Court was in error in enhancing the amount of *mesne* profits.

3. *Per* Raghubar Dayal and Sikri, JJ.

The Judges held as; (i) The High Court was in error in not allowing the appellant to urge the additional ground before it. It was a pure question of law not dependent on the determination of any question of the fact and such questions are allowed to be raised for the first time even at later stages. Even though the High Court has discretion to allow or refuse an application for raising an additional ground, the order refusing permission could be interfered with by the Supreme Court, because, it was not in conformity with the principle that a question of pure law can be urged at any stage of a litigation. [664 H; 666D-F-G] There was no question of the appellant conceding before the Commissioner or electing before the trial court that *mesne* profits could be calculated till the date of delivery of possession when no dispute about the matter had arisen between the parties; *Chittoori Subbanna* v. *Kudappa Subbanna,* AIR 1965 SC 1325: (1965) 2 SCR 661: 1966 (1) SCJ 269.

4. Filing of Appeal and Deposit Decretal Amount

This provision may be read alongwith rule 5(5). Sub-rule (5) of rule 5 specifically refers to rule 1(3). Therefore, the two provisions taken together would clearly show that deposit of the decretal amount or furnishing security is not a condition precedent to filing of the appeal. The word 'shall' used in sub-rule (3) is also not mandatory. This rule by itself does not prescribe any rigour for non-compliance with the direction of the court. But it will be penal for the appellant when he seeks stay of the execution of the decree. In that event rule 1(3) must be taken together with rule (5) and the appellant may not obtain an order of stay so long as the decretal amount is not deposited or a security is not furnished. Sub-rule (5) of rule 5 refers to rule 1(3) and this rule permits the plaintiff to furnish security as an alternative measure, if allowed by the appellate court; *Union Bank of India* v. *Jagannath Radhey Shyam and Co.,* AIR 1979 Del 36: 81 Pun LR (D) 50.

5. Rule 1—Changes in the Rules

Prior to passing of the Amendment Act of 1999, it was imperative for the appellant to file a copy of the decree alongwith the memo of appeal. There was some relaxation regarding filing of copy of the judgment and that too was available only with permission of the appellate court. Now the appellant has to file a copy of the judgment only.

The High Court of Madras held in *L. Vardarajan* v. *Thomos,* AIR 2000 Mad 383 that if a copy of the decree is produced within the time granted the appeal must be deemed as presented properly. Obviously, according to this view filing of copy of the decree is essential. But the provisions laid down by rule 1 of Order XLI, as amended by the Amendment Act of 1999 which came into force w.e.f. 1-7-2002 filing of the copy of the decree is not required. Even regarding filing of copy of the judgment, the rule does not empower the court to grant time. The provision that the memorandum shall be accompanied by a copy of the judgment makes its filing an essential condition of a valid memorandum of appeal.

There were innumerable case-laws regarding filing of the decree and default in doing so alongwith the memorandum of appeal which have no relevance after 1.7.2002.

6. Order XLI, Rule 1 and Order III, Rule 4

Signing of memo of appeal by appellant or pleader Nature of requirement Defects in – Effects of – The Supreme Court held that said deficiencies will not invalidate memo of appeal if such omission or defect is not deliberate *Uday Shanker Triyar* v. *Ram Kalewar Prasad Singh,* AIR 2006 SC 269: 2005 AIR SCW 5851: (2006) 1 SCC 75; *see* also *B.P. Agarwal* v. *Dhanalakshmi Bank Ltd.,* AIR 2008 SC 1431: AIR 2008 SCW 1448: (2008) 3 SCC 397 and *Malwa Strips Pvt. Ltd.* v. *Jyoti Ltd.,* AIR 2009 SC 1581: 2009 AIR SCW 1113: (2009) 1 SCALE 438.

Rule 1—Mere filing of an appeal does not make the unenforceable Centrotrade; *Minerals* v. *Hindustan Copper Ltd.,* 2006 (6) Supreme 519.

In *B.K. Harsha* v. *Bharat Heavy Electricals,* AIR 2008 SC 1267: 2008 AIR SCW 1301: (2008) 4 SCC 48, the Supreme Court held that first appeal may not be dismissed *in limine.*

In *Inderchand Jain* v. *Motilal,* also the Court held that filing of an appeal does not amount to stay of execution of a decree. (2009) 11 SCR 252: 2009 AIR SCW 5364.

7. Order XLI, Rule 1 – Effect of Copy of Decree Filed with Appeal not in Accordance with Order XX, Rule 6

The High Court of Punjab said that where the copy of the decree which is filed with the appeal is not in accordance with Order XX, rule 6, the decree is not capable of execution. Where the appellant is not responsible for the mistake, he cannot be panelized for any fault of the Court and it would be sadly prolonging the litigation, if the appellate, court were to direct that a proper decree be presented and that the appellant should then obtain a copy of the amended decree and file it with the proper and executable decree can be prepared and that the appellant should then obtain a copy of the amended decree and file with the proper appeal to get an executable decree. Appellate court on decision of the appeal can pass direction which would include the decree of the trial court; as well; 59 Punj LR 310: AIR 1957 Punj 238.

8. Copies of Judgment and Decree Obtained by Appellant from Respondent Fraudulently

The High Court of Madhya Pradesh examined effect of a case of obtaining decree fraudulently and used against wishes of respondent- However, no plea has been taken by respondent to restoration of possession of such copies The

Court said that it cannot be held that appeal has been filed without copies of judgment and decree appealed from. *Union of India representing the General Manager, South Eastern Railway, Calcutta* v. *Ibrahim Gulaba Tobacco Merchant*, 1965 MPLJ 572: 1965 Jab LJ 1001: AIR 1966 MP 52 (54) (Pt B) (Pr 9).

9. New Plea

In the case of *New Prakash Transport* under Motor Vehicles Act, it was held that even in a Court of law a party is not entitled to raise the question at the appellate stage that he should have been granted an adjournment which he did not pray for in the Court of first instance. Far less, such a claim can be entertained in an appeal from a Tribunal which is not a Court of justice, but a statutory body functioning in a *quasi*-judicial way. The *New Prakash Transport Co. Ltd.* v. *The New Suwarna Transport Co. Ltd.*, 1957 MPC 205: 1957 SCA 178: 1957 Jab LJ 344: 1957 SCJ 236: 1957 Mad L (Cr) 157: 1957 SCR 98: AIR 1957 SC 232 (241) (Pt E) (Pr 19).

10. New Case in Appeal

A Division Bench of the High Court of Nagpur said that where in a suit for damages for wrongful injury the plaintiff did not plead particular facts constituting negligence in the plaint, the High Court of Nagpur said that he could not be allowed to plead such a new case at the stage of appeal, particularly when the defendant had no opportunity of meeting it in the trial court; *Lal Ramkumar Singh* v. *Governor-General in-Council*, 1950 Nag LJ 351: IL 11 (1950) Nag 473: AIR 1950 Nag 234 (236) (Pt A) (Pr 7) (DB).

A Division Bench of the High Court of Orissa said that plea of want of notice under section 80 cannot be raised for first time in appeal. *See ibid.*, section 80. *Basudeb* v. *Padmanav*, ILR 1959 Cut 258: 25 Cut LT 335, The High Court of Orissa said that case not made out in pleadings or in evidence in lower court cannot be set-up in appellate court. *Chandrasekhar Praharaj* v. *Pitambari Dibya*, ILR (1953) Cut 343: AIR 1953 Ori 315 (325) (Pt H) (Pr 46) (DB).

The High Court of Rajasthan also decided the question whether a particular place was a town sought to be raised in second appeal – Determination dependent on notification by Government and on evidence – It was held that appellant could not raise the plea at such a late stage; *Parbhati* v. *Bhonrelal*, 1955 Raj LW 676: AIR 1954 Raj 285 (286) (Pt A).

11. New Case in Appeal After Remand

Where the plaintiff never pressed the question of adoption before the case was remanded to the lower court by the High Court, he cannot press the question before the appellate court after remand, 1951 RLW 156. An appellant can raise a question of law or jurisdiction for the first time in appeal; *Shah Jagjivau Jetha* v. *Doshi Talakchand Hirachand*, 8 Sau LR 102: AIR 1955 Sau 88 (Pt &) (Pr 3) (DB). A question of law which is not raised either in the Court below or in the memorandum of appeal and which requires for its decision additional or fresh evidence cannot be raised in appeal, and the appellate Court will not on that ground ask the trial Court to have a *de novo* trial of the suit. *Eapen Cherian* v. *Manacheekhan Meerakhan*, 1950 Trav Co LR 683: (1950) Ker LT 383: AIR 1951

Trav Co 101 (102, 103) (Pr 4). Point not considered by lower court nor raised in grounds of appeal cannot be urged or argued at hearing; *B. Meerakutty* v. *K. Meerakutty*, 1951 Ker LT 574: AIR 1952 Trav Co 91 (92) (Pt B) (Pr 2) (DB).

12. Right to Raise Question of Law in Appeal

An another Division Bench of the said High Court held that where a pure question of law arises, it is not open to the party to object to the raising of that question for the first time in first appeal; *Reghu Singh* v. *Government of Orissa*, 18 Cut LT 176: AIR 1951 Ori 95 (100) (Pt G) (Pr 14) (DB).

13. Rules 1 and 2 – New Point in the Matter of Mixed Question of Law and Facts

Question of abatement of suit as widow was not brought on record along with minor son of deceased plaintiff-Question was not raised in lower court or in memorandum of appeal although defendant was aware of presence of widow. The High Court of Patna held that the question being mixed question of law and fact, defendant will be estopped from raising it in appeal, Evidence Act (1872), section 115; *Balgajan Rai* v. *Sukhu Rai*, ILR 26 Pat 249: AIR 1948 Pat 288 foll. *Jaggernath Singh* v. *Narayan Sarogi*, AIR 1965 Pat 300 (301) (Pt A) (Pr 6), rules 1 and 2.

14. Rules 1 and 2 – New Point in Reply

A Division Bench of the High Court of Calcutta stressed that when the Counsel for the appellant had not even mentioned a point in his opening address it is not open to respondent too to raise a new point in the course of his reply; *Hindustan Motors Ltd.* v. *Union of India*, 58 Cal WN 209: AIR 1954 Cal 151 (156) (Pt G) (Pr 13) (DB).

15. Right of Defendant to Raise Question

A Division Bench of the High Court of Patna said that where the defendant intends to raise question of want of notice for the first time in appeal, the High Court of Patna said "Plea cannot be allowed to be raised in appeal for the first time"; *Abdul Rahim* v. *Azimuddin*, AIR 1965 Pat 156 (DB).

16. New Point in Letters Patent Appeal

A Division Bench of the Patna High Court directed in an LPA that question of fact about Intention of parties cannot interfere for the first time in appeal. The Bench said that question that intention of parties was that lease would become operative after entire nazrana money had been paid to lessor, cannot be pleaded in defence for first time in Letters Patent Appeal; *Purna Nand Puri* v. *Kamala Sinha*, AIR 1965 Pat 39 (43) (Pt D) (Pr 14) (DB).

17. New Plea of Waiver

Another Division Bench of the said Court held that where there was nothing either in the plaint or the issues to give any indication that the question of "waiver" was ever raised on the side of the respondent, he cannot raise it for the first time in appeal in support of the judgment under appeal; *Baldeo Narain Singh* v. *State of Bihar*, 1959 Pat LR 103: ILR 38 Pat 788: AIR 1959 Pat 442 (445) (Pt EP) (Pr 9) (DB).

18. New Point

Where the point as to maintainability of suit against Dominion of India for want of contract in accordance with section 175(3), Government of India Act, 1935, was neither raised in the written statement nor in the memorandum of appeal the High Court refused to entertain it at the time of arguments in appeal; *Kalyanpur Lime Works Ltd.* v. *State of Bihar*, 1954 SCJ 99: 1954 SCR 958: AIR 1954 SC 165, rel. on. *Union of India* v. *Dwarkadas Radhakrishna*, 1958 BLIB 504: ILB 37 Pat 468: AIR 1959 Pat 39 (46) (Pt D) Pr 31.

19. New Plea as to Adverse Possession

New plea as to adverse possession cannot be allowed for the first time in appeal. Where the defendant has not raised the plea of adverse possession in his written statement and no issue on the point has consequently been framed, the appellate court would not be justified in making out a new case of adverse possession for the defendant which the plaintiff had no time to meet or rebut; *Siri Ram* v. *Bishan Singh*, AIR 1952 Pepsu 46 (47) (Pt B) (Pr 4).

20. New Plea About Question of Possession

When in connection with a question of law regarding the effect of the proviso to section 42 of the Specific Relief Act, no specific issue as to possession is raised or decided by the trial court, the question of possession which is a question of fact cannot be allowed to be raised in appeal. 1951 AWR (Rev.) 190: 1951 RD 239. New question sought to be raised, being pure question of law – Neither raised in lower appellate court, nor referred to in pleadings – Point was allowed to be raised because it was a pure question of law. (1965) 2 An LT 402: (1966) 1 Andh WR 62.

21. New Plea – Grounds of Objection – Question of Law

The question whether the trial court should have dismissed the suit as being one for partial partition is a question of law, the High Court of Ajmer had said that the objection could be raised in first appeal even though no objection was taken on that point before the trial court and no issue was got framed, if it arose out of facts admitted or proved to the satisfaction of the Court. *Sohanlal* v. *Maganlal*, AIR 1954 Ajmer 78 (79) (Pt A) (Pr 4). The High Court of Allahabad said that where claimant did not claim interest before District Judge, he cannot claim it in appeal when he has not taken it as a ground of appeal. *See* Land Acquisition Act (1894), section 34 *Maharaj Kumar Arfan Rasul Khan* v. *U.P. Govt.*, ILR (1960) 2 All 71. If facts admitted or established give rise to certain questions of law, the Court is not debarred from giving effect to such pleas by any technicality of procedure. *Lakshmi Ratan Cotton Mills Co. Ltd.* v. *J.K. Jute Mills Co. Ltd., Kanpur*, (1957) 27 Com Cas 660: AIR 1957 All 311 (316) (Pt D) (Pr 32) (1313). A Division Bench of the High Court of Allahabad held that where plea is raised by respondent in reply to a new plea adduced on behalf of appellant himself, such plea should be allowed, (1957) 27 Com Cas 660: AIR 1957 All 311 (316) (Pt E) (Pr 32) (DB).

22. Rule 1 and Order VI, Rule 2 – New Plea – Ratification

Question of ratification is a Mixed question of law and fact. Hence, it cannot be allowed for the first time in appeal. *Board of Directors, Y.M.C.A., Allahabad* v. *R.H. Niblett*, AIR 1957 All 219 (232) (Pt F) (Pr 57).

23. Reopening of Point Conceded by Lawyer, in Appeal

The High Court of Patna held in a case where the lawyer intended to re-open the point conceded by him that where a lawyer, feeling that the evidence on his side on a point in issue does not establish his case, concedes the point, the concession is not intended to bind his clients in a later stage of the case and to prevent another lawyer, who might take a different view of the evidence, from re-opening the point in appeal; *Dundbahadur Singh* v. *Durga Prasad Singh*, 1953 BLJR 234: AIR 1953 Pat 346 (348) (Pt A) (Pr 7) (DB).

24. Order XLI, Rule 1 and U.P. Agriculturists' Relief Act (27 of 1934), Section 12

Application under—Mortgagor urging that mortgagee being able, with the exercise of ordinary diligence, to realize the amounts of the decree for arrears of *theka* money and he having nonetheless failed to recover the same from the mortgagor, was not entitled to claim the profits in respect of the period covered by the decree in the case. Failure to plead that the mortgage could have realised the amount with the exercise of ordinary diligence, a Division Bench of the High Court of Allahabad said that question being one of fact could not be allowed to be raised in appeal. *Tajpal Singh* v. *Ganga Sahai*, 1952 All LJ 172: 1952 All WR (HC) 209: 1951 BD (BR) 325: AIR 1952 All 808 (809) (Pt C) (Pr 12) (DB). In a case where the party claimed to be hereditary tenant by virtue of contract, he cannot set up new case that he became hereditary tenant under section 180 (2); *See Tenancy Laws—U.P. Tenancy* Act (17 of 1939), section 180(2). 1952 BD (BR) 235.

25. New Plea of Jurisdiction

The plea of want of jurisdiction of the Commissioner under section 265(3) of the U.P. Tenancy Act though not taken in the grounds of appeal can be permitted to be argued as it requires no further investigation of facts. *See* U.P. Tenancy Act, section 265(3). 1952 RD (BR) 165: 1952 All LJ Rev 136.

26. Plea of *Res Judicata*

A Full Bench of the High Court of Andhra Pradesh held that where plea of *res judicata* is not raised by pleadings or in the issues, plea could not be raised in appeal for the first time; *Katragadda China Anjaneyulu* v. *Kattragadda China Ramayya*, (1965) 1 Andh WR 159: (1965) 1 Andh LT 149: AIR 1965 AP 177 (FB).

27. New Plea under Madras Rivers Conservancy Act; (6 of 1884), Sections 11, 12, 13 – Contravention of

It was held that application of the sections depended upon survey under section 3 and notification under section 7 – Whether river was so surveyed and notified or not is question of fact – Question not investigated in lower Court – Party cannot raise question in appeal — Madras Rivers Conservancy Act (6 of 1884), sections 3, 7, 11, 12, 13; *State of Andhra Pradesh* v. *Koneru Suryanarayana*, (1962) 2 Andh WR 401: AIR 1963 AP 94 (103) (Pt B) (Pr 37).

28. New Plea – Important Plea not Taken by Defendant Appellant in Written Statement – Plea not Taken Even in Memo of Appeal

The High Court of Madras held that plea could not be raised at the time of arguments in appeal, based upon a few answers given by witnesses during their examination – Need for formulating a claim with precision and particularity present in all cases is even more so in a case where rights are made to rest upon lateral accretions and reformation *in situ*; rel. on: AIR 1945 Mad 396: (1962) 2 Andh WR 401: AIR 1963 AP 94 (104) (Pt E) (Pr 41).

29. New Point of Limitation

According to a Division Bench of the High Court of Andhra Pradesh a question of limitation can be raised in appeal for the first time where the parties proceeded on that footing in the Court and far from raising any objection on the ground of lack of definite pleading in that behalf, both sides invited the Court to go into that matter and to give a decision on that issue; *Anantam Veeraju* v. *Valluri Venkayya*, (1960) 1 Andh WR 340: ILB 1959 AP 951: AIR 1960 AP 222 (228) (Pt G) (Pr 20) (DB).

30. Plea of Jurisdiction in a Suit for Restitution of Conjugal Rights Instituted before Commencement of Hindu Marriage Act

Court clothed with jurisdiction under Act – Objection that remedy available to aggrieved party was not by way of regular suit but by way of application under Order IX – Such objection held could not be raised for first time in appeal – Court held competent to entertain suit – Decree held was not nullity – *See* Hindu Marriage Act, (1955), section S (b); *B. Sivanandy* v. *P. Bhagavathyamma*, AIR 1962 Mad 400: 75 Mad LW 161.

31. New Plea of *Estoppel*

Plea of *estoppel* is mixed question of fact and law – Plea cannot be permitted to be raised for the first time in appeal. *Union of India* v. *R. Akbar Sheriff*, 1961 Mad WN 321: (1961) 3 PLR 35: 1901 Mad LI (Cri) 180: 74 Mad LW 293: (1961) 1 Mad LJ 273: ILR (1461) Mad 747: AIR 1961 Mad 486 (494) (Pt C) (Pr 29) (DB). Where a plea raising a pure question of law on the facts admitted in the plaint was taken during the trial of the suit and the trial court has considered the plea and given a finding thereon, the question can be considered and decided in the appeal, although no such express plea was taken in the defendant's written statement; *M. Vedachala Mudaliar* v. *S. Rangaraju Naidu*, 73 Mad LW 315: (1960) 39 ITR 308: ILR 1960 Mad 455: (1960) 1 Mad LJ 445: AIR 1960 Mad 457 (459) (Pt A) (Pr 9).

Where the point was not raised in the written statement filed by the appellant but for the first time in the memo of appeal, it was held that it would not be just and proper that the appellants should be allowed to raise this plea in appeal when they did not choose to raise it at the trial and when the person interested, did not contest the plaintiff's claim in the Court below and had not chosen to contest his claim in appeal; *Kokila* v. *K.M. Rajabather*, (1957) 2 Mad LJ 123: 70 Mad LW 457: ILR (1957) Mad 968: 1957 Mad WN 370: AIR 1957 Mad 470 (471) (Pt B) (Pr 4) (DB).

32. New Point – If can be Urged

Here the appellant-villagers filed a suit clearly claiming an easement of pasturage over certain land by prescription, they cannot be allowed to change their case by claiming customary easement in appeal when they found that their case based on prescription must fail.

Consequently where the pleadings did not set up clearly the custom alleged, even if the appellants are allowed to raise the plea in appeal they cannot succeed. *Hidangmayum Achou Sarma* v. *Union Territory of Manipur,* AIR 1960 Manipur 18 (19) (Pt B) (Pr 9).

33. New Point Abandoned in Lower Court

A Division Bench of the High Court of Andhra Pradesh held that it is no doubt true that on questions of law, there cannot be any question of *estoppel* and the appellant can raise this as a ground of objection in the appeal, but when the appellant as a matter of fact had given up a point he cannot be allowed to agitate the same in appeal; *Dippala Suri Dora* v. *V.V. Giri,* (1958) 2 Andh WR 226: ILR 1958 AP 343: 1958 Andh LT 1095: AIR 1958 AP 724 (732) (Pt G) (Pr 26) (DB).

34. Order XLI, Rules 1, 2 – Second Appeal – Appeal Confined to One Part – Case Abandoned in Lower Court – Effect

It is indeed well-settled that it is open to the parties or their counsel in the trial of civil suits to abandon such issues as they like and if that is done, they cannot be revived. It was held that the appellants could not, by reason of their own abandonment, raise any other point in the appeal save that of interest; *Sukhlal* v. *Deepchand,* ILR (1953) 3 Raj 373: AIR 1954 Raj 58 (63) (Pt B) (Pr 22) (DB).

35. Plea that Suit was Premature

Plea abandoned in trial court – Cannot be entertained in first appeal; *Dhan Singh Yadav* v. *Badri Prasad,* 1963 Raj LW 304: ILR (1963) 13 Raj 668: AIR 1963 Raj 198.

36. Point not Raised in Lower Court

According to a Division Bench of the High Court of Andhra Pradesh a point of law not raised in the lower court can be allowed to be raised in the appeal for the first time; *Chunduru Seshamma* v. *Chunduru Ramakoteswara Rao,* (1957) 2 Andh WR 287: AIR 1958 AP 280 (282) (Pt A) (Pr 8) (DB).

37. Letters Patent (Mad), Cl. 15

Regarding a plea raised in LPA, the High Court of Andhra Pradesh said that a new plea which is inconsistent and contrary to the admissions made by a party in the counter-affidavit filed by it in a writ petition before a Single Judge cannot be allowed to be raised for the first time in Letters Patent Appeal against the order of the Single Judge; *Commissioner, Municipal Council, Guntur* v. *Basu Venkateswara Rao,* 1956 Andh LT 605: 1956 Andh WR 616: ILR 1956 Andh 622: AIR 1957 AP 103 (104) (Pt A) (Pr 6) (DB).

38. New Plea of Validity of Security Bond

The validity of a security bond was not challenged on the ground that it was not prepared on a duly stamped paper in the objections raised by the respondent under section 47 of the Code.

A Division Bench of the High Court of Assam held that the question did not strictly arise before the High Court in appeal; *Jagannath Prosad Jayaswal* v. *Ramprosad Jayaswal,* AIR 1958 Assam 15 (17) at C) (Pr 6) (DB).

39. New Plea – Question of Fact

Nature of property sold in execution sale.—According to another Division Bench of the Assam High Court it is a question of fact in each case whether what was sold in an execution sale was the property itself or merely the right, title and interest of the judgment-debtor. Where that question was not raised in the trial court and no finding on it was given by that Court, it cannot be raised at the appellate stage; *Girija Sankar Sukul* v. *Nayan Chandra Das*, ILR (1951) 3 Assam 332: AIR 1952 Assam 5 (10) (Pt B) (Pr 26) (DB).

40. Appeal – Objection to Admissibility of a Document cannot be Raised for the First Time

A Division Bench of the High Court of Assam held that question as to the admissibility of a document cannot be raised for the first time in appeal; *Alkash Ali Khalifa* v. *Nath Bank Ltd.*, ILR (1951) 3 Assam 1: AIR 1951 Assam 56 (59) (Pt C) (Pr 7) (DB).

41. Suit Against Railway Administration

Plea that plaintiff without alleging and proving misconduct could not claim compensation not raised in written statement – Plea, if can be allowed to be raised in appeal – Railways Act (1890), section 72.

42. *Per* Barn Labhaya, J.

Where the defendant admits a material fact in no mistake or misapprehension in his written statement, he cannot be allowed to convert his admission into a denial for the first time in appeal. Thus, where there is an omission in the written statement to raise the plea that as the consignment was admittedly booked under Risk Notes A and B, the plaintiffs could not claim compensation without alleging and proving, misconduct on the part of the Administration or its servants and the liability to pay compensation is admitted, the plea cannot be allowed to be raised in appeal for the first time as it involves a total denial of liability to pay compensation. *Governor-General of India in-Council* v. *Jesraj Tilokchand Labhchand*, ILR (1950) 2 Assam 489: AIR 1950 Assam 175 (181) (Pt C) (Pr 33, 34) (DB). New point of law can be allowed to be argued for the first time in appeal. *Ulhasibari Jethmal Bagman* v. *S. Bhagchand*, ILR (1959) Bom 680: 61 Bom LR 103.

Pleadings in the *mofusil* are not always artistically drawn and should not be construed too strictly. If it is open to the party on the admitted facts to rely upon a particular contention it would be open to the Court to allow him to do so though that is raised only as an alternative plea in appeal during the hearing, when it can be allowed without any prejudice to the opposite party. *Karam Chand* v. *Firm Mian Mir Ahmad Aziz Ahmad*, AIR 1938 PC 121: 32 Sind LR 462, foll. *Ramlaxmi Ranchhodlal* v. *Bank of Baroda Ltd.*, (1952) 54 Bom LR 667: ILR 1953 Bom 339: AIR 1953 Bom 50 454, 55) (Pt B) (Prs 2, 3) (DB).

43. Question of Waiver of Notice under Section 77, Railways Act, is a Mixed Question of law and fact and cannot be raised for first time in appeal. *Jibanram Agarwalla* v. *Union of India*, (1965) 69 Cal WN 692.

Plea as to Bailment not taken in Trial Court

Plea not allowed to be raised in appeal in absence of sufficient material on record. *Hanutmal Bhutoria* v. *Dominion of India*, AIR 1961 Cal 54 (58) (Pt C) (Pr 14) (DB).

The question whether or not the appellants were willing to take the properties of the dissolved firm at a valuation fixed by the arbitrator is entirely a question of fact. The appellants cannot be allowed to raise a new question of fact for the first time in the appellate court; *Pannalal Paul* v. *Padmabati Paul*, 64 Cal WN 816: ILR (1961) 1 Cal 931: AIR 1960 Cal 693 (696) (Pt F) (Pr 9) (DB).

44. New Plea in Land Acquisition Act (1894), Sections 5A and 6

Whether the acquisition has been made on the strength of section 89 of the Calcutta Improvement Act or not is a question of fact. If the plaintiff wanted to make a case that section 5A, Land Acquisition Act, 1894, was applicable to these proceedings, and so the declaration under section 6 was invalid in law, having been made without waiting for the period of thirty years, which is allowed under section 5A to interested parties to object to the acquisition, it was necessary, that he should have raised this point definitely. This point was not raised in the plaint and rightly no issue was framed. In that state of things, the plaintiff could not be allowed to urge the point, that in view of the provisions of section 5A, the declaration under section 8 was invalid in law; *Jivandas Khimji* v. *Narbada Bai*, AIR 1959 Cal 519 (524) (Pt C) (Pr 17) (DB).

Ordinarily, an appellant will not be allowed to set up in appeal a plea not taken by him in the lower court, but if the objection is one which goes to the very root of the case, it may be taken for the first time even in second appeal, and an objection to jurisdiction may be taken for the first time in second appeal, if it is patent on the face of the record; IL 136 Mad 76 and AIR 1921 All 290 (2), rel. on. *Rajkumar Lukhoisana Singh* v. *Ayekpam Ango Singh*, AIR 1958 Mani 7 (11) (Pt C) (Pr 32). A party cannot be allowed to travel beyond the pleadings and make out a totally new case in appeal; *Durga Das Janak Raj* v. *Preete Shah Sant Ram*, 61 Puni LR 434: ILR 1959 Punj 817: AIR 1959 Punj 530 (531) (Pt B) (Pr 3) (DB).

45. Order XLI, Rule 1 – Mode of Proof

Certified copy of statement of accounts bearing certificate of General Manager of Bank – Objection to its admissibility not taken in trial court – It cannot be taken in appeal. *See* Bankers' Books Evidence Act (1881), section 4; *Kalipada Sinha* v. *Mahaluxmi Bank Ltd.*, (1962) 32 Com Cas 511: AIR 1961 Cal 191 (DB).

46. Necessity of Plea of Waiver

The High Court of Calcutta said that the case of waiver and implied agreement involves question of law and fact and in the absence of specific pleading and specific issue, such pleas cannot be allowed to be raised in appeal; *S. Mohd. Naim Mohd. Alam* v. *Rouraffic and Far Eastern Ltd.*, ILR (1960) 2 Cal 427: AIR 1960 Cal 146 (150) (Pt C) (Pr 34) (DB).

47. Rules 1 and 11, Sections 2(2), 96, 100 and 115 – 'Decree' – Time-barred Appeal – Refusal to Extend Time – Appeal Dismissed but Decree not Drawn up – Remedy – Appeal or Revision – [Limitation Act (1908), Section 5]

Where the first appellate court refused to extend time under section 5, Limitation Act, and dismissed the appeal as time-barred, a revision petition to set aside the order refusing to extend time is not competent. The dismissal of appeal as time-barred is a decree as defined in section 2(2), C.P. Code. Therefore what is competent is an appeal; *Keshomal Basantlal* v. *Panchulal Motilal,* AIR 1953 Ajmer 32, rel. on.

A Division Bench of Nagpur said that in such a case, if the first appellate Court has not drawn up a decree, the revision filed in the High Court cannot be treated as an appeal for, in no case, can a party come up in appeal unless a formal decree is drawn up and signed; *Baliram Ganpatrao* v. *Manohar Damodar,* ILR 1943 Nag 241: AIR 1943 Nag 204 (FB), relied on; *Mangal Ballav Roaza* v. *Nihar Prava Mutsuddi,* AIR 1959 Tripura 6 (7) (Prs 2, 4).

Memorandum of appeal against appellate decree under Order XLI, rule 11(1) must be accompanied by copy of appellate decree. It is, therefore, incumbent on lower appellate court to prepare decree and supply copy of it to appellant; *Ganga Singh* v. *Jagjit Singh,* AIR 1955 VP 39 (40) (Pt A) (Pr 2).

48. Date of Presentation for Purposes of Limitation

Receipt of memorandum of appeal is date of filing appeal and not the date of posting the memorandum – Limitation. *See* Sea Customs Act (1878), section 180. AIR 1957 SC 48. Date of presentation for purposes of limitation where copy of appellate judgment appealed against is filed after limitation – In excluding time taken for obtaining copy of judgment, time taken in respect of the trial court's judgment can be excluded. *See* Limitation Act (1908), section 12, AIR 1955 NUC 2516.

49. Rule (3) (Madras) – Appeal Filed after Period of Limitation – Application for Condoning Delay also Filed with Appeal

Appeal is not admitted unless application is decided in favour of appellant – Court has no jurisdiction to pass interlocutory order in appeal until it is admitted.

After the insertion of sub-rule (3) in rule 1 of Order XLI, where an appeal is presented after the period of limitation and an application to excuse the delay in filing the appeal has also been filed, the appeal is not admitted unless the application for condoning the delay is disposed of in appellant's favour. Until the respondent is heard, after a notice is issued to him, on the petition for condoning the delay, and the appeal is admitted, the Court has no jurisdiction to pass an interlocutory order in the appeal itself. The practice of posting the application for delay for hearing along with the appeal is not warranted after the incorporation of sub-rule (3) in rule 1 of Order XLI; *Bayya Reddy* v. *Gopalarao,* AIR 1934 Mad 303: 66 Mad LJ 486, rel. on. *Ramayyan* v. *Ashtamoorthi Namboodri,* (1962) Ker LJ 681: 1962 Ker LT 500.

50. Order under Section 47 – Second Appeal not Accompanied by Copy of Decree – Copy Produced After Limitation – Appeal is Incompetent

A judgment-debtor's objection that the execution was barred by limitation was dismissed and an appeal therefrom was also dismissed. The judgment-debtor filed a second appeal accompanied by only the copy of judgment. When he produced the copy of the decree under orders of court the limitation for appeal had already expired. It was held that under Order XLI, rule 1, it was imperative on the appellant to file the copy of the decree along with the memorandum of appeal and as it was filed beyond limitation the appeal was incompetent; *Hafijan* v. *Imaman*, AIR 1951 MB 61 (62) (Prs 12, 13).

51. Patna High Court Rules, Part 2 'r' Chapter 7, Rule 7

Power of Deputy Registrar under rule 7 to grant time for production of copies of judgment beyond period of limitation – [Limitation Act (1908), section 5].

When an appeal is not accompanied by necessary copies of the judgments, the Registrar or the Deputy Registrar under rule 7 of the Patna High Court Rules, cannot grant time for production of the same beyond the period of]imitation. It is only when an application under section 5, Limitation Act, is filed that the question of condoning the delay can be considered by the Bench. The Bench even, therefore, by merely extending the time granted by the Registrar, or the Deputy Registrar, under rule 7, beyond the period of limitation, for filing the copy of the judgment appealed against cannot extend the period of limitation fixed by the statute. Rule 7 of the Patna High Court Rules cannot override the provisions of the Limitation Act; *Moinuddin* v. *Ajodhya Sahu*, 1955 BLJR 724: AIR 1957 Pat 135 (Pr 3).

52. Appellant Instead of Filing Copy of Judgment Filing Last Order in the Order Sheet of Trial Court Alongwith Memo of Appeal

Last order mistakenly taken to be judgment of trial court by the appellant as well as copying department which supplied its copy-Held, that there was no defect in form of appeal so as to make the appeal incompetent; (56) 00 Cal WN 754

53. Railways Act (1890), Section 145 – Three Persons Authorised to Plead and Act for Governor-General

Only one of them signing memorandum of appeal – Other two allowed to sign memorandum after appeal was filed – Appeal could not be held to be filed without authority; *P.C. Verma* v. *Governor-General in-Council*, AIR 1950 EP 160 (161, 162) (Pt A) (Pr 3).

54. Presentation of Appeal

Appeal has to be presented during Court hours. An appellant is entitled to present an appeal during the hours that the Courts are open. Simply because limitation may not expire until 12 p.m. it would be hard on officers if they were liable to be raised at mid-night by a person who had not been able to present his appeal within court hours. Court hours are fixed under the provisions of the Revenue Court Manual and the appeals have to be filed during these hours. It cannot, therefore be said that there would be any illegality in refusing to accept the appeal when it was presented at house of the officer after Court hours; 1932 RD 185, rel. on. 1952 RD (BR) 9: 1952 All WR 11-lev) 22: 1952 All LJ (Rev) 5. Presentation after office hours is improper and wrong; *Javariah* v. *Abdul Rahiman*, 31 Mys LJ 32: AIR 1952 Mys 66 (67) (Pr 2).

55. Person Not Party to Proceedings – Power of Appellate Court to Grant Leave to Appeal

It is manifest from sections 96, 148 and Order XLI, rule 1 that none of these provisions bars the filing of an appeal by an aggrieved person who was not actually party to the proceeding. But it may now be taken as settled that a person not a party to a proceeding cannot, as a matter of right, present an appeal against the decree. This does not, however, preclude the appellate court from according leave to file an appeal to a person against the decree or order if he is affected by the decision though he was not actually impleaded as a party; *Dimmiti Pullayya* v. *Abdebolu Nagabhushanam*, (1961) 2 Andh WR 204: 1961 Andh LT 736: ILB (1962) AP 127: AIR 1962 AP 140 (142, 145) (Prs 9, 14, 32) (FB).

56. Presentation to Wrong Court

It is true that an appeal must be presented by an authorized person, and if it is presented by a person who is not authorized to do so, it shall be rejected. But, where an appeal is presented by an authorized person, but in a wrong Court and that Court instead of returning the appeal to the appellant, itself sends it to the proper court which accepts the presentation, the appellant should not be made to suffer for the mistakes of the Court on the principle *'actus curiae neminem gravabit'*, and the appeal should not be dismissed; *Gangu* v. *Lassa Zargar*, AIR 1954 J&K 44 (Pt A) (Pr 3).

57. Proper Presentation – Appeal Filed by Advocate for Municipality – Supersession of Municipality – Presentation is Proper

A counsel appointed by a Municipal Committee will continue to have an authority on its behalf and on behalf of the Administrator who is appointed on the supersession of the Committee unless his powers are revoked under the provisions of Order III, rule 4.

Appeal signed and presented by advocate for appellant which was described as Municipality – Municipality superseded – Administrator appointed Vakalatnama signed by Administrator subsequently filed – Advocate who presented appeal held had authority on behalf of Administrator to present it and thus there was no defect in presentation; AIR 1955 Ajmer 29 (30): Pt A) (Pr 3).

58. Rule 1 and Order III, Rule 1

Vakalatnama not signed by appellant and memorandum of appeal filed signed by counsel – Appeal cannot be considered as properly presented; AIR 1928 All 252 and *Mohammad Qamar* v. *Mohammad Salamat Ali Khan*, 121 Ind Cas 546: AIR 1930 All 112, rel. on 1952 All L 1 (Rev) 110: 1952 BD (BR) 144 (DB). Memorandum of appeal signed by two advocates not entered on rolls of High Court; but granted conditional permission to appear along with enrolled Advocate – Amendment by filing power of enrolled Advocate after expiry of limitation for appeal – Delay of 43 days condoned on affidavit of Advocates – Limitation Act (1908), section (5). AIR 1955 NUC (Him Era) 5680. Appeal presented by pleader without Vakalatnama—Pleader duly authorised by person on whose behalf appeal is presented—Defect can be cured by filing of Vakalatnama even at later stage. *See ibid.*, Order III, rule 2; *State of Madhya Pradesh* v. *Yatendra Prasad Sharma*, AIR 1963 MB 127.

But the High Court of Madhya Pradesh said that omission to file a Vakalatnama is an irregularity which can be cured. *Moolchand Prop. Firm Lallimal Biharilal* v. *Ram Babu Vaishya*, 1961 MPL (Notes) 313: 1961 Jab LJ 399 AIR 1961 MP 323 (324) (Pt B) (Pr 6).

59. Rules 1 and 3, Order III, Rule 4

Memo of appeal signed by advocate of appellant – Vakalatnama not Filed with Memo – Appeal admitted – On date of hearing advocate offering to produce Vakalatnama – Appeal dismissed on ground that Advocate bad no authority – Order of dismissal invalid.

Where in an appeal against an order of the Revenue Officer, filed before the Taxation Appeal Committee, the appeal memorandum was signed by the Advocate of the assessee and not by the assessee himself, without any Vakalatnama having been filed along with the appeal petition, and the Committee rejected the appeal on the date of hearing on the ground that the advocate had no authority to sign the appeal, despite the Advocates having offered to produce a Vakalatnama.

It was held that the appeal should not have been rejected. It was not necessary that the Vakalatnama should have accompanied the appeal petition. If a person purporting to be the authorised agent of the appellant files an appeal and if he has the necessary authority to so file a petition, it cannot be regarded as defective in any way.

60. Applicability – Writ appeal-Copy of Judgment – If to be Filed

The High Court of Calcutta held that an appellant who seeks to file an appeal against an order of a Single Judge disposing of an application under article 228 of the Constitution in a matter arising outside the ordinary Original Civil Jurisdiction of the High Court, need not annex to the memorandum of appeal either a certified copy of the judgment appealed from or of the formal order which may have been or be drawn up in such cases; *Chairman, Budge Budge Municipality* v. *Mongru Mia,* AIR 1953 Cal 433 (SB), Foil.; F.M.A.T. No. 121 of 1952 (Cal), rel. on. *Surendra Nath* v. *S.M. Murshed,* 58 Cal WN 175: AIR 1954 Cal 189 (191, 192) (Pt B) (Prs 13, 19) (DB).

61. Final Judgment Referring to Previous Order – No Necessity to File Copy of Order

A Division Bench of the High Court of J&K held that the copy of the judgment which is required to be filed under Order XLI, rule 1 is the final judgment on which the decree is founded. If in the final judgment a reference is made to a previous order, it will not be necessary to file the copy of that order as well along with the memorandum of appeal; *Town Area Committee* v. *Nabir Joo Reshi,* AIR 1960 J&K 88 (Pr 4) (DB).

62. Order XLI, Rule 1, Section 115

Memorandum of appeal not accompanied by certified copy of judgment – So prayer for dispensing with such copy made when appeal was filed-appellate court in its discretion not dispensing with such copy – Decision not interfered with in revision – Appeal held incompetent; *Chetanlal* v. *Dan G.S. Gupta,* AIR 1938 Nag 233: 176 IC 33, rel. on. 1961 MPL 151.

The High Court of Madras said that memorandum of appeal not accompanied by decretal order is not maintainable; *Balakrishna Industrial Works* v. *C.S. Venkatachari,* (1954) 2 Mad LJ 290: 1954 Mad WN 347: ILR (1954) Mad 1122: 67 Mad LW 545: AIR 1954 Mad 883 (883, 884) (Prs 2, 6) (DB).

Where the copy of the decree which is filed with the appeal is not in accordance with Order XX, rule 8 and is not capable of execution, as the appellant is not responsible for the mistake he cannot be penalised for any fault of the Court and it would be unnecessarily prolonging the litigation, if the appellate Court were to direct that a proper decree be prepared and that the appellant should then obtain a copy of the amended decree and file it with the appeal. A proper and executable decree can be prepared by the appellate court on decision of the appeal on merits which would include the decree of the trial court, as well. *Hari Chand L. Sharna Mal* v. *Gordhan Das Faqir Chand Vaish*, 59 Punj LR 310: AIR 1957 Punj 238 (239) (Pt A) (Pr 3) (DB).

Two decrees in two cross-appeals or two cross-suits.

63. Proper Presentation – Cross Appeals

Distinct decrees – Appeal against one decree – Memorandum accompanied by copy of one decree only – Order XX, rule 8: AIR 1955 NUC (Pepsu) 2502.

64. Proper Presentation on Behalf of Minor

Presentation of appeal on behalf of minor Power-of-attorney signed by mother without mentioning that she was acting as next friend – Power-of-attorney did not become invalid or ineffective – There was no necessity for her to describe herself as next friend when it was conceded that she was; AIR 1955 NUC (Punj) 2161.

65. Order XLI, Rule 1 – Scope of Two Appeals Arising Out of Same Decree

Two appeals arising from same suit disposed of by one judgment— Two decrees prepared – Second appeal from one decree only – Failure to file copy of other decree—Effect. *See* section 11, *Sukhlal* v. *Deepchand*, ILR (1953) 3 Raj 373: AIR 1954 Raj 58 (DB). Separate copies of judgment are not necessary; *In re R.M. Kandaswami Mudaliar*, (1950) 2 Mad LJ 495: 1950 Mad WN 797: AIR 1951 Mad 275 (Pt B) (Pr 2). [Overruled on another point in *Karur Jai Hind Pictures represented by its Partner Periasami Goundar* v. *A.M. Shahul Hameed*, AIR 1955 Mad 625: (1955) 2 Mad LJ 254: ILR 1955 Mad 1145 (FB).] – Order XLI, rule 1 – Dismissal of appeal for failure to supply summons forms within date fixed – Order passed behind back of party prior to date fixed for hearing of appeal – Order is without jurisdiction. *See ibid.*, section 1&7; *Hemam Thambaltombi Devi* v. *Moirangthem Ibonaha Singh*, AIR 1963 Manipur 48.

66. Misdescription in the Memorandum of Appeal – Effect of Misdescription of Parties

Mewalal was defendant No. 2 in the suit. In the second appeal by the plaintiff, respondent No. 1 was described as 'Tejmal son of Bherunji (died) represented by Mewalal, son of Tejmal.' Tejmal having died could not be made a party to the appeal, Mewalal was a party.

The High Court of Ajmer distinguishing *Prabhu Dayal* v. *Firm Prabhulal Chandmal*, AIR 1954 Ajmer 74; AIR 1948 Mad 368, disting. held that the correct description would have been Mewalal on behalf of himself and as representing Tejmal.' The mistake, however, was not material; *Lal Singh* v. *Tejmal*, 1954 AMLJ 133: AIR 1954 Ajmer 75: (77) (Pt F) (Pr 10).

GROUNDS OF OBJECTION

67. Order XLI, Rules 1 and 16 – Burden of Showing Trial Court's Judgment Wrong 1 – Evidence Act (1872), Sections 101 to 103

In appeals the burden of showing that the judgment appealed from is wrong lies upon the appellant. If all he can show is nicely balanced calculation which leads to the equal possibility of the judgment on either the one side or the other being right, he has not succeeded in discharging the burden; AIR 1922:

68. Plaintiff Raising Plea of Alternative Case Neither in Trial Court nor in Grounds of Appeal

A Division Bench of the High Court of Rajasthan said that he is not strictly entitled to urge it for first time in appeal; *Bapulal* v. *Laxmi Bharat Trading Co.*, ILR (1965) 15 Raj 478: 1955 Raj LW 173: AIR 1966 Raj 14 (17) (Pt B) (Pr 8) (DB).

69. Order XLI, Rules 1 and 2

Question that the successor State is not liable for any wrong committed by its predecessor, raised for first time during argument in appeals point not raised in trial court, nor made subject-matter of any issue, nor raised as ground in memorandum of appeal – Neither party led evidence on that aspect – Point should not be permitted to be argued in appeal; *State of Rajasthan* v. *Dungar Singh*, ILR (1965) 15 Raj 503: 1966 Raj LW 21.

70. New Plea of Point of Law not in Memo of Appeal

The objection that sufficient time has not been allowed between summons and date of hearing according to rules relates to a question of law and the facts necessary to apply that rule of law are only those that will appear on the face of the records of the proceeding about which there will and can be no controversy. Therefore, even if the defendant does not raise it in his application to set aside the *ex parte* decree or in his memorandum of appeal the appellate court has a discretion to permit him to raise it in arguments the same; *Ahmed Ummal Sulaiha Ummal* v. *Abdul Khanni Lebba Noohookannulebba*, 1952 Ker LT 665: AIR 1953 Trav Co 126 (128) (Pt B) (Pr 4).

71. Order XLI, Rule 2 – Cross-objection Entertained by Lower Appellate Court – Objection to Maintainability not Taken before Lower Court

Objection involving investigation – It cannot be allowed to be raised for the first time in second appeal – *See* section 100. (1961) MLJ (Notes) 301.

The question of oral surrender is one essentially not of fact, and cannot be permitted to be raised for the first time in appeal, when there was no pleading, no issue and no trial on that question in the lower Court; *Raju* alias *Srinivasan Chettiar* v. *Lakshmi Ammal*, (1954) 1 Mad LJ 654: 67 Mad LW 291: (1955) Mad 247: 1954 Mad WN 414: AIR 1955 Mad 705 (706) (Pt A) (Pr 3) (313).

72. New Plea of Fraud

The point that a previous foreign judgment which was pleaded as a bar to the suit was already prepared and was ready before the hearing began but was delivered alter the hearing, fraudulently pretending that it had been prepared only after the hearing and therefore was vitiated by fraud and should be treated;

as *null* and *void*, cannot be urged in appeal for the first time if not raised before the trial court previously; *Ruku-ul-Mulk S. Abdul Wazid* v. *R. Viswanathan*, (1953) 1 Mad LJ 56: 65 Mad LW 925: AIR 1953 Mad 261 (260) (Pt D) (Pr 14) (DB).

73. Rule 2—Scope and Application

The rule initially directs that the appellant may not urge any ground not set forth in the memorandum of appeal. It is then provided that the party may do so with leave of the Court. Further, the rule gives wide discretion to the Court to consider any ground set forth in the memorandum of appeal or not even offered by the appellant with leave of the Court. However, the discretion of the party has been restricted by the proviso which gives a mandate to the court to consider those grounds only when the party to be affected by the said grounds have been given opportunity to contest such grounds. Hence, taken into consideration the entire provisions, it is clear that any other ground may be urged and considered after giving opportunity to the parties of having a hearing; *New India Life Assurance Co. Ltd.* v. *Commr. of Income-tax, Bombay E.P. Tax, Bombay City*, AIR 1958 Bom 143: 59 Bom LR 504: ILR 1957 Bom 502 and *Keshavlal Lallubhai Patel* v. *Lalbhai Trikumlal Mills Ltd.*, AIR 1958 SC 512: 1958 SCJ 866: 1959 SCR 213.

The Supreme Court held in *Additional Income Tax Commissioner* v. *East Coast Flour Mills*, that a question of law may be urged as an additional ground. AIR 1994 SC 1513: 1994 AIR SCW 981.

Order XLI, rule 3 – Defect of parties – Memorandum of appeal – Amendment – Respondent dead when appeal was filed – Legal representatives can be brought on record – Amendment permissible. *See ibid*, section; 151 *Doddamallappa Channabasappa Kari* v. *Gangappa Shiddappa Gulganji*, AIR 1962 Mys 44: ILR 1961 Mys 513.

74. Order XLI, Rule 3, Sections 2(2) and 115

Order of dismissal of memo of appeal on ground of limitation, is a "decree" – Revision does not lie from such an order; *Achyuta Dhangadamajhi* v. *Sibram Dhangadamajhi*, ILR 1962 Cut 818. Overruled. section 2(24); *Banwarilal Bhoid* v. *P. Neelkantham*, AIR 1965 Ori 102: ILR 1964 Cut 674 (DB).

75. Order XLI, Rule 3(2) – Insufficient Court-fee on Memorandum of Appeal Conditional Order under Section 149

Validity – Non-payment of deficit Court-fee within time cannot operate as automatic dismissal – Court has discretion to extend time under section 148. *See ibid.* section 148; *Ningombam Tombi Singh* v. *Ningombam Nene Singh*, AIR 1961 Mani 50.

76. Order XLI, Rules 3, 11, Order VII, Rule 11, Section 107(2) – Rejection of Memorandum of Appeal and Dismissal of Appeal under Order XLI, Rule 3 or Order VII, Rule 11 read with (2) – Effect

The rejection of a Memorandum of Appeal, dismissal of the appeal under the provisions of rule 3 or Order VII, read with section 107 (2 is not), dismissal of the appeal under Order XLI, rule 11 and determination of the rights of the parties with regard to all or any of the matters in controversy. The Court expresses no opinion on these matters, rejection would not amount to a decree -elicit is not appealable. Revision is maintainable. (1962) Cot' 818.

[Overruled in *Banwarilal Bhoid* v. *P. Neelkantham*, AIR 1965 Ori 102: ILR 1964 Cut 674 (DB).]

77. Order XLI, Rule 3, Sections 2(2) and 115

Order of dismissal of memo of appeal, on ground of limitation, is a "decree" – Revision does not lie from such an order; *Achyuta Dhangadamajhi* v. *Sibram Dhangadamajhi*, ILR 1962 Cut 818. Overruled. *See ibid.*, section 2(24); *Banwarilal Bhoid* v. *P. Neelkantham*, AIR 1965 Ori 102: ILR 1964 Cut 674 (DB).

78. Rule 3A

The rule deals with the condonation of delay in filing appeal after expiry of the period prescribed for it. Obviously, the provisions of section 5 of Limitation Act may not be invoked. The memorandum of appeal requires an application to be accompanied with it explaining the delay. The High Court of Delhi has held that there is no appeal before the court unless the delay is condoned. *R.C. Chaudhry* v. *Prestige Finance and Chit Fund Co. Pvt. Ltd.*, AIR 1996 Del 382: 1997 (1) Civ LJ 760: 1997 (1) CCC 698. The Supreme Court said that condonation of delay is a condition precedent to the appeal. *State of Madhya Pradesh* v. *Pradeep Kumar*, (2000) 7 SCC 372: JT 2000 (10) SC 349. According to the High Court of Calcutta, such an application may be filed even subsequent to the filing of appeal. *Sipra Dey* v. *Ajit Kumar Dey*, AIR 1988 Cal 28: (1987) 2 Cal LJ 446: (1988) 1 Hindu LR 735. Condonation of delay with imposition of costs – Supreme Court imposing costs of Rs. 10,000 to be paid by demand draft and deposited as a pre-condition for restoring appeal *Ram Chandra* v. *Chandramala*, (2005) 13 SCC 124.

79. Order XLI, Rule 4 and Section 96

Decree for ejectment against lessee and his sub-lessee – Sub-lessee has right of appeal – Decree becoming final as against lessee – Appeal by sub-lessee alone would be incompetent; T.P. Act (1882), section 115; *Shankarrao Govindrao Naik* v. *Kisanlal Nagarmal*, 1 Madh BLR 144: AIR 1950 MB 19 (20, 21) (Pt B) (Pr 4).

80. Order XLI, Rule 4

Lessee not preferring appeal against decree of ejectment passed against him and his licensee – Licensee cannot challenge lessee – Order XLI, rule 4, not applicable. *Madanlal Kothari son of Champalal Kothari* v. *Bank of Maharashtra*, 1964 MPLJ (Notes) 111: 1964 Jab LJ 495: AIR 1964 MP 262.

81. Order XLI, Rules 4 and 38 – Suit for Partition – No Decree can be Passed in the Absence of Even a Single Co-sharer

Decree for partition against *A* and six other defendants – Three of the defendants appealing without impleading *A*. Appealing defendants not only not admitting the possession or share of *A* but also setting up a case that he was not alive – Appeal abates as a whole – Rule 4 does not apply to the case because decree cannot be said to have proceeded on a ground common to all defendants – Rule 33 can be of no help to appellants in as much as it deals only with power of Court to pass decree in an appeal that is maintainable and not with the maintainability of the appeal itself; 1962 All LJ 282: 1962 All WR (HC) 217.

82. Order XLI, Rules 4 and 33

The provisions of Order XLI, rule 4 or rule 33 of the Code can apply only where the appeal is otherwise properly constituted. Those provisions cannot be called in aid to defeat the law relating to joinder of necessary parties; AIR 1957 MP 89, foll.: *Shrikrishan Moolchand* v. *Deokinandan Sardharam*, ILR 1961 MP 597: 1961 Jab LJ 462: 1961 MPLJ 538: AIR 1961 MP 314 (316) (Pt B) (Pr 7).

83. Order XLI, Rule 4 and Order XXII, Rule 3 – Appeal Proceeding on Grounds Common to All Appellants – All Joining in Preferring Appeal – Provisions of Order XXII, Apply

Where an appeal proceeds on grounds common to all the appellants so that any one of them could have prosecuted the appeal without the others, but all the appellants join in preferring the appeal, Order XLI, rule 4 ceases to apply and the appellants cannot claim an exemption from the operation of the provisions contained in Order XXII of the Code. *Lilawati Bai* v. *Gangadhar*, 1952 Nag LJ 421: AIR 1953 Nag 12, fol.l; *Ganeshmull Sahasmull* v. *Sohanlal Punamchand*, AIR 1956 Nag 111: 1955 Nag LJ 224: ILR 1955 Nag 33, disting. *Shivrajsingh* v. *Gaurishankar Baldeo Prasad*, 1960 Jab LJ 530: 1960 MPC 454: 1961 MPLJ 1106: AIR 1961 MP 147 (148) (Pt B) (Pr 5). Where a suit filed against the main defendants and .a Municipal Corporation is decreed in favour of the plaintiff rejecting the plea of the Municipality that the suit was hit by section 508 of the Patna Municipal Corporation Act, and the Municipality has not chosen to appeal against the decision along with principal defendants the appellate court will not exercise its powers under Order XLI, rules 4 and 33 to grant relief to Municipality added as respondent especially when the appellant principal defendants could not take advantage of the provisions of section 508 of that Act; *Ramautar Gope* v. *Sheonandan Mistri*, 1962 BLJR 11: AIR 1962 Pat 273 (275) (Pt D) (Pr 5).

84. Ground Common to All the Defendants

Where a decree passed against several defendants is one and indivisible and proceeds upon a ground common to all the defendants, the entire decree can be set aside on appeal at the instance of one of the defendants. 83 Ind Cas 95 and *Parwati Kuer* v. *Manna Lal Khetan*, AIR 1956 Pat 414: 1956 BLJR 327: 35 Pat 449 (FB), rel. on; *Bir Singh* v. *Budhu Ram*, AIR 1950 Pat 346 and *Venukuri Krishna Reddi* v. *Kota Ramireddi*, (1954) 2 Mad LJ 559: ILR 1954 Mad 1126: AIR 1954 Mad 848, *Dist. Digvijay Narain Singh* v. *Bibhunath Pande*, 1956 BLJR 445. Suit for ejectment of tenant on ground of sub-letting without consent of landlord – Tenant and sub-tenant both made defendants – One decree-against both – Sub-tenant alone can appeal. See Houses and Rents – Delhi and Ajmer Rent Control Act (38 of 1952), section 34; *Karam Singh Sobti* v. *Sri Pratap Chand*, AIR 1964 SC 1305: 66 Pun LR 210: (1964) 4 SCR 647.

In a case where grounds were common to all defendants, the second defendant preferred the appeal against the entire subject-matter of the suit and the grounds were common to all the defendants; and all the other defendants were made respondents to the appeal. The appellate court reversed the decree in favour of all the defendants.

It was held that under Order XLI, rule 4, the appellate decree was proper and the benefit of the appellate decree should go to all the other defendants who had not filed the appeal; *Kapila Annapurnamma* v. *Panchalavarupu Venkata Satya Seeta Ramanjaneyaratnam*, AIR 1959 AP 40 (48) (Pt F) (Pr 20) (DB).

85. Order XLI, Rule 4 – Scope and Application

In execution of a decree for partition and for costs, the judgment-debtor's objection that the decree was not executable as being time-barred was rejected. The judgment-debtors appealed against the order but on account of want of notice on one of the respondents, *A* who was defendant in the suit, the appeal stood dismissed as against him.

Held, that the effect of dismissal of appeal against *A* was to make the whole appeal incompetent. *A* 'being in the position of a plaintiff he had acquired a very valuable right to execute the decree for partition irrespective of the decision that might be made in the appeal. And because there cannot be two inconsistent decrees in one and the same litigation, the appeal cannot be allowed to proceed as against the remaining respondents. In such a case the powers under Order XLI, rule 4 cannot be invoked; *Kali Prasad Srivastava* v. *Tulshi Prasad*, ILR 32 Pat 795: 1953 BLJR 361: AIR 1954 Pat 49 (Pr 3) (DB).

86. Order XLI, Rule 4 – Applicability to Second Appeals

In an appeal by one of several appellants, the principle of Order XLI, rule 4 is applicable to second appeals and where the second appeal preferred proceeds on the ground common to all the appellants (two in this case), one of them is competent to appeal from the whole order and it is open to the Court to reverse it in favour of both, should the Court consider that such a reversal was called for; *Nanha* v. *Baroo*, ILR 1952 Patiala 592: AIR 1952 Pepsu 88 (89) (Pt A) (Pr 4) (DB).

87. Order XLI, Rules 4 and 20 – Appeal by one of the Parties Affected by the Decree

Competency:—Court's discretion – "Necessary party." Reinstatement under sec. 27 of Act 10 of 1947 (U.P.) prayed for by *A* was allowed as against *B, C* and *D* alone appealed from the decision. Held: The criterion to decide if a person is a necessary party in an appeal is whether the interest of that person will be adversely affected if the appeals were to be allowed. Order XLI, rule 4, C.P.C., enables any one of the parties aggrieved by the decree to prefer an appeal for the benefit of others also, if their interests are identical. The option to so prefer an appeal lies with the appellant and it is not in the Court's discretion to entertain it or not. If the Court finds later on that any of the omitted plaintiff or defendant was necessary to be impleaded in the circumstances of the case the discretion of the Court arises to order the impleading of such a party and insist on it. But the mere omission to implead a party is not fatal. The interests of *B, C* and *D* are identical and if the appeal is allowed the reinstatement is refused for the benefit of them all. 1952 ALJ (Rev) 229.

88. Scope of Order XLI, Rule 4; Order XLVII, Rule 1

Appeal by elder brother for himself and for minor brother – Dismissal as incompetent for want of order of appointment of elder brother as guardian Competency – Power to review – Error apparent on face of record.

Appeal purported to be filed on behalf of *A* and minor brothers through guardianship of *A* – Appeal dismissed as not properly filed on ground of *A* not being properly appointed guardian of minors.

Held, that appeal having been filed by *A* on his own behalf also, it was competent at least insofar as his claim was concerned – Therefore dismissal of his appeal was due to an error which could be rectified in review under Order XLI, rule 4, application of *A* made both on his own behalf and on behalf of his minor brother for review of the order of dismissal of appeal was allowed; *Suba Singh Kure Singh* v. *Neki Kishen Sahai*, 55 Punj LR 50: ILR (1953) Punj 379: AIR 1953 Punj 106 (107) (Pt B) (Pr 5) (DB).

"COMMON GROUND"

89. Order XLI, Rule 4

Rule 4 applies only where lower court's decree proceeds on common ground. Order XLI, rule 4 applies only where the lower court's decree proceeds on a common ground to all the defendants and not where the appellate court wishes to proceed on a common ground and reverse or modify the decree appealed from in favour of all the defendants, even though some of the defendants may not be before the appellate court: 14 WR 130, foll.; 20 All 8 and 22 All 388, ref. *Mritunjoy Das* v. *Sabitrimoni Dasi*, AIR 1950 Cal 59 (60) (Pt A) (Pr 8). Order XLI, rule 4 – Scope – Order XLI, rule 4 of the Code of Civil Procedure applies only when all the plaintiffs or defendants are alive at the time when the decree of the appellate court is passed. This provision should not run counter to the provisions of Order XXII, rule 3. A reading of the plaint disclosed that two reliefs were claimed by the plaintiff: (1) as against defendants 1 to 5, he had prayed for specific performance of the contract of sale; (2) as against the sixth defendant he had prayed for recovery of possession on payment of the mortgage money. Held, that the reliefs prayed for were disjunctive and not joint or conjunctive. There was no possibility of a joint decree as against all the defendants. As the reliefs prayed for were disjunctive if one of the defendants died who was not represented, still the appeal as a whole did not abate. Consequently the appeal abated not as a whole but against the heirs of the deceased respondent; *Mallangowda* v. *Gavisiddangowda*, ILR (1958) Mys 746: 37 Mys LJ 261: AIR 1959 Mys 194 (198, 199) (Pt C) (Prs 23. 29) (DB).

90. Decree Against Several Persons but Appeal by One

A brought a suit for ejectment of *B* and *C* from a house and also for arrears of rent. His case was that *B's* husband *D* and *C's* husband *E* were cousins and members of a joint Hindu family and *D* was the *karta*. *E* died in the life-time of *D*. Thereafter, his widow *C* lived jointly with *D*. After *E's* death *D* as *Karta* of the family borrowed some money from the plaintiff *A* and made a usufructuary mortgage of the house in dispute. The possession of the house was transferred to the plaintiff and *D* thereafter took the house on rent. The plaintiff's suit was brought against the two widows as the legal representatives of *D*. *B* did not appear in the trial Court and the suit proceeded *ex parte* against her. *C* contested the suit on two grounds. In the *first* place, it was urged that *D* and *E* were separate and *D* could not mortgage *E's* half share in the house and, therefore,

C was in possession of half the house in her own right as owner and could not be ejected. *Secondly,* it was urged that the tenancy created by the rent note was a tenancy at will which came to an end on the death of *D* and no suit for arrears of rent and ejectment based on the rent note could be maintained. The trial court decided against *C* on the question whether *D* and *E* were joint. It also held that the tenancy terminated at the death of *D* and, therefore, there could be no claim for rent but it granted a decree for ejectment from the whole house against both *C* and *B*. There was no appeal by *B* but *C* appealed to the District Judge. Where a necessary party has not been impleaded in appeal within time, it is liable to be dismissed as the success of the appeal would mean a decision in conflict with the rights already secured by the non-impleaded party. Where the interest of the appellant is not based on a ground common to him and that party, rule 4 of Order XLI, C.P.C., cannot apply. Nor could a decree be given under rule 33, of Order XLI. Though the powers under that rule are very wide, they cannot be used to defeat the provisions of the law of limitation. 1951 RD 40: 1951 AWR (Rev) 143. Where defendants *B* and *C* derived title from defendant *A*. Decree was passed against all. Appeal was filed by *A* making *B* and *C* respondents – *B* and *C* dying during appeal – Appeal does not abate if plaintiff's claim was contested on ground common to all.

91. Order XLI, Rule 4 – Ground Common to All the Defendants

Where a decree passed against several defendants is one and indivisible and proceeds upon a ground common to all the defendants, the entire decree can be set aside on appeal at the instance of one of the defendants. 83 Ind Cas 95 and *Rohtas Industries Ltd.* v. *State of Bihar*, 1958 BLJR 200: ILR 37 Pat 711: AIR 1958 Pat 414 (FB), rel. on; AIR 1950 Pat 348 and *Venukuri Krishna Reddi* v. *Kota Ramireddi*, (1954) 2 Mad LJ 559: ILR 1954 Mad 1126: AIR 1954 Mad 848, disting. *Digvijay Narain Singh* v. *Bibhunath Pande*, 1956 BLJR 445.

Where in a suit in ejectment against two alleged representatives *S* and *T* of the mortgagor-lessee, one of them *S* pleaded a right in herself to a half share of the house in suit and the other remained *ex parte,* the trial Court finding against the right to a half share set up in defence decreed the suit against both. In appeal by *S* her claim as owner of half share was found and the suit dismissed with respect to the same; the point raised by her as to the maintainability of the suit on a tenancy after its expiry was held not necessary as *T* had not appealed. *T* now appealed against the appellate decree that the whole suit ought to have been dismissed in the appellate court. Where appeal is filed by some of the defendants against a suit filed by one of the wives of the deceased for a declaration that the co-wife was excluded from inheritance to any part of the estate of the deceased and that the plaintiff alone was entitled to the entire income of the estate. The Manager of the Court of Wards, in whose possession the estate was intervened. He was added as second defendant to the suit as representing the co-wife who was retained as the first defendant in her personal and independent capacity. The suit was decreed. No appeal was filed by the first defendant but the second defendant appealed on her behalf. The plaintiff raised an objection to the maintainability of the appeal first on the ground that the manager, Court of Wards, had no right to represent the first defendant and, *secondly*, on the ground that the first defendant herself not having appealed as such, the appeal preferred on her behalf by the manager, Court of Wards, was not maintainable. Held, that the appellate court in the circumstances of the case, had ample power under rules 4 and 33, to reverse or vary the decree or pass any order in favour of both the defendants in the appeal preferred by the second defendant alone. If, the manager, Court of Wards could in law represent the first defendant he would then be having independent right of appeal even as against the first defendant because the decree may have some effect on the properties in the hands of the Court of Wards in respect whereof the manager Court of Wards alone could represent her under law. (1957) 100 Cal LJ 27: ILR (1958) 1 Cal 470. If Order XLI, rule 4 and Order XLI, rule 33 are read together, there can be no doubt that one of the defendants can file an appeal without impleading the other defendants, as respondents, and if the appeal proceeds on a ground common to all the defendants, the appellate court may exercise the power of varying the decree in favour of the non-appealing defendants, though they have not been parties to the appeal. The effect of these two rules is that the appellate court is authorised to pass a decree in favour of a party who has not been heard but the appellate court is not authorised to pass a decree against a person who is not a party to the appeal.

92. Rule 4 and Order XLI, Rule 4 of Order XLI and Order XXII, Rule 3 – Appeal Filed by Defendants on Ground Common to All

Death of some defendants pending appeal – Representatives not substituted under Order XXII, rule 3 in time – Power of appellate court in such case—It cannot vary or reverse decree in favour of all defendants. The appellate court has no power to proceed with the hearing of the appeal and to reverse and vary the decree in favour of all the plaintiffs or defendants under Order XLI, rule 4, C.P.C. if all the plaintiff or defendants appeal from the decree and any of them dies and no substitution is effected within time contemplated under Order XXII, rule 3, always assuming that the decree proceeds on a ground common to all the plaintiffs or defendants. The High Court of Bhopal said that where on the death of a party to an appeal his legal representatives are not brought on record the appeal cannot abate as a whole in all cases. If the case is of such a nature that it cannot be disposed of in the absence of the legal representatives of the de-ceased, the whole appeal would abate. But if the lower court's decree under appeal has proceeded on a ground common to the deceased as well as to the survivor or survivors, the latter could under Order XLI, rule 4, C.P.C., appeal from the whole decree, and the absence of the legal representatives of the deceased would not be a bar to the disposal of the appeal. If the appeal succeeds, the success would ensure for the benefit of the appellants, including the deceased appellant or his legal representatives even if they are not on record. The appeal could not in such a case abate as a whole; *Gulam Dastgir* v. *Pannalal*, AIR 1952 Bhopal 20 (21) (Pt B) (Prs 5, 6).

93. Order XLI, Rule 4 – Powers of Court in an Appeal against a Decree for Specific Performance of Contract

A Division Bench of the High Court of Patna examined the nature of a decree for specific performance of contract and powers of the court in an appeal against the said decree and held that a decree for specific performance of contract is a double-edged decree and in essence is in favour of the defendants-appellants also and, so, in the garb of exercising the powers under Order XLI, rule 4, of the Code, the Court cannot reverse or vary the decree in favour of the deceased appellant which is for the benefit of the legal representatives. Setting aside the decree against the remaining appellants as well as the legal representatives of the deceased appellant would be varying the decree in favour of the latter. *Ambika Prasad Singh* v. *Thakur Prasad Singh,* 1958 BLJR 634: AIR 1958 Pat 399 (405) (Pt. B) (Pr. 32) (DB). In a suit for possession of certain property defendants *B* and *C* alleged to have delivered title from defendant *A* and all of them contested the plaintiff's claim on a common ground that he had no title. *A* decree was passed against them all. Defendant *A* appealed making *B* and *C* respondents. *B* and C died during the pendency of appeal and their representatives were not brought on record within the time allowed by law: Held that provisions of Order XLI, rule 4, C.P.C. applied and appeal did not abate as defendant *A* alone was competent to appeal from the whole decree; *Krishna Dei* v. *Governor-General in-Council,* AIR 1950 All 1 (2) (Pt A) (Pr 5).

94. The Provisions of Order XXII, Rules 3 and 4 are Mandatory

There is nothing to indicate either in this Order or Order XLI that the provisions of Order XXII, rule 3 are to be read subject to any exception or subject to Order XLI, rule 4. There is no justification for applying the provisions of Order XLI, rule 4 on grounds of analogy or on *pari materia* considerations when the language of the rule is unambiguous and specific and made expressly applicable to certain contingencies. Order XLI, rule 4 is merely an enabling provision empowering the Court to exercise the discretion to vary or reverse the decree under appeal which was passed on any ground common to all and that it cannot be interpreted to exceed the scope and ambit of that discretion. The High Court of Andhra Pradesh said that to hold that Order XXII, rule 3 does not apply to a case coming under Order XLI, rule 4 would be tantamount to negativing those provisions and making them *otiose*. *Chaladina Venkata Ram Rao* v. *Engu Narayana,* ILR 1964 AP 105: (1962) 2 Andh WR 376: (1962) 2 Andh LT 476: AIR 1963 AP 168 (169, 176, 177) (Pt A) (Prs 1, 24, 25) (FB) In case of death of one of several appellants and appeal abating as against him under Order XXII, rule 3, Court has no power to proceed under Order XLI, rule 4. An appellate Court has no power to proceed with the appeal and to reverse and vary the decree in favour of all the plaintiffs or defendants under Order XLI, rule 4 when the decree proceeds on a ground common to all the plaintiffs or defendants, if all the plaintiffs or the defendants appeal from the decree and any of them dies and the appeal abates so far as he is concerned under Order XXII, rule 3. The Supreme Court approved *Ramphal Sahu* v. *Satdeo Jha,* ILR 19 Pat 870: AIR 1940 Pat 346 (FB) and *Amin Chand* v. *Baldeo Sahai Ganga Sahai,* AIR 1934 Lah 206: 35 Pat LR 92: ILR 15 Lah 667 and *Baij Nath* v. *Ram Bharose,* AIR 1953 All 565 (FB) and *Nanak* v. *Ahmad Ali,* 48 Pun LR 141: AIR 1946 Lah 399 (FB) and *Pyarelal* v. *Modi Sikharchand,* 1957 MPLJ 192: ILR 1957 MP 21: AIR 1957 MP 89 and AIR 1963 AP 188 (FB) and On death of *Ambar Ali his legal heirs Sonahar Ali* v. *Mukbul Ali,* AIR 1956 Assam 164, and overruled

Shripad Balwant v. *Nagu Kushaba,* AIR 1943 Bom 301: 45 Bom LR 109: ILR 1948 Bom 143 and *Satulal Bhattacharjee* v. *Asiruddin,* ILR 61 Cal 879: AIR 1934 Cal 703 and *Somasundaram Chettiar* v. *Vaithilinga Mudaliar,* ILR 40 Mad 846: AIR 1918 Mad 794(2); *Rameshwar Prasad* v. *Shambehari Lal Jagannath,* (1965) 1 SCJ 114: (1964) 3 SCR 549: 1963 SCD 945: 1963 All LJ 109: ILR 1963 Supp 2 SCR 933: AIR 1963 SC 1901: (1904) (Pt C) (Pr 16).

95. Order XLI, Rules 4, 20, Order XXII – Death of Some of Non-appealing Defendants After Filing of Appeal

A Division Bench of the High Court of Patna considered the previous views of the Court and said that remaining non-appealing defendants can take advantage of Order XLI, rule 4. When the decree against the defendants !proceeds on grounds common to all the defendants, Order XLI, rule 4 can be taken advantage of by non-appealing defendants, even where any of the non-appealing defendants dies after the passing of the decree appealed from but before the filing of the appeal and his legal representatives are not brought on the record either as appellants or respondents or where any of the non-appealing defendants dies after the filing of the appeal and during its pendency. There is no provision in the Code under which legal representatives can be brought on record in such a situation. AIR 1948 Pat 480 and *Parwati Kuer* v. *Manna Lal Khetan,* AIR 1956 Pat 414: 1956 BLJR 327: 35 Pat 449, rel. on; *Ramphal Sahu* v. *Satdeo Jha,* ILR 19 Pat 870: AIR 1940 Pat 346 (FB) and *Deo Narain Singh* v. *Bibi Khatoon,* ILR 27 Pat 43: AIR 1949 Pat 401 and *Ambika Prasad Singh* v. *Thakur Prasad Singh,* 1958 BLJR 634: AIR 1958 Pat 399 and AIR 1958 Pat 324, Disting. *Thakur Ram Janki* v. *Jago Singh,* AIR 1962 Pat 131 (133, 134, 137) (Pt A) (Pr, 5, 6, 8) (DB).

96. Rule 1, Order XXXIV, Rules 1 and 33

One defendant mortgagee appealing against decree without impleading other defendant mortgagees – The appellate court can vary decree, provided appeal proceeds on grounds common to all appealing and non-appealing defendants - Redemption suit – All mortgagees – collectively opposing for same reasons – Redemption decree granted against all – Decree held proceeded on grounds common to them all – Appeal by one of mortgagees – Others not impleaded – Appeal can be regarded as one, Held: Order XLI, rule 4, C.P.C., permits the Court, where the decree proceeds on a common ground, to vary it even in favour of the non-appealing defendants. The common ground of the non-maintainability of the suit on the ground that the tenancy relied on had been terminated in law long before suit was not the ground on which the trial Court's decree was based. Nor was this ground, raised by the appellant, decided by the lower appellate Court. Hence the rule is not applicable.

The second appeal by *T* who had not preferred an appeal against the decree of the trial court is not maintainable. AIR 1928 PC 34, foll. 1952 RLW 203: ILR (1952) 2 Raj 13. A Full Bench of the High Court of Patna examined the effect of rules 4 and 33 and said that reading rules 4 and 33 of Order XLI, together it is manifest that if an order in execution proceedings proceeds on a ground common to all the decree-holders, some of the decree-holders can prefer an appeal without making the other decree-holders parties to the appeal and the appellate court can pass an order in favour of those decree-holders also who are not parties to appeal. Hence, the appeal cannot be said to be incompetent for non-joinder of the other decree-holders: *Parwati Kuer* v. *Manna Lal Khetan*, AIR 1956 Pat 414: 1956 BLJR 327: 35 Pat 449 (FB), foll. *Anantalal Daga* v. *Debi Prasad Pandey*, AIR 1959 Pat 258 (259) (Pt. A) (Pr. 4) (DB).

Order XLI, rule 4 Death of one of respondents before hearing of appeal – All heirs who have exactly the same interest impleaded and decree passed against them – Appeal by one of them alone is competent under Order XLI, rule 4. *Misri Lal Nayak* v. *Surji*, 1950 All LJ 113: 63 Mad LW 184: (1950) 1 Mad LJ 294: 1950 All WB 211: 54 Cal WN 508: 52 Bom LR 477: 31 Pat LT 1: AIR 1950 PC 28 (30) (Pt C) (Pr 15).

Where appeal is filed on any ground common to all the plaintiffs or to all the defendants and all or several of the plaintiffs or defendants appeal against the decree, the High Court of Calcutta said that the appellate court can, in view of the provisions of Order XLI, rule 4, proceed with the appeal and reverse the decree of the trial court in spite of the omission to bring on the record the heirs of one of the appellants who dies during the pendency of the appeal. See *Santosh Kumar Mondal* v. *Nandalal Chakrapani*, AIR 1963 Cal 289 (291, 292, 296, 298, 304, 307) (Prs 9, 12, 28, 45, 69, 85) (FB). *Ramphal Sahu* v. *Satdeo Jha*, AIR 1940 Pat 348 (FB) and *Gulab Singh* v. *Collector of, Farrukhabad*, AIR 1953 All 585 (FB), Dist. from *Santosh Kumar Mondal* v. *Nandalal Chakrapani*.

97. Order XLI, Rule 4 – Order of Abatement Recorded – Rule 4 does not Apply

The High Court of Calcutta held that where there is already an order of abatement recorded by the appellate court. Rule 4 is not attracted; *Mritunjoy Das* v. *Sabitrimoni Dasi*, AIR 1950 Cal 59 (61) (Pt B) (Pr 10).

98. Order XLI, Rules 4 and 20 – Decree for Pre-emption against Vendor and Vendee

Appeal by vendee alone – Power of Court to reverse decree as against both. Where in a suit for pre-emption a decree is passed against the vendor and the vendee and the vendee alone appeals against the decree without joining the vendor as party, the appeal does not become incompetent as the vendor is not a necessary party to the appeal. In such a case the appellate Court has power under Order XLI, rule 4 to reverse the decree of the trial court, not only against the vendee who has appealed but also against the vendor who was not a party to the appeal. AIR 1948 Pat 480 and *Gobind Dayal* v. *Inayat Ullah*, ILR 7 All 775: 1885 All WN 182, rel. on. *Suraj Prakash* v. *Sant Lal Singh*, ILR 18 Pat 768: AIR 1940 Pat 137 and *Brij Narain* v. *B.H.K. Dhaon*, 1942 OWN 237: AIR 1942 Oudh 366, Dist. *Ajodhya Dutta Missir* v. *Mohar Kali Kuer*, AIR 1951 Pat 581 (582, 583) (Prs. 7, 9, 10) (DB).

99. Rules 4, 33 and Order XLVII, Rule 1 – Failure to Consider Effect of Order XLI, Rules 4 and 33 by Appellate Court – If Sufficient Ground for Review

In execution of a money decree against the father (defendant 1) and sons (defendants 2 to 4) the properties in the hands of sons were attached. The sons objected that the properties in their hands were not liable to attachment as the suit debt was incurred by their father after a partition had taken place amongst them. The objection was dismissed as barred by *res judicata*. In the appeal filed by defendants 3 and 4 defendant 2 was not even made a party. The appellate court remanded the case for determination of the objection on merits. After taking evidence of all the defendants including that of defendant 2, the trial court held that the partition was subsequent to the suit debt and therefore dismissed the objection. On appeal by defendants 2 to 4, the appellate court reversed the decree in favour of defendants 3 and 4 only and observed that defendant 2 was not entitled to get the benefit of the appellate order of remand as he was not a party to it. Defendant 2 therefore applied for review of this order. Held that the benefit of the order of remand passed by the appellate court must be taken as operating in favour of defendant 2 also though he was not a party to the appeal filed by defendants 3 and 4 as the appellate court had ample powers to pass the order in favour of defendant 2 under Order XLI, rule 4 and rule 33. Held: further that as the appellate court had failed to consider the vital point in the case namely whether defendant 2 was entitled to the benefit of Order XLI, rule 33, C.P.C. there was a mistake or error apparent on face of record or atleast a sufficient ground for review.

RULE 5

100. Stay of Execution

Sub-rule (1) provides for grant of stay of execution by the appellate court and sub-rule (2) empowers the Court which passed the decree to grant it. The provisions contained under sub-rules (3), (4) & (6) are common.

The provisions of sub-rule (2) should be read together with the provisions of rule 26 of Order XXI which empowers the court to which a decree is transferred for execution to grant temporary stay to enable the judgment-debtor to apply for stay before the court which passed the decree or before the appellate court where an appeal has been filed.

Sub-rule (2) does not prescribe any time-limit for which the Court passing decree may grant stay of execution. But the jurisdiction of the Court of first instance cannot be concurrent with jurisdiction of the appellate court. The High Court of Gauhati has also explained that when an appeal is preferred, it is the appellate court alone which is seized of the matter and an application for stay may be made to that court. Therefore, the Court of first instance may grant stay of execution till an appeal is preferred or a period prescribed for filing an appeal expires. A stay order passed by the appellate court has the effect of staying all the proceedings in the trial court and anything done during the time the stay order is operative, is *null* and *void*. The proceedings before the trial judge on the date of the stay order would be without jurisdiction in spite of the fact that the stay order was not communicated to the trial court. 1962 MP LJ (Notes) 195. When stay order is issued to the trial court, proceedings in suit thereafter are without jurisdiction. After the proceedings before the trial court are stayed by the Court of appeal and the stay order is actually received by the trial Court, all further proceedings in suit before the trial court are without jurisdiction. During the trial of a suit plaintiff applied for examining one witness on commission and for issue of a summons to another to produce a document. But the applications were rejected, whereupon the plaintiff filed revision to the High Court. The revision was admitted and all further proceedings in suit were stayed, and the stay order was also received by the trial court. The trial court, however, took up for consideration two more applications of the plaintiff which were filed in the meanwhile, and dismissed them in the absence of plaintiff. Held, that the order passed by the trial court rejecting plaintiff's two applications after the stay order was received was without jurisdiction and illegal. 1961 MPLJ (Notes) 306. C. The High Court of Patna also held that after stay of proceedings by superior Court, further proceedings by lower court are without jurisdiction. AIR 1962 Pat 357 (360) (Pt B) (Prs 15, 16). But a Full Bench of the High Court of Allahabad had said that where the order for stay of execution proceedings before the officer was passed by the transferor Court but before it was communicated to the sale officer the sale had taken place, held, that the sale was valid. *Parsotam Saran* v. *Brahma Nand*, 25 All LJ 430: AIR 1927 All 401 (FB), foll.: *Kunj Behari* v. *Shia College, Lucknow*, 1954 All WR (HC) 351: 1954 All LJ 446: AIR 1955 All 96 (97) (Pt A) (Pr 2).

The High Court of Madras examined the principles to be taken into consideration while granting stay in a case where a Hindu wife institutes suits against her husband for her maintenance and for the maintenance of her minor children and subsequently the husband applies for the custody of the minor children under the Guardians and Wards Act, and also applies for restitution of conjugal rights against his wife, the suits for maintenance filed earlier by the wife ought not to be stayed on the ground that the husband has subsequently filed petitions for the custody of the minor children and for restitution of conjugal rights. It would be proper for the Court to refuse to stay the maintenance suit but in refusing to stay the suits it would be inexpedient to make any observations on the merits of the proceedings pending between the parties; it must take care to avoid any prejudice that might be caused by unnecessary observations on the merits; (1958) 1 Mad LJ 210: 1958 Mad WN 270.

101. Order XLI, Rule 5 and Sections 21 and 23 – Arbitration Act – Stay of Final Decree Granted in Appeal Against Preliminary Decree

Court can refer dispute to arbitration during stay – Waiver of benefit of stay by party entitled occurs by agreement to refer – *See* Arbitration Act, section 21. AIR 1953 Mad 492 (DB). The said Court further said that where in contravention of a stay order passed by the Court passing the decree the decree-holder obtained delivery of possession and this being pointed out an application for stay of execution pending disposal of the appeal was dismissed by the appellate Court: It was held that the proper procedure for the judgment-debtor was to go to the Court which made a wrong order in ignorance of the order of stay to have it corrected by vacating the same and directing re-delivery. The order of the appellate court dismissing the application for stay of execution could not be said to be a bar to directing re-delivery of possession; *Ayyammal* v. *Thangavelu Padayachi*, 1949 Mad WN 799: (1949) 2 Mad LJ 764: AIR 1950 Mad 317.

102. Security Deposit

Sub-rule (3)(c) makes it mandatory to deposit security to obtain a stay order to be granted either by the court of first instance under sub-rule (2) or by the appellate court under sub-rule (1). Sub-rule (5) also lays down a similar provision but adds a new term 'deposit'. This sub-rule first ignores anything contained in sub-rule (3), but again it refers to the said sub-rule and lays down that the appellate court will not grant stay if the appellant fails to make the deposit or furnish the security specified in sub-rule (3) of rule 1, stress may be laid on 'the deposit'. Therefore, sub-rule (5) of rule 5 is disabling provision and the term 'deposit' does not find mention in sub-rule (3) or elsewhere. The High Court of Madhya Pradesh also referred to the term 'security' in *Mannalal Balgovind Mishra* v. *Bhalchandrao Ramchandrarao Bhuskute,* AIR 1960 MP 41: 1959 MPLJ 559: 1959 MPC 584. However, the High Court of Bombay said that where the decree is for payment of money, the party may obtain stay by depositing the amount in Court; *Dhanji Bhai* v. *Lisbea,* (1889) ILR 13 Bom 241. *See* also *Mooka Naicker* v. *A.K. Venkatasami Naidu,* AIR 1950 Mad 807: (1950) 2 Mad LJ 194.

Option of the party is not the same as is 'compulsion'. The High Court of Delhi said that in case of a money decree, so long as the decretal amount is not deposited or security is not furnished, the Court shall not make an order staying the execution of the decree; *Union Bank of India* v. *Jagannath Radhey Shyam and Co.,* AIR 1979 Del 36: 81 Pun LR (D) 50.

Rule 19, Order V, rules 17, 9, & 9A and Order XXII, rules 9 and 4 – Restoration of appeal dismissed for default of appellant in respect of re-service of notice, first notice to certain respondents having been returned unserved – Held, High Court was not justified in restoring to refuse the appeal; *Ramdas Shivram Sattur* v. *Ramchandra Popatlal Sah,* AIR 2007 SC 3018: 2007 AIR SCW 5476: (2007) 8 SCC 400.

103. Rule 5 – Stay of Proceedings – Scope

A Division Bench of the High Court of Orissa said that the Court has no inherent power to stay execution. Court cannot override express provision of law *Purna Chand Sahu* v. *Chamra Bariha,* AIR 1954 Ori 114: 20 Cut LT 424 (DB).

In a case where stay of execution was granted by the High Court on condition of depositing decretal amount and the judgment-debtor deposited it in part, the High Court vacated the stay treating it to be default. The Supreme Court found it to be a good case to grant more time to the judgment-debtor to make the deposit; *Executive Engineer PWD* v. *Balraj Kumar Bansal,* (2005) 12 SCC 460.

The Supreme Court said that the High Court was justified in staying dispossession of the appellant on depositing the monthly instalments; *Pabbathi Venkataramaiah Chetty* v. *Pabbathi N. Rathnamaiah Chetty,* AIR 2007 SC 2333: 2007 AIR SCW 4038: (2007) 3 SCC 151. Similar view was held by the Supreme Court in *Pradeep Kumar* v. *Hajari Lal,* AIR 2008 SC 1689: 2008 AIR SCW 1964: (2008) 3 SCC 299.

The power conferred upon an appellate court under sub-rule 1 of rule 5 of Order XLI, C.P.C. can be exercised if there is an appeal pending in that Court and if sufficient cause is shown for making an order for the stay of the execution of the decree. For the exercise of this power it is not necessary that an application for execution should have been made or be pending at the time when the application for stay of execution is made; *Laxman Ramchandra* v. *Shridhar Vaman*, AIR 1933 Bom 118: 57 Bom 202, foll. *Phusia* v. *Mohammad Tasadduq Husain Khan*, 1952 All WR (HC) 49: 1952 RD (HC) 37: 1952 All LJ 136: AIR 1952 All 684 (686) (Pr 7).

104. Stay of Execution of Money Decree

A Division Bench of the High Court of Andhra Pradesh said that stay of execution of money decree cannot ordinarily be granted. It is an established rule of practice that ordinarily stay of money decree will not be given unless there are special circumstances. *Pamulapati Varadayya* v. *Kommareddi Chinnappareddi*, ILR 1955 Andh 557: 1955 Andh WR 724: 1955 Andh LT 616: AIR 1956 Andh 64 (Pt B) (Pr 5) (DB). A Division Bench of Saurashtra Court said that the power of the Court to stay execution of a decree has to be exercised within the four corners of rule 5 of Order XLI. The reason of the rule appears to be that the rights of the decree-holder having been determined by a competent Court, it is not fair that he should be deprived of the fruits of his decree merely because the judgment-debtor prefers an appeal against the decree. At the same-time if execution of the decree is likely to result in substantial loss to the decree-holder, discretion is given to the Court to stay execution, provided the other two conditions of sub-rule (3) are satisfied. It is impossible to formulate any uniform rule of practice and each case must be decided on its own facts. The discretion of the Court is very much limited and has to be exercised within the limits prescribed by the rule, and in a proper case where substantial loss is likely to result to the judgment-debtor if a decree for payment of money is executed the Court can stay execution of the decree even before the judgment-debtor deposits the amount in Court. Whether the judgment-debtor is a public body or a private person makes no difference in principle in deciding whether execution of the decree should be stayed. That the decree-holder will not suffer any loss if execution is stayed is also no ground because the law is that the decree should be executed unless the judgment-debtor proves specific loss to him if execution is not stayed. Execution cannot be stayed on the ground that the decree-holder will suffer no loss. *Borough Municipality, Jamnagar* v. *Firm Ramji Vasram*, 9 Sau LR 169: AIR 1956 Sau 113 (114) (Prs 2, 3, 4) (DB). Application must have been made without unreasonable delay. Where in a suit for a declaration against the State regarding the propriety of the order passed for the plaintiff's compulsory retirement from the State service, the trial court grants a decree for a bare declaration and pending appeal filed by the State from such a decree, the State applies for suspension of all further proceedings including execution of the decree there is no executable decree passed by the trial court which under Order XLI, rule 5 could be stayed by the appellate court, nor is there any justification in such proceedings for the award of any sum by the appellant (State) to the respondent as there was no claim for the recovery of any sum of money in the suit and the decree does not award any pecuniary relief; *State of Andhra Pradesh* v. *S. Kameswar Rao*, AIR 1959 AP 39 (40) (Pt A) (Pr 4) (DB).

105. Order XLI, Rule 5, Order XXI, Rule 11(3) and Rule 17 – Appeal

Effect on execution of original decree – Where appellate court affirms original decree, fresh execution not necessary. It is no doubt true that when an appellate Court passes a decree the decree of the trial court is merged in it and the appellate decree, is the only decree which can be executed and technically a fresh application for execution should be filed. But it does not necessarily follow that where the decree-holder has, already applied for execution of the decree of the first Court, and if that decree is affirmed by the Court of appeal, then the decree-holder cannot amend his pending application for execution so as to make it one for execution of the decree of the appellate court or that if he makes an amendment in such a case it must be within three years of the date of the appellate decree.

106. Stay – Not a Matter of Right

The High Court of Rajasthan held that though no order of stay of execution can be made under Order XLI, rule 5 yet an order of stay of execution can be made under section 107 read with Order XXI, rule 26: *Bhonreylal* v. *Ram Singh*, ILR (1955) 5 Raj 175: 1954 Raj LW 526: AIR 1956 Raj 49 (50) (Pt C) (Pr 10) The Supreme Court expressed clear views in *Rajaram Prasad Gupta* v. *Ramchandra Prasad*, (2008) 10 SCC 796 and *State of Maharashtra* v. *Super Max International Pvt. Ltd.*, (2009) 9 SCC 772: AIR 2010 SC 722: 2009 AIR SCW 7265 that stay of execution of the decree may not be claimed as of right. In proper case, Court may refuse it while admitting appeal or revision. Apparently, the power is discretionary. The High Court of Rajasthan held that though no order of stay of execution can be made under Order XLI, rule 5 yet an order of stay of execution can be made under section 107 read with Order XXI, rule 26: *Bhonreylal* v. *Ram Singh*, ILR (1955) 5 Raj 175: 1954 Raj LW 526: AIR 1956 Raj 49 (50) (Pt C) (Pr 10) The Court further said that although there is no power under Order XLI, rule 5 yet stay can be ordered under section 107 read with Order XXI, rule 28. AIR 1955 NUC (Raj) 4666. Rule applies only when decree under appeal is capable of execution.

107. Appeal against Preliminary Decree

Passing of final decree stayed – Where the High Court in an appeal against preliminary decree in a partition suit directed that the final decree proceedings shall go on, but there shall be stay restricted only to the passing of the final decree, that means, the trial court will have unfettered and ample jurisdiction to proceed with the final decree proceedings, and every step taken and every direction given by the lower court up to the passing of the final decree will be clearly binding upon both the parties. All orders passed by the lower court, all the steps taken in pursuance thereof towards the framing and passing of the final decree are clearly binding upon the parties and the succeeding judges, unless of course a case for review satisfying the conditions under Order XLVII, C.P.C. is made out. It is elementary and well-established that principles of *res judicata* apply to successive Judges and in successive stages of the same litigation provided there is an adjudication of the rights of parties in the course of the progress of proceedings in a Court of law. *Parthasarathy Apparao* v. *Venkatadri Apparao*, ILR 31 All 153: 113 IC 646: AIR 1929 Mad 121; *Jotindra Mohan Tagore* v. *Bejoy Chand*, ILR (1905) 32 Cal 483; *Nukala Venkatesu* v. *Nanduri Suryanarayana*, ILR 1958 AP 755: 1959 Andh LT 252: AIR 1959 AP 16, rel. on.

Abdul Azeez v. *M.K.P. Kader Mohideen*, (1963) 2 Mad LJ 220: 76 Mad LW 498: AIR 1963 Mad 428 (430, 431) (Pt C) (Prs 6, 8, 9) (DB).

108. Rule 6 – Security under Rule 6

Rule 6, section 145 – Sufficiency of security – A Division Bench of the High Court of Calcutta examined the sufficiency of security under this rule and held that determination of the sufficiency or otherwise of security offered by the parties is a judicial act and such act has to be performed judicially. Mere acceptance of the report of a ministerial officer on the point without applying the judicial mind to the consideration of the various factors bearing on it cannot be said to be a proper or adequate performance of a judicial act. *Ketaki Ranjan Banerjee* v. *Bipradas Mukherjee*, 85 Cal LJ 6: AIR 1950 Cal 325 (326) (Pr 2) (DB).

Force of acceptance of Surety bond by Court.—The High Court of Madhya Pradesh said that a surety bond is not effective until it is accepted by the Court. A security bond is nothing but a contract between the Court and the surety who is personally liable to the Court to pay the amount and unless what has been offered is accepted by the Court it will not have the effect of a binding contract, for, offer and acceptance are necessary to constitute a contract; 1958 MPLJ (Notes) 156.

109. Rule 6 – Scope of – Restitution under – If same as in Section 144 – Security

The word 'restitution' in Order XLI, rule 6, C.P.C., has no reference to restitution order under section 144. Order XLI, rule 6, contemplates cases where a decree-holder seeks to draw out moneys deposited by the other party to avert execution. In such cases, when an appeal is pending, suitable terms may be imposed, such as furnishing security, etc., for such withdrawal. It is quite a different matter where a party is only seeking to draw out of his own money deposited by the other side by way of restitution under section 144. In such cases the Court is not bound to order security for the withdrawal of money due to a party in restitution proceedings merely because the other side has filed an appeal.

110. Rules 6(2) and 5

Court ordering sale of immovable property in execution of decree – judgment-debtor filing appeal against decree and applying for stay of sale under Order XLI, rule 6(2), the High Court of Andhra Pradesh held that Court is bound to stay sale notwithstanding fact that High Court which had granted interim stay order had dissolved it for default. Where an order for sale of immovable property is made in execution of a decree and the judgment-debtor who has preferred an appeal against the decree, applies to such executing Court, under Order XLI, rule 6(2) to stay the order for sale, the Court has no option but to order the stay of the sale even though the interim stay order granted by the High Court under rule 5 was dissolved by it for non-compliance with the terms of the order. Where in such a case the executing Court refuses to stay the sale taking the view that it has become *functus officio* when an interim order for stay was passed and subsequently dissolved by the High Court, and a sale is held in contravention of the embargo placed by rule 6(2), such sale has no existence in the eye of law and hence it must be quashed. The provisions of Order XLI, rule 6(2) are attracted in all cases in which there is an order for the sale of immovable property in execution of a decree and that decree is under appeal. The word "shall" occurring after the words "the sale" in rule 6(2) which has to be given its natural and ordinary meaning does not, admit of any other interpretation than that the Court to which an application is presented for the stay of the sale, has no option but to stay it. The provisions of rule 6(2) are not complementary to those of rule 5. Hence it cannot be said that the stay of the sale under R. 6 (2) is not imperative. *Harnarain* v. *Govind Rai*, AIR 1932 All 551: ILR 54 All 874, Dissented. From the fact that the High Court before which the appeal is pending has dissolved an interim order of stay granted by it previously, it could not be contended that the executing Court had become *functus officio* and hence could not stay the sale on the ground that if such order was passed it would conflict with the order made by the High Court. (1959) 2 Andh WR 939, Dissented. The words *"functus officio"* mean 'has discharged his duty'. The duty imposed by rule 6(2) is discharged only when an order is made under its provisions according to law. That duty does not come to an end by reason of an order made by the appellate court under Order XLI, rule 5, whose provisions do not overlap those of Order XLI, rule 6(2). An order for stay of execution which an appellate Court may make under rule 5 is an order by which every process which may be taken in execution of a decree may be stayed, whereas rule 6(2) does no more than to authorize the stay of the sale of the immovable property belonging to the judgment-debtor when it is brought to sale; *Laxman Omana Muchandi* v. *Ramachandra Omana Muchandi*, (1964) 1 Mys LJ 101: AIR 1964 Mys 232 (234, 235) (Pt A) (Prs 5, 9, 11, 12, 13, 14, 17) (DB).

111. Rule 6 – Transmission of Decree for Execution

In case of limits of jurisdiction of transferor and transferee Court when Certificate under section 41 not received from transferee Court, transferor Court does not altogether lose *seisin* of decree – It has jurisdiction to execute decree in respect of property within its jurisdiction. *See* section 18. *Giridhari Lal* v. *Thakurdas*, (1964) 6 OJD 21: ILR 1964 Cut 556: AIR 1964 Ori 170. Order XLI, rule 6 – Scope - No inherent power to stay execution – Court cannot override express provision of law. *See* section 151; *Purna Chand Sahu* v. *Chamra Bariha*, AIR 1954 Ori 114: 20 Cut LT 424 (DB).

112. Order XLI, Rule 10 – Scope and Application of Discretion

A Division Bench of the High Court of Madras held that the discretion is a very nice one as in giving its reasons appellate Court has to guard against expressing any strong views on the merits which may give the impression that they have been prejudged without hearing the other side. There is of course the ordinary presumption that the findings of the lower court are correct until they are set aside in appeal. An order under Order XLI, rule 10(1) is ordinarily entirely in the discretion of the appellate court and thus High Court sitting in revision would be most reluctant to interfere with the exercise of such discretion. But the fact that the appellant is a minor or a woman should be never taken into consideration in the matter of directing security on the ground that in the event of the appeal being unsuccessful the respondents may not realise their costs. Security should be ordered on other considerations. On the facts of the case, the order of the lower appellate court directing the appellants to deposit security was set aside; *A. Kuttoossa* v. *M.K. Kunhamma*, AIR 1938 Mad 380: (1938) 1 MLJ 142, Foll. *Ramaraju Goundar* v. *Molayan*, 1954 Mad WN 309: (1954) 2 Mad LJ 276: 67 Mad LW 840: AIR 1954 Mad 881 (882) (Prs 3, 4). Order XLI, rule 10 – Order for security for court fees. *See ibid.*, Order XXXIII, rule 13. *Rachabhathuni Brahmam* v. *State of Madras*, (1953) 2 Mad LJ 307: ILR 1954 Mad 200: AIR 1954 Mad 277 (DB).

113. Order XLI, Rule 10 – Compromise

In a case *A*, the vendor refused to accept consideration of sale and suing *M* unsuccessfully for cancellation of deed. In *A's* appeal *M* applied for security of costs – Parties agreeing that costs be deducted from unpaid purchase money – There is binding contract. *See* Contract Act, section 10. 1952 Nag L 3 (Notes) 141.

114. Order XLI, Rule 11, Order XLII, Rule 2 and Sections 100 and 102

Madhya Pradesh High Court in the case of *Food Corporation of India* v. *Munnilal Singh*, 2003 (2) MPLJ 290: AIR 2003 MP 66: 2003 (4) JCR 320 MP examined the maintainability of second appeal. Short facts of the case are that plaintiff entered into an agreement with appellants for transportation of goods from Itarsi railway station to the godowns of appellants. For this purpose respondent No. 1 submitted a guarantee through respondent No. 2 New Bank of India. Contention of the plaintiff was that he has completed the work as per conditions of the agreement and was entitled for refund of bank guarantee and in spite of several requests, appellants have not refunded the guarantee amount. On these grounds suit was filed for recovery of Rs. 16,900.

Appellants denied the claim contending that plaintiff has committed breach of the agreement. He has not transported 120 bags of sugar in time to godown of defendant at Pipariya and there was delay in transporting the aforesaid sugar. He has misused stock of sugar resulting loss to the appellants and, in consequence, the bank guarantee was forfeited. Respondent bank contended that it was unnecessarily made party. There is defect of misjoinder of party. Apart from this, as per condition of bank guarantee, plaintiff is not entitled for refund of amount of bank guarantee and plaintiff is under obligation to return the bank guarantee after due discharge from appellants.

Learned trial court framed issues and after recording the evidence, decreed the suit.

It is pertinent to mention that the valuation of suit in the trial court was Rs. 16,900 and it was a money suit for recovery of the amount.

At the time of hearing, learned counsel appearing for respondent No. 1 raised a preliminary objection that present appeal has not been admitted and in view of amendment in Code of Civil Procedure, in section 102 of the Code, this appeal is not maintainable as the valuation of this appeal and the suit is less than Rs. 25,000.

Learned counsel for the appellants submited that in this appeal this Court had already applied mind and also issued notice to the respondents. In the Code of Civil Procedure, there is no provision for issuing notice to the respondent prior to framing substantial question of law and in the circumstances, the order dated 11-11-1998 will be deemed to be an order of admission of appeal.

To appreciate the rival contention of the parties, the Court felt inclined to quote certain provisions of Code of Civil Procedure in this regard. Earlier section 102 was as under:

> "102. No second appeal in certain suits.—No second appeal shall lie in any suit of the nature cognizable by Court of Small Causes, when the amount or value of the subject-matter of the original suit does not exceed three thousand rupees."

By Code of Civil Procedure (Amendment) Act. 2002, section 102 substituted as under:

> "102. No second appeal in certain cases. No second appeal shall lie from any decree, when the subject-matter of the original suit is for recovery of money not exceeding twenty-five thousand rupees."

Vide notification dated 6th June, 2002 No. SO 604 (V), the Central Government appointed 1st day of July, 2002 as the date on which provisions of the Code of Civil Procedure (Amendment) Act, 2002 came into force. In the circumstances, the newly substituted section 102 by Code of Civil Procedure (Amendment) Act, 2002 came into force with effect from 1st July, 2002 and the second appeal from any decree, when the subject-matter of the original suit was for recovery of money not exceeding twenty-five thousand rupees, will be barred.

Now the question remained whether any appeal which was pending on 1-7-2002 would be governed by the aforesaid section 102 of the Code of Civil Procedure. Code of Civil Procedure (Amendment) Act, 2002, under section 16 provides for repeal and savings. The relevant provision is section 16(2)(a) which reads as under:

> "16(2) Notwithstanding that the provisions of this Act have come into force or repeal under sub-section (1) has taken effect, and without prejudice to the generality of the provisions of section 6 of the General Clauses Act, 1887,
>
> (a) the provisions of section 102 of the principal Act as substituted by section 5 of this Act shall not apply to or affect any appeal which had been admitted before the commencement of section 5; and every such appeal shall be disposed of as if section 5 had not come into force;"

The aforesaid clause provides that the appeals which are pending on 1-7-2002 and already admitted before commencement of section 5 (substitution of section 102) are to be disposed of as if section 5 has not come into force. The word 'admitted' is not used in the Code of Civil Procedure. In Order XLI under heading "Procedure on admission of appeal", rule 9 onwards upto rule 37 are given. The relevant rule is rule 11 which read as under:—

> **"11. Power to dismiss appeal without sending notice to lower court.**—(1) The appellate court after fixing a day for hearing the appellant or his pleader and hearing him accordingly if he appears on that day may dismiss the appeal.

(2) If on the day fixed or any other day to which the hearing may be adjourned the appellant does not appear when the appeal is called on for hearing, the Court may make an order that the appeal be dismissed.

(3) The dismissal of an appeal under this rule shall be notified to the court from whose decree the appeal is preferred.

(4) Where an appellate court, not being the High Court, dismisses an appeal under sub-rule (1), it shall deliver a judgment, recording in brief its grounds for doing so, and a decree shall be drawn up in accordance with the judgment."

Though under rule 11 word "admit" is not used but when this rule is seen with section 100 and Order XLII of Code of Civil Procedure, position becomes clear. Section 100 reads as under:

> "**100. Second Appeal.**—(1) Save as otherwise expressly provided in the body of this Code or by any other law for the time being in force, an appeal shall lie to the High Court from every decree passed in appeal by any Court subordinate to the High Court, if the High Court is satisfied that the case involves a substantial question of law.
>
> (2) An appeal may lie under this section from an appellate decree passed *ex parte*.
>
> (3) In an appeal under this section, the memorandum of appeal shall precisely state the substantial question of law involved in the appeal.
>
> (4) Where the High Court is satisfied that a substantial question of law is involved in any case, it shall formulate that question.
>
> (5) The appeal shall be heard on the question so formulated and the respondent shall, at the hearing of the appeal, be allowed to argue that the case does not involve such question:
>
> Provided that nothing in this sub-section shall be deemed to take away or abridge the power of the Court to hear, for reasons to be recorded, the appeal on any other substantial question of law, not formulated by it, if it is satisfied that the case involves such question."

To appreciate section 100(4), it is necessary to read Order XLII, rule 2 of the Code of Civil Procedure, which reads as under:—

> "2. Power of the Court to direct that the appeal be heard on the question formulated by it. At the time of making an order under rule 11 of Order XLI for the hearing of a second appeal, the Court shall formulate the substantial question of law as required by section 100 and in doing so the Court may direct that the second appeal be heard on the question so formulated and it shall not be open to the appellant to urge any other ground in the appeal without the leave of the Court, given in accordance with the provision of section 100."

While giving harmonious construction to section 100, Order XLI, rule 11. Order XLII, rule 2, Code of Civil Procedure, if all these three provisions are read together then the appeal in which a substantial question of law is not formulated, cannot be heard finally and every such appeal in which the substantial question of law is not involved, then the appeal will be dismissed under Order XLI, rule 11, Code of Civil Procedure, and then there is no question of final hearing of the appeal. The essential requirement for further proceeding when the appeal is not dismissed under Order XLI, rule 11, Code of Civil Procedure is formulation of substantial question of law. Until and unless Court is satisfied that in the appeal any substantial question of law is involved such appeal cannot be entertained. In the circumstances, if in a second appeal substantial question of law is not formulated then it cannot be heard finally. In the circumstances, the formulation of substantial question of law is *sine qua non*. To give effect to section 102, newly amended, it can reasonably be held that until and unless substantial question of law is formulated, an appeal cannot, be deemed to have passed through the stage of Order XLI, rule 11, Code of Civil Procedure. In the circumstances, intention of legislature in section 102 is that when the substantial question of law is formulated as required under section 100 and Order XLII, rule 2 of the Code, appeal shall be deemed to be admitted. If before this, Court has Issued notice to the other side, it is in the stage of determining whether in the appeal any substantial question of law is involved or not. Thereafter, the Court will either formulate such substantial question of law and the appeal will proceed further, otherwise appeal shall be dismissed. Only after admission of appeal, provision of rule 16 of Order XLI will apply. In the circumstances, the word 'admitted' used in section 16(2)(a) of the Code of Civil Procedure (Amendment) Act, 2002 will mean that Court after hearing the appeal on formation of substantial question of law is satisfied that the substantial question of law is involved and formulates such substantial question of law then only appeal would be deemed to have been "admitted". Merely the Court issued notice to other side in the process of admitting the appeal, it cannot be said that the appeal is admitted. In the circumstances, if an appeal is not admitted before 1-7-2002, the saving clause would not apply and the bar created under section 102 of the Code of Civil Procedure would apply.

Another contention of the learned counsel for the appellant was for permission to convert the appeal into civil revision. To appreciate this contention, it is necessary to consider the relevant provisions for necessary contents in memo of second appeal and memo of revision. As per sub-rule (2) of rule 1 of Order XLI memo of appeal shall set forth, concisely and under distinct heads, the grounds of objection to the decree appealed from without any argument or narrative; and such grounds shall be numbered consecutively. In second appeal, memo of appeal shall concisely set forth substantial question of law involved in appeal. In the aforesaid circumstances, the contents for memo of appeal in second appeal are based on different requirements, while the memo of revision has to contend the facts of the case and specific averments that the Court either has exercised jurisdiction not vested in it by law or has failed to exercise a jurisdiction so vested, or has acted in the exercise of its jurisdiction illegally or with material irregularity, without such averments in memo of revision it will be incomplete, and the revisional Court may not entertain a revision. In the circumstances, memo of appeal and memo of revision are based on different requirements. In the circumstances memo of appeal cannot be treated as a memo of revision.

Similar is the position under Order XLI, rule 3 of the Code. If the memorandum of appeal is not drawn up in the manner prescribed under rule 1 of Order XLI, Code of Civil Procedure, the memo of appeal shall be rejected or returned to the appellant for the purpose of being amended within a time to be fixed by the Court or be amended then and there. In the circumstances, it will not be just and proper to convert the memo of appeal into revision. However, appellants who had filed present appeal much before of the amendment in section 102. Code of Civil Procedure, can be permitted to withdraw this appeal with liberty to file a revision or other proceeding as they choose in accordance with law. If the appellants find that the order is revisable as per section 115, Code of Civil Procedure, they may file such a revision before the Court by taking all the grounds as required for revision, by drafting appropriate memorandum of revision within a period of one month. In abovesaid peculiar circumstances their revision will not be dismissed on the ground of limitation and will be heard and decided in accordance with law. But this appeal cannot be permitted to convert into civil revision,

Learned counsel for the appellants prayed that the appellants have paid court-fee which may be refunded to them. In the Code of Civil Procedure (Amendment) Act, 2002, there is no such provision directing refund of court-fee. Even in the Code of Civil Procedure (Amendment) Act. 1999. Section 34 inserted a new section 16 in the Court-fees Act, 1870, in which the refund of court-fee is provided only in case when the Court refers the parties to the suit to any one of the mode of settlement of dispute referred to in section 89 of the Code of Civil Procedure, 1908 the plaintiff shall be entitled to a certificate from the Court authorising him to receive back from the Collector, the full amount of the fee paid in respect of such plaint, but no such provision has been made when the appeal is held to be not maintainable. In the circumstances, the provision of Court-fees Act can be seen. The refund of court-fee is envisaged in sections 13, 14 and 15 of the Court-fees Act, 1870. Under section 13 of the Court-fees Act, the refund of court fees of memorandum of appeal can be ordered in the circumstances when an appeal or plaint, which has been rejected by the lower court on any of the grounds mentioned in the Code of Civil Procedure, is ordered to be received or if a suit is remanded in appeal, on any of the grounds mentioned in section 35 (now Order XLI, rule 23 of the Code) of the same Code, for a second decision by the lower court, the appellate court is authorised to grant the appellant a certificate for refund. Section 14 provides refund of court-fee on application for review of judgment and section 15 provides for refund of court-fee where the Court reverses or modifies its former decision on the ground of mistake. But, in the present case, the right of appeal which was available prior to 1-7-2002 has been taken away by the Code of Civil Procedure (Amendment) Act, 2002 without making any such provision of refund of court-fee. In the circumstances, prayer made by the learned counsel for the appellants for refund of court-fee cannot be accepted.

However, in the interest of justice, appellants were permitted to withdraw the appeal with a liberty to file a revision or any other proceeding which may be available to them under the law. This appeal was found not maintainable and was permitted to be withdrawn with no order as to costs.

The High Court of Jharkhand examined the scope of rule 11 of Order XLI in the case of *Bishnu Bhagat*. The instant appeal had been placed before this Bench for deciding a question as to whether first appeal arising out of original decree was necessary to be placed for hearing under Order XLI, rule 11 of the Code of Civil Procedure.

The instant appeal had been filed challenging the judgment and decree passed by the Additional District Judge, Simdega in Judicial Separation Case No. 9/95 dismissing the case filed by the petitioner/appellant under section 10 of the Hindu Marriage Act.

When the appeal was listed before the Bench for admission a question arose as to whether the appeal ought to be sent up for admission in terms of Order XLI, rule 11 of the Code of Civil Procedure or it should automatically be taken on file by the Registrar of this Court in exercise of power conferred under rule 205 of the High Court of Jharkhand Rules. A Bench of this Court (P.K. Balasubramanyan, C.J. as he then was) answered the question by order dated 2.8.2004 holding that the appeals, whether it be under the Code of Civil Procedure or under any Special enactment, have to be sent up for admission before the Bench in terms of Order XLI, rule 11 of the Code of Civil Procedure notwithstanding the powers conferred on the Registrar by rule 205 of the High Court of Jharkhand Rules, 2001. The learned Court held that the combined effect of rules 11 and 11A of Order XLI is that any appeal filed has to be preliminarily heard by a Judge and order has to be passed on it either issuing notice or admitting the appeal. Even the unfettered right of appeal under section 96 of the Code of Civil Procedure would be governed or curtailed by what is contained in rules 11 and 11A of Order XLI of the Code of Civil Procedure.

The instant appeal was, thereafter, placed before the Division Bench presided over by Hon'ble the Chief Justice (Altmas Kabir, CJ. as he then was) and the following order was passed on 18.8.2005:

> In view of the order passed on 2nd August, 2004, this matter was directed to be listed before the Division Bench presided over by the Chief Justice for consideration as to whether the matter requires hearing under Order XLI, rules 11 of the Code of Civil Procedure.

This is how the instant appeal had been placed before this Bench for consideration as to whether a regular first appeal arising out of an original decree requires hearing under Order XLI, rule 11 of the Code of Civil Procedure.

Before deciding the issue, the Court quoted rule 205 of the High Court of Jharkhand Rules, 2001, which reads as under:

Rule 205: (1) If a memorandum of appeal is not barred by limitation, is sufficiently and properly stamped and complies with the provisions of these Rules and the law relating to the maintainability and filing of such an appeal:

(a) in the case of a First Appeal from a judgment and decree, the Registrar-General in the Lawazima Board shall admit the appeal by passing a formal order of admission and direct issuance of notices to the respondents;

(b) all other appeals shall be posted before the appropriate Bench for consideration of admission and passing of appropriate orders.

(2) Any party seeking stay of the execution of the decree in every appeal of for obtaining any other interim relief shall do so by making an appropriate application before the Court and the Court may pass orders on such application. The mere admission of a First Appeal by the Registrar-General or the pendency of any appeal in the Court shall not be construed or treated as a stay nor shall it amount to the grant of any interim relief in any form.

From bare perusal of the aforesaid Rules, it is manifestly clear that the Registrar-General of the High Court has been conferred power to admit the appeal by passing Page 1409 formal order of admission and appeal is not barred by limitation and is sufficiently and properly stamped irrespective of the fact whether such appeal has merit or not. Now the question that falls for consideration is to whether procedure provided under rule 205 is in conflict with the Code of Civil procedure.

Part VII of the Code of Civil Procedure deals with the appeals from original decree. Section 96 of the Code is worth to be quoted herein below:

Section 96.—Appeal from original decree – (1) Save where otherwise expressly provided in the body of this Code or by any other law for the time being in force, an appeal shall lie from every decree passed by any court exercising original jurisdiction to the court authorized to hear the appeal from the decision of such court.

(2) An appeal may lie from an original decree passed *ex parte*.

(3) No appeal shall lie from a decree passed by the court with the consent of parties.

(4) No appeal shall lie, except on a question of law, from a decree in any suit of the nature cognizable by Courts of small causes, when the amount or value of the subject-matter of the original suit does not exceed (Rs. 10,000)

Section 100 of the Code deals with the procedure of appeals from appellate decrees (Second Appeal) which reads as under:

Section 100(1). Save as otherwise expressly provided in the body of this Code or by any other law for the time being in force, an appeal shall lie to the High Court from every decree passed in appeal by any court subordinate to the High Court, if the High Court is satisfied that the case involves a substantial question of law.

(2) An appeal may lie under this section from an appellate decree passed *ex parte*.

(3) In an appeal under this section, the memorandum of appeal shall precisely state the substantial question of law involved in the appeal.

(4) Where the High Court is satisfied that a substantial question of law is involved in any case, it shall formulate that question.

(5) The appeal shall be heard on the question so formulated and the respondent shall, at the hearing of the appeal, be allowed to argue that the case does not involve such question:

Provided that nothing in this sub-section shall be deemed to take away or abridge the power of the Court to hear, for reasons to be recorded, the appeal on any other substantial question of law, not formulated by it, if it is satisfied that the case involves such question.

Comparing the two provisions, it is manifestly clear that an appeal shall lie from every decree passed by any court exercising original jurisdiction unless the Code or any other law expressly bars it, for the time being in force. On the other hand, a second appeal *i.e.* appeal from appellate decree shall be entertained by the High Court only after the High Court is satisfied that the case involves substantial question of law. Section 100 of the Code further provides that in a second appeal the memorandum of appeal shall precisely state the substantial question of law involved Page 1410 in the appeal. It further provides that the High Court, if satisfied that substantial questions of law are involved, then it shall formulate such questions.

Section 101 of the Code further clarifies that no second appeal shall lie, except on the ground mentioned in section 100 of the Code.

It would also be useful to quote hereinbelow some of the provisions of Order XLI of the Code of Civil Procedure. Order XLI, rule 11 and rule 12 read as under:

Rule 11. Power to dismiss appeal without sending notice to lower court.—(1) Appellate court after fixing a day for hearing the appellant or his pleader and hearing him accordingly if he appears on that day may dismiss the appeal.

(2) If on the day fixed or any other day to which the hearing may be adjourned the appellant does not appear when the appeal is called on for hearing, the Court may make an order that the appeal be dismissed.

(3) The dismissal of an appeal under this rule shall be notified to the Court from whose decree the appeal is preferred.

(4) Where an appellate court, not being the High Court, dismisses an appeal under sub-rule (1), it shall deliver a judgment, recording in brief its grounds for doing so, and a decree shall be drawn up in accordance with the judgment.

Rule 12. Day for hearing appeal.—(1) Unless the appellate court dismisses the appeal under rule 11, it shall fix a day for hearing the appeal.

(2) Such day shall be fixed with reference to the current business of the Court.

Rule 14 of Order XLI provides that those appeals which have not been dismissed at the admission stage under rule 11, a date shall be fixed for hearing the appeal and rule 14 makes provision for issuance of notice. Order XLI, rule 14 reads as under:

Rule 14. Publication and service of notice of day for hearing appeal. (1) Notice of the day fixed under rule 12 shall be affixed in the Appellate Court-house, and a like notice shall be sent by the appellate court to the Court from whose decree the appeal is preferred, and shall be served on the respondent or on his pleader in the appellate court in the manner provided for the service on a defendant of a summons to appear and answer; and all the provisions applicable to such summons, and to proceedings with reference to the service thereof, shall apply to the service of such notice.

(2) Appellate court may itself cause notice to be served.—Instead of sending the notice to the Court from whose decree the appeal is preferred, the appellate court may itself cause the notice to be served on the respondent or his pleader under the provisions above referred to.

(3) The notice to be served on the respondent shall be accompanied by a copy of the memorandum of appeal.

(4) Notwithstanding anything to the contrary contained in sub-rule (1), it shall not be necessary to serve notice of any proceeding incidental to an appeal on any respondent other than a person impleaded for the first time in the appellate court, unless he has appeared and filed an address for the service in the Court of first instance or has appeared in the appeal.

(5) Nothing in sub-rule (4) shall bar the respondent referred to in the appeal from defending it.

Rule 16. Right to begin.—(1) On the day fixed, or on any other day to which the hearing may be adjourned, the appellant shall be heard in support of the appeal.

(2) The Court shall then, if it does not dismiss the appeal at once, hear the respondent against the appeal, and in such case the appellant shall be entitled to reply.

Sub-rule (4) of rule 11 has been inserted in the year 1976 by C.P.C. Amendment Act of, 1976. Sub-rule (4) now made obligatory for the appellate court not being a High Court to deliver judgment recording in brief the grounds for dismissing the appeal under sub-rule (1). By now the legal proposition has been set at rest by the Supreme Court that notwithstanding the provision of sub-rule (4) of rule 11 of Order XLI, C.P.C. High Court is expected to pass a reasoned order even in dismissing appeal on the first day of hearing at the admission stage in absence of the respondents to ensure that justice not only done but appears to be done. Provisions of Order XLI, rule 11(4) of the Code does not do away with its basic obligation of doing justice in deciding rights and liabilities of the contesting parties.

In this connection reference may be made to the report of Justice Malimath Committee, Chapter III, P. 30, which reads as under: Indeed, the provisions of Order XLI, rules 11, 11A and 12 of the Code of Civil Procedure read together make it obligatory for the appellate court to fix a day for the preliminary hearing of appeal as expeditiously as possible and to make endeavour to conclude such hearing within sixty days from the date of which the memorandum of appeal is filed and, unless the appeal is summarily dismissed at preliminary hearing, to fix a day for final hearing. In other words, the question of fixing a day for the final hearing of appeal arises only if the appeal is not summarily dismissed at the preliminary hearing which has to be fixed as expeditiously as possible after the memorandum of appeal is filed. In our view, these provisions should be strictly followed. However, care should be taken that an appeal which raises triable issue is not dismissed *in limine*. We would also like to emphasis that when an appeal is dismissed *in limine*, a brief order giving reasons for dismissal at the preliminary stage should invariably be recorded. A similar recommendation has been made by the Law Commission of India in its 79th report." [Quoted from Sarkars on CPC 10th Edition]

In the case of *Mahadev Tukaram Vetale* v. *Sugandha*, AIR 1972 SC 1932: 1972 SCD 1063: (1973) 3 SCC 746 a suit was filed for partition as well as other reliefs including genuineness of Will. The trial court came to the conclusion that the Will in question was genuine Will and decreed the suit. The defendant went up in appeal to High Court of Bombay. The High Court summarily dismissed the appeal in a single word "Dismissed". The question for decision before the Supreme Court was whether the appeal raised any triable issue. The Supreme Court held that if the appeal did raise any triable issue then the High Court was not justified in summarily dismissing the appeal. Consequently, the appeal was sent back to the High Court for re-admitting the appeal and for disposing the same according to law.

In the case of *Jayanti De* v. *Abani Kanta Barat*, AIR 2000 SC 3578 (2), their Lordships observed:

> The appeal had been dismissed by the High Court with the following order:
>
> "We are not satisfied that the High Court has considered the appeal on merits. Even if the dismissal is under Order XLI, rule 11 and the High Court is not required under sub-rule (4) to record in brief its grounds for doing so it is not a *carte balanche* to enable the appellate court to avoid recording any reason whatsoever. We think that the appeal required consideration on merits. We, therefore, set aside the impugned order and remit the appeal to the High Court for disposal of the same on merits and in accordance with law by stating the reasons. The position which remained as on the date of impugned order will continue till the disposal of the appeal".

In the case of *Devram Bilve* v. *Indumati*, (2000) 10 SCC 540, a suit was filed for restoration of conjugal rights alleging that the appellant had deserted his wife. The suit was contested by the respondents and evidence was adduced by both the parties. The trial court decreed the suit. Learned Single Judge of the High Court allowed First Appeal and the same was upheld by a Division Bench of this Court. In the Supreme Court, it was argued that both the learned Single Judge and the Division Bench have considered the evidence on record which should have enabled it to decide whether respondent was guilty of committing any act of cruelty. The Supreme Court allowed the appeal and remanded the matter to the High Court for deciding the appeal afresh. Their Lordships observed: That learned counsel for the parties have taken us to the record. We find that neither the Single Judge nor has the Division Bench considered the evidence on the record which would have enabled it to decide whether the respondent was guilty of committing any act of cruelty. The letters on the basis of which cruelty was sought to be established have not even been referred by the Division Bench nor do they seem to have been analysed by the Single Judge. Both the Courts did not appear to have gone into this aspect in great detail because they decided the appeal in favour of the respondent on the ground that the parties had lived together at Sugar hotel at Indore and that amounted to an act of condonation. We have some doubt, on the basis of the evidence on record or the lack of it, whether this conclusion is correct and, therefore, it was important for the Single Judge as well as the Division Bench to have examined the evidence on record in order to determine whether the appellant herein had been able to prove that the respondent had committed such acts of cruelty which could entitle the appellant to get a decree of divorce.

In the light of the decisions of Supreme Court, quoted hereinbefore and also considering the provisions of sub-rule (4) of rule 11, I am of the view that notwithstanding the provisions of sub-rule (4) of rule 11 Order XLI, C.P.C. the High Court is expected to pass a reasoned order even in dismissing appeal on the first date of hearing in absence of the respondents to ensure that justice not only done but appears to be dome. Provisions of Order XLI, rule 11(4) of the Code does not do away with its basic obligation of doing justice in deciding rights and liabilities of the contesting parties.

Reading the entire provisions from Order XLI, rule 11 it can safely be held that it is the appellate court and the appellate court only before whom the appeal shall be listed for admission. If the appellate court finds no merit in the appeal then it shall dismiss the appeal without even issuing notices to the respondents. On the first day of hearing at the admission stage if the appellate court finds arguable points in appeal then notices shall be issued to the respondents fixing a date for hearing of the appeal.

Having regard to the law discussed hereinabove, the Court said, I fully agree with the view of a Bench of this Court (P.K. Balasubramanyan, CJ. as he then was) that rule 205 is inconsistent with the provisions of Order XLI, rule 11 of the Code of Civil Procedure. His Lordships in his order dated 2.8.2004 observed:

This Rule enables the Registry to admit an appeal if the appeal is not barred by limitation and it substantially and properly complies with the provisions of the High Court of Jharkhand Rules and the law relating to the mandate for filing of such an appeal. It appears to me that in the context of Order XLI, rule 11 and 11A of the Code, rule 205 of the High Court of Jharkhand Rules would have to be read down lest it conflicts with the mandate of Order XLI, rules 11 and 11A of the Code. Since an appeal filed in the High Court is governed by the Code of Civil Procedure, any Rule of the High Court in respect of that appeal can only be consistent with the provisions relating to appeals in the Code of Civil Procedure. So viewed, rule 205(1)(a) of the High Court of Jharkhand Rules to avoid it being inconsistent with the scheme of Order XLI, rule 11 of the Code of Civil Procedure, has to be read as subject to the procedure in Order XLI, rule 11. In other words, the said Rule cannot prevail over the requirement of Order XLI, rule 11 of the Code. The said Rule has therefore to be read as only enabling the Registrar to register the appeal when the conditions therein are satisfied. The appeal thereafter has to be dealt with in terms of Order XLI, rule 11 of the Code of Civil Procedure.

Section 29 of the Bihar Reorganization Act, 2000 under which the High Court of Jharkhand Rules, 2001 were framed enables the High Court of Jharkhand either to adopt the Rules of the High Court of Patna or to make Rules for itself. This power to make Rules relates to the procedure to be followed in the matter of a proceeding filed in the High Court. This power to regulate the procedure, in my view, has to be understood consistently with the requirement of the Code of Civil Procedure, which governs the filing of an appeal in this Court. So understood, I am of the view that the rule 205 of the High Court of Jharkhand Rules, 2001 cannot prevail over the requirement of Order XLI, rule 11 of the Code of Civil Procedure. I am, therefore, satisfied that appeals, whether it be under the Code of Civil Procedure or any special enactment have to be sent up for admission before the Bench in terms of Order XLI, rule 11 of the Code of Civil Procedure and notwithstanding the power conferred on the Registrar by rule 205 of the High Court of Jharkhand Rules, 2001.

The High Court of Jharkhand held, in the light of the discussions made above, in our considered opinion, rule 205(1)(a) of the High Court of Jharkhand Rules, 2001 needs to be amended to the extent that all appeals arising out of the original decree, if it is sufficiently and properly stamped and complies with the provisions of the Rule and Law regarding maintainability shall be posted before the appropriate Bench for consideration and admission and for passing appropriate order.

The Court ultimately ordered, "Let this appeal be placed for hearing under Order XLI, rule 11 of the Code of Civil Procedure"; *Bishnu Bhagat* v. *Pushpa Devi*, AIR 2006 Jhar 117: 2006 (3) JCR Jha 457: 2006 (3) JLJR 645.

115. Rule 11 – Appeal – Dismissal without Hearing Appellant

Order of dismissal without hearing the appellant cannot be sustained. AIR 1955 NUC (Ajmer) 4154. The High Court of Allahabad said that Revenue Board can summarily dismiss appeal without hearing either appellant or his pleader. *See* Tenancy Laws – U.P. Tenancy Act (1939), section 243: 1964 All WR (HC) 226. Only Revenue Board has power to dismiss appeal summarily without hearing party. The Additional Commissioner's powers to dismiss appeal summarily without hearing parties are vested in the Board of Revenue by virtue of the modification made in rule 11 of Order XLI, C.P.C. by Serial No. 13 of List II of the Second Schedule of the U.P. Tenancy Act. The lower appellate Court must comply with rule 11 of Order XLI, which makes it mandatory on the Court to fix a day for hearing the appellant. 1952 RD (BR) 9: 1952 All WR (Rev) 22: 1952 All LJ (Rev) 5. The High Court of Allahabad said that the mere fact that the order of dismissal was passed before the date fixed for hearing does not deprive the Board of Revenue of its jurisdiction to dispose of an appeal. 1951 RD 109: 1951 All WR (Rev) 91 (92). A Full Bench of the High Court of Bombay said that reasons for dismissal should be given. Regarding Summary dismissal of Appeal under section 29 of Bombay Rents, Hotel and Lodging Houses Rates Control Act (57 of 1947), the said Court also said that Appellate Bench bound to give reasons. *Hanumant Rukhmaji* v. *Annaji Hanmant*, (1913) 15 Bom LR 765: ILR 37 Bom 610 (FB) and CR A 589 of 1955 dated 1st February, 1956 Bom ILR 36 Bom 116 held not good law in view of *Hanumant Rukhmaji* v. *Annaji Hanmant*, (1913) 15 Bom LR 765: ILR 37 Bom 610 (FB). About the order of dismissal of appeal under rule 11 as not maintainable, the High Court of Mysore said that having dismissed appeal appellate court should not proceed to say anything more about the order which was in appeal. He should not make any observation regarding appropriateness of the directions made by the Court in the order. *Mundyappu Hengsu* v. *Sampa Alvathi*, (1965) 1 Mys LJ 728: AIR 1965 Mys 268 (Pt A) (Pr 6). Dismissal under rule 11 is controlled by provisions of rule 31. Order dismissing appeal under Order XLI, rule 11 is a, judgment and falls within mischief of Order XLI, rule 31.

116. Rule 11 – Restoration of Appeal when Dismissal for Default

Considerations for Court – Sufficient cause-Negligence of Advocate. In considering whether there are sufficient grounds for the restoration of an appeal which was dismissed for default, the Courts would ordinarily be inclined to restore it unless there has been gross negligence on the part of the party, because the Courts are there only for the advancement of justice and would not ordinarily deprive a litigant of his right. Courts will not, as far as possible allow the sins of his advocate to visit on the client, as the client should not be made to suffer for the negligence or default of his Advocate. Costs are always a panacea for all ills and the opposite party can be compensated by costs for the inconvenience caused. Without prejudicially affecting the rights of the other party, the Court will subject to costs and restore the appeal. 63 IA 12, ref. *Bansilal* v. *Mukundas*, ILR 1952 Hyd 85: AIR 1952 Hyd 155 (157) (Prs 7, 8) (DB). But in case of dismissal of appeal on merits when appellant not present on day of hearing appellate court has no such jurisdiction – Remedy against dismissal in such a case is application for restoration under rule 19 and not appeal; *Kundha Singh* v. *Punjab State*, ILR (1962) 1 Punj 156: AIR 1962 Punj 82 (83, 85) (Prs 10, 12).

117. Rule 11, Order XLVII, Rule 1 – Order of Dismissal of Appeal under Order XLI, Rule 11

The various High Courts are of the view that order can be reviewed even if no formal judgment had been written if the mistake of law is gross and apparent from the record. *Jamuna Prasad Rai* v. *Rajballam Rai*, AIR 1937 Pat 349: 169 IC 359 and *Makhu Sahu* v. *Kamta Prasad Sahu*, AIR 1934 Pat 341: ILR 13 Pat 540; AIR 1995 Rang 267 and C.R. No. 1031 of 1957, dated 26-10-1959 (All) and *Jamna Kuer* v. *Lal Bahadur*, AIR 1950 FC 131: 1949 FCR 662 and *Govinda Chettiar* v. *Varadappa Chettiar*, AIR 1940 Mad 17: (1939) 2 Mad LJ 809, rel. on; *Ayesha Bai* v. *Daleep Singh*, AIR 1961 Raj 186: 1960 Raj LW 527: ILR (1960) 10 Raj 1271 and *Soosai Anthony D'Costa Nicholas D'Costa* v. *Francis Roche Anthony Kurush Roche*, AIR 1962 Mad 304: (1962) 1 Mad LJ 376: ILR 1962 Mad 804, Disting. *Krishna* v. *Rajeshwar Mishra*, AIR 1964 Pat 474 (476, 477) (Pt A) (Prs 3, 7). 10. Where the Counsel was present but not ready to argue and prayed for adjournment, adjournment was refused and appeal is dismissed, the High Court of MP said that the dismissal is under section 151 – Restoration can only be under section 151 – No appeal against dismissal of application for restoration lies but only revision is competent – 1962 MP LJ (Notes) 158. Where appeal is dismissed as time-barred, order amounts to decree – No revision lies. *Bhagirathi Padhan* v. *Achuta Padhan*, AIR 1965 Ori 193:

31 Cut LT 105: ILR 1965 Cut 4. Order of dismissal of memorandum of appeal on ground of limitation is decree. Revision does not lie from such order. *Achyuta Dhangadamajhi* v. *Sibram Dhangadamajhi*, ILR 1962 Cut 818, *Banwarilal Bhoid* v. *P. Neelkantham*, AIR 1965 Ori 102: ILR 1964 Cut 674 (DB). Order of dismissal of memorandum of appeal on ground of limitation is not decree – Revision lies from such order. Section 107(2) confines itself with regard to the powers and duties of the appellate court and cannot enlarge the statutory definition of the decree itself in course of the exercise of those powers and duties. No distinction in principle can be made between rejection of a memorandum of appeal on the ground of its being insufficiently stamped and its being barred by limitation. An order of dismissal of a memorandum of appeal on the ground that it is barred by limitation does not amount to a decree and is not appealable and a revision is maintainable from such order. *Phaltan Bank Ltd.* v. *Baburao Appajirao*, AIR 1954 Bom 43: 55 Bom LR 762: ILR 1953 Bom 1176, foll.; *Keshomal Basantlal* v. *Panchulal Motilal*, AIR 1953 Ajmer 32; *Mangal Ballav Roaza* v. *Nihar Prava Mutsuddi*, AIR 1959 Tripura 6(7); *Loli Kaikho* v. *Peli Sibo*, AIR 1959 Manipur 13; *Adarpriya Chaudhrani* v. *Ramprotap Agarwalla*, AIR 1926 Cal 1105: 44 Cal LJ 44; AIR 1920 Pat 818; *Gajadhar Bhagat* v. *Moti Chand*, 22 Pat LT 549: AIR 1941 Pat 108, not foll. *Achyuta Dhangadamajhi* v. *Sibram Dhangadamajhi*, ILR 1962 Cut 818. [Overruled in *Ishteyaque Ahamad* v. *Kitawan Bibi*, AIR 1985 Ori 102: 1985 (1) Ori LR 102.]

118. Rules 11 and 12 – Restriction of Grounds of Appeal on Admission

A Court cannot on admission of an appeal under Order XLI, rule 11, restrict the grounds on which the appeal is to be heard finally. There is nothing in the rules to indicate that the Court is entitled to admit the appeal piece-meal. If, however, at the time of admission the appellant abandons any one or more of the grounds taken in the memorandum and confines the appeal to some of the grounds alone, it may be open to the Court to make a record of that fact which may have the effect of limiting the scope of "the appeal", and the day to be fixed under Order XLI, rule 12, would be to hear the appeal as so limited and not as originally presented. In such a case there is no admission of the appeal in part. *Lakhi Narain Sarangi* v. *Ramchandra Bhunya*, 14 Cal LJ 146: 11 IC 212 (Cal): AIR 1918 Cal 741.

119. Order XLI, Rule 20 – Scope and Application

A party who is interested in an appeal can alone be impleaded under rule 20 of Order XLI C.P.C., and a party against whom no appeal has been filed within the period of limitation cannot he impleaded under this rule. 1951 All WR (Rev) 143: 1951 RD 40.

120. Object of Order XLI, Rule 20

The object of rule 20 of Order XLI, C.P.C., is not to empower an appellate court to implead a person who is interested in the decree of the lower court and against whom no appeal has been preferred and who has, therefore, acquired a substantive right and is no longer interested in the result of the appeal, to be impleaded so as to enable the appellate court to pass a decree against him afresh. 1951 RD 36 (2): 1951 All WR (Rev) 22. Appeal by one of the parties affected by the decree – Competency of the party depends upon Court's discretion; 1952 All LJ (Rev) 229.

121. Order XLI, Rule 20 – "Interested in the Result of the Appeal." Meaning and Scope of the Term

Under Order XLI, rule 20 an appellate court is entitled to add as a respondent any party not so impleaded but interested in the result of the appeal. This power would not however be exercised if the period of limitation as against the party sought to be so added has already expired, for, by reason of the appeal having thus become time-barred against him, such a party cannot be said to be interested in the result of the appeal; *Chokalingam* v. *Seethai Ache*, ILR 6 Rang 29: AIR 1927 PC 252: (1928) 54 Mad LJ 88, foll.: AIR 195Z HP 9 (10) (Pt B) (Pr 5).

Delay in joining such party as respondent in appeal.—

> Where a party to the original proceeding against whom the suit is dismissed is proposed to be added as a party to the appeal and the time for appeal against him has expired, the question whether the interest of such person proposed to be added still survives in the appeal must depend on the nature of the litigation, the decree passed, the subject-matter of the appeal and the effect of the decision in appeal in his absence; *Alabhai Vajsurbhai* v. *Bhura Bhaya*, AIR 1937 Bom 401: 39 Bom LR 444, foll.: *Keshorao* v. *Yeshwantrao*, AIR 1957 MB 17 (18): 1956 MBLR Civil 188: 1956 MBLJ 774 (Pt B) (Pr 4) (DB).

122. Order XLI, Rule 20 – Person Interested in Result of Appeal – Joint Decree-holder not Joined in Appeal

It can be joined after limitation – [Limitation Act (1908), section 5].

The plaintiffs, who had lost in the trial court, appealed and failed to implead one of the defendants. Limitation for filing an appeal against that defendant had expired. The District Judge declined to grant the prayer of the plaintiffs who sought permission of the Court to add him under Order XLI, rule 20.

It was held that whether the District Judge had discretion in the matter or not he could not be said to have acted wrongly in refusing to implead the defendant. But apart from the question of discretion that defendant could no longer be said to be an interested party since the decision of the trial court in his favour was unalterable and not open to appeal. In the circumstances the District Judge acted rightly in refusing to implead the defendant; AIR 1944 Lah 76 (FB), rel. on. *Jagan Singh* v. *Panni*, 55 Punj LR 449: AIR 1954 Punj 20 (Pt A) (Prs **2,** 3).

[Overruled in *Notified Area Committee, Buria* v. *Gobind Ram Lachhman Dass*, AIR 1959 Punj 277: 61 Pun LR 326: ILR 1959 Punj 1066 (FB).

A joint decree-holder who has not been joined as a respondent within time is not a person "interested in the result of the appeal" within the meaning of rule 20, O. *Bhojraj Krishnarao* v. *Darsu*, 1958 MPLJ 361: 1957 MPC 398: AIR 1959 MP 52 (54, 53) (Pt A) (Prs 6, 10, 15).

123. Order XLI, Rule 20 and Section 115 Power of the Court

Power to direct addition of party is discretionary – Discretion cannot be questioned in revision. AIR 1955 NUC (Ajmer) 1259. Party whose name was not disclosed in decree not impleaded as respondent in appeal – Power under – Exercise of. *See* Tenancy Laws – Ti. P. Tenancy Act (1939), section 59. 1965 All WR 540.

124. Order XLI, Rule 21 – Time-barred Appeal

Refusal to extend time-bared Appeal dismissed but decree not drawn up – Remedy – Appeal – Revision; *Mungal Bullav Rouza* v. *Nihar Prava Mutsuddi*, AIR 1959 Tri 6.

RULE 22

125. Scope and Application

The respondent may support part of the decree and at the same time, may state that the findings against him in respect of any issue ought to have been in his favour. In other words, the respondent may oppose decree on some ground, though he has not preferred a separate appeal. But the cross-objection to the appeal must be filed within one month from the date of service on him of notice of the day fixed for hearing the appeal, or within such further time as the court may think proper. It is, therefore, manifest that the period of limitation for filing cross-objection will be guided by rule 22 itself and not either by the Limitation Act or by section 148. Therefore, if the decision of the suit goes partially against the respondent, he may feel contended with the rest decided in his favour. But if the appellant prefers an appeal against part of the judgment, the respondent may choose to prefer a cross objection subject to the limitation as prescribed by rule 22 of this Order and all provisions contained in rule 1 will be applicable to his cross objection.

The High Court of Madras directed that cross-objection can be filed only in respect of a finding on which the decree appealed against is based. *Kuppuswami* v. *Krishnaveni*, AIR 1996 Mad 94: 1996 (1) ICC 358: 1995 (2) Mad LW 793. The Supreme Court in *N. Jayaram Reddi* v. *Revenue Divisional Officer and Land Acquisition Officer, Kurnool*, AIR 1979 SC 1393: (1979) 3 SCC 578: (1979) 3 SCR 599 and in *Mahant Dhangir* v. *Madan Mohan*, AIR 1988 SC 54: JT 1987 (5) SC 202: 1987 Rajdhani LR 663 had made it clear that a cross-objection is like a cross-appeal. The distinction between the two lies in the fact that whereas cross-objections form part of the same record, cross-appeals are two independent proceedings. The Court also held that the right to file cross-objection is substantive in nature and not merely procedural.

The High Court of Madhya Pradesh held that cross-objection may be filed not only in the first appeal but also in the second appeal and may also be filed in appeals from orders; *Beniprasad Agarwal* v. *Hindustan Lever Ltd., Bombay*, AIR 1958 MP 348: 1957 MPC 554: 1957 MPLJ 676.

The High Court of Delhi considered the scope of rule 22 of Order XLI in the case of *Delhi Transport Undertaking*. The question for consideration was whether cross-objections are maintainable in a case where an appeal has been preferred under an Act which does not specifically provide for the filing of cross-objection is the main question which has arisen for decision in the two appeals F.A.O. No. 239-D of 1964 and F.A.O. No. 37 of 1971, which are being decided by this judgment.

The facts relating to F.A.O. No. 239-D of 1964 in brief were that Kumari Lalita was run over by a D.T.U. bus on 6-12-1961 and received serious injuries. According to the doctors, she was permanently disabled. She filed a claim for Rs. 1,00,000 under section 110A of the Motor Vehicles Act against the Delhi Transport Undertaking. The Tribunal awarded a sum of Rs. 12,000 to her. The Delhi Transport Undertaking filed the present appeal against the Award. Kumari Lalita filed cross-objections and asked for enhancement of the compensation awarded by the Tribunal. During the course of arguments, Mr. R.L. Tandon, learned counsel for the appellant, raised a contention that no cross-objections were maintainable. His submission was that the Award of the Tribunal did not amount to a decree and the provisions of Order XLI, rule 22 of the Code of Civil Procedure had not been specifically made applicable and so no cross-objections could be preferred. The Award could not be treated as an order since it did not fall under the definition given in section 2(14) of the Code of Civil Procedure. When this matter came up before one of us (V.D. Misra, J.), it was noticed that there was a conflict of decisions and it was decided to refer the following question for the decision of a larger Bench:—

> "Whether cross-objections are maintainable in .a case where an appeal has been preferred under section 110A of the Motor Vehicles Act against the Award of the Motor Claims Tribunal?" (3) In F.A.O. No. 37 of 1971 M/s. Banwari Lal and Sons (Pvt.) Ltd., filed an appeal against the Award of the arbitrator under sections 8 of the Requisitioning and Acquisition of Immovable Property Act, 1952. The Union of India, who was the first respondent in this appeal, filed cross-objections. The appellant objected to the maintainability of the cross-objections on the ground that the Act did not provide for the filing of the same. It was also contended that the principle underlying under Order XLI, rule 22 of the Code of Civil Procedure would not enable the respondent to file cross-objections. When the matter came up before one of us (M.R.A. Ansari, J.), it was noticed that there was a conflict of decisions and it was decided to refer the matter to a larger Bench. (4) The contention of the learned counsel for the respondents, who have filed cross-objections, is that when an appeal lies to the High Court from the decision of a Tribunal the proceedings are governed by the practice and procedure of the High Court. The High Court is a Court of Record to which the provisions of the Code of Civil Procedure are applicable, and so the respondents can file cross-objections. On the other hand, the learned counsel for the appellants contended that the right of filing cross-objections is a substantive right which can be given by a statute only and is not a matter of procedure. Appeals from Tribunals lie to the High Court as *persona designata*, and in any case procedure of High Court gives no right of filing cross-objections. Reliance is also placed on an unreported Division Bench decision of Punjab High Court (Circuit Bench at Delhi) in *Union of India* v. *Mauji Ram*, F.A.O. No. 85D of 1956, decided on 17-12-1965. (i). (5) The relevant provisions of the Motor Vehicles Act and the Requisitioning and Acquisition of Immovable Property Act may be noticed. Sections 110 to 111A were enacted by amendment in 1956 to the Motor Vehicles Act, 1939. Section 110 deals with the constitution of

Motor Accidents Claims Tribunals for the purpose of adjudicating upon claims for compensation arising out of motor accidents. Section 110A lays down the period within which an application for compensation may be made to the Claims Tribunal having jurisdiction over the area within which the accident took place by the persons described in this Section. This application is to be in such form, and is to contain such particulars, as may be prescribed by the rules made under the Act. Section 110-B requires holding of an enquiry into the claim and making an award. Section 110-C provides for the procedure of the Tribunal subject to the rules which may be made and its powers. The procedure to be followed by the Claims Tribunals and its powers are to be laid down by the rules to be framed by State Governments under section 111A. Delhi Motor Vehicles Rules, 1940, were amended by a notification dated 15-11-1960 under section 111A. New rules are 8.5 to 8.24. They lay down the procedure to be followed by the Claims Tribunal in entertaining applications for compensation and their disposal. Provision for examination of parties, summoning of witnesses, local inspection, recording evidence, framing of issues and their determination, judgment and award of compensation has been made. Some provisions of the Code of Civil Procedure have been made applicable by rule 8.22. Section 110D gives to any aggrieved person the right of appeal to the High Court against the award of a Tribunal, and is as under:—

"Section 110D. Appeal.—(1) Subject to the provisions of sub-section (2), any person aggrieved by an Award of a Claims Tribunal may, within ninety days from the date of the Award, prefer an appeal to the High Court: Provided that the High Court may entertain the appeal after the expiry of the said period of ninety days, if it is satisfied that the appellant was prevented by sufficient cause from preferring the appeal in time. (2) No appeal shall lie against any award of a Claims Tribunal, if the amount in dispute in the appeal is less than two thousand rupees." (6) Rule 8.23 only deals with appeals, and is as under:—

"8.23. Form and number of appeals against the decision of Claims Tribunal.—(1) An appeal against the Award of a Claims Tribunal, shall be preferred in the form of a memorandum stating concisely the grounds on which the appeal is preferred. (2) It shall be accompanied by a copy of the judgment and the Award appealed against."

A Division Bench of the Calcutta High Court in *Ramasray Singh* v. *Bibhisan Sinha,* AIR 1950 Cal 372, relying on the observations of Viscount Haldane, L.C., held that the cross-objections were maintainable despite the fact that section 38(3) of the Bengal Money-Lenders Act of 1940 did not provide for the same and observed thus: "The right of appeal, under that section, is given to an establishment Court, namely, the Court of the District Judge. Nothing is stated expressly in the sub-section as to the procedure regulating such appeal. In our view, where nothing is stated expressly as to the procedure of an appeal before a District Judge, the law will import that the ordinary procedure of that Court on appeal will apply. The ordinary procedure on an appeal is that the respondent has the right to file cross-objection and therefore it is quite clear that the respondent has the right to file a cross-objection." Their Lordships of the Supreme Court in *South Asia Industries (P.) Ltd.* v. *S.B. Sarup Singh,* AIR 1965 SC 1442: (1965) 2 SCR 756: 1966 (2) SCJ 69 quoted with approval their following observations in *National Sewing Thread Co. Ltd.* v. *James Chadwick & Bros. Ltd.,* AIR 1953 SC 357: 1953 SCR 1028: 1953 SCJ 509. "Obviously, after the appeal had reached the High Court it has to be determined according to the rules of practice and procedure of that Court and in accordance with the provisions of the charter under which that Court is constituted and which confers on it power in respect to the method and manner of exercising that jurisdiction The rule is well-settled that when a statute directs that an appeal shall lie to a Court already established then the appeal must be regulated by the practice and procedure of that Court." (15) After referring to various decisions of the Judicial Committee with approval, including the case of National Telephone Co., Ltd. (*supra*) (2). it was observed thus: "The following legal position emerges from the said discussion. A statute may give a right of appeal from an order of a Tribunal or a Court to the High Court without any limitation thereof. The appeal to the High Court will be regulated by the practice and procedure obtaining in the High Court."

In *Collector, Varanasi* v. *Gauri Shanker Misra,* AIR 1968 SC 384: 1968 (1) SCJ 857: (1968) 1 SCR 372 the import of section 19(1)(f) of the Defence of India Act, 1939, which is as follows:—

> "An appeal shall lie to the High Court against an Award of an arbitrator excepting in cases where the amount thereof does not exceed an amount prescribed in this behalf by rule made by the Central Government" was considered, and their Lordships of the Supreme Court observed thus: "We were informed that neither the Act nor the rules framed thereunder, prescribed any special procedure for the disposal of appeals under section 19(1)(f). Appeals under that provision have to be disposed of just in the same manner as other appeals to the High Court. Obviously after the appeal had reached the High Court, it had to be determined according to the rules of practice and procedure of that Court. The rule is well-settled that when a statute directs that an appeal shall lie to a Court already established, then that appeal must be regulated by the practice and procedure of that Court." It was also observed: "The fact that the arbitrator appointed under section 19(1)(b) is either a designated person or a Tribunal – as to whether he is a person designated or a Tribunal we express no opinion – does not in any way bear on the question whether the 'High Court' referred to under section 19(1)(f) is a Court or not. Our statutes are full of instances where appeals or revisions to Courts are provided as against the decisions of designated person and Tribunals."
>
> The earlier decision of the Supreme Court in *Hanskumar Kishan Chand* v. *Union of India,* AIR 1958 SC 947: 1959 SCJ 603: 1959 SCR 1177 holding that an appeal to the High Court under section 19(l)(f), Defence of India Act, 1939, against the decision of a *persona designata* is to be "construed" as a reference to it as an authority designated and not as a Court since appeal is a continuation of a proceedings, is no longer good law in view of

Gauri Shanker case (*supra*). (6) The Division Bench (*supra*) (1) had based its decision on *Hanskumar Kishanchand* case (7), since the relevant provisions of the Requisitioning and Acquisition Act, 1952, are an exact parallel to those of Section 19 of the Defence of India Act, 1939, for coming to the conclusion that appeal to the High Court under the former Act lay to it as an authority designated and not a Court. In view of *Gauri Shanker's* case (6) (*supra*), *Mauji Ram's* case (1) cannot be held to be laying down the correct law. A Full Bench of this Court in the *Municipal Corporation of Delhi* v. *Kuldip Lal Bhandari*, AIR 1970 Del 37: 1969 ACJ 276: ILR 1969 Del 497 considered the import of section 110D of the Motor Vehicles Act, and observed thus: "As already stated above, the claim for compensation caused by negligence is well-known to the law of torts, as a part of common law independent of any statute. The claim not being a creation of any particular statute it would be reasonable to suppose that the provisions of the Motor Vehicles (Amendment) Act, 1956 were intended only to expedite the trial of such a claim by the establishment of Claims Tribunal. The statute did not otherwise intend to cut down or modify or change in any way, the common law right. Section 110F barred the jurisdiction of Civil Courts only to entertain the original claim as a trial court. This bar operated only when in the particular area the Claims Tribunal had been established. In the other areas, the Civil Courts continue to entertain such a claim. The appeal to the High Court under section 110D of the Act enables the High Court to consider the claim in its entirety free from any limitations in the same way as the High Court would consider the claim in an appeal from a Civil Court from an area in which a Claims Tribunal has not been established." It was further observed: in hearing the appeal under section 110D of the Act, the High Court must be held to be acting as a High Court and not as a Tribunal, in as much as the claim for compensation for negligence is a common law right not as created by a statute and the claim is considered by the Tribunal in its entirety without limitation with the result that an appeal to the High Court is made in its ordinary Civil Jurisdiction."

The other contention of the learned counsel for the appellants that the Order XLI, rule 22 of the Code of Civil Procedure would not apply since Award is neither a decree nor an order is not well founded. The fact that the impugned Awards are neither decrees nor orders in terms of the Code of Civil Procedure Code (which is not being decided by us) makes no difference. The Awards have been made appealable and the procedure applicable is that of Order XLI, Civil Procedure Code. The word 'decree' used in rule 22 in these circumstances have to be read as 'award' in order to give effect to this order. It is in this fashion that Order XLI, rule 22 is read when an appeal is preferred against an order made appealable under Order XLIII, rule 1 of the Code of Civil Procedure and rule 2 thereof makes Order XLI applicable. (31) The other decisions relied upon by the learned counsel taking opposite views may now be noticed. A Division Bench of Patna High Court in *Bokaro and Ramgar Ltd.* v. *Kathara Coal Co. Ltd.*, AIR 1969 Pat 235 came to the conclusion that cross-objection filed by the respondent in appeal under section 20 of the Coal Bearing Areas (Acquisition and Development) Act, 1957, were not maintainable on the following reasoning: "Except section 20 of the Act there is no other section under which a person aggrieved by any award of a Tribunal constituted under section 14(2) of the Act can come up to the High Court and section 20 specifically provides for an appeal to the High Court by a person aggrieved by the Award of such a Tribunal, in other words, under the Act no right to file a cross-objection appears to have been granted. There is no provision in the Act analogous to those of Order XLI, rule 22 of the Code of Civil Procedure. Right of cross-objection like a right of appeal is a creature of statute.... The only manner in which that determination by the Tribunal, *viz.*, its award can be subjected to a review is by appealing against the whole or part of it under section 20. Cross-objection is thus ruled out." This decision does not refer to any judgment in support of its view. Moreover none of the questions raised before us and discussed above has been discussed.

A Division Bench of the Allahabad High Court in *Zahid Hussain* v. *B. Khairati Lal Jain,* AIR 1954 All 419: 1954 All LJ 90: 1954 All WR (HC) 101 (20) held that cross-objections were not tenable in an appeal filed under section 75 of the Provisional Insolvency Act of 1920, on the following reasons:—

> "Section 75 of the Insolvency Act provides for an appeal within 30 days to the District Court and within 90 days to the High Court. There is no provision for a cross-objection to be filed within 30 days after service of notice as under Order XII, rule 22 of the Civil Procedure Code. So far as we *see* there is nothing in the Provincial Insolvency Act making the provisions of Order XII, rule 22, C.P.C., applicable to an appeal under section 75." This case also does not take note of the various aspects discussed by us. Even the Full Bench decision of the Madras High Court in *A.L.A. Algappa Chettiar* case and Division Beach decision of the Bombay High Court in *Raghunathdas Gopaldas* case (*supra*) (10) have not been taken note of. With great respect to the learned Judges, the Court did not agree with them.

The result was that we hold that cross-objections filed in the present appeals by the respondents were held not maintainable. The appeals will now go back before a Single Bench for decision on merits; *Delhi Transport Undertaking of Delhi Municipal Corporation, Delhi* v. *Kumari Lalita,* AIR 1972 Del 281: 8 (1972) DLT 188: ILR (1972) 2 Del 384.

126. Order XLI, Rule 23 – Scope of Remand

Order XLI, rule 23 does not contemplate an appellate court confirming substantial findings of fact and then remanding the entire suit for fresh disposal because it considers a finding on some other issue is necessary; *Kolandayammal* v. *Krishnaswami Goundan,* (1953) 2 Mad LJ 80: ILR 1953 Mad 1109: 66 Mad LW 1106: 1953 Mad WN 366: AIR 1954 Mad 167 (167; (Pr 4).

Where in an appeal against a decree obtained by a widow whose surrender of her life estate in favour of certain relations of hers was attacked as having been got by collusion and fraud, and the appellate court, on filing of two Wills unregistered and said to have been made in favour of the widow into

Court during appeal, remanded the case to the trial court for further trial with a direction to admit fresh documents and fresh oral evidence: Held, that the procedure adopted by the lower appellate court was illegal and nowhere contemplated by Order XLI, rule 23 of the C.P.C. The lower appellate Court could have only recorded fresh evidence under Order XLI, rule 27, C.P.C. The strict provisions of the Code could not be circumvented and by-passed in a way as this *i.e.*, wholesale remand under rule 23, Order XLI. If additional evidence should be let in, the lower appellate court should have retained the case on its own file instead of remanding it to the trial court; *Pusuluri Puchamma* v. *Sankaramanchi Ramasitamma*, (1953) 2 Mad LJ 392: 1953 Mad WN 531: AIR 1954 Mad 191 (192) (Pt A) (Pr 3).

127. Rules 23, 23A, 25 and 27

The appellate court may remand the case only when it is found that the trial court recorded findings on a preliminary issue, but decided the whole case. The Supreme Court has said that it is obligatory for the appellate court to consider all the issues unless they have been given up, and it is not permissible to deal with one issue and dispose off the appeal. *State of Punjab* v. *Hardyal*, (1985) 2 SCC 629: AIR 1985 SC 920: (1985) 2 Civ LJ 129. The appellate court may direct adducing of further evidence, but the Supreme Court said that the evidence through remand shall not be permitted where no plea has been taken in the written statements. *Peria Nachi Muthu Gounder* v. *Raju Thevar*, (1985) 2 SCC 290: AIR 1985 SC 821: (1985) 2 Civ LJ 1. But many High Courts have said that when additional evidence is tendered in appeal, the appellate court should act under rule 27. See *Chithiah Mudaliar* v. *Govinda Pandithan*, AIR 1949 Mad 394: (1948) 2 Mad LJ 413; *Sudha S. Alva* v. *Sanjeevi R. Shetty*, AIR 1996 Kant 5: 1995 (2) Civ LJ 921: ILR (Kant) 1995 Kar 1302. The High Court of Gujarat said that when some issues have been omitted, the matter should be dealt with under rule 25; *Khant Jadav Naja* v. *Patel Raja Kachra Rakholia*, AIR 1963 Guj 336: (1964) 5 Guj LR 222.

See also *Raghvendra Bose* v. *Sunil Krishna Ghosh*, (2005) 12 SCC 309 and *Hameed* v. *Kumattumal Kunhi P.P. Amma*, 2006 (6) SCJ 318 in which the High Court remanded the case with a liberty to produce document to fill lacuna in evidence and the order was set aside by the Supreme Court. The Court said that Appellate court cannot remand back the case to trial court for taking additional evidence and re-determining a particular issue on; *Kattu Kandi Edathil Krishnan* v. *Kattu Kandi Edathi Valson*, (2006) 9 SCC 166.

128. Rules 23 and 25 – Power of Appellate Court

A Division Bench of the High Court of Mysore considered the scope of remand and held that remand of whole case Legality and propriety. When an appellate court comes to the conclusion that the trial court had omitted to frame or try an important issue arising from the pleadings and essential for a right decision of the suit on merits, it is open to that Court under Order XLI, rule 25, C.P. Code, to frame and refer that issue for trial to the trial court retaining the appeal on its own file and directing the trial court to take additional evidence and submit the same with the finding thereon and on receipt of that finding the appellate court may proceed to judgment. In such a case, no useful purpose will be served by reopening the entire case and remanding the same. The order of remand of the entire case after setting aside the judgment and decree of the trial court is not warranted. *M.H. Krishnappa* v. *D.K. Govindachar*, ILR 1956 Mys 114: AIR 1957 Mys 9(1) (Pr 4) (DB). Where the appellant takes risk of depending on pure question of law, he cannot ask Court for further indulgence for re-hearing of the facts, by remanding the case. 1962 BLJR 809. A Division Bench of the High Court of Patna said that in a case where there are conflicting findings and failure to frame essential issues by lower court, case is fit for remand; *Province of Bihar* v. *Choudhary Balam Singh*, AIR 1950 Pat 356 (357, 358) (Prs 7, 8) (DB).

129. Rule 23 – Effect of Order Remanding the case and Dismissing Appeal

A Full Bench of the High Court of Madras held that where the High Court in an appeal against an order of remand dismissed the appeal and remitted the case to the trial court for fresh disposal with certain directions. Held, that (1) the directions together with the final order dismissing the appeal formed an integral whole and have become final; and. (2) when an appellate court remands a case to the trial court for fresh disposal, it can give directions as to the manner in which the suit when it goes back should be dealt with; *Jainul Abideen Marakayar* v. *Habibullah Sahib*, AIR 1928 Mad 430: 109 IC 130 and *Secretary of State* v. *Jagannadham*, (1941) 2 Mad LJ 47: AIR 1941 Mad 530 (FB).

130. Unnecessary Remand to be Discouraged

In the case of *Sunil Panna Lal Banthia* the Supreme Court held that where no decision is required to be taken on facts, an order of remand is unnecessary *Sunil Pannalal Banthia* v. *City and Industrial Development Corpn. of Maharashtra Ltd.*, AIR 2007 SC 1529: 2007 AIR SCW 2117: (2007) 4 SCALE 216.

131. Adducing Additional Evidence

Two options are left for the appellate court where an application for adducing additional evidence is allowed, either to record the evidence itself or to direct trial court to do so, but cannot direct the court to dispose of after taking evidence; *H.V. Vedavyasachar* v. *Shiv Shanker*, (2009) 8 SCC 231: AIR 2010 SC (Supp) 394: 2010 AIR SCW 468.

132. Where Additional Evidence is Permissible

The provisions do not intend to allow to adduce evidence to pronounce judgment in a particular way; *State of Gujarat* v. *Mahendra Kumar Parshottambhai Desai*, AIR 2006 SC 1864: 2006 AIR SCW 2169: (2006) 9 SCC 772; *Municipal Corpn. of Greater Bombay* v. *Lala Pancham*, AIR 1965 SC 1008: 1966 (1) SCJ 49: (1965) 1 SCR 542 followed.

Similar view was expressed by the Supreme Court in *K.R. Mohan Reddy* v. *Net Work Inc.*, (2007) 10 SCR 872: 2007 AIR SCW 7597: (2007) 12 SCALE 587 and *Jatinder Singh* v. *Mehar Singh*, (2008) 12 SCALE 734: AIR 2009 SC 354: 2008 AIR SCW 7392.

Subsequently also, the Supreme Court examined the desirability of additional evidence and held that where it is necessary, no condition is proper; *Anupam Gupta* v. *Sumeet Gupta*, AIR 2009 SC 918: 2008 AIR SCW 8248: (2009) 1 SCC 254.

133. Additional Evidence Only in the Interest of Justice

The Supreme court ruled in the case of *Shalimar Chemical Works* that additional evidence can be taken only in the interest of justice. (2010) 8 SCC 423. The Supreme Court again expressed the similar view in; *Malyalam Plantations Ltd.* v. *State of Kerala*, AIR 2011 SC 559: 2011 AIR SCW 264: (2010) 11 SCALE 614.

134. Meaning of "And may Further Direct what Issue or Issues shall be Tried in the Case

In a case, the trial court had omitted to decide certain questions, suit remanded by appellate court to trial Court to decide those issues-Remand order held was clearly covered by Order XLI, rule 23 against which an appeal was provided by Order XLIII, rule 1(u) – Order did not come within Order XLI, rule 25: AIR 1955 NUC (Pat) 2487 (DB).

135. Rule 23 Remand – When not Justified

The High Court of Allahabad said that a remand of case would not be justified when it is not desirable that the final decision in the case should be delayed, and *secondly*, the observations of the first appellate court give some indication of his opinion of the evidence led by the defendant. 1965 All LJ 298. A Division Bench of the High Court of Calcutta stressed the powers of the appellate Court as regards remand are not restricted to the cases specified in Order XLI, rules 23 and 25 but the Court by reason of its inherent jurisdiction, recognised and preserved in the Code, under section 151, may order a remand in cases other than the case specified in Order XLI, rules 23 and 25 if it be necessary for the ends of justice; *Abdul Karim Abu Ahmad Khan* v. *Allahabad Bank Ltd.*, AIR 1917 Cal 44: 21 Cal WN 877: ILR 44 Cal 929 (FB) and *Bhairab Chandra* v. *Kali Kumar*, AIR 1923 Cal 606: 37 Cal LJ 491; *Jnanendra Mohan* v. *Profullananda Goswami*, AIR 1928 Cal 812: 32 Cal WN 101 and AIR 1941 Oudh 581, rel. on. The High Court of Allahabad said that where some of the most material propositions of fact and law arising from the pleadings of the parties were not properly considered by the trial court and proper issues had not been framed, the appellate court is perfectly justified in remanding the case for a retrial as it was necessary for the ends of justice. In such a case the appellate court cannot prevent the parties from adducing additional evidence on the matter. 1958 All LJ 299: 1958 All WR (HC) 441 (DB).

RULE 33

136. Non-filing of Cross-Objection or Cross-Appeal

The Supreme Court reversing decision of the High Court, while deciding a dispute under the Bihar Land Reforms Act 1962, held that the part of the decree which is not appealed against or against which no cross-objection is filed becomes final. But the Court held that rule 33 of this Order does not confer on the Court an unrestricted power to re-open decrees which have become final. *Choudhary Sahu* v. *State of Bihar*, AIR 1982 SC 98: (1982) 1 SCC 232: 1982 BLJR 176. The Court also held that the rule confers upon the Court power to avoid inconsistent decisions on the same question in the same suit but, as already stated, this power is not unrestricted. According to the Court, the discretion conferred by rule 33 must be exercised with due care and caution.

137. Recourse to Rule 33

Where the plaintiff prefers an appeal claiming a decree as prayed in the suit, recourse to rule 33 need not be taken; *Nazeer Ahmed* v. *State Bank of Mysore,* AIR 2007 SC 989: 2007 AIR SCW 766: (2007) 2 SCALE 349: (2007) 2 SCC 75.

138. Rule 33 – Meaning of the Term 'Case'

The Supreme Court said in the case of Prahlad that expression 'case' would mean the justice of the case and the expression 'order ought to have been made' would mean an order which justice of the case requires to be made; *Prahlad* v. *State of Maharashtra,* (2010) 10 SCC 58.

The Supreme Court of India examined the scope of rule 33 of Order XLI in the case of *Bihar Supply Syndicate* v. *Asiatic Navigation,* AIR 1993 SC 2054: 1993 AIR SCW 2116: (1993) 2 SCR 425.

The plaintiff had purchased crushed and uncrushed salt from Defendant No. 3 on payment by a charter party agreement defendant No. 2, chartered a vessel to defendant No. 3 for loading salt at Kandla Port in Gujarat and for carrying the same to Calcutta Port. The Plaintiff had directly paid to Defendant No. 2 the freight amount for transport of cargo from Kandla to Calcutta. Defendant No. 2 had inform defendant No. 3 that the Plaintiff is accepted as sub-charteres. The Plaintiff had itself insured the cargo through the Insurance Company for Rs. 9,50,000. The policy was for the voyage from Kandla to Calcutta with Institute Cargo Clauses (FPA) cover attached including warehouse to warehouse risks and sling loss but excluding war and SRCC risks.

The plaintiff loaded the salt on the said Vessel at Kandla for shipment to Calcutta. The vessel left Kandla and the plaintiff received a telex message from Defendant No. 2 informing that the vessel was at an anchorage at sand-heads near Calcutta and was experiencing engine trouble. The vessel was required to be towed from sand-heads to Vishakhapatnam as repairs could not be undertaken at sand-heads. The plaintiff was informed and it in turn informed the Insurance Company about the said development. The vessel could not be repaired as the Hindustan Shipyard who was to carry out the repairs were not paid the requisite charges by the Owner, Defendant No. 1.

The crew members were not paid their wages and they instituted an Admiralty Suit in the High Court, which passed an order arresting the vessel including cargo etc. and appointed a Receiver for the vessel and the cargo. Consent was given by the plaintiff for the sale of the vessel and the cargo. The High Court directed the receiver to sell the vessel along with the cargo. An amount of approximately Rs. 12.5 lakhs was received as sale proceeds of the vessel and the cargo. The plaintiff approached the High Court requesting to direct the receiver to withhold an amount of Rs. 9,50,000 for the benefit of the plaintiff against loss of its goods. High Court declined to grant the request and the appeal preferred by the plaintiff also ended in dismissal.

Plaintiff filed a suit claiming recovery of the loss suffered by him, *viz.* Rs. 9,50,000. The claim was made against the owner of the vessel, the charterer and the Insurance Company.

The trial court passed a decree against all the defendants in the sum of Rs. 10,49,750 *i.e.* 9,50,000 with interest. On an appeal by the Insurance Company, the Division Bench of the High Court dismissed the suit decreed by the Single Judge against the Insurance Company and other defendants. Being aggrieved by the High Court's judgment, the plaintiff and defendant No. 3 in the suit preferred the present appeals before this Court.

Dismissing the appeal of the plaintiff, and allowing the appeal of defendant No. 3, this Court,

HELD 1.1. It is axiomatic that the burden was on the plaintiff to prove the loss due to perils of the sea and on the facts of the case, at no stage, such a burden was shifted on Insurance Company to prove otherwise.

1.2. The cables sent by the Master of the ship do not show that sea water had entered the engine room and it was not a case of loss of goods due to perils of the sea. The expression "warehouse to warehouse" merely indicates the period during which the policy would remain in force and has nothing to do with the type of the risk policy covered. It was not a case of abandonment of the goods because of the perils of the sea. In fact the plaintiff gave the consent for permitting the sale of cargo and to recover the value thereof.

1.3. Since the finding of the High Court is that no sea water entered in the engine room and the fact that the cargo was intact even after the ship was towed to Vishakhapatnam showed that no sea water entered the ship and, therefore, the loss to the plaintiff was not on account of perils of the sea and the suit of the plaintiff against the Insurance Company *i.e.* defendant No. 4 was rightly dismissed by the High Court.

2.1. The plaintiff was dealing itself directly with defendant No. 2. The plaintiff directly paid the freight of the voyage to defendant No. 2. The plaintiff took the Bill of Lading in its own name itself. Thus there was no cause of action whatsoever against defendant No. 3.

2.2. On the facts and circumstance of the case in so far as it relates to defendant No, 3, it was a fit case for the High Court to have exercised power under Order XLI, rule 33, C.P.C. to set aside the decree passed by the trial court against defendant No. 3 without having discussed any issue against defendant No. 3 and to decide the case itself. The facts are simple and lie in narrow compass and show total non-liability of No. 3 to the claim put forward by the plaintiff against it. No cause of action is established against defendant No. 3 who merely sold salt to the plaintiff and introduced defendant No. 2, the Charter Party to the plaintiff. The plaintiff thereafter directly dealt with defendant No. 2 by paying the freight to defendant No. 2 and by staining the Bill of Lading in its own name. The property in goods had already passed on to the plaintiff before it obtained the Bill of Lading. *Choudhary Sahu* v. *State of Bihar,* AIR 1982 SC 98: (1982) 1 SCC 232: 1982 BLJR 176: *Mahant Dhangir* v. *Madan Mohan,* AIR 1988 SC 54: JT 1987 (5) SC 202: 1987 Rajdhani LR 663; *Panna Lal* v. *State of Bombay,* AIR 1963 SC 1516: 66 Bom LR 100: (1964) 1 SCR 980 and *Giani Ram* v. *Ramji Lal,* AIR 1969 SC 1144: (1970) 1 SCA 424: (1969) 3 SCR 944, relied on. (438H, 439AG) 428.

On these pleadings the learned trial court settled separate issues between the plaintiff and defendant No. 2; as many as five issues between the plaintiff and defendant No. 3 (appellant in Civil Appeal No. 4612 of 1992) and between plaintiff and defendant No. 4. The issues settled between the plaintiff and defendant No.4 were as under:—

"(1) Whether the plaint does not disclose any cause of action against the 4th defendants as alleged in para 1 of, the written statement?

(2) Whether the plaintiffs have suffered any loss due to any of the perils insured against by the Policy of Insurance dated 12.7.1972?

(3) Whether the plaintiffs abandoned the goods as alleged in para 38 of the plaint?

(4) Whether the 4th defendant acquiesced in abandonment as alleged in paras 35 and 38 of the plaint?

(5) Whether there was total loss as alleged in para 38 of the plaint?

(6) What relief, if any?

The issues settled between the plaintiff and defendant No. 3 were as under:—

(1) Whether the plaintiffs are a registered partnership firm as alleged in para 1 of the plaint?

(2) Whether the plaint discloses any cause of action as against this defendant as alleged in para 31 of the written statement?

(3) Whether this defendant was liable as sub-charterers to pay the plaintiffs the market value of the said goods at Calcutta being Rs. 9,50,000 as set out in Ex. 'E' of any part thereof as alleged in paragraph 3 of the plaint?

(4) Whether this defendant is absolved from all liabilities of the plaintiffs as alleged in para 28 of the written statement?

(5) Whether the plaintiffs are entitled to any relief against this defendant? If so, what?"

The trial court decreed the suit of the plaintiff against all the four defendants. In the present appeals before us we are not concerned with the rights of the plaintiff *vis-a-vis* defendants 1 and 2 as defendants 1 and 2 did not prefer any appeal against the decision of the trial court. The defendant No. 4, namely the Insurance Company, filed the appeal before the Division Bench of the High Court whereas defendant No. 3, United Salt Works and Industries Ltd., (appellant in Civil Appeal No. 4612 of 1992) preferred cross-objections on receipt of notice of appeal filed by M/s. National Insurance Company Ltd. The trial court while decreeing the suit against the Insurance Company held issue numbers 1, 2, 3 in the affirmative, in favour of the plaintiff and against defendant No. 4. On issue No. 4 it held that it was not necessary. Issue No. 5 was also answered in the affirmative and issue No. 6 as per the order. Consequently the trial court decreed the claim of the plaintiff against all the defendants in the sum of Rs. 10,49,50 with interest on Rs. 9,50,000 at the rate of 12 per cent per annum from 17th June, 1973 till realisation with costs of the suit.

The Court took it as curious that though the trial court found issues as settled between the plaintiff and defendant No. 3 against defendant No. 3 but there is no discussion at all in the trial court judgment for various findings recorded against defendant No. 3. On appeal by the Insurance Company the Division Bench of the Bombay High court examined the oral evidence led by the Insurance Company of its Assistant General Manager Dhirubhai A. Shah and one of its employee Mangaldas Keshavji Jagad. The Division Bench also examined the evidence led on behalf of defendant No. 2 of Sentu Vazirmal Ramchandani who had carried out the work of survey of the damaged vessel at Vishakhapatnam.

Before the Division Bench it was submitted on behalf of the Insurance Company No. 4, that its liability arises out of Marine Insurance Policy and the plaintiff cannot succeed in obtaining a decree against it unless it is established that the goods were lost due to perils of the sea. It was submitted on its behalf that the plaintiff had not even averred in the plaint that the goods were damaged due to perils of the sea. It was also submitted that the trial court entirely misconstrued the terms of policy and erroneously concluded that the loss was caused due to perils of the sea. It was submitted on behalf of the Insurance Company that the trial court was in error in assuming that the term in the policy that the risk is covered from warehouse to warehouse means that the policy covers all kinds of risks to the vessel and the goods. On behalf of the plaintiff/ respondent No. 1 in the appeal before the High Court, it was submitted on the other hand that the finding of the trial court that the loss was caused due to perils of the sea justified. It was also pleaded in the alternative that the policy covered all risks from warehouse at Vishakhapatnam to warehouse at Calcutta and as there was constructive loss of all the goods the plaintiff was entitled to a decree.

In view of these rival contentions, the High Court felt that the question which falls for determination is whether the plaintiff has suffered loss due to any perils of the sea insured against by the policy for insurance dated July 12, 1972.

It may be noticed that in that case no first appeal or even the second appeal was filed on behalf of the daughters and the widow yet this Court thought it fit to grant them relief under Order XLI, rule 33 of the Code of Civil Procedure. The decision in the case of *Pannalal* v. *State of Bombay*, was followed by this Court in *Mahant Dhangir* v. *Madan Mohan*, AIR 1988 SC 54: JT 1987 (5) SC 202: 1987 Rajdhani LR 663.

It was held that if the relief can be granted by the appellate court even when no appeal or cross-objections were filed by the respondent, surely relief can be granted by the appellate court when cross-objections have been filed by the respondent against a co-respondent. Order XLI, rule 33 of the Code of Civil Procedure reads as under:

"33. Power of Court of Appeal.—The appellate court shall have power to pass any decree and make any order which ought to have been passed or made and to pass or make such further or other decree or order as the case may require, and this power may be exercised by the Court notwithstanding that the appeal is as to part only of the decree and may be exercised in favour of all or any of the respondents or parties, although such respondents or parties may not have filed any appeal or objection and may, where there have been decrees in cross-suits or where two or more decrees are passed in one suit, be exercised in respect of all or any of the decrees, although an appeal may not have been filed against such decrees."

Really speaking, the Rule is in three parts. The first part confers on the appellate court very wide powers to pass such orders in appeal as the case may require. The second part contemplates that this wide power will be exercised by the appellate court notwithstanding that the appeal is as to part only of the decree and may be exercised in favour of all or any of the respondents or parties, although such respondents or parties may not have filed any appeal or objection. The third part is where there have been decrees in cross-suits or where two or more decrees are passed in one suit, this power is directed to be exercised in respect of all or any of the decrees, although an appeal may not have been filed against such decrees.

The present case falls within the third part of rule 33 of Order XLI of the Code of Civil Procedure.

The Court held the view that on the facts and circumstances of this case it was a fit case for the High Court to have exercised power under Order XLI, rule 33 to set aside the decree passed by the trial court against defendant No. 3 without having discussed any issue against defendant No. 3 and to decide the case itself. We also thought of remanding back the matter to the High Court but we find that the facts are simple and lie in narrow compass and show total non-liability of defendant No. 3 to the claim put forward by the plaintiff against it. As we have noticed earlier no cause of action is established against defendant No. 3 who merely sold salt to the plaintiff and introduced defendant No. 2, the Charter Party to the plaintiff. The plaintiff thereafter directly dealt with defendant No. 2 by paying the freight to defendant No. 2 and by obtaining the Bill of Lading in its own name. The property in goods had already passed on to the plaintiff before it obtained the Bill of Lading.

The result was that Civil Appeal No. 4611 of 1992 was dismissed and Civil Appeal No. 4612 of 1992 is accepted and suit of the plaintiff filed against defendant No. 3 is dismissed. The judgments of the trial court and High Court were modified further to the extent that the suit against defendant No. 3 is also dismissed. In both the appeals the parties are left to bear their own costs.

139. Supreme Court of India

Respondent No. 5, who was the Managing Director of a limited company, resigned his post and in his capacity as a shareholder filed an application in the District Court for compulsory winding-up of the company, which was ordered. The Official Liquidator made an application before the District Judge that as the four Directors, respondents 1 to 4, had illegally, withheld or retained certain amounts, they became liable to refund them. Contesting this application respondents 1 to 4 requested that they might be allowed to cross-examine respondent No. 5, which application was rejected. On appeal the High Court set aside the order of the District Judge and remanded the case to the City Civil Court, Bombay to record additional evidence under Order XLI, rule 27, Code of Civil Procedure.

On appeal it was contended in this Court that the High Court was wrong in directing additional evidence to be allowed under this Order.

Dismissing the appeal,

HELD: The High Court rightly ordered that additional evidence be recorded in this case. There was no justification whatsoever for the District Court to reject the evidence which the respondent had intended to lead or to disallow the production of documents. [895 H; 896 A] under Order XLI, rule 27 it is only where the Court had improperly refused to admit evidence or where the appellate court required additional evidence to be recorded in order to enable it to pronounce judgment that it could make such an order. Under cl. (b) of this rule the Court may require additional evidence either to enable it to pronounce judgment or when it may require additional evidence to be recorded for any other substantial cause, [894 A-B] *Arjan Singh* v. *Kartar Singh*, AIR 1951 SC 193: 1951 ALJ SC 78: 1951 (1) MLJ 556: 1951 SCJ 274: 1951 SCR 258; *State of Uttar Pradesh* v. *Manbodhan Lal Srivastava*, 1958 SCR 533: 1958 SCJ 150: 1958 SCR 533; *Municipal Corporation of Greater Bombay* v. *Lala Pancham*, AIR 1965 SC 1008: 1966 (1) SCJ 49: (1965) 1 SCR 542 (548) referred to.

It is no one's case that the commission according to this letter was not paid, and as the Nagpur Company has received this commission it cannot claim any additional commission. Insofar as Item (4) is concerned, it has reference to four amounts, namely Rs. 7,689/12; Rs. 2,184; Rs. 9,827 and Rs. 2,100. Nothing has been shown as to why these claims were not properly allowed. The appellant, however, challenges the item for Rs. 9,827 as not being the correct amount. In fact the book value is Rs. 39,309/4/9. The High Court took the difference between the book value and the stock purchased by the Bombay Company after August 23, 1952, since the date of resignation of Shantilal Shah. Accordingly it took the opening stock as per the balance sheet dated March, 31, 1953 at Rs. 53,574-4-0, The closing stock as per audit report dated March, 13, 1953, reduced to the extent of 7/9 was Rs. 24,092-0-0 leaving an amount of Rs. 29,482-4-9. This amount was transferred to the Bombay office and the difference between the above amounts amounted to Rs. 9,827. Shantilal Shah was questioned about this but he did not know how it was made up of. No explanation was also given on behalf of the Official Liquidator as to how the item was made up. For this reason this item was not allowed. Similarly no exception can be taken to the amount of Rs. 2,100 which was allowed because within few months of its purchase the scooter was sold to the Delhi Branch for only Rs. 6,001. These two items, namely Rs. 9,827 and Rs. 2,100 which are allowable to the Liquidator come to Rs. 11,927 the other two items for Rs. 7,689/12 and Rs. 2,184 which relate to the purchases actually made by the Bombay Company in pursuance of their offer and in pursuance of the majority resolution of April 25, 1953 and the difference between the book value and the purchase value of the car by the Bombay Company were also allowed. Apart from this, Item (5) for a sum of

Rs. 2,686/3 in connection with the wrongful remission to the Hyderabad Company was also allowed. There seemed to be no dispute on this account because the whole of the amount as claimed has been allowed.

In the result the Court found no reason to interfere with the Judgment of the Bombay High Court under appeal. Accordingly the appeal was dismissed with costs.

140. Supreme Court of India Rules, 1966 – Views of the Supreme Court

Supreme Court of India in the case of *Sita Ram* v. *State of Uttar Pradesh,* examined nature and scope of the rules. Supreme Court Rules, 1966, Order XXI, rule 15(1)(c), Constitutional India, 1950. Articles 134, 136, 145, Criminal Procedure Code, 1898, section 384 and Supreme Court (Enlargement of Criminal Appellate Jurisdiction) Act, 1970, J, 2(a) – Procedure of the Supreme Court hearing appeals in criminal matters at the admission stage *ex parte* – Whether *ultra vires.*

141. Meaning of Words and Phrases 'Appeal' and Procedure

Rule 15(1)(c) of Order XXI of the Supreme Court Rules, 1966 envisages that the petition of appeal under sub-clause (a) or sub-clause (b) of clause (1) of article 134 of the Constitution or under the Supreme Court (Enlargement of Criminal Appellate Jurisdiction) Act, 1970 or under section 379 of the Code of Criminal Procedure 1973, on being Registered shall be put up for hearing *ex parte* before the court which may either dismiss it summarily or direct issue of notice to all necessary parties or make such orders, as the circumstances of the case may require.

The appellants in the appeal who were acquitted by the Sessions Court had been convicted and sentenced by the High Court and awarded life imprisonment under section 302 read with section 149, IPC.

When their appeal under the Supreme Court (Enlargement of Criminal Appellate Jurisdiction) Act, 1970 was listed for preliminary hearing under rule 15(1)(c) of Order XXI of the Supreme Court Rules, 1966 it was contended (1) that the said provision empowering the court to dismiss the appeal summarily was *ultra vires* the Enlargement Act, 1970, (2) the power of the Supreme Court to frame rules under article 145 of the Constitution can not be extended to annul the rights conferred under an Act of Parliament, and (3) that an appeal under the Enlargement Act, 1970 cannot be dismissed summarily without calling for the records, ordering notice to the State and without giving reasons.

142. Per Krishna Iyer, Shinghal & Desai, JJ.

1. Article 134(1)(c) spells a measure of seriousness because the High Court which has heard the case certifies that it involves questions of such moment that the Supreme Court itself must resolve them. To dispose of such a matter by a preliminary healing is to cast a reflection on the High Court's capacity to understand the seriousness of a certification.

2. Article 136 vests a plenary discretion in the Supreme Court to deign or decline to grant leave to appeal against any conviction or sentence. Before deciding to grant or reject such leave the court accords an oral hearing after 1086

In the case of *Rajendra Singh Yadav* v. *Chandra Sen,* AIR 1979 SC 882: (1979) 4 SCC 111: 1979 (2) SCJ 234 the Court said:

> The proviso to article 134(1) enables this Court to make provisions subject to which appeals under sub-clause (c) of article 134 shall lie. These provisions are to be made under clause (1)(d) of article 145 which, in specific terms, deals with rules as to the entertainment of appeals under sub-clause (c) of clause (1) of article 134. We are not concerned with these rules which relate to the entertainment of appeals or provisions subject to which the appeal may be instituted and do not trench upon the right of appeal or the manner of hearing. But article 145(1)(b) enables the Supreme Court to make rules; *inter alia,* as to the procedure for hearing appeals. One such rule is Order XXI, rule 15 which warrants preliminary hearing and disposal of all categories of cases in the territory of India if the High Court – (a) has on appeal reversed an order of acquittal of an accused person and sentenced him to death; or (b) has withdrawn for trial before itself any case from any court subordinate to its authority and has in such trial convicted the accused person and sentenced him to death; or (c) certifies that the case is a fit one for appeal to the Supreme Court;
>
> Provided that an appeal under sub-clause (c) shall lie subject to such provisions as may be made in that behalf under clause (1) of article 145 and to such conditions as the High Court may establish or require. (2) Parliament may by law confer on the Supreme Court any further powers to entertain and hear appeals from any judgment, final order or sentence in a criminal proceeding of a High Court in the territory of India subject to such conditions and limitations as may be specified in such law. No argument is needed to realise the gravity of the subject covered by the first two clauses of the article-death sentence for the first time or in reversal of an acquittal. Human life is too dear obligate dragging the opposite side to court involving expense and delay. Fullness of hearing of the proponent is not incompatible with non-hearing of the opponent where after appreciating all that could be urged in support of the cause there is no need felt to call upon the other side, as where the proposition is groundless, frivolous or not *prima facie* statable. The ambit of appellate hearing may have to be explored in the constitutional context to which we will advert later.

Plainly, this rule clothes the court with power to shorten the life of an appeal even under article 134 by dismissing it *ex parte,* summarily. Is this abbreviatory power absonent with the appellate scheme envisaged in article 134 and, therefore, excessive or offensive and void? Or is the rule valid because it does not bear upon the substantive right of appeal but relates to the procedure for hearing and fall squarely within article 145(1)(b)? This is the main crux of the debate; *Sita Ram* v. *State of Uttar Pradesh,* AIR 1979 SC 745: (1975) 2 SCC 656: (1979) 2 SCR 1085; *Rajendra Singh Yadav* v. *Chandra Sen*, AIR 1979 SC 882: (1979) 4 SCC 111: 1978 UJ (SC) 862.

143. *Per* Sinha, J.

The Constitution while laying down clause (3) of article 145, contemplates the whole matter in controversy arising in a case, which may include substantial questions of law as to the interpretation of the Constitution as also other questions. The main clause (3), excepting cases coming within the purview of the proviso, does not contemplate a splitting-up of a case into parts, one part involving substantial questions of law as to the interpretation of the Constitution and another part or parts not involving such questions.

The language of clause (3) of article 145 does not warrant the hearing of a case piecemeal by different Benches unless it comes within the purview of the proviso. The proviso is meant to cover only a limited class of cases which otherwise would have come within the purview of the main clause (3). But the proviso cannot have a larger effect than is justified by its language, *viz.*, that only a question of that description has to be referred for the opinion of the larger Bench, the case itself remaining on the file of the smaller Bench. The proviso thus makes a clear distinction between a "case" and a "question". *Maulvi Muhammad Abdul Majid* v. *Muhammad Abdul Aziz,* (97) 24 IA 22: 19 All 155; *Burrowes* v. *High Commission Court,* (3 Bulst 48) and *Habibar Rahman* v. *Saidannessa Bibi,* AIR 1924 Cal 473: ILR 51 Cal 331, referred to. *Rao Shiva Bahadur Singh* v. *State of Madhya Pradesh,* AIR 1955 SC 446: (1955) 2 SCR 206: 1955 SCJ 483.

ORDER XLI

A LETTERS PATENT APPEAL

1. The rules of Order XLIA shall apply, so far as may be, to appeals to the High Court of Madras under clause 15 of the Letters Patent of the said Court:

Provided that it shall not be necessary to file copies of the judgment and decree appealed from.

2. Notice of the appeal shall be given in manner prescribed by Order XLIA, rule or if the party to be served has appeared in person in manner prescribed by rule 5 of the said Order,"

[*Vide* GO No. 2128-Home (Judi.), dated 18th October, 1917.]

144. Order XLI, Rule 31 – Challenge to preliminary decree

In *V. Venkatakrishna Reddy* v. *Chevireddigari Chinna Changa Reddy (died) per L.Rs.,* 2014 (3) ALD 713: 2014 (3) ALT 38 (AP) Preliminary decree was wrongly reversed by Single Judge.

Though the suit was filed for partition, in effect, it was aimed at annulling the sale deed dated 27-06-1973 marked as Ex.A-1. By that time, both the plaintiffs were minors. The litigation was being pursued by their mother. The principal contention on behalf of the plaintiffs was that their father, the 2nd defendant, was addicted to vices and to meet the expenditure therefore, he sold away the property.

The Trial Court passed a preliminary decree directing the property to be divided into three (03) equal shares and for allotment of one share each to the plaintiffs. It was also observed that the 1st defendant shall be entitled to retain 1/3rd of the property, representing the share of the 2nd defendant.

In the appeal preferred by the plaintiffs, no points as such were framed. The learned Single Judge took the view that the 2nd defendant was not possessed of any joint family funds nor any nucleus of the joint family, to utilize the same for purchase of the property. On that basis, preliminary decree passed by the Trial Court was set aside.

Basically, the learned Single Judge did not frame any point for consideration in the appeal as required under rule 31 of Order XLI of the Code of Civil Procedure, 1908. Though the Hon'ble Supreme Court, in certain precedents held that failure to frame point is fatal to the judgment in an appeal, we do not propose to rest over on that proposition. The discussion by framing of points had its own advantage, wherein the relevant facts and provisions of law can be analysed objectively. Be that as it may, the learned Single Judge did not take into account, the fact that long before the suit, scheduled property was acquired; the 2nd defendant purchased a large extent of Acs.14-00 of land under Ex.A-10 by utilizing the sale proceeds under Exs.A-6 to A-8. In addition to that, he had the benefit of his share of consideration under Ex.A-12. Therefore, the finding recorded by the learned Single Judge that the 2nd respondent did not have the benefit of any jointly family properties or nucleus cannot be sustainable in law. The point is accordingly answered.

The Division Bench said, there is some uncertainty as to the nature of relief claimed in relation to the mesne profits. As the litigation started almost four decades ago, we do not want to keep it pending any longer. We clinch the issue by directing that the legal representatives of the 1st defendant shall be under the obligation to pay Rs. 50,000 (Rupees fifty thousand only) to the plaintiffs towards past mesne profits and damages.

Hence, the appeal is allowed. The preliminary decree passed by the Trial Court is upheld subject to the direction as to payment of Rs. 50,000 to the plaintiffs. There shall be no order as to costs.

145. Order XLI, Rule 4 – Necessary parties to the suit

In *Valluri Srinivasa Rao* v. *Valluri Vijaya Ramachandra Murty,* 2013 4 ALD 704: 2013 4 ALT 565 (AP) the appeal was laid against the defendants 2, 5 and 12. The defendants 2, 5 and 12 indeed contested the suit by entering appearance and by filing written statements. However, there are as many as 23 defendants out of whom, the defendants 1 to 3 are said to be the father, and half brother and half sister of the plaintiffs. Nevertheless, appeal was not laid against the 3rd defendant. Indeed, the 1st defendant is no more. At the same time, the legal representatives of the 1st defendant ought to have been brought on record in the appeal. More important, the 10th defendant claims possession over part of the plaint schedule property as a lessee whereas the defendants 6 to 8 and 14 claimed simple mortgages over parts of the plaint schedule property. I am afraid that this appeal without the defendants 6 to 8, 10 and 14 and without the 3rd defendant and the legal representatives of the 1st defendant is not maintainable merely against the defendants 2, 5 and 12. I agree with the contention of the learned counsel for the respondents in the appeal that the appeal is misconceived and is liable to be dismissed for non-joinder of necessary parties. I therefore do not wish to go into the merits of the appeal as the appeal deserves to be dismissed in limine for the technical reasons of not impleading all or the material defendants.

The Court further said, it may be noticed that Order XLI, rule 4 C.P.C envisages that some of the defendants or some of the plaintiffs may file the appeal. It however does not empower such some of the plaintiffs or some of the defendants, as the case may be, to appeal against some of the parties only. While the appellants can be only some of the parties to the suit, every party whose interest is at stake shall be arrayed as a respondent. It therefore is not open for the learned counsel of the appellants-plaintiffs to contend that the appeal is maintainable as it is laid against the defendants 2, 5 and 12. As already pointed out, all the mortgagees and the lessee as well as the 3rd defendant and the legal representatives of the 1st defendant are necessary parties. Failure to implead them in the appeal shall result in not suing the plaintiffs in the appeal.

In that view of the matter, this appeal is found to be devoid of merits and is accordingly dismissed for non-joinder of necessary parties as respondents. However, there shall be no order as to costs.

146. Order XLI, Rule 27 and Section 96 – Appeal

In *Gudivada Sankara Rao* v. *Gudivada Venkata Ramana*, 2013 (5) ALD 452 (AP) the High Court said, the 6th defendant alone filed the written statement and some of the defendants including the 2nd defendant adopted the same. The suit was instituted originally way back in the year 1987. The 2nd defendant was set ex parte on 12.11.1992, when the suit was pending before the Court of Principal Subordinate Judge, Visakhapatnam. It is not as if the 2nd defendant did not have any opportunity to pursue the matter before that Court. It was pending before it till the year 1995. It was only thereafter that it was transferred to the Court of III Additional District Judge, Visakhapatnam. Seven years after he was set ex parte, the 2nd defendant filed an application being I.A.No.196 of 1999. The Trial Court was not at all convinced with the reasons offered by him and dismissed the I.A.

In case, the 2nd defendant was serious enough to participate in the suit, he could have assailed the order in I.A.No.196 of 1999. He did not take any steps in that direction. The result is that he was kept out of the trial of the suit and he did not feel any grievance about it. The suit remained on the file of the trial Court for more than one year after the I.A. was dismissed. The preliminary decree was passed only on 28.07.2000. It is at that stage that the 2nd defendant filed the appeal

147. Order XLI, Rule 3A(3) – Courts not to stay from execution of decree

In *Smt. Ajudhya Devi* v. *Shri Pramod Kumar Sharma*, 2017 Him L R 1631 the High Court of Himachal Pradesh said, Order 41, rule 3A (3) C.P.C. prohibits Courts from staying execution of decree under challenge in appeal before deciding to hear the appeal after hearing it under Order XLI, rule 11 C.P.C., but this provision is to be interpreted with reference to entire scheme of this provision.

Order XLI, rule 3A(3) C.P.C. relates to a situation where application under Order 41, rule 3A sub-rule (1) explaining delay in filing appeal has been allowed under sub-rule (2) but appeal is yet to be heard for admission under Order XLI, rule 11 C.P.C. In such eventuality Court shall not make an order for the stay of execution of decree against which the appeal is preferred to be filed, so long as the Court does not, after hearing under rule 11, decide to hear the appeal. Question of passing of interim order in appeal under Order XLI, rule 1 3A(3) shall arise only after deciding the application under sub-rule (2) preferred under sub-rule (1). Therefore, sub-rule (3) will come in to play only after completion of process under sub-rule (2).

Order XLI, rule 3A C.P.C. ensures that filing of time barred appeal must be accompanied by application for condonation of delay explaining sufficient cause which prevented filing of appeal in time and final decision on the said application prior to proceeding to deal with the appeal and also considering the said appeal under rule 11 C.P.C. before staying execution of impugned decree is mandatory. But it does not deal a situation of application pending adjudication under section 5 of the Limitation Act and application for interim stay filed therein.

Order XLI, rule 3A C.P.C. provides procedure of filing time barred appeal but does not empower the Court for condonation of delay. Substantive provision empowering Court to condone delay is in section 5 of the Limitation Act. There is no specific provision dealing with grant of interim relief during pendency of application under section 5 of Limitation Act. Therefore, in separate and distinct proceeding under section 5 of Limitation Act, independent of appeal, applicant can prefer an application under section 151 C.P.C. for interim order during pendency of this proceeding and Court is not prohibited from passing any interim order in such application exercising its inherent powers for ends of justice or prevent abuse of the process of the Court, in such proceeding pending application for condonation of delay, for the reason that prohibition under sub-rule (3) of Order XLI, rule 3A C.P.C, for staying impugned decree, will be operative only at the stage when appeal, before Court, is pending for hearing and that situation will come only in case application, as prescribed under sub-rule (1), filed under section 5 of Limitation Act for condonation of delay, has been allowed. Sub-rule (3) prescribes procedure to be followed after allowing application under sub-rule (2) preferred in compliance of procedure provided in sub-rule (1).

Order XLI, rule 3A C.P.C. does not prohibit Court from passing an interim order staying execution of order in an application under section 151 C.P.C. filed in application under section 5 of Limitation Act which in itself provides complete mechanism for condonation of delay in preferring remedy available within prescribed time and in such proceeding a separate application for grant of interim stay under section 151 C.P.C. is also maintainable and such an application is not to be governed by Order XLI, rule 3A C.P.C. and for ends of justice or to prevent abuse of process of law, if Court thinks necessary to stay execution of impugned decree pending hearing of application for condonation of delay, it can certainly stay execution during pendency of application for condonation of delay prior to admission of appeal. There is no prohibition for the Court to pass an interim order in an application independent of appeal filed in distinct proceeding under section 5 of Limitation Act to do substantial justice.

Proceeding under section 5 of Limitation Act is an independent proceeding and condonation of delay is precondition for registration of time barred appeal and in absence of appeal, application for stay filed with appeal does also not exist. In present case, there was no appeal pending before Sub Divisional Collector, as the appeal was yet to be registered, only after condonation of delay, if any, and as such there was no application for interim stay pending before him. Admittedly, there is no separate application for stay, filed in proceeding under section 5 of Limitation Act by petitioners, praying for interim stay of impugned order during pendency of the application for condonation of delay. There was no occasion for Sub Divisional Commissioner to pass an order granting interim stay against order dated 21.6.2016. Therefore, interim order dated 19.1.2017 passed by Sub Divisional Collector was without an application pending before him and as such he had no alternative, except to review and suspend the said order vide order dated 30.5.2017.

148. Power of Sub-divisional Collector

About power of the Sub divisional Collector the High Court said, I find no force in another contention raised on behalf of petitioners that Sub Divisional Collector was not competent to review his own order for want of necessary sanction under section 16 of H.P. Land Revenue Act as the said section 16 provides that for correction of a mistake or error apparent on face of record, a revenue officer either of his own motion or on the application of any party interested, is empowered to modify, reverse or confirm any order passed by himself or by any of his predecessor in office by reviewing the same. As per proviso (a) to this section, Commissioner or Collector is not required to obtain sanction of immediately superior Revenue Officer to review any order passed by himself. In present case order has been reviewed by the same officer passed by him as Sub Divisional Collector and there was error apparent on the face of record as without existence of appeal and application for stay, interim order dated 19.1.2017 was passed and the said mistake/error was apparent on face of record. Therefore, I find no material irregularity, illegality or perversity in the impugned order passed by Sub Divisional Collector.

149. Order XLI, Rule 3A – Limitation Act, 1963 and Section 5 Delay in filing appeal

In *Kishor Kumar Lala* v. *Shrimatya Sandhya Lala*, 2017 (2) ICC 80: 2017 (1) Cal LJ 578 (Cal) the High Court of Calcutta said, at the very outset, it can be said that the provision adumbrated in rule 3A Order 41 of the Code of Civil Procedure is virtually a replica of section 5 of the Limitation Act, 1963 in some elucidated form with additional 3 separate clauses. But in both the cases the main matter must have to be accompanied with an application supported by affidavit explaining the reasons of delay in filing the main matter, be it an appeal, or, application. In turn the Court accepts the reasons to condone the delay if the Court is satisfied about sufficient cause. These cardinal principles are to be followed by the litigants in seeking reliefs from the Court so long such provisions are appearing in the Code or in the Act. The ratio of the above noted decisions though have been formulated on different facts and circumstances, which will be dealt with at the appropriate stage, those are sounding in the same voice that for substantial justice prayer of condonation of delay should be construed liberally, so that, a meritorious case be not defeated under such technical bar of limitation. The principle also has been formulated that for the purpose of condonation of delay, length of the period is not a matter, provided the cause behind such delay is sufficient and acceptable to the Court.

The High Court further said, that apart, even if any worst view is assumed about impugned deed of gift dated January 17, 1985, challenge on which was taken in the grounds of Title Appeal 1 of 2014 under reference since it was executed by guardian mother for self and her minor son (Nemai Lala) at best the same could have been a voidable document so far as share of the then minor which would have been actionable under Law. Article 60 of the Limitation Act, 1963 provides:—

> "60. To set aside a transfer of property made by the guardian of a ward (a) by the ward who has attained majority."

The opposite party No. 2 was born in 1973.

Thereby he attained majority sometime in 1991. So he had opportunity also to challenge said deed of gift, at least so far as his own share within 1994. Therefore, from angle of this vision the allegation against the deed, has become hopelessly otherwise barred under article 60 of the Limitation Act. Therefore, there was also no vitiation of trial of the suit for not appointing Court guardian on behalf of opposite party No. 2. Learned Court below when weighing the grounds of appeal should not ignore all these aspects. The statements of opposite parties in the name of "better particulars" made in Para-15 onwards can be some pleas to make attempt in filling up lacunas, but, those pleas do not earn credence as sufficient cause, far to speak of incurring satisfaction of the Court, since prior to taking steps on December 18, 2008 in another Title Suit No. 276 of 1996 filed by some other, the opposite party Nos.1 and 2 in the instant Title Suit No. 45 of 1988 attempted unsuccessfully to reject their earlier written statement dated March 2, 1989 since last part of March, 2007, and having suffered by rejection Order of the Trial Court one after another upto December 20, 2007, all of those were accepted without making challenge. Those all unsuccessful attempts were also made beyond the prescribed period of limitation, which cannot speak about their bonafideness.

In view of above, the consideration of prayer of the opposite parties, who had no defence at all in the suit in opposition to the prayer of partition, does not have anything to justify on merit. Rather learned Court below in such peculiar nature of fact and circumstance has misplaced the concept of justice oriented approach. When there was no defence in opposition to the suit for partition, and when the petitioner by virtue of the contested decree against others has accrued an executable right enforceable through process of law, admitting an appeal by condoning the deliberate delay to their knowledge would only mean either a remand bound fate of the suit by setting the contested judgment, or dismissal of the appeal for want of no case or evidence led by the opposite parties in opposition to the prayer of partition. Learned Judge also failed to take note that the opposite party Nos.1 and 2 asserted themselves on March 2, 1989 as unnecessary parties to the partition suit and they had no share in the suit property. So, what they would say more in appeal if after its admission it would continue for some years to come. Alternatively if such an application with all above circumstances, is to answer in the affirmative extending liberal approach only for admitting Title appeal 1 of 2014 at the instance of such opposite party Nos.1 to 4 then I am afraid of whether there is any further necessity of keeping existence of the relevant provision either in the Limitation Act or in the Code.

150. Order XLI, Rule 23A – Remand – Decree passed by trial Court

In *Balaji Singh* v. *Diwakar (Cal) Cole,* 2017 (3) MLJ 839: AIR 2017 (SCW) 2402 (SC) the Apex Court held, coming to the facts of the case, we are of the considered opinion that once the first Appellate Court allowed the application under Order XLI, rule 27 of Code and took on record the additional evidence, it rightly set aside the judgment/decree of the Trial Court giving liberty to the parties to lead additional evidence in support of their case which, in turn, enabled the Trial Court to decide the civil suit afresh on merits in the light of entire evidence. The first Appellate Court was, therefore, justified in taking recourse to powers conferred on the Appellate Court under Order XLI, rule 23A for remanding the case to the Trial Court. We find no fault in exercise of such power by the first Appellate Court.

In our considered view, the only error which the first Appellate Court committed was that it went on to record the findings on merits. In our view, it was not necessary to do so while passing the order of remand. The reason is that once the first Appellate Court formed an opinion to remand the case, it was required to give reasons in support of the remand order as to why the remand is called for in the case. Indeed, the remand was made only to enable the Trial Court to decide the case on merits. Therefore, there was no need to discuss much less record findings on several issues on merits. It was totally uncalled for.

151. Rules 27 and 28 – Production of additional evidence

So far as the impugned order is concerned, the High Court, in our view, committed jurisdictional error when it again examined the case on merits and set aside the judgment of the first Appellate Court and restored the judgment of the Trial Court. The High Court, in our opinion, should not have done this for the simple reason that it was only examining the legality of the remand order in an appeal filed under Order XLIII, rule 1 (u) of the Code. Indeed, once the High Court came to a conclusion that the remand order was bad in law then it could only remand the case to the first Appellate Court with a direction to decide the first appeal on merits.

The High Court failed to see that when the first Appellate Court itself did not decide the appeal on merits and considered it proper to remand the case to the Trial Court, a fortiori, the High Court had no jurisdiction to decide the appeal on merits. Moreover, Order XLIII, rule 1 (u) confers limited power on the

High Court to examine only the legality and correctness of the remand order of the first Appellate Court but not beyond that. In other words, the High Court should have seen that Order XLIII, rule 1 (u) gives a limited power to examine the issue relating to legality of remand order, as is clear from Order XLIII, rule 1 (u) which reads thus:—

> *"1(u) an order under rule 23 or rule 23A of Order* XLI *remanding a case, where an appeal would lie from the decree of the Appellate Court"*

It is well settled law that the jurisdiction to decide the appeal on merits can be exercised by the Appellate Court only when the appeal is filed under section 96 or 100 of the Code against the decree. Such was not the case here.

In the light of above mentioned discussion, we are of the opinion that the High Court had no jurisdiction to consider much less deciding the entire case of the parties on merits in such appeal.

We are also unable to agree with the High Court when it held that the first Appellate Court instead of remanding the case to the Trial Court should have heard the appeal on merits. This finding, in our view, is bad in law for the reason that firstly, it was not possible for the first Appellate Court to have recorded the evidence at the appellate stage. Secondly, having regard to the nature of factual controversy involved and keeping in view the nature of additional evidence filed which too needed to be proved in evidence, it was not possible to retain the appeal to itself and invite finding only on additional evidence by taking recourse to powers under rule 25; and lastly, wholesome remand, as directed by the first Appellate Court, would enable the Trial Court to appreciate the entire evidence in its proper perspective while deciding the suit afresh on merits.

152. Order XLI, Rules 27 and 28 – Application for producing Additional evidence

In *Alamelu Ammal* v. *S. Rani*, AIR 2017 (SC) 2612: 2017 (3) Jhr 340 the Supreme Court said, from the aforesaid, it transpires that the High Court has not questioned the order passed by the First Appellate Court in allowing the application of the appellants under Order XLI, rule 28 of the Code of Civil Procedure, 1908. It means that insofar as exercise of the discretion by the First Appellate Court on this aspect was concerned, no fault was found there with and though the High Court rightly held that once the application under Order 41, rule 27 of the Code of Civil Procedure, 1908 was allowed, the procedure contemplated under Order 41, rule 28 of the Code of Civil Procedure, 1908 should have been followed by the First Appellate Court and the document in question, which was Exhibit - A10, should have been proved in accordance with law. This was not done and the First Appellate Court simply acted upon the said Exhibit - A10 and on that basis passed the decree in favour of the appellants. However, thereafter the manner in which the High Court proceeded is also blemished to some extent. The High Court has set aside the decree passed by the First Appellate Court simply because the procedure contemplated under Order XLI, rule 28 of the Code of Civil Procedure, 1908 was not followed. In a situation like this more appropriate course of action for the High Court was to remit the case to the First Appellate Court with a direction to follow the procedure as contemplated under Order XLI, rule 28 of the Code of Civil Procedure, 1908 and thereafter decide the first appeal which was filed by the appellants herein.

For the aforesaid reasons, we set aside the impugned judgment of the High Court and remit the case to the First Appellate Court. The First Appellate Court shall follow the procedure contained in Order XLI, Rules 28 and29 of the Code of Civil Procedure, 1908 by permitting the appellants to adduce the necessary evidence to prove Exhibit-A10 and also give an opportunity to the respondents herein to lead any evidence and thereafter decide the first appeal of the appellants.

The appeals are, accordingly, disposed of.

153. Section 100 and Rule 27 of Order XLI – Specific Relief Act, 1963 and Sections 6, 34 and 37

In *Srimati Pramila Deka* v. *Sri. Prasanta Deka,* 2017 (3) Gau LT 413 the High Court of Gauhati said about the application of the above noted provisions, Now the question that may arise is, whether the said additional evidence had any impact on the decision of the appeal and the findings arrived at by the learned first appellate court concurring with the finding of the trial court. So far as the sale deed executed by the vendor of the plaintiff or his vendors vendor, there was no dispute, inasmuch as, the defendant never denied in his pleadings the existence of the sale deed in question. Specific plea of the defendant was that those deeds were only paper works incapable of conveying title in absence of delivery of possession. It is now settled position, that mutation entry neither creates or extinguish title. Therefore, even if, there was some error or anomaly in the mutation order or mutation entry, that could be of no consequence in view of the fact that the deed in question having bearing on the title of the plaintiff were never in dispute.

No doubt, granting or refusing leave to adduce additional evidence is a judicial discretion of the appellate court to be exercise within the parameter of Order 41 Rule 27 of the CPC. In the instant case, learned appellate court appears to have traveled beyond the scope of Order XLI, rule 27 CPC, while allowing the additional evidence. When additional evidence is allowed to be adduced at the appellate stage going beyond the scope of Order XLI, rule 27 CPC, such evidence is to be ignored as has been held by the Apex Court in the case of *Natha Singh* v. *The Financial Commissioner, Taxation, Punjab, (1976)* 3 SCC 28: AIR 1976 SC 1053: [1976] 3 SCR 620

> "So far as the application of the appellants for additional evidence is concerned, it cannot be allowed in view of the well settled principles of law that the discretion given to the appellate court to receive and admit additional evidence is not an arbitrary one but is a judicial one circumscribed by the limitations specified in OrderXLI, rule 27 of the Code of Civil Procedure. If the additional evidence is allowed to be adduced contrary to the principles governing the reception of such evidence, it will be a case of improper exercise of discretion and the additional evidence so brought on the record will have to be ignored. The true test to be applied in dealing with applications for additional evidence is whether the appellate

court is able to pronounce judgment on the materials before it, without taking into consideration the additional evidence sought to be adduced. (See *Arjun Singh Alias Puran* v. *Kartar Singh,* AIR 1951 SC 193: (1951) 1 MLJ 556 (SC). In the instant case, we have not been able to experience any difficulty in rendering the judgment on the material already before us. Instead we feel that the prayer for adducing additional evidence has been made merely to fill up gaps on the basis of some revenue record which has been found by the Collector and the Commissioner to the spurious."

154. The legal status of mutation

The Court also examined the effect of mutation and held, keeping in mind the legal proposition that mutation neither creates nor extinguishes title, even if the additional evidence of which learned appellate court took judicial notice, is totally ignored or obliterated, there could be no scope for coming to a finding different from the one, arrived at by the trial court and also concurred by the first appellate court on the basis of the evidence available on record as discussed hereinbefore.

In view of the above discussion, the appeal is found devoid of merit and substantial questions of law are answered accordingly. The appeal stands dismissed. No Cost.

Registry shall send down the record.

155. Order XLI,Rule 27 – Application for additional evidence

In *Bhisham Lal Garg* v. *Hardei,* 2017 (2) Him LR 1029: 2017 Latest HLG HP 571 the High Court of Himachal Pradesh said, close scrutiny of record made available to this Court clearly suggests that while deciding the main appeal, learned lower appellate Court failed to take note of the application filed under Order XLI, rule 27 as well as documents accompanying the same. This court was unable to find any mention with regard to the pendency of aforesaid application in the impugned judgment. Learned first appellate Court without caring to look into the merits of the aforesaid application, proceeded to decide the appeal in slipshod manner.

By now, it is well settled that application filed under Order XLI, rule 27 is required to be decided along with the main appeal but as has been observed above, there is no consideration of the application for leading additional evidence by the learned trial Court while passing the final judgment in the appeal having been preferred by the appellant plaintiff. Once an application under Order XLI, rule 27 Civil Procedure Code was filed and thereafter entertained by the first appellate Court, it was incumbent upon the first appellate Court to consider/ deal with the same on merits but impugned judgment having been passed by the learned first appellate Court nowhere suggests that above referred application was ever considered by the Court while deciding the main appeal.

It has been repeatedly held by the Hon'ble Apex Court that dismissal of appeal without deciding the application of additional evidence is improper and in all eventualities, application for additional evidence under Order XLI, rule 27

CPC should be dealt with on merits at the first instance. In this regard, reliance is placed on judgment passed by the Hon'ble Supreme Court in case titled "*Jatinder Singh (Minor through mother)* v. *Mehar Singh* with *Balbir Singh* v. *Jatinder Singh,* AIR 2009 (Vol. 96) SC 354: 2008 (12) SCALE 734, the relevant paragraphs are being reproduced herein below:—

> "3. In our view, this appeal can be decided on a very short question. The trial court as well as the appellate court and finally the High Court in the second appeal dismissed the suit filed by the plaintiffs/appellants for declaration challenging the sale deed dated 29th of May, 1989, executed by the respondent Nos. 1 to 3 in favour of respondent Nos. 9 and 10 as well as the compromise (Exhibit No. C1) dated 7th of April, 1986 in a suit title *Ujagar Singh* v. *Puran Singh,* AIR 1930 Lah 961 But it is an admitted position that before the High Court, the appellants filed an application under Order XLI, rule 27 of the Code of Civil Procedure for acceptance of additional evidence, namely, documents such as certificate of Military service, voter list of concerned assembly segment for the year 1982, receipt of house tax 1988-89, payment of chaowkdra of khariff 1986, rabi 1990, rabi 1991, khariff 1992, identity card issued by Election Commission of India, Ration Card etc.
>
> While deciding the second appeal, however, the High Court had failed to take notice of the application under Order XLI, rule 27 of the Code of Civil Procedure and decide whether additional evidence could be permitted to be admitted into evidence. In our view, when an application for acceptance of additional evidence under Order XLI, rule 27 of the Code of Civil Procedure was filed by the appellants, it was the duty of the High Court to deal with the same on merits. That being the admitted position, we have no other alternative but to set aside the judgment of the High Court and remit the appeal back to it for a decision afresh in the second appeal along with the application for acceptance of additional evidence in accordance with law.
>
> For the reasons aforesaid, the impugned Judgment is set aside. The appeal is thus allowed to the extent indicated above. There will be no order as to costs."

156. Order XLI, Rule 27 – Power to be used very sparingly

Raveendranadhan v. *State of Kerala Represented by Chief Secretary, Govt. of Kerala, Thiruvananthapuram,* 2017 (1) ILR (Ker) 256: 2017 AIR CC 1134 a Division bench of the High Court of Kerala held, it is well settled that normally the appellate court should not travel outside the records produced before the trial court and cannot take any evidence in appeal. Order XLI, rule 27 of CPC enables the court to take additional evidence only in the circumstances specifically enumerated therein. The first point to be established by a person seeking introduction of additional evidence is that even after due diligence such evidence was not within his knowledge or could not after exercise of due diligence be produced by him at the time when the decree appealed against was passed. Therefore, the appellate court is entitled to call for fresh evidence only on satisfaction of the conditions laid down in the rules. Here, it is to be noted that in the appeal memorandum, there is no mention that the documents produced along with the petition were not within their knowledge or could not produce before the trial court even after exercise of due diligence. It is also well established that the power under Order XLI, rule 27 of CPC should be used sparingly and only if the party is able to establish that even after their best efforts, such additional evidence could not be adduced at the first instance and the documents are relevant for deciding the issue. Here it is to be noted that there is no whisper regarding the same in the appeal memorandum, but they have simply produced the documents, without any satisfactory explanation for not having produced it before the trial court. So, it is not just and proper to accept Exts.A1 to A6 produced along with the appeal memorandum in evidence as prayed for by the appellants. Moreover, most of the documents have been obtained only much later after disposal of the O.As. by the learned Forest Tribunal. So, the prayer for acceptance of additional documents under Order XLI, rule 27 is rejected. In short, we find absolutely no justification to interfere with the findings of the learned Forest Tribunal.

157. Order XLI, Rule 27 – Second appeal – Application for acceptance of additional evidence

In *Jatanmal Fofaliya s/o Late shri Chhuttan Lal (Deceased during pendency of appeal)* v. *Smt Chameli Devi@ Atto Devi Widow of Late Shri Jugal Kishore,* 2017 (1) WLC (Raj) (UC) 720: 2017 (3) WLN 426 Rajsthan High Court considering question of remand said, it is not in dispute that applications under Order XLI, rule 27 CPC were filed by both the parties in the lower appellate Court but the same are left undecided by the lower appellate Court.

In *Hakam Singh* v. *State of Haryana,* AIR 2008 SC 2990: 2008 (6) SCALE 127 Hon'ble Apex Court has observed as under:—

> "That being the position, without going into the legality and propriety of the impugned order of the High Court passed in the aforesaid appeals, we set aside the same and remit back the case to the High Court for decision of the Appeals afresh on merits and in accordance with law along with the application for acceptance of additional evidence under Order XLI, rule 27 of the Code."

In *Jatinder Singh* v. *Mehar Singh,* (2009) 17 SCC 465: AIR 2009 SC 354 Hon'ble Apex Court in para No. 4 has observed as under:—

> "While deciding the second appeal, however, the High Court had failed to take notice of the application under Order XLI, rule 27 of the Code of Civil Procedure and decide whether additional evidence could be permitted to be admitted into evidence. In our view, when an application for acceptance of additional evidence under Order XLI, rule 27 of the Code of Civil Procedure was filed by the appellants, it was the duty of the High Court to deal with the same on merits. That being the admitted position, we have no other alternative but to set aside the judgment of the High Court and remit the appeal back to it for a decision afresh in the second appeal along with the application for acceptance of additional evidence in accordance with law."

In the light of the aforesaid, the judgment and decree impugned are liable to be set aside and the matter is liable to be remitted to the appellate Court for a decision afresh.

In the result, the appeal is allowed. The judgment and decree dated 01.09.2009 passed by Additional District Judge No.9, Jaipur City, Jaipur in civil regular appeal No.64/2006 is set aside and the matter is remitted back to the appellate Court to decide it afresh on merits along with the applications under Order XLI, rule 27 of the Civil Procedure Code in accordance with the law. The parties are directed to remain present before the appellate Court on 5th July, 2017.

158. Order XLI, Rule 27(b) – Appeal – Additional Evidence – Permissibility

In *Basant Kumar Mehrotra* v. *Ram Laxman Janki Virajman Mandir* 2017 (4) All LJ190: 2017 (122) Air 795 (All) learned counsel for the petitioner has assailed the order passed by the court below on the ground that the document was necessary for doing complete justice between the parties and it was required for the purpose of pronouncing the judgment therefore the court should have accepted the document as an additional evidence under clause (c) of sub rule (1) of Rule 27 Order 41 of the Code, as applicable in U.P., which is pari materia clause (b) of the Code. In support of the aforesaid submission, a decision of the Apex Court in *Wadi* v. *Amilal,* 2015 (1) SCC 677, has been cited, in which, in paragraph 5 of the report, it has been held that the general principle incorporated in sub rule (1) of Rule 27, Order XLI is that the parties to an appeal are not entitled to produce additional evidence (oral or documentary) in the appellate court to cure a lacuna or fill up a gap in a case. The exceptions to that principle are enumerated thereunder in clauses (a), (aa) and (b) (in the context of State of Uttar Pradesh should be read as (a), (b) and (c)). The court observed that while considering whether clause (b) is applicable to the facts of a case, the court must have regard to the ends of justice and if the court feels that pronouncing a judgment in the absence of such evidence would result in a defective decision and to pronounce an effective judgment, admission of such document is necessary, the said clause enables it to adopt that course. It was observed that for invocation of the said clause, the vigilance or negligence of the parties would not be relevant.

A bare perusal of the judgment which has been cited by the learned counsel for the petitioner would go to show that the said clause is applicable in a case where the court is of the view that pronouncing a judgment in the absence of such evidence would result in a defective decision and to pronounce an effective judgment, the document/evidence is necessary.

The apex court in *K.R. Mohan Reddy* v. *Net Work Inc.,* (2007) 14 SCC 257: AIR 2008 SC 579, while dealing with clauses (aa) and (b) of sub rule (1) of Rule 27, Order XLI of the Code, which should be read as clauses (b) and (c) in the context of State of U.P., held as under:

> "17. It is now a trite law that the conditions precedent for application of clause (aa) of sub-rule (1) of Rule 27 Order XLI is different from that of clause (b). In the event the former is to be applied, it would be for the applicant to show that the ingredients or conditions precedent mentioned therein are satisfied. On the other hand if clause (b) to sub-rule (1) of Rule

27 Order XLI CPC is to be taken recourse to, the appellate court is bound to consider the entire evidence on record and come to an independent finding for arriving at a just decision; adduction of additional evidence as has been prayed by the appellant was necessary. The fact that the High Court failed to do so, in our opinion, amounts to misdirection in law. Furthermore, if the High Court is correct in its view that the respondent-plaintiff had proceeded on the basis that the suit is entirely based on a cheque, where-for, it was not necessary for it to file the books of accounts before the trial court, finding contrary thereto could not have been arrived at that the same was in fact required to be proved so as to enable the appellate court to arrive at a just conclusion.

The appellate court should not pass an order so as to patch up the weakness of the evidence of the unsuccessful party before the trial court, but it will be different if the court itself requires the evidence to do justice between the parties. The ability to pronounce judgment is to be understood as the ability to pronounce judgment satisfactorily to the mind of the court. But mere difficulty is not sufficient to issue such direction. While saying so, however, we do not mean that the court at an appropriate stage would be precluded from considering the applicability of clause (b)."

Further, the Apex Court in *State of Gujarat* v. *Mahendrakumar Parshottambhai Desai,* (2006) 9 SCC 772: AIR 2006 SC 1864, relying upon *Municipal Corpn. of Greater Bombay* v. *Lala Pancham,* AIR 1965 SC 1008: [1965] 1 SCR 542, held as under:

> "10. ... though the appellate court has the power to allow a document to be produced and a witness to be examined under Order XLI, rule 27 CPC, the requirement of the said Court must be limited to those cases where it found it necessary to obtain such evidence for enabling it to pronounce judgment. This provision did not entitle the appellate court to let in fresh evidence at the appellate stage where even without such evidence it can pronounce judgment in the case. It does not entitle the appellate court to let in fresh evidence only for the purposes of pronouncement of judgment in a particular way."

In *Mahavir Singh* v. *Naresh Chandra,* (2001) 1 SCC 309: 2000 (7) SCALE 356, the Apex Court while dealing with the import of clause (b) (should be read as clause (c) in the context of the State of Uttar Pradesh), observed as follows:

> "5... In the third circumstance, the appellate court may require any document to be produced or any witness to be examined to enable it to pronounce the judgment, or for any other substantial cause. The expression "to enable it to pronounce judgment" has been the subject of several decisions including *Syed Abdul Khader* v. *Rami Reddy,* (1979) 2 SCC 601: AIR 1979 SC 553 wherein it was held that when the appellate court finds itself unable to pronounce judgment owing to a lacuna or defect in the evidence as it stands, it may admit additional evidence. The ability to pronounce a judgment is to be understood as the ability to pronounce a judgment satisfactory to the mind of the court delivering it. It is only

a lacuna in the evidence that will empower the court to admit additional evidence (see: *Municipal Corpn. of Greater Bombay* v. *Lala Pancham,* AIR 1965 SC 1008: 1965 1 SCR 542). But a mere difficulty in coming to a decision is not sufficient for admission of evidence under this rule. The words "or for any other substantial cause" must be read with the word "requires", which is set out at the commencement of the provision, so that it is only where, for any other substantial cause, the appellate court requires additional evidence, that this rule would apply as noticed by the Privy Council in *Kessowji Issur* v. *G.I.P. Rly,* ILR 31 Bom 381 (PC). It is under these circumstances such a power could be exercised. Therefore, when the first appellate court did not find the necessity to allow the application, we fail to understand as to how the High Court could, in exercise of its power under section 115 CPC, have interfered with such an order, particularly when the whole appeal is not before the Court. It is only in the circumstances when the appellate court requires such evidence to pronounce the judgment the necessity to adduce additional evidence would arise and not in any other circumstances. When the first appellate court passed the order on the application filed under Order XLI, rule 27 CPC, the whole appeal was before it and if the first appellate court is satisfied that additional evidence was not required, we fail to understand as to how the High Court could interfere with such an order under section 115 CPC."

From the law noticed herein above, the legal position, as it stands, is that the parties to an appeal are not entitled to produce additional evidence (oral or documentary) in the appellate court except on the principles enumerated in clauses (a), (b) and (c) of sub rule (1) of Rule 27 Order XLI of the Code, as applicable in the State of Uttar Pradesh, which are pari materia clauses (a), (aa) and (b) of the Code. Clause (c), which is pari materia clause (b) of the Code, is applicable where the appellate court requires a document to be produced or any witness to be examined to enable it to pronounce the judgment, or for any other substantial cause. The expression "to enable it to pronounce judgment" has been interpreted so as to mean that when the appellate court finds itself unable to pronounce judgment owing to a lacuna or defect in the evidence as it stands, it may admit additional evidence. But that does not mean that the clause should be resorted to patch up the weakness of the evidence of the unsuccessful party before the trial court, though, if the court itself requires the evidence to do justice between the parties, it may accept it. The ability to pronounce a judgment is to be understood as the ability to pronounce a judgment satisfactory to the mind of the court delivering it. But a mere difficulty in coming to a decision is not sufficient for admission of evidence under this rule. This provision does not entitle the appellate court to let in fresh evidence at the appellate stage where even without such evidence it can satisfactorily pronounce judgment in the case. It does not entitle the appellate court to let in fresh evidence only for the purposes of pronouncement of judgment in a particular way. The words "or for any other substantial cause" must be read with the word "requires", which is set out at the commencement of the provision, so that it is only where, for any other substantial cause, the appellate court requires additional evidence, that this clause would apply. Furthermore, if recourse is to be taken to the said clause, that is clause (c), which is pari materia clause (b) of the Code, the appellate court is required to consider the entire evidence on record to come to an independent conclusion whether for arriving at a just decision, adduction of additional evidence, as has been prayed for, is necessary. Therefore, ordinarily, an application seeking adduction of additional evidence by taking recourse to the aforesaid clause is to be considered at the time of hearing by taking a conspectus of the entire evidence on record for drawing satisfaction whether the evidence, the adduction of which is sought, is necessary for pronouncing a judgment.

In the instant case, the parties were aware of the issues on which they were required to lead evidence. The first issue itself was as to whether the defendant had sublet the premises without a written permission of the landlord. Under the circumstances, if the defendant had in his possession the document in respect of written permission for subletting, then he ought to have brought the same on record. In the event such document was not produced before the trial court, then for its adduction in appellate court, it ought to have been demonstrated that after exercise of due diligence, the document was not within his knowledge or could not be produced by him at the time when the decree under appeal was passed. But, in the instant case, the application seeking adduction of the document does not disclose that the document was not within the knowledge of the petitioner or could not have been produced before the trial court despite exercise of due diligence. Accordingly, the application was clearly not maintainable under the second clause that is clause (b), which is pari materia clause (aa) of the Code. In so far as applicability of clause (c), which is pari materia clause (b) of the Code, is concerned, suffice to say that it is not the case of the petitioner that the Court would be unable to pronounce a satisfactory judgment in absence of the said document. This court has already noticed that recourse to the said clause is not to be used to patch up the weakness of the evidence of the unsuccessful party before the trial court. Accordingly and in view of the discussion made above, this court is of the view that the order rejecting the application to adduce additional evidence does not suffer from any legal infirmity and the same calls for no interference.

159. Order XLI, Rule 27 – Order of remand back to produce certified copies and to adduce additional evidence with respect to Will pertaining to mutation

In *Satnam Singh* v. *Malook Singh*, 2017 AIR SC 3749: 2017 AIR (SCW) 3749 it transpires that original will was filed by the defendant-appellant in the case pertaining to mutation, the record of the said case, was requisitioned and had been produced in the Court by Charan Singh but unfortunately the record was not retained. The District Court has allowed the evidence by making following discussion:

> "...14. Perusal of record of civil suit shows that on 18.10.2000 Charan Singh Office Kanungo Tehsil Samana produced some record of mutation no.903 of village Dhainthal in which registered Will No. 34 dated 30.11.1987 was available. After recording such statement of Charan Singh

and obtaining his signatures on his statement, thee [sic:there] is one more endorsement about receiving back file by said Charan Singh but such endorsement does not bear any date. When record was called from Charan Singh and he brought the record and produced the same and material document registered Will was lying on record of mutation no. 903 brought by Charan Singh Office Kanungo, trial court out to have retained, why it was allowed to be taken back by Charan Singh is not understandable.

15. Perusal of statement of DW-3 Banjit Singh shows that be deposted that he had seen Will meant for original Will and he identified his signature thereon. He deposed that such Will was scribed by Ashok Kumar document writer. When Ranjith Singh DW-3 deposed so on 9.02.01 obviously original Will was available that is why he could identify his signatures on original Will but from the file it could not be understood who produced when statement of DW3 Ranjith Singh was recorded, then it should not be recorded in his statement that he had seen Will and identified his signature thereon.

16. Perusal of statement of DW-4 Ashok Kumar shows that he deposed he had seen original Will which was scribed by him. He had seen such original Will on the record of file. When he deposed so it infers that he had seen the original Will and identified his hand-writing on 2.6.01 when his statement was recorded. But it could not be spelt out from record who had brought such original Will, where original Will had gone and how original Will came in the hands of Balkar Singh or defendant-appellants. When such is the position of record of trial court, I am unable to maintain the judgment and decree of trial court when original Will is not on record and it could not be spelt out how original Will has gone in the hands of Balkar Singh or defendant-appellants. Perusal of para 13 of judgment shows that trial court observed that neither original Will nor its certified copy produced on record. When trial court made up mind to hold such findings of trial court generated from its own fault as to why it did not retain Will on record and how original Will slip from record of civil suit and how DW3 and DW4 could depose having seen original Will. Perusal of page 10 of judgment shows that trial court was overwhelmingly convinced against the Will due to reason of non-production of its certified copy. Such findings cannot be maintained at all.

(i) Opportunities to lead addl. evidence to defendant appellants will be afforded for production of certified copies of orders of Asstt. Collector 1st Grade, Samana and Collector, Patiala. Trial court should afford opportunity to them to place original Will on record which is lying on record of present appeal tagged along with application dated 8.1.03;

(ii) Trial Court shall afford opportunity to defendant-appellants to lead addl. evidence to prove Will dated 30.11.87 by allowing them to place on record original registered Will of Hasura Singh dated 30.11.98;

(iii) After evidence of contesting defendant so led trial court shall afford opportunities to plaintiffs for leading rebuttal evidence;

(iv) After completion of such exercise trial court should re-decide all the issues in accordance with law;

(v) Contesting defendant s are at liberally to either collect the original Will against proper identification and verification in accordance with law or the can summon the record of appeal for producing original Will on record of civil suit.

Parties are directed to put appearance before trial court on 17.2.2003. Thereafter trial court shall endeavour to dispose of the suit as early as possible after giving due opportunities of leading evidence accordingly to both parties."

We find that the District Court was justified in giving opportunity to adduce the additional evidence in the peculiar fact and circumstances of the case which was discretionary order and legally justified one. Litigant could not have punished for no fault on his part. Thus the High Court has erred in setting aside the order of the remand passed by Additional District Judge on 21.5.2003. The judgment and order of the High Court cannot be said to be justified in the facts and circumstances of the case.

160. Order XLI, Rule 27 - Additional evidence

In *Mohan Mahto* v. *State of Jharkhand, (Jharkhand),* 2017 (2) JBCJ 522: 2017 (2) AIR R Jhar 795 the learned appellate court of Additional District Judge-XII, Hazaribag in Title Appeal No. 47/2012 has refused to accept additional evidence under Order XLI, rule 27 of the Code of Civil Procedure preferred by the plaintiffs-appellants to adduce copy of the writ petition of the private respondents being W.P. (C) No. 6923/2004.

The respondent - Divisional Forest Officer has, however, contested the case by filing counter affidavit and claimed that the land in question is a forest land over which forest pillar nos. 13, 14, 15 and 16 are in existence. The forest demarcated land has never been released by the department. Therefore, claim of the said petitioners is baseless and on the basis of forged and fabricated papers including the documents of Hukumnama. Learned appellate court, however, has observed that the writ petition is simply pending and no final judgment has been passed in that respect. It has also been observed that both the parties had produced their evidence after sufficient opportunity before the trial court, leading to passing of the impugned judgment and decree. Mere filing of the pleadings of the writ petition, when no final decision has been taken thereupon by this Court, could not be of any consequence of being adduced as an additional evidence. Accordingly, the prayer has been rejected.

The High Court after hearing the parties held, the opinion of the learned appellate court in disallowing the evidence adduced by the appellants at this stage when the appeal is ripe for hearing, cannot be held to be suffering from error in law for the reasons that the plaintiffs have, during pendency of the suit from 2001 itself till 2012, never ventured to adduce these documents before the learned trial court. If it appears to the appellate court, however, that it requires any such documents to be produced or witness to be examined to enable it to pronounce judgment or for any substantial cause as per the provisions of Order XLI, rule 27 (1)(b) it is always open for the appellate court to do so. The appellate court in that context may keep it in mind whether the stand of the State in the matter is necessary for final adjudication of the dispute between the parties. In that event it may resort to the provisions of Order XLI, rule 27 (1)(b) of the Civil Procedure Code.

161. Application under Order XLI, Rule 27 – Additional evidence – Sections 96 and 100

In *Latif Khan* v. *Civil Judge, S.D., Bulandshahar*, 2017 (8) ADJ 498 (All): 2017 (123) AIR 544 the court below rejected the application 101 C2 by a detailed order by holding that no good ground has been disclosed by the applicant to satisfy the conditions on which additional evidence could be accepted on record, during pendency of an appeal, under Order XLI, rule 27 C.P.C.

Learned counsel for the petitioners has assailed the order passed by the court below by submitting that once it is stated in the application that the applicant was not aware of the documents from before and claims that he is a simple illiterate villager, it is a sufficient ground to accept additional evidence on record particularly when the documents are part of public record.

In support of the above contention, the learned counsel for the petitioners has placed reliance on a judgment of the Apex Court in *Government of Karnataka* v. *K.C. Subramanya* 2014 (2) AWC 1155 to contend that where the documents were not within the knowledge of the applicant, then that is sufficient ground to take documents on record.

The High Court held, Order XLI, rule 27 of the C.P.C. provides for production of additional evidence in Appellate Court. This rule is an exception to the general principle that Appellate Court should not travel outside the record of the Lower Court. The rule lays down the conditions under which the Appellate Court is empowered to allow the additional evidence either oral or documentary to be taken on record. The rule provides that the Appellate Court is empowered to accept additional evidence if either of the specified three conditions exist. That is:—

(i) if the evidence in question was tendered in Lower Court but was improperly or illegally rejected by it; or

(ii) the party seeking to produce additional evidence establishes that notwithstanding the exercise of due diligence, such evidence was not within his knowledge or could not, after the exercise of due diligence, be produced by him at the time when the decree appealed against was passed; or

(iii) where the Appellate Court itself requires the additional evidence to enable it to pronounce judgment, or for any other substantial cause.

The case at hand does not deal with condition no. (i) and in so far as condition. (iii) is concerned that, according to several pronouncements of the Apex Court, is for the court to consider at the time of hearing of the matter whether it requires the additional evidence to enable to it to pronounce judgment, or for any other substantial cause. Therefore, at this stage what has to be seen is whether from the allegations made in the application requirements of condition no. (ii) were satisfied.

For applicability of condition no.(ii), the applicant has to satisfy the court that despite the exercise of due diligence, either (a) such evidence was not within his knowledge; or (b) he could not produce it before the court below by the time decree was passed. Accordingly to enable the court to admit additional evidence under this clause, the applicant has to demonstrate that despite the exercise of due diligence he could not learn about the document or the evidence or could not produce the same at the earlier stage. The judgment cited by learned counsel for the petitioner nowhere holds that mere statement made in the application that the document was not within the knowledge of the applicant is sufficient to accept the document as additional evidence. The facts of each case have to be examined to ascertain whether the explanation offered is bona fide or not.

162. Order XLI, Rule 33 – Execution of decree - Objection - Appeal – Section 100 - Framing of Substantial question of law

In *Delhi Transport Corporation* v. *Vidya Mandir Classes Ltd.*, 2017 (239) DLT 564: 017 (176) AIC 534 (Del) Delhi High Court examined the scope of rule 33 of Order XLI together with section 100 of CPC. The Court said, I am not only perturbed and disturbed by the impugned judgment dated 22.1.2016, but this Court would like to go on to observe that if courts pass judgments such as the impugned judgment, then there will result a rule of jungle and not the rule of law. This Court even after going through the impugned judgment repeatedly has not been able to understand as to how the first appellate court has demonstrated complete lack of knowledge of basics of law, and, the first appellate court is not a junior judicial officer but holds the rank of an Additional District Judge. In sum and substance the first appellate court by its impugned judgment holds that though it is not hearing an appeal against the main judgment and decree dated 14.5.2012 but simply because the entire record of the suit is before the court, therefore the court since it finds the reasons given by the suit court for passing the judgment and decree dated 14.5.2012 are unsustainable, hence the first appellate court cannot sit as a mute spectator and shut its eyes to patent illegality and that consequently it was bound to set aside the judgment dated 14.5.2012. Not only the course of action taken by the first appellate court in the impugned judgment is against all canons of law and justice, but the first appellate court has for setting aside the judgment and decree dated 14.5.2012 invoked its assumed powers under Order XLI, rule 33 CPC. I am really amazed as to how the first appellate court could have invoked Order XLI, rule 33 CPC because the provision of Order XLI, rule 33 CPC even on a plain reading thereof would only apply when the first appeal is filed against the main judgment and decree. Order XLI, rule 33CPC when used in execution proceedings can only be confined to the scope of the execution proceedings. There is nothing whatsoever in Order XLI, rule 33 CPC which empowers an appellate court in execution proceedings to set aside a final judgment and decree passed by a trial court and that too allegedly on the ground that the reasoning and conclusion of the trial court while passing the judgment and decree dated 14.5.2012 were erroneous.

I am forced to say that the first appellate court has travelled totally beyond its jurisdiction and assumed powers which no law of this country gives.

The Court further said, since this is an execution second appeal, learned counsel for the appellant states that a substantial question of law be framed, however, in my opinion a substantial question of law is only to be framed in a regular second appeal against a judgment of the first appellate court passed in the first appeal against a judgment of the trial court passed in a suit. Learned counsel for the respondent also argues that he does not press for framing of any substantial question of law. I may also note that the present judgment in any case notes the necessary serious question of law and also answers them.

In view of the above position, the following conclusions emerge:—

(i) The judgment and decree of the appellant/plaintiff/decree holder dated 14.5.2012 decreeing the suit of a sum of Rs. 1,34,400/- along with interest had become final because not only the judgment was not taken in challenge in the appeal but even the application under Order IX, rule 13 CPC stood dismissed.

(ii) Once a judgment and decree is final, an executing court has no power under any provision of law not only to not go behind the decree much less have any power to set aside a judgment and decree which has achieved finality.

(iii) By no stretch of imagination can Order XLI, rule 33 CPC be applied by an appellate court in execution proceedings to set aside a final decree passed in the suit and which has become final.

(iv) Observations by the first appellate court in the impugned judgment that it cannot remain as a mute spectator and shut its eyes to illegality are only an apology for acting beyond any and every principle of law known in this country and with which the first appellate court was undoubtedly bound by.

163. Order XLI, Rules 24 to 31 – Remand of case

In *Seethappa* v. *Lakshmamma,* 2017 (2) ICC 528: 2017 (3) AIR Kar R 654 (Kar) the High Court of Karnataka examined the provisions of rules 24 to 31 and said, the Court below, instead of considering the record and deciding the controversy between the parties finally by keeping in view the provision tinder Order XLI, Rule 24 CPC, has on account of the misdirection adopted and in ignorance of the record of the suit and also earlier judgment of remand, has passed the Judgment of remand i.e., for the second time. It is apparent that provisions of Order XLI, rules 24 to 27 CPC has not been kept in view. As a short-cut, Judgment of remand has been passed without reversing/setting aside the findings entered by Trial Court on the issues/additional issues raised and answered.

I.A. No. 3 filed for grant of permission to produce additional evidence having been objected, has not been considered by keeping in view the mandatory provision under Order XLI, rule 27 of CPC and the principles of law laid down in para Nos. 36 to 48 in the case of *Union of India* v. *Ibrahim Uddin,* (2012) 8 SCC 148: [2013 (1) RLR (SC) 354: 2012 (2) HLR (SC) 197: 2012 (3) ICC (SC) 539],

Even if additional evidence is permitted, then the Appellate Court should keep in view the provision made in rule 28 Order XLI CPC.

Without assigning the cogent reasons, Appellate Court cannot and should not exercise the power under Order XLI, rule 27 of CPC. The exercise of such power should be for valid reasons i.e., upon the fulfilment of the conditions precedent, which is not forthcoming in the present case. The impugned Judgment is capricious and perverse.

For the foregoing reasons, the appeal is allowed and the impugned Judgment and Decree set aside. R.A. No. 216/2011 is restored for consideration afresh. Both parties shall appear in the Court of Senior Civil Judge, Malur, on 03.04.2017 and receive orders. Court below shall keep in view the observation made supra and decide the appeal and I.A.No.3 on or before 31.08.2017.

In the said case it was also felt that the remand of the case leads to delay and causes prejudice to the parties to the *lis*, as an unwarranted order of remand gives the litigation an undeserved lease of the life and, therefore, must be avoided. When the evidence is available, the Court should decide the appeal one way or the other. If necessary issue has not been raised, issues can be re-casted or additional issue raised and the appeal should be decided. Appellate Court being headed by the Senior and experienced judicial Officer should keep in view the power under Section 107 of CPC and the guidelines provided as per Order XLI, Rules 24 to 31 of CPC and decide the matter.

164. Order XLI, Rule 31 and Order VII7, Rule 3 – Eviction from disputed property

In *Mohd. Hanif* v. *Syed Khan,* R 2017 (8) ADJ 461: 2017 (124) ALR 330, the plaintiffs filed a suit being Original Suit No. 47 of 1977 with a prayer for eviction of the defendant from the disputed land and for arrears of rent amounting to Rs. 600/- along with Rs. 80/- as damages. The further relief for mandatory injunction for the removal of certain illegal constructions as had been erected by the defendant over the disputed land was also there. Permanent injunction was also prayed for to restrain the defendants from making any further constructions. The suit was dismissed. However, the First Appellate Court allowed the appeal and decreed the suit.

The plaintiffs-respondents had come up with a case that the disputed property was situate in Kasba Bhula Shahari, Pargana Mohammadabad, District Ghazipur and was numbered as plot no. 107/2 having an area of 2 Biswas and 4 Dhurs. The property, as per the plaint case, belonged to the father of the plaintiffs, Tayyab Khan who was the owner in possession of the suit property. The further averment was that 20 years prior to the filing of the suit, the plaintiffs along with their father had erected a verandah and a room to the west of the disputed property and the remaining land in the east of the built up portion was kept vacant for their use as sehan and land appurtenant. The further allegation was that 15 years prior to the institution of the suit, the father of the plaintiffs, Tayyab Khan died and thereafter, the plaintiffs became bhoomidhars of plot no. 107/ 2. As per the plaint allegations, the defendant had requested the plaintiffs for letting out the room at the rate of Rs. 20/- per month for running a shop and ever since then the defendants had been continuing in possession and had been paying regular rent. However, the plaintiffs alleged that when they had gone out of their home town in connection with their jobs then the defendant had inducted an outsider by the name of Panna and the defendant further had opened a door on the eastern side of the room and had begun to use the vacant land by putting his Nad and Chhappar etc. The further allegation was that upon having found the illegal entry of the defendant over the land in question and the concomitant mutation in revenue records plaintiffs sent a registered notice to the defendant for eviction and for arrears of rent. The defendant denied his status of a1-13 tenant and in his reply, stated that in fact, the defendant was the owner of the property in question. This necessitated the filing of the suit. The written statement of the defendant was filed denying the allegations of the plaint, specially that t1-13he disputed land was situate in plot no. 107/2.

The defendant also stated that in fact the owner of the disputed plot was the father of the plaintiffs namely Tayyab Khan and that around 25 years prior to the filing of the suit, Tayyab Khan had orally gifted the property in question to the defendant in the presence of various witnesses.

The further case of the defendant was that he had constructed the room and verandah in question in 1953 and the land east of the verandah and the room was used by him as his sehan and that after 1952-53 when the plaintiffs' father, Tayyab Khan had gifted the property to the defendant, he had lost all interest in the property. Further, it was stated that the suit itself was barred by limitation, especially when before 1976 and after 1952, no objection was made by either the plaintiffs or their father regarding the possession of the defendant.

The Trial Court after framing 16 issues, while deciding issues no. 1, 14 and 15, very categorically held, after taking into account all the oral and documentary evidence, that the property in dispute was gifted by Tayyab Khan, father of the plaintiffs to the defendant and that the defendant was not a tenant in the disputed property in question but was an owner in possession of it. Still further, while dealing with issue no. 2, which was, as to whether the disputed property was situate in plot no. 107/2, the Trial Court categorically found that only some portion of the land and house in question was situate in the northern portion of plot no. 107/2 of Kasba Bhula Shahari, Pargana Mohammadabad.

The First Appellate Court however, reversed the judgment of the Trial Court and after reassessing the evidence which was available on the record gave its own finding and allowed the appeal and decreed the suit. However, with regard to issue no.2 i.e. about the location of the disputed plot, as to whether it was situate on plot no. 107/2 the finding of the Trial Court was affirmed as the same had also not been challenged by the appellant in the first appeal.

The Court said, having heard the learned counsel for the parties and after having gone through the record, I am of the view that the first appeal was wrongly allowed. When the property itself was not identifiable and it was vaguely found that some portion of the disputed property fell in plot no. 107/2, then the further exercise of dealing with the remaining issues, which has been undertaken by the two courts below, was an exercise in futility.

The Courts could have proceeded with the case had they found that the suit property was contained in the boundaries as were given in the plaint map. This finding also was not arrived at by the First Appellate Court. Also the reversal of the findings of fact as were arrived at by the Trial Court was done on absolutely irrelevant consideration.

The submission of the appellant-defendant that the judgement of the court below was in contravention of Order 41, Rule 31 also appears to be correct in view of the law laid down in 2017 (2) SCC 415: 2016 (12) SCALE 902 (*Laliteshwar Prasad Singh* v. *S.P. Srivastava (D) Thr. Lrs.*).

Upon finding that the judgment of the First Appellate Court was in contravention of the provisions of Order XLI, rule 31 C.P.C., this Court ought to have remanded the matter but in view of the fact that the property was not properly identifiable (as per Order VII, rule 3 CPC) as it was not found to be situate in plot no. 107/2 but was only found to have been located in some northern portion of it, I do not think that the case could be proceeded with and in such circumstances, there is no other option but to allow the appeal, set aside the judgment and decree dated 20.3.1990 and dismiss the suit.

165. Order XLI, Rule 22 – Limitation Act, 1963 Section 5 – Rajasthan Motor Vehicles Rules, 1990, Rule 10.28

In *Kailash Chand Meena* v. *Suresh Yadav*, 2017 (2) TAC 339: 2017 (3) RLC 2282 (Raj) the High Court considered whether the remedy for cross objection was available to the respondent cross objector or not.

Learned counsel for the appellant further contended that the appeal has not been admitted as yet thus, the cross objections are not maintainable. The owner has remedy to file appeal under section 173 of Motor Vehicles Act with pre- requisite condition of depositing 50% of the awarded amount or Rs.25,000/-, which ever is less. As such the remedy of cross-objections is not available to the owner, because he cannot bye pass mandatory condition incorporated in Section 173 of the Act of 1988. The learned counsel prayed to allow the appeal and liability of the awarded amount may be imposed upon all the non complaint/ respondents jointly and severally and to dismiss the cross-objections filed by the owner of the vehicle. In support of his contentions, learned counsel for the appellant placed reliance on:—

A. *Khenyei* v. *New India Assurance Co. Ltd.*, 2015 ACJ 1441: AIR 2015 SC 2261

B. *Pawan Kumar* v. *Harkishan Dass Mohal Lal*, 2014 (1) ACTC (SC) 270: 2014 (10) SCALE 27

C. *R.D. Hattangadi* v. *Pest Control (India) Pvt. Ltd.*, 1995 ACJ 366: AIR 1995 SC 755.

D. *Mahadev Govind Gharge* v. *The Special Land Acquisition Officer*, (2011) 6 SCC 321: AIR 2011 SC 2439

E. *East India Hotels (The) Ltd.* v. *Smt. Mahendra Kumari, Since deceased, through her LR Jitendra*, [2008] 3 RLW (Raj) 2345: AIR 2008 Raj 131

F. *Lata* v. *United India Insurance Co. Ltd.*, 2005 ACJ 857: I (2005) ACC 788

G. *Abhilasha Bai* v. *Arvind Kumar*, 2003 ACJ 49: 2002 (2) MPLJ 493.

H. *Ram Chandra Singh* v. *Savitri Devi*, (2003) 8 SCC 319: 2003 (8) SCALE 505

I. *Smt. Shrisht Dhawan* v. *Shaw Brothers*, AIR 1992 SC 1555.

The High Court said, we have given anxious consideration, to the contentions of learned counsel for the parties and perused the record of the case. First of all, we have to decide whether the remedy of cross objections envisaged under Order XLI, rule 22 of CPC is available to the respondent/cross-objector or not?

It is contended by of learned counsel for the appellant that the owner has remedy to file appeal under Section 173 of the Motor Vehicles Act and before filing the appeal there is a pre requisite condition for depositing the amount, as such the remedy of cross-objections is not available to him because he cannot byepass the mandatory condition incorporated in section 173 of the Motor Vehicles Act, 1988. It is also contended that provisions of cross-objections under Order XLI, rule 22 of CPC are not applicable to the appeal filed under section 173 of the Act 1988, as the concerned Rules does not provide so. Learned counsel attracted our attention to Rule 10.28 of Rajasthan Motor Vehicle Rules, 1990 (hereinafter referred to as "the Rules of 1990") and submitted that provisions of Order XLI, rule 22 of CPC have not been made applicable to the claim proceedings and therefore, the cross-objections are liable to be dismissed, on this score alone.

We are not persuaded with the contention of learned counsel for the appellant. Rule 10.28 of the Rules of 1990 makes provisions for procedure to be followed by the Claims Tribunal in holding inquiries. Certain sections and provisions of First Schedule of the Code, 1908 envisaged in Rule 10.28, have been made applicable to the proceedings before the Claims Tribunal. For filing and hearing of appeals, provisions have been made in Rule 10.31 of Rules of 1990, which are as under:—

> 10.31. *Form of Appeal and Contents of Memorandum.*—(1) Every Appeal against the award of the Claims Tribunal shall be preferred in the form of a memorandum signed by the appellant or an Advocate or Attorney of the High Court duly authorised in that behalf by the applicant and presented to the High Court or to such officer as it appoints in this behalf. This memorandum shall be accompanied by a copy of the award.
>
> (2) The memorandum shall set forth concisely and under distinct heads the grounds of objection to the award appealed from without any argument or narrative, and such grounds shall be numbered consecutively.
>
> (3) Save as provided in sub-rule (1) and (2) the provisions of Order XXI and Order XLI1 in the First Schedule to the Code of Civil Procedure, 1908 (V of 1908) shall *mutatis mutandis* apply to appeals preferred to High Court under section 173.

From the above provisions, it is crystal clear that provisions of Order XLIin the First Schedule to the Code of Civil Procedure, 1908 *mutatis mutandis* applies to appeals preferred to High Court under section 173 of the Motor Vehicles Act, 1988.

In view of the discussions made above, the judgments relied upon by the appellant passed in *Lata* v. *United India Insurance Company Ltd.* (supra), *Abhilasha Bai* v. *Arvind Kumar* (supra), are not of much help to the appellant and we are of the considered opinion that provisions of Rule 22 Order XLI of CPC regarding filing of cross objections by the respondents, also applies in the appeals preferred under section 173 of the Motor Vehicles Act, 1988.

25. It is also contended by learned counsel for the appellant that the cross objections filed by the respondent/cross-objector are barred by limitation, because the cross objections can be filed within 30 days from the date of hearing. It is argued that the appeal has still not been admitted. Moreover, the appellant came to know of the filing of appeal on 15/02/2014, when first vakalatnama was filed on his behalf before this Hon'ble Court and the cross objections have been filed by the respondent No. 2 on 16/10/2015, as such the cross objections cannot be considered being filed within the period of limitation, prescribed for.

166. Order XLI., Rule 5 – Section 106 TP Act – Open Land – Termination of Tenancy

In *Mr. Mujibur Rehman Haji Israr Alam Siddiqui* v. *M/s K.T. Kubal and Co.*, 2017 (5) AIR Bom R 301, this suit was contested by the Defendant by filing its written statement. Thereafter, issues were framed by the Trial Court and on the basis of these issues, the parties led their respective evidence. The Trial Court, thereafter, after hearing the parties, by it judgment and order dated 3rd May 2016 decreed the suit and ordered eviction of the Defendant. The Trial Court further also ordered an inquiry into mesne profits under the provisions of Order XX, Rule 12 of the CPC.

Being aggrieved by this judgment and order of the Trial Court, the Defendant preferred an Appeal before the Appellate Bench of the Small Causes Court, Mumbai viz. PSCC Appeal No.303 of 2016.

I must mention here that as there was some bona fide error in the judgment and decree dated 3rd May, 2016 regarding the description of the suit property, the Plaintiff moved the Trial Court for modification/clarification of the said judgment and decree. The Trial Court by its order dated 1st July, 2016 accordingly corrected/modified the description of the suit property as mentioned in its earlier judgment and decree of 3rd May, 2016.

Be that as it may, along with the Appeal filed by the Defendant challenging the decree dated 3rd May 2016, the Defendant also preferred a Stay Application (Exh.7) seeking a stay of the execution of the decree. The order impugned in this Writ Petition (dated 22nd September, 2016) has been passed in this Stay Application (Exh.7). By the impugned order, the execution of the decree against the Defendant was stayed subject to the Defendant depositing compensation at the rate of Rs. 1,50,000 per month from May 2016 to September 2016 within a period of three months from the date of the order. Further monthly compensation at the same rate was also to be deposited on or before the 10th day of each month, pending the hearing and final disposal of the Appeal. Over and above this, the

Defendant was also directed to deposit arrears of rent which the Petitioner herein was allowed to withdraw.

167. Rule 5 – Refusal to stay execution proceeding – Challenged

In *Noor Bandi* v. *Ajijul Haque,* (Patna), 2017 (2) PLJR 54: 2017 (175) AIC 366 Patna High Court considered the order passed by the learned lower court and said, perused the impugned order dated 08.04.2016 whereby the learned 6th Additional District Judge, Gopalganj in Title Appeal No.28 of 2014 rejected the stay application filed by the petitioners under Order XLI, Rule 5 of the Code of Civil Procedure and refused to stay the further proceeding of Execution Case No.06 of 2014.

The learned counsel for the petitioners submitted that the final decree has been passed in partition suit and now the respondents are taking steps for delivery of possession of the property, which are in possession of the petitioners.

The learned counsel for the respondents referred to the Division Bench decision of this Court in the case of *Mostt. Ramkali Devi* v. *Jagdish Prasad,* 2001 (4) PLJR 273 and submitted that delivery of possession of the properties, which are either agricultural or orchard cannot be stayed as no prejudice will be caused to the judgment-debtor.

It may be mentioned here that this Court in the case of *Byasdeo Mandal* v. *Smt. Longi Devi* in Second Appeal No. 392 of 2009 on 16.08.2012 relying on this Division Bench decision of the High Court wherein it has been held that it is not the practise of Patna High Court to stay delivery of possession of the properties which are either agricultural or orchard rejected the stay application filed before this court in the aforesaid Second Appeal. Against this order dated 16.08.2012 the appellant therein filed Civil Appeal No. 8775 of 2013 arising out of S.L.P.(C) No. 26142 of 2012. The Supreme Court granted leave and the Hon'ble Supreme Court held that having regard to the fact that Second Appeal is pending before the High Court and the appellant is in possession of the subject property, we are satisfied that if the decree of the first appellate court is allowed to be executed during pendency of the Second Appeal, the appellant may be put to irreparable loss and accordingly the Supreme Court allowed the appeal and directed that during the pendency of the Second Appeal status quo with regard to subject property shall be maintained. In other words, it can very safely be held that impliedly the Division Bench decision has already been overruled because the order of this Court was on the basis of Division Bench decision. The order of this court was set aside by allowing the Special Leave Petition meaning thereby the Division Bench decision has been overruled.

In view of the above facts and circumstances of the case this civil miscellaneous application is allowed. The impugned order dated 08.04.2016 passed by 6th Additional District Judge, Gopalganj in Title Appeal No. 28 of 2014 is hereby set aside. The stay application under Order XLI, Rule 5 CPC filed by the petitioners herein is allowed. The further proceeding in Execution Case No. 06 of 2014 is stayed till the disposal of the title appeal.

168. Order XLI, Rule 11 – Order of High Court set aside and remanded

In *Kanailal* v. *Ram Chandra Singh,* 2017 (11) SCALE 163 the Apex Court directed, it is clear from mere reading of the Rule 31(a) to (d) that it makes it legally obligatory upon the Appellate Court (both-first and second Appellate Court) as to what should the judgment of the Appellate Court contain. Sub-clause(a) provides that the judgment must formulate and state the points arising in the case for determination. Sub-clause (b) provides that the Court must give decision on such points and sub- clause(c) provides that the judgment shall state the reasons for the decision. So far as sub-clause (d) is concerned, it applies in those cases where the Appellate Court has reversed the decree. In such case, the Court has to specify the relief to which the appellant has become entitled to as a result of the decree having been reversed in appeal at his instance.

While deciding the second appeal which lies only to the High Court, the Court has to further ensure compliance of the requirements of Section 100 of the Code in addition to the requirements of Order XLI, Rule 31 of the Code set out above.

In other words, the High Court while hearing the second appeal at the time of its admission has to first find out whether the second appeal involves any substantial question(s) of law and if the Court finds that the appeal does involve any substantial question(s) of law then such question(s) is/are required to be formulated. The appeal can be then heard finally only on such formulated question(s). (See Santosh Hazari).

If however, the Court, at the time of hearing the appeal on the question of admission, comes to a conclusion that the appeal does not involve any such question within the meaning of section 100 of the Code, then it has to pass a reasoned order keeping in view the requirements of Order XLI, Rule 31 set out above. Indeed, this being the mandatory requirements of law, its non-compliance by the Appellate Court render their judgment bad in law.

169. Order XLI, Rule 23 – Karnataka Land Reforms Act, 1961 – Section 21

In *B.S. Mahabala* v. *Gopala Krishna,* 2017 AIR SC 3046:v 2017 (5) SCALE 145 the High Court said, the argument of the Appellant that the order passed by the Land Tribunal on 04.10.1980 cannot be allowed to be challenged at this distance of time, in our opinion, is misplaced. We agree with the view expressed by the Division Bench of the High Court that the Land Tribunal committed manifest jurisdictional error by passing an order in favour of the Appellant behind the back of the legal representatives of the deceased tenant/applicant. For, it could not have proceeded with the inquiry behind the back of the legal representatives of the deceased tenant without bringing them on record in the proceedings pending before it. Such exercise of jurisdiction is bordering on passing an order which is nullity in the eyes of law. It would have been a different matter if the Land Tribunal had consciously proceeded on being satisfied that the deceased tenant Applicant has not left behind any legal representative who could espouse his or their cause further. No attempt was made by the Land Tribunal to ascertain about the possibility of any objection from any legal representative of the deceased tenant/Applicant before bestowing occupancy rights in favour of the Appellant on the basis of the alleged Will executed by Channappa Poojary.

As the order passed by the Land Tribunal is vitiated due to failure to bring on record the legal representatives of deceased Applicant Channappa Poojary and also without considering the mandate of section 21 of the Act, the objection regarding the manner of interference by the Learned Single Judge of the High Court does not commend to us. The Respondent No. 1 in his writ petition had offered explanation about the circumstances in which he could file the writ petition only after getting knowledge of the order in the 1st week of April, 2004. Further, the plea of laches cannot be countenanced in light of the assertion of the Respondent No. 1 that, taking advantage of his minority, the Appellant succeeded in misleading the Land Tribunal to pass an order in his favour on the basis of an alleged Will executed by Channappa Poojary. This technical plea has been rightly negatived by the High Court in the fact situation of the present case involving the permissibility of transfer of tenancy by a Will to third person who is not covered by the excepted category of persons. Thus, the legal principle expounded in the case of *State of Rajasthan* v. *D.R. Laxmi,* (1996) 6 SCC 445: 1996 (7) SCALE 316 and *Tayabbhai M. Bagasarwalla* v. *Hind Rubber Industries Pvt. Ltd.,* 1997 (2) RCR (Civil) 473: 1997 (2) RCR (Rent) 682: (1997) 3 SCC 443, will be of no avail to the Appellant. The Respondent No. 1 has justly relied on the decisions in the case of Hasham Abbas Sayyad (supra) to buttress his plea that the objection regarding procedural matters cannot come in the way in a case where an order passed by the Tribunal is without jurisdiction as in this case and that issue can be raised at any stage [see Zuari Cement Limited.

As aforesaid, the Tribunal must and will have to first consider the legal position as to whether the Appellant can legitimately claim to be a legal heir of the deceased tenant within the meaning of Section 21 read with 2(12) and other applicable provisions of the said Act; and only on recording finding on that issue in favour of the Appellant, further inquiry into the matter regarding the admissibility and genuineness of the alleged Will may become necessary. Since the parties have been relegated before the Land Tribunal, all questions about the genuineness and the legitimacy of their claim can be and will have to be considered by the said Authority in the first place on its own merit and in accordance with law without being influenced by any observation made by the learned Single Judge or the Division Bench of the High Court or for that matter, in the present judgment.

ORDER XLII

APPEALS FROM APPELLATE DECREES

1. Procedure.—The rules of Order XLI shall apply, so far as may be, to appeals from appellate decrees.

High Court Amendment.—

Allahabad.—In Order XLII, for rule 1, substitute the following rule, namely:—

> "1. The rules of Order XLI and Order XLIA shall apply, so far as may be, to appeals from appellate decrees, subject to the following proviso:

Every memorandum of appeal from an appellate decree shall be accompanied by a copy of the decree appealed from unless the Court sees fit to dispense with either or all of them—

(1) a copy of the judgment on which the said decree is found,—

(2) a copy of the judgment of the Court of the first instance, and

(3) a copy of the finding of the Civil or the Revenue Court, as the case may be, where an issue was remitted to such Court for decision."

[*Vide* Notification No. 14186/VII-d-147, dated 22nd December, 1951.]

Calcutta.—In Order XLII, for rule 1, substitute the following rule, namely:—

"1. The rules of Order XLI shall apply, so far as may be, to appeals from appellate decrees:

Provided that every memorandum of appeal from an appellate decree shall be accompanied by a copy of the decree appealed from and also (unless the Court sees fit to dispense within any or all of them), by copies of the judgment on which the said decree is founded and of the judgment and decree of the Court of first instance."

[*Vide* Notification No. 1750-G, dated 15th February, 1938.]

Gauhati.—Same as in Calcutta.

Kerala.—In Order XLII, in rule 1,—

(a) after the words "Order XLI", insert the words "as modified by Order XLIA".

[*Vide* Notification No. 1-32897/68, dated 5th January, 1970.]

(b) after rule 1, insert the following rule, namely:—

"2. Memo to be typed or printed. What to accompany memorandum.- (1) The memorandum of appeal shall be printed or type written and shall be accompanied by a certified copy of the decree and judgment of the appellate court and (unless the Court dispenses therewith) a certified copy of the decree and judgment of the Court of first instance.

(2) Copies of documents to be construed.—If any ground of appeal is based upon the construction of a document, a true copy of such document shall be presented with the memorandum of appeal. (w.e.f. 9-6-1959)"

Punjab.—In Order XLII, after rule 1, insert the following rule, namely:—

"2. In addition to the copies specified in Order XLI, rule 1, the memorandum of appeal shall be accompanied by a copy of the judgment of the Court of first instance, unless the appellate court dispenses therewith."

[*Vide* Notification No. 4685-G, dated 17th October, 1919 and Notification No. 138-G, dated 19th March, 1926.]

Rajasthan.—In Order XLII, for rule 1, substitute the following rule, namely:—

"1. Procedure.—The rule of Order XLI shall apply, so far as may be, to appeals from appellate decree, subject to the following proviso;

Every memorandum of appeal from an appellate decree shall be accompanied by a copy of the decree appealed from and unless the Court sees fit to dispense with either or all of them—

(1) a copy of the judgment on which the said decree is founded,

(2) a copy of the judgment of the Court of the first instance, and

(3) a copy of the finding of the Civil or Revenue Court, as the case may be, whereas issue was remitted to such Court for decision."

2. Power of Court to direct that the appeal be heard on the question formulated by it.—At the time of making an order under rule 11 or Order XLI for the hearing of a second appeal, the Court shall formulate the substantial question of law as required by section 100 and in doing so, the Court may direct that the second appeal be heard on the question so formulated and it shall not be open to the appellant to urge any other ground in the appeal without the leave of the Court, given in accordance with the provision of section 100.

3. Application of rule 14 of Order XLI.—Reference in sub-rule (4) of rule 14 of Order XLI to the Court of first instance shall, in the case of an appeal from an appellate decree or order, be construed as a reference to the Court to which the appeal was preferred from the original decree or order.

HIGH COURT AMENDMENT

Andhra Pradesh.—Same as in Madras.

Delhi.—Same as in Punjab.

Haryana.—Same as in Punjab.

Himachal Pradesh.—Same as in Punjab.

Karnataka.—For Order XLII, substitute the following Order, namely:—

1. The Rules contained in Order XLI and Order XLIA shall apply, so far as may be, to appeals to the High Court of Mysore from appellate decrees with the modifications contained in this Order.
2. The memorandum of appeal shall be accompanied by one certified copy each of the decree and judgment of the Court of the first instance and one certified copy each of the decree and judgment of the appellate court.
3. If any ground of appeal is based upon the constriction of a document a copy of such document shall be presented with the memorandum of appeal, and if such document is not in the language of the Court a translation thereof or of a material portion thereof certified to be a true translation by the appellant's Advocate shall be presented."

Madras.—For Order XLII, substitute the following Order, namely:—

Order XLII, Rule 1—Scope and Application.—In a case where second appeal was dismissed without notice to the respondent the High Court of Madhya Pradesh held that where Second appeal is dismissed summarily without notice to respondent, dismissal cannot be assailed when its admission would have merely prolonged litigation. 1961 MPLJ (Notes) 189. A Division Bench of the

High Court of Nagpur held that order rejecting application for restoration is not a decree. Hence, no L.P.A. lies —Letters Patent (Nag) O. 110 1952 Nag LJ (Notes) 28 (DB).

Order XLII, rule 1, C.P.C., provides that the rules of Order XLI, shall apply, so far as may be, to appeals from appellate decree. Order XLI, rule 22 which allows the respondent to support the decree on any of the grounds decided against him in the Court below, is a rule governing first appeals wherein questions of fact as well as law can be agitated. This rule applies "so far as may be" to appeals from appellate decrees. It clearly means that if any other provision prohibits him from agitating any of the grounds he would not be able to support the decree on those grounds. Sections 100 and 101, C.P.C., lay down such prohibition. What these sections permit the Court of second appeal to do is to set aside that decision which comes within the provisions of clauses (a), (b) or (c) of section 100 and no other decision. So a Court of second appeal cannot interfere with a finding of fact either at the instance of the appellant or at the instance of the respondent if there is evidence to support it. It follows, therefore, that a respondent in second appeal is not entitled to support the decree of the first appellate court by contesting a finding of fact of that Court. Per Mya Bu, J. in AIR 1939 Rang 59, dist. from; ILR 17 Cal 291 (PC); *Durga Chowdhrani* v. *Jawahir Singh*, 17 IA 122: ILR 18 Cal 23 (PC); *Ramratan Shukul* v. *Mussumat Nandu*, 19 IA 1: ILR 19 Cal 249 (PC) and *Nafar Chandra Pal* v. *Shukur*, AIR 1918 PC 92: 45 IA 183, referred to; *Kesheo* v. *Tukaram*, ILR 1951 Nag 301: 1951 Nag LJ 167: AIR 1951 Nag 8 (9)(Pt C) (Pr 5).

Order XLII, rule 1 and Order XLI, rule 22—Second appeal—Respondent's right to contest finding of fact.—The Privy Council had examined the scope of Order XLI and XLII and held that Order XLII, rule 1, C.P.C., provides that the rules of Order XLI, shall apply, so far as may be, to appeals from appellate decree. Order XLI, rule 22 which allows the respondent to support the decree on any of the grounds decided against him in the Court below, is a rule governing first appeals wherein questions of fact as well as law can be agitated. This rule applies "so far as may be" to appeals from appellate decrees. It clearly means that if any other provision prohibits him from agitating any of the grounds he would not be able to support the decree on those grounds. Sections 100 and 101, C.P.C., lay down such prohibition. What these sections permit the Court of second appeal to do is to set aside that decision which comes within the provisions of cls. (a), (b) or (c) of section 100 and no other decision. So a Court of second appeal cannot interfere with a finding of fact either at the instance of the appellant or at the instance of the respondent if there is evidence to support it. It follows, therefore, that a respondent in second appeal is not entitled to support the decree of the first appellate court by contesting a finding of fact of that Court. Per Mya Bu, J. in AIR 1939 Rang 59, dist. from; *Pertab Chunder Ghose* v. *Mohendra Nath Purkait*, 16 IA 233: ILR 17 Cal 291 (PC); *Durga Chowdhrani* v. *Jawahir Singh*, 17 IA 122: ILR 18 Cal 23 (PC); *Ramratan Shukul* v. *Mussumat Nandu*, 19 IA 1: ILR 19 Cal 249 (PC) and *Nafar Chandra Pal* v. *Shukur*, AIR 1918 PC 92: 45 IA 183, referred to; *Kesheo* v. *Tukaram*, ILR 1951 Nag 301: 1951 Nag LJ 167: AIR 1951 Nag 8 (9)(Pt C) (Pr 5).

Order XLII, rule 1—Limitation—The High Court of Punjab examined the effect of filing of copy after expiry of the period of limitation and said that where Second appeal presented without copy of judgment appealed against and the copy is filed after limitation—Time taken, for obtaining trial court's judgment, if can be excluded under section 12, Limitation Act. *See* Limitation Act (1908), section 12. AIR 1955 NUC (Punj) 2516. Application under section 5, Limitation Act, to excuse delay necessary—Power of Registrar to grant time for filing copies on oral request can be availed of. *Mool Chand* v. *Kamta Prasad*, AIR 1961 All 595 (597, 598) (Prs 8, 14, 16, 17). A Full Bench of the High Court of Punjab said that where plea of limitation is not raised in grounds of second appeal, it can be allowed at stage of hearing before Full Bench. *Santa Singh Gopal Singh* v. *Rajinder Singh Bur Singh*, AIR 1965 Punj 415: ILR (1965) 2 Punj 97 (FB).

Second Appeal to High Court—Power of Court to dispense with printed copies of judgment and to receive typed copies instead.—The High Court of Andhra Pradesh said that printed copies of the judgment had to he filed and that type-written copies of judgment were not sufficient to meet the requirements of law. Printed copies of judgment cannot be dispensed with in such a way as to allow typed copies to be filed in their place. Unreported decision in C.M.P. No. 9886 of 1980, M.-3-1-1981 (AP), followed. Obiter:—The power of the appellate court to dispense with copies of the judgment on which the appeal is founded is not positively given by Order XLI, rule 1, Civil Procedure Code, but is only referred to in Order XLI, rule 1, as existent even independent of Order XLI, rule 1. So that, under Order XLII, Civil Procedure Code also, the High Court has power to dispense with copies of the lower courts' judgments in suitable cases. Also held that this is not a fit case for dispensing with copies of judgment altogether or of printed copies in particular; *Kallappa* v. *Sangamma*, (1965) 2 Andh WR 472: (1965) 2 Andh LT 367: AIR 1966 AP 181.

Order XLII, rule 1 and Order XLI, rule 22 and rule 2.—Second appeal.— Respondent's right to contest finding of fact. Order XLII, rule 1, C.P.C., provides that the rules of Order XLI, shall apply, so far as may be, to appeals from appellate decree. Order XLI, rule 22 which allows the respondent to support the decree on any of the grounds decided against him in the Court below, is a rule governing first appeals wherein questions of fact as well as law can be agitated. This rule applies "so far as may be" to appeals from appellate decrees. It clearly means that if any other provision prohibits him from agitating any of the grounds he would not be able to support the decree on those grounds. Sections 100 and 101 C.P.C., lay down such prohibition. What these sections permit the Court of second appeal to do is to set aside that decision which comes within the provisions of cls. (a), (b) or (c) of section 100 and no other decision. So a Court of second appeal cannot interfere with a finding of fact either at the instance of the appellant or at the instance of the respondent if there is evidence to support it. It follows, therefore, that a respondent in second appeal is not entitled to support the decree of the first appellate court by contesting a finding of fact of that Court. *Per* Mya Bu, J. in *Ma Lon* v. *Ma Mya May*, AIR 1939 Rang 59: 179 IC 946, diss. from; *Pertab Chunder Ghose* v. *Mohendra Nath Purkait*, 16 IA 233: ILR 17 Cal 291 (PC); *Durga Chowdhrani* v. *Jawahir Singh*, 17 IA 122: ILR 18

Cal 23 (PC); *Ramratan Shukul* v. *Mussumat Nandu*, 19 IA 1: ILR 19 Cal 249 (PC) and *Nafar Chandra Pal* v. *Shukur*, AIR 1918 PC 92: 45 IA 183, referred to; *Kesheo* v. *Tukaram*, ILR 1951 Nag 301: AIR 1951 Nag 8: 1951 Nag LJ 167: *Kesheo* v. *Tukaram*, ILR 1951 Nag 301: 1951 Nag LJ 167: AIR 1951 Nag 8 (9) (Pt C) (Pr 5).

"ORDER XLII

APPEALS FROM APPELLATE DECREE

1. The rules of Order XLI and Order XLIA shall apply, so far as may be, to appeals to the High Court of Judicature at Madras from appellate decrees with the modifications contained in this Order.

2. (1) The memorandum of appeal shall be printed or type-written and shall be accompanied by the following papers;

(2) One certified copy of the decrees of the Court of first instance and of the appellate court and four printed copies of each of the judgments of the said Courts, one copy of each judgment being a certified copy;

(3) If any ground of appeal is based upon the construction of a document, a printed or type-written copy of such document shall be presented with the memorandum of appeal:

Provided that if such document is not in the English language and the appellant appears by a pleader, an English translation of the document certified by the pleader to be a correct translation shall be presented.

3. If the appellant fails to comply with this rule, the appeal may be dismissed." (w.e.f. 18-10-1917).

Punjab.—In Order XLII, after rule 1, insert the following, namely:—

> "2. In addition to the copies specified in Order XLI, rule 1, the memorandum of appeal shall be accompanied by a copy of the judgment of the Court of first instance, unless the Appellate Court dispenses therewith", (w.e.f. 9-6-1959)

Kerala.—After Order XLII, insert the following Order, namely:—

ORDER XLII

APPEALS FROM DECREES AND ORDERS OF SINGLE JUDGE DIVISION BENCH OF THE HIGH COURT

Procedure.—The Rules of Orders XLI and XLIA shall apply, so far as may be, to appeals from decrees and orders of a Single Judge to a Division Bench." (w.e.f. 9-6-1959).

1. Section 100 Civil Procedure Code, Order XLII, Rule 2 and 11- Second appeal before High Court

In *D.N. Joshi (D)* v. *D.C. Harris*, (SC) 2017 AIR SC 3105: 2017 (7) SCALE 216: 2017 (3) Jharkhand R 532: 2017 (6) MLJ 113 On 13.03.1980, the appeal was listed for hearing under Order LXI, Rule 11. It was summarily dismissed for default with the observation that no question of law, much less substantial question of law, was involved. By this time, the C.P.C. was amended in the year 1976 whereby substantial question of law was required to be formulated in the memo of second appeal and by the High Court whilst admitting such appeal.

As the second appeal was dismissed for default, the respondents moved an application for restoration of the appeal. The said appeal was restored on 7th May, 1980, after recalling the earlier order. That order reads thus:

> "Heard learned counsel for the appellants. I recall my order dated 13.03.1980."

Thereafter, the learned Single Judge by a separate order admitted the second appeal on the same day, with one word, "Admit". After establishment of the High Court of Uttarakhand at Nainital, the second appeal stood transferred to that High Court and was assigned a new number being Second Appeal No. 1269 of 2001.

Under the amended section 100 of C.P.C., substantial questions of law were required to be framed. Therefore, an application for amendment of the second appeal was filed before the High Court of Uttarakhand by the respondents (appellants in the said appeal) for adding substantial questions of law.

The said application was opposed by the appellants. But, after hearing both the parties, the High Court allowed the application for amendment and observed that the court would frame questions of law at the time of hearing of the appeal. The said order dated 15th July, 2006, reads thus:

> "15.07.2006
>
> Sri S.P. Dubey Learned Counsel for the appellant has submitted an Amendment Application before this Court and the copy of the said application has been served to Sri Arvind Vashisht learned Counsel for the respondents(s).
>
> It has been alleged that the substantial question of law as shown in para 2 of the Amendment Application may be added in the Memo of Appeal.
>
> Sri Vashist learned Counsel for the respondent objected that the questions mentioned in the Amendment application do not arise in the present appeal. No substantial question of law has been framed by this Court.
>
> The Court will have to frame the question afresh at the time of hearing. This point will be considered at the time of framing of substantial question of law.
>
> Amendment application is allowed. Let the amendment be incorporated within a week.

At the stage of hearing of the appeal, the Learned Single Judge of the High Court, being conscious of the earlier order dated 15th July, 2006, in the impugned judgment, has noted thus:

> "9. Section 100 of Code of Civil Procedure, 1908, was amended vide Act No. 104 of 1976 w.e.f. 01.02.1977 whereafter it became necessary to formulate the substantial question of law at the time of admitting the Second Appeal. Since the Second Appeal was presented before Allahabad High Court on 20.05.1974 and admitted there, as such at that point of time it was not necessary to formulate substantial question of law that is why it

appears that in this appeal no substantial question of law was formulated. However, following question of law is involved in this appeal, which requires to be answered:—

Whether both the Courts below erred in law in holding that Hiba (gift) by Akhtari Begum in favour of Zamir Ahmad was not valid for want of delivery of possession with the same, if so, its effect?"

The High Court of Uttarakhand, by its impugned judgment and decree, allowed the appeal filed by the respondents herein by holding that the gift deed dated 31.05.1949 was valid and was accompanied by possession. The High Court also referred to the judgment dated 15.02.1978 passed by the High Court of Judicature at Allahabad in relation to a dispute between the respondents herein and another tenant, in which the High Court found the selfsame gift deed dated 31.05.1949 as valid. Significantly, the said decision was challenged before this Court. That petition for special leave was dismissed on 24.04.1978.

Aggrieved, the appellants-defendants have challenged the impugned judgment, whereby the suit was decreed in favour of the respondents-plaintiffs and ordering eviction of the appellants-defendants from the suit premises with consequential directions.

The principal argument of the appellants-defendants is that: the High Court has exceeded its jurisdiction, firstly, by deciding the second appeal filed by the respondents-plaintiffs which was admitted without formulating the substantial question of law and secondly, because the High Court has re-appreciated the evidence to overturn the concurrent findings of facts on merit as recorded by two courts below. As regards the first point, reliance has been placed on the decisions of this court in *Kanai Lal Garari And Others* v. *Murari Ganguly*, (1999) 6 SCC 35: 2000 (38) ALR 283, *Narayanan Rajendran* v. *Lekshmy Sarojini*, 2009 (2) RCR (Civil) 286: 2009 (1) Recent Apex Judgments (RAJ) 278: (2009) 5 SCC 264, *Biswanath Ghosh (Dead) by Legal Representatives* v. *Gobinda Ghosh Alias Gobindha Chandra Ghosh*, 2014 (2) RCR (Civil) 407: 2014 (2) CDR 418 (SC): (2014) 11 SCC 605, *Ashok Rangnath Magar* v. *Shrikant Govindrao Sangvikar*, 2015 (4) RCR (Civil) 948: (2015) 16 SCC 763 and *Syeda Rahimunnisa* v. *Malan Bi (Dead) By Legal Representatives*, 2016 (4) RCR (Civil) 774: AIR 2016 SC 4653: (2016) 10 SCC 315. Reliance is also placed on section 97 of the Code of Civil Procedure Amendment Act 104 of 1976, in particular, clause (m) of sub-section (2) thereof. This is repeal and saving clause. Sub-section (2) opens with a non-obstante clause. The said provision including clause (m) thereof, reads thus:

The Court referred to the provisions of section 97 and said reliance is also placed on the provisions of Order XLI, rule 11 and Order 42, Rule 1 and 2 of the C.P.C. to contend that the High Court has acted without jurisdiction to admit the second appeal without formulating substantial question of law and also because it unjustly interfered with concurrent findings of facts.

The moot question is: whether the judgment under appeal rendered by the High Court should be treated as nullity and *non est*, as contended by the appellants? It is an admitted position that the second appeal was filed in the High Court of Judicature at Allahabad in 1974 and was admitted by the Registrar of the High Court on 20.05.1974 with further direction to list it for hearing before the court under Order XLI, Rule 11 on 08.07.1974. The second appeal was in fact, taken up for such hearing by the learned Single Judge on 13.03.1980, albeit after the amendment of section 100 of C.P.C. (vide Act 104 of 1974) which had already come into force on 01.02.1977. The appellants-defendants may be justified in relying on clause (m) of section 97 (2) of the Act 104 of 1976 which uses the expression "appeal had been admitted" on or before 01.02.1977. In the present case, the order of admitting the second appeal was passed by the Registrar on 20.05.1974. That order, however, has been passed by the Registrar in exercise of delegated powers under the High Court Rules and is not ascribable to an order passed under Order XLI, Rule 11 of C.P.C., which reads thus:

> ***"11. Power to dismiss appeal without sending notice to Lower Court-*** (1) The Appellate Court after fixing a day for hearing the appellant or his pleader and hearing him accordingly if he appears on that day may dismiss the appeal.
>
> (2) If on the day fixed or any other day to which the hearing may be adjourned the appellant does not appear when the appeal is called on for hearing, the Court may make an order that the appeal be dismissed.
>
> (3) The dismissal of an appeal under this rule shall be notified to the Court from whose decree the appeal is preferred.
>
> (4) Where an Appellate Court, not being the High Court, dismisses an appeal under sub-rule (1), it shall deliver a judgment, recording in brief its grounds for doing so, and a decree shall be drawn up in accordance with the judgment."

Sub-rule (1) of Rule 11 envisages fixing a day for hearing when the appellants or his pleader will be heard. Further, it is an enabling provision entitling the court to dismiss the appeal. Rule 11A postulates that every appeal shall be heard under Rule 11 preferably within sixty days from the date on which the memorandum of appeal is filed. Rule 12 provides that if the appeal is not dismissed after hearing under Rule 11, the court must fix a day for hearing the appeal. Neither Rule 11, 11A nor 12 prescribe that the court shall formulate substantial question of law before fixing a day for hearing the appeal. That duty of the court is spelt out from Order 42 dealing with appeals from Appellate Decrees.

We may now usefully refer to the provisions of Order XLII of C.P.C., which applies to the case on hand. It contains three Rules. The same read thus:

> "1. ***Procedure***—The rules of Order XLI shall apply, so far as may be, to appeals from appellate decrees.
>
> 2. ***Power of Court to direct that the appeal be heard on the question formulated by it.***—At the time of making an order under rule 11 of Order XLI for the hearing of a second appeal, the Court shall formulate the substantial question of law as required by section 100, and in doing so, the Court may direct that the second appeal be heard on the question so formulated and it shall not be open to the appellant to urge any other ground in the appeal without the leave of the Court, given in accordance with the provision of section 100.

3. ***Application of rule 14 of Order XLI***—Reference in sub-rule (4) of rule 14 of Order XLI to the Court to first instance shall, in the case of an appeal from an appellate decree or order, be construed as a reference to the Court to which the appeal was preferred from the original decree or order."

On a conjoint reading of Rule 2 Order 42 with Rule 11, Order 41, it is evident that the court is obliged to formulate substantial question of law on the day of hearing of the appeal (for admission under Rule 11) so that the second appeal can be heard on the question of law so formulated. The latter part of Rule 2 Order 42 presupposes that the grounds of challenge by the appellants will be circumscribed by the substantial question of law so formulated. At the same time, it gives enough discretion to the High Court to permit the parties to argue any other ground, only with the leave of the court. The purport of Section 100 has already been delineated by this court in several decisions, after the Amendment Act of 1976. The appellants-defendants have rightly invited our attention to those decisions.

In the facts of the present case there have been substantial compliance of section 100 of C.P.C., as amended. Significantly, the proviso to section 100 (5) read with the latter part of Rule 2 Order XLII enables the High Court to reframe the substantial question of law already formulated and even permit any other substantial question of law not formulated, after recording reasons, if it is satisfied that the case involves such question. This discretion has been bestowed on the High Court to ensure full, complete and effectual adjudication of all the matters in issue between the parties and to do complete justice. In our opinion, therefore, in the facts of the present case, there has been compliance of section 100 of C.P.C. as also Order XLII of C.P.C. It is not open to the appellants-defendants to now raise an issue of non-formulation of substantial question of law while admitting the appeal, having failed to challenge the order dated 07.05.1980 (admitting the second appeal) and dated 15.07.2006 (allowing the respondents-plaintiffs to amend the memorandum of second appeal with an observation that the court will formulate the substantial question of law at the time of hearing of the appeal). Suffice it to note that the High Court, has, in fact, formulated a substantial question of law and heard the parties on that question, as can be discerned from paragraph 9 of the impugned judgment. Therefore, we do not find any merit in the first contention raised by the appellants-defendants.

2. Order XLII, Rule 2 – Additional substantial question – Permissibility – Objection raised by respondent

In *Emkay Medicare Services* v. *The President, Rajasthan Medicare Relief Society*, 2017 AIR (Raj) 123 (Raj) during arguments advanced by learned counsel for the appellant, submission has been made that the tender forms submitted by defendant No. 4 - M/s Ganpati Diagnostic Center were not on the formats prescribed and issued by the President, RMRS. Tender forms were not signed by the proprictor of defendant No. 4 but only initials were affixed thereon. It has also been submitted that the notice inviting tender was issued by RMRS, which is a registered society and there was no role of the Government of Rajasthan in the tender process but with the intention to extend undue advantage to defendant No. 4, a committee under the Chairmanship of District Collector, Bikaner was constituted to finalize the tender process on the basis of political intervention and malice. After holding an unauthorized and unwarranted meeting of the committee, recommendation was made to the State Government for approval of the defendant No. 4 as lowest bidder and to finalize the tender in his favor. All the proceedings undertaken by the said committee in regard to the tender process were without any authority and to extend undue benefit to the defendant No. 4. While duly appreciating the evidence, learned trial Court passed the judgment and decree in favor of plaintiff, which was quashed and set aside by learned lower appellate Court without any basis and without taking the relevant facts and evidence into consideration. In support of the contentions raised, learned counsel for the appellant has placed reliance on number of judicial authorities.

The Court said, I may mention here that learned counsel for the appellant has referred to various judgments (48 in numbers) on various aspects of this case. Learned counsel for the respondent No.4 has also placed reliance on 22 judicial pronouncements in the submissions made in reply. Pains taking efforts put in by both learned Senior Advocates are worth appreciation. When there is an ambiguity in the legal proposition about any aspect, the judicial pronouncements are always required to be taken into consideration and prove helpful to form the view. But if the factual aspect is explicitly clear as per the ocular and documentary evidence, the provisions of law are directly applicable in the facts and circumstances of the case and the legal proposition is well settled and crystallized, then, to my view making extra efforts in referring multiple authorities on such aspects can only be an extravagance. It consumes the time and energy of the Courts and members of the Bar as well. When courts at all levels, more particularly the trial Courts, are clogged with arrears of cases and huge pendency, the time and energy can be invested more usefully in taking up more number of cases for hearing and disposing them. This may give more relief to the litigants waiting for their turn to come for disposal of pending cases. With this view, I feel inclined not to encumber this judgment with multiple reference of judicial pronouncement on the same point. But of course, it will be enlightening for me to take help of the relevant and most suitably applicable citations, wherever need arises to do so.

Since, these are civil second appeals, their hearing is required to be governed as per the provisions contained in section 100 and Order XLII CPC. Sub-section (5) of section 100 CPC is reproduced below:—

> "The appeal shall be heard on the question so formulated and the respondent shall, at the hearing of the appeal, be allowed to argue that the case does not involve such question.
>
> Provided that nothing in this sub-section shall be deemed to take away or abridge the power of the Court to hear, for reasons to be recorded, the appeal on any other substantial question of law, not formulated by it, if it is satisfied that the case involves such question."

Similarly Rule 2 Order XLII CPC is also required to be taken into consideration, which is as follows:—

> "Power of Court to direct that the appeal be heard on the question formulated by it.—At the time of making an order under Rule 11 Order 41 for the hearing of a second appeal, the Court shall formulate the substantial question of law as required by Section 100, and in doing so, the Court may direct that the second appeal be heard on the question so formulated and it shall not be open to the appellant to urge any other ground in the appeal without the leave of the Court, given in accordance with the provision of Section 100."

Both the provisions reiterated above restrict the scope of the hearing of second appeal on the substantial question of law formulated by the Court while admitting the appeal. As per Section 100(5) CPC, it is however left at the discretion of the Court, for the reasons to be recorded, to hear the appeal on any other substantial question of law not formulated by it, if it is satisfied that the case involves such question. Rule 2, Order XLII, CPC also speaks that it shall not be open to the appellant to urge any other grounds without leave of the Court. In light of these provisions, I find myself under legal obligation to restrict the scope of discussion in regard to these appeals, to the substantial questions of law mentioned hereinabove.

On perusal of the record, it appears that the objection raised by learned counsel for respondent No. 4 regarding suit having been filed by power of attorney of the plaintiff without any mention of this fact in the plaint as also the objection that the power of attorney has not been signed by its holder was never raised earlier before learned trial Court or first appellate Court. It has been laid down by Hon'ble Supreme Court in *Santosh Hazari* v. *Purshottam Tiwari (Deceased) by LRs,* reported in 2001 (3) SCC 179: AIR 2001 SC 965, that entirely new point raised for the first time before the High Court is not a substantial question involved in the case unless it goes to the root of the matter. It has also been observed by Hon'ble Supreme Court in *Kondiba Dagadu Kadam* v. *Savitribai Sopan Gujar,* reported in 1999 (3) SCC 722: AIR 1999 SC 2213, that where a point of law has not been pleaded or is found to be arisen between the parties in the absence of any factual format, litigants should not be allowed to raise that question as substantial question of law in second appeal.

3. Order XLII, Rule 1 – Evidence Act, 1872 Section 114 – Marriage – Presumption

In *Seenappa* v. *Smt. Gowramma, (Karnataka),* 2016 (1) Kant J 415 The substance of the plaintiff's case was that, she was the legally wedded wife of the defendant and their marriage was solemnised as per Hindu religious and customs 20 years back. After living together for two years, defendant started quarrelling with the plaintiff and demanded dowry, since the parents of the plaintiff are poor, they could not meet the demand of the defendant. Defendant deserted the plaintiff and got the second marriage with Padmavathamma without consent of the plaintiff. Defendant who is earning more than Rs. 10,000/- is capable to maintain and he is duty bound to maintain plaintiff. The substance of the entire case of the defendant is that, he never married plaintiff and his only wife is Padmavathamma and therefore, the question of paying maintenance to her does not arise.

In order to establish plaintiff's case to prove that she is the legally wedded wife of the defendant, she examined herself as P.W. 1 and stated on oath that, she is the legally wedded wife of the defendant. In support of her case, she has also examined two witnesses as P.Ws. 2 and 3 who are the eye-witnesses to the marriage between the plaintiff and defendant and who have stated on oath that, the marriage of the plaintiff and defendant took place about 22 years back and they have attended the marriage. Nothing contrary has been elicited in their cross-examination by the defendant. Ex. P. 1 is the legal notice issued by the plaintiff through her Counsel stating that she is the legally wedded wife of the defendant and she is entitled for maintenance. Though notice was received by the defendant, he has not given any reply. The said circumstance clearly indicates that defendant knowingly well that plaintiff is his wife, has not replied to the said legal notice. Exs. P. 2 and P. 3 are Voters list for the years 2002 and 2005 pertains to Tharabanahalli and at SI. No. 643 depicts the name of plaintiff and her husband's name is shown as Seenappa who is none other than the defendant. The plaintiff approached the Court at the age of 45 years seeking maintenance and according to the Hindu customs, no woman will falsely state her husband's name as she is having respect to her husband. The defendant has not produced any material documents to disprove the contents of Exs. P. 1 to P. 3. This is another circumstance that shows that plaintiff is the legally wedded wife of the defendant.

The High Court held, it is well-settled principles of law that, the continuous cohabitation of a man and woman as husband and wife and others treating them as such for number of years gives rise to a presumption of marriage between them. In the present case, P.Ws. 2 and 3 who were the eye-witnesses of the marriage between the plaintiff and defendant have categorically stated on oath that there was a marriage between the plaintiff and defendant and the same is reiterated by the plaintiff as P.W. 1. The said presumption is not rebutted by the defendant by producing any material documents and does not appear in the witness-box and states his own case on oath and does not offer himself to be cross-examined by the plaintiff; a presumption would arise that the case set up by him is not correct in view of the dictum of the Hon'ble Supreme Court in the case of *Vidhyadhar* v. *Mankikrao,* (1999) 3 SCC 573: AIR 1999 SC 1441 held at para 17 as under:

> "17. Where a party to the suit does not appear in the witness-box and states his own case on oath and does not offer himself to be cross-examined by the other side, a presumption would arise that the case set up by him is not correct as has been held in a series of decisions passed by various High Courts and the Privy Council beginning from the decision in *Sardar Gurbakshsh Singh* v. *Gurdial Singh,* AIR 1927 PC 230: 32 CWN 119. This was followed by the Lahore High Court in *Kirpa Singh* v. *Ajaipal Singh,* AIR 1930 Lahore 1: ILR 11 LAH 142 and the Bombay High Court in *Martand Pandharinath Chaudhari* v. *Radhabai Krishnarao Deshmukh,* AIR 1931

Bom 97: 1930 (32) Bom LR 924. The Madhya Pradesh High Court in *Gulla Kharagjit Carpenter* v. *Narsingh Nandkishore Rawat,* AIR 1970 MP 225: 1970 MPLJ 586 also followed the Privy Council decision in Sardar Gurbakhsh Singh's case. The Allahabad High Court in *Arjun Singh* v. *Virendra Nath,* AIR 1971 All 29, held that if a party abstains from entering the witness-box, it would give rise to an inference adverse against him. Similarly, a Division Bench of the Punjab and Haryana High Court in *Bhagwan Dass* v. *Bhishan Chand,* AIR 1974 P&H 7, drew a presumption under Section 114 of the Indian Evidence Act, 1872 against a party who did not enter into the witness-box."

When both the Courts, considering the pleadings and oral and documentary evidence have come to the definite conclusion that there is a valid marriage between the plaintiff and the defendant, the defendant being the husband of the plaintiff is duty bound to maintain the plaintiff, in view of the dictum of the Hon'ble Supreme Court in the case of *Bhuwan Mohan Singh* v. *Meena,* AIR 2014 SC 2875: 2014 (8) SCALE 573 wherein the Apex Court in para 2 has observed as under:

"2. Be it ingeminated that Section 125 of the Code of Criminal Procedure, 1973 (for short, "the Code") was conceived to ameliorate the agony, anguish, financial suffering of a woman who left her matrimonial home for the reasons provided in the provision so that some suitable arrangements can be made by the Court and she can sustain herself and also her children if they are with her. The concept of sustenance does not necessarily mean to lead the life of an animal, feel like an unperson to be thrown away from grace and roam for her basic maintenance somewhere else. She is entitled in law to lead a life in a similar manner as she would have lived in the house of her husband. That is where the status and strata come into play, and that is where the obligations of the husband, in case of a wife, become a prominent one. In a proceeding of this nature, the husband cannot take subterfuges to deprive her of the benefit of living with dignity. Regard being had to the solemn pledge at the time of marriage and also in consonance with the statutory law that governs the field, it is the obligation of the husband to see that the wife does not become a destitute, a beggar. A situation is not to be maladroitly created whereunder she is compelled to resign to her fate and think of life "dust unto dust". It is totally impermissible. In fact, it is the sacrosanct duty to render the financial support even if the husband is required to earn money with physical labour, if he is able-bodied. There is no escape route unless there is an order from the Court that the wife is not entitled to get maintenance from the husband on any legally permissible grounds."

4. Order XLII, Rule 1 – Review – Exercise of jurisdiction

In *Hindustan Petroleum Corporation Ltd.* v. *Sanjay Kumar Singh,* 2016 (2) PLJR 843 (Pat): 2016 (165) AIC 413 the High Court after hearing the parties and considering the case the Court said, having heard the parties and on consideration of the materials on record, this Court finds the review petition to be devoid of merit. It is not in dispute that even though circular No. R- 30024/33/2012-MC dated 23.06.2014 had come into existence during the pendency of the writ petition, the Corporation failed to bring the same before this Court and as such the said circular did not form part of the record of proceedings of the writ petition. In that view of the matter, it cannot be said that the judgment under review suffers from any error apparent on the face of the record.

The parameters and restricted scope for interference in review jurisdiction are well known. In *Thungabhadra Industries Ltd.* v. *The Government of Andhra Pradesh,* AIR 1964 SC 1372: (1964) 5 SCR 174, it was held as follows:

> "There is a distinction which is real, though it might not always be capable of exposition, between a mere erroneous decision and a decision which could be characterised as vitiated by "error apparent". A review is by no means an appeal in disguise whereby an erroneous decision is reheard and corrected, but lies only for patent error."

In *Aribam Tuleshwar Sharma* v. *Aribam Pishak Sharma,* (1979) 4 SCC 389: AIR 1979 SC 1047, it was held as follows:

> "There are definitive limits to the exercise of power of review. The power of review may be exercised on the discovery of new and important matter or evidence which, after the exercise of due digilence was not within the knowledge of the person seeking the review or could not be produced by him at the time when the order was made; it may be exercised where some mistake or error apparent on the face of the record is found; it may also be exercised on any analogous ground. But, it may not be exercised on the ground that the decision was erroneous on merits. That would be the province of a Court of appeal. A power of review is not to be confused with appellate power which may enable an Appellate Court to correct all manner of errors committed by the Subordinate Court."

In *Northern India Caterers (India) Ltd.* v. *Lt. Governor of Delhi,* (1980) 2 SCC 167: AIR 1980 SC 674, it was explained as follows:

> "Whatever be the nature of the proceeding, it is beyond dispute that a review proceeding cannot be equated with the original hearing of the case and the finality of the judgment delivered by the Court will not be reconsidered except where a glaring omission or patent mistake or like grave error has crept in earlier by judicial fallibility."

In *Haridas Das* v. *Smt. Usha Rani Banik,* (2006) 4 SCC 78: AIR 2006 SC 1634, it was held as follows:—

> "The parameters are prescribed in Order XLVII of the CPC and for the purposes of this *lis,* permit the defendant to press for a rehearing "on account of some mistake or error apparent on the face of the records or for any other sufficient reason". The former part of the rule deals with a situation attributable to the applicant, and the latter to a jural action which is manifestly incorrect or on which two conclusions are not possible. Neither of them postulate a rehearing of the dispute because a party had not highlighted all the aspects of the case or could perhaps have argued

them more forcefully and/or cited binding precedents to the Court and thereby enjoyed a favourable verdict."

A cumulative reading of the aforesaid authoritative pronouncements makes it abundantly clear that review jurisdiction is not available to re-hear the matter by taking on record any fresh documents or materials at the stage of review which could have, but were not, produced in the original proceedings. Moreover, the circular dated 23.06.2014 sought to be relied on by the Corporation is merely in the nature of a guideline and thus non-consideration of the same by reason of the Corporation not having brought it on record, would not constitute an error of law, much less an error apparent on the face of the record.

Learned counsel for the petitioner has relied upon the decision in the *High Court of Judicature at Patna* v. *K.K. Chaubey reported in* 2015 (4) PLJR 328 (FB), as also on *Chairman & MD, Central Bank of India* v. *Central Bank of India SC/ST Employees Welfare Association*, 2016 (1) PLJR 506, to submit that review jurisdiction may be exercised in a situation where the Court's attention was not drawn to a material statutory provision during the original hearing as an act of court shall prejudice none, as well as to prevent miscarriage of justice. It may however be observed that the present case is not one of oversight of any statutory provision rather merely of a guideline and its non-consideration is not such as is likely to result in miscarriage of justice.

5. Section 100 read with Order XLII, Rule 2 – Second appeal – Substantial question of law

In *Jotsna @ Jyoti* v. *Lakhpat Rai*, 2016 (235) DLT 633 (Del) the High Court of Delhi explaining the provisions of section 100 said, Section 100 of the Code of Civil Procedure was amended by Amending Act No. 104 of 1976. After the amendment, section 100 of the Code of Civil Procedure reads as under:—

> *S. 100. Second appeal.*—(1) Save as otherwise expressly provided in the body of this Code or by any other law for the time being in force, an appeal shall lie to the High Court from every decree passed in appeal by any Court subordinate to the High Court, if the High Court is satisfied that the case involves a substantial question of law.
>
> (2) An appeal may lie under this section from an appellate decree passed ex parte.
>
> (3) In an appeal under this section, the memorandum of appeal shall precisely state the substantial question of law involved in the appeal.
>
> (4) Where the High Court is satisfied that a substantial question of law is involved in any case, it shall formulate that question.
>
> (5) The appeal shall be heard on the question so formulated and the Respondent shall, at the hearing of the appeal, be allowed to argue that the case does not involve such question:
>
> Provided that nothing in this Sub-section shall be deemed to take away or abridge the power of the Court to hear, for reasons to be recorded, the appeal on any other substantial question of law, not formulated by it, if it is satisfied that the case involves such question.'

In the case *Municipal Committee, Hoshiarpur* v. *Punjab State Electricity Board,* (2010) 13 SCC 216: 2010 (11) SCALE 69, the legal position as to when the Second Appeal can lie has been summarised in paragraph 16 as under:

> '... The existence of a substantial question of law is a condition precedent for entertaining the second appeal; on failure to do so, the judgment cannot be maintained. The existence of a substantial question of law is a sine qua non for the exercise of jurisdiction under the provisions of Section 100 Code of Civil Procedure....'

It is settled law that in second appeal the High Court cannot set aside concurrent finding of fact given by the Courts below unless a substantial question of law is raised. Where there is a clear enunciation on a question of law the appellant cannot claim that the case involves substantial question of law.

The concurrent finding of the Courts below regarding the suit property being self-acquired, the father-in-law is under no legal obligation to maintain the appellant No. 1 and her adult son i.e. appellant No. 2 in his self acquired property in view of the legal position enunciated in the decision *S.R. Batra* v. *Taruna Batra,* 2007 (3) SCC 169: AIR 2007 SC 1118.

The respondent/plaintiff filed a Civil Suit claiming himself to be the absolute owner of the suit property by virtue of documents executed by DDA in his favour, Ex. PW-1/3, claiming it to be the self-acquired property. The appellants/defendants on the other hand failed to place on record any document to controvert the said plea of the plaintiff by showing that the suit property was purchased out of the sale proceeds of any ancestral property in which the husband of the appellant No.1 has right, title or interest. The appellant No.1 being the daughter-in-law, her right would be dependent on the rights of her husband. Her husband could have resided in the said house as a matter of right only if it could be established to be an ancestral house in which he can claim his share by seeking partition. Her husband has neither contributed towards purchase of the suit property nor he had been residing in that house. The appellant No.1 who got married in the year 1987 and her son who was born in 1988 are independent and the respondent in his capacity as father-in-law or grandfather is under no legal obligation to maintain them. Out of love and affection he provided shelter to them temporarily when the appellants/defendants approached him in the year 2001 requesting for shelter as their financial position was not permitting them to stay in a rented accommodation. The litigations going on, the police complaints against the father-in-law who is 84 years old by the appellants/defendants when he is suffering from various ailments with no support system even from his son who is not residing with him, the respondent cannot be compelled to remain under constant threat of false implication and face humiliation at the hands of his daughter-in-law and grandson. The parents in such a case when their life has been made miserable by their daughter-in-law can always ask such son, daughter-in-law or grandson to leave the house and lead their life so that the parents can live in peace. The concurrent finding given by the Courts below are in accordance with the law settled by the judgment of the Supreme Court in *S.R. Batra* v. *Taruna Batra* (supra) case which has been followed by the Division Bench of this Court in *Shumita Didi Sandhu* v. *Sanjay Singh Sandhu,* 174 (2010) DLT 79.

ORDER XLIII

APPEALS FROM ORDERS

1. Appeals from orders.—An appeal shall lie from the following orders under the provisions of section 104, namely:—

(a) an order under rule 10 of Order VII returning a plaint to be presented to the proper Court [except where the procedure specified in rule 10A of Order VII has been followed;

(b) Omitted

(c) an order under rule 9 of Order IX rejecting an application (in a case open to appeal) for an order to set aside the dismissal of a suit;

(d) an order under rule 13 of Order IX rejecting an application (in a case open to appeal) for an order to set aside a decree passed *ex parte;*

* * * * *

(f) an order under rule 21 of Order XI;

* * * * *

(i) an order under rule 34 of Order XXI on an objection to the draft of a document or of an endorsement;

(j) an order under rule 72 or rule 92 of Order XXI setting aside or refusing to set aside a sale;

(ja) an order rejecting an application made under sub-rule (1) of rule 106 of Order XXI, provided that an order on the original application, that is to say, the application referred to in sub-rule (1) of rule 105 of that Order is appealable.]

(k) an order under rule 9 of Order XXII refusing to set aside the abatement or dismissal of a suit;

(l) an order under rule 10 of Order XXII giving or refusing to give leave;

* * * * *

(n) an order under rule 2 of Order XXV rejecting an application (in a case open to appeal) for an order to set aside the dismissal of a suit;

(na) an order under rule 5 or rule 7 of Order XXXIII rejecting an application for permission to sue as an indigent persons:]

* * * * *

(p) orders in inter-pleader-suits under rule 3, rule 4 or rule 6 of Order XXXV; (q) an order under rule 2, rule 3 or rule 6 of Order XXXVIII; (r) an order under rule 1, rule 2 [rule 2A], rule 4 or rule 10 of Order XXXIX; (s) an order under rule 1 or rule 4 of Order XL;

(t) an order of refusal under rule 19 of Order XLI to re-admit, or under rule 21 of Order XLI to re-hear, an appeal;

(u) an order under rule 23 [or rule 23A] of Order XLI remanding a case, where an appeal would lie from the decree of the appellate court;

* * * *

(w) an order under rule 4 of Order XLVII granting an application for review.

HIGH COURT AMENDMENT

Allahabad.—In Order XLIII, in rule 1, omit clauses (g), (i) and (o).

[*Vide* Notification No. 43/VII-d-29, dated 1st June, 1957.]

Andhra Pradesh.—In Order XLIII, in rule 1,—

(i) after clause (i) insert the following clause, namely:-

"(ii) an order under rule 106 of Order XXI;"

[*Vide* Notification No. P Dis. 229/56, dated 2nd April, 1956.]

(ii) in clause (r), after the words and figure "rule 2", insert the words and figures "rule 3A, rule 3B". (w.e.f. 12-7-1962)

Bombay.—In Order XLIII, in rule 1,—

(i) in clause (r), for the words and figures "or rule 10", substitute the words and figures v "rule 10 and rule 11"; (w.e.f. 1-11-1966)

(ii) omit clause (w).

[*Vide* Notification No. 1646, dated 9th March, 1926.]

Calcutta.—In Order XLIII, in rule 1, after clause (i), insert the following clause, namely:—

"(i) (a) An order under rule 57 of Order XXI, directing that an attachment shall cease or directing or omitting to direct that an attachment shall continue."

[*Vide* Notification No. 3516-G, dated 3rd February, 1933.]

Gauhati.—Same as in Calcutta.

Gujarat.—Same as in Bombay (ii).

Kerala.—In Order XLIII, in rule 1, same as in Madras (b). (9-6-1959)

Madras.—In Order XLIII, in rule 1,—

(a) after clause (i) insert the following clause, namely:—

"(ii) an order under rule 106 of Order XXI." (w.e.f. 19-5-1954)

(b) in clause (s), at the end, insert the words "except an order under the proviso to sub-rule (2) of rule 4."

[*Vide* P Dis. No. 60 of 1933.]

Patna.—In Order XLIII, in rule 1, after clause (i), insert the following clause, namely:—

"(ii) an Order in *garnishee* proceedings other than an order referred to in rule 63 H(1) of Order XXI." (w.e.f. 7-1-1936)

1A. Right to challenge non-appealable orders in appeal against decree.—(1) Where any order is made under this Code against a party and thereupon any judgment is pronounced against such party and a decree is drawn up, such party may, in an appeal against the decree, contend that such order should not have been made and the judgment should not have been pronounced.

(2) In an appeal against a decree passed in a suit after recording a compromise or refusing to record a compromise, it shall be open to the appellant to contest the decree on the ground that the compromise should, or should not, have been recorded.

2. Procedure.—The rules of Order XLI shall apply, so far as may be, to appeals from orders.

HIGH COURT AMENDMENT

Allahabad.—In Order XLIII, in rule 2, after the words and figures "Order XL1", insert the words and figures "and Order XLIA".

[*Vide* Notification No. 14186/VII-d-147, dated 22nd December, 1951.]

Andhra Pradesh.—Same as in Madras;

Karnataka.—In Order XLIII, for rule 2, substitute the following rules, namely:—

"2. The rules contained in Orders XLI and XLIA shall apply, so far as may be, to appeals from the orders specified in rule 1 and other orders of any subordinate Court from which an appeal to the High Court is allowed under the provisions of any law:

Provided that in the case of appeals against interlocutory orders made prior to decree or final order, the Court which passed the order appealed from need not send the records of the case unless an order has been made by the High Court for stay of further proceedings in that Court but send only such records as may be called by the High Court.

Rules contained in Order XLII shall apply, so far as may be, to appeals from appellate Orders."

[*Vide* Notification No. ROC 2296/59, dated 5th November, 1959.]

Kerala.—In Order XLIII, for rule 2, substitute the following rule, namely:—

"2. The rules of Order XLI, Order XLIA and Order XLII, rule 2(2) shall apply, so far as may be, to appeals from the Orders specified in rule I and other orders of any Civil Court from which an appeal to the High Court is allowed under any provision of law:

Provided that in the case of appeals against interlocutory orders made prior to decree, the Court which passed the order appealed from shall not send the records of the case unless an order has been made for stay of further proceedings in that Court." (w.e.f. 9-6-1959)

Madras.—In Order XLIII, for rule 2,—

(a) substitute the following rule, namely:—

"2. The rules of Order XLI and of Order XLIA shall apply, so far as may be, to appeals from the orders specified in rule 1 and other orders of any Civil Court from which an appeal to the High Court is allowed under any provision of law:

Provided that in the case of appeals against interlocutory orders made prior to decree, the Court which passed the order appealed from shall not send the records of the case unless an order has been made for stay of further proceedings in that Court."

(b) after rule 2, insert the following rule, namely:—

"3. Appeals from Appellate Orders.—(1) The provisions of Order XLII shall apply, so far as may be, to appeals from appellate orders.

(2) A memorandum of appeal from an appellate order shall be accompanied by a certified copy of the judgment and of the order of the Court of first instance, and by a certified copy of the judgment and of the order of the appellate court.

(3) If any ground of appeal is based upon the construction of a document, a printed and a type-written copy of such document shall be presented with the memorandum of appeal:

Provided that, if such document is not in the English language and the appellant appears by a pleader, an English translation of the document certified by the pleader to be a correct translation shall be presented."

[*Vide* P Dis. No. 788 of 1932.]

Punjab, Haryana and Chandigarh.—In Order XLIII, for rule 2, substitute the following rule, namely:—

"2. The rules of Order XLI shall apply, so far as may be, to appeals from order:

Provided that in case of appeals against interlocutory orders, the Court which passed the order appealed from shall not sent the records of the case unless summoned by the appellate court." (w.e.f. 28-1-1993)

Comments

1. Scope and Application.—Order XLIII, Rule 1(j) – Order Refusing to Set Aside Sale

The High court of Madhya Pradesh said that Second appeal not maintainable whether the order is passed by Civil Court or Revenue Officer. *See* Order XXI, rule 90. 1952 MP LJ (Notes) 321.

2. Order XLIII, Rule 1 – Order Refusing Installments – Appealability

Both the orders fixing instalments or refusing to fix installments for the payment of the decretal amount by the executing Court would be made under sub-rule (2) of rule 11 of Order XX and an order under this sub-rule would be appealable under Order XLIII, rule 1(ii) (Jammu and Kashmir), if it is passed without the consent of the parties. It would be doing nothing short of violence to the language of sub-rule (ii) of rule 1 of Order XLIII (Jammu and Kashmir) to confine its application to those orders alone by which fixation of instalments for payment of the decretal amount is made. *Om Prakash* v. *Jammu and Kashmir Bank Ltd., Jammu*, 12 JKLR 131: AIR 1954 J&K 39 (Pr 2) (DB). 9. Clause (j) – Order under Order XXI, rules 72 or 92. Order refusing to set aside sale – Second appeal not maintainable whether the order is passed by civil Court or Revenue Officer. 1952 MPLJ (Notes) 321.

3. Order XLIII, Rule 1(d) – Arbitration Act (1940) Section 17 and Section 115 of CPC – Proper Remedy

Decree passed under section 17 of the Arbitration Act in absence of defendant cannot be said to be *ex parte* – Not open to appeal for purposes of Order XLIII, rule 1(d) Civil P.C. According to the High Court of Rajasthan revision is the proper remedy available to the aggrieved.—Principles of O. 9, R. 13, Civil P.C., can, however, be applied to such decrees. *Ram Chander* v. *Jamna Shankar*, AIR 1962 Raj 12: ILR (1961) 11 Raj 76. A Division Bench of the Court referred to a case where on 15-2-1952 the Court passed a conditional order allowing an application to set aside an *ex parte* decree on certain terms. The matter was put up again on 25-3-1952 and the Court passed an order actually dismissing the application on that day. The applicant having appealed against the order of 25-3-1952. It was held, that in the circumstances, the real order was the order of 25-3-1952 dismissing the application and, therefore, an appeal lay from that order. Held, further that, even if no appeal lay, a revision would lie from the order of 15-2-1952 if that was treated as a complete order in itself allowing the application on certain terms; *Chhagan Raj* v. *Sugan Mal*, ILR (1958) 8 Raj 295: 1957 Rai LW 631: AIR 1958 Raj 237 (238) (Pt A) (Prs 4, 5) (DB). According to a Division Bench of the High Court of Nagpur order refusing to set aside sale is passed and the decision is passed with material irregularity – Revision is competent section 115: AIR 1957 Nag 97 (DB).

4. Order XLIII, Rule 1(D) – Scope – Execution Sale

Purchase money— No deposit within time prescribed by Order XXI, rule 85 – Sale set aside and re-sale ordered – Appeal and no revision lies. *See ibid.*, section 47; *Nand Lal* v. *Siddiquan*, AIR 1957 All 558.

5. Order XLIII, Rule 1(j); Order XXI, Rule 92

The High Court of Andhra Pradesh held that where order under rule 92 of Order XXI, is passed merely directing judgment-debtor to furnish security and no order dismissing the application for non-compliance with the direction – Appeal against order passed is incompetent. (1963) 2 Andh WR 127: (1963) 2 Andh LT 70. According to a Division Bench of the said Court dismissal of application under Order XXI, rule 90 for failure to deposit sale warrant amount, appeal may be maintained; AIR 1959 AP 667 (DB).

6. Order XLIII, Rule 1(j) and Order XXI, Rule 92 – Necessary Party

Appeal challenging auction sale — Auction-purchaser is necessary party – Omission is fatal. In a case three houses belonging to the petitioner were sold in auction for arrears of income-tax, Petitioner applied for setting aside the sale on the ground that there were material irregularities in conducting the sale. The application was rejected by Deputy Commissioner. Petitioner filed an appeal before the Board of Revenue in which he impleaded only the State Government. Subsequently he sought leave to implead the auction-purchasers as respondents to the appeal, The Board held that the auction purchasers were necessary parties to the appeal and they having not been impleaded within time, the appeal was dismissed. Held, that in view of the express provision in Order XXI, rule 92(2), C.P.C., enjoining the executing Court to give a notice to the parties affected.

7. Order XLIII, Rule 1(0), Order XI, Rule 21 and Section 105 – Appeal against order under Order XI, Rule 21 after Disposal of Suit

The High court of Calcutta said that Order XLIII, rule 1(f), confers a right of appeal against an order passed under Order XI, rule 21. An additional right is conferred by sub-section (1) of section 105, C.P.C. and a litigant without filing an appeal from the order may in an appeal from the decree challenge the order as erroneous. The right of appeal conferred by Order XLIII, rule 1(f) is not cut down by section 105(1). The right does not cease although a decree has subsequently been passed and although no appeal has been filed from the decree. The decree disposing of the suit is dependent upon the order passed under Order XI, rule 21 and if the order is set aside in appeal, the decree will stand superseded; ILR (1957) 3 Cal 167.

8. Order XLIII, Section 104 – Delhi High Court Act, 1966, Section 10 – Commercial dispute – Appeal

In *HPL (India) Limited* v. *QRG Enterprises*, 2017 (238) DLT 123: 2017 (162) DRJ 80 (Del) (DB), the appeal was directed against the order dated 20.12.2016 passed by a learned single Judge of this court in I.A. No.15867/2016 in CS (Comm) 1218/2016. The said application was filed by the plaintiffs, inter alia, praying that new documents filed along with the affidavits by way of examination-in-chief of new witnesses of the plaintiffs be taken on record. The learned single Judge permitted the said documents to be taken on record, subject to the plaintiffs/respondents herein paying costs. The appellants are aggrieved by this order.

At the commencement of the hearing of this appeal, the respondents took a preliminary objection as to its maintainability. It was contended that the impugned order was not an appealable order specified in Order XLIII of the Code of Civil Procedure, 1908 (hereinafter referred to as 'the CPC'). It was further contended that this being an order passed by the Commercial Division of this High Court, an appeal therefrom was governed by Section 13 of the Commercial Courts, Commercial Division and Commercial Appellate Division of High Courts Act, 2015 (hereinafter referred to as 'the said Act'). It was contended that the proviso to Section 13(1) of the said Act limited appeals from orders to such orders which were specifically enumerated under Order XLIII CPC and Section 37 of the Arbitration and Conciliation Act, 1996. Reliance was also placed on Section 13(2) of the said Act which is a non-obstante provision specifying that notwithstanding anything contained in any other law for the time being in force or Letters Patent of a High Court, no appeal shall lie from any order or decree of a Commercial Division or Commercial Court otherwise than in accordance with the provisions of the said Act. Relying upon these provisions, it was contended that the present appeal was not maintainable.

The Court said in the case, in fact, in our view, sub-section (1) of Section 13 not only provides the forum of appeal (i.e., Commercial Appellate Division of a High Court) but also prescribes a period of limitation for an appeal from a decision of the Commercial Court or the Commercial Division of a High Court. If we look at the Limitation Act, 1963 and, in particular, Article 116 of the Schedule to the Limitation Act, 1963, it would be evident that an appeal under the CPC to a High Court from any decree or order would have to be filed within 90 days of the date of the decree or order. Article 117 of the said Schedule stipulates a period of 30 days for an appeal from a decree or order of any High Court to the same Court, from the date of the decree or order. If we look at Section 13(1), we find that it provides for a period of limitation of 60 days for an appeal in respect of a decision of a Commercial Court or Commercial Division of a High Court. There is a clear departure from the normal procedure in respect of not only the specification of an Appellate Court but also with regard to the period of limitation for filing an appeal. This is clear from the fact that all appeals under the said Act have to be heard by the Commercial Appellate Division which, in terms of Section 5 thereof, has to comprise of Division Benches of a High Court. While in respect of disputes which are not commercial disputes of a specified value, an appeal to the High Court from any decree or order could be heard by a Single Judge of the High Court, an appeal from any decree or order of a Commercial Court would have to be heard by a Division Bench which forms part of the Commercial Appellate Division of the High Court. Moreover, in respect of disputes which are not covered by the said Act, the period of limitation for an appeal from any decree or order to a High Court is 90 days, in respect of commercial disputes of a specified value if a person is aggrieved by a decision of a Commercial Court, the appeal would have to be preferred before the Appellate Division of the High Court within a period of 60 days from the date of the decision. In case the decision appealed against is that of a Commercial Division of a High Court, the appeal before the Commercial Appellate Division of that High Court would also to be filed within 60 days. This can be easily contrasted with Article 117 of the Limitation Act, 1963, where the period of 30 days is provided for an appeal from a decree or order of any High Court to the same Court. The sum and substance of this discussion is that the provisions of Articles 116 and 117 of the Limitation Act, 1963, which provided for appeals to the High Court from any decree or order and of a subordinate court and appeals to the High Court from a decree or order passed by the original Side of that High Court to be filed within 90 days and 30 days, respectively from the date of the decree or order, have now been combined into one period of limitation and, that is, 60 days from the date of 'judgment' or order', as the case may be.

Viewed in this context, it becomes immediately apparent that Section 13(1) prescribes a different forum of appeal and a different period of limitation thereof.

We now come to the meaning to be ascribed to the proviso in Section 13(1). It clearly stipulates that an appeal shall lie from such orders passed by a Commercial Division or a Commercial Court that are specifically enumerated under Order XLIII of the CPC, as amended by the said Act, and section 37 of the Arbitration and Conciliation Act, 1996. We have seen that 'orders' as understood under the CPC are different and distinct from 'decrees'. And, orders are nothing but the formal expression of any decision of a Civil Court not amounting to a decree. Therefore, the amplitude and width of the expression 'order' is very wide under the CPC itself but not all orders are appealable. The appealable orders are enumerated in Order XLIII of the CPC. We have already pointed out above, that there are only two kinds of appeals recognised under the CPC, namely, – 'Appeals from decrees' and 'Appeals from orders'. Section 104, which has been extracted earlier in this judgment, specifies the orders from which appeals lie. It clearly provides that an appeal shall lie from the orders enumerated in the said provision itself and, save as otherwise expressly provided in the body of the CPC or by any law for the time being in force, from no other orders. This means that appeals from orders are restricted to those orders which are either specified in Section 104 itself or expressly provided in the body of the Code or by any law for the time being in force. Insofar as the impugned order is concerned, it is clear that it does not fall within the orders specified under Section 104. We now have to look at Order XLIII, Rule 1 which stipulates that an appeal shall lie from the orders enumerated therein under the provisions of Section 104. In other words, only an order specified under Order XLIII, Rule 1 would be appealable and, read with the provisions of Section 104, no other order would be an appealable order under the CPC. In this backdrop, the proviso to Section 13(1) makes it abundantly clear that an appeal shall lie from such orders passed by a Commercial Division or a Commercial Court that are 'specifically enumerated' under Order XLIII of the CPC, as amended by the said Act and Section 37 of the Arbitration and Conciliation Act, 1996. Clearly, in our view, this restricts the appealable orders to only those orders which are specifically enumerated in Order XLIII. In the present case, the impugned order is admittedly not one specified under Order XLIII.

Judgment Its meaning —We would also like to examine the scope and function of a 'proviso'. In *CIT* v. *Indo-Mercantile Bank Ltd.,* 1959 Supp (2) SCR 256: AIR 1959 SC 713, the Supreme Court held:—

> "The proper function of a proviso is that it qualifies the generality of the main enactment by providing an exception and taking out as it were, from the main enactment, a portion which, but for the proviso would fall within the main enactment. Ordinarily it is foreign to the proper function of a proviso to read it as providing something by way of an addendum or dealing with a subject which is foreign to the main enactment. 'It is a fundamental rule of construction that a proviso must be considered with relation to the principal matter to which it stands as a proviso.' Therefore it is to be construed harmoniously with the main enactment. (Per Das, C.J.) in *Abdul Jabar Butt* v. *State of Jammu & Kashmir,* (1957) 1 SCR 51 (59): AIR 1957 SC 281.
>
> Bhagwati, J., in *Ram Narain Sons Ltd.* v. *Assistant Commissioner of Sales Tax,* (1955) 2 SCR 483 (493): AIR 1955 SC 765 said: 'It is a cardinal rule of interpretation that a proviso to a particular provision of a statute only embraces the field which is covered by the main provision. It carves out an exception to the main provision to which it has been enacted as a proviso and to no other.

Lord Macmillan in *Madras & Southern Maharatta Railway Co.* v. *Bezwada Municipality*, (1944) LR 71 IA 113 (122): AIR 1944 PC 71] laid down the sphere of a proviso as follows:

> 'The proper function of a proviso is to except and deal with a case which would otherwise fall within the general language of the main enactment, and its effect is confined to that case. Where, as in the present case, the language of the main enactment is clear and unambiguous, a proviso can have no repercussion on the interpretation of the main enactment, so as to exclude from it by implication what clearly falls within its express terms.'
>
> The territory of a proviso therefore is to carve out an exception to the main enactment and exclude something which otherwise would have been within the section. It has to operate in the same field and if the language of the main enactment is clear it cannot be used for the purpose of interpreting the main enactment or to exclude by implication what the enactment clearly says unless the words of the proviso are such that is its necessary effect. (Vide also *Corporation of City of Toronto* v. *Attorney-General for Canada*, (1946) AC 32 (37)"

(underlining added)

In *Ali M.K.* v. *State of Kerala*, (2003) 11 SCC 632: AIR 2003 SC 4006, the Supreme Court made similar observations:—

> "10. The normal function of a proviso is to except something out of the enactment or to qualify something enacted therein which but for the proviso would be within the purview of the enactment. As was stated in *Mullins* v. *Treasurer of Surrey*, (1880) 5 QBD 170: 42 LT 128] (referred to in *Shah Bhojraj Kuverji Oil Mills and Ginning Factory* v. *Subhash Chandra Yograj Sinha*, AIR 1961 SC 1596: (1962) 2 SCR 159 and *Calcutta Tramways Co. Ltd.* v. *Corpn. of Calcutta*, AIR 1965 SC 1728: (1965) 3 SCR 354), when one finds a proviso to a section the natural presumption is that, but for the proviso, the enacting part of the section would have included the subject-matter of the proviso. The proper function of a proviso is to except and to deal with a case which would otherwise fall within the general language of the main enactment and its effect is confined to that case. It is a qualification of the preceding enactment which is expressed in terms too general to be quite accurate. As a general rule, a proviso is added to an enactment to qualify or create an exception to what is in the enactment and ordinarily, a proviso is not interpreted as stating a general rule...'

Presumption in interpreting a proviso—

From the above, it is evident that the natural presumption that can be raised while interpreting a proviso is that but for the proviso, the enacting part of the Section would have included the subject matter of the proviso. In sub-section (1) of Section 13, the word 'order' would have very wide amplitude and that could have included even orders which are not specifically enumerated in Order XLIII of the CPC. The proviso has taken out those orders and carved out an exception by limiting the appeal from orders to those which are specifically enumerated under Order XLIII of the CPC (apart from an Order under Section 37 of the Arbitration and Conciliation Act, 1996).

9. Meaning of the term 'Judgment' in section 13(1) of the said Act

The above analysis reveals that:—(a) the word 'judgment' appearing in Section 13(1) of the said Act actually relates or has a reference to a 'decree'; (b) the word 'order' in that provision would have to be construed in the light of Section 2(14) of the CPC as meaning 'a formal expression of a decision of a Civil Court which is not a decree; (c) the appealable orders would be only those which are specifically enumerated under Order XLIII, as provided in the proviso to Section 13(1) of the said Act.

Now, let us examine sub-section (2) of section 13 of the said Act. As noticed above, it begins with the non obstante expression "notwithstanding anything contained in any other law for the time being in force or Letters Patent of a High Court ..". The words – 'any other law for the time being in force' – would include the Delhi High Court Act, 1966. The portion after the non obstante expression specifically cautions that 'no appeal shall lie from any order or decree of a Commercial Division or Commercial Court otherwise than in accordance with the provisions of this Act'. In other words, whatever may be contained in, inter alia, the Delhi High Court Act, 1966, an appeal from any order or decree of a Commercial Division or Commercial Court 'shall lie' only in accordance with the provisions of the said Act. To be clear, if an appeal from a particular kind of order or decree were to be provided under the Delhi High Court Act, 1966 but not under the said Act then, such an order or decree would not be appealable. Therefore, even if, by virtue of section 10 of the Delhi High Court Act, 1966, an appeal lay from a particular kind of an order, no appeal could be preferred there against unless the said Act itself provided for such an appeal.

10. Order XLIII, Rule 1, Order VII, Rule 11 – Appeal – Maintainability

In *Vaijinath* v. *Shankramma*, 2017 (2) ICC 1311 (Karn): 2017 ILR Karn 1089 the respondents are the plaintiffs and the appellants are the defendants in O.S.171/2004 on the file of the Additional Senior Civil Judge, Bidar. The suit was filed on 21.08.2004 to pass a decree of declaration of title and perpetual injunction in respect of the plaint schedule property. Written Statement was filed on 25.10.2004 and the suit contested. Issues were raised. Issue No.3 "Whether the suit is improperly valued and the court fee paid is insufficient ?" was treated as a preliminary issue and was subjected to trial. Both sides having adduced evidence, an Order dated 29.06.2010 was passed and the plaintiffs directed to furnish fresh valuation slip and pay court fee on the actual market value of the suit property. Said order remained unchallenged. Despite granting sufficient time and the case adjourned on 24 occasions, there being non compliance, on 08.08.2011, the suit was dismissed.

Aggrieved, the plaintiffs preferred Miscellaneous Appeal No. 67/2011 under Order XLIII, Rule 1 CPC, which came up for hearing before the Presiding Officer, FTC-II, at Bidar. On hearing the parties, appeal was allowed, impugned order set aside and suit remanded to the Trial Court by a Judgment dated 31.10.2012. Assailing the judgment of remand, the defendants preferred this appeal.

The High Court said, heard the learned Advocates on both sides and perused the record. Substantial question of law required to be considered is "Whether an appeal under Order XLIII, Rule 1 CPC against an order passed under Order VIII, Rule 11 CPC is maintainable?"

Issue No. 3 raised in the suit was rightly treated as a preliminary issue in view of the mandate of section 11(2) of Karnataka Court Fees and Suits Valuation Act, 1958. After trial, wherein, both parties adduced evidence, valuation made by the plaintiffs was found to be incorrect, and by an order dated 29.06.2010 the plaintiffs were directed to furnish fresh valuation and pay requisite court fee. Even after 24 adjournments, plaintiffs having not furnished the correct valuation and failed to pay correct court fee, by an order dated 08.08.2011, in exercise of power under Order VI, Rule 11 CPC. suit was dismissed.

There is no sub rule under Order XLIII, Rule 1 CPC, which makes provision for preferring an appeal against the dismissal of the suit by invocation of power under Order VII, Rule 1 CPC. That being so, remedy to the plaintiff was only by filing an appeal under Section 96 read with Order XLI, Rule 1 CPC. There being absolutely no scope for the plaintiffs to have preferred an appeal under Order XLIII, Rule 1 CPC, the Court below has erred in allowing the miscellaneous appeal in exercise of its jurisdiction under Section 104 read with Section 107 CPC.

ORDER XLIV

APPEALS BY INDIGENT PERSON

1. Who may appeal as an indigent person.—(1) Any person entitled to prefer an appeal, who is unable to pay the fee required for the memorandum of appeal, may present an application accompanied by a memorandum of appeal, and may be allowed to appeal as an indigent person, subject, in all matters, including the presentation of such application, to the provisions relating to suits by [indigent persons], insofar as those provisions are applicable.

HIGH COURT AMENDMENT

Andhra Pradesh.—In Order XLIV, in rule 1, in sub-rule (1), insert the following proviso, namely:—

> "Provided that in case where the appeal is presented to the High Court, the application for permission to appeal as pauper may be presented by the applicant in person or by his or her authorised agent or by an Advocate." (w.e.f. 30-4-1970)

2. Grant of time for payment of Court-fee.—Where an application is rejected under rule 1, the Court may, while rejecting the application, allow the applicant to pay the requisite Court-fee, within such time as may be fixed by the Court or extended by it from time to time; and upon such payment, the memorandum of appeal in respect of which such fee is payable shall have the same force and effect as if such fee has been paid in the first instance.

3. Inquiry as to whether applicant is an indigent person.—(1) Where an applicant, referred to in rule 1, was allowed to sue or appeal as an indigent person in the Court from whose decree the appeal is preferred, no further inquiry in respect of the question whether or not he is an indigent person shall be necessary if the applicant has made an affidavit stating that he has not ceased to be an indigent person since the date of the decree appealed from; but if the Government pleader or the respondent disputes the truth of the statement made in such affidavit, an inquiry into the question aforesaid shall be held by the appellate court, or, under the orders of the appellate court, by an officer of the Court.

(2) Where the applicant, referred to in rule 11, is alleged to have become an indigent person since the date of the decree appealed from the inquiry into the question whether or not he is an indigent person shall be made by the appellate court or, under the orders of the appellate court, by an officer of that Court unless the appellate court considers it necessary in the circumstances of the case that the inquiry should be held by the Court from whose decision the appeal is preferred.]

HIGH COURT AMENDMENT

Allahabad.—In Order XLIV, for rule 3, substitute the following rule, namely:—

> "**3. Inquiry as to whether applicant is an indigent person**.—The inquiry into the question whether or not the applicant referred to in rule 1, is an indigent person shall be made by the appellate court or under the orders of the appellate court by an officer of that Court unless the appellate court considers it necessary, in the circumstances of the case, that the inquiry should be held by the Court from whose decision the appeal is preferred:
>
> Provided that if such applicant was allowed to sue or appeal as an indigent person in the Court from whose decree the appeal is preferred, no further inquiry in respect of the question whether or not he is an indigent person shall be necessary if the applicant has made an affidavit stating that he has not ceased to be an indigent person since the date of the decree appealed from, but if the Government pleader or the respondent disputes the truth of the statement made in such affidavit, an inquiry into the question aforesaid shall be made in the manner stated above." (w.e.f. 25-4-1987)

In exercise of powers vested by article 145 of the Constitution of India, the Supreme Court has framed rules for filing of an appeal before it by an indigent person. The Rules framed under Order XVII of the Supreme Court Rules, 1966 are as follows:—

ORDER XLIV

APPEALS AND APPLICATION BY INDIGENT PERSON

1. An application for leave to proceed as [an indigent person] shall be made on a petition. It shall be accompanied by:

(a) a copy of the petition of appeal and the documents referred to in rule 3 of Order XV, or of the petition for special leave and the documents mentioned in rule 5 of Order XVI, as the case may be; and

(b) an affidavit from the petitioner disclosing all the property to which he is entitled and the value thereof other than his necessary wearing apparel and his interest in the subject-matter of the intended appeal and stating that he is unable to provide security or surety for the cost of respondent and pay Court-fees.

2. The Registrar shall, on satisfying himself that the petition is in order, direct that the petition shall be [registered] and set down for hearing before the Chamber Judge on a date to be fixed for the purpose.

3. The application shall be posted before the Judge in Chambers who may himself inquire into the [indigency] of the petitioner after notice to the other parties in the case and to the Attorney-General, or make an order directing the High Court either by itself or by a Court subordinate to the High Court, to investigate the [indigency] after notice to the parties interested and submit a report thereon within such time as may be fixed by the order. On receipt of the report, the petition shall again be posted before the Judge in Chambers for further orders:

Provided that, if the applicant was allowed to sue or appeal as [an indigent person] in the Court from whose decree the appeal is preferred, no further inquiry in respect of his [indigency] shall be necessary, unless this Court sees cause to direct such inquiry.

4. In granting or refusing leave to appeal as [an indigent person], the Court shall ordinarily follow the principles set out in sub-rule (2) of rule 1 of Order XLIV of the Code.

5. Where a petitioner obtains leave of the Court to appeal as [an indigent person] he shall not be required to pay Court-fees [on the documents filed in the case or fees payable for service of process. He shall, however, be required to pay fees for obtaining copies of any documents or orders].

6. The Judge in Chambers may assign an advocate on record to assist [an indigent person] in the case, unless the [indigent person] has made his own arrangement for his representation. Such assignment shall ordinarily be from a panel of advocates willing to assist [indigent persons] and chosen by the Judge in Chambers. It shall however be open to the Judge in Chambers in his discretion to assign an advocate outside the panel in any particular case.

7. (a) No fees shall be payable by [an indigent person] to his advocate, nor shall any such fees be allowed on taxation against the other party except by an order of Court. The advocate may however receive from the [indigent person] money for out of pocket expenses, if any, properly incurred in the case.

(b) It shall be open to the Court, if it thinks fit, to award costs against the adverse party or out of the property decreed to [an indigent person] and direct payment of such costs to the advocate for the [indigent person].

(c) Save as aforesaid no person shall take or agree to take or seek to obtain from [an indigent person] any fee, profit or reward for the conduct of his case, and any person who takes, agrees to take or seeks to obtain, any such fee, profit.

[11A. The record of the appeal arising out of the petition for special leave shall normally consist of the petition of appeal and the paper book of the Court below, if available, plus such additional documents that the parties may file from the record of the case, if the printed record of the Court below be not available. In that event, no fresh printing of the record shall be necessary, and the original record will be called for, from the Court below for reference of the Court:

Provided, however, that where in a particular case the Court feels that fresh printing of record is necessary, a specific order to that effect shall be made by the Court at the time of granting special leave to appeal, the provisions contained in Order XV relating to preparation of record shall with necessary modification and adaptation apply.]

[12. While granting special leave in all matters in which the Bench granting special leave is of the opinion that the matter is capable of being disposed of within a short time, say within an hour or two, it will indicate accordingly. The office shall maintain a separate register of such matters to enable the Chief Justice to constitute a Bench for the disposal of such matters.]

[13. (1) Respondent to whom a notice in a Special Leave Petition is issued or who had filed a caveat shall be entitled to oppose the grant of leave or interim orders, without filing any written objections. He shall also be at liberty to file his objections within 30 days from the date of receipt of notice or not later than 2 weeks before the date appointed for hearing, whichever be earlier, but shall do so only by setting out the grounds in opposition to the questions of law or grounds set out in the SLP and may produce such pleadings and documents filed before the Court.

Tribunal against whose order the SLP is filed and shall also set out the grounds for not granting interim order or for vacating interim order if already granted.]

(2) No separate application for vacating interim order need be filed. The respondent shall, however, be at liberty to file application for vacating stay separately before or after filing objections.

(3) (a) Where any statement of objection is filed by the respondent, it shall be supported by an affidavit of the party or any person authorised by him verifying to the correctness of the statements made therein and also to the effect that annexures produced are the true copies of the originals which formed part of record in the Court below.

(b) If respondent wants to produce any document which was not part of the record in the Court below, he shall file an application seeking permission of the Court to produce such documents setting out the reason as to why it was not produced in the Court below as also the necessity of producing it before the Court.

(4) The respondent may, if considered necessary, file additional list of dates with material facts in addition to those furnished by the petitioners if he considers that the list of dates and facts by the petitioner is inaccurate or incomplete.

Comments

1. Order XLIV – Scope and Application

44. Rule 1 – Scope of inquiry – Application for leave to appeal – Notice – Opposite party if can show that judgment sought to be appealed against is not *prima facie* contrary to law. Both under the original proviso and the new sub-rule (2) it is clearly the duty of the Court to examine the judgment straightway and decide whether it is *prima facie* right or wrong. If the judgment is prima facie correct, then the application must be dismissed without any further ado. If the Court comes to the conclusion that the judgment is *prima facie* wrong it will issue notice to the opposite party, and it is quite wrong and unjustified to hold that the judgment has only to be considered after the question whether the applicant is a pauper or not has been decided. Once the Court has perused the judgment and found it *prima facie* wrong and has issued notice, the respondent ought not to be heard at all on the merits of the case unless and until leave has been granted and the appeal is heard as such. *Panchu Bala Dasi* v. *Nikhil Rajan Pal,* 60 Cal WN 835: AIR 1956 Cal 530, rel. on. *Mohd-un-Nisa Begum* v. *Fayaz Ali Hashmi,* ILR 1958 Punj 663: 60 Punj LR 587: AIR 1958 Punj 437 (440) (Pt A) (Prs. 10, 12, 14) (DB). When an application for leave to appeal in *forma pauperis* is presented ordinarily the appellate court must make up its mind at once whether the decree is contrary to law or to some usage having the force of law or is otherwise erroneous or unjust. The mere fact, however, that the application is not rejected at once and a notice is issued to the opposite party would not mean that the Court would be precluded from rejecting the application if the opposite party is able to satisfy the Court that the applicant's contention was wrong and that the decree is really not contrary to law or to some usage having the force of law or that it is not otherwise erroneous or unjust. The Court should proceed to enquire into the pauperism of the applicant only after it has definitely come to the conclusion that the application is not fit to be rejected on the above grounds; *Nagarattamma* v. *Nagayya,* AIR 1933 Mad 658: 65 Mad LJ 362; *Somasundaram Chettiar* v. *Arunachalam Chettiar,* AIR 1932 Mad 523: ILR 55 Mad 982; *Panchu Bala Dasi* v. *Nikhil Rajan Pal,* 60 Cal WN 835: AIR 1956 Cal 530; Dissented from: *Narsingh Dass* v. *Mool Raj,* ILR (1958) 8 Raj 44: 1958 Raj LW 295: AIR 1958 Raj 133 (136) (Pr 15) (DB).

2. Order XLIV, Rule 1 – Scope – Rejection of Application for Leave to Appeal in *Forma Pauperis*—Power of Court

The High Court of Madras examined the scope of an appeal as *pauperis* and held that a Court is bound to reject an application for leave to file on appeal in forma pauperis, if on a perusal thereof and of the judgment and decree appealed from, it sees no reason to think that the decree is contrary to law or to some usage having the force of law or is otherwise erroneous or unjust. It is not even necessary for the appellate court to hear the petitioner in a pauper appeal before rejecting the appeal or to grant appellant time for paying the Court-fee. So, where the appellate court hears the counsel for the petitioner and rejects the petition it must be presumed to have applied its mind to the arguments of the learned counsel and the facts of the case and the mere fact that no detailed reasons were given for rejection is no proof that the appellate court did not apply its mind to the facts of the case or the arguments urged. Any interference in revision under section 115 of the Civil P.C. with such an order would not be justified. Case-law reviewed; *Swaminatha Pillai* v. *Balasubrahmanya Udayar*, (1951) 64 MLW 333: (1951) 1 Mad LJ 472: 1951 Mad WN 273: AIR 1952 Mad 178 (Pr 4). A Division Bench of the High Court of Andhra Pradesh said that when once an application under Order XLIV, rule 2, C.P.C., is accepted, it is not competent for the Court, to reject that application unless it be by way of review. The question whether an application comes within the purview of Order XLIV, rule 2 or not is one that has to be decided before the application under Order XLIV, rule 1, is allowed. But when once an order has been passed finally, it is not open to impeach that order, except by way of review. In an application under Order XLIV, rule 2, it is permissible for the High Court to issue notice before the application is allowed. But that is not the same thing as saying that after the appellant is permitted to file an appeal in forma pauperis it is open to the respondent who had received the notice after the admission of the appeal to reopen the question. The two situations are different and distinct; *Abdul Azeem* v. *Syed Miram*, (1960) 2 Andh WR 303: 1960 Andh LT 772: AIR 1961 AP 65 (65, 66) (Prs 6, 7) (DB).

3. Order XLIV, Rule 1 – Conditional Leave to Defend Granted under Order XXXVII, Rule 2 – Condition not Observed

Suit decreed—Leave to appeal in *forma pauperis* – If can be granted—Where the judgment appealed against was simply a formal order to the effect that since the defendant had failed to deposit the sum in suit and costs in Court within the specified period, on which condition alone she was allowed to defend the suit under Order XXXVII, rule 3, C.P. Code, the suit was decreed. Held, that even if the order by which this condition of deposit of suit amount and cost was imposed on the defendant were to be treated as part of the judgment under appeal, there was nothing prima facie contrary to lax/or otherwise erroneous or unjust in it, in order to entitle the defendant to appeal in *forma pauperis;* ILR 1958 Punj 663: 60 Punj LR 587: *Mohd-un-Nisa Begum* v. *Fayaz Ali Hashmi*, ILR 1958 Punj 663: 60 Punj LR 587: AIR 1958 Punj 437 (440) (Pt C) (Pr 15).

4. Order XLIV, Rule 1 – Time Given for Payment of Court-fee on Rejection of Leave to Appeal as a Pauper – Right of Respondent to Challenge Admission of Appeal

When time is given for payment of Court-fee on rejection of leave to appeal as a pauper, the appeal though deemed to have been filed when the appeal memo was filed along with the application for leave to sue as a pauper, it is subject to the right of the respondent to challenge the admission of the appeal where it is made *ex parte*. But it can be challenged only on the ground that the original application for leave to appeal as a pauper was itself *mala fide* or fraudulent, the burden of proving which is on the respondent. *Shivji Kunvarji* v. *Kalianji Ratanshi*, AIR 1951 Kutch 87 (Pr 4). Where application for leave to appeal as pauper is filed by clerk of appellant's counsel and application is found not *mala fide* or fraudulent—Appellant subsequently paying requisite court-fees—Effect —Court can accept appeal section 149. 1959 MPLJ (Notes) 94. O. 44, R. 1 and section 149.

Where permission to file appeal as pauper is rejected for non payment of court fees, Court can grant time to pay court-fee. The dismissal of an application for permission to file an appeal in forma pauperis does not entail dismissal of the appeal. The Court has power under section 149, C.P. Code, to grant time to pay necessary Court-fee. ILR 22 Bom 849: AIR 1918 Mad 1039 and *Mohommed Farzand Ali* v. *Rahat Ali*, 40 All 381: AIR 1918 All 194, Foil.; *Vertannes* v. *R.G.B. Lawson*, AIR 1935 Rang 336: ILR 13 Rang 50, not foll. 1959 NI P LJ (Notes) 6.

5. Order XLIV, Rules 2 and I – Application Accepted – Rejection – Power of Court

A Division Bench of the High Court of Andhra Pradesh said that when once an application under Order XLIV, rule 2, Civil P.C., is accepted, it is not competent for the Court, to reject that application unless it be by way of review. The question whether an application comes within the purview of Order XLIV, rule 2 or not is one that has to be decided before the application under Order XLIV, rule 1, is allowed. But when once an order has been passed finally, it is not open to impeach that order except by way of review. In an application under Order XLIV, rule 2, it is permissible for the High Court to issue notice before the application is allowed. But that is not the same thing as saying that after the appellant is permitted to file an appeal in *forma pauperis* it is open to the respondent who had received the notice after the admission of the appeal to reopen the question. The two situations are different and distinct; *Abdul Azeem* v. *Syed Miram*, (1960) 2 Andh WR 303: 1960 Andh LT 772: AIR 1961 AP 65 (65, 66) (Prs 6, 7) (DB).

6. Order XLIV, Rule 1, Proviso – Scope

Where the Court is not satisfied that the decree is contrary to law or to some usage having the force of law or is otherwise erroneous or unjust, leave to appeal as pauper cannot be granted under Order XLIV, rule 1 AIR 1955 VP 4 (5) (Pt B) (Prs 1, 3).

7. Order XLIV, Rule 2 – Whether Respondent is Entitled to Notice

The High court of Kerala said that on an application for leave to appeal as pauper being filed, the respondent is not entitled to notice. Even if a notice to respondent is issued, the respondent is not entitled to say that decree sought to be appealed against is contrary to law. He can only contest the fact of pauperism of applicant. *See ibidi*, Order XLIV, rule 1. *Krishna Bhatta* v. *Ananta Bhatta*, AIR 1961 Ker 309: 1960 Ker LJ 1177: 1961 Ker LT 38. The High Court of Calcutta said that where the respondent files appeal in *forma pauperis*, appellant disposing will have the opportunity and the right to challenge of property immediately after decree against him. Permission for hearing of the appeal. *Arunendra Nath* v. *Sanat Kumar*, 58 Cal WN 367: 93 Cal LJ 165, overruled cannot be granted. *Dass Bank Ltd.* v. *Kali Kumari Debi*, AIR 1958 Cal 530: 62 Cal WN 493: ILR (1959) 1 Cal 423, approved; *Tilak Mahto* v. *Akhil Kishore*, ILR 10 Pat 606: AIR 1931 Pat 183; The defendants who filed an appeal from a decree *Pawdhari* v. *Ram Sanwari*, AIR 1934 All 1004: ILR 57 All 440: 1934 All LJ 961 (FB); *Mohd-un-Nisa Begum* v. *Fayaz Ali Hashmi*, ILR 1958 Punj 663: 60 Punj LR 587: AIR 1958 Punj 437; AIR 1958 against them made an application under Order XLIV, rule 1 for Raj 133;

Habshi Mian v. *Mehdi Hasan,* AIR 1937 Oudh 222: ILR 13 Luck 31, diss. from Shib permission to file the appeal in *forma pauperis*. *Shib Krishna Das* v. *Panchanan Ganguly,* 65 Cal WN 576: ILR (1961) 2 Cal 688 appeared that immediately after the decree was passed 576: AIR 1981 Cal 346 (351) (Pr 13) (FB) the defendant sold away, by registered deed certain immovable properties.

8. Order XLIV, Rule 3 (1) – Second appeal by indigent person – Application for leave to appeal as pauper

In *Late Bhajan Bai* v. *Dilsai,* 2017 AIR CC 959 (Chhattisgarh) learned counsel for the applicant mentioned the judgment and decree passed by the Court below filed by the then plaintiff, i.e. present applicants who are the legal heirs of the then plaintiff Bhajan Bai, their names were duly incorporated during hearing of FA No.19A/14. And as the first appellate court set aside the judgment and decree passed by the trial Court, the plaintiff of the original suit/respondents of the first appeal/present applicants have filed instant Miscellaneous Civil Case followed by the second appeal for consideration, hence, prayed that instant MCC may be allowed and the second appeal may be heard on admission and to proceed further in the matter.

As the applicants have complied with the provisions of law contained in Order XLIV, Rule 3(1) CPC there is no need to examine their status regarding pauperism from Registrar (Judl.). With this, prayer of the applicants is allowed and the matter is considered on the basis of affidavit filed by the applicants and the documents annexed.

The High Court said, a perusal of the entire material and in absence of any counter affidavit on behalf of the respondents it appears that the plaintiffs were granted liberty to file a suit as pauper which reflects from the judgment at para 26 last two lines and also in the decree of the trial Court. Before the first appellate court, as the present applicants were arrayed as respondents, they were not required to pay any court fee. The first appellate Court allowed the appeal and set aside the judgment and decree passed by the trial Court in favour of the appellant. The present applicants were aggrieved with the said judgment and decree passed by the first appellate court and then only occasion arises for payment of court fee. On perusal of the affidavit applicant No.1(A), he has stated on oath that the plaintiffs were allowed to sue the civil suit as indigent persons and were granted live to sue the civil suit as indigent person since the date of decree appealed from. In absence of any counter affidavit the statement of oath is prima facie acceptable.

Provisions of Order XLIV, Rule 3 (1) CPC is also applicable in the second appeal as there is no separate provision for the same.

On due consideration and also with the fact that delay in filing the instant MCC has already been condoned vide order dated 19.7.2016, the MCC is allowed and the applicants are permitted to sue the matter as pauper without paying court fee as required for the moment. It is further observed that if subsequently anything contrary to the above fact is surfaced, then the applicants may be asked to pay the requisite court fee as required.

9. Order XLIV, Rule 1 – Application under - Indigent Person

In *Shalender Kumar* v. *Umesh Kumar Mittal,* (P&H) 2017 (1) Law Herald 767; 2017 (3) ICC 325: LNIND 2017 PNH 963 relevant part of the impugned order passed by learned first appellate court, read as under:—

> "There is an application under Order XLIV, Rule 1 CPC seeking permission to file the appeal as indigent persons. Appellant No. 1 Shalender Kumar, present in Court, made statement to the effect that he is employed at a shop and use to repair bags and getting Rs. 8500/- per month as salary. Appellant No. 2 Ravi Shankar, present in Court, also made statement to the effect that he is working in a factory, which manufactures surgical instruments and getting Rs. 7000/- per month as salary. Considering the statements made by appellants, this Court is of the view that appellants are in a position to pay the Court fee and they cannot be allowed to pursue their appeal as indigent persons. Accordingly, application is dismissed. Case is adjourned to 5.12.2015."

The High Court said, during the course of hearing, learned counsel for the petitioners could not point out any patent illegality or perversity in the impugned order, which may warrant interference at the hands of this Court, while exercising its revisional jurisdiction. So far as judgment of this Court in *Santa* v. *Jarnail Singh,* 2010 (5) Law Herald 3962, relied upon by learned counsel for the petitioners is concerned, there is no dispute about the observations made therein. However, a close perusal of the cited judgment would show that it is of no help to the petitioners, being distinguishable on facts.

It is the settled principle of law that peculiar facts of each case are to be examined, considered and appreciated first, before applying any codified or judge-made law thereto. Sometimes, difference of even one circumstance or additional fact can make the world of difference, as held by the Hon'ble Supreme Court in *Padmausundara Rao* v. *State of Tamil Nadu,* 2002 (3) SCC 533: AIR 2002 SC 1334, *Union of India* v. *Amrit Lal Manchanda,* 2004 (3) SCC 75: AIR 2004 SC 1625, *State of Orissa* v. *Md. Illiyas,* 2006 (1) SCC 275: AIR 2006 SC 258 and *State of Rajasthan* v. *Ganeshi Lal,* 2008 (2) SCC 533: AIR 2008 SC 690.

Once the petitioners have been found to be persons of means, having regular monthly source of income, learned first appellate court was well within its jurisdiction to pass the impugned order and the same deserves to be upheld. Under the circumstances of the case, noticed herein above, it can be safely concluded that neither the impugned order has been found suffering from any patent illegality, nor learned court committed any error of law, while passing the impugned order and the same deserves to be upheld, for this reason also.

ORDER XLV

APPEALS TO THE SUPREME COURT

The provisions contained in Part VII of the Code deal with the substantive provisions relating to appeals, the provisions contained under Order XLI to Order XLV deal with the rules to enforce the said provisions. It may be noted here that out of these provisions Order XLV deals with the rules regarding appeal to the Supreme Court.

It is pertinent to note here that rules under Order XLV have been framed by the Code of Civil Procedure, but apart from it, the Constitution of India under article 145 empowers the Supreme Court to frame its own rules for regulating the practice and procedure of the Court as and when required (with the approval of the President). Article 145 of the constitution says:

(1) Subject to the provisions of any law made by Parliament the Supreme Court may from time to time, with the approval of the President, make rules for regulating generally the practice and procedure of the Court including:

(a) rules as to the persons practising before the Court;

(b) rules as to the procedure for hearing appeals, and other matters pertaining to appeals including the time within which appeals to the Court are to be entered;

(c) rules as to the proceedings in the Court for the enforcement of any of the rights conferred by Part III;

(cc) rules as to the proceedings in the Court under article 139A;

(d) rules as to the entertainment of appeals under sub-clause (c) of clause (1) of article 134;

(e) any judgment pronounced or order made by the Court may be received and rules as to the conditions the procedure for such review including the time within which applications to the Court for such review are to be entered;

(f) rules as to the costs of and incidental to any proceedings in the Court and as to the fees to be charged in respect of proceeding therein;

(g) rules as to the granting of bail;

(h) rules as to stay of proceedings;

(i) rules providing for the summary determination of any appeal which appears to the Court to be frivolous or vexatious or brought for the purpose of delay;

(j) rules as to the procedure for inquiries referred to in clause (1) of article 317.

(2) Subject to the provisions of clause (3), rules made under this article may fix the minimum number of Judges who are to sit for any purpose, and may provide for the powers of Single Judges and Division Courts.

(3) The minimum number of Judges who are to sit for the purpose of deciding any case involving a substantial question of law as to the interpretation of this Constitution or for the purpose of hearing any reference under article 143 shall be five:

Provided that, where the Court hearing an appeal under any of the provisions of this chapter other than article 132 consists of less than five Judges and in the course of the hearing of the appeal the Court is satisfied that the appeal involves a substantial question of law as to the interpretation of this Constitution the determination of which is necessary for the disposal of the appeal, such Court shall refer the question for opinion to a Court constituted as required by this clause for the purpose of deciding any case involving such a question and shall on receipt of the opinion dispose of the appeal in conformity with such opinion.

(4) No judgment shall be delivered by the Supreme Court save in open Court, and no report shall be made under article 143 save in accordance with an opinion also delivered in open Court.

(5) No judgment and no such opinion shall be delivered by the Supreme Court save with the concurrence of a majority of the Judges present at the hearing of the case, but nothing in this clause shall be deemed to prevent a Judge who does not concur from delivering a dissenting judgment or opinion. Accordingly, "Supreme Court Rules, 1950" were framed. They were replaced by the present rules called as "Supreme Court Rules, 1966".

1. "Decree" defined.—In this Order, unless there is something repugnant in the subject or context, the expression "decree" shall include a final order.

2. Application to Court whose decree complained of.—[(1)] Whoever desires to appeal to the Supreme Court shall apply by petition to the Court whose decree is complained of.

(2) Every petition under sub-rule (1) shall be heard as expeditiously as possible and endeavour shall be made to conclude the disposal of the petition within sixty days from the date on which the petition is presented to the Court under sub-rule (1).

STATE AMENDMENT

Uttar Pradesh.—In its application to the State of Uttar Pradesh, in rule 2 after sub-rule (2) the following sub-rule be inserted, namely:—

> "(3) Notwithstanding anything contained in sub-rule (1), whoever desires to appeal to the Supreme Court, may apply orally to the Court whose decree is to be complained of, immediately before or after the pronouncement of the judgment by the Court, for a certificate contemplated in sub-rule (1) of rule 3, and the Court may either grant or refuse the certificate, or direct the applicant to file petition as required by sub-rule (1):

Provided that if an oral application is entertained and rejected, no written petition under sub-rule (1) shall lie." [U.P. Act 57 of 1976].

HIGH COURT AMENDMENT

Andhra Pradesh.—In Order XLV, for rule 2, substitute the following rules, namely:—

> "2. Application of Court whose decree or judgment complained of.—Whoever desires to appeal to the Supreme Court under clause (1) of article 133 of the Constitution shall apply for a certificate by petition to the Court whose decree or judgment is complained of:
>
> Provided that an application may be made orally for the purpose, immediately after the judgment had been delivered:

Provided further where the certificate has been refused on an oral application no subsequent petition for the certificate shall lie."

[*Vide* Andhra Pradesh Gazette, Pt. II, (R.S.), p. 132, dated 10th February, 1977.]

Bombay.—In Order XLV, in rule 2, after sub-rule (2), insert the following sub-rule, namely:—

"3. Application to Court whose decree is complained of.—(1) Whoever desires to appeal to the Supreme Court shall apply by petition to the Court whose decree is complained of.

(2) Notwithstanding anything contained in sub-rule (1) a party desiring to appeal to the Supreme Court may apply orally immediately after the pronouncement of the judgment by the Court, and the Court may grant or refuse leave to the party to appeal to the Supreme Court or direct the party to file a petition as required by sub-rule (1):

Provided, however, that if an oral application for leave under sub-rule (2) is made and rejected, no written petition under sub-rule (1) shall lie." (w.e.f. 1-10-1983)

Madras.—In Order XLV, in rule 2, for sub-rule (1), substitute the following sub-rule, namely:—

"(1) whoever desires to appeal to the Supreme Court, may, make an oral application to the Court whose decree is complained or, immediately after the pronouncement of the judgment and in such a case, it shall be heard and disposed of immediately, or may apply by petition to the Court, whose decree is complained of."

[*Vide* Tamil Nadu Government Gazette, Pt. III, section 2, p. 136, dated 16th November, 1988.]

Patna.—In Order XLV, for rule 2, substitute the following rule, namely:—

"2. Application to Court whose judgment, decree or final order is complained of.—(1) Whoever desires to appeal to the Supreme Court may apply by petition to the Court whose judgment, decree or final order is complained of.

(2) Notwithstanding anything contained in sub-rule (1) a party desiring to appeal to the Supreme Court may apply orally immediately after the pronouncement of the judgment or final order by the Court and the Court may grant or refuse leave to the party to appeal to the Supreme Court or direct the party to file a petition as required by sub-rule (1):

Provided that if an oral application for leave under the sub-rule (2) is made and rejected, no written petition under sub-rule (1) shall lie."

[*Vide* Bihar Gazette, Pt. III, p. 3, dated 11th January, 1978.]

3. Certificate as to value or fitness.—[(1) Every petition shall state the grounds of appeal and pray for a certificate—

(i) that the case involves a substantial question of law of general importance, and

(ii) that in the opinion of the Court the said question needs to be decided by the Supreme Court.]

(2) Upon receipt of such petition, the Court shall direct notice to be served on the opposite party to show cause why the said certificate should not be granted.

HIGH COURT AMENDMENT

Allahabad.—In Order XLV, in rule 3, in sub-rule (2), at the end, omit full stop and insert the words "unless it thinks fit to refuse the certificate."

[*Vide* Notification No. 1/VII-d-158, dated, 4th January, 1960.]

Andhra Pradesh.—In Order XLV, for rule 3, substitute the following rule, namely:—

"3. Contents of the petition.—Every such petition shall state the grounds of appeal and pray for a certificate to appeal to the Supreme Court under clause (1) of article 13 of the Constitution."

[*Vide* Andhra Pradesh Gazette, Pt. II, (R.S.), p. 132, dated 10th February, 1977.]

Bombay.—In Order XLV, in rule 3, in sub-rule (2), at the end, omit the full stop and insert the words "unless it thinks fit to refuse the certificate."

[*Vide* Notification No. P 1614/45, dated 26th June, 1951.]

Gujarat.—Same as in Bombay.

Kerala.—In Order XLV, in rule 3,—

(i) for sub-rule (2), substitute the following sub-rule, namely:—

"(2) Upon receipt of such petition, the Court, after fixing a day for hearing the applicant or his pleader and hearing him, if he appears, may dismiss the petition."

(ii) after sub-rule (2), insert sub-rule (3) as in Madhya Pradesh (b).

[*Vide* Notification No. Bl-3312/58, dated 7th April, 1959.]

Madhya Pradesh.—In Order XLV, in rule 3,—

(a) for sub-rule (2), substitute the following sub-rule, namely:—

"(2) Upon receipt of such petition, the Court, after sending for the record, and after fixing a day for hearing the applicant or his pleader and hearing him accordingly if he appears on that day, may dismiss the petition."

(b) after sub-rule (2), insert the following sub-rule, namely:—

"(3) Unless the Court dismisses the petition under sub-rule (2), it shall direct notice to be served on the opposite party to show cause why the said certificate should not be granted." (w.e.f. 16-9-1960)

Madras.—In Order XLV, in rule 3, in sub-rule (2), insert the following proviso, namely:—

"Provided that where leave to appeal is sought from a decree dismissing a proceeding *in limine*, notice shall not be necessary unless the Court otherwise directs." (w.e.f. 19-6-1969)

Orissa.—In Order XLV, in rule 3, for sub-rule (2), substitute the following sub-rules, namely:—

"(2) Upon receipt of such petition, the Court may, after giving the applicant or his pleader an opportunity of being heard dismiss the petition summarily.

(3) Unless the Court dismisses the petition under sub-rule (2) it shall direct notice to be served on the opposite party to show cause why the said certificate should not be granted:

Provided that where a party has appealed through a pleader in the High Court, service of notice on such pleader either in the manner provided in this Code or by sending a copy of such notice by registered post shall be deemed to be sufficient notice to the party." (w.e.f. 14-5-1984)

4. Consolidation of suits.—*Rep. by the Code of Civil Procedure (Amendment Act, 1973 (49 of 1973) section 4 (w.e.f. 29-11-1973).*

5. Remission of dispute to Court of first instance.—[*Rep. by section 4, ibid., (w.e.f. 29-11-1973).*]

6. Effect of refusal of certificate.—Where such certificate is refused, the petition shall be dismissed.

7. Security and deposit required on grant of certificate.—(1) Where the certificate is granted, the applicant shall, within ninety days or such further period, not exceeding sixty days, as the Court may upon cause shown allow; from the date of the decree complained of, or within six weeks from the date of the grant of the certificate whichever is the later date,—

(a) furnish security in cash or in Government securities for the costs of the respondent, and

(b) deposit the amount required to defray the expense of translating, transcribing indexing, printing, and transmitting to the Supreme Court a correct copy of the whole record of the suit, except—

(1) formal documents directed to be excluded by any Rule of the Supreme Court in force for the time being;

(2) papers which the parties agree to exclude;

(3) accounts, or portions of accounts, which the officer empowered by the Court for that purpose considers unnecessary, and which the parties have not specifically asked to be included; and

(4) such other documents as the High Court may direct to be excluded:

Provided that the Court at the time of granting the certificate may, after hearing any opposite party who appears, order on the ground of special hardship that some other form of security may be furnished:

Provided further, that no adjournment shall be granted to an opposite party to contest the nature of such security.

HIGH COURT AMENDMENT

Allahabad.—In Order XLV, in rule 7,—

(a) in sub-rule (1), in clause (a), between the words "the respondent" and the word "and" insert the words "except when the Government is the applicant"

(b) in sub-rule (1), in the first proviso, for the words "at the time of granting the certificate", substitute the words "at any time before expiry of the period for furnishing security".

[*Vide* Notification No. 3713-454(7), dated 20th June, 1936 and Notification No. 676/35(a)-1, dated 4th February, 1939.]

Andhra Pradesh.—In Order XLV, omit rule 7. (w.e.f. 4-8-1975)

Bombay.—In Order XLV, after rule 7 insert the following rule, namely:—

"7A. Security not to be demanded from Union or State Government or Government servant defended by Government.—No such security as is mentioned in clause (a) of sub-rule (1) of rule 7 above shall be required from the Union of India or [a State Government or where] Government has undertaken the defence of the suit, from any public officer sued in respect of an act alleged to [have been] done by him in his official capacity." (w.e.f. 1-10-1983)

Gujarat.—In Order XLV, after rule 7, insert the following rule, namely:—

"7A. No such security as is mentioned in clause (a) of sub-rule (1) of rule 7, shall be required from the Union of India, or, where the State Government has undertaken the defence of the suit from any public officer sued in respect of an act alleged to be done by him in his official capacity." (w.e.f. 17-8-1961)

Kerala.—In Order XLV, in rule 7, after sub-rule (1) insert the following sub-rule, namely:—

"(2) No such security as is mentioned in rule 7(1) clause (a) shall be required from the Government or, where State Government has undertaken the defence of the suit, from any public officer and in respect of an Act purporting to be done by him in his official capacity."

[*Vide* Notification No. Bl-3312/58, dated 7th April, 1959.]

Madhya Pradesh.—In Order XLV, insert rule 7A as in Gujarat.

[*Vide* Notification No. 3409, dated 29th June, 1943.]

8. Admission of appeal and procedure thereon.—Where such security has been furnished and deposit made to the satisfaction of the Court, the Court shall—

(a) declare the appeal admitted,

(b) give notice thereof to the respondent,

(c) transmit to the Supreme Court under the seal of the Court a correct copy of the said record, except as aforesaid, and

(d) give to either party one or more authenticated copies of any of the papers in the suit on his applying therefor and paying the reasonable expenses incurred in preparing them.

HIGH COURT AMENDMENT

Andhra Pradesh.—In Order XLV, for rule 8, substitute the following rule, namely:—

"8. On receipt from the Supreme Court of the copy of the petition of appeal, the Registrar of the Court shall—

(i) cause notice of the lodgment of the petition of appeal to be served on the respondent personally or in such manner as provided for service of its own processes or as the Court may prescribe or order;

(ii) unless otherwise ordered by the Supreme Court, transmit to the Supreme Court at the expense of the appellant the original record of the case; and

(iii) as soon as notice as aforementioned is served, to send a certificate as to the date or dates on which the said notice was served." (w.e.f. 4-8-1975)

Madras.—In Order XLV, in rule 8,—

(i) for clause (b), substitute the following clause, namely:—

"(b) give notice to such of the respondents as have entered appearance at the hearing, of the appeal in the High Court and such of the respondents who have entered appearance in pursuance of notice issued under rule 3(2) *supra*";

(ii) in clause (c), at the end, insert the words "give notice of such transmission to the respondents specified in rule 8(b) above, and". (w.e.f. 28-1-1959).

9. Revocation of acceptance of security.—At any time before the admission of the appeal the Court may, upon cause shown, revoke the acceptance of any such security, and make further directions thereon.

HIGH COURT AMENDMENT

Andhra Pradesh.—In Order XLV, omit rule 9. (w.e.f. 4-8-1975)

9A. Power to dispense with notices in case of deceased parties.—Nothing in these rules requiring any notice to be served on or given to an opposite party or respondent shall be deemed to require any notice to be served on or given to the legal representative of any deceased opposite party or deceased respondent in a case, where such opposite party or respondent did not appear either at the hearing in the Court whose decree is complained of or at any proceedings subsequent to the decree of that Court:

Provided that notices under sub-rule (2) of rule 3 and under rule 8 shall be given by affixing the same in some conspicuous place in the court-house of the Judge of the district in which the suit was originally brought, and by publication in such newspapers as the Court may direct.

HIGH COURT AMENDMENT

Kerala.—In Order XLV, in rule 9A, in the proviso after the words "sub-rule", for the figure "(2)" substitute the figure "(3)".

[*Vide* Notification No. Bl-3312/58, dated 7th April, 1959.]

10. Power to order further security or payment.—Where at any time after the admission of an appeal but before the transmission of the copy of the record, except as aforesaid, to the Supreme Court such security appears inadequate,

or further payment is required for the purpose of translating, transcribing, printing, indexing or transmitting the copy of the record, except as aforesaid,

the Court may order the appellant to furnish, within a time to be fixed by the Court, other and sufficient security, or to make, within except as aforesaid.

HIGH COURT AMENDMENT

Andhra Pradesh.—In Order XLV, omit rule 10. (w.e.f. 4-8-1975)

11. Effect of failure to comply with order.—Where the appellant fails to comply with such order, the proceedings shall be stayed, and the appeal shall not proceed without an order in this behalf of the Supreme Court and in the meantime execution of the decree appealed from shall not be stayed.

HIGH COURT AMENDMENT

Andhra Pradesh.—In Order XLV, omit rule 11. (w.e.f. 4-8-1975)

12. Refund of balance deposit.—When the copy of the record, except as aforesaid, has been transmitted to the Supreme Court, the appellant may obtain a refund of the balance (if any) of the amount which he had deposited under rule 7.

HIGH COURT AMENDMENT

Andhra Pradesh.—In Order XLV, omit rule 12. (w.e.f. 4-8-1975)

13. Powers of Court pending appeal.—(1) Notwithstanding the grant of a certificate for the admission of any appeal, the decree appealed from shall be unconditionally executed, unless the Court otherwise directs.

(2) The Court may, if it thinks fit, on special cause shown by any party interested in the suit, or otherwise appearing to the court,—

(a) impound any movable property in dispute or any part thereof, or

(b) allow the decree appealed from to be executed, taking such security from the respondent as the Court thinks fit for the due performance of any order which the Supreme Court may make on the appeal, or

(c) stay the execution of the decree appealed from, taking such security from the appellant as the Court thinks fit for the due performance of the decree appealed from, or of any decree or order which the Supreme Court may make on the appeal, or

(d) place any party seeking the assistance of the Court under such conditions or give such other direction respecting the subject-matter of the appeal, as it thinks fit, by the appointment of a receiver or otherwise.

14. Increase of security found inadequate.—(1) Where at any time during the pendency of the appeal the security furnished by either party appears inadequate, the Court may, on the application of the other party, require further security.

(2) In default of such further security being furnished as required by the Court,—

(a) if the original security was furnished by the appellant, the Court may, on the application of the respondent, execute the decree, appealed from as if the appellant had furnished no such security;

(b) if the original security was furnished by the respondent, the Court shall, so far as may be practicable stay the further execution of the decree, and restore the parties to the position in which they respectively were when the security which appears inadequate was furnished, or give such direction respecting the subject-matter of the appeal as it thinks fit.

HIGH COURT AMENDMENT

Andhra Pradesh.—In Order XLV, omit rule 14. (w.e.f. 4-8-1975)

15. Procedure to enforce orders of the Supreme Court.—(1) Whoever desires to obtain execution of any decree or order of the Supreme Court shall apply by petition, accompanied by a certified copy of the decree passed or order made in appeal and sought to be executed, to the Court from which the appeal to the Supreme Courts, was preferred.

(2) Such Court shall transmit the decree or order of the Supreme Court to the Court which passed the first decree appealed from, or to such other Court as the Supreme Court by such decree or order may direct and shall (upon the application of either party) give such directions as may be required for the execution of the same; and the Court to which the said decree or order is so transmitted shall execute it accordingly, in the manner and according to the provisions applicable to the execution of its original decrees.

[* * *]

(4) Unless the Supreme Court otherwise directs, no decree or order of that Court shall be inoperative on the ground that no notice has been served on or given to the legal representative of any deceased opposite party or deceased respondent in a case, where such opposite party or respondent did not appear either at the hearing in the Court whose decree was complained of or at any proceedings subsequent to the decree of that Court, but such order shall have the same force and effect as if it had been made before the death took place.

HIGH COURT AMENDMENT

Allahabad.—In Order XLV, in rule 15, for sub-rule (1), substitute the following sub-rule, namely:—

"(1) Whoever desires to obtain,—

(a) execution of any order of any Supreme Court; or,

(b) where an appeal has been dismissed by the Supreme Court for want of prosecution, an order of the Court from which the appeal to [the Supreme Court] was preferred terminating proceedings and determining the costs, shall apply to the said Court by a petition, accompanied by a certificate copy of the decree passed or order made by the Supreme Court of which execution is desired or to which the effect is to be given and a memorandum of all costs incurred in India that are claimed in pursuance thereof."

[*Vide* Notification No. 1591/35(a), dated 7th April, 1928.]

Andhra Pradesh.—In Order XLV, in rule 15,—

(i) for sub-rule (1), substitute the following sub-rule, namely:—

"(1) Whoever desires to obtain execution of any appellate decree or order of the Supreme Court shall apply by petition accompanied by a certified copy of the said decree or order, to the Court of first instance.

Explanation.—The Court of first instance in this rule shall mean the Court in which the suit or proceedings was first instituted and where such Court has ceased to exist or to have jurisdiction to execute it, the Court which if the suit wherein the decree was passed was instituted at the time of making the application for the execution of the decree, would have jurisdiction to try such suit."

(ii) omit sub-rule (2);

(iii) re-number sub-rule (4) as sub-rule (2).

[*Vide* Notification No. ROC No. 6842/51-B-l, dated 9th August, 1957.]

Bombay.—In Order XLV, for rule 15, substitute the following rule, namely:—

"15. Procedure to enforce order of the Supreme Court.—(1) (a) Any decree passed or order made by the Supreme Court in exercise of the appellate jurisdiction including any order as to the costs of, and incidental to, any proceedings in that Court shall be enforceable in accordance with the provisions of law for the time being in force relating to the enforcement of the decrees or orders of the Court or Tribunal from which the appeal to the Supreme Court was preferred or sought to be preferred.

(b) The costs incurred in the High Court as incidental to the Supreme Court Appeal including the costs in the application for leave to appeal to the Supreme Court shall be recoverable where awarded, by execution of the order of the High Court in the same manner in which the decree or order of the High Court from which the appeal to the Supreme Court was preferred or sought to be preferred would have been executed.

(2) Unless the Supreme Court otherwise directs no decree or order of that Court shall be inoperative on the ground that no notice has been served on or given to the legal representative of any deceased opposite party or deceased respondent in a case, where such opposite party or respondent did not appear either at the hearing of the Court whose decree was complained of or at any proceedings subsequent to the decree of that Court but such order shall have the same force and effect as if it had been made before the death took place." (w.e.f. 1-10-1983).

Karnataka.—In Order XLV, in rule 15, omit sub-rules (1) and (2). (w.e.f. 30-3-1967)

Madras.—Same as in Andhra Pradesh. (w.e.f. 28-5-1958)

16. Appeal from order relating to execution.—The orders made by the Court which executes the decree or order of the Supreme Court, relating to such execution, shall be appealable in the same manner and subject to the same rules as the orders of such Court relating to the execution of its own decrees.

HIGH COURT AMENDMENT

Allahabad.—In Order XLV, after rule 16, insert the following rule, namely:—

> "17. The provisions of sub-rules (1) and (2) of rule 15 and the provisions of rule 16 shall apply *mutatis mutandis*, to the execution of decrees or orders for costs passed by the Supreme Court in appeals from the High Court"

[*Vide* Notification No. 3922/VII-d 107, dated 14th August, 1948.]

Andhra Pradesh.—Same as in Madras.

Kerala.—In Order XLV, after rule 16, insert the following rule, namely:—

> "***16A. Appeals to Federal Court.***—The provisions of sub-rules (1) and (2) of rule 15 and the provisions of rule 16 shall apply, *mutatis mutandis*, to the execution of decrees or orders for costs passed by the Federal Court in appeals from the High Court."

Madhya Pradesh. In Order XLV, insert rule 17 which is same as in Allahabad with insertion of the words "in accordance with the declaration or order made" after the words "orders for costs passed".

[*Vide* Notification No. 3409, dated 20th June, 1943.]

Madras.—(1) In Order XLV, after rule 16, insert the following rule, namely:—

> "16A. The provisions of sub-rules (1) and (2) of rule 15 and the provisions of rule 16 shall apply *mutants mutandis* to the execution of decrees or orders for costs passed in the Federal Court in appeals from the High Court."

[*Vide* ROC No. 280 of 1945.]

(2) After Order XLV, insert the following Order, namely:—

"ORDER XLVA

APPEALS TO THE SUPREME COURT

1. Decree defined.—In this Order, unless there is something repugnant in the subject or context, the expression "decree" shall include a final order.

2. Application to Court whose decree is complained of.—Whoever desires to appeal to the Supreme Court shall apply by petition to the Court whose decree is complained of.

3. Certificate as to value or fitness.—(1) Every petition shall state the grounds of appeal and pray for a certificate either that, as regards amount or value and nature, the case fulfils the requirements of section 110, or that it is otherwise a fit one for appeal to the Supreme Court.

(2) Upon receipt of such petition, the Court shall direct notice to be served on the opposite party to show cause why the said certificate should not be granted:

Provided that where leave to appeal is sought from a decree dismissing a proceeding *in limine* notice shall not be necessary unless the Court otherwise directs.

4. Consolidation of suits.—For the purpose of pecuniary valuation, suits involving substantially the same questions for determination and decided by the same judgment may be consolidated; but suits decided by separate judgments shall not be consolidated, notwithstanding that they involve substantially the same questions for determination.

5. Remission of dispute to Court of first instance.—In the event of any dispute arising between the parties as to the amount or value of the subject-matter or the suit in the Court of first instance, or as to the amount or value of the subject-matter in dispute on appeal to the Supreme Court, the Court to which a petition for a certificate is made under rule 2, may, if it thinks fit, refer such dispute for report to the Court of first instance, which last mentioned Court shall proceed to determine such amount or value and shall return its report together with the evidence to the Court by which the reference was made.

6. Effect of refusal of certificate.—Where a certificate is refused, the petition shall be dismissed.

7. Powers of Court pending appeal.—(1) Notwithstanding the grant of leave to appeal to the Supreme Court, the decree appealed from shall be unconditionally executed, unless the Court otherwise directs.

(2) The Court may, if it thinks fit on special cause shown by any party interested in the suit, or otherwise appearing to the Court.

(a) impound any movable property in dispute or any part thereof, or

(b) allow the decree appealed from to be executed, taking such security from the respondent as the Court thinks fit for the due performance of the decree appealed from or of any decree or order which the Supreme Court may make on appeal, or

(c) stay the execution of the decree appealed from, taking such security from the appellant as the Court thinks fit for the due performance of the decree appealed from, or of any decree or order which the Supreme Court may make on the appeal, or

(d) place any party seeking the assistance of the Court under such conditions or give such other direction respecting the subject-matter of appeal, as it thinks fit by the appointment of a receiver or otherwise, till the petition for leave to appeal is disposed of or till the appeal is filed in the Supreme Court.

8. Procedure to enforce orders of the Supreme Court.—(1) whoever desires to obtain execution of any appellate decree or order of the Supreme Court shall apply by petition accompanied by a certified copy of the said decree or order to the Court of first instance.

Explanation.—The Court of first instance in this rule shall mean the Court in which the suit or proceeding was first instituted and where such Court has ceased to exist or to have jurisdiction to execute it, the Court, which, if the suit wherein the decree was passed was instituted at the time of making the application for the execution of the decree, would have jurisdiction to try the suit.

(2) Unless the Supreme Court otherwise directs, no decree or order of that Court shall be inoperative on the ground, that no notice has been served on or given to the legal representative of any deceased opposite party or deceased respondent in a case, where such opposite party or respondent did not appear either at the hearing in the Court whose decree was complained of or at any proceedings subsequent to the decree of that Court, but such order shall have the same force and effect as if it had been made before the death took place.

9. Appeal from order relating to execution.—The orders made by Court which executes the decree or order of the Supreme Court relating to such execution, shall be appealable in the same manner as the orders of such Court relating to the execution of its own decree." (w.e.f. 21-4-1971 and 21-8-1974)

17. [Appeals to Federal Court].—Rep. by the Federal Court Act, 1941 (21 of 1941), section 2.

HIGH COURT AMENDMENT

Punjab and Haryana.—For Order XLV, substitute the following Order, namely:—

"ORDER XLV

APPEALS TO THE SUPREME COURT

1. "Decree defined.—In this Order, unless there is something repugnant in the subject or context, the expression "decree" shall include a final order.

2. Application to Court whose decree complained of.—Whoever desires to appeal to the Supreme Court shall apply by petition to the Court whose decree is complained of.

3. Certificate as to the fitness.—(1) Every petition shall state the grounds of appeal and pray for a certificate—

(i) that the case involves a substantial question of law of general importance, and

(ii) that in the opinion of the Court the said question needs to be decided by the Supreme Court.

(2) On receipt of such petition, the Court shall, unless it dismisses the petition at the preliminary hearing, direct notice to be served on the opposite-party to show, cause why the said certificate should not be granted.

4. [Omitted]

5. [Omitted]

6. Effect of refusal of certificate.—Where such certificate is refused, the petition shall be dismissed.

7. Deposit required on grant of certificate.—(1) Where the certificate is granted the applicant shall within ninety days of the order of the Supreme Court under rule 14(1) of the Supreme Court Rules for the time being in force or such further period not exceeding sixty days as the Court may, upon cause shown, allow from the date of the Supreme Court Order under rule 14(1), whichever is later:

(a) deposit the amount required to defray the expense of translating, transcribing, indexing, printing and transmitting to the Supreme Court three copies of the whole record of the suit except—

(1) formal documents directed to be excluded by any rule of the Supreme Court in force for the time being;

(2) papers which the parties agree to exclude;

(3) accounts or portions of accounts which the officer empowered by the Court for that purpose considers unnecessary, and which the parties have not specifically asked to be included;

(4) such other documents as the High Court may direct to be excluded.

8. Power to order further payment.—Where at any time after the admission of an appeal but before the transmission of the copy at the record to the Supreme Court further payment is required for the purpose of translating, transcribing, printing, indexing or transmitting the copy of the record, except as aforesaid, the Court may order the appellant to make, within a time to be specified by the Court, the required payment.

9. Effect to failure to comply with order.—Where the appellant fails to comply with such order, the proceedings shall be stayed, and the appeal shall not proceed without an order in this behalf of the Supreme Court, and in the meantime execution of the decree appealed from shall not be stayed.

9A. Power to dispense with notice in case of deceased.—Nothing in these rules requiring any notice to be served on or given to an opposite-party or respondent shall be deemed to require any notice to be served on or given to the legal representative of any deceased opposite-party or deceased respondent in a case, where such opposite-party or respondent did not appear either at the hearing in the Court whose decree is complained of or at any proceedings subsequent to the decree of that Court:

Provided that notice under sub-rule (2) of rule 3 shall be given by affixing the same on some conspicuous place in the Court-house of the Judge of the district in which the suit was originally brought, and by publication in such newspaper as the Court may direct.

10. Refund of balance deposit.—When the copy of the record, except as aforesaid, has been transmitted to the Supreme Court, the appellant may obtain a refund of the balance, if any, or the amount which he has deposited under rule 7.

11. Power of Court pending appeal.—(1) Notwithstanding the grant of a certificate for the admission of any appeal, the decree appealed from shall be unconditionally executed, unless the Court otherwise directs.

(2) The Court may, if it thinks, fit, on special cause shown by any party interested in the suit, or otherwise appearing to the Court,—

(a) impound any movable property in dispute or any part thereof, or

(b) allow the decree appealed from to be executed, taking such security from the respondent as the Court thinks fit for the due performance of any order which the Supreme Court may make on the appeal, or

(c) stay the execution of the decree appealed from, taking such security from the appellant as the Court thinks for the due performance of the decree appealed from, or of any decree or order which the Supreme Court may make on the appeal, or

(d) place any party seeking the assistance of the Court under such conditions or give such other direction respecting the subject-matter of the appeal, as it thinks fit, by the appointment of a receiver or otherwise.

12. Procedure to enforce orders of the Supreme Court.—(1) Whoever desires to obtain execution of any decree or order of the Supreme Court shall apply by petition, accompanied by a certified copy of the decree passed or order made in appeal and sought to be executed, to the Court from which the appeal to the Supreme Court was preferred.

(2) Such Court shall transmit the decree or order of the Supreme Court to the Court which gassed the first decree appealed from, or to such other Court as the Supreme Court by such decree or order may direct, and shall upon the application of either party give directions as may be required for the execution of the same, and the Court to which the said decree or order is so transmitted shall execute it accordingly, in the manner and according to the provisions applicable to the execution of the original decrees.

(3) Unless the Supreme Court otherwise directs, no decree or order of that Court shall be inoperative on the ground that no notice has been served on or given to the legal representative of any deceased opposite-party or deceased respondent in a case, where such opposite-party or respondent did not appear either at hearing in the Court whose decree was complained of or at any proceeding subsequent to the decree of that Court, but such order shall have the same force and effect as if it had been made before the death took place.

13. Appeal from order relating to execution.—The orders made by the Court which executes the decree or order of the Supreme Court, relating to such execution, shall be appealable in the same manner and subject to the same rules as the orders of such Court relating to the execution of its own decrees,"

[*Vide* G.S.R. CA/5/1908/S/122/73, dated 21st December, 1973, published in the Punjab Government Gazette, L.S. dated 4th January, 1974.]

Besides the provisions contained in Order XLV of CPC, the Supreme Court also has framed its own rules known as the Supreme Courts Rules 1966. The provisions contained in Order XVI of the said rules are as follows:—

ORDER XLV

APPEALS BY SPECIAL LEAVE

2. Where [certificate of fitness] to appeal to the Court was refused in a case by the High Court, a petition for special leave to appeal to the Court shall, subject to the provisions of sections 4, 5, 12 and 14 of the Limitation Act, 1963 (36 of 1963) be lodged in the Court within sixty days from the date of the order of refusal and in any other case within ninety days from the date of the Judgment or Order sought to be appealed from:

> Provided that where an application for leave to appeal to the High Court from the Judgment of a Single Judge of that Court has been made and refused, in computing the period of limitation in that case under this rule, the period from the making of that application and the rejection thereof shall also be excluded.

Explanation.—For purposes of this rule, the expression 'order of refusal' means the order refusing to [grant the certificate under article 134A of the Constitution being a certificate of the nature] referred to in article 132 or article 133 of the Constitution on merits and shall not include an order rejecting the application on the ground of limitation or on the ground that such an application is not maintainable.

2. Where the period of limitation is claimed from the date of the refusal of a certificate under article 134A of the Constitution, being a certificate of the nature referred to in article 132 or article 133 of the Constitution, it shall not be necessary to file the order refusing the certificate, but the petition for special leave shall be accompanied by an affidavit stating the date of the judgment sought to be appealed from, the date on which the application for a certificate of fitness to appeal to the Court was made to the High Court, the date of the order refusing the certificate, and the ground or grounds on which the certificate was refused and in particular whether the application for the certificate was dismissed as being out of time. 1. Subs. by G.S.R. 272, dated 17th June, 1997 (w.e.f. 28-6-1997). 2. Subs. by G.S.R. 506, dated 21st May, 1981 (w.e.f 30-5-1981).

[***]

4. [(1)] (a) The petition for seeking special leave to appeal (SLP) filed before the Court, under article 136 of the Constitution shall be in Form No. 28 appended to the rules. No separate application for interim relief need be filed. Interim prayer if any should be incorporated in Form No. 28.

(b) Alongwith the petition, list of dates in chronological order with relevant material facts or events pertaining to each of the dates shall be furnished.

(c) SLPs shall be confined only to the pleadings before the Court/Tribunal whose order is challenged. However, the petitioner may, with due notice to the respondent, and with leave of the Court urge additional grounds, at the time of hearing.

(d) (i) The petitioner may produce copies of such petition/documents which are part of the record in the case before the Court/Tribunal below if and to the extent necessary to answer the question of law arising for consideration in the petition or to make out the grounds urged in the SLP, as Annexures to the petition-numbering them as Annexures 1, 2, 3 and so on.

(ii) If the petitioner wants to produce any document which was not part of the records in the Court below he shall make a separate application stating the reasons for not producing it in the Court/Tribunal below and the necessity for its production in the Court and seek leave of the Court for producing such additional documents.

(e) Every petition shall be supported by the affidavit of the petitioners or one of the petitioners as the case may be or by any person authorised by the petitioner in which the deponent shall state that the facts stated in the petition are true and the statement of dates and facts furnished along with the SLP are true to his knowledge and/or in formation and belief.

(f) The papers of the SLP shall be arranged in the following order:

(i) List of dates in terms of clause (b) of sub-rule (1).

(ii) Certified copies of the judgment and order against which the leave has been sought

(iii) The special leave petition in the prescribed Form No. 28.

(iv) Annexures, if any, filed alongwith the SLP.

(g) If notice is ordered on the special leave petition, the petitioner should take steps to serve the notice on the respondent:

Provided in the case of a special leave petition against an interlocutory order, the notice may be served on the advocate appearing for the party in the Court/Tribunal against whose order the leave to appeal is sought for.

[(2) No petition shall be entertained by the Registry unless it contains a statement as to whether the petitioner had filed any petition for special leave to appeal against the impugned judgment or order earlier and if so, with what result, duly supported by an affidavit of the petitioner or his Pairokar only.

(3) The Court shall, if it finds that the petitioner has not disclosed the fact of filing a similar petition earlier and its dismissal by this Court, dismiss the second petition if it is pending or, if special leave has already been granted therein, revoke the same.]

[(4) The petition shall also contain a statement as to whether the matter was contested in the Court appealed from and if so, the full name and address of all the contesting parties shall be given in the statement of facts in the petition.]

5. The petition shall be accompanied by.—(i) a certified copy of the judgment or order appealed from; and

(ii) an affidavit in support of the statement of facts contained in the petition.

6. No annexures to the petition shall be accepted unless such annexures are certified copies of documents which have formed part of the record of the case in the Court sought to be appealed from; provided that uncertified copies of documents may be accepted as annexures if such copies are affirmed to be true copies upon affidavit.

7. The petitioner shall file at least seven spare sets of the petition and of the accompanying papers.

8. Where any person is sought to be impleaded in the petition as the legal representative of any party to the proceedings in the Court below, the petition shall contain a prayer for bringing on record such person as the legal representative and shall be supported by an affidavit setting out the facts showing him to be the proper person to be entered on the record as such legal representative.

9. Where at any time between the filing of the petition for special leave to appeal and the hearing thereof the record becomes defective by reason of the death or change of status of a party to the appeal or for any other reason, an application shall be made to the Court stating who is the proper person to be substituted or entered on the record in place of or in addition to the party on record. Provisions contained in rule 33 of Order XV shall apply to the hearing of such applications.

10. (1) Unless a caveat as prescribed by rule 2 of Order XVIII has been lodged by the other parties, who appeared in the Court below, petitions for grant of special leave shall be put up for hearing *ex parte*, but the Court, if it thinks fit, may direct issue of notice to the respondent and adjourn the hearing of the petition:

Provided that where a petition for special leave has been filed beyond the period of limitation prescribed therefor and is accompanied by an application for condonation of delay, the Court shall not condone the delay without notice to the respondent.

(2) A caveator shall not be entitled to costs of the petition, unless the Court other wise orders.

Where a caveat has been lodged as aforesaid, notice of the hearing of the petition shall be given to the caveator; but a caveator shall not be entitled to costs of the petition, unless the Court otherwise orders.

(3) Notwithstanding anything contained in sub-rules (1) and (2) above, the Respondents who contested the matter in the Court appealed from shall be informed about the decision on the petition after it is heard *ex parte*, if the petition stands dismissed.

11A The record of the appeal arising out of the petition for special leave shall normally consist of the petition of appeal and the paper book of the Court below, if available, plus such additional documents that the parties may file from the record of the case, if the printed record of the Court below be not available. In that event, no fresh printing of the record shall be necessary, and the original record will be called for, from the Court below for reference of the Court:

Provided however, that where in a particular case the Court feels that fresh printing of record is necessary, a specific order to that effect shall be made by the Court at the time of granting special leave to appeal, the provisions contained in Order XV relating to preparation of record shall with necessary modification and adaptation apply.]

12. While granting special leave in all matters in which the Bench granting special leave is of the opinion that the matter is capable of being disposed of within a short time, say within an hour or two, it will indicate accordingly. The office shall maintain a separate register of such matters to enable the Chief Justice to constitute a Bench for the disposal of such matters.]

13.

14.

[(1) Respondent to whom a notice in a Special Leave Petition is issued or who had filed a caveat shall be entitled to oppose the grant of leave or interim orders, without filing any written objections. He shall also be at liberty to file his objections within 30 days from the date of receipt of notice or not later than 2 weeks before the date appointed for hearing, whichever be earlier, but shall do so only by setting out the grounds in opposition to the questions of law or grounds set out in the SLP and may produce such pleadings and documents filed before the Court.

Tribunal against whose order the SLP is filed and shall also set out the grounds for not granting interim order or for vacating interim order if already granted.]

(2) No separate application for vacating interim order need be filed. The respondent shall, however, be at liberty to file application for vacating stay separately before or after filing objections.

(3)(a) Where any statement of objection is filed by the respondent, it shall be supported by an affidavit of the party or any person authorised by him verifying to the correctness of the statements made therein and also to the effect that annexures Court below.

(b) If respondent wants to produce any document which was not part of the record in the Court below, he shall file an application seeking permission of the Court to produce such documents setting out the reason as to why it was not produced in the Court below as also the necessity of producing it before the Court.

(4) The respondent may, if considered necessary, file additional list of dates with material facts in addition to those furnished by the petitioners if he considers that the list of dates and facts by the petitioner is inaccurate or incomplete.)

Comments

1. Scope

The Order deals with provisions for an appeal to the Supreme Court with a certificate to appeal as mentioned in rules 2 and 3. Hence, it is the certificate itself, not the Order or grounds mentioned in the Order for granting certificate, which is to be examined by the Supreme Court while deciding whether the certificate was granted properly or not. *Radha Krishan Das* v. *Rai Krishn Chand,* ILR (1901) 23 All 415: (1901) 28 IA 182. The Supreme Court made it clear that it may revoke a certificate granted by the High Court, if it does not fulfill the requisite requirements for granting it. But the appellant may support the certificate on grounds other than those mentioned in the order; *Jethanand and*

Sons v. *State of Uttar Pradesh,* AIR 1961 SC 794: 1962 (1) SCJ 713: (1962) 3 SCR 751 and *Deputy Commr., Hardoi* v. *Rama Krishna Narain,* 1954 SCR 506: AIR 1953 SC 521: 1953 SCJ 664.

2. Order XLV, Rule 1 – Order XLV, Rule 1, 13; Section 109 – Meaning of Final Order

Order quashing certain proceedings passed by High Court in writ petition — (Constitution of India, Article 215.)

3. *Per* Desai, J.

A 'final order' within the meaning of Order XLV, rule 1 must be an order as defined in section 2(14) of the Code, *i.e.,* it must be a formal expression of a decision of a Civil Court. Where the High Court in a writ petition passes an order quashing certain orders of the consolidation authorities under U.P. Consolidation of Holdings Act (5 of 1954), it is not an order of a Civil Court, because a High Court is a Court of record created by the Constitution, and not a civil Court. Civil Courts are inferior Courts created by the States through their local Acts. *Phul Kumari* v. *State,* AIR 1957 All 495: (1957) 2 Lab LJ 225: 1958 All WR (HC) 330, rel. on. The word "decree" includes a final order, but an order is not final if it does not bind parties. *State of Uttar Pradesh* v. *Mukhtar Singh,* 1957 All WR (HC) 268: AIR 1957 All 505 (517) (Pt K) (Pr 21) (DB). As per a Division Bench of the High Court of Punjab an order in Letters Patent Appeal held not a judgment-decree or final order within the meaning of artless 133 - Leave to appeal to Supreme Court not granted. *See* Constitution of India, article 133; AIR 1955 NUC (Punj) 5394 (DB).

4. Order XLV, Rule 2 – Certificate cancelled under Order XII, Rule 3, Supreme Court Rules

When once leave to file an appeal to the Supreme Court has been granted, the further stages of the appeal are governed by the Supreme Court Rules except in relation to matters specifically mentioned in Order XLV, Civil P.C. Thereafter the High Court is divested of jurisdiction to deal with anything connected with the appeal except as provided in Order XLV. Order XXXVIII of the Supreme Court Rules vests power of review only in the Supreme Court while Order XLV of these Rules clothes that Court with inherent jurisdiction. No such power is extended to the High Court under the Supreme Court Rules. There is nothing in the Civil P.C. which warrants the conclusion that a second application could be filed for leave to appeal to the Supreme Court after certificate was cancelled under Order XII, rule 3, Supreme Court Rules. Therefore, a second petition is inadmissible under Order XLV, rule 2, Civil PC Deities of *Sri Audinarayana Swamy and Anjenayaswami Temples of Donepudi* v. *R. Hanumacharyulu,* 1961 Andh LT 926: (1962) 1 Andh WR 24: AIR 1962 AP 245 (246, 247) (Prs 6, 12, 14, 16) (DB).

5. Order XLV, Rule 2 – Appeal to Supreme Court – Procedure Laid Down in Code must be followed

A Division Bench of the High court of Calcutta held that article 179, Limitation Act which applies to applications under sections 109 and 110, Civil

P.C. also applies to application under article 133 of Constitution; *Azamabad Tea Co. Private Ltd.* v. *Suraj Ratan Thirani*, 62 Cal WN 155: AIR 1958 Cal 296 (297) (DB).

6. Order XLV, Rule 2; Order XLVII, Rule 1 – Procedure – Application for Review or for Leave to Appeal to Supreme Court – Maintainability – Proper Procedure

Scope of review application and application for leave to appeal. It is not permissible for a party to file an application asking for a review of judgment or leave to appeal against that judgment to the Supreme Court. If the applicant is advised that he has sufficient grounds to ask for leave to appeal to the Supreme Court he has to file a separate application therefor. Such leave has to be asked for on grounds which are altogether different from those on which a review can be sought. The two reliefs cannot be sought in one and the same application; AIR 1952 VP 19 (20) (Pt A) (Pr 1).

7. Order XLV, Rule 3; Order I, Rule 10; Sections 100, 109(c) – Suit for Declaration of Title to Stolen Articles Recovered by Police

Suit valued at sum over five thousand – Suit triable by Sub-Judge and not Additional Sub-Judge under administrative order although latter had pecuniary jurisdiction to try under section 9, Ajmer Courts Regulation – Suit transferred by Sub-Judge to Additional Sub-Judge in ignorance of order – Case re-transferred to Sub-Judge – Framing of issues and further proceedings in Court of Sub-Judge – Order impleading persons claiming as pledgees as defendants under Order I, rule 10 before transfer – Irregularity if any curable under section 99 – Case not fit for appeal under section 109(c) or Order XLV, rule 3. *See ibid.*, sections 99-109(c). *Beni Gopal* v. *Damodar Das*, AIR 1950 Ajmer 33.

8. Order XLV, Rule 3 – Application for Leave to Appeal to Supreme Court – Certificate of Fitness – Valuation of Subject-matter in Suit and Appeal

A Full Bench of the High Court of Madras explained the question of valuation of subject-matter in suit and appeal and said that valuation adopted in plaint and accepted for appeal by defendant – Party applying for certificate can show higher and real value of subject-matter – He is not precluded from doing so by provision of section 11, Order VII, rule 1; Order VIII, rule 2 or Order XLI, rule 1(2), Civil P.C. or section 115 of Evidence Act. *See* Constitution of India, article 133(1)(a): *Kuppanna Gounder* v. *Peruma Gounder*, AIR 1961 Mad 511: ILR (1961) Mad 1143: (1962) 1 Mad LJ 65 (FB).

9. Order XLV, Rule 4 – Writ Petition Dismissed on Ground that Petition is Concluded by Judgment in Previous Day's Writ Petition – Decision not by Same Judgment

No consolidation will be allowed. In a case for examination before a Division Bench of the High Court of Allahabad Plaintiffs in the six suits filed six different writ petitions. They were numbered differently. The High Court dismissed one of them on 8-10-1958. The other five petitions were dismissed on the next day by a short order. Each petition involved the same question for determination, but different petitioners, different respondents, different land, different leases granted in favour of the petitioners and different entries in the village papers in favour of the different respondents. The cause of action in each suit was different. Value of the subject-matter in each petition was below Rs. 20,000 but taken together it exceeded Rs. 20,000. In an application for leave to appeal to the Supreme Court, it was sought to consolidate these petitions in one petition under Order XLV, rule 4.

It was held that it was not possible to hold that the six writ petitions were decided by the same judgment and it follows that these writ petitions could not be ordered to be consolidated under Order XLV, rule 4, Civil P.C. The appropriate meaning of the word 'same' in rule 4 seems to be 'one'. The identity of two separate judgments will not make them one and the same; *Hari Lal* v. *Board of Revenue Uttar Pradesh*, 1959 All LJ 594: ILR (1959) 2 All 245: AIR 1960 All 133 (134, 135, 136) (Prs 6, 7, 12, 15) (DB).

10. Order XLV, Rule 4 – Meaning of the Phrase 'Involving Substantially the Same Questions'

A Division Bench of the High Court of Calcutta explained the meaning of the term 'substantially the same question' and held that the expression 'involving substantially the same questions' means, not that the principal question is common or that the majority of the questions are so, but that all the questions are common and basically the same, raising the same issue of law and fact. The fact that there is a question common to all of a number of suits, would not entitle an appellant to an order for consolidation, if there are other questions which are not common. Where three suits for setting aside three different sales were disposed of by a common judgment and the regularity of each sale was sought to be proved by separate evidence which had necessarily to be separately adjudged and each of the three proposed appeals to the Supreme Court related to the sufficiency and regularity of the service and validity of the sale. Held, that the appeals did not involve substantially the same questions so as to allow consolidation under Order XLV, rule 4. *Balanagayya Ghetto* v. *Varadarajulu Chetti*, AIR 1939 Mad 734: ILR 1939 Mad 593, *Prabirendra Mohan* v. *Berhampore Bank Ltd.*, 57 Cal WN 933: AIR 1954 Cal 289 (291) (Pt B) (Pr 11) (DB). [Overruled on another point in *Garikapati Veeraya* v. *N. Subbiah Choudhry*, AIR 1957 SC 5403: 1957 SCJ 439: 1957 SCR 399.

11. Order XLV, Rule 4 – Consolidation of Suits

The power to order consolidation conferred by Order XLV, rule 4 is only discretionary and when a petitioner has prayed for consolidation of appeals, which could not possibly be consolidated, and insisted on an order for consolidation by a lengthy argument when at last in the course of his reply offers to prune and edit his appeals, the Court will not permit him to do so, only to enable him to take appeals of small value to the Supreme Court which the Constitution does not intend ordinarily to be taken there. In such a case, therefore the prayer for consolidation must be rejected; *Prabirendra Mohan* v. *Berhampore Bank Ltd.*, 57 Cal WN 933: AIR 1954 Cal 289 (291) (Pt C) (Pr 11) (DB).

12. Order XLV, Rule 4, Article 133 – Applicability

A Division Bench of the Nagpur High Court decide the scope of rule 4 and discussed the term 'same judgment' and said that If the judgments are substantially the same consolidation can be ordered. When a Judge writes a single statement of the grounds and makes those grounds applicable to different decrees, it is the same judgment for the purposes of the 4th Rule of the 45th Order of the Code. The word 'same' does not always mean 'identical' only. The emphasis in the rule is not on different cases or suits but on different judgments that is to say, the statement of the reasons for the decision; *Kishanlal Nandlal* v. *Vithal Nagayya*, 1956 Nag LJ 617: 1956 MPLJ 97: AIR 1956 Nag 276 (277) (Pt A) (Prs 3, 4) (DB).

13. Order XLV, Rule 7 – Security Deposited not in Accordance with Order XLV, Rule 7 – Effect

Supreme Court Rules (1950), The High Court has no jurisdiction to extend the time for depositing the proper security under Order XLV, rule 7 even though the bond was furnished in time but was found defective. In such cases the certificate granting leave to appeal must be cancelled under Order XII, rule 3 of the Supreme Court Rules. (50) 54 Cal WN 479 (DB). [Overruled in AIR 1961 Cal 483 (FB)] Where money was deposited in Court, and appeal was preferred to Privy Council which was rejected by a Division Bench of the High Court of Punjab relying on the decision of a Full Bench of the Oudh High Court held that the loss of money deposited in Court under the provisions of Order XLV, rule 7 of the Code should be borne by the person for whose benefit the deposit was made when he becomes entitled to it by the appeal preferred by the other party being rejected. If on account of the partition of the country the money has been lost or has ceased to become available to the person for whose benefit it was deposited the loss must be borne by him for there is no known principle of law or equity which would exempt him from liability to bear the loss, if any loss has in fact been sustained. *Jai Inder Bahadur Singh* v. *Brij Inder Kaur*, 5 Luck 80: AIR 1929 Oudh 231 (FB), rel. on. *Mehar Chand* v. *Shiv Lal*, ILR 1955 Punj 1341: 57 Punj LR 350: AIR 1956 Punj 12 (Pt A) (Pr 4) (DB). The High Court of Punjab also said that money deposited by a party to an action under the provisions of a statute or in compliance with an order of the Court to await the outcome of litigation is deemed to be in the custody of the law and is not liable either to attachment or to execution. It ceases to be the property of the person by whom it was paid and is said to belong to the person who is found eventually to be 'entitled thereto; (1874) 9 Ch A 379: *Roop Chand* v. *Gulzari Lal*, AIR 1954 Punj 257: ILR 1954 Punj 916, rel. on. *Mehar Chand* v. *Shiv Lal*, ILR 1955 Punj 1341: 57 Punj LR 350: AIR 1956 Punj 12 (Pt B) (Pr 3) (DB).

14. Order XLV, Rule 7 – Security by Deposit – Object of

Right of decree-holder to .proceed against other property. The security deposit under rule 7 of Order XLV of the Code is the property of the appellant and in case of the success of the appeal has to be returned to him. It is taken merely by way of security for liability for costs which might arise in case the appeal failed and hence it is open to the decree-holder to relinquish security and recover the costs of the appeal awarded to him under the order of His Majesty in Council from the judgment-debtor by proceeding against his person and property. *Shiv Lal Ghanaya Lal* v. *Mehr Chand Gaind,* AIR 1952 Punj 42 (43) (Pr 10).

4. Form of security-Proviso. Order XLV, rule 7(1) – Supreme Court Rules (1950), Order XII, rule 3 – Power to accept security other than cash or Government securities. The High Court has power to accept security in immovable property instead of cash or Government securities, if that is tendered in time permitted by Order XLV, rule 7 and if it is an order which the justice of the case requires, though no application was made to the Court for permission to deposit such security in accordance with the proviso to Order XLV, rule 7(1); *Purnendu Nath Tagore* v. *Sree Sree Radha Kanta Jew*, 54 Cal WN 476: ILR (1951) 1 Cal 472: AIR 1950 Cal 318 (319) (Prs 5, 9, 7′ 6, 10) (DB).

15. Order XLV, Rule 7, Proviso – Form of Security for Costs

Order as to-Time for passing. A Division Bench of the High Court of Orissa said that an order under the first proviso to Order XLV, rule 7, Civil P.C. can only be made at the time of passing the order for granting the certificate. If an appellant wishes to furnish a security in any other form than in cash or Government securities he must apply for an order to that effect and obtain it at the time of passing the order for granting the certificate. If he fails to apply at the time it cannot be granted afterwards; *Arunachala Naidu* v. *Balakrishna and Company*, AIR 1925 Mad 449: 48 Mad 559 and *Pitamhari Dibya* v. *Chandrasekhar Praharaj*, AIR 1954 Ori 71: ILR 1952 Cut 649: 19 Cut LT 520, rel. on. *Hiralal* v. *Kundanmal*, MBLJ 1956 (Civ) 608: 1956 Madh BLBJ 1479: AIR 1957 Madh B71 (72) (Prs 10, 16, 17) (DB). The High Court of Madras examined the question of crucial date for an application to vary the nature of security and said that the crucial date for making an application to the Court to vary the nature of the security under Order XLV, rule 7(1), Proviso, is the date on which the order granting the certificate is passed, as distinguished from the date on which the actual certificate is signed. AIR 1925 Mad 449. A Full Bench of the High Court of Calcutta examined the scope of the rules framed under clause 37 of the Letters Patent and said that the said Rules are not confined in their application to suits and proceedings on the Original Side only. An application for a certificate under article 133 of the Constitution is a proceeding in a civil case brought before the High Court and the High Court has power to frame Rules relating to such an application. The restriction upon the power of the Court as contained in the proviso to clause 37 of the Letters Patent is that the rules framed under that clause should, 'as far as possible' be in conformity with the provisions of the Civil Procedure Code. Consequently, if any rule framed by the High Court under clause 37 be inconsistent with or confers any additional power besides what is granted by the Code of Civil Procedure, the rule framed under clause 37 will prevail over the corresponding provisions of the Code of Civil Procedure. The rules framed by the High Court under Chapter 33A of the Original Side Rules are within the rule-making powers of the Calcutta High Court under clause 37 of the Letters Patent. Rule 5 of Chapter 33A of the Original Side Rules authorises the appellate court to extend time beyond the limits provided for by Order XLV, rule 7 of the Code of Civil Procedure. AIR 1948 Bom 174 and In re, Ram Dayal De, AIR 1932 Cal 1: ILR 59 Cal 370, rel. on. *Manickchand Durgaprasad* v. *Pratabmull Rameswar*, ILR (1962) 1 Cal 132: AIR 1961 Cal 483 (488, 489) (Pt B) (Prs 12, 13) (FB).

16. Order XLV, Rule 13 and Section 151 – Powers of Court

Order in writ petition declaring certain provisions of statute unconstitutional and quashing orders passed thereunder – Application for certificate for leave to appeal to Supreme Court pending – Power of High Court to grant interim relief in form of stay order – (Constitution of India, articles 226, 227.) In a petition for a writ of *certiorari* the High Court held that certain provisions of the U.P. Consolidation of Holdings Act (5 of 1954), were unconstitutional and quashed certain orders of the consolidation authorities as a matter of course. The State filed an application under article 133(1), Constitution of India, for certificate for leave to appeal to the Supreme Court. Pending that application, it asked for stay of the operation of the order passed by the High Court. The question was whether the High Court had any jurisdiction to stay the operation of the order either under Order XLV, rule 13 or under any other. Held (*Per* Desai, J.); that the operation of the impugned order cannot be stayed under article 228 or 227, Constitution of India, or under Order XLV, rule 13 or under section 151, Civil P.C. (*Per* Beg, J., dissenting): The High Court in a proper case had powers to issue a stay order. (On the merits, however, his Lordship held agreeing with Desai, J., that no case for grant of interim stay had been made out.) Both from the point of view of the subject-matter as well as from the point of view of their object, the proceedings taken in the present case were clearly of a civil nature. A proceeding, which deals with right of a civil nature and is otherwise civil, does not cease to be so just because a party chooses to resort to article 226 of the Constitution for the enforcement of such a right; *State of Uttar Pradesh* v. *Mukhtar Singh*, 1957 All WR (HC) 268: AIR 1957 All 505 (517) (519, 521, 522, 526) (Pt H) (Prs 24, 27, 32, 33, 61) (DB).

17. Order XLV, Rule 13(2)(d) – Object of – Party Unsuccessful in High Court – Right to Apply for Directions

Justice Desai explained the object of Power to give direction under clause (d) of rule 13(2) only a particular party can be placed under conditions, *e.g.*, the party seeking the assistance of the Court. Only the party successful in the High Court could have an occasion for seeking its assistance through either execution (if a decree was passed in his favour) or enforcement (if an order was passed in his favour). The party which is unsuccessful in the High Court cannot apply under Order XLV, rule 13(2)(d). Moreover, the Court has to act only when the party seeks its assistance; so long as it does not do so, it cannot be placed under any condition. The power to give any other direction is exactly similar to that of placing him under conditions, so no direction also can be given if he does not seek its assistance. The direction can be only in respect of the subject-matter of the appeal. The subject-matter contemplated by the legislature seems to be tangible property; the reference to appointment of a receiver is indicative of this intention. Where the constitutionality of an Act was the only dispute sought to be raised in the appeal. It is not possible to give any direction respecting that subject-matter of appeal. The object behind clause (d) was certainly not to stay execution or operation of an order completely but to allow it under certain conditions or to provide a substitute for it. *State of Uttar Pradesh* v. *Mukhtar Singh*, 1957 All WR (HC) 268: AIR 1957 All 505 (517) (517) (Pt M) (Pr 20). Order XLV, rule 13(2)(d)

– Applicability. Order XLV, rule 13(2)(d) only enables the High Court to place a party seeking assistance of the Court under any conditions which the Court may think fit to impose or to give a direction other than a direction placing under any condition, respecting the subject-matter of the appeal by the appointment of a receiver. It does not enable a Court to give temporary relief to a party in respect of a matter which was not pressed and adjudicated upon; *Gwalior Sugar Co. Ltd.* v. *State*, ILR 1955 MB 361: MBLR 1956 Civil 638: MBLJ 1955 HCR 1364: AIR 1955 MB 210 (212) (Ft B) (Pr 6) (DB).

There is nothing in Order XLV, in general or in rule 13, in particular restricting the exercise of the powers under [Vol. 3] Fn. D. 39. Rule 13, to only where the certificate for leave to appeal to the Supreme Court has been granted. The filing of an application for leave to appeal to the Supreme Court invests the Court with the jurisdiction to pass such orders as it may become necessary to pass in connection with such an application, including orders in exercise of powers pending appeal provided by rule 13. *Girja Prasad Sunder Lal* v. *Divisional Forest Officer, Dudhi*, 1955 All LJ 838: ILR (1955) 2 All 743: AIR 1955 All 589 (591) (Pt A) (Pr 9) (DB). [Overruled in AIR 1981 All 619 (FB).] The High Court of Madhya Pradesh said that grant of leave does not operate as stay order against decision of High Court. Stay can be given only by the Supreme Court. 1963 MPLJ (Notes) 51. Examining the scope of power under rule 13 the High Court of Madras said that Order XLV, rule 13(2)(d) only enables the High Court to place the party seeking the assistance of the Court under any conditions which the Court may think fit to impose, it also enables that Court to give such other direction, that is to say, direction other than a direction placing under any condition respecting the subject-matter of the appeal, such as for instance, by an officer directing the appointment of a Receiver. But it does not enable the Court to give any direction to the successful party by way of restricting or preventing him from exercising the rights to which he has become entitled under its final order; *Rajahmundry Electric Supply Corporation Ltd.* v. *State of Madras represented by the Secretary to the Government*, 1952 Mad WN 823: (1952) 2 Mad LJ 732: ILR 1952 Mad 980: 65 Mad LW 1023: AIR 1953 Mad 475 (475) (Pt A) (Pr 2) (DB).

18. Order XLV, Rule 13(2)(d) – "To Give Such other Directions"

The High Court of Allahabad examined the meaning of the term in a case where the petitioner sold to the opposite parties some land and disputes having arisen in the Revenue Department as to the mutation. The Chief Commissioner ordered the mutation to be set aside and mutation proceedings to be started *de novo*. Against this order the opposite parties brought a petition to the High Court under article 226 of the Constitution. This petition was allowed, but the petitioner was granted leave to appeal to the Supreme Court. The petitioner thereafter applied under Order XLV, rule 13 praying that the operation of the order of the High Court be suspended and the opposite parties be restrained from alienating the property sold to them. Held, that clause (d) of rule 13 did not cover the prayer made by the petitioner. *Rajahmundry Electric Supply Corporation Ltd.* v. *State of Madras represented by the Secretary to the Government*, AIR 1953

Mad 475: (1952) 65 Mad LW 1023: ILR 1952 Mad 980: 1952 Mad WN 823 and *Lalitessur Singh* v. *Bhabessur Singh*, 13 Cal WN 690: 1 IC 812 (Cal) (IT) and *Chet Ram* v. *Ram Singh*, 64 Ind Cas 152 (All).

19. Order XLV, Rule 13 – Pendency of Appeal from Decision under Article 226, Constitution of India

Applicability of rule 13—There is no warrant for the view that Order XLV, rule 13 does not apply to cases where the appeal, during the pendency of which the Court is asked to exercise powers under that rule, is an appeal from a decision under article 228 of the Constitution. A final order is a decree within the special definition of that term in rule 1 of Order XLV. That being so, the provisions of that order are applicable where the appeal contemplated is one from a decision under article 226 of the Constitution. *Abdul Rahman* v. *Cassim and Sons*, AIR 1933 PC 58: 60 IA 76, rel. on. *Girja Prasad Sunder Lal* v. *Divisional Forest Officer, Dudhi*, 1955 All LJ 838: ILR (1955) 2 All 743: AIR 1955 All 589 (591) (Pt B) (Pr 10) (DB). *Overruled in Kalyan Singh* v. *State of Uttar Pradesh*, 1961 All LJ 571: ILR (1961) 2 All 246: AIR 1961 All 619 (FB).] A Division Bench of the High Court of Allahabad said that the High Court is empowered under Order XLV, rule 13(2)(d), Civil P.C., to restrain the respondents from interfering with the petitioner's right pending disposal of the petitioner's application for leave to appeal to the Supreme Court, provided the interests of the respondents are at the same time sufficiently safeguarded. *Girja Prasad Sunder Lal* v. *Divisional Forest Officer, Dudhi*, 1955 All LJ 838: ILR (1955) 2 All 743: AIR 1955 All 589 (591) (Pt C) (Pr 12) (DB). [Overruled in *Kalyan Singh* v. *State of Uttar Pradesh*, 1961 All LJ 571: ILR (1961) 2 All 246: AIR 1961 All 619 (FB). The High Court of Madras dissenting from 1955 All LJ 838 held that power of High Court under rule 13(2)(d). Order XLV, rule 13(2), clause (d) consists of two parts under both of which the Court might pass such orders as it thinks fit respecting the subject-matter of the appeal but while the first part speaks of placing the party seeking the assistance of the Court under such conditions as the Court thinks fit, the other part, which is quite independent of the part does not speak of any such part but only generally of the Court giving such other direction as it thinks fit. There is nothing in the second part of the clause to restrict the powers of the Court. *Government*, 1952 Mad WN 823: (1952) 2 Mad LJ 732: ILR 1952 Mad 980: 65 Mad LW 1023: AIR 1953 Mad 475, dissented from; *Girja Prasad Sunder Lal* v. *Divisional Forest Officer, Dudhi*, 1955 All LJ 838: ILR (1955) 2 All 743: AIR 1955 All 589 (592) (Pt D) (Pr 16) (DB), overruled in *Kalyan Singh* v. *State of Uttar Pradesh*, 1961 All LJ 571: ILR (1961) 2 All 246: AIR 1961 All 619 (FB).]

20. Order XLV, Rule 13; Section 151 – Application for Leave to Appeal to Supreme Court – Stay of Proceeding

Inherent power of High Court. Even if it were construed that Order XLV, rule 13 does not give specifically the power to grant stay before the admission of the appeal, still the High Court has inherent jurisdiction under section 151 of the Code to stay execution after receipt of a petition for leave to appeal to Supreme Court.

However, the inherent powers of the Court to stay execution should be sparingly used. Under Order XLV, rule 13 also stay can be granted only when specific cause is shown even after the grant of the certificate. *Narumall* v. *Jagatmal,* AIR 1925 Sind 216: 82 IC 739, rel. on. *Ukusana Singh* v. *Union of India,* AIR 1957 Mani 35 (Prs 6, 9). The High Court of Orissa said that even if no application for leave to Supreme Court yet filed still High Court has jurisdiction under section 151 to pass interim orders, ordering the parties to maintain *status quo* regarding the matters in dispute. AIR 1964 Ori 72 (DB). The Court further said that stay of execution after rejecting leave to appeal. Under section 11, 13 special provision is made for granting stay of execution of the decree only after the grant certificate. The High Court therefore cannot grant stay when the leave to appeal is rejected, for allowing the appellant to apply for special leave to the Supreme Court and obtain stay; *Purna Chand Sahu* v. *Chamra Bariha,* AIR 1954 Ori 114 (116): 20 Cut LT 424 (Pt C) (Pr 6) (DB).

The High Court of Calcutta in *Standard Vacuum Oil Co.* v. *Commercial Tax Officer,* AIR 1957 Cal 528: 61 CWN 600 examined the scope of certificate granted under article 133 of the Constitution.

The petitioner, the Standard Vacuum Oil Company, wanted to appeal to the Supreme Court from an order passed by Sinha, J., whereby he discharged a rule *nisi* issued by himself at the instance of the petitioner upon an application made under article 226 of the Constitution. The prayer in the petition is that if necessary, a certificate be granted in terms which appear to be the terms contemplated by both article 132 and article 133.

It appears that a certificate under article 132 had already been granted by the learned trial judge himself by an observation made by him at the end of his judgment. He has certified that the case involves a substantial question of law as to the interpretation of the Constitution. No particular form is required for a certificate under article 132. It is also well-settled that on questions covered by article 132, an appeal lies directly to the Supreme Court from the decision of even one learned judge sitting singly, if he gives the necessary certificate. The prayer in the present petition for a certificate that the proposed appeal involved a substantial question of law as to the interpretation of the Constitution appeared to be misconceived and a surplusage.

There is, however, a prayer for a certificate which would seem to be a certificate of the kind contemplated by article 133. The grounds which are intended to be taken in the proposed appeal are set out in para. 16 of the petition and at least one of them, namely, ground (d), does not seem to have any concern with the interpretation of the Constitution. The proposed, appeal, therefore, is intended to cover grounds contemplated by article 132 and also other grounds which are outside the ambit of that article. It need hardly be said that the latter grounds would not be covered by the certificate granted by the learned trial judge under article 132 and, therefore, the first question which arises is whether a further certificate from this Court is required in order to enable the petitioner to take before the Supreme Court grounds oilier than those covered by article 132.

The Court said, it appears to me that no such further certificate is required. Clause (3) of article 132 provides as follows;—

> "Where such a certificate is given"—that is to say, a certificate under article 132(1)—"or such leave is granted"—that is to say, special leave by the Supreme Court under article 132(2)—"any party in the case may appeal to the Supreme Court on the ground that any such question as aforesaid has been wrongly decided and, with the leave of the Supreme Court, on any other ground." It would appear from the terms of clause (3) of article 132 that if any appellant to the Supreme Court who has obtained from the High Court a certificate under clause (1) wishes to urge other grounds in his appeal, he can do so if the Supreme Court gives him the necessary leave and only if such leave is given. There would seem to be no scope for the High Court granting a further certificate under article 133 for the purpose of authorising the further grounds to be taken in the appeal.

From the facts stated, it was clear that before the order is made on the petition, made to the Court taking Supreme Court matters, that a formal certificate be issued, there can be no question of demanding or depositing the amount of security or the amount of costs for the preparation and transmission of the paper book. Order XLV, rule 7, which says that "where the certificate is granted, the applicant shall, within ninety days or such further period, not exceeding sixty days, as the Court may upon cause shown allow from the date of the decree complained of, or within six weeks from the date of the grant of the certificate, whichever is the later date, furnish security in cash" etc., will have to be applied by reference to the date of the order made for the issue of a formal certificate as the date of the grant of the certificate and not the date on which the certificate was recorded by the trial judge in his judgment.

The Court expressed the view that owing to a misconception on the part of all parties, the amount of security and a sum of Rs. 440 by way of costs have already been deposited. Mr. Meyer prayed that we should not only make a formal order on the present petition, but should also direct the appeal to be admitted, in as much as the provisions of Order XLV, rule 8, had already been complied with. Although the moneys may have been deposited, to make the order prayed for by Mr. Meyer would be to put the cart before the horse. There can be no question of making any deposit of security or depositing any costs before an appeal has come into existence. At the stage when the moneys were paid and received, there was only a certificate, but yet no appeal. A petition of appeal came into existence when the present petition was filed and an appeal will come into existence only after we make the order that we are going to make.

The present petition had been made within the period of limitation. The necessary parties had been impleaded. Accordingly, the order was that a formal certificate under article 132(1) be drawn up and issued to the intending appellant.

There was also a prayer for a stay of all further proceedings and levy on realisation of tax in respect of sales of aviation spirit to be made by the petitioner to foreign-bound aircraft. In compliance with an order made by us when the application came up as a new Motion, the petitioner has already submitted the necessary returns to respondent. No. 1 for the period up to the date of the petition and also placed in deposit with its own solicitors, Messrs Fowler & Co., a sum of Rs. 2,00,000 as the amount of tax payable on these returns. The respondents do not insist that for the period during which the appeal to the Supreme Court may remain pending, the petitioner should be required to make further payments. They only pray that the petitioner shall go on submitting monthly returns, as required by the Bengal Motor Spirit Sales Taxation Act, 1941, as amended up to date.

The Court accordingly directed that Messrs Fowler & Co., shall hold the sum of Rs. 2,00,000 (two lakhs of rupees), already deposited with them, free of lien and until further orders and that of long as the appeal to the Supreme Court may remain pending, the petitioner shall submit to respondent No. 1 returns of its sales of aviation spirit to foreign-bound aircraft month by month, as required by the Bengal Motor Spirit Sales Taxation Act, 1941, as amended up to date.

The respondents have agreed before us by their learned counsel, Mr. Mukherjee, that they will have no objection to accepting the returns without payment of the tax payable thereon. The Court ordered accordingly. In the case of *State of Uttar Pradesh* the High Court of Allahabad examined the provisions contained in rule 13 of Order XLV. In the said case an application was filed purporting to be under Order XLV, rule 13, C.P.C., for the issue of an order staying operation of the Order passed by this Court on October 8, 1956, in Writ Petition No. 252 of 1956 and maintaining the *status quo* as regards possession over the land covered by the orders of the consolidation authorities. The facts leading to this application are as follows:

Under section 26 of the U.P. Consolidation of Holdings Act, 1953 (No. 5 of 1954) possession of some land belonging to opposite parties Nos. 1 to 11 was transferred to other tenants of the village, who are opposite parties 12 to 16. After exhausting the remedy as provided in the Act against the transfer they filed a petition for a writ of *certiorari, Mukhtar Singh* v. *State of Uttar Pradesh,* Petn. No. 252 of 1956: (AIR 1957 All 297: 1956 All WR (HC) 643: 1956 All LJ 878) (A). A Bench of this Court quashed the orders of the consolidation authorities regarding transfer of possession of the Opposite parties' land on 8th October, 1956 on the ground that section 14(ee) of the Act was unconstitutional. The State of U.P. has filed an application "for certificate for leave to appeal to the Supreme Court" and the application is pending. Opposite parties Nos. 1 to 11 are trying to get back possession over their land on which crops have been sown by opposite parties 12 to 16 after possession was transferred by the consolidation authorities. The State apprehends that a grave situation would arise if the *status quo* were not maintained and if the opposite parties 1 to 11 were allowed to take back possession from opposite parties 12 to 16; therefore, it asks for stay of the operation of the order passed by the Bench on 8-10-1956. The application is contested by opposite parties 1 to 11; who contend that this Court has no jurisdiction to stay the operation of the order either under Order XLV, rule 13, C.P.C., or under any other law.

The Court said that before deciding whether we have any jurisdiction to stay the operation of the Order passed by this Court it is essential to determine what proceeding is pending before us, because our jurisdiction depends upon its nature. The proceeding is undoubtedly one connected with an appeal desired to be preferred by the applicant to the Supreme Court from the Court's order. Under article 132 an appeal lies to the Supreme Court from any final order of a High Court "whether in a civil, criminal or other proceeding", if the High Court certifies that the case involves a substantial question of law as to the interpretation of the Constitution. Where the High Court has refused to give a certificate, the Supreme Court may grant special leave to appeal. Where such a certificate is given or such leave is granted, any party in the case may appeal to the Supreme Court on the ground that such question has been wrongly decided and, with the leave of the Supreme Court, on any other ground. Three facts emerge from these provisions of article 132(1) that proceedings are divisible into three classes, "Civil", "Criminal" and "other" proceedings, (2) that the appeal must be filed after the certificate is given by the High Court and not before; and (3) that it must be filed in the Supreme Court and not in the High Court. The grounds of appeal may, with the leave of the Supreme Court, include grounds other than that the question of law as to the interpretation of the Constitution has been wrongly decided; it follows that they are expected to be prepared after the certificate is given or the leave is granted. If the appellant wants to appeal on any other ground, he must after receiving the certificate from the High Court or the special leave from the Supreme Court obtain the leave of the Supreme Court for the same. Article 133 provides that "an appeal shall lie to the Supreme Court from any judgment, decree or final order in a civil proceeding of a High Court" if the High Court certifies that the case is a fit one for appeal to the Supreme Court; but no appeal shall lie from the judgment, decree or final order of one judge of a High Court. Article 134 provides for an appeal to the Supreme Court from any judgment, final order or sentence in a criminal proceeding of a High Court. Under article 135 the Supreme Court has jurisdiction and powers with respect to any matter to which the provisions of article 133 or 134 do not apply if jurisdiction and powers in relation to that matter were exercisable by the Federal Court immediately before the Constitution came into force, article 136 empowers the Supreme Court to grant special leave to appeal from any judgment, decree, determination, sentence or order in any cause or matter passed or made by any court or Tribunal. In civil and criminal proceedings a party has a right of appeal to the Supreme Court if he has obtained a certain certificate; but no party in any other proceedings has a right of appeal to the Supreme Court except when a question of law as to the interpretation of the Constitution is involved.

If a party to a proceeding that is neither civil nor criminal desires to appeal, even though the proceeding does not involve a question of law as to the interpretation of the Constitution he can do so only after obtaining special leave from the Supreme Court. In other words an order in a proceeding that is neither civil nor criminal can be appealed from either if it involves a question of law as to the interpretation of the Constitution or special leave has been obtained from the Supreme Court.

The Supreme Court is authorised by article 145(1) to make rules "as to the procedure for hearing appeals and other matters pertaining to appeals'", "as to the entertainment of appeals under sub-clause (c) of clause (1) of article 134", "as to stay of proceedings" and as to other matters relating to the practice and procedure of the Court Chapter XII of the Supreme Court Rules, 1950, made by the Supreme Court in exercise of these powers, contain rules regarding "civil appeals" on certificate by a High Court. Rule 1 applies the provisions of Order XLV of the Civil Procedure Code and any rules made for the purpose by the High Court, in relation to appeals under articles 132(1) and 133.

In support of the contrary view strong reliance was placed by the learned counsel on *Tobacco Manufacturers (India) Ltd.* v. *State*, ILR 30 Pat 174: AIR 1951 Pat 29 (FB) (Z-42), and other cases under the Sales Tax and Income-tax Acts in which the opinion given by the High Court was not held to be given in a civil proceeding. These cases, in my opinion are distinguishable. They were decided on the footing that the High Court did not pass any judgment at all in those cases hence article 133 of the Constitution was inapplicable to them. As observed in AIR 1951 SC 14 (Z), in such cases the High Court acts merely in an advisory or consultative capacity and the order passed by it cannot be said to be passed either in its original or its appellate jurisdiction. About the writ proceedings, it cannot be said that the High Court does not pass any judgment in them or that it exercises neither its original nor its appellate jurisdiction in disposing of the same. In the order dated 10-1-1957 in the recent Full Bench case of this Court arising out of *Aidal Singh* v. *Karam Singh*, Special Appeals Nos. 53, 57 and 76 and 105 of 1956: (S) AIR 1957 All 414: 1957 All LJ 389: ILR (1957) 1 All 299 (Z-43), it has already been held that an order of a Single Judge in a writ matter is applicable to a Bench. It is, however, not necessary for me to go into this matter or to express any opinion on it as this question does not arise here.

In this connection learned counsel for the contesting parties also argued that the original jurisdiction exercised in Insolvency, Matrimonial, Probate and Company matters of a like nature by the High Court was not civil jurisdiction. Again, for the reasons given by me already, I find it difficult to uphold this contention. Learned counsel further relied on the separate mention of the Testamentary, Intestate and Matrimonial jurisdictions in the Letters Patent as indicating that these were not embraced in the civil jurisdiction and were not a part of it. I do not think that from the premises postulated by him the conclusion that he wants me to draw necessarily follows. The mention of these types of jurisdiction in the Letters Patent is not on the basis that they are exclusive of or contrasted with civil jurisdiction. These jurisdictions might be inclusive within the broader genus of civil jurisdiction. They had to be mentioned separately and specifically with a view to single them out, because the specific areas covered by them had to be carved out from the larger area of civil jurisdiction and demarcated as particular fields of civil jurisdiction in which the High Court could function on the original side, and further, these had to be denominated as special spheres in which the newly erected High Court of Allahabad as inheritor of the old Court was continuing to function in place of its predecessor with the like power and authority as the latter had.

In *Ba Thaw Moung* v. *Ma Pin*, 61 IA 158: 1934 All LJ 358: AIR 1934 PC 81 (Z-44), it was held that once a proceeding, even though under a special Act like the Provincial Insolvency Act (1920), reached the High Court, the procedure, orders and decrees of the Court as well as the right of appeal to the Privy Council was governed by the provisions of the Civil Procedure Code. Similarly in *Pramatha Nath* v. *Sanat Kumar*, 1948 FCR 228: AIR 1949 FC 60 (Z-45), it was held that once a proceeding under a Special Act like the Bengal Money Lenders Act (Act X of 1940) reached the High Court, "further rights of appeal are governed by the provisions of the Civil Procedure Code."

Article 28 of the Letters Patent gave power to the High Court to adopt rules of the C.P. Code from time to time. Section 129 of the Civil Procedure Code entitles the High Court to frame rules regulating its original civil jurisdiction. In Chapter XV, of the High Court Rules, this Court has framed rules regulating its original and extraordinary original civil jurisdiction.

Chapter XXIII, rule 26 of the Rules of Court lays down that:

> "In cases not governed by the Code, the provisions of Order XLV of the Code shall, so far as may be and with such adaptations and modifications as may be found necessary, apply."

Order XII, rule 1, of the Supreme Court Rules (1950) runs as follows:—

> "Subject to any special directions which the Court may give in any particular case, the provisions of Order XLV of the Code, and of any rules made for the purpose by the High Court or other authority concerned, so far as may be applicable, shall apply in relation to appeals preferred under articles 132(1), 133(1) and 135 of the Constitution."

In *Nand Kishore Singh* v. *Rani Golam Sahu*, ILR 40 Cal 955: 16 Cal LJ 508 (Z-7), the Calcutta High Court went to the extent of holding that even if no application for leave to appeal were pending, stay could under its inherent powers, be granted by the High Court.

For the above reasons, as at present advised, I am inclined to hold that this Court has in a proper case powers to issue a stay order.

In this connection, the question of the amplitude and scope of article 227 of the Constitution was also raised. In regard to this matter I may mention that I am of opinion that the power of superintendence granted to the High Court under article 227 is extensive enough to cover not only the administrative, but also the judicial power. I have already given reasons for the same in my judgment in *Jodhey* v. *State*, 1952 Cr LJ 1282: 1952 All LJ 493: AIR 1952 All 788 (Z-46) and my judgment dated 10-1-1957, in the Full Bench case arising out of Special Appeals Nos. 53, 57, 76 and 105 of 1956: (S) *Aidal Singh* v. *Karam Singh*, AIR 1957 All 414: 1957 All LJ 389: ILR (1957) 1 All 299) (Z-43). I do not, therefore, think it necessary to repeat the same. As, however, I agree with my learned brother, on the question of merits, I am of opinion that the application should be dismissed.

The Court held, "For the reasons given in our respective judgments we dismiss this application. The costs will be borne by the parties themselves. The interim stay order is discharged". *State of Uttar Pradesh* v. *Mukhtar Singh*, 1957 All WR (HC) 268: AIR 1957 All 505 (517).

In the case of *Lalmina Singh* v. *Kumar Kamal Singh*, AIR 1952 Pat 450: ILR 30 Pat 1274 the High Court of Patna also decide the scope granting certificate under article 133.

Two applications were directed, against a judgment of a Division Bench of this Court dated the 16th May 1951, passed in First Appeal No. 202 of 1946 and in Civil Revision, No. 610 of 1946, by which the first appeal was dismissed and the civil revision was allowed, the two cases being heard together.

The petitioner in these two applications was the same; the opposite party was also the same. The facts giving rise to the dispute may shortly be stated as follows: The petitioner had an occupancy holding measuring 99.46 acres, being '*khata*' No. 13 of village Jahua, under the opposite party. There was default in the payment of rent and the opposite party instituted a suit against the petitioner for recovery of arrears of rent in respect of the holding and a decree was obtained. The decree was executed in execution case No. 883 of 1936 in the Court of the Second Munsif of Buxar. The petitioner filed an objection under section 47 of the Code of Civil Procedure on the ground, '*inter alia*', that the execution was time-barred. The objection was dismissed by the Munsif and thereupon an appeal was preferred by him to the District Judge. During the pendency of the appeal the holding was put up to sale and auction-purchased by the decree-holder on 17th May, 1937. On 16th June, 1937, the petitioner deposited the amount under Order XXI, rule 89, Code of Civil Procedure, and prayed that the amount deposited by him be not allowed to be withdrawn by the decree-holder, and although the prayer was rejected, the money was not withdrawn by the decree-holder.

The appeal filed by the petitioner against the order dismissing his application under section 47 of the Code of Civil Procedure was, however, allowed and the application for execution was held to be time-barred. Thereupon the decree-holder preferred a second appeal to this Court, and before the appeal was finally decided the Munsif set aside the sale and held that the judgment-debtor "will get back the money deposited," and on the 22nd April, 1938, a payment order for the sum deposited was issued to the judgment-debtor and he withdrew the money.

According to this rule, it is argued, the certificate is to be granted with reference to the provisions of section 110. And it has been held by this Court in the aforesaid case 'AIR 1951 Pat 177', that the requirements of section 110 as to valuation are not fulfilled if the value of the subject-matter of the dispute in the Court of first instance is less than Rs. 10,000, now Rs. 20,000. Consequently, it is said, the present case does not satisfy the requirements of section 110. But, as already pointed out, the certificate, since the Constitution came into force, is to be granted under article 133(1) of the Constitution. If there is any conflict between the provisions of this article with those of Order XLV, rule 3 and section 110, Code of Civil Procedure the Constitution will prevail. The present case is fully covered by article 133(1)(b) of the Constitution as the judgment indirectly involves questions respecting property of the value of not less than Rs. 20,000. Therefore, as the judgment is one of affirmance, leave can be granted under clause (b) if we are satisfied that the appeal involves a substantial question of law.

There would have been difficulty in granting a certificate if leave to appeal had been refused from the order in the civil revision; but leave having been granted in that matter, it ought not to be refused in this case. If the judgment of this Court in the civil revision be reversed by the Supreme Court, the very foundation of the claim for *mesne* profits in the appeal will disappear; the plaintiff would not be entitled to *mesne* profits if he has no title to the property. Therefore, if leave is refused in this matter, he will get a decree without having title in respect of the property for which *mesne* profits have been claimed. The question of title is a substantial question of law as between the parties. In such circumstances, we think leave must be granted in this case also.

The Court accordingly certified that a substantial question of law is involved in Supreme Court Appeal No. 116 of 1951, which arises out of First Appeal No. 202 of 1946, and it fulfils the requirement of clause (b) of article 133(1) of the Constitution, and Supreme Court Appeal No. 117 of 1951, which arises out of Civil Revision No. 610 of 1946, fulfils the requirements of clauses (a) and (b) of article 133(1) of the Constitution, and grant leave to appeal to the Supreme Court in both these cases. The petitioner is entitled to costs: hearing fee five gold mohurs; *Lalmina Singh* v. *Kumar Kamal Singh*, AIR 1952 Pat 450: ILR 30 Pat 1274.

21. Order XLV, Rule 15 – Rules of Orissa High Court, 1948, Chapter XXVII

In *State of Orissa* v. *Biranchi Narayan Das*, 2017 (1) Ori Law Rev 964: 2017 (171) AIC 351 (Ori) (Cuttack), the High Court of Orrisa said, reading of the provisions contained in Chapter XXVIII of the Rules of the High Court of Orissa, 1948 makes way for execution of decrees in shape of judgment or orders passed by the High Court in exercise of the original jurisdiction including the cases decided under Articles 226 and 227 of the Constitution of India or under some other provisions, as mentioned therein and in the case of execution of orders in exercise of power under Articles 226 and 227 of the Constitution of India, the applications for execution shall have to be presented before the Registrar in terms of Rule 11(2) of Order XXI of C.P.C. and following the provision contained in Rule 7 of Chapter XXVIII unless the payment involved is made within the time fixed, the Registrar is required to proceed to realize the amount in accordance with the provision of the Order XXI of C.P.C. and following Sub-Rule (2) of Rule 7 for the purpose of execution, the Registrar taking up the execution shall be deemed to be the Court, which passed the decree or order as the case may be and any order of the Registrar is appealable to a Division Bench of the same Court.

Now following the provisions contained in Order XLV, rule 15, this is a mechanism for enforcing the orders of the Hon'ble apex Court by way of execution. Following this procedure, an application for execution of the Hon'ble apex Court's orders is required to be made to the Court, from which the appeal to the Hon'ble apex Court was preferred and following Sub-Clause (2) therein upon the direction of the Court and transmission of the record to the Court, which passed the first decree appealed or to such other Court as the Hon'ble apex Court may direct and the Court, to which the said decree or order is so transmitted shall execute it accordingly.

Now coming back to the facts involved in the case and the directions therein, more particularly, looking to the prayer made in the Execution Petition, it appears, the opposite parties sought for execution of the direction contained in the order dated 9.1.2013 passed in S.L.P.(C) No. 32998/2009. Hon'ble Supreme Court though dismissed the S.L.P. but by order dated 9.1.2013 passed the following:

> "Heard learned senior counsel for the petitioner State, respondents and perused the relevant material.
>
> We do not find any valid and legal ground for interference. The special leave petition is dismissed.
>
> However, the petitioner is granted three months' time to comply with the order of the High Court.
>
> In case if the State finds no suitable land, as suggested by the High Court, they are permitted to pay the market value prevailing as on date to the parties concerned."

Reading of this order, it appears, Hon'ble apex Court going ahead of the final direction of the High Court specifically, directed the State Government in the event it is unable to find out any suitable land, it is permitted to pay market value as on date of the order to the parties concerned. This direction is a positive direction and available for execution and there is no dispute, thus, that order of the Hon'ble apex Court is put to execution. Since the order of the Hon'ble apex Court was sought to be executed, this Court finds, there was no question of application of the provision of the Chapter XXVIII of the Rules of the Orissa High Court, 1948 in the present case. It is, on the other hand, the provision contained in Order XLV, Rule 15 of C.P.C. has a direct application. Assuming that nomenclature in the body of the Execution Petition is immaterial for the settled position of law and since the Execution Petition is filed in the High Court from which the appeal was preferred to Hon'ble apex Court can be treated as an application under Order XLV, Rule 15 of the Code of Civil Procedure. It is now to be seen, if the Registrar is competent to deal with such Execution Petition ? Under the admitted circumstance specifically for the admission of the opposite parties that the Execution Petition is directed involving the direction of Hon'ble apex Court dated 9.1.2013 being permitted by order of the Hon'ble apex Court in the contempt proceeding in its order dated 28.1.2015, the execution, if any, was only maintainable under Order XLV, Rule 15 of C.P.C. Reading of the provision at Order XLV, Rule 15 of C.P.C., it makes clear that the Execution Petition is not only to be made to High Court, from which the appeal to the Hon'ble Supreme Court was preferred and such Court which for all purpose in the case at hand here will be this High Court. In such event, this Court was required to transmit the decree or order of the Hon'ble Supreme Court to the Court which passed the decree appealed from and the Court to which the record is transmitted should have executed it accordingly in the manner and according to the provision applicable to the execution of its original decrees/ orders. In the given circumstance, the execution application since maintainable applying provision at Order XLV, Rule 15 is required to be dealt by the High Court not by the Registrar and the Registrar has absolutely no power to sit over it. This Court finds, the Registrar exercising power involving the present execution proceeding was without jurisdiction.

Considering the challenge of the opposite parties with regard to maintainability of the Civil Miscellaneous Petition and also framed by this Court at the admission of the Civil Miscellaneous Petition, this Court finds, under the facts scenario of the case, the Registrar taking up the Execution Proceeding, since involved execution of the direction of the Hon'ble apex Court, was incompetent to exercise its power under Order XLV, Rule 15 of C.P.C. and therefore, its action being an action of a Court subordinate to the High Court is coming well within the scope of Article 227 of the Constitution of India, as such this Court finds, the Civil Miscellaneous Petition under Article 227 of the Constitution of India where the High Court exercises its power of superintendence over the subordinate courts, is very much maintainable.

Deciding the scope of High Court in exercise of power under Article 227 of Constitution of India the Hon'ble Apex Court in the case of *Radhey Shyam* v. *Chhabi Nath,* (2015) 5 SCC 423: AIR 2015 SC 3269, has held in paragraph-25 as follows:—

> 25. It is true that this Court has laid down that technicalities associated with the prerogative writs in England have no role to play under our constitutional scheme. There is no parallel system of King's Court in India and of all other courts having limited jurisdiction subject to supervision of King's Court. Courts are set up under the Constitution or the laws. All courts in the jurisdiction of a High Court are subordinate to it and subject to its control and supervision under Article 227. Writ jurisdiction is constitutionally conferred on all High Courts. Broad principles of writ jurisdiction followed in England are applicable to India and a writ of certiorari lies against patently erroneous or without jurisdiction orders of Tribunals or authorities or courts other than judicial courts. There are no precedents in India for High Courts to issue writs to subordinate courts. Control of working of subordinate courts in dealing with their judicial orders is exercised by way of appellate or revisional powers or power of superintendence under Article 227. Orders of civil court stand on different footing from the orders of authorities or Tribunals or courts other than judicial/civil courts. While appellate or revisional jurisdiction is regulated by statutes, power of superintendence under Article 227 is constitutional. The expression "inferior court" is not referable to judicial courts, as rightly observed in the referring order in paras 26 and 27 quoted above.

Looking to the dispute herein as decision of the Hon'ble Apex court is under execution, this Court finds the decision (Supra) has a direct bearing in the present case and the Civil Miscellaneous petition, since directed against the order of the Registrar of the High Court being subordinate to this Court the Civil Miscellaneous petition is maintainable.

Under the circumstance and for the reason assigned in paragraph-14 herein, this Court finds the execution petition No. 2/2015 in the present form is maintainable under Order XLV, Rule 15 of C.P.C. forgetting the nomenclation be treated as a proceeding under Order XLV, Rule 15 of the Code of Civil Procedure but the Registrar exercising his power under Chapter XXVIII of the Rules of the High Court of Orissa is incompetent and as such, all orders passed by the Registrar of High Court of Orissa become void and inoperative. Thus, while holding that the present Civil Miscellaneous Petition under Article 227 of the Constitution of India maintainable, this Court finds, all the orders passed by the Registrar are without competency and as such, this Court sets aside all the orders passed by the Registrar of High Court of Orissa involving E.P. No. 2/2015 and directs the Registry to place the Execution Proceeding before the assigned Bench taking the permission of the Bench for its proceeding in accordance with law. Dealing with the deposit made by the State on the orders in the execution side, this Court directs the deposit made here will be treated as a deposit involving the Execution Case and release of the same shall be dependent on the orders to be passed in the Execution Proceeding by the Court of competency.

22. Order XLV, Rule 2 read with Section 151 – Karnataka High Court Act, 1962, Section 4 – Karnataka High Court Rules, 1959

In *Ryatar Sahakari Sakkarre Karkhane Niyamit* v. *Principal Commissioner of Income Tax*, 2016 (4) KCCR 3797: 2016 (4) AIR Kar R 812 (Karn) (DB) (Dharwad Bench) this petition was filed under Order XLV, rule 2 read with Section 151, CPC with a prayer to grant a 'Fitness Certificate' for filing an appeal before the Hon'ble Supreme Court under Article 133 of the Constitution of India against common order dated 26.2.2016 in ITAs. No. 100111 to 100120/2015 c/w. 100012 to 100017/2016 (T-IT) passed by this Court.

Grant of certificate by an High Court for filing an appeal before the Hon'ble Supreme Court is provided under Article 134A of the Constitution of India and the same reads as follows:—

> "**134A. Certificate for appeal to the Supreme Court.**—Every High Court, passing or making a judgment, decree, final order, or sentence, referred to in clause (1) of Article 132 or clause(1) of Article 133, or clause (1) of Article 134—
>
> (a) may, if it deems fit so to do, on its own motion; and
>
> (b) shall, if an oral application is made, by or on behalf of the party aggrieved, immediately after the passing or making of such judgment, decree, final order or sentence, determine, as soon as may be after such passing or making, the question whether a certificate of the nature referred to in clause (1) of Article 132, or clause (1) of Article 133 or, as the case may be, sub-clause (c) of clause (1) of Article 134, may be given in respect of that case."

Chapter XIX of the High Court Rules also deals with appeals to Hon'ble Supreme Court and Rules 1 to 3 read as follows:—

> "1. Civil appeals on the certificate of the High Court, Rules contained in this Chapter shall be read as supplemental to Order XLV of the Code of Civil Procedure. 1908, and to the Supreme Court Rules and shall not be read in derogation of either of them.

ORDER XVI

HEARING OF APPEALS

1. At the hearing of an appeal not more than one advocate shall be heard on behalf of the appellant/appellants and not more than one Advocate on behalf of each respondent/each set of respondents, unless directed otherwise by the Court.

2. No party shall, without the leave of the Court, rely at the hearing on any ground not specified in the statement of the case filed by him.

3. Where the Court, after hearing an appeal, decides to reserve its Judgment thereon, the date of pronouncement shall be notified by the Registrar in the daily cause list.

4. (1) An appellant whose appeal has been dismissed for default of appearance may, within thirty days of the order, present a petition praying that the appeal may be restored and the Court may, after giving notice of such application to the respondent who has entered appearance in the appeal, restore the appeal if good and sufficient cause is shown, putting the appellant on terms as to costs or otherwise as it thinks fit, or pass such other order as the circumstances of the case and the ends of justice may require.

(2) Where an appeal is heard *ex-parte* and Judgment is pronounced against the respondent, he may apply to the Court to re-hear the appeal, and if he satisfies the Court that the appeal was set down *ex-parte* against him without notice to him or that he was prevented by sufficient cause from appearing when the appeal was called on for hearing the Court may re-hear the appeal on such terms as to costs or otherwise as it thinks fit to impose upon him.

ORDER XVII

MISCELLANEOUS

1. The filing of a special leave petition or an appeal shall not prevent execution of the decree or order appealed against but the Court, may, subject to such terms and conditions as it may think fit to impose, order a stay of execution of the decree or order, or order a stay of proceedings, in any case under appeal to the Court.

2. A party to a special leave petition or an appeal who appears shall furnish the Registrar complete postal address (and e-mail address, if any) which shall be treated as his registered address for service and all documents left at that address, or sent by registered post to that address, shall be deemed to have been duly served. If the party does not have an e-mail address, a statement to that effect shall be made.

3. In cases where intervention is allowed by the Court, the intervener or interveners shall be entitled to receive documents produced and relied upon by the petitioner(s), unless directed otherwise by the Court. The intervener(s) may make oral submissions with the leave of the Court.

ORDER XVIII

APPEALS AND APPLICATIONS BY INDIGENT PERSON

1. An application for leave to proceed as an indigent person shall be made on a petition. It shall be accompanied by:

(a) a copy of the petition of appeal and the documents referred to in rule 3 of Order XIX, or of the petition for special leave and the documents mentioned in rule 4 of Order XXI, as the case may be, and

(b) an affidavit from the petitioner disclosing all the property to which he is entitled and the value thereof other than his necessary wearing apparel and his interest in the subject-matter of the intended appeal and stating that he is unable to provide security or surety for the cost of respondent and pay Court fees.

2. The Registrar shall, on satisfying himself that the petition is in order, direct that the petition shall be registered and set down for hearing before the Chamber Judge on a date to be fixed for the purpose.

3. The application shall be posted before the Judge in Chambers who may himself inquire into the indigency of the petitioner after notice to the other parties in the case and to the Attorney-General, or make an order directing the High Court either by itself or by a Court subordinate to the High Court, to investigate the indigency after notice to the parties interested and submit a report thereon within such time as may be fixed by the order. On receipt of the report, the petition shall again be posted before the Judge in Chambers for further orders:

Provided that, if the applicant was allowed to sue or appeal as an indigent person in the Court from whose decree the appeal is preferred, no further inquiry in respect of his indigency shall be necessary, unless this Court sees cause to direct such inquiry.

4. In granting or refusing leave to appeal as an indigent person, the Court shall ordinarily follow the principles set out in Order XXXIII of the Code.

5. Where a petitioner obtains leave of the Court to appeal as an indigent person he shall not be required to pay Court fees on the documents filed in the case or fees payable for service of process. He shall, however, be required to pay fees for obtaining copies of any documents or orders.

6. The Judge in Chambers may assign an advocate-on-record to assist an indigent person in the case, unless the indigent person has made his own arrangement for his representation. Such assignment shall ordinarily be from a panel of advocates willing to assist indigent persons and chosen by the Judge in Chambers. It shall however be open to the Judge in Chambers in his discretion to assign an advocate outside the panel in any particular case.

7. (1) No fees shall be payable by an indigent person to his advocate, nor shall any such fees be allowed on taxation against the other party except by an order of Court. The advocate may however receive from the indigent person money for out of pocket expenses, if any, properly incurred in the case.

(2) It shall be open to the Court, if it thinks fit, to award costs against the adverse party or out of the property decreed to an indigent person and direct payment of such costs to the advocate for the indigent person.

(3) Save as aforesaid no person shall take or agree to take or seek to obtain from an indigent person any fee, profit or reward for the conduct of his case, and any person who takes, agrees to take or seeks to obtain, any such fee, profit or reward, shall be guilty of Contempt of Court.

(4) Soon after an appeal by an indigent person has been heard and disposed of, the advocate for the indigent person shall file in the Registry a statement of account showing what moneys, if any, were received by him in the case on any account from the indigent person or from any person on his behalf and the expenditure incurred. If no moneys had been received, a statement shall be filed to that effect. The Taxing Officer may, where he thinks it necessary, place the statement filed before the Judge in Chambers for his perusal and orders.

8. Where the appellant succeeds in the appeal, the Registrar shall calculate the amount of Court-fees which would have been paid by the appellant if he had not been permitted to appeal as an indigent person and incorporate it in the decree or order of the Court; such amount shall be recoverable by the Government of India from any party ordered by the Court to pay the same, and shall be the first charge on the subject-matter of the appeal.

9. Where the appellant fails in the appeal or the permission granted to him to sue as an indigent person has been withdrawn, the Court may order the appellant to pay the Court-fees which would have been paid by him if he had not been permitted to appeal as an indigent person.

10. The Central Government shall have the right at any time to apply to the Court to make an order for the payment of Court-fees under rule 8 or rule 9.

11. (1) Where the party is not represented by an Advocate of his choice, the Court may in a proper case, direct the engagement of an Advocate from panel of Supreme Court Legal Services Committee or at the cost of the State. The fee of the Advocate engaged at the cost of State shall be such as may, from time to time, be fixed by the Chief Justice, unless otherwise directed by the Court.

(2) After the hearing of the matter is over, the Registrar, the Additional Registrar or the Deputy Registrar shall issue to the Advocate where engaged at the cost of State, a certificate in the prescribed form, indicating therein, the name of the said Advocate and the amount of fees payable to him.

(3) The State concerned shall pay the fees specified in the certificate issued under sub-rule (2) to the Advocate named therein within three months from the date of his presenting before it his claim for the fees supported by the certificate. If the fees are not paid within the period above-said, the Advocate shall be entitled to recover the same from the State concerned by enforcement

of the certificate as an Order as to costs under the Supreme Court (Decrees and Orders) Enforcement Order, 1954.

Explanation.—For the purposes of this rule, the term "State" shall include a Union Territory.

12. All matters arising between the Central Government and any party to the appeal under the three preceding rules shall be deemed to be questions arising between the parties to the appeal.

13. In every appeal by an indigent person the Registrar shall, after the disposal thereof, send to the Attorney-General for India a memorandum of the court fees payable by the indigent person.

14. No appeal or other proceeding begun, carried on or defended by an indigent person shall be compromised or discontinued without the leave of the Court.

15. Any respondent, who desires to defend, may be allowed to set up the defence as an indigent person, and the rules contained in this Order shall, so far as may be, apply to him as if he were a petitioner moving the petition for leave to proceed as an indigent person.

ORDER XIX

APPEALS ON CERTIFICATE BY HIGH COURT

1. Where a certificate of the nature referred to in clause (1) of article 132 or clause (1) of article 133 has been given under article 134A of the Constitution or a certificate has been given under article 135 of the Constitution or under any other provision of law the party concerned shall file a petition of appeal in the Court.

2. Subject to the provisions of sections 4, 5 and 12 of the Limitation Act, 1963 (36 of 1963), the petition of appeal shall be presented within sixty days from the date of the grant of the certificate of fitness:

Provided that in computing the said period, the time requisite for obtaining a copy of the certificate and the order granting the said certificate, shall also be excluded.

3. (1) The petition shall recite succinctly and in chronological order with relevant dates, the principal steps in the proceedings leading up to the appeal from the commencement thereof till the grant of the certificate of leave to appeal to the Court, and shall state the grounds on which the judgment under appeal is assailed as well as the amount or value of the subject-matter of the suit in the Court of first instance and in the High Court, and the amount or value of the subject-matter in dispute before the Court with particulars showing how the said valuation has been arrived at. Where the appeal is incapable of valuation, it shall be so stated.

(2) The petition shall be accompanied by a certified copy of—

(i) judgment and decree or order appealed from;

(ii) certificate granted by the High Court; and

(iii) the order granting the said certificate.

In cases where according to the practice prevailing in the High Court, the decree or order is not required to be drawn up it shall be so stated upon affidavit. In appeals falling under any of the categories enumerated in rule 6, however, in addition to the documents mentioned above, a certified copy (or uncertified copy if such copy is affirmed to be true copy upon affidavit) of the judgment or order and also of the decree of the Court immediately below or such a copy of the order of the Tribunal, Government authority or person, as the case may be shall also be filed before the appeal is listed for hearing *ex-parte*. At least seven copies of the aforesaid documents shall be filed in the Registry.

(3) Where at any time between the grant by the High Court of the Certificate for leave to appeal to the Court and the filing of the petition of appeal, any party to the proceeding in the Court below dies, the petition of appeal may be filed by or against the legal representative, as the case may be, of the deceased party, provided that the petition is accompanied by a separate application, duly supported by an affidavit, praying for bringing on record such person as the legal representative of the deceased party and setting out the facts showing him to be the proper person to be entered on the record as such legal representative.

4. The Registrar, after satisfying himself that the petition of appeal is in order, shall endorse the date of presentation on the petition and register the same as an appeal in the Court.

5. Where a party desires to appeal on grounds which can be raised only with the leave of the Court, it shall lodge along with the petition of appeal a separate petition stating the grounds so proposed to be raised and praying for leave to appeal on those grounds.

6. Each of the following categories of appeals, on being registered, shall be put up for hearing *ex-parte* before the Court which may either dismiss it summarily or direct issue of notice to all necessary parties or may make such orders as the circumstances of the case may require, namely:—

(a) an appeal from any judgment, decree or final order of a High Court summarily dismissing the appeal or the matter, as the case may be before it;

(b) an appeal on a certificate granted by a High Court under article 134A of the Constitution being a certificate of the nature referred to in clause (1) of article 132 or clause (1) of article 133 of the Constitution or under any other provision of law if the High Court has not recorded the reasons or the grounds for granting the certificate.

(c) an appeal under clause (b) of sub-section (1) of section 19 of the Contempt of Courts Act, 1971 (70 of 1971).

APPEARANCE BY RESPONDENT

7. As soon as the petition of appeal has been registered and in the case of categories of appeals falling under rule 6 as soon as notice is directed to be issued the Registrar of the Court shall—

(i) require the appellant to furnish as many copies of the petition of appeal as may be necessary for record and for service on the respondent; and

(ii) send to the Registrar of the Court appealed from a copy of the petition of appeal for record in that Court who shall serve upon the respondent or each of the respondents the notice of lodgment of appeal:

Provided that the Registrar of the Court may on an application made for the purpose, dispense with service of the petition of appeal on any respondent who did not appear in the proceedings in the Court appealed from or on his legal representative:

Provided however that no order dispensing with service of notice shall be made in respect of a respondent who is a minor or a lunatic:

Provided further that an order dispensing with service of notice shall not preclude any respondent or his legal representative from appearing to contest the appeal.

8. On receipt from the Court of the copy of the petition of appeal, the Registrar of the Court appealed from shall—

(i) cause notice of the lodgment of the petition of appeal to be served on the respondent personally or in such manner as the Court appealed from may by rules prescribe;

(ii) unless otherwise ordered by the Court transmit to the Court at the expense of the appellant the original record of the case, including the record of the Courts below:

Provided that where a transcript is to be prepared in accordance with the proviso to sub-rule (1) of rule 11, no original record shall be transmitted until specifically requisitioned; and

(iii) as soon as notice as aforesaid is served, to send a certificate as to the date or dates on which the said notice was served.

9. A respondent shall enter appearance in the Court within thirty days of the service on him of the notice of lodgment of the petition of appeal.

10. The respondent may within the time limited for his appearance deliver to Registrar of the Court and to the appellant a notice in writing consenting to the appeal, and the Court may thereupon make such order on the appeal as the justice of the case may require without requiring the attendance of the person so consenting.

PREPARATION OF RECORD

11. (1) The record shall be printed in accordance with the rules contained in the First Schedule to these rules and, unless otherwise ordered by the Court, it shall be printed under the supervision of the Registrar of the Court:

Provided that where the proceedings from which the appeal arises were had in courts below in a language other than English, the Registrar of the Court appealed from shall within six months from the date of the service on the respondent of the notice of petition of appeal transmit to the Court in triplicate a transcript in English of the record proper of the appeal to be laid before the Court, one copy of which shall be duly authenticated. The provisions contained in rules 12 to 17 shall apply to the preparation and transmission to the Court of the said transcript record:

Provided further that where the records are printed for the purpose of the appeal before the High Court and the said record be in English, the High Court shall prepare 10 extra copies in addition to the number of copies required by the High Court for use in the Court.

(2) Upon receipt from the Court appealed from of the English transcript of the record as aforesaid, the Registrar of the Court shall proceed to cause an estimate of the costs of preparing the printed copies of the records to be made and served on the appellant in accordance with the provisions contained in rule 16 and with all convenient speed arrange for the preparation thereof.

(3) Unless otherwise ordered by the Court, at least twenty copies of the record shall be prepared.

12. (1) As soon as the original record of the case is received in the Court, the Registrar shall give notice to the parties who have entered appearance of the arrival of the original record and the parties shall, thereafter be entitled to inspect the record and to extract all necessary particulars therefrom.

(2) The appellant shall within four weeks of the service upon him of the notice referred to in sub-rule (1), file a list of the documents which he proposes to include in the paper book, a copy whereof shall be served on the respondent. The respondent may within three weeks of the service on him of the said list, file a list of such additional documents as he considers necessary for the determination of the appeal.

13. After the expiry of the time fixed for the filing of the additional list by the respondent, the Registrar shall fix a day for the settlement of list of documents to be included in the appeal record and shall give notice thereof to the parties who have entered appearance. In settling the lists the Registrar, as well as the parties concerned, shall endeavour to exclude from the record all documents that are not relevant to the subject-matter of the appeal and generally to reduce the bulk of the record as far as practicable.

14. Where the respondent objects to the inclusion of a document on the ground that it is not necessary or is irrelevant and the appellant nevertheless insists upon its inclusion, the record as finally printed shall, with a view to subsequent adjustment of cost of and incidental to the printing of the said document, indicate in the index of papers or otherwise the fact that the respondent has objected to the inclusion of the document and that it has been included at the instance of the appellant.

15. Where the appellant objects to the inclusion of a document on the ground that it is not necessary or is irrelevant and the respondent nevertheless insists upon its inclusion, the Registrar, if he is of opinion that the document is not relevant, may direct that the said document be printed separately at the expense

of the respondent and require the respondent to deposit within such time as he may prescribe, the necessary charges therefor, and the question of the costs thereof shall be dealt with by the Court at the time of the determination of the appeal.

16. As soon as the index of the records is settled, the Registrar concerned shall cause an estimate of the costs of the preparation of the record to be prepared and served on the appellant and require him to deposit within thirty days of such service the said amount. The appellant may deposit the said amount in lump sum or in such installments as the Registrar may prescribe.

17. Where the record has been printed for the purpose of the appeal before the High Court and sufficient number of copies (if it is in English) are available, no fresh printing of the record shall be necessary except of such additional papers as may be required.

18. Where an appeal paper book is likely to consist of two hundred or less number of pages, the Registrar may, instead of having it printed, have the record photocopied under his supervision.

19. If at any time during the preparation of the record the amount deposited is found insufficient, the Registrar shall call upon the appellant to deposit such further sum as may be necessary within such further time as may be deemed fit but not exceeding twenty-eight days in the aggregate.

20. Where the appellant fails to make the required deposit, the preparation of the records shall be suspended and the Registrar concerned shall not proceed with the preparation thereof without an order in this behalf of the Court and where the record is under preparation in the Court appealed from, of the Court appealed from.

21. When the record has been made ready the Registrar shall certify the same and give notice to the parties of the certification of the record and append to the record a certificate showing the amount of expenses incurred by the party concerned for the preparation of the record.

22. Each party who has entered appearance shall be entitled to three copies of the record for his own use.

23. Subject to any special direction from the Court to the contrary, the costs of, and incidental to, the printing of the record shall form part of the costs of the appeal, but the costs of, and incidental to, the printing of any document objected to by one party in accordance with rule 15 or rule 16, shall, if such document is found, on taxation of costs, to be unnecessary or irrelevant, be disallowed to, or borne by the party insisting on including the same in the record.

24. Where the record is directed to be prepared under the supervision of the Registrar of the Court appealed from, the provisions contained in rules 12 to 22 shall apply *mutatis mutandis* to the preparation thereof.

SPECIAL CASE

25. Where the decision of the appeal is likely to turn exclusively on a question of law, any party, with the sanction of the Registrar of the Court, may submit such question of law in the form of a special case, and the Registrar may call

the parties before him, and having heard them and examined the record, may report to the Court as to the nature of the proceedings and the record that may be necessary for the discussion of the same. Upon perusing the said report, the Court may give such directions as to the preparation of the record and hearing of the appeal, including directions regarding the time within which or otherwise, the parties shall lodge their respective statements of case:

Provided that nothing herein contained shall in any way prevent this Court from ordering the full discussion of the whole case if the Court shall so think fit.

WITHDRAWAL OF APPEAL

26. Where at any stage prior to the hearing of the appeal an appellant desires to withdraw his appeal, he shall present a petition to that effect to the Court. At the hearing of any such petition a respondent who has entered appearance may apply to the Court for his costs.

NON-PROSECUTION OF APPEALS – CHANGE OF PARTIES

27. If an appellant fails to take any steps in the appeal within the time fixed for the same under these rules, or if no time is specified, it appears to the Registrar of the Court that he is not prosecuting the appeal with due diligence, the Registrar shall call upon him to explain his default and, if no Explanation is offered, or if the Explanation offered appears to the Registrar to be insufficient, the Registrar may issue a summons calling upon him to show cause before the Court why the appeal should not be dismissed for non-prosecution.

28. The Registrar shall send a copy of the summons mentioned in the last specified rule to every respondent who has entered appearance. The Court may, after hearing the parties, dismiss the appeal for non-prosecution or give such other directions thereon as the justice of the case may require.

29. Where at any time between the filing of the petition of appeal and the hearing of the appeal the record becomes defective by reason of the death or change of status of a party to the appeal, or for any other reason, an application shall be made to the Court, stating who is the proper person to be substituted or entered on the record in place of, or in addition to the party on record.

30. Upon the filing of such an application the Registrar of the Court shall, after notice to the parties concerned, determine who in his opinion is the proper person to be substituted or entered on the record in place of, or in addition to the party on record, and the name of such person shall thereupon be substituted or entered on the record:

Provided that no such order of substitution or revivor shall be made by the Registrar—

(i) where a question arises as to whether any person is or is not the legal representative of the deceased party, or

(ii) where a question of setting aside the abatement of the cause is involved;

and in such a case he shall place the matter before the Court for orders:

Provided further that where during the course of the proceedings it appears to the Registrar that it would be convenient for the enquiry that investigation in regard to the person who is to be substituted on record, be made by the Court appealed from or a Court subordinate thereto, the Registrar may place the matter before the Judge in Chambers and the Judge in Chambers may thereupon make an order directing to the Court appealed from to investigate into the matter either itself or cause an enquiry to be made by a Court subordinate to it, after notice to the parties, and submit its report thereon to this Court within such time as may be fixed by the order. On receipt of the report from the Court below the matter shall be posted before the Judge in Chambers again for appropriate orders.

31. Save as aforesaid the provision of Order XXII of the Code relating to abatement shall apply *mutatis mutandis* to appeals and proceedings before the Court.

32. (1) Within forty-five days of the service on him of the notice of authentication of the record, the appellant shall lodge in the Court the statement of his case and serve a copy thereof on the respondent. The respondent shall lodge statement of case within thirty-five days thereafter. In appeals where printing of record is dispensed with, the appellant shall file statement of case within 45 days from the date of order dispensing with the printing of appeal record or from the expiry of period granted by the Court for filing additional papers or record, whichever is later and the respondent shall file statement of case within 35 days either from the date on which the period of 30 days from the date of service of notice of lodgment of petition of appeal expires or from the date of service of statement of case of the appellant, whichever is later.

(2) If the appellant does not file a statement of case within the time, as provided for in sub-rule (1), it shall be presumed that the appellant has adopted the list of dates/synopsis containing chronology of events as filed at the time of presentation of petition for seeking special leave to appeal (SLP)/Appeal, as statement of case, and does not desire to file any further statement of case:

Provided that where a respondent, who has entered appearance, does not file a statement of case within the time, as provided in sub-rule (1), it shall be presumed that the respondent does not desire to lodge statement of case in the appeal.

33. (1) The statement of a case shall consist of two parts as follows:

Part I shall consist of a concise statement of the facts of the case in proper sequence. A list of the dates of the relevant events leading up and concerning the litigation in chronological order and pedigree tables, wherever necessary, shall be given at the end of the part.

Part II shall set out the contentions of facts and law sought to be urged in support of the claim of the party lodging the statement of case and the authorities in support thereof. Where authorities are cited, reference shall be given to the Official Reports, if available, where text books are cited, the reference shall if possible, be to the latest available editions. Where a statute, regulation, rule, ordinance or bye law is cited or relied on, so much thereof as may be necessary to the decision of the case shall be set out. At the end of the part shall ordinarily be set out a table of cases cited.

(2) The statement of case shall consist of paragraphs numbered consecutively. Reference shall be given by page and line to the relevant portions of the record in the margin and care shall be taken to avoid, as far as possible, the re-producing in the statement of case of long extracts from the Record. The statement of case shall not travel beyond the limits of the certificate or the special leave, as the case may be, and of such additional grounds, if any, as the Court may allow to be urged on application made for the purpose. The Taxing Officer in taxing the costs of the appeal shall, either of his own motion, or at the instance of the opposite party, enquire into any unnecessary prolixity in the case, and shall disallow the costs occasioned thereby.

34. Two or more respondents may, at their own risk of costs, lodge separate statement of cases in the same appeal.

35. A respondent who has not entered appearance shall not be entitled to receive any notice relating to the appeal from the Registrar of the Court, nor allowed to lodge a statement of case in the appeal.

36. The appeal shall be set down for hearing one month after the expiry of the time prescribed for lodging the statement of case by the respondent.

37. If the printing of record has not been dispensed with, the appellant shall, within two weeks of the receipt of the notice setting down the appeal for hearing, attend at the Registry and obtain eight copies of the record and the statements of case to be bound in cloth or in one-fourth leather with paper sides, and six leaves of blank paper shall be kept for the use of the Court. The front cover shall bear a label stating the title and Supreme Court number of the appeal, the contents of the volume and the name and address of the advocates-on-record. The several documents indicated by inducts shall be arranged in the following order:—

(1) Appellant's Statement of Case;

(2) Respondent's Statement of Case;

(3) Record (if in more than one Part, showing the separate Parts by inducts, all Parts being paged at the top of the page);

(4) Supplemental Record (if any) and the short title and Supreme Court number of appeal shall also be shown on the back.

38. The appellant shall lodge the bound copies not less than ten clear days before the date fixed for the hearing of the Appeal.

39. The provisions of rule 11 of Order XVIII of the rules shall, so far as may be, apply to the parties in matters to which this Order applies.

40. Except where specifically otherwise provided in these Rules, the provisions of this Order with necessary modifications and adaptations, shall apply to Statutory Appeals filed under any enabling Act or provision.

SUBJECT INDEX

•••